Portugal

THE ROUGH GUIDE

There are more than sixty Rough Guide titles covering
destinations from Amsterdam to Zimbabwe & Botswana

Forthcoming titles include
Bali • Costa Rica • Goa • Hawaii • Majorca
Rhodes • Singapore • Vietnam

Rough Guide Reference Series
Classical Music • World Music

Rough Guide Phrasebooks
Czech • French • German • Greek • Italian • Spanish

ROUGH GUIDE PORTUGAL CREDITS

Series editor:	Mark Ellingham
Text editor:	Jules Brown
Editorial:	Martin Dunford, Jonathan Buckley, Graham Parker, Jo Mead, Samantha Cook, Amanda Tomlin, Alison Cowan, Annie Shaw, Lemisse al-Hafidh, Catherine McHale
Production:	Susanne Hillen, Andy Hilliard, Melissa Flack, Alan Spicer, Judy Pang, Link Hall, Nicola Williamson
Finance:	John Fisher, Celia Crowley, Simon Carloss
Publicity:	Richard Trillo (UK), Jean-Marie Kelly (US)
Administration:	Tania Hummel

Acknowledgments

Special thanks to Don Grisbrook for research above and beyond the call of duty, to Jules Brown for pulling it all together, to Kevin Rose and James Allen for their work on Lisbon, Pilar Pereira of the Portuguese National Tourist Office in London, Amanda Tomlin and Matthew Hancock for their border exertions, Roberta Fox for her expertise and local knowledge, David Reed for trans-Atlantic contributions, Colette Doyle who walked all the way to Portugal, Paul Doyle for Algarvian browsing and sluicing, Jonathan Buckley and Susanne Hillen for road-testing the guide, John Pare for handsteadying assistance, Capt. I. Little for his expert guidance in port wine matters, Sam Kirby for her excellent maps, and Amanda Tomlin (again) for proofreading.

In Portugal, thanks to Jorge Bochechas, Luís Miguel da Costa and Fernanda Valente for all their help past and present; and to António Carona of *ICEP Porto*, Isabel Oliveira of *ICEP Algarve*, *Hotel de Lagos* in Lagos, *Hotel Cerro Alagoa* in Albufeira, *Hotel Faro* and *Hotel Eva* in Faro, Isabel Gonçalves, Francisco da Palma, Maria Natércia Espinho, José Manuel Nobre, Filomina Morgado, Raquel Luza, Maria Manuel Magahães, Maria Manuela, Yussef Abdul Sacur, Abbas Madatali Rajabali, Maria Helena Raposo Antunes, João José Rodrigues de Freitas and Assunção Pelayo.

And we'd like to say a big thankyou to the **readers of the previous edition** of the guide who took time to annotate our errors, omissions and lapses of taste; the roll of honour appears on p.431 – apologies to anyone whose name we missed or whose signatures we couldn't quite decipher.

The publishers and authors have done their best to ensure the accuracy and currency of all the information in *The Rough Guide to Portugal;* however, they can accept no responsibility for any loss, injury, or inconvenience sustained by any traveller as a result of information or advice contained in the guide.

This sixth edition published in 1994 by Rough Guides, 1 Mercer Street, London WC2H 9QJ. Reprinted July 1994 and May 1995.

Distributed by the Penguin Group:

Penguin Books Ltd, 27 Wrights Lane, London W8 5TZ
Penguin Books USA Inc., 375 Hudson Street, New York 10014, USA
Penguin Books Australia Ltd, 487 Maroondah Highway, PO Box 257, Ringwood, Victoria 3134, Australia
Penguin Books Canada Ltd, 10 Alcorn Avenue, Toronto, Ontario, Canada M4V 1E4
Penguin Books (NZ) Ltd, 182–190 Wairau Road, Auckland 10, New Zealand

Previous editions published in the UK by Routledge & Kegan Paul and by Harrap Columbus.
Previous edition published in the United States and Canada as *The Real Guide Portugal.*

Typeset in Linotron Univers and Century Old Style to an original design by Andrew Oliver.
Printed in the United Kingdom by Cox & Wyman, Reading.

Illustrations in Part One and Part Three by Ed Briant; Basics illustration by Andrew Harris;
Contexts illustration by Helen Manning.

A catalogue record for this book is available from the British Library.

ISBN : 1-85828-084-2

Portugal

THE ROUGH GUIDE

Written and researched by
**Mark Ellingham, John Fisher,
Graham Kenyon and Alice Martin**

This edition updated by
Don Grisbrook with Jules Brown

With additional research by
Matthew Hancock, Amanda Tomlin,
Kevin Rose and James Allen

THE ROUGH GUIDES

CONTENTS

Introduction vi

INTRODUCTION

I am very happy here, because I loves oranges, and talks bad Latin to the Monks, who understand it as it is like their own. And I goes into society (with my pocket pistols) and I swims in the Tagus all across at once, and I rides on an ass or a mule and swears Portuguese, and I have got a diarrhoea, and bites from the mosquitoes. But what of that? Comfort must not be expected by folks that go a-pleasuring.

Byron in Portugal, July 1809.

P ortugal is an astonishingly beautiful country, the rivers, forests and lush valleys of the north a splendid and complementary contrast to its contorted southern coastline of beaches, cliffs and coves. If you've come from the arid plains of central Spain, Portugal's dry southern Alentejo region doesn't promise any immediate relief, but – unlike Spain – you don't have to travel very far to witness so total a contrast that it's hard, at first, to take in. Suddenly the landscape is infinitely softer and greener, with flowers and trees everywhere. Life also seems easier-paced and the people more courteous; the Portuguese themselves talk of their nation as a land of *brandos costumes* – gentle ways.

For so small a country, Portugal sports a tremendous cultural diversity. There are highly sophisticated resorts along the coast around Lisbon and on the well-developed Algarve in the south, upon which European tourists have been descending for almost thirty years. Lisbon itself, in its idiosyncratic, rather old-fashioned way, has enough diversions to please most city devotees; as 1994 European City of Culture it's endured an infrastructural overhaul that locks it into modern Europe without quite jettisoning its most endearing, ramshackle qualities. But in the rural areas – the Alentejo, the mountainous Beiras, or northern Trás-os-Montes – this is often still a conspicuously underdeveloped country. Tourism and European Community membership have changed many regions – most notably in the north, where new road building scythes through the countryside – but for anyone wanting to get off the beaten track, there are limitless opportunities to experience smaller towns and rural areas that still seem rooted in the last century.

In terms of population, and of customs, differences between the **north and south** are particularly striking. Above a roughly sketched line, more or less corresponding with the course of the Rio Tejo (River Tagus), the people are of predominantly Celtic and Germanic stock. It was here, in the north at Guimarães, that the "Lusitanian" nation was born, in the wake of the Christian reconquest from the North African Moors. South of the Tagus, where the Roman, and then the Moorish, civilisations were most established, people tend to be darker-skinned (*moreno*) and maintain perhaps more of a "Mediterranean" lifestyle (though the Portuguese coastline is, in fact, entirely Atlantic). **Agriculture** reflects this divide as well, with oranges, figs, and cork in the south, and more elemental corn and potatoes in the north. Indeed, in the north the methods of farming date back to pre-Christian days, based on a mass of tiny plots divided and subdivided over the generations.

More recent events are also woven into the pattern. The 1974 **revolution**, which brought to an end 48 years of dictatorship, came from the south – an area of vast estates, rich landowners and a dependent workforce – while the later conservative backlash came from the north, with its powerful religious authorities and individual smallholders wary of change. But more profoundly even than the revolution, it is **emigration** that has altered people's attitudes and the appearance of the countryside. After Lisbon, the largest Portuguese community is in Paris, and there are migrant workers spread throughout France, Germany and North America. Returning, these emigrants have brought in modern ideas and challenged many traditional rural values. New ideas and cultural life have arrived, too, through Portugal's own recent **immigrants** from the old African colonies of Cape Verde, Mozambique and Angola.

The greatest of all Portuguese influences, however, is **the sea**. The Atlantic seems to dominate the land not only physically, producing the consistently temperate climate, but mentally and historically, too. The Portuguese are very conscious of themselves as a seafaring race; mariners like Vasco da Gama led the way in the discovery of Africa and the New World, and until comparatively recently Portugal remained a colonial power, albeit one in deep crisis. Such links long ago brought African and South American strands into the country's culture: in the distinctive music of *fado*, blues-like songs heard in Lisbon and Coimbra, for example, or the Moorish-influenced Manueline, or Baroque "Discovery", architecture that provides the country's most distinctive monuments.

This "glorious" history has also led to the peculiar national characteristic of *saudade*: a slightly resigned, nostalgic air, and a feeling that the past will always overshadow the possibilities of the future. The years of isolation under the dictator Salazar, which yielded to democracy after the 1974 revolution, reinforced such feelings, as the ruling elite spurned "contamination" by the rest of Europe. Only in the last decade or so, with Portugal's entry into the European Community, have things really begun to change. A belated industrial revolution is finally underway, and the Portuguese are becoming increasingly geared toward Lisbon and the cities. For those who have stayed in the countryside, however, life remains traditional – disarmingly so to outsiders – and social mores seem fixed in the past. Women still wear black if their husbands are absent, as many are, working in France, or Germany, or at sea.

Where to go and when

Since Portugal is so compact, it's easy to take in something of each of its elements – northern river valleys, southern coast, and mountains – even on a brief visit, whether you rent a car or make your own way by public transport.

Scenically, the most interesting parts of the country are in the north: the **Minho**, green, damp, and often startling in its rural customs; the sensational gorge and valley of the **Rio Douro**; the remote **Trás-os-Montes**; and the wild, mountainous *serras* of **Beira Alta**. For contemporary interest, spend at least some time in both **Lisbon** and **Porto**, the only two cities of real size. And if it's monuments you're after, the whole centre of the country – above all **Coimbra**, **Évora** and the **Estremadura** region – retains a faded grandeur dating from the Age of the Discoveries in the sixteenth century and from the later gold and diamond wealth of Brazil.

The **coast** is virtually continuous beach – some 800km of it – and only on the **Algarve** and in a few pockets around Lisbon and Porto has there been large-scale tourist development. Elsewhere, a number of beach areas have seen casual development on a relatively small scale, these resorts remaining thoroughly Portuguese, with great stretches of deserted sands between them. Perhaps the loveliest beaches are along the northern **Costa Verde**, around Viana do Castelo, or, for isolation, the wild stretches of **southern Alentejo**. It must be added, however, that the Portuguese coast *is* the Atlantic and can often be windswept and exposed. If you like your swimming warm, the only area where the water approaches Mediterranean temperatures is the **eastern Algarve**, where a series of sandbank islands, the *ilhas*, protect the shore.

Swimming aside, **when you go** matters little. The entire country is warm from **April to October**, if slightly erratically so in the rainy north, while the Algarve is amazingly mild throughout the year – it hardly has a winter and January can be delightful when the almond blossom is out. The **Serra da Estrêla**, in contrast, features winter snow for skiers, while further north winter is wet and the wind bitingly cold – this is no time for extended journeys around Trás-os-Montes. Throughout the year, escaping the crowds, outside the Algarve and Lisbon, is little problem. Especially on the Algarve, booking accommodation is essential in high season; elsewhere, however, you should find rooms with little difficulty throughout the year.

AVERAGE DAYTIME TEMPERATURES (°F)						
	JAN	MARCH	MAY	JULY	SEPT	NOV
LISBON	53	57	63	70	70	59
PORTO (Costa Verde)	49	53	59	67	65	53
COIMBRA (Costa da Prata)	50	56	60	67	67	56
FARO (Algarve)	54	57	65	75	72	60

PART ONE

THE
BASICS

GETTING THERE FROM BRITAIN

You need at least two full days to travel overland from Britain to Portugal, so for most visitors flying is the most viable option. There are scheduled year-round flights to Lisbon, Porto and Faro (in the Algarve) from London and from five regional British airports – Birmingham, Edinburgh, Glasgow, Manchester and Newcastle. Numerous package companies also sell charter flights (mostly to Faro) from a variety of British regional airports. Alternatively, if time isn't the most important factor, you can approach Portugal overland from Spain, to which there are many more, and often cheaper, charter deals.

Road or rail alternatives are worth considering if you plan to visit Portugal as part of an extended trip through Europe. There is no direct ferry from Britain to Portugal but drivers can knock off much of the journey by taking the ferry from Plymouth or Portsmouth to Santander in northern Spain.

BY PLANE

Most of the cheaper flights to Portugal are **charter** deals, sold either with a package holiday or as a flight-only option. They have fixed and unchangeable outward and return dates, and allow a maximum stay of one month. Obviously the more flexible you can be about departure dates, the better your chances of a rock-bottom fare. Last-minute summer flights go for as little as £90 return, though more realistically you'll pay around £140.

Travel agents throughout Britain sell charter flights to Portugal (see p.4 for agents' addresses) and even the major high street chains frequently promote "flight-only" deals, or heavily discount their all-inclusive holidays. The greatest variety of flights, however, tends to be from the **London airports to Faro**; there are fewer charters to Lisbon and Porto. Flying from other **British regional airports**, you'll find flights often have a connection in London or Manchester.

Student/youth charters are also sporadically available to Lisbon, though it's usually easier (and cheaper) to pick up flights to Madrid or Málaga (see below). The main student/youth operator for charters is *Campus Travel* (see p.4 for address).

Scheduled flights (with *British Airways* or *TAP*, the Portuguese national airline) are generally more expensive than charters, but can be booked well in advance and remain valid for three months, sometimes longer. There are various types of scheduled ticket and occasional special offers, but with most you'll have to stay at least one Saturday night; the cheapest tickets won't allow you to change your flight once it's booked. As with charters, discount deals are available from high street travel agents, as well as specialist flight and student/youth agencies.

TAP flies from London (Heathrow) to Lisbon, Porto and Faro, and from Manchester to Lisbon, with connections to Porto and Faro. **British Airways** also flies to Lisbon and Porto from London (Heathrow), and from Manchester to Faro in summer. *TAP* and *BA* work in conjunction with each other, so you can book a flight to Portugal from any airport in Britain, with a low-cost add-on fare for the routing through London or Manchester. There is a bewildering fare structure, with **fares** ranging from around £110 to £400 return, depending on class, ticket status and season. For a summer flight reckon on £120–160 return from London for the cheapest flight; a little more from elsewhere in Britain.

An alternative is to **fly to Spain** and travel on to Portugal from there. You can pick up relatively inexpensive charter flights to Madrid or Málaga throughout the summer (and scheduled flights year-round), from where train connections to Portugal are simple enough – see the feature on p.5 for more details. However, the closest Spanish airport is at Santiago de Compostela, in Galicia, in northwestern Spain, under two hours by train from the northern border town of Valença. *Iberia*, the Spanish airline, has regular flights here for £170–220 depending on the time of year.

Besides the operators below, try the classified sections of newspapers like *The Independent* and *The Guardian*, *The Sunday Times* and *Observer* or, in London, *Time Out* and *The Evening Standard*.

AIRLINES, AGENTS AND OPERATORS

AIRLINES

British Airways, 156 Regent St, London W1 (☎081/897 4000); 19–21 St Mary's Gate, Market St, Manchester (personal callers only).

Iberia, 130 Regent St, London W1 (☎071/437 5622).

TAP, 19 Regent St, London SW1 (☎071/839 1031).

FLIGHT AGENTS

Campus Travel, 52 Grosvenor Gardens, London SW1 (☎071/730 3402); 541 Bristol Rd, Selly Oak, Birmingham (☎021/414 1848); 39 Queen's Rd, Clifton, Bristol (☎0272/292 494); 5 Emmanuel St, Cambridge (☎0223/324 283); 53 Forest Rd, Edinburgh (☎031/668 3303); 166 Deansgate, Manchester (☎061/273 1721); 13 High St, Oxford (☎0865/242 067); also in YHA shops and on university campuses throughout Britain. Student/youth specialists.

Destination Portugal, 37 Corn St, Witney, Oxfordshire (☎0993/773 269). Specialist in discount fares to Portugal.

South Coast Student Travel, 61 Ditchling Rd, Brighton (☎0273/570226). A good agent with plenty to offer non-students as well.

Springways Travel, 71 Oxford St, London W1 (☎071/734 0393). Reliable discounted flight agent.

STA Travel, 74 Old Brompton Rd, London W7 (☎071/937 9962); 25 Queen's Rd, Bristol (☎0272/294 399); 38 Sidney St, Cambridge (☎0223/669 66); 75 Deansgate, Manchester (☎061/834 0668); and personal callers at 117 Euston Rd, London NW1; 28 Vicar Lane, Leeds; 36 George St, Oxford; and offices at the universities of Birmingham, London, Kent and Loughborough. Discount fares and special deals for students and young people.

SPECIALIST OPERATORS

Abreu, 109 Westbourne Grove, London W2 (☎071/229 9905/9906/9907). Portuguese-run agency – always worth a call for flights or coaches.

Allegro Holidays, Vanguard House, 277 London Rd, Burgess Hill, West Sussex (☎0444/248 222). Holidays in the Lisbon area, Minho and Algarve.

Beach Villas, 8 Market Passage, Cambridge (☎0223/311 113). Costa Verde, Sintra and Algarve.

Caravela Tours, 38–44 Gillingham St, London SW1 (☎071/630 5148). Charter wing of *TAP*. Offers stays in manor houses in the north, plus *pousadas* throughout the country.

Destination Portugal, 37 Corn St, Witney, Oxfordshire (☎0993/773 269). A most unusual agent, who claims to accommodate literally any Portuguese needs, from a flight-only deal, to car rental, villa and manor house lets, and national park hiking holidays. Highly recommended.

Explore Worldwide, 1 Frederick St, Aldershot (☎0252/344 161). Hiking specialist that offers small group tours in the Douro and Gerês.

Portugalicia, 110 Ladbroke Grove, London W10 (☎071/221 0333). Another agency run by (and

principally for) Portuguese nationals living in London.

Portugal Travel, 84 York St, London W1 (☎071/723 7774). Offers a full range of flights and holidays.

Portuguese Options, 26 Tottenham St, London W1 (☎071/436 3246). Tailor-made holidays.

Portuguese Travel Centre, 13 Beauchamp Place, London SW3 (☎071/581 3104). Flights, car rental, hotels and villas.

Something Special, 10 Bull Plain, Hertford, Herts (☎0992/552 231). Algarve villas.

Sunvil Holidays, 7–8 Upper Square, Isleworth, Middlesex (☎081/568 4499). Tailor-made itineraries to suit most budgets.

Travel Club of Upminster, Station Rd, Upminster, Essex (☎07082/25000). Long-established villa operator.

Travelscene, 11–15 St Ann's Rd, Harrow, Middlesex (☎081/427-8800). Weekend breaks.

Unicorn Holidays, 34–35 Cam Centre, Wilbury Way, Hitchin, Herts (☎0462/422 223). *Pousadas*, manor houses and fly-drive.

PACKAGE HOLIDAYS

Package holidays tend to concentrate on the Algarve, but there's a fair range of other possibilities, too. In addition to beach-and-villa or beach-and-hotel holidays, there are companies which arrange rooms in manor houses and *pousadas* (see p.23–24) and others which operate weekend breaks to Lisbon or organise sporting (mainly tennis and golf) holidays.

Standard villa/hotel breaks to the Algarve start at around £227 per person for a week in high season; in winter, you can get some very good deals and may pay around £50–60 less than this. **Specialist holidays** come a little pricier, say from around £400 for a week's golfing holiday based in a four-star hotel; though a three-night **weekend break** in Lisbon can be had for as little as £160 in winter, more like £250–300 in high season.

Virtually every UK holiday company operates in Portugal. There's a list of recommended specialist operators above, most of which are smaller companies, whose holidays tend to be directed towards individuals; all should be able to arrange flights and car rental. For a full list of companies offering holidays in Portugal, contact the Portuguese National Tourist Office (see p.15).

BY TRAIN

From London to Lisbon by train takes a minimum of 40 hours: setting out from Victoria Station, crossing the Channel at either Newhaven–Dieppe (the cheapest route) or Dover–Calais, changing trains in Paris (and transfering stations, from Nord to Austerlitz) and again at the Spanish border (at Hendaye/Irún or Cerbère/Port Bou). It's a good way to travel if you want to stop off in France or Spain on the way. But even if you qualify for under-26 or over-65 discounts, you are likely to pay more than if you just bought a charter flight.

There are two main **routes into Portugal**: from Paris via Irún, San Sebastian, Vilar Formoso, Guarda and Pampilhosa to Porto, Coimbra and Lisbon; and from Madrid via Cáceres to Marvão-Beirã, Abrantes and Entroncamento (where the line splits to Lisbon, or to Coimbra and Porto). A secondary route runs across northwestern Spain, through Santiago de Compostela and Vigo in Galicia, crossing the border at Tuy-Valença, from where it's an easy journey south to Porto.

The current standard **fare** from London to Lisbon is £218 return (Newhaven/Dieppe crossing included). If you're under-26, a **discounted ticket** (available from *Eurotrain* or *Wasteels*, see below) on the same route is £209, or £215 via Dover/Calais; in winter *Eurotrain* tickets are £25 cheaper as long as you don't travel out on a Friday. For trains direct to Faro, on the Algarve, add on another £15–20 to the above prices. All these tickets are valid for two months and stops are allowed anywhere along the way on a pre-specified route.

TRAIN CONNECTIONS FROM SPAIN

Flying to **Madrid** or **Málaga** may well work out cheaper than flying to Portugal and from either place train connections west are routine, with rewarding stops en route.

From Madrid, the most direct trains leave from the Estacion Atocha, reaching **Lisbon** (Santa Apolónia station) six to ten hours later. The fastest route is **via Badajoz**, the "gateway to Portugal", a close neighbour of the star-shaped fortress town of Elvas (see p.329), the first stop the train makes in Portugal. Other stops along this line, such as the lofty towns of Portalegre (p.333) and Abrantes (p.144) make this the recommended route through the country. Another attractive route from Madrid goes **via Valencia de Alcantara**, reaching Lisbon in nine to ten hours.

From Málaga you are well placed to head for the **Algarve** and if you have the time, you could take in a loop through the great Andalucian cities of Granada, Córdoba and Seville (though note that the Málaga–Granada and Granada–Córdoba journeys are quicker and easier by bus). At Córdoba, you're back on the main train line to Seville, with services to Huelva, from where buses run to the Portuguese border at Ayamonte–Vila Real de Santo António. Buses from Ayamonte, or a ferry ride across the Guadiana river, put you across the border at the Portuguese town of Vila Real, where you can join the Algarve train line, towards Faro and Lagos.

If you're working your way around Spain first, longer routes cross **from Old Castile** at Fuentes de Onoro (6hr to Lisbon) or, at more sociable hours, **from Vigo** in Galicia (3hr to Porto, 9hr to Lisbon).

However, none are a particularly good deal when compared to an **InterRail pass**. If you're under-26, this costs £249 for a month and gives unlimited travel on all European (and Moroccan) railways, and 30 percent discounts in Britain, on the English Channel ferries, and on ferries from Spain to the Balearic Islands or Morocco. For older travellers, there's an **InterRail 26-plus pass** at £269 for a month; however, this doesn't include travel in Spain, nor discounts on ferries nor travel within Britain. To qualify for either pass, you have to have been resident in Europe for six months. Less useful than these, given the distances involved in train travel to Portugal, is the **Eurail Flexipass**, valid for any five, ten, or fifteen days' travel on European trains within two months. Currently, for five days this costs £163 for under 26s, £219 for over 26s; ten days, £257/£365; and fifteen days, £343/£497.

Senior citizens holding a Senior Citizen Railcard can purchase a **Rail Europe Senior Card** for £5. This allows 30 percent discounts on rail fares throughout Europe, plus 30 percent off most ferry crossings. More details and tickets from British Rail stations.

BY BUS

If you can tolerate the long journey (40–45hr depending on your destination), the cheapest means of getting to Portugal is **by bus**. **Eurolines**, the foreign travel wing of *National Express*, operates a once-weekly service from London to Lisbon, Coimbra, Porto, Viseu, Guarda, Faro and Lagos. The current fare to Lisbon is £129 return (£91 for children aged 4–12); there are no student discounts. Tickets are available in Britain from any *National Express* or *Eurolines* agent (in effect most travel agents), or from Victoria Coach Station in London. You have to change in Paris from the London terminus at Place Stalingrad to the southbound one at Porte de Charenton – there should be a transfer bus, but it's an easy enough journey on the metro.

Alternatively, if you make your own way to **Paris**, there are buses six days a week (not Mon) to Lisbon, and fairly regular services to most other towns in Portugal. Coming back, providing you've made bookings in advance, you can join these buses at any stage. In Paris, tickets are sold at the Porte de Charenton terminus, and by a Portuguese agent at Boulevard Poniatowski 75, Paris (☎43 07 44 58).

TRAIN AND BUS INFORMATION

British Rail European Travel Centre, Victoria Station, London SW1 (☎071/834 2345).

Eurotrain, 52 Grosvenor Gardens, London SW1 (☎071/730 3402).

National Express Eurolines (☎071/730 0202).

Wasteels, 121 Wilton Rd, London SW1 (☎071/834 7066).

Tiring though these journeys are, they're comfortable enough, and broken by frequent rest and meal stops. As long as you take plenty to eat, drink and read, as well as a certain amount of French and Spanish currency to use along the way, you should emerge relatively unscathed.

BY CAR: THE FERRIES

The only way of substantially cutting down on the driving time to Portugal is to take the ferry from **Plymouth** (Nov–March) or **Portsmouth** (April–Oct) to **Santander** in northern Spain, though this is an expensive route – and it still means a long day's drive before you reach Portugal itself. The ferry crossing takes 24 hours and the boat runs twice weekly for most of the year (once a week in January, and with a three-week gap around Christmas) carrying cars and passengers. Seat prices for a one-way trip cost up to £80 according to the season, cars from £85–155. Details and tickets are available from most travel agents or direct from **Brittany Ferries**, Plymouth (☎0752/221321).

Driving through France, your route obviously depends on what you want to see along the way. The quickest route is to take the coast road via Nantes and Bordeaux, entering Spain at Irún. This can be followed from the standard **channel ports** (Calais, Boulogne or Dieppe) or, further to the west, off the **ferries** from Portsmouth–Cherbourg (4hr 30min; *P&O*), Poole–Cherbourg (4hr; *Brittany Ferries*), Weymouth–Cherbourg (4hr; March–Oct only; *Sealink*), Portsmouth–Caen (5hr 45min; *Brittany Ferries*), Portsmouth–St Malo (9hr; *Brittany Ferries*) or Plymouth–Roscoff (6hr; *Brittany Ferries*).

Ferry costs vary enormously and depend on the size of car, number of passengers and, especially, the season – from October to March there are very good deals on all the longer crossings. You're looking at around £50 return for a cross-

Channel foot-passenger fare and from £140–320 return for a car (plus up to five passengers), depending on the season. Crossing from Portsmouth or Plymouth is a little more expensive, but may of course be much more convenient if you live west of London. Full details can be obtained from travel agents or from **Sealink** (☎0233/647 047), **P&O** (☎0304/203 388) and **Brittany Ferries** (☎0752/221 321).

HITCHING

If you're **hitching** the best plan is to get as far south into France as you can afford by some other means. Hitching out of the channel ports is a nightmare, as it is from Paris and the 100km or so around the capital. Try taking the bus as far as Tours or the train to Chartres. From there it's not too far to Irún, and once in Spain local buses and trains are cheap fallbacks if necessary.

Freewheelers (☎071/738 6861) is a London-based **lift-sharing service** which is free to drivers and costs passengers a few pounds in fees plus any arrangements they make with the driver – typically about 3p per mile. Lifts to Portugal (but more frequently Spain) are most common in summer and work out at around half the price of a bus fare. Alternatively, *Allostop*, the French hitch-hiking association, will enrol you for a single journey and put you in touch with a driver going your way (to whom you contribute petrol costs). The Paris *Allostop* office is at Passage Brady 84 (☎42 46 00 66: open Mon–Fri 9am–1pm & 2–6pm).

GETTING THERE FROM IRELAND

Summer charter flights to Faro are easy to pick up from either Dublin or Belfast, while year-round scheduled services operate to Lisbon. However, the cheaper flights, including the majority of the youth/student offers, are often via London or Manchester, with an add-on fare from Ireland for the connection.

TAP has direct **scheduled** flights in the summer only from Dublin to Portugal; all *BA* flights to Portugal are via London. Summer **charters** from Dublin to Faro cost around £IR80–200 return; £IR250 return on scheduled services to Lisbon. Or you can fly from Belfast to Faro for around £230 return. Taking a **package holiday** is one way to cut these costs, with one week's villa or hotel holiday in the Algarve costing from around £IR240–260.

If you're really trying to get there in the cheapest possible way, you might find that budget flights from Dublin (with *Ryanair*, *Aer Lingus* and *British Midland*) or Belfast (*British Airways* and *British Midland*) to London, plus a last-minute London–Faro charter flight, will save you a few pounds, but don't count on it. Buying a *Eurotrain* ticket from Dublin to London will slightly undercut the plane's price, but by this time you're starting to talk about a journey of days and not hours.

GETTING THERE FROM NORTH AMERICA

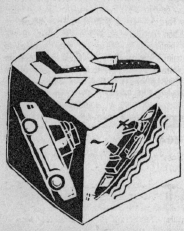

Flying to Portugal directly from North America is more feasible than it used to be. *TAP* **(the Portuguese national airline) has a range of flights available, while deals and routes have opened up in general as it dawns on both the travel industry and consumers that Portugal is one of the few European countries where the dollar is still worth something.**

However, unless time is your only consideration, you can, on the whole, get better-priced tickets to Spain, making your own way on to Portugal by train or bus. Similarly, you may want to consider flying first to London and then picking up one of the cheap British charters on to Portugal. For Canadians, in particular, this can make a large saving on travel budgets. See "Getting There from Britain", above, for all the relevant details; and see "Getting Around", p.20, for details of the *Eurail* pass, which can get you from London or elsewhere in Europe to Portugal by train.

FROM THE US

Most scheduled and charter flights to Portugal originate in New York, Boston, Montréal or Miami, and if you want to travel direct you'll generally do best to buy an add-on ticket to one of these "gateway" cities. The choice is greater (but the fares are no cheaper) if you're prepared to fly **via Madrid** or one of several other European hubs.

TAP (the Portuguese national airline), *TWA* and *Delta* are the main scheduled operators to Lisbon, and the ones most often used by discount flight brokers; *TAP* also offers flights to Porto and Faro (via Lisbon). *Iberia* flies to Porto (via Madrid), and also to Santiago de Compostela in northwestern Spain, just a couple of hours by car or train from the Portuguese border. Various other European carriers fly on to Porto and Faro via their respective capitals.

Discounted tickets aside, the cheapest way to go is with an **Apex** (Advance Purchase Excursion) ticket, although this carries certain restrictions: you have to book – and pay – at least 21 days before departure, spend at least seven days abroad (maximum stay three months), and face penalties if you change your schedule. There are also winter **Super Apex** tickets, sometimes known as "Eurosavers" – slightly cheaper than an ordinary Apex, but limiting your stay to between 7 and 21 days. Some airlines issue **Special Apex** tickets to those under 24, often extending the maximum stay to a year.

However, discount outlets, advertised in Sunday newspaper travel sections such as that in the *New York Times*, can usually do better than any Apex fare. They come in several forms. **Consolidators** buy up large blocks of tickets that airlines don't think they'll be able to sell at their published fares, and sell them at a discount. Besides being cheap, consolidators normally don't impose advance purchase requirements (although in busy times you'll want to book ahead to be sure of getting a ticket), but they do often charge very stiff fees for date changes. Also, these companies' margins are tiny, so they make their money by dealing in volume – don't expect them to entertain lots of questions. **Discount agents** also wheel and deal in blocks of tickets offloaded by the airlines, but they typically offer a range of other travel-related services such as travel insurance, rail passes, youth and student ID cards, car rental, tours, and the like. These agencies tend to be most worthwhile to students and under-26s, who can often benefit from special fares and deals. **Travel clubs** are another option for those who travel a lot – most charge an annual membership fee, which may be worth it for discounts on air tickets and car rental.

Regardless of where you buy your ticket, the **fare** will depend on the season. Fares to Portugal (like the rest of Europe) are highest from around early June to the end of August; they drop during the "shoulder" seasons (Sept–Oct and April–May), and you'll get the best deals during the low season, November through March (excluding Christmas). Note that flying on weekends ordinarily adds $50 to the round-trip fare. **Price ranges quoted in the sections below assume midweek travel.**

FROM EASTERN AND CENTRAL USA

Currently, *TAP*'s cheapest round-trip fare **from New York/Boston** to Lisbon is around $630 in low season, $860 in high season; fares to Porto or Faro are around $40 more. **From Miami** to Lisbon, *Iberia* charges $720 in low season, $1150 in high (and the same price for Santiago in Spain). There are no direct scheduled flights **from central US cities** to Lisbon, but it's easy enough to pick up a flight to New York, which will typically add $200–400 to the New York–Lisbon fare.

USEFUL ADDRESSES IN NORTH AMERICA

TOUR OPERATORS

Abreu Tours, 317 E. 34th St., New York, NY 10016 (☎800/223-1580). *Pousada* bookings and tailor-made holidays.

Altamira Tours, 860 Detroit St., Denver, CO 80206 (☎800/747-2869). Specialises in wine tours to the north of Portugal.

American Express, World Financial Center, New York, NY 10285 (☎800/241-1700). Packages, city breaks, etc, all over Europe.

Contiki Holidays, 300 Plaza Alicante, Suite 900, Garden Grove, CA (☎800/466-0610). Coach tours for under-35s through Europe.

Cosmos/Global Gateway, 92-25 Queens Blvd, Rego Park, NY 11374 (☎800/221-0090). The leading US budget tour operators to Europe. Bookable through travel agents only.

Cycling Through The Centuries, PO Box 877, San Antonio, FL 33576 (☎800/245-4226). Cycling holidays in Alentejo, Minho and the Algarve.

Discovery Vacations, 399 Market St., Newark, NJ 07105 (☎800/221-7370). *TAP*'s tour arm.

Europe Through the Back Door Tours, 109 4th Ave. N, Box C-20009, Edmonds, WA 98020 (☎206/771-8303). Excellent travel club which publishes a regular newsletter packed full of travel tales and advice, sells its own guides and travel accessories, *Eurail* passes, and runs good-value bus tours taking in the biggest European cities.

Europe Train Tours, 198 Boston Post Rd, Mamaroneck, NY 105431 (☎800/551-2085). Rail specialist.

Jet Vacations, 1775 Broadway, New York, NY 10019 (☎800/538-2999). European package specialist.

Marsans International, 19 W 34th St, Suite 302, New York, NY 10001 (☎800/777-9110). Major packager of Portuguese tours.

AIRLINES

Air France, (☎800/237-2747). Flies from many cities to Paris and then on to Lisbon, Porto and various Spanish destinations.

American Airlines, (☎800/433-7300). Dallas and Miami to Madrid.

British Airways, (☎800/247-9297; in Canada, ☎800/668-1059). Flies from many cities to London, with connections to Lisbon, Faro and Porto and Spanish cities.

Continental Airlines, (☎800/231-0856). Newark to Madrid.

Delta Airlines, (☎800/241-4141). New York to Lisbon, Atlanta to Madrid.

Iberia, (☎800/772-4642). Flights from many cities to Madrid, with connections to Lisbon, Porto and Spanish cities.

KLM, (☎800/374-7747). Numerous flights, via Amsterdam, to Lisbon, Porto, Faro and Spanish cities.

Lufthansa, (☎800/645-3880). Flights from many cities to Lisbon, Porto, Faro and Spain, all via Frankfurt.

Sabena, (☎800/955-2000). Flights from East Coast cities to Brussels and on to Lisbon, Porto and Spain.

TAP Air Portugal, (☎800/221-7370). New York, Boston, Toronto and Montréal to Lisbon, Porto, and Faro.

TWA, (☎800/892-4141). New York to Madrid and Lisbon.

United Airlines, (☎800/538-2929). Washington, DC to Madrid.

DISCOUNT AGENTS, CONSOLIDATORS & TRAVEL CLUBS

Council Travel, Head Office, 205 E 42nd St, New York, NY 10017 (☎800/743-1823); offices at 312 Sutter St, Suite 407, San Francisco, CA 94108; 14515 Ventura Blvd, Suite 250, Sherman Oaks, CA 91403; 1138 13th St, Boulder, CO 80302; 1210 Potomac St NW, Washington, DC 20007; 1153 N Dearborn St, Chicago, IL 60610; 729 Boylston St, Suite 201, Boston, MA 02116; 1501 University Ave SE, Room 300, Minneapolis, MN 55414; 2000 Guadalupe St, Suite 6, Austin, TX 78705; 1314 Northeast 43rd St, Suite 210, Seattle, WA 98105. Nationwide US student travel organisation.

Discount Travel International, Ives Bldg, 114 Forrest Ave, Suite 205, Narberth, PA 19072 (☎800/334-9294). Discount travel club.

Encore Travel Club, 4501 Forbes Blvd, Lanham, MD 20706 (☎301/459-8020). East Coast travel club.

Interworld, 800 Douglass Rd, Miami, FL 33134 (☎305/443-4929). Southeastern US consolidator.

Moment's Notice, 425 Madison Ave, New York, NY 10017 (☎212/486-0503). Discount travel club.

New Frontiers/Nouvelles Frontières, 12 E 33rd St, New York, NY 10016 (☎800/366-6387); 1001 Sherbrook East, Suite 720, Montréal,H2L 1L3 (☎514/526-8444). French discount firm. Other branches in LA, San Francisco and Quebec City.

STA Travel, ☎800/777-0112 (nationwide); 48 E 11th St, Suite 805, New York, NY 10003 (telesales ☎212/986 9470); 7202 Melrose Ave, Los Angeles, CA 90046 (tele-sales ☎213/937 5781); 82 Shattuck Sq, Berkeley, CA 94704 (☎510/841

1037); 166 Geary St, Suite 702, San Francisco, CA 94108 (☎415/391 8407); 273 Newbury St, Boston, MA 02116; (☎617/266-6014). Worldwide specialist in independent travel.

Stand Buys, 311 W Superior St, Chicago, IL 60610 (☎800/255-0200). Midwestern travel club.

Travel Cuts, Head Office: 187 College St, Toronto, ON M5T 1P7 (☎416/979-2406). Others include: MacEwan Hall Student Centre, University of Calgary, Calgary, AL T2N 1N4 (☎403/282-7687); 12304 Jasper Av, Edmonton, AL T5N 3K5 (☎403/488 8487); 6139 South St, Halifax, NS B3H 4J2 (☎902/494-7027); 1613 Rue St Denis, Montréal, PQ H2X 3K3; (☎514/843-8511); 1 Stewart St, Ottawa, ON K1N 6H7 (☎613/238 8222); 100–2383 CH St Foy, St Foy, G1V 1T1 (☎418/654 0224); Place Riel Campus Centre, University of Saskatchewan, Saskatoon S7N 0W0 (☎306/975-3722); 501–602 W Hastings, Vancouver V6B 1P2 (☎604/681 9136); University Centre, University of Manitoba, Winnipeg R3T 2N2 (☎204/269-9530). Canadian student travel organisation.

Travelers Advantage, 49 Music Sq. West, Nashville, TN 37204 (☎800/344-2334). Reliable travel club.

Travac, 989 6th Ave., New York NY 10018 (☎800/872-8800). US consolidator.

Unitravel, 1177 N Warson Rd, St Louis, MO 63132 (☎800/325-2222). US consolidator.

Worldwide Discount Travel Club, 1674 Meridian Ave, Miami Beach, FL 33139 (☎305/534-2082). Florida-based travel club.

Booking through a discount agent, you can expect the following minimum fare ranges to Lisbon: from New York, $550–750, depending on season; Miami, $630–820; Chicago, $600–800; and Denver or Houston, $660–850. By comparison, the cheapest round-trip flights from New York to Madrid run about $100 less.

FROM THE WEST COAST

All flights to Portugal from the West Coast involve changing planes, either in New York or somewhere in Europe. *TAP*'s APEX fares **from Los Angeles**, **San Fransisco** or **Seattle** (using feeder flights on other carriers to get to New York) cost at least $800 in low season, $1250 in high season. *Iberia* offers a nonstop service from Los Angeles to Madrid or Santiago for the same price.

Most of the discount travel brokers can't do much better than the airlines from the West Coast to Lisbon, but they're generally able to turn up cheaper deals **to Madrid**: figure $600–1000.

FROM CANADA

In Canada, you'll always get the best deals flying **from Toronto** and **Montréal**. *TAP* flies nonstop from Montréal to Lisbon, and many other European airlines fly from both cities to London, with connections to Lisbon. APEX fares from Toronto/Montréal to Lisbon typically run in the region of CDN$780 low season, $1070 high (*TAP* provides connecting flights to Faro and Porto at no extra charge). Discount agents, which deal mainly in flights via London, charge roughly the same.

West of the Rockies you're probably better off flying **from Vancouver** to London (from $750–$1050 return) and then continuing on to Lisbon, or alternatively getting a flight from Seattle to Madrid. Note that neither *Air Canada* nor *Canadian Airlines* flies to Portugal or Spain.

GETTING THERE FROM AUSTRALASIA

There are no direct flights to Portugal from Australia or New Zealand, but changing planes a couple of times can get you there surprisingly quickly, via stopovers in Europe, Asia or the Pacific.

Air France, Aeroflot or combined services with *KLM/Singapore Airlines*, and *Qantas/Alitalia/BA*, can all get you to Lisbon in around 24 hours flying time. Alternatively, you can find a rock-bottom fare to Amsterdam, London or other European hub city and then either pick up a cheap charter flight or travel overland – see "Getting There from Britain" above for more details. However, with the high living and transport costs in north-western Europe, this rarely works out any cheaper in practice. **Round-the-World** (RTW) tickets (valid for a year) are a better choice; they are usually priced according to the number of stopovers you make, but extras are not always expensive. A *Qantas/BA Global Explorer* RTW ticket, allowing six stopovers in any city the airlines fly to (including Lisbon), currently costs

---

USEFUL ADDRESSES IN AUSTRALASIA

AIRLINES

Aeroflot, 388 George St, Sydney (☎02/233 7911). Sydney to Moscow and Lisbon once a week.

Air France, 12 Castlereagh St, Sydney (☎02/233 3277); 57 Fort St, Auckland (☎09/303 1229). Once weekly from Sydney and Auckland via the Pacific islands and Paris to Lisbon.

Qantas, corner of Hunter and Phillip St, Sydney (☎02/952 9555); Qantas House, 154 Queen St,

Auckland (☎09/303 2506). Sydney to London, and regular connecting *BA* flights to Lisbon; Auckland to Rome for a connecting *Alitalia* flight to Lisbon three times a week.

Singapore Airlines, 5 Elizabeth St, Sydney (☎02/231 6333). Four flights a week from Sydney to Amsterdam, with connecting *KLM* services to Lisbon.

AUSTRALIAN DISCOUNT AGENTS

Anywhere Travel, 345 Anzac Parade, Kingsford, Sydney (☎02/663 0411).

Brisbane Discount Travel, 360 Queen St, Brisbane (☎07/229 9211).

Discount Travel Specialists, Shop 53, Forrest Chase, Perth (☎09/221 1400).

Flight Centres, Circular Quay, Sydney (☎02/241 2422); Bourke St, Melbourne (☎03/650 2899); plus branches nationwide except Northern Territory.

STA Travel, 732 Harris St, Sydney (☎02/212 1255); 256 Flinders St, Melbourne (☎03/347 4711); other offices in Townsville and state capitals.

Topdeck Travel, 45 Grenfell St, Adelaide (☎08/410 1110).

Tymtro Travel, Suite G12, Wallaceway Shopping Centre, Chatswood, Sydney (☎02/411 1222).

Passport Travel, 320b Glenfarrie Rd, Malvern, Melbourne (☎03/824 7183).

NEW ZEALAND DISCOUNT AGENTS

Budget Travel, PO Box 505, Auckland (☎09/309 4313).

Flight Centres, National Bank Towers, 205–225 Queen St, Auckland (☎09/309 6171); Shop 1M, National Mutual Arcade, 152 Hereford St, Christchurch (☎09/379 7145); 50–52 Willis St,

Wellington (☎04/472 8101); other branches countrywide.

STA Travel, Traveller's Centre, 10 High St, Auckland (☎09/309 9995); 233 Cuba St, Wellington (☎04/385 0561); 223 High St, Christchurch (☎03/379 9098); other offices in Dunedin, Palmerston North and Hamilton.

from A$2200–2700, or from around NZ$2500, depending on the season.

Fares to Portugal vary according to the season. December and January is high season; February and October to mid-November low season; rest of the year is shoulder season. **Standard low/high season fares to Lisbon** are currently around A$2000/2200 from eastern Australia; AS$1990/2200 from Perth; and NZ$2200/2600 from

Auckland. **Discount agents** can get you far better prices – from AS$1700/NZ$2155 for a low-season fare – but alterations and cancellations incur huge penalties.

Full-time students, and those under 26 or over 60, can also make big savings by contacting a specialist agent. Some agents are listed above, or check the travel pages of the weekend newspapers.

VISAS AND RED TAPE

Citizens of European Community states need only a valid passport or identity card for entry to Portugal, and can stay for up to ninety days. Australian and New Zealand nationals may also stay up to ninety days on

production of a passport; American and Canadian nationals can stay up to sixty days.

For **longer stays** you can apply for an extension once you're in the country. These are issued by the nearest District Police headquarters or the Foreigner's Registration Service (Avda. António Augusto de Aguilar 20, Lisbon; ☎01/52 33 24) which has branch offices – *Serviço de Estrangeiros* – in most major tourist centres. You should apply at least a week before your time runs out and be prepared to prove that you can support yourself without working (for example by keeping your bank exchange forms every time you change money). One well-used way around the bureaucracy is simply to leave the country for a couple of days and get a new sixty- or ninety-day stay stamped in your passport when you return.

Visas or extended stay visas are also available through any **Portuguese Consulate** abroad; see below for addresses.

PORTUGUESE CONSULATES AND EMBASSIES ABROAD

Australia
Embassy: 6 Campion Street, 1st floor, Canberra, ACT 2600 (☎06/852 084).

Britain
Consulate: 62 Brompton Road, London SW3 (☎071/581 8722/8723/8724).

Canada
Embassy: 645 Island Park Drive, Ottawa K1Y OB8 (☎613/729-2922). Consulates in several other cities.

Ireland
Embassy: Knock Sinna House, Fox Rock, Dublin 18 (☎01/289 4416).

Netherlands
Embassy: Willenskade 18, 3016 TL, Rotterdam (☎010/411 1540).

New Zealand
Embassy: 117 Armey Rd, Remuera, Auckland 5 (☎09/548 266).

Sweden
Embassy: Fredrikshovagadam 5/3, PO Box 27004, Stockholm (☎8/662 6028).

USA
Embassy: 2125 Kalorama Rd. NW, Washington DC 20008 (☎202/328-8610). Consulates in nearly a dozen other cities.

HEALTH AND INSURANCE

No inoculations are required for Portugal, though, as throughout southern Europe, it's a sensible precaution to have a typhoid shot and an up-to-date polio booster. A hepatitis jab is also worth considering, as there have been recent outbreaks along parts of the coastline around Porto.

Whatever you might hear from hypochondriacs, water is drinkable from the tap anywhere in the country, and from some freshwater sources. too. Be wary, however, of pools and streams in the south of the country. Otherwise, Portugal poses few health problems. **Mosquitoes** can be an intolerable menace at certain times of year and in certain areas, but there seems to be no pattern to this, though the north is often cited as being particularly bad. December and January are usually mosquito-free. Mosquito-repellent lotion and coils are widely sold in towns and resorts.

MEDICAL MATTERS

For minor health complaints in Portugal you should go to a **farmácia** (pharmacy), which you'll find in almost any village; in larger towns there's usually one where English is spoken. Pharmacists are highly trained and can dispense many drugs that would be available only with a prescription in Britain or North America.

In the case of serious illness, you can get the address of an **English-speaking doctor** from a British or American consular office or, with luck, from the local police or tourist office, or a major hotel. There's a *British Hospital* in Lisbon (see "Listings", p.84); other hospitals in major towns

are given in the text. In an **emergency** dial ☎115 (free).

TRAVEL INSURANCE

As an EC country, Portugal has free reciprocal health agreements with other member states. To take advantage EC citizens will need form E111, available from main post offices. Reassuring as the EC health agreements may sound, however, some form of **travel insurance** is still worthwhile – and essential for North Americans and Australasians, who must pay for any medical treatment in Portugal.

In many parts of Portugal public health care lags behind much of northern Europe and you may well prefer to get private treatment. With insurance you have to pay on the spot, but will be able to claim back the cost – along with any drugs prescribed by pharmacies. Be sure to keep all your receipts. Travel insurance usually provides cover for your **baggage, money and tickets**, too, should they be stolen, though to reclaim from your insurance company you must register any theft with the police within 24 hours.

EUROPEAN COVER

In Britain and Ireland, insurance schemes are sold by almost every travel agent and bank, or consider using a specialist insurance firm. Policies issued by *Campus Travel* (see p.4 for address), *Endsleigh* (Cranfield House, 97–107 Southampton Row, London WC1; ☎071/436 4451), or *Columbus Travel Insurance* (17 Devonshire Square, London EC2; ☎071/375 0011), are all good value, costing around £15 for two week's basic cover.

Be aware, too, of the cover offered by various **credit card companies** for holidays bought on their account; *Visa* and *American Express* offer some medical and theft coverage against items and travel arrangements paid for with their cards.

NORTH AMERICAN COVER

North Americans should check on existing cover (including bank and charge card benefits) before buying special travel insurance. For example, **Canadians** are usually covered for medical expenses by their provincial health plans. Holders of **ISIC** student identity cards are entitled to accident coverage and sixty days of hospital inpatient benefits for the period during which the card is valid. **University students** will often find that their student health coverage extends for one term beyond the date of last enrolment. **Company** plans may take care of most contingencies, and **homeowners' or renters'** insurance may cover overseas theft or loss of documents, money, and valuables.

If, after exhausting the above possibilities, you feel you still need additional travel insurance, your travel agent can recommend a policy. Most

offerings are quite comprehensive, though **premiums** vary widely, starting at around US$50 for 15 days, $80 a month; it's worth knowing that policies offered through student/youth agencies are often available to everyone.

If you are travelling for some length of time in Europe, or if you are stopping en route in Britain, it is worth considering taking out a British travel insurance policy, which routinely cover thefts – sometimes excluded from the more health-based American policies.

DISABLED TRAVELLERS

Portugal is only slowly coming to terms with the needs of travellers with disabilities and you should not expect much in the way of special facilities. That said, the Portuguese themselves always seem ready to help and people will go out of their way to make your visit as straightforward as possible.

Facilities that do exist include adapted WCs and wheelchair facilities at airports and main train stations; a "dial-a-ride" system for wheelchair users in Lisbon (call ☎01/63 20 44); and reserved disabled parking spaces in main cities.

Portuguese national tourist offices abroad can supply a list of wheelchair accessible hotels and campsites. Once there, your first port of call in

any town should be the local tourist office, or *Turismo*, which will invariably find you a suitable hotel and, in smaller towns, may personally organise your needs.

As far as **airlines** go, *British Airways* has a better-than-average record for treatment of disabled passengers, and coming from North America, *Virgin* and *Air Canada* come out tops in terms of disability awareness (and seating arrangements) and might be worth contacting first for any information they can provide.

For other **information**, contact one of the organisations listed below; and see *Nothing Ventured: Disabled People Travel the World* (a *Rough Guide* special), published in North America as *Able to Travel* (Penguin).

USEFUL ADDRESSES

PORTUGAL

ARAC, Rua Dr António Candido 8, 1097 Lisbon (☎01/56 37 37). Provides rental cars with hand controls, though you're advised to write or call first.
Institute for the Promotion of Tourism (*IPT*), Rua Alexandre Herculano 51, 1200 Lisbon (☎01/68 11 74). Publishes a list of hotels that are "without

barriers or with few obstacles to wheelchair users".
Secretariado Nacional de Reabilitação, Avda. Conde de Valbom 63, 1000 Lisbon (☎01/76 10 81). Provides information on transport facilities and Lisbon access, but in Portuguese only.

BRITAIN

Holiday Care Service, 2 Old Bank Chambers, Station Rd, Horley, Surrey RH6 9HW (☎0293/774535). Information on all aspects of travel.
Mobility International, 228 Borough High St, London SE1 1JX (☎071/403 5688). Information,

access guides, and a variety of tours and exchange programmes.
RADAR, 25 Mortimer St, London W1N 8AB (☎071/637 5400). A good source of advice on holidays and travel abroad.

NORTH AMERICA

Mobility International USA, PO Box 3551, Eugene, OR 97403 (☎503/343 1248). Provides

information, access guides, tours and exchange programmes.

INFORMATION AND MAPS

You can pick up a wide range of brochures and maps, for free, from the Portuguese National Tourist Office (see below for addresses). Though some of their descriptions are best taken with a grain of salt, it is well worth contacting one of their offices for information before you leave home.

In Portugal itself you'll find a tourist office, or *Turismo*, in almost every town and village of any size. Most are detailed in the guide and the vast majority are exceptionally helpful and friendly. Aside from the help they can give you in finding a room (some will make bookings, others simply supply lists), they often have useful local maps and leaflets that you won't find in the national offices. Local tourist office **opening hours** are

generally Monday to Saturday 9am–12.30pm and 2–6pm, though in Porto, Lisbon, the Algarve and other resorts they often stay open later than this, and open on Sunday, too. In more out-of-the-way towns and villages, offices will be closed at weekends.

MAPS

The Portuguese National Tourist Office can provide you with a reasonable **map** of the country. However, if you're doing any real exploration, or driving, it's worth investing in a good **road map**. The best maps available abroad are *Michelin*'s 1:400,000 "Portugal" (#440); or *Geo Centre*'s *Euro Map* "Portugal and Galicia" at 1:300,000. *Geo Centre* also produces a 1:200,000 map of the Algarve and a 1:250,000 map of the Lisbon area; *Bartholomew's Algarve Holiday Map* (1:100,000) is good, too. If you're planning on spending more than a day or two in Lisbon, the German *Falk Plan* of the city is unequalled.

More detailed topographic **maps for walkers** can be obtained in Lisbon at the *Serviços Cartográficos do Exército* (Avda. Dr. Alfredo Bensaúde, Olivais Norte), and in Porto at *Porto Editora*, Rua da Fábrica. Many of these topographic maps are disastrously out of date – none have been revised since Portugal began its motorway programme – but they're the best you'll get.

Most general and regional Portuguese maps can be ordered through one of the map suppliers in Britain and North America detailed in the box below.

PORTUGUESE TOURIST OFFICES ABROAD

Britain
22/25a Sackville Street, London W1 (☎071/494 1441).

Canada
500 Sherbooke West #930, Montréal, Québec H3A 3C6 (☎514/843 4623); 60 Bloor St West, Suite 1005, Toronto, Ontario M4W 3BS (☎416/921 7376).

Ireland
c/o Portuguese Embassy, Knock Sinna House, Fox Rock, Dublin 18 (☎01/289 4416).

Netherlands
Stadhouderskade 57, 1072 AC Amsterdam (☎20/675 0301).

Spain
Gran Via 27, Madrid 28013 (☎91/522 4408).

Sweden
Linnegatan 2S, 11447, Stockholm (☎08/660 2654)

USA
590 Fifth Avenue, 4th floor, New York NY10036 (☎212/354 4403).

There are no offices in Australia or New Zealand.

MAP OUTLETS IN THE UK

London

National Map Centre, 22–24 Caxton St, SW1
(☎071/222 4945);

Stanfords, 12–14 Long Acre, WC2
(☎071/836 1321);

The Travellers Bookshop, 25 Cecil Court, WC2
(☎071/836 9132).

Edinburgh

Thomas Nelson and Sons Ltd, 51 York Place, EH1
3JD (☎031/557 3011).

Glasgow

John Smith and Sons, 57–61 St Vincent St
(☎041/221 7472).

Maps by **mail or phone order** are available from *Stanfords* (☎071/836 1321).

MAP OUTLETS IN NORTH AMERICA

Chicago

Rand McNally, 444 N Michigan Ave, IL 60611
(☎312/321-1751).

Montréal

Ulysses Travel Bookshop, 4176 St-Denis
(☎514/289-0993).

New York

British Travel Bookshop, 551 5th Ave, NY 10176
(☎1-800/448-3039 or ☎212/490-6688)

The Complete Traveler Bookstore, 199 Madison
Ave, NY 10016 (☎212/685-9007

Rand McNally, 150 East 52nd St, NY 10022
(☎212/758-7488);

Traveler's Bookstore, 22 West 52nd St, NY 10019
(☎212/664- 0995).

San Francisco

The Complete Traveler Bookstore, 3207 Filmore St,
CA 92123 (☎415/923-1511)

Rand McNally, 595 Market St, CA 94105 (☎415/
777-3131).

Seattle

Elliot Bay Book Company, 101 South Main St, WA
98104 (☎206/624-6600).

Toronto

Open Air Books and Maps, 25 Toronto St, M5R
2C1 (☎416/363-0719).

Vancouver

World Wide Books and Maps, 1247 Granville St.

Washington DC

Rand McNally, 1201 Connecticut Ave NW,
Washington DC 20036 (☎202/223-6751).

Note that *Rand McNally* now have 24 stores across the US; phone ☎1-800/333-0136 (ext 2111) for the
address of your nearest store, or for **direct mail** maps.

MAP OUTLETS IN AUSTRALIA

Adelaide

The Map Shop, 16a Peel St, Adelaide, SA 5000
(☎08/231 2033).

Brisbane

Hema, 239 George St, Brisbane, QLD 4000 (☎07/
221 4330).

Melbourne

Bowyangs, 372 Little Bourke St, Melbourne, VIC
3000 (☎03/670 4383).

Sydney

Travel Bookshop, 20 Bridge St, Sydney, NSW 2000
(☎02/241 3554).

Perth

Perth Map Centre, 891 Hay St, Perth, WA 6000
(☎09/322 5733).

COSTS, MONEY AND BANKS

The cost of living in Portugal has been edging up since entry into the EC in 1986 but as a tourist, you're unlikely to feel the pinch. Accommodation, transport, food and drink are much cheaper than in northern Europe – or North America – and, on the whole, better value than in Spain.

In most places you can get by on a budget of **around £25/US$40 a day**, which will get you a room for the night, picnic lunch, dinner with drinks in a restaurant, a bus or train ride, and a beer or two. By camping and being a little more frugal, you could reasonably expect to survive on less than this; while on £30–40/$45–60 a day you'll be living pretty well. It's worth noting that prices in the Algarve are higher than anywhere else in the country; expect things to cost up to 10 percent more in all the main tourist resorts.

SOME BASIC COSTS

Costs for a **double room** in the cheaper pensions work out at about £10–15/$15–23, rising to around £20–30/$30–45) in two- or three-star hotels and from £40–80/$60–120 in four-star places and *pousadas*. **Campsites** are a bargain at around £2–3/$3–5 a night per person, tent included, in all but the fanciest coastal sites.

You should always be able to get a substantial basic **meal** for around £5/$7.50; even dinner in the smarter restaurants is unlikely to cost more than £15/$23 a head. **Drink** costs are more than reasonable, too – a bottle of house wine rarely comes to more than £3/$5, a glass of the local brew in a bar around 30p/50c. Even **transport** is

hardly going to break the bank, especially since most distances you'll travel are fairly small and fares (especially on trains) low. From Porto to Lisbon, or Lisbon to the Algarve, for example, costs around £10/$15.

To some extent all these prices depend on **where and when you go** – the cities and developed tourist areas are invariably more expensive than elsewhere. As always, too, if you're travelling alone you'll spend considerably more than you would in a group of two or more people, sharing rooms and meals.

An **International Student Identity Card (ISIC)** is well worth having if you're eligible – it'll get you free or reduced admission to many museums and sights as well as other occasional discounts. The cards are available through *STA* and *Campus Travel/USIT* in Britain and Ireland, *Council Travel* in the US and *Travel CUTS* in Canada (see the relevant "Getting There" sections for addresses). Also of some use, giving similar discounts, is a **Federation of International Youth Travel Organisations (FIYTO)** youth card. This is available to anyone under 26, from the same outlets.

CURRENCY

The Portuguese currency unit is the **escudo ($)**, which is divided into 100 **centavos**. It is written with the $ sign in the middle: thus 100$50 is 100 *escudos* and fifty *centavos*. For the last few years, exchange rates have hovered around 250$00 to the pound sterling, 170$00 to the American dollar. You can buy *escudos* in advance at most European, US and Canadian banks. **Notes** come in denominations of 500$00, 1000$00, 2000$00, 5000$00 and 10,000$00; **coins** as $50, 1$00, 2$50, 5$00, 10$00, 20$00, 50$00, 100$00 and 200$00.

When travelling in rural areas, don't get stranded without **small notes and change**. A 10,000$00 note can be hard to change on a bus or at a small village market.

BANKS AND EXCHANGE

Recently introduced regulations have made it very expensive to change **travellers' cheques** in Portugal, but they're still the safest and easiest way to carry money. You can buy them at most banks (even if you don't have an account), or from offices of *Thomas Cook* and *American Express*. They are accepted by all Portuguese banks and by exchange bureaux (*cambios*) at airports and major train stations. Alternatively, most British banks can issue current account holders with a **Eurocheque** card and chequebook, with which you can pay for things in some shops and get cash from the majority of Portuguese banks; you'll pay a few pounds service charge a year but usually no commission on transactions.

Visa, *American Express*, and *Mastercard* are the most useful **credit cards** in Portugal, though many smaller places and even some upmarket hotels have no facilities to take payment with them. In the banks of large towns, however, there are increasing numbers of *Multibanco* Automatic Teller Machines (ATMs) for credit card **cash advances** (don't forget your PIN number). They charge interest on the withdrawal from day one,

plus a currency conversion fee, as do the banks which give cash advances on the cards over the counter. Among banks offering this service are *Banco Fonsecas & Burnay* and *Banco Pinto & Sotto Major*.

All banks now charge a hefty 2000$00 **commission** on changing travellers' cheques – so it is worth changing a reasonable amount of money at a time. There are much lower commissions on foreign currency exchanges at *caixas* – savings banks or building societies – though this of course means carrying around large amounts of foreign cash.

You'll find a **bank** in all but the smallest towns. Standard **opening hours** are Monday to Friday 8.30am–3pm. In Lisbon and in some of the Algarve resorts they may also open in the evening to change money, while some banks have installed **automatic exchange machines** for various currencies and denominations.

GETTING AROUND

Portugal is not a large country and you can get almost everywhere easily and efficiently by train or bus. Trains are often cheaper, and some lines highly scenic, but it's almost always quicker to go by bus – especially on shorter or less obvious routes. Approximate times and frequencies of most journeys are given in the "Travel Details" section at the end of each chapter; local connections and peculiarities are pointed out in the text.

Car rental is also worth considering if time is limited and you want to cover a lot of ground, though you may find you need nerves of steel to drive on some Portuguese roads.

TRAINS

CP, the Portuguese railway company, operates all trains. Most are designated *Regional*, which means they stop at most stations en route and have first- and second-class cars. The next category up, *Intercidades*, are twice as fast and twice as expensive, and you should reserve your seat in advance if using them. The fastest, most luxurious and priciest services are the *Rápidos* (known as "Alfa"), which speed between Lisbon, Coimbra and Porto – sometimes they have only first-class seats. Both these latter classes charge supplements for rail pass holders (see below).

Always turn up at the station with time to spare since long queues often form at the ticket desk. On certain trains, even with a rail pass, you'll need to queue up for seat reservations, too. If you end up on the train without first buying a ticket you could be liable for a huge supplement, payable to the ticket controller, or be kicked off the train by the guard at the next stop.

Complete **train timetables**, and timetables for individual lines, are available from information desks at main stations.

Sadly, several of the old narrow-gauge **mountain railways** of the north have been phased out, with the Tâmega, Corgo and Tua lines terminating, respectively, at Amarante, Vila Real and

PORTUGAL: TRAINS

To Tuy & Vigo

Valença
Caminha
Viana do Castelo
Barcelos
Braga
Bragança
Póvoa de Varzim
Guimarães
Vila Real
Mirandela
Amarante
Lousado
Porto
Régua
Tua
Pocinho
Espinho

Atlantic Ocean

Sernada
Vouzela
Viseu
Vilar Formoso
Aveiro
Nelas
To Salamanca & Paris
Cantanhede
Sta. Comba Dão
Guarda
Pampilhosa
Figueira da Foz
Coimbra
Covilhã
Lousã
Fundão

Pombal
Castelo Branco
Leiria
Tomar
Abrantes
Marvão
To Madrid
Caldas da Rainha
Entroncamento
Portalegre
Torres Vedras
Santarém
Setil

Sintra
Vendas Novas
Estremoz
Elvas
To Sevilla
Cascais
LISBON
Badajoz
Casa Branca
Évora
Vila Viçosa
Setúbal
Alcácer do Sal
Moura
Ermidas-Sado
Beja
Sines
Funcheira

SPAIN

1. Tâmega Line
2. Corgo Line
3. Tua Line
4. Douro Line
5. Vouga Line
6. Norte Line
7. Minho Line
8. Póvoa Line
9. Beira-Alta Line
10. Beira-Baixa Line
11. Leste Line
12. Portalegre Line
13. Oeste Line
14. Sul Line
15. Sado Line
16. Algarve Line

0   100 km

Silves
Tunes
Lagos
Tavira
Portimão
Faro
Vila Real de Sto. António
To Huelva & Sevilla

------ Lines replaced with CP buses

Mirandela. Several other minor lines have been closed, too, though some have at least been replaced by buses operated by *CP*. Regular train tickets and passes are valid on these bus lines.

Lastly, it's as well to note that train stations can be some miles from the town or village they serve — Portalegre station and town are 12km distant, for example — and there's no guarantee of connecting transport.

TICKETS AND PASSES

Train travel is relatively inexpensive and most visitors simply buy a ticket every time they make a journey; **children** under four go free, under 12s pay half price. **Senior citizens** (over-65s) can get half-price travel if they produce their passport (or other form of ID proving their age). It' est to travel on the main routes if you called "Blue Days" – ie Fridays, Sun noons, Monday mornings, national holidays and the day preceding a national holiday.

If you're planning on a lot of train travel, using a **rail pass** will probably save you money, though note that pass holders pay **supplements** on *Intercidades* and *Rápidos*. CP sells its own *Bilhete Turístico* rail pass (valid for first-class travel on all trains except the Lisbon–Madrid Talgo) for 15,200$00 (£60/$90) for 7 days, 24,200$00 (£97/$145) for 14 days, and 34,600$00 (£140/$210) for 21 days. There's also a *CP* family card (*cartão de família*) and group tickets (*bilhetes de grupo*), which offer varying reductions on tickets – more information from local stations.

You're more likely to be travelling on an *InterRail* or *Eurail* pass, both of which will get you across Europe to Portugal in the first place. For details of **InterRail**, see p.6, though note that unless you're planning to travel extensively by train you're unlikely to be able to make it pay on a short trip just to Portugal. What might be a Portugal **Eurodomino** pass (available in Britain from *Eurotrain*, see p.6), valid for three, five or ten days' unlimited travel on the Portuguese train network – the under-26 and over-26 prices are £62/£80, £77/£100 and £116/£151 respectively.

The North American equivalent of *InterRail* is the **Eurail Pass**, which is nowhere near as good a deal, unless you're planning to virtually live on European trains for the entire duration of the pass. The pass, which must be purchased before arrival in Europe, allows unlimited free train travel in Portugal and sixteen other countries. The *Eurail Youthpass* (for under-26s) costs US$578 for one month or $768 for two; if you're 26 or over you'll have to buy a first-class pass, available in 15-day ($498), 21-day ($648), one-month ($798), two-month ($1098) and three-month ($1398) formats. You stand a better chance of getting your money's worth out of a *Eurail* **Flexipass**, which is good for a certain number of travel days in a two-month period. This, too, comes in under-26 and first-class versions: 5 days cost $255/ $3498; 10 days, $398/$560; and 15 days, $540/ $740. North Americans are also eligible to purchase the more specific **Portuguese Railpass**, allowing 4 days' travel out of 15 ($95, all ages) or 7 days out of 21 ($145). All these passes can be reserved through *Rail Europe*, 226 Westchester Ave., White Plains, NY 10604 (☎800/438-7245) or youth-oriented travel agents (see the list on p.9).

BUSES

Buses shadow many of the main train routes as well as linking most of the country's smaller towns and villages. It's almost always quicker to go by bus if you can, though you'll pay slightly more than for the equivalent train ride. Comfortable express buses operate on longer routes, for which you'll usually have to reserve tickets in advance – certainly for the Lisbon–Algarve routes in summer.

Most services were operated until recently by the state-owned *Rodoviaria Nacional* (*RN*). This has now been privatised, though a national network of expresses (*Rede Expressos*) has been maintained. However, tourists remain largely unaffected by the organisational changes: although there are now many other private companies operating in competition, most have retained the same fleet of *RN* buses and staff.

The local bus station – detailed wherever possible in the text – is the place to pick up time-tables and reserve seats on long-distance journeys. Failing that, local tourist offices can usually help with bus information. It's as well to be aware that bus services are considerably less frequent – occasionally non-existent – at weekends, especially on rural routes; while at other times, you'll find that departures can be frighteningly early in the morning. This is because bus services are often designed to fit around school and market hours rather than for the needs of tourists.

DRIVING, CAR RENTAL AND HITCHING

With car rental rates among the lowest in Europe driving around Portugal is an option worth thinking about, even for just a part of your travels. **Petrol** (*super*), however, is relatively expensive: about 25 percent more than in Britain, and nearly twice the US equivalent. Unleaded petrol is now widely available (and most rental cars run on it).

Before you set out, bear in mind that Portugal has one of the highest **accident** rates in Europe. Portuguese driving can be crazy – no one seems to recognise the same set of rules and you'll find people driving at you at night on full beam, or coasting down the middle of the road and never observing a right-of-way. Even on motorways, you'll need to check your mirror every few seconds to make sure someone isn't right up your exhaust pipe. August is especially lethal, with Portuguese emigrant workers returning home in fast cars to show off to relatives.

The **motorway network** is gradually expanding outwards from a central spine that links Setúbal and Lisbon with Porto. Recent developments include the completion of stretches heading east, from Porto to Bragança, and from Aveiro to the Spanish border at Vilar Formoso. In the south, it's now possible to travel between Lisbon and the Algarve by motorway, and construction of the IP1 across the eastern Algarve to the Spanish border is well underway. The motorways are all **toll roads**, which adds to the cost of a journey (around £15/$23 from Lisbon to Porto) but has one distinct advantage for foreign visitors. Because of the relatively high tolls, local drivers have been priced off the motorways, making them the least congested in Europe and easily the quickest way to cover long distances.

Conversely, on **smaller roads**, you'll find the traffic much heavier: slow journeys stuck behind trucks on potholed roads are common. In addition, as car ownership has increased massively over recent years, towns can no longer cope with the traffic. Travelling by car, you'll have endless problems finding central parking spaces – Coimbra is notoriously awful. Only the top hotels have carparks; otherwise you can expect to spend ages looking for a space, often ending up on the outskirts of town and having to walk to the centre.

Traffic drives on the right; **speed limits** are 60km/hr in towns and villages; 90km/hr on normal roads; 120km/hr on motorways. At road junctions, unless there's a sign to the contrary, vehicles coming from the right have priority. If you're **stopped by the police**, they'll want to see your documents – carry them in the car at all times and be courteous to the officers (see "Police and Trouble", p.35).

If you **break down** you can get assistance from the *Automóvel Clube de Portugal* which has reciprocal arrangements with foreign automobile clubs. The head office is at Rua Rosa Araújo 24 (☎01/56 39 31); in the north, phone their Porto service on ☎02/31 67 32; in the south, phone Lisbon ☎01/942 50 95.

CAR RENTAL

Car rental agencies can be found in all the major towns and at the airports in Lisbon, Porto and Faro. Local agencies usually charge less than the big three – *Hertz, Avis* and *Europcar* – and we've listed addresses and phone numbers for some of them in the Lisbon, Porto and Algarve chapters; tourist offices can give details of others.

CAR RENTAL AGENCIES

Britain
Avis ☎081/848 8733.
Budget ☎0800/181 181.
Europcar/InterRent ☎0345/222 525
Hertz ☎081/679 1799.
Holiday Autos ☎071/491 1111.

North America
Europe by Car ☎800/223-1516.
Holiday Autos ☎800/442-7737.
National Car Rental ☎800/CAR-RENT.

Rates are reasonable, from around £100–120/$150–180 a week for the cheapest category car with unlimited mileage, though prices are inflated on the Algarve in high season. It's often a much better deal to **arrange rental before setting out**. In Britain, several of the specialist holiday companies detailed on p.4 will arrange car rental in conjunction with flights; or call one of the major car rental outfits listed in the box above. When picking up your car, check such important details as brakes and, if you're renting locally, **insurance coverage**. As you might have gathered, collision insurance is a good idea and unless you pay a separate supplement the initial several thousand *escudos'* worth of damage may be on your head. If you make any repairs along the way, keep the receipts – you may be able to get some money back from the company.

HITCHING

It can take hours to **hitch** out of Lisbon or Porto because there's nowhere good to stand – and, quite often, there's competition from Portuguese national servicemen. But most other towns are very small, their centres within easy reach of the main highways, and present no problems. The main difficulty – in a predominantly rural, village-oriented country – is that drivers tend not to be driving very far.

BIKES, MOPEDS AND MOTORBIKES

Bicycles are a great way of seeing the country, though everywhere north of Lisbon is hilly and you'll find pedalling hard work in mountainous Beira Alta or across the burned plains of southern Alentejo. It's inexpensive to transport t[...] trains (about 200$00), but the proced[...]

require some patience – you should arrive at the baggage office a good hour and a half before your train, and be prepared to pester someone into opening up the office. On long-distance international trains allow three days for the bike to arrive.

Although it's a hassle taking your own **bike by plane**, it really is worth it to have a decent machine with gears and brakes you can trust. Take sufficient **spares**, as you're not likely to find what you need except in large cities.

If all that legwork is not to your taste, you can rent **mopeds** and low-powered (80cc) **motorbikes** in many tourist areas, especially on the Algarve. Go easy, wear a helmet, and check all the cables before setting off.

ACCOMMODATION

In almost any Portuguese town you can find a pension offering a double room for around 3000$00 (£12/$18). You'll rarely find anything much cheaper than this – but then you're unlikely to have to pay much more either, except in Algarve resorts in high season, or in Lisbon. If you have the money to move upmarket, you're often spoilt for choice, with some wonderful manor houses in the north and a network of state-run *pousadas* scattered about the country.

Even in high season you shouldn't have much of a problem finding a bed in most of the Portuguese regions. However, parts of the Algarve are often a very different matter, with all rooms booked up for days ahead. Try and reserve in advance where you can, especially if you're arriving late in Faro.

YOUTH HOSTELS

There are 21 **youth hostels** (*Pousadas de Juventude*) in Portugal, open all year round. The price for a dormitory bed runs from around 900–1700$00 a night, depending on the location and season, a little extra if you need to hire sheets and blankets. The most expensive hostels are in Lisbon, Porto and on the Algarve.

Most have a curfew (usually 11pm or midnight) and all demand a valid *IYHF* card – available from your home-based youth hostel association (see below). In Portugal, the head office of the **Portuguese Youth Hostel Association** (*Associação de Utenes das Pousadas de Juventude*) is at Avenida Duque de Ávila 137, Lisbon (Mon–Fri 9.30am–12.45pm & 2–5.45pm; ☎01/355 98 01).

YOUTH HOSTEL ASSOCIATIONS

Australia *Australian Youth Hostels Association*, Level 3, 10 Mallett St, Camperdown, NSW (☎02/565-1325).

Canada *Canadian Hostelling Association*, 1600 James Naismith Drive, Suite 608, Gloucester, ON K1B 5N4 (☎613/748-5638).

England and Wales *Youth Hostel Association* (*YHA*), Trevelyan House, 8 St Stephen's Hill, St Alban's, Herts AL1 (☎07278/45047). London shop and information office: 14 Southampton St, London WC2 (☎071/836 1036).

Ireland *An Oige*, 39 Mountjoy Square, Dublin 1 (☎01/363111).

New Zealand *Youth Hostels Association of New Zealand*, PO Box 436, Christchurch 1 (☎03/799-970).

Northern Ireland *Youth Hostel Association of Northern Ireland*, 56 Bradbury Place, Belfast, BT7 (☎0232/324733).

Scotland *Scottish Youth Hostel Association*, 7 Glebe Crescent, Stirling, FK8 2JA (☎0786/51181).

USA *American Youth Hostels* (*AYH*), PO Box 37613, Washington, DC 20005 (☎202/783-6161).

All of the hostels are detailed in the guide. Among the best are those at Vilarinho das Furnas (in the Gerês National Park), Penhas de Saúde (in the Serra de Estrêla), São Martinho do Porto, Areia Branca, Oeiras (on the seafront near Lisbon), Coimbra, Alcoutim (northeastern Algarve), Portalegre (in a monastery) and Leiria (perhaps the best of the lot).

ROOMS AND PENSIONS

After hostels, the next rung up the accommodation ladder consists of **rooms** (*quartos* or *dormidas*) let out in private houses. Most commonly available in the seaside resorts, these are sometimes advertised, or more often hawked at bus and train stations. Rates should be a little below that of a pension, say 2000–3000$00 (£8–12/$12–18), though on the Algarve, in high season, you can expect to pay up to twice as much. It's always worth haggling over prices, especially if you're prepared to commit yourself to a longish stay. And always ask where the room is before you agree to take it – in the resorts you could end up miles from the town centre or beach.

The main budget travel standby is a room in a pension – a **pensão** (plural, *pensões*) – which are officially graded from one to three stars (often, it seems, in quite random fashion). Most serve meals, usually in a bargain-priced, all-inclusive package, but they rarely insist that you take them. Pensions that don't serve meals are sometimes called **residencials**., though in price and all other respects they are virtually identical. Similar to *pensões*, and generally at the cheaper end of the scale, are **hospedarias** or **casas de hóspedes** – boarding houses – which can be characterful places, though you don't see very many of them around these days.

Pension **prices** for a double room range from around 3000–7000$00 (£12–28/$18–42), depending on the season, and their location and facilities. Always ask to see the room before you take it, and don't be afraid to ask if there's a cheaper one – especially if you're travelling alone, in which case you'll frequently be asked to pay more or less the full price of a double. *Tem um quarto mais barato?* ("Do you have a cheaper room?") is the relevant phrase.

HOTELS AND POUSADAS

A one-star **hotel** usually costs about the same as a three-star *pensão*, though quirks abound in the official grading systems and establishments classified as one-star hotels often don't show any notable differences to pensions. Indeed, it's not uncommon to find a two- or three-star *pensão* offering much better quality rooms than a one-star hotel. Prices for two- and three-star hotels, though, see a notable shift upscale, with doubles running from 10,000$00 (£40/$60) upwards.

There's a further and more dramatic shift in rates as you move into the four- and five-star hotel league, where you'll pay anything from 15,000–30,000$00 (£60–120/$90–180) for a double. The very fanciest places, on the Algarve and in Lisbon, can pretty much charge what they like. **Estalagens** and **albergarias** are other designations of hotels in the same range.

One fairly surprising bargain is the chain of 32 government-run **pousadas**, often converted from old monasteries or castles, or located in dramatic countryside settings. They're rated in three categories, and charge different prices in low-, middle- and high-season; in some you'll pay as little as 7000$00 a double a night in winter, $10,000$00 in summer, though on average you

---

ACCOMMODATION PRICE CODES

All the accommodation prices in this book have been coded using the symbols below. The symbols represent the prices for the **cheapest available double room in high season**. Effectively this means that most rooms in places with a ① or ② category will be *without* private bath or shower, though there's usually a washbasin in the room. In places with a ③ category and above, you'll probably be getting private facilities; while many of the cheaper places may also have more expensive rooms with bath/shower if you ask.

Note that price codes are not given for youth hostels; see "Youth Hostels", p.22, for the rates at those.

① Under 3000$00 (under £12/$18)	② 3000$00–4000$00 (£12–16/$18–24)
③ 4000$00–5500$00 (£16–22/$24–33)	④ 5500$00–8500$00 (£22–34/$33–51)
⑤ 8500$00–12,500$00 (£34–50/$51–75)	⑥ 12,500$00–20,000$00 (£50–80/$75–120)
⑦ Over 20,000$00 (over £80/$120)	

can expect to pay more like 12,000–15,000$00 a night. We've detailed some of the most interesting places in the guide, like those at Évora, Estremoz and Óbidos. For a full list of *pousadas*, contact the Portuguese National Tourist Office in your home country, or *ENATUR*, Avenida Santa Joana Princesa 10, 1700 Lisbon (☎01/848 1221).

MANOR HOUSES AND VILLAS

An attractive alternative in the three- to four-star hotel price range is the accommodation marketed as **manor and country houses**: in effect upmarket B & B, offered by owners of "houses of distinction", ranging from great homes to more modest farmhouses. There are various schemes in operation around the country, most widely in Minho and around Sintra, where they are known as **Turihab** (*Turismo de Habitação*). Some of the best places are detailed in the text; otherwise, local tourist offices usually have information and leaflets. If you want to book in advance, several of the specialist holiday operators detailed on p.4 or p.9 can make arrangements for you, or the Portuguese National Tourist Office can send you a short *Guide to Manor and Country Houses*. In Portugal, you can contact the *Associação do Turismo de Habitação* (*Turihab*) at Praça da República, 4990, Ponte de Lima (☎058/94 23 35).

Holiday and tour operators are also the best sources if you want to rent a **villa** for your stay in Portugal. Summer sees most places booked solid months in advance, especially on the Algarve, but either side of the peak period you should be able to turn up in more out-of-the-way resorts like Tavira or Sagres and bag a self-catering apartment. The local Turismo will probably be able to help. In winter, prices can be very reasonable indeed.

CAMPING

Portugal has over a hundred authorised **campsites**, most of them small, low-key and attractively located. Charges are per person and per tent, with showers and parking extra; even so, it's rare that you'll end up paying more than 500–600$00 a person. Some are even cheaper than this; while those operated by the *Orbitur* chain are usually a little more expensive. The most useful are detailed in the text but you can get a fairly complete list from any Portuguese tourist office, or a detailed booklet called *Roteiro Campista* (with prices, exact locations, facilities, etc) from Portuguese bookshops.

You'll need an **international camping carnet** to stay on most sites in Portugal. It's available from home motoring organizations, or, in Britain, from the *Camping and Caravan Club*, 32 High St, London, E15 2PF (☎081/503 0426), in the US from the *National Campers and Hikers Association*, 4804 Transit Rd, Building 2, Depew, NY 14043 (☎716/668-6242). It serves as useful identification and covers you for third party insurance when camping.

Camping outside official grounds is legal, but with certain restrictions. You're not allowed to camp "in urban zones, in zones of protection for water sources, or less than 1km from camping parks, beaches, or other places frequented by the public". What this means in practice is that you can't camp on tourist beaches, but with a little sensitivity you can pitch a tent for a short period almost anywhere in the countryside.

However, the **Algarve** is an exception. This is the only region where freelance camping is banned and where campsite thefts are a regular occurrence. Over most of the rest of the country the locals are extremely honest and you can leave equipment without worrying.

EATING AND DRINKING

Portuguese food is excellent, inexpensive and served in quantity. Virtually all cafés, whatever their appearance, will serve you a basic meal for around 1250$00 (£5/$8), while for 1500–3000$00 (£6–12/S$9–18) you have the run of most of the country's restaurants. Only a handful of top-class restaurants in Lisbon and the Algarve will cause a credit card crisis. Do beware, however, of eating anything you haven't explicitly asked for and expecting it to be free, or included: it won't be.

CAFÉS, SNACKS AND MARKETS

You'll often find a whole range of dishes served at a café, but classic Portuguese **snacks** include *prego no pão* (steak sandwich), which is usually served with a fried egg (*prego no prato*) or with sliced ham (*prego no fiambre*); *rissóis* (deep-fried meat patties); and *pastéis de bacalhau* (cod fish-cakes). In the north you may also find *lanches* (pieces of sweetish bread stuffed with ham) and *pastéis de carne* or *pastéis de chaves* (puff pastries stuffed with sausage meat). If cafés cook in a big way you'll probably see blackboard lists of dishes, or perhaps just a sign reading *Comidas* (meals).

Among **sandwiches** (*sandes*) on offer, the most common fillings include *queijo* (cheese), *fiambre* (ham), *presunto* (smoked ham) and *chouriço* (smoked sausage). *Sandes mistas* are usually a combination of ham and cheese. If

there's food displayed on café counters and you see anything that looks appealing, just ask for *uma dose* (a portion). *Uma coisa destas* (one of those) can also be a useful phrase.

Markets – often held in indoor covered sites – are always good hunting grounds for snacks. At many of them you'll find stands serving complete meals, or at least some local delicacy. In the north, especially, the most delicious standby is a chunk of *broa* (corn/rye bread) with local cheese and *marmelada* (thick quince spread).

RESTAURANTS

Even those on the tightest of budgets won't need to depend exclusively on snacks and picnics. The country is awash with accessible and affordable **restaurants** and, in addition, servings tend to be huge. Indeed, you can usually have a substantial meal by ordering a *meia dose* (half portion) or *uma dose* between two. Meals are often listed like this on the menu and it's normal practice; you don't need to be a child.

It is worth checking out the *ementa turística*, too – not necessarily a "tourist menu" as such, but more like the French *menu du jour*. It can be very good value, particularly in pensions that serve meals, or in the cheaper workers' cafés. Smarter restaurants, however, sometimes resent the law that compels them to offer the *ementa turística*, responding with stingy portions or, where there's any deviation from the set fare, declaring your meal to be *à lista* (*á la carte*) and consequently twice as expensive.

Otherwise, the one thing to watch for when eating out in Portugal – especially if you've grown happily complacent in Spain on a regular intake of free *tapas* – is the plate of **starters** usually placed before you when you take a table and before you order. These can be quite elaborate little dishes of olives, cheese, sardine spread and *chouriço*, or can consist of little more than rolls and butter, but what you eat is counted and you will be charged for every bite. Each item should be itemised on the menu, so you can see what you're spending.

Apart from straightforward restaurants – **restaurantes** – you could end up eating a meal in one of several other venues. A **tasca** is a small neighbourhood tavern; a **casa de pasto**, a

A LIST OF FOODS AND DISHES

Basics and Appetisers

Acepipes	Hors d'oeuvres	*cozido*	boiled
Almoço	Lunch	*mexido*	scrambled
Arroz	Rice	*estrelado*	fried
Azeitonas	Olives	*Pão*	Bread
Batatas fritas	French fries	*Pequeno almoço*	Breakfast
Jantar	Dinner	*Pimenta*	Pepper
Legumes	Vegetables	*Sal*	Salt
Manteiga	Butter	*Salada*	Salad
Ovos	Eggs	*Queijo*	Cheese

Soups

Caldo verde	Cabbage/potato broth	*Sopa de feijão verde*	Green bean soup
Canja de galinha	Chicken broth with rice and boiled egg yolks	*Sopa de grão*	Chickpea soup
		Sopa de legumes	Vegetable soup
Gaspacho	Chilled vegetable soup	*Sopa de marisco*	Shellfish soup
Sopa à alentejana	Garlic/bread soup with poached egg on top	*Sopa de peixe*	Fish soup

Fish (*peixe*) and shellfish (*mariscos*)

Ameijoas	Clams	*Linguado*	Sole
Anchovas	Anchovies	*Lulas*	Squid
Atum	Tuna	*Mexilhões*	Mussels
Camarões	Shrimp	*Ostras*	Oysters
Caranguejo	Crab	*Pargo*	Sea bream
Carapau	Mackerel	*Peixe espada*	Swordfish
Cherne	Sea bream	*Perceves*	Goose barnacles
Chocos	Cuttlefish	*Pescada*	Hake
Enguia	Eel	*Polvo*	Octopus
Espadarte	Scabbard fish (a long, thin, silver fish)	*Robalo*	Sea bass
		Salmão	Salmon
Gambas	Prawns	*Salmonete*	Red mullet
Garoupa	(Like) bream	*Sarda*	Mackerel
Lagosta	Lobster	*Sardinhas*	Sardines
Lampreia	Lamprey (similar to eel)	*Truta*	Trout

Meat (*carne*), poultry (*aves*) and game (*caça*)

Almondegas	Meatballs	*Fígado*	Liver
Borrego	Lamb	*Lombo*	Loin of pork
Cabrito	Kid	*Morcela*	Blood pudding
Carne de porco	Pork	*Pato*	Duck
Carneiro	Mutton	*Perdiz*	Partridge
Chouriço	Spicy sausage	*Perú*	Turkey
Coelho	Rabbit	*Presunto*	Smoked ham
Cordoniz	Quail	*Salsicha*	Sausage
Costeleta	Chop	*Tripas*	Tripe
Dobrada	Tripe	*Vitela*	Veal
Fiambre	Cooked ham		

Specialities

Açorda (de marisco)	Bread-based stew (cooked with shellfish and spices)	*Cataplana*	Shellfish or fish cooked with strips of ham, pepper and onion
Arroz de marisco	Seafood paella		
Bacalhau	There are reputedly 365 ways of cooking dried salt cod, including *com batatas e grão* (with boiled potatoes and chickpeas), *à brás* (with egg, onions and potatoes), *na brasa* (roasted with sliced potatoes), *à Gomes de Sá* (sliced, with boiled eggs and potatoes), and *à minhota* (with fried potatoes)	*Chanfana*	Casserole of lamb or kid
		Cozido à Portuguesa	Boiled casserole of chicken, lamb, pork, beef, sausages, offal and beans, served with rice and vegetables.
		Espedeta mista	Mixed meat kebab
		Frango na churrasca	Barbecued chicken, nearly always superb; eat with the *piri-piri* (chili) sauce provided
Bife á Portuguesa	Beef steak, topped with mustard sauce and a fried egg	*Leitão assado*	Roast suckling pig
		Porco à alentejana	Pork cooked with clams, an oily and salty dish from the Alentejo
Caldeirada	Fish stew, with a base of onions, tomatoes and potatoes	*Tripas à moda do Porto*	Tripe with beans and vegetables

Terms

Assado/no speto	Roasted/spit-roasted	*Guisado*	Stew
Cozido	Boiled/stewed	*Molho*	Sauce
Ensopado de . . .	Soup or stew of . . .	*Na brasa*	Charcoal-grilled
Frito	Fried	*No forno*	Baked
Fumado	Smoked	*Piri-piri*	With chilli sauce
Grelhado	Grilled	*Salteado*	Sautéed

Vegetables (*legumes*) and Salad (*salada*)

Alcachofra	Artichoke	*Espargos*	Asparagus
Alface	Lettuce	*Espinafre*	Spinach
Alho	Garlic	*Favas*	Broad beans
Batatas	Potatoes	*Feijão*	Beans
Cebola	Onion	*Grão*	Chickpeas
Cenoura	Carrot	*Pepino*	Cucumber
Cogumelos	Mushrooms	*Pimenta*	Pepper
Ervilhas	Peas	*Salada*	Salad

Fruit (*fruta*)

Ameixas	Plums	*Maçã*	Apple
Ananás	Pineapple	*Melão*	Melon
Cerejas	Cherries	*Morangos*	Strawberries
Figos	Figs	*Pêra*	Pear
Laranja	Orange	*Pêssego*	Peach
Limão	Lemon	*Uvas*	Grapes

cheap, local dining room usually with a set three-course menu, mostly served at lunch only. A *cervejaria* is literally a "beer house", more informal than a restaurant, with people dropping in at all hours for a beer and a snack. In Lisbon they are often wonderful old tiled caverns, specialising in seafood. Also specialising in seafood is a *marisqueria*, occasionally very upmarket, though as often as not a regular restaurant with a superior fishy menu.

Meal times are earlier than in Spain, with lunch usually served from noon–3pm, dinner from 7.30pm onwards; don't count on being able to eat much after 10pm outside the cities and tourist resorts. Simple cafés and restaurants don't charge for service, though you'll have paid a **cover charge** for bread and appetisers if you had any. People generally leave just small change as a **tip** in these places, though in more upmarket restaurants, you'll either be charged, or should leave, around 10 percent.

DISHES AND SPECIALITIES

It's always worth taking stock of the *prato do dia* (dish of the day) if you're interested in sampling **local specialities**. Some of the more common dishes are detailed in the food lists on p.27.

Soups are extraordinarily inexpensive, and the thick vegetable *caldo verde* – cabbage and potato broth sometimes with pieces of ham – is as filling as dishes come. The other soup served everywhere is *sopa à alentejana*, a garlic and bread soup with a poached egg in it. Otherwise, fish and shellfish soups are always worth sampling.

On the coast, **fish and seafood** are preeminent: crabs, prawns, crayfish, clams and huge barnacles are all fabulous, while fish on offer always includes superb mullet, tuna and swordfish. The most typical Portuguese fish dish is that created from *bacalhau* (dried, salted cod), which is much better than it sounds. It's virtually the national dish with reputedly 365 different ways of preparing it. Running it a close second are *sardines* (*sardinhas*), which – when grilled or barbeuced outside – provide one of the country's most familiar and appetising smells. On the Algarve, you shouldn't miss trying a *cataplana* – pressure-cooked seafood and strips of ham, named after the copper vessel in which it's cooked – or *arroz de marisco*, a bumper serving of mixed seafood served with a soupy rice. These are nearly always served for a minimum of two people, though.

On the whole, **meat** dishes are less special, though they're often enlivened by the addition of a fiery *piri-piri* (chilli) sauce, either in the cooking or provided on the table. Simple grilled or fried steaks of beef and pork are common; while **chicken** is on virtually every menu – at its wonderful best when barbecued (*no churrasco*); certain restaurants specialise in this and little else. Other, more exotic, specialities include smoked hams (*presunto*) from the north of the country (especially Chaves), and the ubiquitous and extremely tasty *porco à alentejana* (pork cooked with clams) – perhaps Portugal's most enterprising contribution to world cuisine – which originated, as its name suggests, in the Alentejo. However, don't be fooled by a couple of special dishes that local Portuguese people might entice you into trying: Porto's *tripas* (tripe) dishes incorporate beans and spices but the heart of the dish is still recognisably chopped stomach-lining; while *Cozido à Portuguesa*, widely served in restaurants on a Sunday, is a stomach-challenging boiled "meat" stew in which you shouldn't be surprised to turn up a pig's ear or worse. And it's worth paying good money to avoid eating the unspeakable *Papas de Sarrabulho*.

Accompanying most dishes will be potatoes (boiled or fried) and/or rice – calorific overkill is a strong feature of Portuguese meal times. Other **vegetables** rarely make an appearance, though you might find sliced fresh tomato served with your fish, and boiled carrots or cabbage and the like accompanying meat stews.

If you've had enough rich food, any restaurant will fix a *salada mista* (mixed salad), which usually has tomatoes, onions and olives as a base, and you can ask for it to be served *sem óleo* (without oil), though it's nowhere near as tasty if you do. Otherwise, strict **vegetarians** are in for something of a hard time outside Lisbon and the Algarve, where there's a bigger choice of non-Portuguese food. Eggs are mostly free-range in Portugal, but out in the sticks you'll soon tire of omlettes or fried eggs, chips and salad – though every restaurant will be happy to prepare this for you if you ask.

PASTRIES, SWEETS AND CHEESES

Pastries – *bolos* or *pastéis* – are usually at their best in *casas de chá* (tea-rooms), though you'll also find them in cafés and in *pastelarias* (pastry shops), which themselves often serve drinks, too. Here, pastries are serious business and enthusiasts won't be disappointed. Among the best are the Sintra cheesecakes (*queijadas de Sintra*), *palha de ovos* (egg pastries) from Abrantes, *bolo de anjo* (angel food cake), *pastéis de nata* (delicious little custard tarts), and a full range of marzipan cakes from the Algarve. The incredibly sweet egg-based *doces de ovos* – most infamously from Aveiro – are completely over-the-top.

Unfortunately, few of these delicacies are available in restaurants as **desserts**. Instead, you'll almost always be offered either fresh fruit, the ubiquitous *Ola* ice cream price list, *pudim flan* (crème caramel), *arroz doce* (rice pudding) or *torta da noz* (almond tart). **Cheese** is widely available in restaurants, the best the *Queijo da Serra* (from the Serra da Estrela). *Cabreiro* or *queijo de cabra* is a goat's cheese like Greek *feta*; and also worth looking out for are the soft cheeses of *Tomar* and *Azeitão*.

ALCOHOLIC DRINKS

Portuguese table wines are dramatically inexpensive and of a good overall quality. Even the standard *vinho da casa* that you get in the humblest of cafés is generally a very pleasant drink. But it's fortified port, of course, and madeira that are Portugal's best known wine exports – and you should certainly sample both.

Beer choices are far less varied, with just two or three brands available country-wide, while the typical Portuguese measure of spirits is equivalent to at least two shots in Britain or North America, making drunkenness all too easy. Low prices, too, are an encouragement, as long as you stick to local (*nacional*) products.

WINES

The best-known of Portuguese table wines are reds from the **Dão** region, a roughly triangular area between Coimbra, Viseu and Guarda, around the River Dão. Tasting a little like burgundy, and produced mainly by local cooperatives, they're available throughout the country. Among other smaller regions offering interesting wines are **Colares** (near Sintra), **Bucelas** in the Estremadura (crisp, dry whites), **Valpaças** from Trás-os-Montes, **Reguengos** from Alentejo and **Lagoa** from the Algarve.

The light, slightly sparkling **vinhos verdes** – "green wines", in age not colour – are again produced in quantity, this time in the Minho. They're drunk early and don't mature or improve with age, but are great with meals, especially shellfish. There are red and rosé *vinhos verdes*, though the whites are the most successful – *Casal Garcia* is the one you'll find most often in restaurants. Otherwise, Portuguese **rosé wines** are known abroad mainly through the spectacularly successful export of *Mateus Rosé*. This is too sweet and aerated for most tastes, but other rosés – the best is *Tavel* – are definitely worth sampling.

Portugal also produces an interesting range of sparkling, champagne-method wines, known as **espumantes naturais**. They are designated *bruto* (extra dry), *seco* (fairly dry), *meio seco* (quite sweet) or *doce* (very sweet). The best of these come from the Bairrada region, northwest of Coimbra, though *Raposeira* wines are the most commonly available.

Even the most basic of restaurants usually has a decent selection of wines, many of which are available in half-bottles, too. The *vinho da casa* (house wine) is nearly always remarkably good value, but even ascending the scale and choosing from the wine list, you'll be surprised at the quality wines on offer at very moderate prices. Most **wine lists** don't just distinguish between *tinto* (red) or *branco* (white); they'll also list wines as either *verdes* (ie, young and slightly sparkling) or *maduros* (mature) – choose from the latter if you're after a red with a kick or a white with no bubbles.

FORTIFIED WINES: PORT AND MADEIRA

Port (*vinho do Porto*) – the famous fortified wine – is produced from grapes grown in the valley of the Douro and stored in huge wine lodges at Vila Nova de Gaia, a riverside suburb of Porto. You can visit these for tours and free tastings; see p.217 for all the details. Alternatively, you can try any of 300 types and vintages of port at the *Instituto do Vinho do Porto* (Port Wine Institute) bars in Lisbon (p.76) and Porto (p.215). But even if your quest for port isn't serious enough to do either, be sure to try the dry white aperitif ports, still little known outside the country.

Madeira (*vinho da Madeira*), from Portugal's Atlantic island province, has been exported to Britain since Shakespeare's time – it was Falstaff's favourite tipple, known then as sack. Widely available, it comes in three main varieties: *Sercial* (a dry aperitif), *Verdelho* (a sweeter aperitif) and *Bual* or *Malmsey* (sweet, heavy dessert wines). Each improves with age and special vintages are greatly prized and priced.

SPIRITS (*LICOR*)

The national **brandy** is arguably outflanked by its Spanish rivals – which are sold almost everywhere – but the native spirit is available in two varieties (*Macieira* and *Constantino*), each with loyal followings. It's frighteningly cheap. Portuguese **gin** is weaker than international brands but again ridiculously inexpensive.

Local **firewaters** – generically known as *aguardente* – are more impressive. They include *Bagaço* (the fieriest), *Figo* (made from figs, with which it shares similar qualities when drunk to excess), *Ginginha* (made from cherries), and the very wonderful *Licor Beirão* (a kind of cognac with herbs). *Aguardente velha* (old) and *velhissima* (very old) are smoother versions of the basic hooch.

BEER

The most common Portuguese **beer** (*cerveja*) is *Sagres*, but there are a fair number of local varieties. If you're curious, they can all be tasted at the Silves Beer Festival, held in the town's castle for a week every June. If you don't get the chance, note that probably the best Portuguese beer is the blue-labelled *Super Bock*, which is rivalled only by *Sagres Europa*. For something unusual (and not recommended on a hot afternoon) try the green-labelled *Sagres Preta*, which is a dark beer, resembling British brown ale.

When **drinking draft beer** order *um imperial* if you want a regular glass; *uma caneca* will get you a half-litre. And when **buying bottles**, don't forget to take your empties back: they can represent as much as a third of the price!

COFFEE, TEA AND SOFT DRINKS

Coffee (*café*) comes either black, small, and espresso-strong (*uma bica* or simply *um café*); small and with milk (*um garoto* or *um pingo* in some parts of the north); or large and with milk but often disgustingly weak (*um galão*). For white coffee that tastes of coffee and not diluted warm milk, ask for "*um café duplo com um pouco de leite*".

Tea (*chá*) is usually plain; *com leite* is with milk, *com limão* with lemon, but *um chá de limão* is hot water with a lemon rind. *Chá* is a big drink in Portugal (which originally exported tea-drinking to England) and you'll find wonderfully elegant *casas de chá* dotted around the country.

All the standard **soft drinks** are available. *Tri Naranjus* is a good local range of fruit drinks (excellent *limão*, lemon), and the fizzy *Sumol*, is extremely fruity and appetising. Fresh orange juice is *sumo de laranja*. Lastly, **mineral water** (*água mineral*) is available almost anywhere in the country, either still (*sem gás*) or carbonated (*com gás*).

COMMUNICATIONS: POST, PHONES AND THE MEDIA

POSTAL SERVICES

Portuguese postal services are reasonably efficient. Letters or cards take under a week to arrive at destinations in Europe, and a week to ten days to North America.

Post offices (*correios*) are normally open Monday to Friday 9am–6pm, larger ones sometimes on Saturday mornings, too. The main Lisbon branches have much longer opening hours; see "Listings", p.84. **Stamps** (*selos*) are sold at post offices and anywhere that has the sign of a red horse on a white circle over a green background and the legend *Correio de Portugal – Selos*.

You can have **poste restante** (general delivery) mail sent to you at any post office in the country. Letters should be marked *Posta*

Restante, and your name, ideally, should be written in capitals and underlined. To collect, you need to take along your passport – look for the counter marked *encomendas*. If you are expecting mail, ask the postal clerk to check for letters under your first name and any other initials (including Ms, etc) as well as under your surname – filing can be erratic.

TELEPHONES

International calls can be made direct from almost any telephone booth in the country, but in most of them, you'll need a good stock of coins and a great deal of patience; the international lines are often blocked. In busy tourist areas, especially the Algarve and Lisbon, it's easier to use the **credifones** which you can use with the **phonecards** (for 750$00 and 1725$00) available from post offices. To call abroad from pay phones in Portugal, you need to insert at least 200$00 to make the connection.

You'll find **pay phones** in bars and cafés (and, increasingly, in Turismo offices and newsagents),

usually indicated by the sign of a red horse on a white circle over a green background and the legend *Correio de Portugal – Telefone*. Otherwise, the best bet for long-distance calls is to go to the main post office in most towns, which almost always have phone cabins – just tell the clerk where you want to phone, and pay for your call afterwards. Except in Lisbon and Porto, most telephone offices are closed in the evening, which can be inconvenient, but there is no cheap-rate period anyway for international calls.

Reverse charge (collect) calls can be made from any phone, dialing ☎099 for a European connection and ☎098 for the rest of the world.

NEWSPAPERS, TV AND RADIO

The two most established **Portuguese daily newspapers** are the Lisbon-based *Diário de Notícias* and the *Jornal de Notícias* from Porto. They have their uses for listings information, even if you only have a very sketchy knowledge of the language. The stylish *Público* has good

---

TELEPHONE CODES AND USEFUL NUMBERS

To phone abroad *from Portugal*

Dial the country code (given below) + area code (minus initial zero) + number

Australia 0061	Ireland 00353	UK 0044
Canada 001	New Zealand 0064	USA 001

To phone Portugal *from abroad*

Dial the international access code (see below) + 351 (country code) + area code (minus intitial zero; see below) + number.

International Access Code

Australia 0011	Ireland 00	UK 010
Canada 011	New Zealand 00	USA 011

Portuguese Area Codes

Braga 053	Guarda 071	Tavira 081
Coimbra 039	Lagos 082	Viana do Castelo 058
Évora 066	Lisbon 01	Vila Real 059
Faro 089	Porto 02	Viseu 032
	Setúbal 065	

Useful Telephone Numbers

Directory enquiries 166	Operator (rest of the world) 098
Emergency services 115	Speaking clock 151
Operator (Europe) 099	

foreign news and regional inserts. Another informative read – on the entertainment front – is Lisbon's weekly paper *SE7E* (*sete* means "7"), and, for a view of the country's culture, *JL* (*Jornal de Letras*).

The *International Herald Tribune*, and most British **newspapers**, can be bought in the major cities and resorts, usually a day late. One or two domestic English-language magazines and newspapers pop up from time to time on the Algarve, none of them especially informative but occasionally useful for finding work.

Portuguese **television** imports many American and British shows – nearly always subtitled rather than dubbed. Increasingly, too,

European **satellite TV** stations are spawning their dishes around the country; sports channels are popular in bars, showing televised bullfights among other things. You also get *telenovelas* – soaps – often from Brazil, and compelling viewing even if you don't understand a word.

On the **radio**, you can pick up the *BBC World Service*, with hourly news, on 648 KHz medium wave and 15.07 MHz short wave; *Voice of America* is sporadically audible on 6040 on the 49m short wave band. Portuguese radio also puts out an **English-language programme** for tourists at 8.30am or 10am (between 558 and 720 KHz/87.9 and 95.7FM depending on where you are).

OPENING HOURS AND PUBLIC HOLIDAYS

Like Spain, Portugal has held onto the institution of the *siesta*. Most stores and businesses, plus smaller museums and post offices, close for a good lunchtime break – usually from around 12.30pm to 2.30 or 3pm.

Banks are a rare exception, opening Monday to Friday 8.30am to 3pm. **Shops** generally open around 9am, and upon re-opening after lunch keep going until 7 or 8pm; except in larger cities, they tend to close for the weekend at Saturday lunchtime. **Museums, churches and monuments** open from around 10am–12.30pm and 2–6pm, though the larger ones stay open through lunchtime. Almost all museums and monuments, however, are closed Mondays. The other thing to watch out for are national **public holidays** (see below) when almost everything is closed and transport services reduced. There are also **local festivals** and holidays (see opposite), when entire town, cities and regions grind to a halt: for example June 13 in Lisbon and June 24 in Porto.

PUBLIC HOLIDAYS

January 1.

March/April; Good Friday.

April 25 (commemorating the 1974 revolution).

May 1 (Labour Day).

June; Corpus Christi (usually early June).

10 (*Dia de Camões e das Comunidades* – Camões day: the community part was added after the Revolution).

August 15 (Feast of the Assumption).

October 5 (Republic Day).

November 1 (All Saints Day).

December 1 (celebrating independence from Spain in 1640).

December 8 (Immaculate Conception).

December 25.

FESTIVALS, BULLFIGHTS AND SPORTS

Portugal maintains a remarkable number of folk customs which find their expression in local carnivals (*festas*) and traditional pilgrimages (*romarias*). Some of these have developed into wild celebrations lasting days or even weeks and have become tourist events in themselves; others have barely strayed from their roots.

Every region is different, but in the **north** especially there are dozens of village festivals, everyone taking the day off to celebrate the local saint's day or the harvest, and performing ancient songs and dances in traditional dress for no one's benefit but their own. Look out, too, for the great **feiras**, especially at Barcelos (p.259). Originally they were markets, but as often as not nowadays you'll find a combination of agricultural show, folk festival, amusement park and, admittedly, tourist bazaar.

The festival list is potentially endless and only the major highlights are picked out below. For more **details** on what's going on around you, check with the local Turismo or buy the monthly *Borda d'Água*, an information leaflet detailing saints' days, star signs, gardening tips and, most importantly, all the country's annual fairs. It is often the obscure and unexpected event which turns out to be the most fun.

Among major, national celebrations, **Easter Week** and **St. John's Eve** (June 23/24) stand out. Both are celebrated throughout the country with religious processions. The former is most magnificent in Braga, where it is full of ceremonial pomp, while the latter tends to be a more

---

MAJOR POPULAR FESTIVALS

Among the biggest and best known of the country's **popular festivals** are:

May
Queima das Fitas, celebrating the end of the academic year in Coimbra (mid-May).

Fátima (13 May); Portugal's most famous pilgrimage; also in October; see p.131.

June
Feira Nacional at Santarém lasts for ten days, starting on the first Fri). Dancing, bullfighting and an agricultural fair; see p.137.

Festa de São Gonçalo in Amarante (1st weekend); see p.229.

Santos Populares (Popular Saints) in Lisbon – celebrations in honour of St Anthony (June 13), St John (24) and St Peter (29). Festival, too, in Porto for St John on the same date.

July
Festa do Colete Encarnado in Vila Franca de Xira, with Pamplona-style running of bulls through the streets (first two weeks); see p.140.

August
Romaria da Nossa Senhora da Agonia in Viana do Castelo (third weekend); see p.267.

September
Romaria de Nossa Senhora dos Remédios in Lamego (pilgrimage on 8 Sept, though events start in last week of Aug and run through to mid-Sept); see p.235.

"New Fairs" in Ponte de Lima (2nd and 3rd weekend); see p.277.

October
Feira de Outubro in Vila Franca de Xira (first two weeks); more bull-running and fighting.

Fátima (13 Oct); second great pilgrimage of the year; see p.131.

November
Feira Nacional do Cavalo (National Horse Fair) in Golegã; see p.141.

joyous affair. In Porto, where St. John's Eve is the highlight of a week of celebration, everyone dances through the streets all night, hitting each other over the head with leeks.

BULLFIGHTS

The Portuguese **bullfight** is neither as common-place nor as famous as its Spanish counterpart, but as a spectacle it's marginally preferable. In Portugal the bull isn't killed, but instead wrestled to the ground in a genuinely elegant, colourful and skilled display. After the fight, however, the bull is usually injured and it is always slaugh-tered later in any case.

If you choose to go – and we would urge visi-tors not to support the events put on simply for tourist benefit on the Algarve – these are the basics.

A *tourada* opens with the bull, its horns padded, facing a mounted *toureiro* in elaborate eighteenth-century costume. His job is to provoke and exhaust the bull and to plant the dart-like *farpas* (or *bandarilhas*) in its back while avoiding the charge – a demonstration of incredible riding prowess. Once the beast is tired the *moços-de-forcado*, or simply *forcados* move in, an eight-man team which tries finally to immobilise it. It appears a totally suicidal task – they line up behind each other across the ring from the bull and persuade it to charge them, the front man leaping between the horns while the rest grab hold and try to subdue it.

The great Portuguese bullfight centre is **Ribatejo**, where the animals are bred. If you want to see a fight, it's best to witness it here, amid the local *aficionados*, or as part of the festivals in Vila Franca de Xira and Santarém. The season lasts from around April to October. Local towns and villages in the Ribatejo also feature **bull-running**, through the streets, at various of their festivals; see Chapter Two for further details.

SPORTS

Soccer is the Portuguese national sport, with a long and often glorious tradition of international and club teams. The leading clubs, inevitably, hail from Lisbon (Benfica and Sporting) and Porto (FC Porto). Just about every Portuguese supports one of these three teams, paying scant attention to the lesser, local teams. Of these, F.C. Guimarães are the most consistent challengers to the big league boys. If you want to see a league match, the season runs from September through to May. Tickets are inexpensive, and matches given due prominence in the local press. The spectacle of a packed capacity football stadium somewhat puts bullfights in the shade.

PARTICIPATORY SPORTS

Participatory sports on offer in Portugal include windsurfing, golf and tennis – all of which are promoted mainly on the Algarve. **Windsurfing boards** are available for rent on most of the Algarve beaches and at the more popular north-ern and Lisbon coast resorts. The biggest wind-surfing destination is **Guincho**, north of Lisbon (see p.88), though the winds and currents here require a high level of expertise.

Tennis courts are a common feature of most larger Algarve hotels – their attraction being that you can play year-round. If you want to improve your game, the best intensive coaching is under the instruction of ex-Wimbledon pro Roger Taylor at the **Vale do Lobo** resort complex. Arguably the country's best **golf course**, designed by Frank Penninck, is just up the road from here at **Vilamoura**, and several others are within reach.

Anyone interested in **fishing** should head to the trout streams of the Minho and other northern regions; licenses are available from local town halls. For further information – and addresses of operators promoting **sporting holidays** – contact the Portuguese National Tourist Office for a copy of their *Sportugal* brochure.

POLICE AND TROUBLE

Portugal is a remarkably crime-free country, though there's the usual petty theft in larger tourist resorts and Lisbon is developing a reputation for pickpockets on public transport. Rental cars, too, are always prey to thieves: wherever you park, don't leave anything visible in the car – preferably, don't leave anything in the car at all.

CRIME AND THE POLICE

Although Lisbon is one of the safer European capitals, you should take care in the Alfama and parts of the Bairro Alto after dark; if you are robbed, whatever you do, don't resist. Hand over your valuables and run.

If you do have anything stolen while in Portugal, you'll need to go the **police** – primarily to file a report which your insurance company will require before they'll pay out for any claims made on your policy. Police stations in Lisbon and other major towns are detailed in the various "Listings" sections throughout the guide.

You can't count on English being spoken by most of the local police personnel you may have occasion to meet, and since tourists can usually muster only a few basic words of Portuguese, confusion can easily arise. To this end, showing deference to a police officer is wise: the Portuguese still hold respect dear, and the more respect you show a figure in authority, the quicker you will be on your way.

In an emergency, dial ☎115 for the police.

There are three different authorities with which you might come into contact, though in an emergency, the first policeman you see will be able to point you in the right direction. In major towns, the police force most likely to be of assistance will be the **PSP** (*Polícia de Segurança Pública*), responsible among other things for incidents involving tourists. They wear distinctive blue uniforms, a beret and a badge on their jackets identifying themselves. Once you're away from the larger conurbations, you will have to rely on the **GNR** (*Guarda Nacional Republicana*) for help: they police the rural areas, patrol the motorways, and are responsible for overseeing all ceremonial occasions, like state visits, at which time they deck themselves out in magnificent dress uniforms. Ordinarily, though, they wear blue-grey uniforms and highly polished knee-length boots. If you require specialist help – work permits and the like – the local office of the **Serviço de Estrangeiros e Fronteiras** is the place to go.

SEXUAL HARASSMENT

The ruralism and small-town life of Portugal make it one of the most relaxed of Latin countries for **women travellers**. Which is not to say that the Portuguese *machismo* is any less ingrained than in Spain or Italy: simply that it gets rather less of an outlet.

Portugal is rarely a dangerous place for women travellers, and only in the following few areas do you need to be particularly wary: parts of Lisbon (particularly the Cais do Sodré and the Bairro Alto by night), streets immediately around train stations in the larger towns (traditionally the red light districts), and the Algarve, where aggressive males congregate on the pick-up.

On the whole it's a rural country, intensely traditional and formal to the point of prudishness. People may initially wonder why you're travelling on your own – especially inland and in the mountains, where Portuguese women never travel unaccompanied – but once they have accepted that you are a crazy foreigner you're likely to be welcomed, adopted, and even offered food and lodging in their homes.

As far as transport goes, **hitching** is reasonably safe as long as there are two or more of you – but absolutely not recommended for lone women travellers. If you are on your own, get around at night by **taxi**, which are very cheap anyway. By day **public transport** is good and quite safe; but take the usual precautions at night on Lisbon's Metro and on the Cais do Sodré–Cascais coastal train line.

WORKING IN PORTUGAL

Portugal has employment problems of its own, and without a special skill you're unlikely to have much luck finding any kind of long-term work. One realistic option though is **teaching English**. For this a TEFL certificate is a distinct advantage, though not absolutely essential. Work is best arranged before you leave as this prevents work permit hassles. But if you're already in Portugal you could just apply to individual schools or advertise your services privately.

WORKING ON THE ALGARVE

As far as temporary jobs go, the only real opportunities are in tourist-related work **on the Algarve**, which offer a range of ways of getting money, all of them dependent to some extent on your self-confidence and/or lack of scruples.

Most obvious of the jobs is **bar work**. This is not easy to find – you'll stand the best chance in one of the many British-owned places – and even when you do, it often brings in barely enough money to live on. Better, at least in terms of time involved, is to try your hand walking the streets at night **giving out disco invitations** to holiday makers. This work is available in most major resorts and is paid solely on a commission basis, but 'it does leave you free during the day – and much of the night – to seek your own entertainment.

Which leads nicely into the biggest scam in the country – perhaps in Europe – of **selling time shares**. Here possibilities exist for making really big bucks, though not everyone, of course, strikes it rich. The work involves walking the streets in the major resorts inviting British tourist couples to view time-share resorts and villas. It is extremely tiring, soul-destroying, and, at its most successful, pretty disreputable work, but earnings are on a commission basis and this can add up to a fair living if you're the type who enjoys selling your own grandmother. Just ask the people who are already doing the job on the street what to do. They'll tell you how to find work and how depressing it is.

One last option is to head for the huge yacht marina at **Vilamoura**, which holds around a thousand craft and is slowly being surrounded by trendy bars, boutiques and cafés. You could try some of these, but it's even better to approach the yachties themselves. Almost all boat owners have hundreds of little tasks that need doing and, given the opportunity, will pay a few thousand *escudos* to anyone presenting themselves as a handyman/woman. Mostly it's **painting** or **scrubbing down** decks – hardly skilled labour – but if you can convince someone you know what you're doing the quality of work you'll be given may improve. Between late September and early November, however, there's the chance of **crewing** to the Canaries or the Caribbean; for this sort of angle try the local bars as well as word of mouth. For the more menial odd-jobs you just need persistence and a thick skin: spend a couple of days asking around and something should turn up.

If you do decide to stay on in the Algarve to work, the easiest (if unofficial) way to **extend** your sixty or ninety days is to cross the border at Vila Real de Santo António. The official way, if reliable long-term employment beckons, is to go to one of the *Serviço de Estrangeiros* offices in Portimão, Albufeira or Faro.

DIRECTORY

ADDRESSES Most addresses in Portugal consist of a street name and number followed by a storey number, eg, Rua de Afonso Henriques 34-3°. This means you need to go up to the third floor of no. 34 (US, fourth floor). An "esq" or "E" (standing for *esquerda*) after a floor number means you should go to the left; "dir" or "D" (for *direita*) indicates the apartment or office you're looking for is on the right.

BAGGAGE You can often leave bags at a train or bus station for a small sum while you look for rooms. On the whole the Portuguese are highly trustworthy, and even shopkeepers and café owners will keep an eye on your belongings for you. Or try the local Turismo, which may agree to look after your bags for a while.

BEACHES Beware of the heavy undertow on many of Portugal's western Atlantic beaches and don't swim if you see a red or yellow flag. The EC Blue Flag indicates that the water is clean enough to swim in – sadly, not always the case at many of Portugal resorts. The sea is warmest on the eastern Algarve (ie, the beaches east of Faro).

CHILDREN Portugal is child-friendly and families should find it as easy a place to roam as any other country. Cheap hotels and *pensões* will only rarely charge extra for children in their parents' room, and in restaurants small portions and extra plates are absolutely the norm for all who require them. Lastly, museums and most sights don't usually charge for small children.

CONTRACEPTION Condoms – *preservativos* – are rarely on display in pharmacies, but always available. Ask, and the pharmacist will set out an array on the counter, in the best formal Portuguese manner.

DRESS Churches often require "modest dress" – which basically just means you shouldn't wear shorts or very flimsy tops.

DUTY-FREE GOODS If you're in the market for duty-free goods, try to check out prices when you arrive at the airport. Apart from standard *licor* brands, there are no great savings to be made. For national specialities – including wine, port, and brandy – you're better off buying from local groceries and *licor* stores.

EMERGENCIES Phone ☎115 for the emergency services. If you're involved in a road accident, use the nearest roadside orange-coloured SOS telephone – press the button and wait for an answer.

FILM Going to the movies in Portugal is extremely cheap, and films are often shown with the original (usually English-language) soundtrack with Portuguese subtitles. Listings can be found in the local newspaper or on boards, invariably placed somewhere in the central square of every small town. Screenings are cheap, with reduced price matinées and at all Monday shows.

GAY LIFE The gay scene isn't especially prominent, or at least commercialised, though there's a fair sprinkling of clubs, and a gay beach, in Lisbon and one or two places to meet in Porto and the Algarve. Attitudes in the capital are fairly tolerant; elsewhere a gay consciousness has yet to make much impact. There is no explicit law against homosexuality.

LAUNDRY There are few self-service launderettes, but loads of *lavandarias*, where you can get your clothes washed, mended, and ironed (overnight) at a fairly low cost.

NATIONAL PARKS The head office in Lisbon (Rua Ferreira Lapa 29-1°) has details on Portugal's parks and reserves, but generally neither head nor district offices have much time for foreign visitors, concentrating on awakening a spirit of wildlife conservation and protection in their compatriots.

SWIMMING POOLS Every sizeable town has a swimming pool, usually outdoors, but you'll find that they are often closed from September to May.

TIME Portugal is one hour ahead of Britain, five hours ahead of Eastern Standard Time and eight hours ahead of Pacific Standard Time. Clocks go forward one hour on the last Sunday in March and back one hour on the last Sunday in September.

TIPPING Hotels and restaurants include a service charge but porters and maids expect something; cab drivers don't.

TOILETS "Ladies" often charge and are clean, "Gentlemen" may look more aesthetic (lots of ironwork) and are free, but usually pretty unat-tractive inside. A sign that says *Retretes* will head you in the right direction, then it's *homens* for men and *senhoras* for women; the doors will generally have the usual block figure wearing a skirt or trousers.

WOMEN'S MOVEMENT There are relatively few women's organisations in Portugal. The best contact points are the *IDM* centre and the feminist bookshop *Editora das Mulheres*, both in Lisbon (see p.85). Also of interest is the *Comissão da Condição Feminina* (Avenida da República 32-2° esq, Lisbon), which maintains a watching brief on all aspects of women's lives in Portugal; members organise conferences and meetings, are very active in areas of social and legal reform, and are linked with feminists throughout the country.

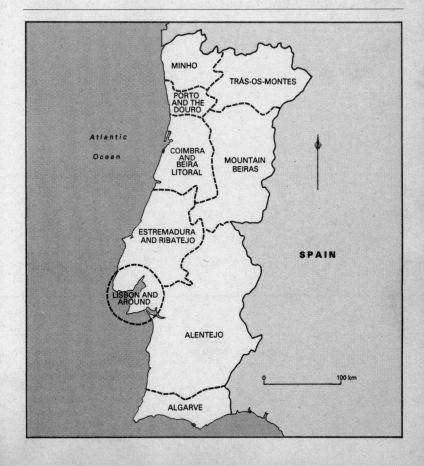

CHAPTER ONE

LISBON AND AROUND

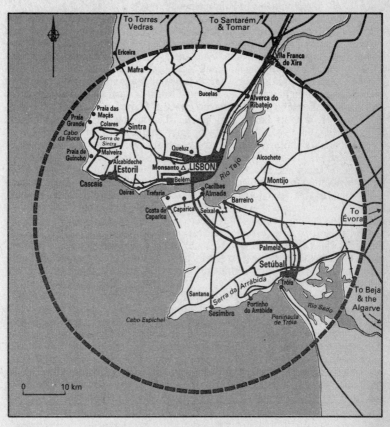

To Torres Vedras
To Santarém & Tomar
Ericeira
Vila Franca de Xira
Mafra
Bucelas
Alverca do Ribatejo
Praia das Maçãs
Praia Grande
Colares
Sintra
Cabo da Roca
Serra de Sintra
Queluz
Praia de Guincho
Malveira
Alcochete
Alcabideche
Monsanto △ LISBON
Rio Tejo
Estoril
Belém
Cacilhas
Almada
Montijo
Cascais
Oeiras
Trafaria
Barreiro
To Évora
Costa de Caparica
Caparica
Seixal
Palmela
Setúbal
Santana
Serra da Arrábida
Tróia
To Beja & the Algarve
Rio Sado
Sesimbra
Portinho da Arrábida
Cabo Espichel
Península de Tróia

0   10 km

There are few cityscapes as startling and eccentric as that of **Lisbon**. Built on a switchback of hills above the broad **Tejo** (Tagus) estuary, its quarters are linked by an amazing network of cobbled streets, up whose outrageous gradients crank trams and funiculars. Down at the river, you are lured across towards the sea by a vast, Rio-like statue of Christ, arms outstretched, whose embrace encompasses one of the grandest of all suspension bridges and a fleet of cross-river ferries. For visitors, it's hard not to see the city as an urban funfair: a sense heightened by the castle poised above the Alfama district's medieval, whitewashed streets; by the fantasy Manueline architecture of Belém; and by the mosaics of the central Rossío square and the Art Nouveau shops and cafés.

For Americans, San Francisco is an obvious counterpart: a city that has parallels in both its physical make-up and its fault-line position – Lisbon's Great Earthquake in 1755 levelled most of the old lower town. The two cities stand a further comparison since Lisbon, too, is immediately likable, gentler than any port or capital should expect to be, almost provincial in feel and defiantly human in pace and scale. For much of the present century, the city stood apart from the European mainstream, an isolation which ended abruptly with the 1974 revolution, and still more so with integration into the European Community a decade later.

Over the past hundred years, Lisbon's population has doubled to nearly a million, a tenth of all Portuguese, and following on from the revolution the capital absorbed a vast influx of **refugees** – *retornados* – from Portugal's former African colonies of Angola, Cabo Verde, São Tomé e Principe, Guinea Bissau and Mozambique. The *retornados* imposed a heavy burden on an already strained economy, especially on housing, but their overall integration is one of the chief triumphs of modern Portugal. Like the city's Brazilian contingent, the Portuguese Africans have also brought a significant **cultural** buoyancy. Alongside the traditional *fado* clubs of its Bairro Alto quarter, Lisbon now has superb Latin and African bands, and a panoply of international restaurants and bars.

Conventional sights and monuments are arguably thin on the ground, largely as a result of the 1755 earthquake. The Romanesque **Sé** (cathedral) and the Moorish walls of the **Castelo de São Jorge** are fine early survivors, though hardly unique in Portugal. But there is one building from Portugal's Golden Age – the extraordinary **Mosteiro dos Jerónimos** at Belém – that is the equal of any in the country. Two museums demand attention, too: the **Fundação Calouste Gulbenkian**, a museum and cultural complex with superb collections of ancient and modern art, and the **Museu de Arte Antiga**, effectively Portugal's national art gallery. Beyond these, it's the central streets, avenues and squares, and their attendant comings and goings, that keep the interest level topped up; keep an eye out, too, for some adventurous contemporary architecture, such as Tómas Taveira's shopping complex at **Amoreiras**.

All of this makes for a city that demands at least a few days out of anyone's Portuguese itinerary. Better still, make the capital a base for a week or two's holiday, with day trips and excursions into the surrounding area. The sea is close by, half an hour's journey taking you to the beach suburb of **Cascais**, or to the miles of dunes along the **Costa da Caparica**. Slightly further afield lie the lush wooded heights and royal palaces of **Sintra**, Byron's "glorious Eden". And if you become interested in Portuguese architecture, there are the rococo delights of the **Palácio de Queluz** and its gardens en route, or the extraordinary monastery of **Mafra** – a good first step into Estremadura, the region immediately to the north.

LISBON (LISBOA)

Physically, **LISBON** is an eighteenth-century city: elegant, open to the sea and carefully planned. The description does not cover its modern expanse, of course – there are suburbs here as poor and inadequate as any in Europe – but is accurate within the old central boundary of a triangle of hills. This "lower city", the **Baixa**, was the product of a single phase of building, carried out in less than a decade by the dictatorial minister, the Marquês de Pombal, in the wake of the earthquake which destroyed much of central Lisbon in 1755.

The **Great Earthquake** – which was felt as far away as Scotland and Jamaica – struck Lisbon at 9.30am on November 1, All Saints' Day, when most of the city's population was at mass. Within the space of ten minutes there had been three major tremors and fires, spread by the candles of a hundred church altars, were raging throughout the capital. A vast tidal wave swept the seafront, where refugees sought shelter: in all, 40,000 of a 270,000 population died. The destruction of the city shocked the continent, with Voltaire, who wrote an account of it in his novel *Candide*, leading an intense debate with Rousseau on the operation of providence. For Portugal, and for the capital, it was a disaster that in retrospect seemed to seal an age. Previously, eighteenth-century Lisbon had been arguably the most active port in Europe.

It had been a prosperous city since **Roman**, perhaps even Phoenician, times. In the Middle Ages, as **Moorish** *Lishbuna*, it thrived on its wide links with the Arab world, while exploiting the rich territories of the south, the Alentejo and Algarve. The country's reconquest by the Christians in 1147 was an early and dubious triumph of the Crusades, its one positive aspect the appearance of the first true Portuguese monarch in **Afonso Henriques**. It was not until 1255, however, that Lisbon took over from Coimbra as capital.

Over the following centuries, Lisbon was twice at the forefront of European development and trade, on a scale that is hard to envisage today. The first phase came with the great Portuguese **discoveries** of the late fifteenth and sixteenth centuries, such as Vasco da Gama's opening of the sea route to India. The second was in the opening decades of the **eighteenth century**, when a colonised Brazil was found to yield both gold and diamonds. It is these that are the great ages of Portuguese patronage. The sixteenth century is dominated by the figure of **Dom Manuel I**, under whom the flamboyant national style known as Manueline developed. Lisbon takes its principal monuments, the tower and monastery at Belém, from this era. The eighteenth century, more extravagant but with less brilliant effect, produced **Dom João V**, best known as the obsessive builder of Mafra, which he created in response to Philip II's El Escorial in Spain.

Orientation

It could hardly be easier to get your bearings in central Lisbon. At the southern end of the **Baixa**, opening onto the River Tejo, is the broad, arcaded **Praça do Comércio** (also known as **Terreiro do Paço**), with its ferry stations for crossing the river, tram terminus for Belém, and grand triumphal arch. At the other end – linked by almost any street you care to take – stands Praça Dom Pedro IV, popularly known as **Rossío**, merging with **Praça da Figueira** and **Praça dos Restauradores**. These squares, filled with cafés, occasional buskers, lost-looking tourists and streetwise dealers, form the hub of Lisbon's daily activity. At night the focus shifts to the **Bairro Alto**, high above and to the west of the Baixa, and best reached by funicular (the *Elevador da Glória*) or by the great street elevator, the *Elevador Santa Justa*. Between the two districts, halfway up the hill, **Chiado** is still Lisbon's most elegant shopping area, despite suffering severe damage in the fire of 1988. East of the Baixa, the **Castelo de São Jorge**, a brooding landmark, surmounts a still taller hill, with the **Alfama** district – the oldest, most fascinating part of the city – sprawled below.

LISBON

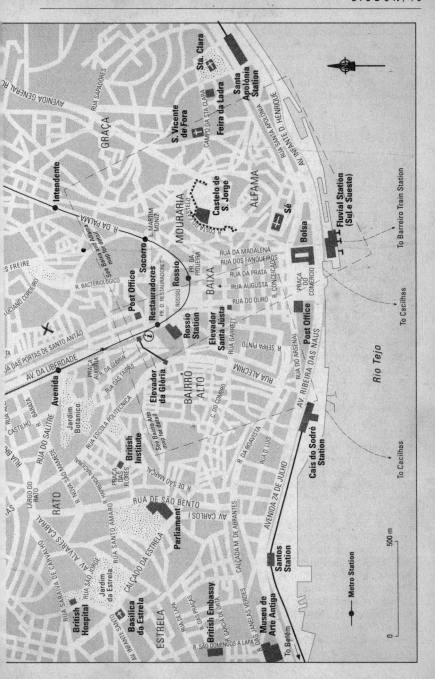

From Rossío, the main, tree-lined **Avenida da Liberdade** runs north to the city's central park, **Parque Eduardo VII**, beyond which spreads the rest of the modern city: the **Amoreiras** complex is to the west, the **Gulbenkian** museum to the north, and mundane shopping streets to the east. Out of the centre, the interest is in **Belém**, 6km to the west, en route to which lies Lisbon's other main museum, the **Museu de Arte Antiga**, in the suburb of Lapa.

Arrival and Information

The first place to head for is **Rossío**, which is easily accessible from all points of arrival, either on foot, or by bus and taxi. Most of the city's pensions are within walking distance of the square, and on the western side of the adjoining Praça dos Restauradores the English-speaking **Turismo** (Mon–Sat 9am–8pm, Sun 10am–6pm; ☎346 33 14)), in the Palácio da Foz, can provide you with accommodation lists, bus timetables and a good, semi-three-dimensional **map** of the city.

By air

The **airport** is just twenty minutes' north of the centre, where there's a small 24-hour tourist office, an exchange bureau and a hotels desk (see "Accommodation" below). There are also car rental agencies at the airport; details in "Listings" on p.84.

The easiest way into the centre is by **taxi**, which should cost 1500–20000$00 to Rossío, depending on traffic conditions. Note that you'll be charged up to 300$00 extra for baggage. Alternatively, catch the **Linha Verde (#90) express bus**, which departs every 15 minutes (7.30am–10pm; 250$00) from outside the terminal, running to Praça Marquês de Pombal, Rossío, Praça do Comércio and Santa Apolónia train stations. Cheaper **local buses** – #44 or #45 – leave from the other side of the car park to Praça dos Restauradores and Cais do Sodré station (every 10–15min, 6am to 1am; 160$00).

By train

Long-distance trains – from Coimbra, Porto and the north (and from Badajoz, Madrid and Paris) – use **Santa Apolónia station**, about fifteen minutes' walk east of Praça do Comércio, or a short ride on buses #9 or #46 from Rossío. At the station there's a helpful information office (Mon–Sat 9am–7pm) and an exchange bureau. The *Linha Verde* #90 bus (see "By air", above) also operates from here, running past Fluvial station (see below), Rossío, Saldanha and the airport.

Trains from the Algarve and south involve a slightly more involved approach. The railway lines from the south terminate at the suburb of Barreiro, on the far bank of the river, where you catch a ferry (included in the price of the train ticket) to the **Fluvial** (or *Sul e Sueste*) station, next to Praça do Comércio. Buses #1, #2, #9, #32, #39, #44 and #45 run up from Fluvial to Rossío.

Local trains – from Sintra or anywhere else in Estremadura – emerge right in the heart of the city at the **Rossío station**, a mock-Manueline complex with the train platforms an improbable escalator-ride above the street-level entrances. It is complete with shops, bank exchange counters and left luggage cabins. The other local station, **Cais do Sodré**, is fairly central, too, a ten-minute walk west of Praça do Comércio, for trains to and from Cascais and Estoril.

The telephone code for the Greater Lisbon area is ☎01.

By bus

Various bus companies have terminals scattered about the city, but the main one is at **Avenida Casal Ribeiro** (metro *Saldanha*), newly refurbished and with an information office that can help with all bus arrival and departure details. This terminal is also where most international bus services arrive. You can usually buy tickets if you turn up half an hour or so in advance, though for the summer express services to the Algarve it's best to book a seat (through any travel agent) a day in advance. For destinations not covered from Avenida Casal Ribeiro, check with the Turismo for the latest details; and see "Listings" (p.84) for a list of other bus terminals in the city.

By car

Driving into Lisbon can take years off your life, and at the beginning or end of public holiday weekends is to be avoided at all costs. Heading to or from the south on these occasions, it can take over an hour just to cross the Ponte 25 de Abril, a notorious traffic bottleneck. **Parking** is also very difficult in the centre; the best place for which to head for space is Campo Pequeno, next to the bullring. Wherever you park, do not leave valuables inside: the break-in rate is extremely high. If you are **renting a car** on arrival, the best advice is to wait until the day you leave the city and then head out to the airport to pick up your rental car; see "Listings" for car rental companies. You really don't need your own transport to get around Lisbon and its surroundings.

City transport

Most places of interest are within easy walking distance of each other, and transport connections – by tram, bus or Metro – are detailed in the text for those that are further away. Taxis are among the cheapest in Europe and a useful complement at all hou further away. Note that although it's one of the safer cities in Europe, Lisbon has its share of **pickpockets**. Take special care on buses and the metro, and walking around the main squares.

If you're staying for more than a few days, the **tourist pass** (*Passe Turístico*; 1350$00 for four days, 1900$00 for seven) might be worth considering. It's valid on trams, buses, *elevadors* and the metro, and is available, on production of a passport, at the booth by the *Elevador Santa Justa*. For longer stays, there is the *Passe Social*, renewable each calendar month (currently 2670$00); it can also be obtained at the *elevador* or at any metro station with a *venta de passes* sign; you'll need a photograph. Otherwise, just buy a ticket each time you ride: all the details are given below.

Trams, elevadors and buses

At the slightest excuse you should ride one of the city's **trams** (*eléctricos*). Ascending some of the steepest gradients of any city in the world, many are worth taking for the pleasure of the ride alone; a few of the best routes are detailed below. Two funicular railways and one street lift – all known as an **eleva-**

USEFUL TRAM AND FUNICULAR ROUTES

Trams

#12: São Tomé in the Alfama to Largo Martim Moniz, near Praça da Figueira.

#15/#17: From Praça do Comércio to Belém; #17 doesn't run on Sundays.

#28: The best ride in the city, from São Vicente to the Estrêla gardens, passing through Rua da Conceição in Baixa.

Elevadors

Elevador Santa Justa: A lift, rather than a funicular, taking you from Rua do Ouro, on the west side of the Baixa, up to a walkway by the Carmo church.

Elevador da Bica: Funicular linking Rua do Loreto/Rua Luz Soriano in Bairro Alto to Rua de São Paulo near Cais do Sodré station.

Elevador da Glória: A funicular to the Bairro Alto from Praça dos Restauradores.

dor – are also exciting forms of transport, offering quick access up to the Bairro Alto. **Buses** (*carris*) run just about everywhere in the Lisbon area and can prove valuable for getting to and from the more outlying attractions. Most of the trams, buses and *elevadors* run every ten to fifteen minutes throughout the day, from around 6.30am to midnight: stops are indicated by a sign marked *paragem*, which usually carries route details.

Individual **tickets** for a bus, tram or *elevador* bought on board cost 140$00; it's 135$00 for a ticket valid for two journeys if you buy them from a kiosk in advance (there's one at the *Elevador Santa Justa*). Or you can buy a one-day (350$00) or three-day (820$00) **pass**, which you validate by punching in the machine by the driver the first time you ride; it's then valid for 24 or 72 hours.

A couple of **tourist tram tours** run during the summer months, departing from Praça do Comércio: the *Linha das Colinas* ("hills line"; May, June & Oct 2 daily; July & Aug 5–7 daily; Sept 3 daily; 2600$00, children under 10, 1400$00) and the *Linha do Tejo* ("Tagus line"; July & Aug Tues–Fri at 2pm; 3000$00, children under 10, 1000$00. For more information on these routes, call ☎363 93 43.

The Metro, trains and ferries

Lisbon's **Metro** – the *Metropolitano* – covers a few useful routes (to the Gulbenkian museum, for example), though as a visitor you're unlikely to make extensive use of it. The most central stations are at Praça dos Restauradores and Rossío, and the **hours of operation** are from 6am to 1am. **Tickets** are 55$00 a journey; or 500$00 for a ten-ticket *caderneta* – sold at all stations.

There is a **local train** line west along the coast through Belém, to Estoril and Cascais, departing from Cais do Sodré station, west of Praça do Comércio. Tickets to Estoril/Cascais are currently 155$00 one-way.

Finally, **ferries** cross the Tejo at various points. From Praça do Comércio (*Sul e Sueste*), there are crossings to Cacilhas (daily 6am–10.30pm; 95$00 one way), Barreiro and Montijo (daily 6am–10.30pm; 275$00), worth doing for the terrific views of Lisbon alone. From Cais do Sodré, ferries also cross to Cacilhas (5.30am–2.30am; 95$00), while from Belém there are services to Trafaria (daily 7am–9pm; 200$00), from where you catch buses to Caparica.

Taxis

Lisbon's **taxis** are inexpensive, so long as your destination is within the city limits; there's a minimum charge of 250$00 and an average ride will run to around 500–600$00 (a little more at night). All taxis have meters, which are generally switched on, and tips are not expected; a green light means the cab is occupied. The only problem is persuading a taxi to stop. They can be found quite easily by day – there are **ranks** in Rossío, as well as at the southern end of Avenida da Liberdade and at Cais do Sodré. At night, going home from a bar or restaurant, it's usually best to phone *Rádio Taxis* (☎82 50 61 – or 62/63/64/65/66/67/68/69).

Accommodation

If you have money for mid-range pensions and the more expensive categories of hotels, you're probably best off using the **booking service** at the Turismo in Praça dos Restauradores, which operates during normal office hours (Mon–Sat 9am–8pm, Sun 10am–6pm); there is no commission charge. The airport hotel desk, facing you as you pass through customs on arrival, will establish whether or not there's space at a city pension or hotel – but they won't reserve the room for you.

Lisbon has scores of small, inexpensive **pensions**, often grouped one on top of the other in tall tenement buildings in all the central parts of the city. The most obvious and accessible accommodation area, with dozens of possibilities, is around Rossío station, in the streets and alleys between Praça dos Restauradores and Praça da Figueira. Among cheaper pensions here, the most likely to have space at busy times of year are those on either side of Avenida da Liberdade and on parallel streets, such as Rua Portas de Santo Antão and Rua da Glória – though some of the pensions on the latter double up as brothels. The Baixa grid, to the south, has a fair selection of places, too, with a couple of more upmarket choices in the Chiado's shopping streets. Bairro Alto is probably the most atmospheric part of the city to stay in – though rooms in its few pensions can be hard to come by – and there are a couple of attractive places on the periphery of the Alfama, climbing up towards the castle. Finally, a number of more expensive places are located some way out from the historic centre: either in the prosperous streets around Parque Eduardo VII; or further east, in the area around Avenida Almirante Reis – in particular the streets between Anjos and Arroios metro stops.

When doing the rounds, be warned that the pensions tend to occupy upper stories (leaving one person with all your bags is a good idea if you're in company). **Addresses** – written below as 53-3°, etc – specify the street number followed by the storey number. Don't be put off unduly by some fairly unsalubri-

---

ACCOMMODATION PRICE CODES

All the accommodation prices in this book have been coded using the symbols below. The symbols represent the prices for the cheapest available double room in high season; for a full explanation, see p.23.

① Under 3000$00   ② 3000$00–4000$00   ③ 4000$00–5500$00
④ 5500$00–8500$00   ⑤ 8500$00–12,500$00   ⑥ 12,500$00–20,000$00
⑦ Over 20,000$00

ous staircases; though do beware that rooms facing onto the street in Lisbon can be pretty noisy.

At Easter, and even more so in midsummer, room **availability** is often stretched to the limit, with many single rooms "converted" to doubles, and prices artificially inflated. At this time you should be prepared to take anything vacant and look around next day, if need be, for somewhere better, or possibly cheaper. Fortunately, during most of the year you should have little difficulty in finding a room, and you can always try to knock the price down at quieter times, especially if you can summon a few good-natured phrases in Portuguese.

Lisbon has two **youth hostels**, one in the city centre and one out at Oeiras, overlooking the sea. For details of these, and the city's **camping** possibilities, turn to p.52–53.

Around Restauradores, Rossío and Praça da Figueira

Pensão Arco da Bandeira, Rua dos Sapateiros 226-4° (☎342 34 78). Highly recommended and friendly *pensão* with half a dozen comfortable rooms, some overlooking Rossío. The separate bathrooms are spotless. The entrance is just through the arch at the southern end of the square. ③.

Hotel Avenida Palace, Rua 1° de Dezembro (☎346 01 51). Lisbon's best downtown hotel, tucked away off Praça dos Restauradores. Elegant nineteenth-century style, very comfortable and correspondingly expensive. ⑦.

Pensão Beira Minho, Praça da Figueira 6-2° (☎886 74 12). Tiny place, entered through a flower shop. Some rooms (with and and without bath) have been recently renovated, though singles without windows may put off lone travellers. ②–③.

Pensão Cidre, Trav. Nova de São Domingos 9-4°. One block north of Praça da Figueira, the *Cidre* offers bargain hostel-type accommodation and other rooms at variable rates. The showers are cold, but there's no curfew and the friendly Brazilian owners will look after luggage and change money. ①.

Pensão Coimbra e Madrid, Praça da Figueira 3-3° (☎342 17 60). Fairly upmarket *pensão*, next to the *Pastelaria Suíça*, with superb views of Rossío and Praça da Figueira. Rooms (and there are lots of them) come with shower or bath; there's a TV room, too. ③–④.

Pensão Dona Maria II, Rua Portas de Santo Antão 9-3° (☎347 11 28). Large airy rooms (with washbasin) and nice views over Rossío, though single rooms don't always come up to scratch. ②.

Pensão Estação Central, Calçada do Carmo 17-2° (☎342 33 08). To the side of Rossío station; climb the flight of stairs and head up the road to the left. Small and musty rooms, but just about acceptable for the price. ②.

Pensão Flor da Baixa, Rua Portas de Santo Antão 81-2° (☎342 31 53). Almost opposite the *Coliseu*, and entered through an electrical supply shop. A modern, efficiently run *pensão* with pleasant rooms. ②.

Residencial Florescente, Rua Portas de Santo Antão 99 (☎342 66 09). Despite the uniformed staff at reception, which suggests high prices, this is one of the street's best-value establishments. There's a large selection of rooms, so if you don't like the look of the one you're shown, ask about alternatives. ③–④.

Pensão Ibérica, Praça da Figueira 10-2° (☎886 70 26). Central location and lots of rooms but a bit ramshackle. The rooms overlooking the praça are best, but you'll find them very noisy. ③.

Pensão Imperial, Praça dos Restauradores 78-4° (☎342 01 66). Securing a room with a view up the avenue makes this place worthwhile; otherwise nothing special. ③.

Pensão Iris, Rua da Glória 2a-1° (☎32 31 57). An extremely off-putting entrance does this place a disservice: up the stairs and through the door are large, clean rooms (triples available), some with shower and a couple overlooking the main avenue. Ones at the side are a bit too close to the clanking street funicular for comfort. ②.

Pensão Monumental, Rua da Glória 21 (☎346 98 07). A backpackers' favourite with a mixed bag of rooms in a rambling old building; the hot water supply is a little erratic. ②.

Pensao Pemba, Avda. da Liberdade 11-3° (☎342 50 10). Decent value rooms on the avenida, most with private showers. ③.

Pensão Portuense, Rua Portas de Santo Antão 153 (☎346 17 49). Singles and doubles available in a family run place that takes good care of its guests. The spacious bathrooms are meticulously clean, the water stays hot, and breakfast is provided. ②.

The Baixa and Chiado

Hotel Borges, Rua Garrett 108–110 (☎346 19 53). Nice position above the *Brasileira* café in Chiado's main street, though the rooms are very ordinary and the hotel itself rather musty. ④–⑤.

Hotel Duas Nações, Rua da Vitória 41 (☎346 20 82). Classy, pleasantly faded, nineteenth-century hotel in the Baixa grid. Rooms with bath are more attractive in every way, but cost quite a bit more. ③–④.

Pensão Galicia, Rua do Crucifixo (☎342 84 30). Clean rooms and a fine Baixa location. Given the good prices, you'll need to ring ahead to be certain of a room. ②.

Residencial Insulana, Rua da Assunção 52 (☎342 76 25). One of the most opulent in the Baixa: fine deep-pile carpet comfort and good breakfasts. ⑤.

Pensão Marinho, Rua dos Correeiros 205-2° (☎346 09 40). Unprepossessing exterior but reasonable enough inside. ②.

Pensão Moderna, Rua dos Correeiros 205-4° (☎346 08 18). Above the *Marinho*, big clean rooms, crammed with elderly furniture. Atmospheric and recommended. ③.

Residencial Nova Silva, Rua Vítor Cordon 11-2° (☎342 43 71). A very comfortable hotel. Small rooms with good, firm beds, kind staff and wonderful views out across the river. ③.

Pensão Prata, Rua da Prata 71-3° (☎346 89 08). Clean and friendly place with showers in the rooms. ②–③.

Residencial Primavera, Rua dos Correeiros 161-2° (☎342 59 83). Quiet and reasonably welcoming, but not the most inspiring rooms you'll see in the Baixa. ③.

Bairro Alto

Casa de Hóspedes Atalaia, Rua da Atalaia 150-1° (☎346 44 59). At the lower, river end of the Bairro Alto, near Cais do Sodré station. Tolerable at the price, but standards vary and you can find yourself uncomfortably remote from the shared bathrooms. Very active nocturnal life – mostly human rather than insect. ②.

Residencial Bragança, Rua do Alecrim 12 (☎342 70 61 or 342 11 14). Very large – the clean rooms come with private bath and phone. ③.

Residencial Camões, Trav. do Poço da Cidade 38 (☎346 40 48). Right in the heart of Bairro Alto, for which you pay quite dearly. But this is a friendly place, with clean, light rooms, the more expensive ones with private bathroom. ③.

Pensão Duque, Calçada do Duque 53, (☎346 34 44). Near São Roque church and consequently just outside the nightclub zone, which means comparatively quiet nights. Fairly basic rooms but reasonably priced. ②.

Pensão Globo, Rua do Teixeira 37 (☎346 22 79). Just behind the famous Port Wine Institute and across the road from the Jardim São Pedro de Alcântara and the *Elevador da Glória*. Rooms are clean, management fine and the location, in a quiet Bairro Alto street, superb. Shared shower and toilet at the top. ③.

Pensão Londres, Rua Dom Pedro V 53 (☎346 55 23). Another nice location: turn right as you leave the *Elevador da Glória*. Pleasant rooms spread across several floors. ③.

Residencial Santa Catarina, Rua Dr Luis de Almeida e Albuquerque 6 (☎346 61 06). Nicely located in a small street just off Calçada do Combro. Very good value for its price, with accommodating staff. ④.

LAPA

Residencial York House, Rua das Janelas Verdes (☎396 25 44); tram #19. West of the Bairro Alto, this four-star hotel is installed in a sixteenth-century convent, packed with antiques and with its best rooms grouped around a beautiful interior courtyard. The *York House Annexe*, at no. 4, is a pleasant townhouse but not really so special – better to book ahead for the real thing. ⑥.

Alfama

Pensão Ninho das Águias, Costa do Castelo 74 (☎886 70 08). Rather surly management, and unremarkable rooms (with and without bath), but beautifully sited in its own view-laden garden on the street looping around the castle. ③–④.

Pensão São João de Praça, Rua São João de Praça (☎86 25 91). Clean, quiet and friendly choice on one of the lower streets. Breakfast costs an extra 200$00. ②.

Albergaria Senhora do Monte, Calçada do Monte 39 (☎886 60 02). Comfortable, modern hotel in a beautiful location with lovely views of the castle and Graça convent from the south-facing rooms; breakfast included. ⑤.

Around Praça Marquês de Pombal and Saldanha

Residencial Avenida Alameda, Avda. Sidónio Pais 4 (☎353 21 86). Very pleasant hotel in a top location; breakfast included. ⑤.

Residencial Canada, Avda. Defensores de Chaves 35-1° (☎352 14 41). Excellent value for money, with private bathrooms (and satellite TV) in all rooms. Kept immaculate by a bevy of charming ladies. Recommended. ④.

Hotel Eduardo VII, Avda. Fontes Pereira de Melo 5 (☎353 51 41). Smart old choice with a rooftop bar and restaurant and recently renovated rooms. ⑥.

Pensão Embaixatriz, Rua Pedro Nunes 45-2° (☎353 10 29). Welcoming management make this a perennially popular place. Inexpensive (even less for a room with a shower instead of a bath) and, while old, it's clean and respectable. ②.

Hotel Fenix, Praça Marquês de Pombal 8 (☎386 21 21). Large four-star hotel with all the associated comforts and a decent location. ⑥–⑦.

Pensão Pátria, Avda. Duque d'Ávila 42-6° (☎315 06 20). Highly convenient for the main bus station if you're leaving town; less obviously recommendable if you're staying, though the rooms are quite large and cheerful. ④.

Around Avenida Almirante Reis

Pensão Fernandina, Rua António Pedro 52-1° (☎353 63 79). Just off Praça do Chile near Arroios metro. Spick and span, but contains rather alarming faded 1960s' furnishings. ②.

Pensão Lar do Areeiro, Praça Dr. Francisco de Sá Carneiro 4-1°; metro Areeiro (☎849 31 50). Very respectable, if old-fashioned, and well-run pension, whose rooms all have attached bath. It's right on the praça, which means it's noisy; ask for a room at the back. Breakfast is included. ④.

Residencial Luena, Rua Pascoal de Melo 9; metro Arroios (☎355 84 26). A competent management maintains neat, welcoming rooms with private bathrooms; breakfast included. It's also handy for the bus station. ④.

Residencial Pascoal de Melo, Rua Pascoal de Melo 127–131; metro Arroios. Three-star *residencial* whose clean rooms all have attached bathrooms.

Residencial Paradouro, Avda. Almirante Reis 106-7° (☎815 32 56). Not overpriced for its high standard. ④.

Youth Hostels

Pousada de Juventude de Lisboa, Rua Andrade Corvo 46 (☎53 26 96). This is the main city hostel, with 200 beds. It's not a bad location, near Parque Eduardo VII; to get there, take the metro to Picoas and walk a block south.

Pousada de Juventude de Catalazete, Forte do Catalazete, Oeiras (☎443 06 28). An attractive small hostel, overlooking the beach at Oeiras, between Belém and Cascais. To reach it, take any train from Cais do Sodré and follow signs from Oeiras station under the coast road (*Estrada Marginal*) and through the park – around 1km. Phone before setting out.

Campsites

The choice comes down to the major municipal campsite, northwest of the centre in the rambling woods of the Parque Florestal de Monsanto, the little campsite at Oeiras on the Estoril coast, or making your base across the river from the city at one of the beach campsites along the Costa da Caparica.

Parque Municipal de Turismo e Campismo (☎70 20 61). The main city campsite – with a swimming pool and shops – is 6km west of the city centre, though buses run every 15min or so. The entrance is on Estrada da Circunvalação on the park's west side. Either take a train from Cais do Sodré to Algés, then bus #50 to the campsite; or bus #43 from Praça da Figueira.

Costa da Caparica. There are several small and lively campsites here, 30–50min away by bus from the Praca de Espanha terminal, or by a ferry from Cais do Sodré to Cacilhas and then local bus on from there. See p.99.

Oeiras (☎243 03 30). A tiny site on the Estoril coast, overlooking the sea.

The City

Eighteenth-century prints show a pre-quake Lisbon of tremendous opulence and mystique, its skyline characterised by towers, palaces and convents. There are glimpses of this still – the old Moorish hillside of **Alfama** survived the destruction, as did Belém – but these are isolated neighbourhoods and monuments. It is instead Pombal's perfect Neoclassical grid that covers the centre. Given orders, following the earthquake, to "Bury the dead, feed the living and close the ports", the king's minister followed his success in restoring order to the city with a complete rebuilding. The **Baixa**, still the heart of the modern city, adheres to his strict ideals of simplicity and economy. Individual streets were assigned to each craft and trade and the whole enterprise was shaped by public buildings and squares. Only **Rossío**, the main square since medieval times, remained in its original place, slightly off-centre in the symmetrical design.

Lisbon's contemporary interest lies as much in the everyday aspects of the city as in any specific sights. The cafés, markets, trams, ferries across the Tejo: all these are sufficient stimulation for random wanderings. The most rewarding areas, as you'd expect, are the oldest: the upper and lower towns of Baixa and **Bairro Alto**, and the winding lanes and anarchic stairways of Alfama. However, other outlying areas of the city provide strong attractions in their museums – above all the **Gulbenkian** and **Arte Antiga** – gardens and palaces. And no stay in Lisbon should neglect the waterfront suburb of **Belém**, to the west, dominated by one of the country's grandest monuments, the **Jerónimos** monastery.

The Baixa

The lower town – the **Baixa** – is very much the heart of the capital, housing many of the country's administrative departments, banks and business offices. Europe's first great example of Neoclassical design and urban planning, it remains an imposing quarter of rod-straight streets, cobbled underfoot and either streaming with traffic or turned over to pedestrians, street performers and pavement artists. A major appeal of the Baixa is the survival of tradition. Many of the streets in the grid maintain their crafts and businesses as Pombal devised: in Rua da Prata (Silversmiths' St), Rua dos Sapateiros (Cobblers' St), Rua do Ouro (Goldsmiths' St), Rua do Comércio (Commercial St). These, along with the mosaic-sidewalked squares, are a visual delight, with tiled Art Deco shopfronts and advertising boards still surviving here and there.

At the waterfront end of the Baixa, the **Praça do Comércio** was intended as the climax to Pombal's design, surrounded by classical buildings and centred on an exuberant bronze of Dom José, monarch during the earthquake and the capital's rebuilding. Seen from the river – from ferries crossing from Barreiro and Cacilhas – the design is graceful and impressive, with the streets of the Baixa extending into the distance beyond. Close up, however, it seems less substantial and less glamourous, having been largely requisitioned as a car park. Lisbon town planners are working on projects to bring the square back into the hub of city life, by pedestrianising the area and opening more cafés, but the only sign of life is still the dimly lit, old-world café of *Martinho da Arcada*, one of the poet Pessoa's haunts.

The Praça do Comércio has a popular name – **Terreiro do Paço**, after the old royal palace which stood here and whose steps still lead up from the Tejo – and has played an important part in the country's history. In 1908, alongside the Central Post Office, King Carlos I and his eldest son were shot and killed, opening the way to the declaration of the Republic two years later.

Rossío

Architecturally, and as points toward which to gravitate, the most interesting places in the Baixa are the squares, and **Rossío** – at the northern end of the Baixa grid – is no exception. The square itself is modest in appearance, but very much a focus for the city, sporting several lively cafés, most of which have outdoor seating. Two of the best are the *Pastelaria Suíça*, on the east side, famous for its cakes and, opposite, the beautifully decorated *Nicola*. The square's single concession to grandeur is the **Teatro Nacional**, built along the north side in the 1840s. Here, prior to the earthquake, stood the Inquisitional Palace; bullfights, public hangings and *autos-da-fé* (ritual burnings of heretics) used to take place in the square. The nineteenth-century statue atop the central column is of Dom Pedro IV (after whom the square is officially named), though curiously it's a bargain adaptation: cast originally as Maximilian of Mexico, it just happened to be in Lisbon en route from France when news came through of his assassination.

The church beyond the square, **São Domingos**, was where the Inquisition actually read out its sentences; though blackened and gutted by a fire in the 1950s, the building is still in religious use.

Chiado

On the west side of the Baixa, stretching up the hillside towards the Bairro Alto, the area known as **Chiado** – the *nom de plume* of the poet António Ribeiro – suffered much damage from a fire that swept across the Baixa in August 1988. This destroyed the *Grandella* department store and many old shops in Rua do Crucifixo, and though the damage is slowly being made good it still makes for a mouth-opening stroll past gutted buildings and jagged holes in the ground as if left by giant pulled teeth.

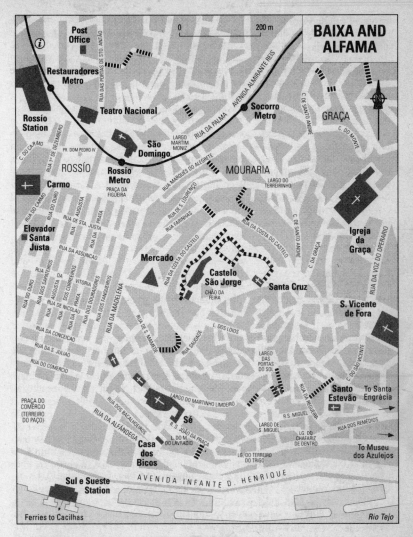

Chiado, however, remains one of the city's most affluent quarters, focused on the fashionable shops and old café-tearooms of the Rua Garrett. Of these, **A Brasileira**, Rua Garrett 120, is the most famous, having been frequented by generations of Lisbon's literary and intellectual leaders – the very readable Eça de Queiroz and Portugal's greatest twentieth-century poet, Fernando Pessoa, among them. While on Rua Garrett, take a stroll past **Igreja dos Mártires**, which occupies the site of the Crusader camp during the Siege of Lisbon. As its name suggests, the church was built on the site of a burial ground, created for the English contingent of the besieging army.

Around Cais do Sodré

Ten minutes' walk west of the Baixa grid, along the riverfront, is **Cais do Sodré** station, from where trains run out to Estoril and Cascais, and ferries cross to Cacilhas. It's not the most elegant, or inviting, of areas, but its various **markets** are particularly wonderful. A good case in point is the huge **fish market** which takes place, daily except Sundays, from dawn behind the station, where you can still see *varinas*, fishwives from Alfama, who were joined a few years ago by groups from Cabo Verde, bargaining for and carting off great baskets of wares on their heads.

Take a look inside the **Ribeira market**, too, the domed building on the right of Cais do Sodré. Even if you're not tempted by the arrays of food – least of all perhaps by the gruesome slabs of flesh and innards – the fruit, flower, spice and vegetable displays on the upper story are impressive. Rua do Arsenal, just behind the market, is packed with stalls selling fresh fish and dried cod, while grocers here are stocked with everything, including unbelievably cheap wines and spirits.

Just as diverting, and perhaps more desirable after a long night out, is the **fruit and vegetable market** down by the waterfront further west, toward Belém. Four in the morning is the perfect time to share a glass of hot *cacão* with the traders in the market bar.

East to the Sé

A couple of blocks east of Praça do Comércio is the church of **Conceição Velha**, severely damaged by the earthquake but retaining its flamboyant Manueline doorway, an early example of this style and hinting at the brilliance that emerged at Belém. It once formed part of the Misericórdia (almshouse) – you'll find one of these impressive structures in almost every Portuguese town or city. Nearby, at Campo das Cebolas, stands the curious **Casa dos Bicos**, set with diamond-shaped stones and again offering an image of the richness of pre-1755 Lisbon. The building is not routinely open, though it sees fairly regular use for cultural exhibitions.

The Sé

Lisbon's cathedral – the **Sé** (daily 8.30am–6pm) – stands very stolidly above the Baixa grid. Founded in 1150 to commemorate the city's reconquest from the Moors, it has a suitably fortress-like appearance, similar to that of Coimbra, and in fact occupies the site of the principal mosque of Moorish *Lishbuna*. Like so many of the country's cathedrals, it is Romanesque – and extraordinarily restrained in both size and decoration. The great rose window and twin towers form a simple and effective facade, but inside there's nothing very exciting: the building was once splendidly embellished on the orders of Dom João V, but his rococo whims were swept away by the earthquake and subsequent restorers. All that remains is a group of Gothic tombs behind the high altar and the decaying thirteenth-century **cloister**.

For admission to this you must buy a ticket (Tues–Sun 10am–1pm & 2–6pm; 120$00, free on Sun), which also covers the Baroque *Sacristia* with its small museum of treasures – including the relics of Saint Vincent, brought to Lisbon in 1173 by Afonso Henriques in a boat piloted by ravens (see "Sagres", p.390). For centuries the descendants of these birds were shown to visitors but the last one, despite great care from the sacristan, died in 1978. Nevertheless, ravens are still one of the city's symbols.

DEVELOPMENT AND DESTRUCTION

In recent years Lisbon has experienced some of the most radical **redevelopment** since the Marquês de Pombal rebuilt the shattered capital after the 1755 earthquake. This is mainly the result of Portugal's relative economic stability – and extensive grants – since joining the European Community in 1986. As a result of cheap labour costs, foreign investment has been pouring into the capital, necessitating a rapid reconstruction programme. This investment has pulled Portugal off the bottom rung of the EC prosperity ladder, above Greece, but at a price: much of old Lisbon has shrunk – including huge swathes of the lovely Parque Eduardo VII; many of the city's beautiful pre-war mansions are being demolished to make way for towering office buildings; and it's likely that most of the trams will eventually disappear to provide space for faster roads.

Ironically, it is beyond Pombal's statue at Rotunda that the worst of the damage is being done. Avenida da República's beauty has all but disappeared and as the green gauze goes up across the graceful façades, the labourers set to, dismantling the buildings with hammers and picks, piece by piece – a dangerous process for both workers and passers-by, who are often showered with lumps of masonry escaping the protective nets. The concrete blocks that take the place of the old houses (supposedly more earthquake-proof than their predecessors) are erected with similar disregard for pedestrians: iron girders and stacks of bricks swing perilously over pavements from rickety cranes.

Much of the blame for the scandalous demolition of the grand mansions can be laid at the door of an inconsistent planning department. The city's highly bureaucratic **planning regulations**, which could be used to safeguard old buildings, are rumoured to be easily bypassed with some financial persuasion. At the same time, pre-revolutionary **rent laws** have contributed to appalling living conditions in Lisbon's older tenements, some of which are literally falling apart and have no chance of being repaired. Only the property developers are prepared to take on such slums – provided they're in prime sites.

The cause of this state of affairs is simple. In Lisbon, **rents** set before the revolution were fixed for life. This means that pre-revolution tenants are still paying miniscule amounts while rents on new accommodation spiral to northern European levels. Landlords of old buildings find themselves with unremovable tenants, and receive such a small income for their property that they can't afford renovations. Nor can they sell, as no one will buy property with tenants already installed; and the slum-bound tenants themselves can't afford to move out to new properties. This impasse has brought about a tidal wave of destruction.

But not all of old Lisbon is lost and at least the **city centre** will retain its elegance. EC funding is helping a renovation scheme in Lisbon's protected areas, including Lisbon's oldest quarter, the **Alfama**. Residents are temporarily rehoused while crumbling buildings are refaced and hot water and reliable electricity are put in. Parts of the **Baixa** and the wealthy **Lapa** areas have already been preserved, while European Community protection orders have also been slapped on some of Lisbon's finest buildings. The most obvious sign of renovation is in the streets of the **Chiado**, burned out in the 1988 fire and currently the subject of an ambitious redevelopment plan to restore the original design.

Up to the Castelo

From the Sé, Rua do Limoeiro winds upward toward the castle, past sparse ruins of a Roman theatre to the well-positioned Igreja da Santa Luzia and the adjacent **Miradouro da Santa Luzia**, from where there are fine views down to the river.

Just beyond, in Largo das Portas do Sol, is the *Espírito Santo Foundation*, home of the **Museu das Artes Decorativas**, a seventeenth-century mansion, stuffed with period furnishings and with a handful of truly beautiful pieces. It's been closed for restoration for some time, but should be open again in the near future: previously, compulsory guided tours used to point out *everything* – "traditional Portuguese, Indian, Brazilian", etc – making for something of an endurance test for any but the most committed tourists.

Castelo de São Jorge

The conquest of Lisbon from the Moors – and the siege of the **Castelo de São Jorge** – are depicted in *azulejos* on the walls of the church of Santa Luzia. An important victory, leading to Muslim surrender at Sintra and throughout the surrounding district, this was not, however, the most Christian or glorious of Portuguese exploits. A full account survives, written by one Osbern of Bawdsley, an English priest and crusader, and its details, despite the author's judgmental tone, direct one's sympathies to the enemy.

The attack, in the summer of 1147, came through the opportunism and skillful management of Afonso Henriques, already established as "King" at Porto, who persuaded a large force of French and British Crusaders to delay their progress to Jerusalem for more immediate goals. The Crusaders – scarcely more than pirates – came to terms and in June the siege began. Osbern records the Archbishop of Braga's demand for the Moors to return to "the land whence you came" and, more revealingly, the weary and contemptuous response of the Muslim spokesman: "How many times have you come hither with pilgrims and barbarians to drive us hence? It is not want of possessions but only ambition of the mind that drives you on". For seventeen weeks the castle and inner city stood firm but in October its walls were breached and the citizens – including a Christian community coexisting with the Muslims – were forced to surrender.

The pilgrims and barbarians, flaunting the diplomacy and guarantees of Afonso Henriques, stormed into the city, cut the throat of the local bishop and sacked, pillaged and murdered Christian and Muslim alike. In 1190 a later band of English Crusaders stopped at Lisbon and, no doubt confused by the continuing presence of Moors, sacked the city a second time.

The Castelo

A triumphant statue of Afonso Henriques – who alone emerges from the account with honour – stands at the entrance to the **Castelo** (daily 9am–sunset; free). Beyond stretch gardens and terraces, walkways and pools, all lying within the old Moorish walls. At first the Portuguese kings had taken up residence within the castle – in the *Alcáçova*, the Muslim palace – but by the time of Manuel I this had been superseded by the new royal palace on Terreiro do Paço. Of the *Alcáçova* only a much-restored shell remains, in which a small, rather insignificant museum (of Roman and Islamic tombstones) has been installed. But the castle as a whole is an enjoyable place to spend a couple of hours, wandering amid the ramparts and towers to look down upon the city. Crammed within the castle's outer walls is the tiny medieval quarter of **Santa Cruz**, once very much a village in itself, while to the north sprawls the old **Mouraria** quarter, to which the Moors were relegated on their loss of the town. This, despite a few grand old houses, is largely in decay, though currently undergoing substantial redevelopment.

Alfama

The oldest part of Lisbon, stumbling from the walls of the castle down to the Tejo, **Alfama** was buttressed against significant damage in the 1755 earthquake by the steep, rocky mass on which it's built. Although none of its houses dates from before the Christian conquest, many are of Moorish design and the kasbah-like layout is still much as Osbern described it, with "steep defiles instead of ordinary streets . . . and buildings so closely packed together that, except in the merchants' quarter, hardly a street could be found more than eight foot wide".

In Arab-occupied times Alfama was the grandest part of the city but following subsequent earthquakes the new Christian nobility moved out, leaving it to the local fishing community. Today, it is undergoing some commercialisation, with its cobbled lanes and "character", but although antique shops and restaurants are moving in, they are far from taking over. The quarter retains a largely traditional life of its own: you can eat at local prices in the cafés; the flea market engulfs the periphery of the area twice a week; and this is very much the place to be during the June "Popular Saints" festivals (above all on June 12), when makeshift *tavernas* appear on every corner.

The steep defiles, alleys and passageways are known as *becos* and *travessas* rather than *ruas*, and it would be impossible (as well as futile) to try and follow any set route. At some point in your wanderings around the quarter, though, head for the **Rua de São Miguel** – off which are some of the most interesting *becos* – and for the (lower) parallel **Rua de São Pedro**, the main market street leading to the lively **Largo do Chafariz de Dentro**.

The Feira da Ladra

The **Feira da Ladra**, Lisbon's rambling and ragged flea market, fills the Campo de Santa Clara, at the edge of Alfama, on Tuesday mornings and all day Saturday. Though it's certainly not the world's greatest – "you will find stalls with shabby ready-made clothes" advises the cautious Turismo pamphlet – it does turn up some interesting things: oddities from the former African colonies, old prints of the country, and army-surplus gear. Out-and-out junk – broken alarm clocks and old postcards – is spread on the ground above Santa Engrácia, and half-genuine antiques at the top end of the *feira*.

To get here, tram #28 runs from Rua da Conceição in the Baixa to São Vicente (see below), and bus #12 runs between Santa Apolónia station and Praça Marquês de Pombal.

Santa Engrácia and São Vicente de Fora

While at the flea market, take a look inside **Santa Engrácia**, the loftiest and most tortuously built church in the city. Begun in 1682 and once a synonym for unfinished work, its vast dome was finally completed in 1966. If you ask nicely, you may be allowed to take the elevator to the dome, from where you can look down on the empty church and out over the flea market, port and city.

More interesting, architecturally, is nearby **São Vicente de Fora**, whose name – "of the outside" – is a reminder of the extent of the sixteenth-century city. It is also where Afonso Henriques pitched camp during his siege and conquest of Lisbon. Built during the years of Spanish rule by Philip II's Italian architect, Felipe Terzi, its severe geometric facade was an important Renaissance innovation. Through the **cloisters**, decorated with *azulejos*, you can visit the old monastic refectory, which since 1855 has formed the **pantheon of the Bragança dynasty** (daily 10am–5pm; 200$00). Here, in more or less complete (though unexciting) sequence, are the bodies of all Portuguese kings from João IV, who restored the monarchy, to Manuel II, who lost it and died in exile in England in 1932. Among them is Catherine of Bragança, the widow of Charles II and (as the local guide points out) "the one who took the habit of the fifth o'clock tea to that country".

Further east: two museums

There's not much call to head east beyond the Alfama, unless you're leaving by train from the dockside **Santa Apolónia station**. Opposite here, a couple of blocks south of Santa Engrácia, is the city's military museum, the **Museu de Artilharia** (Tues–Sat 10am–4pm, Sun 11am–5pm; 150$00), though this is very traditional in lay-out – old weapons in old cases – and lacks much appeal.

Considerably more interesting is the **Museu dos Azulejos** (Tues–Sun 10am–5pm; 200$00) at Rua Madre de Deus 4, a little under a kilometre to the east (tram #3 or #16) of Santa Apolónia. It is installed in the church and cloisters of Madre de Deus, whose own eighteenth-century tiled scenes of the life of Saint Anthony are among the best in the city. The highlight, however, is Portugal's longest *azulejo* – a wonderfully detailed 120-foot panorama of Lisbon, completed in around 1738.

Bairro Alto

High above the central city, to the west, **Bairro Alto**, the upper town, is the natural place to wind up at night – in its *fado* houses, bars, excellent restaurants, or even the refined and somewhat dauntingly named *Instituto do Vinho do Porto* (Port Wine Institute). By day, the quarter's narrow seventeenth-century streets have a very different character, with children playing and the old sitting in doorways. It is well worth a morning or afternoon's exploration, with two of the city's most interesting churches – Carmo and São Roque – on the fringes and a couple of approaches to the quarter that are a treat in themselves.

Raul Mésnier's **Elevador Santa Justa**, just off the northern end of Rua do Ouro on Rua de Santa Justa, is the most startling approach to the Bairro Alto. A lift, built in 1902, it's one of the city's most extraordinary and eccentric structures, which whisks you up through metal latticework, depositing you on a platform high above the Baixa. Alternatives, and hardly more conventional feats of engineering, are the two funicular-like trams. One, the **Elevador da Glória**, links the quarter directly with Praça dos Restauradores, taking off just behind the tourist office on the left; the other, **Elevador da Bica**, climbs up to Rua do Loreto (west of Praça de Camões) from Rua de São Paulo/Rua da Moeda, northwest of Cais do Sodré. Tickets for all these services cost 140$00 each way and the *elevadors* operate from 7am to midnight daily.

Around the quarter

The *Elevador da Glória* drops you at the top of the hill on Rua de São Pedro de Alcântara, across the road from the **Instituto do Vinho do Porto** (see "Drinking, nightlife and live music", p.76). Turn left, down the road, and round the corner for the church of **São Roque**, in Largo Trindade Coelho, which looks from the outside like the plainest in the city, its bleak Renaissance facade (by

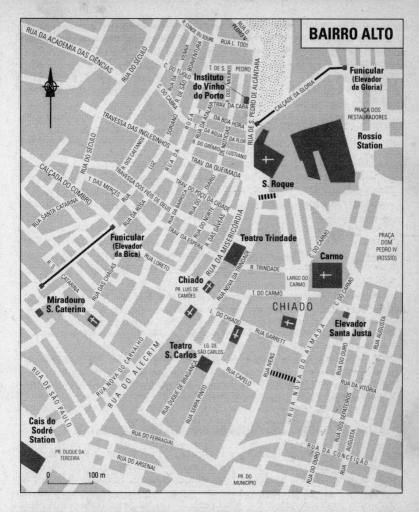

Filipo Terzi, architect of São Vicente) having been further simplified by the earth-quake. Nor does it seem impressive when you walk inside. But hang around in the gloom and the sacristan will come and escort you around, turning on lights to a succession of side chapels, each lavishly crafted with *azulejos* (some emulating reliefs), multicoloured marble, or Baroque painted ceilings.

The climax – to which you're proudly directed – is the **Capela de São João Baptista**, last on the left. This chapel, for its size, is estimated to be the most expensive ever constructed and was certainly one of the most bizarre commissions of its age. It was ordered from Rome in 1742 by Dom João V to honour his patron saint and, more dubiously, to requite the pope, whom he had persuaded to confer a patriarchate upon Lisbon. Designed by the papal architect, Vanvitelli, and using the most costly materials available (including ivory, agate, porphyry and lapis lazuli), it was actually erected at the Vatican for the pope to celebrate mass before being dismantled and shipped to Lisbon. The cost – then – was about £250,000 sterling, which is perhaps its chief curiosity. But there are other eccentricities. Take a close look at the four "oil paintings" of John the Baptist's life and you'll find that they are in fact mosaics, intricately worked over what must have been years rather than months.

Further south, the ruined Gothic arches of the **Convento do Carmo** hang almost directly above the exit of Mésnier's *elevador*. Once the largest church in the city, this was half-destroyed by the earthquake but is perhaps even more beautiful as a result. In the nineteenth century its shell was adapted as a chemical factory. These days it houses a small **archaeological museum** (Oct–March Mon–Sat 10am–1pm & 2–5pm; April–Sept Mon–Sat 10am–6pm; 300$00) with a very miscellaneous collection of medieval tombs and *azulejos* – barely a museum in fact, but no less atmospheric for that. At night, in summer, free classical concerts are often held here.

Estrêla

A third church, the **Basílica da Estrêla**, 2km to the west of Bairro Alto, is also worth a visit; it is half an hour on foot (or take tram #28 from Chiado). The church is memorable not so much for the building itself – a vast monument to late-eighteenth-century Neoclassicism – as for the view across the city from its dome, and for the **public gardens** below. Lisbon takes its gardens seriously, even the small patches amid squares and avenues, and these are among the most enjoyable, a quiet refuge often graced with an afternoon brass band. It has a pool of giant carp, too, and a café.

Through the park and on Rua de São Jorge is the gate to the post-Crusader **English Cemetery** (ring loudly for entry) where among the cypresses lies Henry Fielding, author of *Tom Jones*, whose imminent demise may have influenced his verdict on Lisbon as "the nastiest city in the world".

Parque Eduardo VII, Amoreiras and the Aqueduto

North of Praça dos Restauradores is the city's principal park – the **Parque Eduardo VII**. The easiest approach is by metro (to *Rotunda*), though you could walk up (energetically) in about twenty minutes along Avenida da Liberdade or take any bus going to the Rotunda. The big attractions here are the **Estufas** (9am–6pm, erratically closed at lunchtime; 75$00), huge and wonderful glass-houses at the top end of the park, filled with tropical plants, flamingo pools and endless varieties of palms and cacti. At the *Estufa Fria*, rock and classical concerts and an antiques fair are occasionally held.

Useful **bus links** from the park are #31, #41 and #46 to the Gulbenkian museum; #27 and #49 west to Belém; and #51, which runs to Belém from the top of the park near the *Estufa Fria*.

Amoreiras

West of the park, up Avenida Duarte Pacheco from the Rotunda, is Lisbon's post-Modernist shopping centre, **Amoreiras**, visible on the city skyline from almost any approach. The complex, designed by Tomás Taveira, is Portugal's most adventurous – and most entertaining – modern building: a wild fantasy of pink and blue, sheltering 10 cinemas, 60 cafés and restaurants, 370 shops and a hotel. Most of the shops here stay open until 11pm, seven days a week; Sunday sees the heaviest human traffic, with entire families descending for an afternoon out.

The Aqueduto das Águas Livres

Buses #11 (from Rossío) and #23 go past Amoreiras and then on past the **Aqueduto das Águas Livres**, just to the south. So, too, does the bus from Praça de Espanha to Caparica – affording enough of a view for most people. The aqueduct was opened in 1748, bringing reliable drinking water to the city for the first time. However, it gained a more notorious reputation through one Diogo Alves, a eighteenth-century serial murderer who threw his victims off the arches – a 200-foot drop. To visit the structure, check first at the Turismo that it's open; you can reach the entrance by walking to the left from the top of Parque Eduardo VII along Rua Marquês de Fronteira, Rua Carlos Mascarenhas and Calçada da Quintinha, up to Travessa da Quintinha. Once inside and up, you can walk across the aqueduct to the Parque Monsanto and return back via the Alcântara valley – a very scenic walk. En route, don't miss the former **Mãe d'Água cistern** at Rua das Amoreiras, close to Largo do Rato.

The Fundação Calouste Gulbenkian

The **Fundação Calouste Gulbenkian** is *the* great cultural centre of Portugal – and it is a wonder that it's not better known internationally. Housed in a superb complex, ten minutes' walk north of Parque Eduardo VII, the foundation is set in its own park, and features a museum whose collections seem to take in virtually every great phase of Eastern and Western art – from Ancient Egyptian scarabs to Art Nouveau jewellery, Islamic textiles to French Impressionists. In a separate building, across the park, a modern art museum sports excitingly displayed works, exclusively Portuguese, which touch on most styles of twentieth-century art. The complex has its main entrance at Avenida de Berna 45; to reach it, take bus #31, #41 or #46 from Rossío, or the metro to *Pahlavã* or *São Sebastião*.

Astonishingly, all the main museum exhibits were acquired by just one man, the Armenian oil magnate **Calouste Gulbenkian** (1869–1955), whose legendary art-market coups included buying works from the Leningrad Hermitage after the Russian Revolution. In a scarcely less astute deal made during the last war, Gulbenkian literally auctioned himself and his collections to the European nations: Portugal bid security, an aristocratic palace home (a Marquês was asked to move out) and tax exemption, to acquire one of the most important cultural patrons of the century.

Today the Gulbenkian Foundation runs an orchestra, three concert halls and two galleries for temporary exhibitions in the capital alone. It also finances work in all spheres of Portuguese cultural life – there are Gulbenkian museums and libraries in the smallest towns – and makes charitable grants to a vast range of projects. The admissions desk of the museum has a schedule of current activities.

Anyone travelling with children may be equally impressed to know that the Gulbenkian maintains a **Centro Artístico Infantil** in its gardens (entrance just off Rua Marquês de Sá de Bandeira), well-stocked with toys and offering free **childcare sessions** for 4–12-year-olds between 9am and 5pm.

The Museu Gulbenkian

The **Museu Gulbenkian** (Oct–May Tues–Sun 10am–5pm; June–Sept Tues, Thurs, Fri & Sun 10am–5pm, Wed & Sat 2–7.30pm; 200$00; free on Sun and to *ISIC* card holders) is the foundation's public showplace. It is divided into two complete and distinct halves – the first devoted to Egyptian, Greco-Roman, Islamic and Oriental arts, the second to European art – and ideally you'll want to take them in on separate visits. The collections aren't immense in numbers but each contains pieces of such individual interest and beauty that you need frequent unwinding sessions – well provided for by the basement **café-bar and gardens**.

CLASSICAL AND ORIENTAL ART

It seems arbitrary to hint at highlights, but they must include the entire contents of the small **Egyptian room**, which covers almost every period of importance from the Old Kingdom (2700 BC) to the Roman period. Particularly striking are a carved ivory spoon from the time of Amenophis III and an extraordinarily lifelike *Head of a Priest* from the penultimate, Ptolomaic period. **Mesopotamia** produced the earliest forms of writing and two cylinder seals, one from before 2500 BC, are on display here, along with architectural sculpture from the Assyrian civilisation.

Fine statues, silver and glass from the **Romans** and intricate gold jewellery from ancient **Greece** come soon after. There's also a particularly extensive collection of Greek coins, followed by remarkable illuminated manuscripts and ceramics from **Armenia**, porcelain from **China**, and beautiful **Japanese** prints and lacquer-work. Islamic arts are magnificently represented by ornamented texts, opulently woven carpets, glassware (such as the fourteenth-century mosque lamps from Syria) and precious bindings from **Persia** and **India**.

EUROPEAN ART

In the **European art** section you'll find work from all the major schools. The section starts with a group of French medieval ivory diptychs (particularly six scenes depicting the *Life of the Virgin*) and a thirteenth-century copy of Saint John's prophetic *Apocalypse*, produced in Kent and touched up in Italy under Pope Clement IX. From fifteenth-century Flanders, there's a pair of panels by Van der Weyden; while from the same period in Italy comes Ghirlandaio's *Portrait of a Young Woman*. The seventeenth century yields two exceptional portraits – Rubens' of his second wife, *Helena Fourment*, and Rembrandt's *Figure of an Old Man* – plus works by van Dyck, Frans Hals and Ruisdael. Eighteenth-century works featured include a good Fragonard, and a roll-call which then incorporates Gainsborough, Sir Thomas Lawrence and – most impressively, with no fewer than 19 paintings – Francesco Guardi. Finally Corot, Manet, Monet, Degas and Renoir supply a good showing from nineteenth- to twentieth-century France.

Sculpture is poorly represented on the whole, though a French sixteenth-century religious statue of *Mary Magdalene*, a fifteenth-century medallion of *Faith* by Luca della Robbia, a 1780 marble *Diana* by Jean-Antoine Houdon, and a couple of Rodins all stand out. Elsewhere, you'll find **ceramics** from Spain and Italy; **furniture** from Louis XV to Louis XVI; eighteenth-century works from **French goldsmiths;** fifteenth-century Italian bronze **medals** (especially by Pisanello); and assorted Italian tapestries and textiles. An Art Nouveau collection with 169 pieces of fantasy jewellery by **René Lalique** is the best of the tail-end of this great collection.

The Centro de Arte Moderna

To reach the **Centro de Arte Moderna** (same hours as main museum; 200$00; free on Sun), cross the gardens with their specially commissioned sculptures. Big names on the twentieth-century Portuguese scene include Almada Negreiros, the founder of *modernismo* (his portrait of Fernando Pessoa in the Museu da Cidade is particularly well known), Amadeu de Sousa Cardoso and Guilherme Santa-Rita (both of Futurist inclinations), Vieira da Silva (a crisscross of lines) and Paula Rego (who paints creepy kids).

North of the Gulbenkian

Few visitors explore anything of Lisbon **north** of the Gulbenkian, unless for a trip to the Sporting or Benfica football stadiums or the Campo Pequeno bullring. Out past the Cidade Universitária, though, are a couple of mildly diverting museums, devoted to the city's **history** and to **costume**. They are both on the route of the #1 and #7 buses, which start, respectively, from Rossío and Praça da Figueira. Over to the northwest of the Gulbenkian, further peripheral attractions are provided by the **Jardim Zoológico** (the city's zoo), and by the nearby **Palácio dos Marquêses da Fronteira**. Buses #31, #41 and #46 (or the metro, to *Sete Rios*) link the Rotunda with the Jardim Zoológico.

The Museu da Cidade and Museu do Traje

The **Museu da Cidade** (Tues–Sun 10am–1pm & 2–6pm; 200$00) is installed in the eighteenth-century Palácio Pimenta, in the northwestern corner of Campo Grande. Its principal interest lies in an imaginative collection of prints, paintings and models of pre-1755 Lisbon. Pessoa enthusiasts might also want to make the homage for Almada Negreiros' famous portrait of the poet.

The **Museu do Traje** (Tues–Sun 10am–1pm & 2.30–5pm; 300$00) occupies another eighteenth-century palace, the Palácio do Monteiro-Mor, some 2km further north of the city museum. The museum's extensive collections are drawn upon for temporary thematic exhibitions – excellent if costume is your subject, less gripping if you're not an aficionado of faded fabrics. For more casual visitors, the surrounding park is at least as big an attraction – one of the lushest areas of the city, open daily until 5pm and with a good restaurant and café. A small **Museu de Teatro** (Tues–Sun 10am–1pm & 2.30–5pm; 200$00), of truly specialist interest, is also sited in the grounds.

The Jardim Zoológico

The **Jardim Zoológico** (daily 9am–7pm; 390$00) is one of the least inspiring of European zoos, exhibiting particularly unhappy captives in utterly miserable conditions. On the other hand it's really as much a rambling garden as anything else and in this, and in its peculiarly Portuguese eruptions of kitsch (an extraordinary dogs' cemetery), makes for an enjoyable afternoon's ramble, if you're able to ignore the context. You can get there by metro, to *Sete Ríos*.

The Palácio dos Marquêses da Fronteira

Palace enthusiasts might like to visit the **Palácio dos Marquêses da Fronteira**, which is around twenty minutes' walk west from the zoo. After passing the bland housing development on Rua de São Domingos de Benfica and crossing the little-used railway line, the fantastic gardens of this small, pink country house feel like an oasis. Have a look at the tiled conversation piece that the Marquês built for messing around in boats. The allegorical panels on the lower level, taken from Camões' tale of the *Doze da Inglaterra*, mark an historic moment in the history of *azulejos* when, in the mid-seventeenth century, the Portuguese dropped the formal Moorish methods of design (as in the upper level) and turned to painting straight onto tiles.

Because the palace is still inhabited, **visiting hours** are limited. The gates open at 10.45–11am (Mon–Fri only), when an accompanied visit costs 300$00 (gardens only) or 1000$00 (palace and gardens). On Saturday, at the same time, there's a full **guided tour**; 1000$00 to the gardens, 1500$00 to both.

The Museu de Arte Antiga

The **Museu de Arte Antiga** (Tues–Sun 10am–1pm & 2–5pm; 250$00, free on Sun morning), Portugal's national gallery, is the one Lisbon museum that stands comparison with the Gulbenkian. The core of the museum – comprising fifteenth- and sixteenth-century Portuguese works by such artists as Nuno Gonçalves – is excellent and well displayed in a beautiful converted palace of the period. It is situated at Rua das Janelas Verdes 95 in the wealthy suburb of Lapa, two kilometres west of Praça do Comércio. To get there, take tram #19 from Praça do Comércio, bus #40 from Rua do Comércio, or bus #27 or #49 on the way to or from Belém.

Gonçalves and the Portuguese School

Gonçalves and his fellow painters of the so-called "Portuguese school" span that indeterminate and exciting period when Gothic art was giving way to the Renaissance. Their works, exclusively religious in concept, are particularly interesting in their emphasis on portraiture – transforming any theme, even a martyrdom, into a vivid observation of local contemporary life. Stylistically, the most significant influences upon them were those of the Flemish, "Northern Renaissance" painters: Jan van Eyck, who came to Portugal in 1428, Memling and Mabuse (both well represented here) and Roger van der Weyden.

The acknowledged masterpiece, however, is Gonçalves' *Panéis de São Vicente* (Saint Vincent Altarpiece; 1467–1470), a brilliantly marshalled canvas depicting the saint, Lisbon's patron, receiving homage from all ranks of its citizens. On the two left-hand panels are Cistercian monks, fishermen and pilots; on the opposite side the Duke of Bragança and his family, a helmeted Moorish knight, a Jew (with book), a beggar, and a priest holding Saint Vincent's own relics (a piece of his skull, still possessed by the cathedral). In the epic central panels the mustachioed Henry the Navigator, his nephew Afonso V (in green) and the youthful (future) Dom João II pay tribute to the saint. Among the frieze of portraits behind them, that on the far left is reputed to be Gonçalves himself; the other central panel shows the Archbishop of Lisbon.

The rest of the collection

After Gonçalves and his contemporaries (notably Gregório Lopes, with a Martyrdom of São Sebastião, and Frei Carlos), the most interesting works are by **Flemish and German** painters – Cranach, Bosch (represented by a fabulous *Temptation of St Anthony*) and Dürer – and miscellaneous gems by Raphael,

Zurbarán, and, rather oddly, Rodin. **Later Portuguese painters** – from the sixteenth to the eighteenth century – are displayed too, most notably António de Sequeira and Josefa de Óbidos (for more on whom, see p.114).

But exhibits more likely to delay you are those in the extensive applied art sections. Here you'll find **Portuguese furniture and tapestries** – including Arraiolos carpets – to rival the European selection in the Gulbenkian and an excellent collection of **glassware** and **ceramics**, with many pieces showing the influence of Indian and Oriental designs derived from the new trading links of the time. Other colonially influenced exhibits include inlaid furniture from Goa and a supremely satisfying series of late-sixteenth-century **Japanese screens**, showing the Portuguese landing at Nagasaki.

Belém

It was from **Belém** in 1497 that Vasco da Gama set sail for India, and here too that he was welcomed home by Dom Manuel "the Fortunate" (*O Venturoso*). Da Gama brought with him a small cargo of pepper, enough to pay for his voyage sixty times over. The monastery subsequently built here – the **Mosteiro dos Jerónimos** – stands as a testament to his triumphant discovery of a sea route to the Orient, which amounted to the declaration of a "golden age". It was built in honour of a vow Dom Manuel made to the Virgin in return for a successful voyage, on the site of the old *Ermida do Restelo* or *Capela de São Jerónimo*, a hermitage founded by Henry the Navigator, where Vasco da Gama and his companions had spent their last night ashore in prayer. Its funding also was a levy on the fruits of his discovery – a five percent tax on all spices other than pepper, cinnamon and cloves, whose import had become the sole preserve of the Crown.

The River Tejo at Belém has receded with the centuries, for when the monastery was built it stood almost on the beach, within sight of caravels moored ready for expeditions, and of the **Torre de Belém**, guarding the entrance to the port.

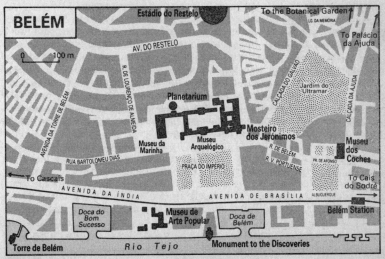

It's worth noting that all the monuments and museums in Belém are **closed on Monday**.

This, too, survived the earthquake and is the other showpiece Manueline building in Lisbon. Both monastery and tower lie in what is now a pleasant waterfront suburb, 6km west of the centre, close by a small group of museums, and with some fine **cafés and restaurants** if you want to make a day of it. Make time, in particular, for the *Antiga Confeitaria de Belém*, in Rua de Belém, by the tram stop, which bills itself as the "única fábrica de pasteis de Belém" – *pasteis de Belém* being delicious flaky tartlets filled with custard-like cream.

Belém is easily reached by **tram** – #15 and #17 run from Praça do Comércio, taking about twenty minutes – or any slow train from Cais do Sodré. If you feel like escaping to a beach you can get a **ferry** across the Tejo from Belém to Trafaria – only 3km by bus from Costa da Caparica (see p.98); ferries run on the hour and half hour (daily 6.30am–12.30am) from a terminus right by the train station. Alternatively, **trains** from here continue to Cascais (see p.87).

The Mosteiro dos Jerónimos

Even before the Great Earthquake, the **Mosteiro dos Jerónimos** (Oct–May Tues–Sun 10am–1pm & 2.30–5pm; June–Sept Tues–Sun 10am–6.30pm; monastery free, cloister 400$00, free to *ISIC* card holders) was Lisbon's finest monument: since then, it has stood quite without comparison. Begun in 1502 and substantially complete when its funding was withdrawn by João III in 1551, the monastery is the most ambitious and successful achievement of Manueline architecture. It is less flamboyantly exotic than either Tomar or Batalha – the great culminations of the style in Estremadura – but, despite a succession of master-builders, it has more daring and confidence in its overall design. This is largely the achievement of two outstanding figures, **Diogo de Boitaca**, perhaps the originator of the Manueline style with his Igreja de Jesus at Setúbal, and **João de Castilho**, a Spaniard who took over the construction from around 1517.

It was Castilho who designed the **main entrance** to the **church**, a complex, shrine-like hierarchy of figures centered around Henry the Navigator (on a pedestal above the arch). In its intricate and almost flat ornamentation, it shows the influence of the then-current Spanish style, Plateresque (literally, the art of the silversmith). Yet it also has distinctive Manueline features – the use of rounded forms, the naturalistic motifs in the bands around the windows – and these seem to create both its harmony and individuality. They are also unmistakably outward-looking, evoking the new forms discovered in the East, a characteristic that makes each Manueline building so new and interesting – and so much a product of its particular and expansionary age.

This is immediately true of the church itself, whose breathtaking sense of space alone places it among the great triumphs of European Gothic. Here, though, Manueline developments add two extraordinary fresh dimensions. There are tensions, deliberately created and carefully restrained, between the grand spatial design and the areas of intensely detailed ornamentation. And, still more striking, there's a naturalism in the forms of this ornamentation that seems to extend into the actual structure of the church. Once you've made the analogy, it's difficult to see the six central columns as anything other than palm trunks, growing both into and from the branches of the delicate rib-vaulting.

Another peculiarity of Manueline buildings is the way in which they can adapt, enliven, or encompass any number of different styles. Here, the basic structure is thoroughly Gothic, though Castilho's ornamentation on the columns is much more Renaissance in spirit. So too is the semicircular apse (around the altar), added in 1572, beyond which is the entrance to the remarkable double cloister.

Vaulted throughout and fantastically embellished, the **cloister** is one of the most original and beautiful pieces of architecture in the country. Again, it holds in balance Gothic forms and Renaissance ornamentation and is exuberant in its innovations – such as the rounded corner canopies and delicate twisting divisions within each of the arches. These lend a wavelike, rhythmic motion to the whole structure, a conceit extended by the typically Manueline motifs drawn from ropes, anchors and the sea. In this – as in all aspects – it would be hard to imagine an art more directly reflecting the achievements and preoccupations of an age.

The monastery's museums

In the wings of the monastery are two museums. The enormous **Museu da Marinha** (Tues–Sun 10am–5pm; 300$00, free Wed), in the west wing, is more interesting than most of its kind, packed not only with models of ships, naval uniforms and a surprising display of artefacts from Portugal's oriental trade and colonies, but also with real vessels – among them fishing boats and sumptuous state barges – a couple of seaplanes and even some fire engines.

In contrast, the **Museu de Arqueologia** (same hours; 250$00), in the east wing, seems sparse and, apart from a few fine Roman mosaics unearthed in the Algarve, thoroughly unexceptional. A third museum, the **Museu Agrícola do Ultramar** – of tropical agriculture – is close to the eastern corner of the monastery, and speaks for itself.

The Torre de Belém

The **Torre de Belém** (Oct–May Tues–Sun 10am–1pm & 2.30–5pm; June–Sept Tues–Sun 10am–6.30pm; 400$00), still washed on three sides by the sea, is just a couple of hundred metres down from the monastery. Whimsical, multi-turreted and with a real hat-in-the-air exuberance, it was built over the last five years of Dom Manuel's reign (1515–20). As such, it is the one completely Manueline building in Portugal, the rest having been adaptations of earlier structures or completed in later years.

Its architect, Francisco de Arruda, had previously worked on Portuguese fortifications in Morocco and a Moorish influence is very strong in the delicately arched windows and balconies. Prominent also in the decoration are two great symbols of the age: Manuel's personal badge of an armillary sphere (representing the globe) and the cross of the military Order of Christ, once the Templars, who took a major role in all Portuguese conquests. The tower's interior is unremarkable except for a "whispering gallery"; it was used into the nineteenth century as a prison, notoriously by Dom Miguel (1828–34), who kept political enemies in the waterlogged dungeons.

More museums and the Monument to the Discoveries

Close by are a number of museums. The best is the **Museu de Arte Popular** (Tues–Sun 10am–12.30pm & 2–5pm; 400$00, free Sun morning), a province-by-province display of Portugal's still very diverse folk arts, housed in a shed-like building on the waterfront. Also well worth a look is the **Museu de Etnologia**

(Tues–Sun 10am–12.30pm & 2–5pm), north of the monastery on Avenida Ilha da Madeira, with its displays from the old African colonies.

Almost adjacent to the Museu de Arte Popular is the **Monument to the Discoveries** (Tues–Sun 9.30am–7pm; 275$00), an angular slab of concrete erected in 1960 to commemorate the 500th anniversary of the death of Henry the Navigator. Henry appears on the prow with Camões and other Portuguese heroes. Within the monument is a small exhibition space, with interesting and changing exhibits on the city's history; while the entrance fee also lets you climb right up to the top for some fine views of the Tejo and Belém tower.

Over the way, the controversial new **Centro Cultural de Belém** puts on regular photography exhibitions and concerts as well as hosting some kind of live entertainment over the weekend – jugglers, mime artists and the like. For the best views of the surroundings, drop into the café, whose esplanade overlooks the river and the Discoveries monument.

At the corner of Belém's other main square – Praça Afonso de Albuquerque, a few minutes' walk from the monastery along Rua de Belém – there's the **Museu dos Coches** (Oct–May Tues–Sun 10am–1pm & 2.30–5.30pm; June–Sept Tues–Sun 10am–1pm & 2.30–6.30pm; 400$00; Sun free), oddly the most visited tourist attraction in Lisbon. It consists of an interminable line of royal coaches – Baroque, heavily gilded and sometimes beautifully painted.

Jump on bus #14, on the Calçada da Ajuda behind the coach museum, for the short ride uphill to the **Palacio da Ajuda** (half-hour tours 10am–5pm, closed Wed; 250$00). The palace was built by those crashingly tasteless nineteenth-century royals, Dona Maria II and Dom Ferdinand, and like their Pena Palace folly at Sintra is all over-the-top aristocratic clutter. The banqueting hall, however, is quite a sight; likewise the lift, decked out with mahogany and mirrors. Tram #18 will get you back from the palace to Praça do Comércio.

Eating

Lisbon has some of the best-value **cafés and restaurants** of any European city, serving large portions of good Portuguese food at sensible prices. A set menu (an *ementa turística*) at lunch or dinner will get you a three-course meal for 1500–2500$00 across the city, though you can eat for considerably less than this by sticking to the ample main dishes and choosing the daily specials. **Seafood** is widely available – there's an entire central street, Rua das Portas de Santo Antão, as well as a whole enclave of restaurants across the River Tejo at Cacilhas, that specialise in it. This is the only time you'll need to be careful what you eat, since seafood is always pricier than the other menu items. Several traditional restaurants still survive in Lisbon, most notably beautifully tiled *cervejarias* (literally beer halls) where the emphasis is often as much on drinking as eating; while the capital, naturally, also features some of the country's best (and most expensive) restaurants – specialising for the most part in a hybrid French-Portuguese cuisine. If you tire of all this, Lisbon has a rich vein of inexpensive **foreign restaurants**, in particular those featuring food from the former colonies: Brazil, Mozambique, Angola and Goa.

There are plenty of restaurants scattered around the Baixa, where a multitude of set lunches are on offer to office employees, and there are some good places, too, in all the other areas you're likely to be sightseeing, up in the Alfama and out in Belém. **By night** the obvious place to be is Bairro Alto, which hosts several of the city's trendiest restaurants, as well as other more basic venues that offer fine value for money.

Note that many restaurants are **closed on Sundays**, while on Saturday nights in midsummer you may need to book for the more popular places: phone numbers are given below where neccessary, or pass by during the day to reserve a table. Assume moderate **prices** at all the places listed below – around 2000$00 per person – unless otherwise stated.

Restaurants aside, you can get snacks and sandwiches in most bars and cafés (for which see the following section); for **markets** turn to p.83, and for the where-abouts of central **supermarkets**, see "Listings", p.84.

Baixa and Chiado

Avis, Rua Serpa Pinto 12 (☎342 83 91). Turn-of-the-century splendour – heavy curtains, oils and chandeliers – forms a backdrop to one of the city's most respected Portuguese restau-rants. Portions are not all they could be, though, considering the high prices – around 6000$00 and upwards. Closed Sat. lunch and Sun.

O Cantinho do Aziz, Rua de São Lourenço 3–5. A little hard to find, up a couple of flights of stairs just to the east of Rossío, but well worth the search. Owned and run by a congenial Mozambican family, it offers a selection of African and Indian food (try the curried goat) at fairly low prices. Closed Sun.

O Coradinho, Rua de Santa Marta 4a. On the northern extension of Rua das Portas de Santo Antão, this is very friendly and has an excellent value *ementa turística* for 1500$00.

Montenegro, Rua das Portas de Santo Antão 38. One of the less expensive places on this street, and worth trying. *Chick'n' Good*

Rei dos Frangos/Bom Jardim, Trav. de Bom Jardim 7–11. On an alleyway connecting Restauradores with Rua das Portas de Santo Antão, this is *the* place for spit-roast chicken – whole ones with fries for about 1000$00. You may have to wait for a table; it's worth it.

Solar da Padaria, Rua da Padaria 18–20. A great, reasonably priced restaurant in the Baixa, off Rua de São Julião, with a tempting seafood menu.

Solmar, Rua das Portas de Santo Antão 108 (☎346 00 10). A vast showpiece seafood restau-rant, with fountain and marine mosaics, and generally deserving of its reputation. Very slick service and fine seafood for up to and around 4000$00 a head.

Tágide, Largo Academia das Belas Artes 18–20 (☎342 07 20). One of Lisbon's priciest restau-rants, serving superb regional dishes in a dining room with sweeping city views. Book ahead, especially for a window seat. At least 6000$00 per person. Closed Sat and Sun.

Bairro Alto, Estrela and Lapa

O Bichano, Rua da Atalaia 78. Imaginative menu, including a very special *Bacalhau à Braz*. Go early or book – it's always crowded. Around 3000$00.

Bota Alta, Trav. da Queimada 37. Old tavern restaurant that pulls in the punters for its large portions of traditional Portuguese food – cod cooked in cream, amongst other things. Closed Sat lunch and Sun.

Brasuca, Rua João Pereira da Rosa 7 (☎342 85 42). A lively restaurant set in an ageing mansion, with great Brazilian food (and *caipirinhas*) as well as Portuguese standards. Busy at the weekends; you may want to book. Up to and around 3000$00.

O Cantinho do Bem Estar, Rua do Norte 46. Inexpensive Alentejan restaurant that's as freindly and authentic as you can get.

Casa Faz Frio, Rua Dom Pedro V 96. A beautiful, very traditional restaurant, replete with tiles. Huge portions and average prices.

Casa de Pasto Flores, Praça das Flores 40. A little to the northwest of the heart of Bairro Alto; classic Portuguese dishes. Around 3000$00.

Cervejaria da Trindade, Rua Nova da Trindade 20. Huge, vaulted beer hall-restaurant, with some of the city's loveliest *azulejos* on the walls. It stays open till 2am (last orders at 1.30am) and specialises in seafood. Around 2000–3000$00.

Farah's Tandoori, Rua de Santana à Lapa 73. Out to the west of Bairro Alto, in Estrela, this is one of the more reliable Indian restaurants in town, and not expensive. Closed Tues.

Fidalgo, Rua da Barroca 27 (☎342 29 00). A fashionable and cosy hangout for arts and media types, who are rewarded by delicious seafood creations. Around 3000$00. Closed Sun.

Final Vermelha, Rua das Gaveas 89. Very popular and – currently – a haunt of the city's trendier element. Recommended Portuguese food.

Mamma Rosa, just off Rua São Pedro de Alcântara, near the top of the *Elevador da Glória*. Cramped, popular pizza place with famously cheeky waiters. Open late, with last orders around 1am. Closed Sun.

Pap'Açorda, Rua da Atalaia 57–59 (☎346 48 11). Popular in-crowd restaurant with a dining room converted from an old bakery. An *açorda* – the house speciality – is a bread and shellfish stew, eaten here from clay bowls. Closed Sat night and Sun. Up to 4000$00 for the works.

Patô Baton, Trav. Fiéis de Deus 28 (☎362 63 72). One of the most stylish interiors in Bairro Alto provides a backdrop for pleasant, French-inspired cooking. The *Bife Dijonais* is splendid. Around 3500$00.

Sua Excelência, Rua do Conde 42 (☎60 36 14). Small, intimate restaurant in the heart of Lapa. There's no menu and the proprietor's camp digressions as he talks you through what's on offer will either delight or enrage. Marvellously inventive Portuguese cooking, though, worth the high prices. A good 5000–6000$00 per head; reservations advised. Closed Wed, Sat and Sun lunch, and Sept.

Vamos ao Norte, Rua do Norte 13. Thoroughly recommended northern Portuguese cooking, with dishes starting at around 900$00.

Velha Goa, Rua Tomás da Anunciação, Campo de Ourique. Out to the northwest of the Bairro Alto; slightly pricey Goan cooking (around 3000$00) but very fine all the same. Closed Mon, and Sat lunchtime.

Alfama

Restaurante Malmequer-Bemmequer, Rua de São Miguel 23–25. Cheery decor, moderate prices and some of the best seafood in the city, all overseen by a friendly owner who learned his craft aboard cruise liners.

Mestré André, Calçadinha de Santo Estevão 4–6. A fine neighbourhood tavern, with superb pork dishes and good *churrasco* (grills). Outdoor seating in summer. Closed Sun.

Rio Coura, Rua Augusta Rosa 30. A couple of hundred metres up from the Sé, this place offers amazing value, with full meals including wine for under 2000$00.

Túnel de Alfama, Rua dos Remedios 132. Cheap and very substantial meals, but open lunchtime only.

Avenida da Liberdade and the modern city

Restaurante Chimarrão, Praça do Chile 8. If you're looking for quantity, 3000$00 spent here gets you unlimited stabs at 12 types of barbecued meat and various salads – you'll need to pace yourself. On Wed and Sat nights, Brazilian *feijoada* is served.

Cervejaria Choupal, Rua do Salitre 9. Very basic, but with tasty food and pleasant service.

O Madeirense, Loja 3027, Amoreiras Shopping Centre, Avda. Eng. Duarte Pacheco. Sunday lunch is especially popular in this Madeirense restaurant; it's about the best of the bunch inside the shopping centre.

Cervejaria Portugália, Avda. Almirante Reis 117; *Arroios* metro. Top quality *mariscos* in a busy beer hall-restaurant that's open until 1.30am. Around 3000$00 to eat.

Cervejaria Ribadouro, Avda. da Liberdade 155; *Avenida* metro. Big, bustling *cervejaria* on the main avenue, in an area surprisingly short on decent places to eat. The shellfish is all good; it's cheaper if you eat at the bar.

VEGETARIAN RESTAURANTS

Celeiro

Rua 1° de Dezembro 65. Conveniently just off Rossío, this health food supermarket with basement restaurant is like a school canteen – and like a school canteen the best things get eaten early. Open Mon–Sat noon–3pm.

Centro Macrobiótico Vegetariano

Rua Mouzinho da Silveira 25; metro *Rotunda*. The food is much more digestible than the name; in the summer, tables are set outside in a small courtyard. Open Mon–Sat noon–8pm.

Espiral

Praça Ilha do Faial 14a, off Largo de Dona Estefânia; metro *Saldanha*. Lisbon's "centre for alternatives" has a pleasant and inexpensive macrobiotic restaurant (plus vegetarian, Chinese and fish dishes) with adjacent bookshop and noticeboard detailing information on the city's alternative/

green/therapy scene. Often has live music at the weekend. Open daily noon–2pm & 6.30–9.30pm.

Instituto Kushi

Avda. Barbosa du Bocage 88, off Avda. da República; metro *Campo Pequeno*. Cheap, wholesome food in a friendly place behind a macrobiotic shop.

Restaurante do Sol

Calçada do Duque 25. Former workers' co-op restaurant with fantastic fruit juices and good, if unexciting, meals. Open Mon–Fri 9am–10pm, Sat 9am–3pm.

O Terraço do Finisterra

Rua do Salitre 117; metro *Avenida*. Located in the Buddhist Centre, this stripped pine restaurant has superb, unusual veggie food and features an inexpensive set lunch. Open Mon–Sat noon–2.30pm & 7–9.30pm

Belém

O Alexandre, Rua Vieira Portuense 84. Tiny fish restaurant with a pavement terrace and views of the monastery. Go for one of the daily specials, all immensely good value and popular with a lunchtime office crowd.

Carvoeiro, Rua Vieira Portuense 66–68. A little *tasca*, with good grilled fish and jugs of wine. A good-value choice. Closed Mon.

Dionísios, Rua de Belém 124. Dependable Greek restaurant that's been around for years.

Drinking, nightlife and live music

Drinking, at its most prosaic level, is done in bars and cafés throughout Lisbon; some of the older **cafés** and *pastelerias* (specialising in cakes) in particular are worth dropping in on at some stage during the day. For nighttime drinking, the densest concentration of designer **bars and clubs** is found in two main areas. Traditionally, **Bairro Alto** has been the centre of Lisbon's nightlife, with its cramped streets still sheltering around fifty or so bars and clubs, in addition to the fado houses and restaurants. Recently, though, the hip nightlife venues, and the punters, have started to shift to **Avenida 24 de Julho** and its surroundings, the avenue running west from Cais do Sodré to the more outlying **Alcântara** district.

Although tourist brochures tend to suggest that **live music** in Lisbon begins and ends with fado, the city's most traditional music, there's no reason to miss out on other forms, from jazz to African or Brazilian music from the former colonies. For **listings and previews** of new bars, clubs and forthcoming events, get hold of a copy of the weekly entertainment paper *Se7e* – a typographical pun, *sete* meaning seven in Portuguese. It's published on Tuesday and available throughout the city; Turismo staff should be able to help if you can't decipher the details.

Cafés

Antiga Casa dos Pasteis, Rua de Belém 90, Belém. Excellent tiled pastry shop-café with scrumptious *pasteis de Belém*.

Café a Brasileira, Rua Garrett 120. Marked by a bronze of Pessoa outside, this is the most famous of Rua Garrett's old-style coffee houses. Livens up at night with a more youthful clientele swigging beer outside until 2am.

Cerca Moura, Largo das Portas do Sol. Nice views up in the Alfama; a good resting place as you climb up and down the hilly streets.

Café Nicola, Praça Dom Pedro IV 26. On the west side of Rossío, this grand old place is a good stop for breakfast. Outdoor seats are always at a premium.

Café Pastelaria Bernard, Rua Garrett 104. Superb cakes and an outdoor terrace on Chiado's most fashionable street.

Café Suiça, Praça Dom Pedro IV 96. Famous for its cakes and pastries, you'll have a hard job getting an outdoor table here, though there's plenty of room inside – the café stretches across to Praça da Figueira.

Bars and clubs

The **Bairro Alto** hosts one of Europe's biggest weekly street parties, with up to 50,000 people descending on the maze of streets over the weekend, drifting from bar to club. Several clubs are extremely low key, revealing their presence simply by a streetlight and a slot in the door for the attendant to inspect customers. Don't be intimidated by this: just knock and walk in – and straight out, if you don't like the look of the place. Although the Bairro Alto is also something of a sex centre, most people are there just to eat, drink, or listen to music and beyond the usual whistles, it's not too threatening for women. Also in Bairro Alto, and on the periphery, over towards Rato, is located much of the city's gay scene.

Recently, much of the action has moved to **Avenida 24 de Julho**, west of Cais do Sodré. In part, this is inkeeping with the local authority's intention to "gentrify" the run-down Cais do Sodré and Alcântara districts: bar and club owners have been encouraged to move out of residential Bairro Alto (where establishments are obliged to close at 3am or so) and into the Avenida 24 de Julho district, lured by the prospect of staying open until 6am. As soon as some of the trendiest operators made the move, the transformation gathered pace and now the district attracts a largely upmarket crowd of young guns, flitting from bar to bar.

The competition for custom involves a high casualty rate among new bars. Some change hands, names, decor and clientele every other week, so you're almost certain to come across good places not in our listings. Generally, where there's an **admission charge** to a bar or club, you can expect to pay around 1500–2000$00, which usually includes a drink or two; if you're handed a ticket on entry, keep hold of it and present it when you buy your first drink. **Friday and Saturday nights** tend to be overcrowded and expensive everywhere; while on Sunday, especially in Bairro Alto, places tend to close and sleep off the weekend excesses.

Bairro Alto

The map on the opposite page shows the whereabouts of most of the Bairro Alto's main bars and clubs (including fado establishments; see p.79). The pick of the bunch is reviewed below.

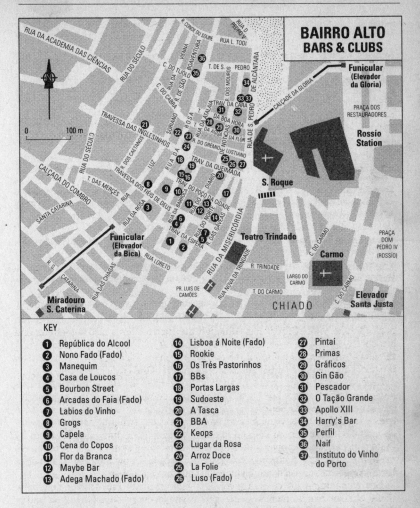

BAIRRO ALTO BARS & CLUBS

Funicular
(Elevador
da Gloria)

PRAÇA DOS
RESTAURADORES

Rossío
Station

S. Roque

Teatro Trindade

PRAÇA
DOM
PEDRO IV
(ROSSÍO)

Carmo

LARGO DO
CARMO

Funicular
(Elevador
da Bica)

Miradouro
S. Caterina

Elevador
Santa Justa

CHIADO

KEY

❶ República do Alcool
❷ Nono Fado (Fado)
❸ Manequim
❹ Casa de Loucos
❺ Bourbon Street
❻ Arcadas do Faia (Fado)
❼ Labios do Vinho
❽ Grogs
❾ Capela
❿ Cena do Copos
⓫ Flor da Branca
⓬ Maybe Bar
⓭ Adega Machado (Fado)

⓮ Lisboa á Noite (Fado)
⓯ Rookie
⓰ Os Trés Pastorinhos
⓱ BBs
⓲ Portas Largas
⓳ Sudoeste
⓴ A Tasca
㉑ BBA
㉒ Keops
㉓ Lugar da Rosa
㉔ Arroz Doce
㉕ La Folie
㉖ Luso (Fado)

㉗ Pintaí
㉘ Primas
㉙ Gráficos
㉚ Gin Gão
㉛ Pescador
㉜ O Tação Grande
㉝ Apollo XIII
㉞ Harry's Bar
㉟ Perfil
㊱ Naif
㊲ Instituto do Vinho
do Porto

Apollo XIII, Trav. da Cara 8. A young, boisterous student crowd careers around one of the few Bairro Alto bars with plenty of room.

Bar Ártiste, Rua do Diário de Notícias 95. Jazz decor and music, and a fine range of snacks and dishes. Closed Mon.

BB's, Rua do Norte 86. Young and hip, though a little expensive; pool table and MTV keep the punters occupied.

Bourbon Street, Trav. da Espera 24. In this *Casa da Cerveja*, there's a "pay when you leave" system – 700$00 for the first hour and cheaper thereafter for as much beer as you can consume, jollied along by live music.

Casa de Loucos, Rua da Barroca 30. Subdued, intimate and ultimately relaxing bar.

Cena de Copos, Rua da Barroca 103–105. Not a club to frequent unless you're under-25 and bursting with energy. If you are, this is the place. A "tourist menu" gets you three cocktails for 750$00.

Frágil, Rua da Atalaia 126. This is one of the few clubs in the country that maintains a door policy of admitting only its own kind: it's very trendy, partly gay and can be oppressively pretentious. Pricey drinks, too, though free entry.

Gin Gão, Trav. da Boa Hora 12. Raucous punk and heavy metal venue; only go in if you can hold your own in rough company.

Gráficos, Trav. da Água de Flor 40. Fashionable, techno-style bar with loud music.

Grogs, Trav. dos Fiéis de Deus 82. A thoroughly unpretentious tavern – stone walls, wooden benches and regular-priced beers.

Harry's Bar, Rua de São Pedro de Alcântara 57. A tiny little front-room bar, with waiter service, bar snacks and an eclectic clientele – often including a late-night contingent from the nearby gay discos. Open all night; ring bell for admission.

Incógnito, Rua dos Poiais de São Bento 37. Appropriately named – the only indication is a pair of large metallic doors. Once within, you'll find downstairs a low-lit, plush, dance floor with interesting music. Closed Mon and Tues.

Instituto do Vinho do Porto, Rua de São Pedro de Alcântara 45. A good, if odd, place to precede more serious drinking, or round off an early meal. Over 300 types and vintages of port, from around 150$00 a glass upwards, served at low tables in a comfortable old mansion. It's not as forbidding as it looks. Open Mon–Sat 10am–10pm.

Keops, Rua da Rosa. Small nightspot with Egyptian decor and modern music. Distinctly fashionable but also rather pleasant.

Labios do Vinho, Rua do Norte 52. Small blues bar, usually with room to spare.

Maybe Bar, Rua do Diário de Notícias 68. Very 1980s in decor and style, and attracting a gay crowd on certain nights.

Pavilhão Chinês, Rua Dom Pedro V 89. A wonderfully decorated bar, completely lined with mirrored cabinets of ludicrous and bizarre tableaux of artefacts from around the world. Drinks include a long list of speciality cocktails.

Perfil, Calçada do Tijolo 8. A predominantly teenage hangout with loud pop played from 11.30pm nightly.

Pintaí, Largo Trindade Coelho 22. Bouncy Brazilian music and cocktails.

República do Alcool, Rua do Diário de Notícias 3. Jazz and laid-back dance music in a basic bar with a heavy gay presence.

Sudoeste, Rua da Barroca 135. Small club, recently renovated, and staying in the fast lane with Seattle grunge sounds. Ring for admission. Closed Tues.

O Tacão Grande, Trav. da Cara. Quiet, low-lit bar with beer, snacks, pop and funk.

A Tasca, Trav. da Quiemada 13. Cheerful and welcoming American-owned *salsa* bar, serving cocktails and Mexican specialities.

Os Três Pastorinhos, Rua da Barroca 111. A good-time place, when it's full: music treads the line between dance and listenability, with lashings of soul and reggae; decor is a rather neat pinball-theme.

Around Cais de Sodré

Despite the trendiness further west, it's still a bit rough around Cais do Sodré station. This is not an area that feels very comfortable late at night, but committed clubbers, drinkers and low-life enthusiasts might try one of a dozen places along Rua Nova do Carvalho, ranging from atmospheric to downright seedy.

Casa Cid, Rua da Ribeira Nova 32. An institution, serving food and drinks to market workers and down-at-heel nightlife stop-outs from 4am onwards.

Jamaica, Rua Nova do Carvalho 6. Disco with predominantly reggae/hard rock sounds.

Shangri-la, Rua Nova do Carvalho 49/51. Less crowded than *Jamaica* or *Tokio* and playing nostalgic 1980s' sounds.

Tokio, Rua Nova do Carvalho 12. A younger scene; more modern sounds than most along here.

GAY AND LESBIAN BARS, CLUBS AND DISCOS

While the Lisbon **gay and lesbian** scene doesn't yet have the high profile common to some other European capitals, there are quite lively goings-on around the borders of the Bairro Alto and the Rato quarter to its northwest. All listings below are in this area.

Bar 108
Rua de São Marçal 33. More upbeat than neighbouring *Tatoo*, with a younger and less self-conscious crowd.

Bric-a-Bar
Rua Cecílio de Sousa 84. Regular disco.

Finalmente
Rua da Palmeira 38. Very busy, with first-class disco but lashings of kitsch. Weekend drag shows feature skimpily dressed young *senhoritas* camping it up to high-tech sounds.

Memorial
Rua Gustavo de Matos Sequeira 42a. The best scene the city has – and as rewarding for lesbians as gay men. It gets absolutely packed, though, and the doorstaff can be dismissive, not to say downright rude.

Tatoo
Rua de São Marçal 15. A favourite haunt with cloney types, but more sophisticated and lively at weekends.

Trumps
Rua da Imprensa Nacional 104b. The biggest gay disco in Lisbon with a reasonably relaxed door policy. Mostly soul, rap and house. Packed with a broad mix of people from Thursday to Saturday, a bit cruisy midweek. Closed Mon.

Xeque-Mate
Rua de São Marçal 170. Exclusive and obnoxiously cruisy bar and disco, though it gets a bit more cosmopolitan in summer.

Avenida 24 de Julho and around

Although Avenida 24 de Julho starts at Cais do Sodré, most of the action itself is around Santos station, 800m or so to the northwest; for Escadinhas da Praia, coming from Santos station, turn left down the avenue and it's second on the right.

Absoluto, Rua Dom Luís 1 5. Entertainment complex with bar, restaurant and disco – and occasional live music. The street is parallel to the avenue.

Alté Enfim, Rua das Janelas Verdes 10. Live music every night, from Portuguese folk to rock cover versions, served up to a local crowd.

Café 24 de Julho, Avda. 24 de Julho 114. Extremely upmarket Italian restaurant downstairs, in conjunction with a designer bar full of the beautiful rich. Tricky to get into if you're neither.

Café Central, Avda. 24 de Julho 110. Techno design, loud blues and rock and video-screen-sized MTV.

Cargo, Avda. 24 de Julho 88. Enjoyable bar with nautical design and strange ceiling; cheapish beer, too.

Chave d'Ouro, Rua das Janelas Verdes 8. Nothing special as bars go, but always crowded at weekends early in the evening before the avenue scene hots up.

Decibel, Avda. 24 de Julho 92. Grunge comes to the avenida; there's a balcony overlooking the street for when it all gets too much.

Kapital, Avda. 24 de Julho, opposite Santos station. One of the seriously trendy spots, with three floors full of bright young things paying high prices for drinks. And that's if you get past the style police on the door.

Kremlin, Escadinhas da Praia 5. One of the city's most fashionable nightspots, this is packed with flash young, raving Lisboetas. Tough door rules, and don't bother showing before 1am. Open until 4am, and then re-opening 7–10am for those still standing.

Plateau, Escadinhas da Praia 3. Gentler admission policy here, with more of a rock orientation – and the all-around beaming of MTV as you bop. Open until 7am.

Alcântara

Some of the city's most exclusive discos are in the far-flung area of Alcântara, west of Avenida 24 de Julho, by the Ponte 25 de Abril; to reach them you'll need to take a taxi.

Alcântara Café, Rua Maria Luísa Holstein 15. Bar-restaurant that is currently among the city's trendiest, in decor, clientele – and prices.

Alcântara Mar, Rua Cozinha Económica. Near the bridge, this big, glitzy disco is usually full of business types.

Alcântara Terra, Centro Comercial Lusíadas, Rua Lusíadas 5. Mostly rap and soul here for a distinctly younger crowd.

Banana-Power, Rua de Cascais 51–53. A club owned and designed by Tomás Taveira, architect of the Amoreiras complex. The clientele is dauntingly well-heeled and the prices outrageous, but design enthusiasts will at least want to take a look at the bar and restaurant.

Baixa and Alfama

Wandering around the main Baixa grid toward midnight you would imagine that the city had closed up and gone to bed; a single exception is the bar Bora-Bora *at Rua da Madalena 201. In Alfama most of the action is to be found in the fado clubs (see below), though a few notable bars exist.*

Cerca Moura, Largo das Portas do Sol. One of a cluster of bars on the square, with a nice view of the Tejo and a large esplanade.

Chapitô, Costa do Castelo 1/7. Multi-media centre, incorporating an open-air bar with a marvellous river view, recording studios, circus tent, exhibition areas, a small theatre, a restaurant, and surreal decoration in the downstairs bar interior. It is youthful, highly fashion-conscious and there's no charge for admission. Open all day.

Sua Excelência O Marquês, Largo Marquês do Lavradio, behind the Sé. A surprisingly trendy bar for this neck of the woods.

Live music

Fado is offered in thirty or so nightclubs in the Bairro Alto, Alfama and elsewhere. It can be a fairly pricey night out these days – there's always a cover charge and most clubs insist you eat as well – but at best it can prove a real highlight of your stay. Of the other possibilities, Portuguese **jazz** can be good, and **rock** an occasional surprise, while there's a good chance of catching **African music** from the former colonies of Cabo Verde, Guinea Bissau, Angola and Mozambique. **Brazilian** artists tour frequently, too.

Fado

Fado is thought to have originated, via the Congo, in the Alfama. It is often described as a kind of working-class blues – although musically it would perhaps be more accurate to class it as a kind of light operetta, sung to a vaguely flamenco accompaniment. Alongside Coimbra (which has its own distinct tradition), Lisbon is still the best place to hear it, either at a *Casa de Fado* or in an *Adega Típica*. There's no real distinction between these places: all are small, all serve food (though you don't always have to eat), and all open around 9–10pm, get going toward midnight, and stay open until maybe 3 or 4am.

Their drawbacks are inflated minimum charges – rarely, these days, below 3000$00 – and, in the more touristic places, extreme tackiness. Uniformed bouncers are fast becoming the norm, as are warm-up singers crooning Beatles songs and photographers snapping your table. Ask around to discover which are the most authentic current experiences.

Adega Machado, Rua do Norte 91, Bairro Alto (☎346 00 95). One of the longest-standing Bairro Alto joints; the minimum consumption of 2500$00 isn't too hard to notch up; you'll end up paying more like 5000$00 a head for fine Portuguese cooking and several styles of fado. Closed Mon.

Adega do Ribatejo, Rua Diário de Noticias 23, Bairro Alto. Enjoyable both for the food and fado, this remains a genuine *adega*, popular with locals. The singers include a couple of professionals, plus the doorman, the manager and – best of all – the cooks.

A Cesária, Rua Gilberto Rola 20, Alcântara. Reckoned by experts to be the real McCoy.

Fado Menor, Rua das Praças 18, Estrêla. Intimate place with a moderate cover charge and good music.

Lisboa á Noite, Rua das Gaveas 69, Bairro Alto. Pricey, touristy fado bar-restaurant. Closed Sun.

Mil e Cem, Trav. da Espera 38, Bairro Alto. Good atmosphere and with one of the cheaper minimum charges in the city.

Parreirinha d'Alfama, Beco do Espírito Santo 1, Alfama. Just off Largo do Chafariz de Dentro, this has reasonable music and food at fairly moderate prices.

O Senhor Vinho, Rua do Meio a Lapa 18, Bairro Alto (☎397 74 56). Famous Bairro Alto club sporting some of the best singers in Portugal, which makes the 3000$00 minimum charge pretty good value.

A Severa, Rua das Gáveas 55, Bairro Alto (☎346 40 06). A city institution, with big fado names and big prices.

Timpanas, Rua Gilberto Rola 24, Alcântara. Out in the suburbs, this is one of Lisbon's most authentic options. Closed Mon.

African music

There's a charge to get into these clubs, which usually covers your first drink. They stay open until around 4am, often later.

Bom Tom, Rua São João da Praça, Alfama. Features occasional sets by Angolan bands.

Monte Cara, Rua do Sol ao Rato, off Largo do Rato, Rato. Northwest of Bairro Alto, there's a lively and relaxed atmosphere in this club, with dancing until 6.30am. You get sporadic live music – mainly Cabo Verdean bands – otherwise there's a disco; and a restaurant on the ground floor serves Cabo Verdean food.

Ritz Clube, Rua da Glória 55. Lisbon's largest African club occupies the premises of an old brothel-cum-music hall, one block west of Avda. da Liberdade. It's a great place, with a resident band, plus occasional big-name concerts.

Brazilian music

The top visiting Brazilian singers – like the wonderful Milton Nascimento, Maria Bethânia, Gilberto Gil – tend to play stadium gigs (see "Rock, Folk and Jazz" below), but there are three smaller venues with regular live sounds:

Chafarica, Calçada de São Vicente 81, Alfama. Brazilian bar with live music till late most nights.

Johnny Guitar, Calçada do Marquês de Abrantes 72, Santos. Regular live music, though a fair way out.

Pê Sujo, Largo de São Martinho 6/7, Alfama. The "Dirty Foot" is five minutes' walk from the Sé in Alfama; ring to gain admission. Drinks feature *caipirinhas*, the lethal Brazilian concoction of rum, lime, sugar and ice, which regularly results in massive audience participation in table-banging samba sessions. Closed Mon.

Rock, Folk and Jazz

Rock music is a chancier business in Lisbon, though there are a handful of established bands who often play the capital – among them Sétima Legião, Madredeus, GNR, Rádio Macau, Xutos e Pontapés, Rui Veloso and Heróis do Mar. There's only one **jazz** venue, the *Hot Clube*, which in addition to jazz bands, sometimes hosts **folk** singers, products of the new "political music" that emerged with the 1974 revolution. Names to watch out for include Sérgio Godinho, Vitorino, Fausto and the band Trovante. There is a big annual **International Jazz Festival** at the Gulbenkian in the summer; information from the reception desk.

Other than the couple of places listed below, venues for all rock, folk and jazz performances are highly erratic, so check *Se7e* for possibilities. Big **American and British rock bands** on tour play at a variety of local stadiums (listed below); you can usually get advance tickets from the kiosk in Praça dos Restauradores.

CLUBS

Anos Sessenta, Largo do Terreirinho 21, Alfama. This small club is one of the few regular rock venues. It's located a few minutes' walk from Largo Martim Moniz, near the castle.

Hot Clube de Portugal, Praça da Alegria, off Avda. da Liberdade. The city's only regular jazz venue – a tiny basement club which hosts local and visiting artists. Open Thurs–Sat 10pm–2am; 800$00 cover charge.

STADIUM VENUES

Coliseu dos Recreios, Rua das Portas de Santo Antão, Baixa (☎346 19 97).

Estádio José Alvalade (the sporting stadium), *Campo Grande* metro.

Pavilhão do Restelo, Restelo, Belém.

Pavilhão de Cascais, Cascais.

The arts and other entertainments

Most major **cultural events**, including just about every classical music concert in the city, are sponsored by the *Fundação Calouste Gulbenkian*. You can pick up a schedule of events from the reception desk (see p.63), or check forthcoming events with the tourist office. Music aside, there's a fair amount of other entertainment in Lisbon: over seventy **cinemas**, two above-average **soccer** teams, summer season **bullfights**, and a host of cultural and traditional **festivals** with which your visit might coincide.

To find out **what's on**, *Se7e* has current details of all events, exhibitions and concerts; the kiosk at the corner of Restauradores, near the post office, has ticket and programme details for all the city's cinemas and theatres.

Classical music and the performing arts

There are three concert halls at the Gulbenkian, and regular **classical music** concerts also take place at the *Teatro Nacional de São Carlos*, at Rua Serpa Pinto 9 (☎346 59 14). Tickets range from 500$00 to 3000$00, though there are also free concerts and recitals at the Carmo and São Roque churches in Bairro Alto (every Sat night at the latter), the Sé and the Basílica da Estrêla.

There are performances of Portuguese and foreign **plays** at the *Teatro Nacional de Dona Maria II* in Rossío (☎342 22 10; Aug–June) and an **opera** season (Sept–June) at the *Teatro Nacional de São Carlos* (see above).

Throughout July and August the **Estoril Festival** takes place, with sometimes adventurous performances by internationally known orchestras, musicians and dance groups.

Film

Cinema is an unsung glory of a stay in Lisbon. The city and its environs have dozens of **cinemas**, virtually all of them showing original-language films with Portuguese subtitles. Ticket prices are low (500$00; 350$00 on Mondays) and some of the theatres are beautiful in themselves – Art Nouveau and Art Deco palaces, often with original period bars. The tourist office should be able to tell you what's on, or consult the kiosk at the corner of Restauradores.

Among the most interesting venues are *Quarteto*, Rua Flores do Lima (☎797 13 78), off Avenida Estados Unidos (*Entre Campos* metro), an art cinema with four screens; and the *Instituto da Cinemateca Portuguesa*, Rua Barata Salgueiro 39 (*Avenida* metro), the national film theatre, with daily shows at 6.30pm and 9.30pm, ranging from contemporary Portuguese films to anything from Truffaut to Valentino. Mainstream movies are on show at a clutch of cinemas around Praça dos Restauradoes and Avenida da Liberdade; while at the Amoreiras complex (☎69 12 75), on Avenida Eng. Duarte Pacheco, there are no fewer than ten screens; all, unfortunately, are modest-sized.

Sports

Soccer is the biggest game in Lisbon, and Benfica – Lisbon's most famous football team – have a glorious past (the great Eusébio played for the team in the 1960s). Games take place at the huge *Estádio da Luz*, north of the city centre and you can buy tickets in advance from the kiosk in Praça dos Restauradores (at a small commission), or at kiosks (not the turnstiles) at the ground on the night; bring a cushion for the bench seats. The best way to get to matches is on the metro – the Benfica stop is right outside the stadium. Sporting Club de Portugal, Benfica's traditional rivals, play at the *Estádio José Alvalade* – metro *Campo Grande* or bus #1 or #36. For somewhat less illustrious action, a trip out to watch lower league F.C. Estoril or Belenenses of Belém can also be fun. Details of all matches – most of the regular league fixtures take place on Sunday afternoons (Sunday evening for a few big events) – are printed in the daily papers.

Bullfights take place most Thursdays and Sundays (April–Sept) at the principal Campo Pequeno bullring (metro *Campo Pequeno*), just off Avenida da República; tickets cost 2000–8000$00, depending on where you sit. There are less frequent fights at Cascais in summer; or travel out of Lisbon to Vila Franca de Xira (see p.140) and surrounding towns and villages for more traditional events.

Festivals and events

Lisbon's main **popular festivals** are in June, with fireworks, fairground rides and street-partying to celebrate the **Santos Populares** – Saints Anthony (June 13),

John (June 24), and Peter (June 29). Celebrations of each begin on the previous evening; Saint Anthony's is the largest, taking over just about every square in Alfama.

Also in June, the **Festas da Lisboa** are a series of city-sponsored events, including free concerts, exhibitions and culinary contests, while from May to September there's a permanent fairground, the **Feira Popular**, opposite the *Entrecampos* metro station: eats, rides and a thoroughly Portuguese night out (until 1am, when the metro closes down too).

On the cultural front, there's the annual Estoril Festival (see "Classical music and the performing arts", above); various summer events in Cascais, mostly held in the Parque Palmela; and – again at Estoril, and a lot better than it sounds – the state-run **Handicrafts Fair**. Here, crafts of all kinds are displayed from every region of the country along Avenida Amaral: if you buy anything, bargain at length. The fair runs through July and August, from around 5pm until midnight, with foodstalls included in the attractions.

Shops and markets

The more interesting **shopping areas** are detailed in the preceding pages: the Chiado district (p.54); the markets around Cais do Sodré (p.56); the Amoreiras complex (p.62); and the Alfama flea market (p.59). The Bairro Alto is fast becoming a centre for designer clothes and furniture; some of the better **shops** are picked out below, along with a handful of specialist **markets**. Other than traditional **ceramics and carpets**, perhaps the most Portuguese of items to take home is a **bottle of port**: check out the vintages at the *Instituto do Vinho do Porto* (see p.76), where you can also sample the stuff, and buy either from there or from any delicatessen or supermarket.

SHOPPING HOURS

Traditionally, **shopping hours** have been Monday–Friday 9am–1pm and 3–7pm or 8pm, Saturday 9am–1am. That said, many of the **Bairro Alto** shops are open afternoons and evenings only, usually from 2–9pm or so; while the **Amoreiras** shops stay open daily from 9am–11pm.

Antiques, arts and crafts

Cheapish antique/junk shops are concentrated along **Rua do Alecrim and Rua Dom Pedro V** in the Bairro Alto – none stand out above the others, but they make for some good browsing. Other interesting shops throughout the city include:

Adro, Rua Diario de Noticias 126, Bairro Alto. Wall hangings, glassware and furniture.

A Bilha, Rua do Milagre de Santo António 10, Alfama. Fine metalwork, lace and jewellery.

Casa Quintão, Rua Ivens 30, Chiado. Traditional Portuguese carpets – *arraiolos*.

Casa Ribeiro da Silva, Trav. Fieis de Deus 69, Bairro Alto. Hand-crafted pottery and rugs.

Cri d'Assis, Rua da Barroca 116, Bairro Alto. Sculpture, vases and furniture.

De Natura Decorocões, Rua da Rosa 164, Bairro Alto. Unusual collection of "natural" furniture.

Fábrica Santana, Rua do Alecrim 95, Bairro Alto. If you're interested in Portuguese tiles – *azulejos* – check out this factory-shop, which sells copies of traditional designs.

Fábrica Viúva Lamego, Largo do Intendente 25; metro *Intendente*. Another *azulejo* factory shop.

Filartesanato, Feira Internacional de Lisboa, on the waterfront, west of Ponte 25 de Abril. General Portuguese regional crafts emporium. Closed Mon.

Tin Tin, Rua do Século, Bairro Alto. Strange-looking tea pots and bric-a-brac.

Books, newspapers and maps

International Press Centre, by the Turismo, west side of Praça dos Restauradores, Baixa. The best place for English-language newspapers.

Livraria Bertrand, Rua Garrett 75, Chiado. Good general bookshop with novels in English, plus a range of foreign magazines.

Livraria Britânica, Rua São Marçal 168, opposite the Jardim Botânico, Rato. Exclusively English-language bookshop – pricey but well stocked.

Livraria Portugal, Rua do Carmo 70–74, Baixa. Excellent Portuguese bookshop which features – among other fine books – *Rough Guides*.

Ouriarte, Rua da Rosa 237, Bairro Alto. Second-hand comic shop.

Serviços Cartográficos do Exército, Avda. Dr. Alfredo Bensaúde, Olivais Norte (bus #25 from Praça do Comércio to *Laboratório Química Militar*). The army's map office is the place to go for ordnance survey maps for hiking. If at all possible, take a Portuguese friend along to facilitate the operation. Open Mon–Fri 9–11.30am & 1–4.30pm.

Valentim de Carvalho, Rossío. A record and video shop downstairs with a bookshop above; good for browsing.

Clothes

The main shopping area for clothes is in the modern city, from Praça de Londres north along **Avenida de Roma**. Portuguese designers also have outlets in Amoreiras shopping centre and in various fashionable stores in the Bairro Alto.

Atalaia 31, Rua da Atalaia 31, Bairro Alto. Mostly Calvin Klein underwear and aftershave.

Eldorado, Rua do Norte 25, Bairro Alto. Expensive antique classic clothing and bric-a-brac.

Latão, Rua Diario de Noticias 69, Bairro Alto. Designer labels and accessories.

Manuel Alves & José Manuel Gonçalves, Rua da Rosa 39 & 85–87, Bairro Alto. Portuguese designers selling menswear at the first shop, women's clothing at the second.

Sempabrir-Compra, Rua das Gaveas 9, Bairro Alto. Designer gear and accessories aimed at the young.

Markets

31 Janeiro market (Mon–Sat). A food and fancies market opposite the *Sheraton* hotel on Avda. Fontes Pereira de Melo; metro *Picoas* or *Saldanha*.

Cais do Sodré (daily). Fish and flowers.

Feira da Ladra, Campo de Santa Clara, Alfama (Tues morning and all day Sat). Flea market.

Numismatists' market, Praça do Comércio, Baixa (Sun morning). Old coins and notes from Portugal and its former colonies.

Praça do Chile, off Avda. Almirante Reis; metro *Arroios* (Mon–Sat). An interesting general market in a large circular building.

Praça de Espanha; metro *Palhavā*. Daily market (not Sun) for clothes and groceries.

Rotunda do Aeroporto (Sun morning). The main rag-trade market, with complete wardrobes of clothing for a few thousand *escudos*. Take an airport bus to get there.

Listings

Airlines *Air France*, Avda. da Liberdade 244a (☎356 21 71); *Alitalia*, Avda. da Liberdade 225 (☎353 61 41); *British Airways*, Avda. da Liberdade 36-2° (☎346 09 31); *Iberia*, Rua Rosa Araujo 2 (☎356 28 15); *Swissair*, Avda. da Liberdade (☎347 30 61); *TAP*, Praça Marquês de Pombal (☎386 10 20).

Airport For flight information call ☎80 20 60.

American Express The local agent is *Top Tours* Avda. Duque de Loulé 108 (☎315 58 77).

Banks Most main branches are in the Baixa and surrounding streets and standard banking hours are Mon–Fri 8.30–3pm, though *Banco Borges & Irmão* (Avda. da Liberdade 9a) is open until 7.30pm. There's a currency exchange office at the airport (open 24hr) 'and at Santa Apolónia station (daily 8.30am–8.30pm). *Marcus & Harting*, Rossío 45 (☎346 92 71), currently exchange travellers' cheques without charging commission, though their rates are slightly lower than usual.

Buses Terminals at: Avda. Casal Ribeiro (metro *Saldanha*) for international and most domestic departures, including express services to the Algarve; Praça de Espanha (metro *Palhavã*) and Avda. 5 de Outubro 75 (metro *Saldanha*) for *Rodoviária da Lisboa* departures; Campo Pequeno for *AVIC* services to the northwest coast and *SolexPresso* to the Alentejo and Algarve; Campo das Cebolas, near Praça do Comércio, for destinations in the Minho; and Largo Martim Moniz, northeast of Rossío, for *Empresa Mafrense* services to Mafra and Ericeira. You can buy advance bus tickets at most major travel agents; try *Marcus & Harting*, Rossío 45 (☎346 92 71).

Car rental *Auto Jardim* (☎851 48 71); *Avis*, Avda. Praia da Vitória 12c (☎356 11 76); *Europcar*, airport (☎801 11 76), Santa Apolónia station (☎86 15 73) and Avda. António Augusto Aguiar 24 (☎53 51 15); *Kenning*, Rua Luciano Cordeiro 6a (☎54 91 82); *Thrifty*, Rua Visconde de Seabra 12a (☎793 79 24).

Embassies *Australia*, Avda. da Liberdade 244-4° (☎52 33 50); *Canada*, Avda. da Liberdade 144-3° (☎347 48 92); *Ireland*, Rua da Imprensa à Estrêla 1-4° (☎396 15 69); *Netherlands*, Rua do Sacramento à Lapa 4-1° (☎396 23 06); *UK*, Rua São Domingos à Lapa 37 (☎396 11 91); *USA*, Avda. das Forças Armadas (☎726 66 00).

Emergencies The general emergency number is ☎115. For police, see below.

Hospital *British Hospital*, Rua Saraiva de Carvalho 49 (☎395 50 67). For an appointment, call ☎397 63 29.

Laundry *Lava Neve*, Rua de Alegría 37, Bairro Alto, is excellent, or try the one at Rua Saraiva de Carvalho 117, a little west of Rato (bus #9 from Rossío).

Left luggage Lockers at Rossío and Santa Apolónia stations, and at the bus terminal on Avda. Casal Ribeiro.

Lost Property The police lost property office is at Rua dos Anjos 56a.

Newspapers There are news stands around Rossío, several of which sell foreign-language papers. And see "Shops and markets" above.

Police If you need help, or have something stolen, go to the 24-hour office at Rua Capelo 13 (☎346 61 41), west of the Baixa near the *Teatro São Carlos*. You need to report here in order to make a claim on your travel insurance.

Post offices The main post office is on Praça do Comércio (Mon–Fri 9am–7pm); its poste restante section has a separate entrance at Rua do Arsenal 27 (closes at 2pm). More convenient is the post office at Praça dos Restauradores 58 (east side; daily 8am–10pm), from where you can send Airmail and *Correio Azul* (Express Mail – the fastest service).

Supermarket There's a huge supermarket in the Amoreiras centre (open daily, 9am–11pm); more central is the late-night supermarket just off Rossío in Rua Jardim do Regedor (Mon–Fri 8am–midnight; Sat 9am–midnight; Sun 9am–11pm).

Students The *Centro Nacional de Informação Juvenil*, Avda. da Liberdade 194, (open 9.30am–7pm) offers practical advice and a library.

Swimming pools *Piscina dos Olivais* is quite a way out of the centre, but enjoyable – take bus #31 from Rossío (45min) or #10 from Areeiro (20min). Turismo can advise about alternatives – the *Piscina do Areeiro*, closer in, may be open again by now.

Telephones For international calls, it's easiest to use the telephone office next to the post office in Praça dos Restauradores (see above). There's a second office on the corner of Rossío (no. 65; 8am–11pm). You can also, in theory, make international calls from any phone booth. Phonecards, available in denominations of 500$00 from any post office, make calls from cabins a lot easier.

Trains See "Arrival and Information", p.46, for details of Lisbon's various stations. Timetables and train information are available at Rossío station information office, on the ground floor, or call ☎87 60 25.

Travel Agencies Specialists include: *Turismo Juvenil*, Praça de Londres 9B (*Alameda* metro; ☎848 49 57), for youth deals; *Intercentro*, Avda. Casal Ribeiro 18b (☎57 17 45), the main international bus agents; *Transalpino*, Avda. Guerra Junqueiro 28 (☎848 22 79); and well-established charter agents *Abreu*, Avda. da Liberdade 160 (☎347 64 41).

Women's Movement The best contact points are the *Editora das Mulheres* bookshop, Rua da Conceição 17 (Baixa), and *IDM* (*Informação e Documentação das Mulheres*) at Rua Filipe da Mata 115a (metro *Palhavã* or bus #31 from Rossío or Praça de Espanha). *IDM* is a women's centre incorporating a small library and café – very eager to welcome foreign travellers.

AROUND LISBON

The most straightforward escape from the city is to the string of beach resorts along the coast from Belém, reached on the train from Cais do Sodré. At places like **Oeiras** and **Carcavelos**, and above all at **Estoril** and **Cascais**, the beaches are good even if the water quality leaves a lot to be desired. For better sands and a cleaner ocean you'll have to head north to **Guincho**; or cross the Tejo by ferry to reach the **Costa da Caparica**, a 30-kilometre expanse of dunes south of the capital. There's reasonably priced accommodation at all these places, as well as a youth hostel at Oeiras and campsites at Guincho and Caparica. But as you might imagine, all the beach-resorts in the Lisbon area get very crowded at weekends and throughout August.

Basing yourself in Lisbon, you also could take in a fair part of the provinces of Estremadura (Chapter Two) and Alentejo (Chapter Eight) on daytrips. Indeed, some of those regions' greatest attractions lie within a 50-kilometre or so radius of the capital – such as the palaces of **Queluz** or **Mafra** – and are best seen on a daytrip. The beautiful town of **Sintra**, the most popular excursion from Lisbon, demands a longer look, revealing a different side if you can stay overnight. However you decide to see them, bear in mind that most of the Sintra palaces are closed on Mondays, and those at Queluz and Mafra on Tuesdays. Further afield, south of the Tagus, the large town of **Setúbal** is noted for its Igreja de Jesus, the earliest of all Manueline buildings, while the coast to the southwest sports a succession of small resorts and beaches of varying degrees of popularity.

West to Estoril and Cascais

Stretching for over 30km west of Lisbon, the **Estoril coast** – from Oeiras to Cascais – makes for an enjoyable day out, drifting from beach to bar and strolling along the lively seafront promenades. Sadly, the water itself has suffered badly from pollution and many locals regard a dip in the sea as too much of a health hazard. Nonetheless, the coast retains its attractions and **Cascais**, in particular, makes a pleasant alternative to staying in Lisbon, and is well placed for trips to Sintra or the wild Guincho beach.

Access to the resorts could hardly be easier. The *Linha de Cascais* electric train leaves every twenty minutes or so (from 5.30am–2.30am) from **Cais do Sodré** station, stopping first at Belém en route to Cascais. Beware, though, that some trains terminate in Oeiras, while others stop only at Alcântara, Oeiras and stations beyond. By road, the **N6** is the coastal highway, passing through most of the centres along the seafront, often as the Avenida Marginal; the faster **motorway** (*Auto-Estrada da Oeste*) runs to Estoril, starting in Lisbon – drive west past Amoreiras and follow the signs.

Oeiras to São João

The first suburb of any size after Belém is **OEIRAS**, where the Tejo river officially turns into the sea. The beach here is nothing special and, unless you're staying at the youth hostel or campsite (see p.53 for both), the only reason for a stop would be to see the **Palácio do Marquês de Pombal**, erstwhile home of the rebuilder of Lisbon. The house is now an adult education centre and the park is not technically open to visitors. However, if there's nothing special going on, the guard should be able to show you the gardens, or at least let you peer over the walls at its massive grotto. For **meals**, try the inexpensive *Adega* on Rua Marquês de Pombal, or the *Vai Vem* on the same street.

Carcavelos

Next stop along the coast is **CARCAVELOS**, popular for its kilometre of beach and plethora of bars and cafés. The water here, though far from clean, doesn't appear to do lasting damage and it's a busy surfing area. The other possible motivation for a visit is the huge Thursday **market**, which sprawls between the train station and town centre, a great place to pick up cheap clothing. There's a superb and inexpensive Mozambiquan restaurant, *O Palheiro*, on Rua Santarém. *The Pub*, right by the station in an old train carriage, is the one late-night haunt, open till 2am.

Parede

PAREDE, like Carcavelos, boasts a clutch of culinary highlights, though a rather less impressive beach. If you stop off, don't under any circumstances miss the superb *Lua de Mel* pastelaria – 50 metres up from the station on Avenida da República – nor *Eduardo's*, right by the station (open until 2am), which draws gastronomes from Lisbon for its seafood. Other enjoyable feasts are to be had at the nearby *Churrasqueira Brito*, a typical Portuguese *frango* joint; *Limo Verde*, a massive and exuberant *cervejaria;* and *O Junco*, an unexpectedly marvellous Chinese restaurant; all of these are along Avenida da República.

São Pedro and São João

Beyond Parede, the beaches improve rapidly and you reach the beginning of an esplanade which stretches virtually uninterrupted to Cascais. **SÃO PEDRO**, the first stop, has a superb beach, just down from the station, and **SÃO JOÃO** is flanked by two lovely stretches of sand. The whole seafront here is pretty animated in the summer months, swarming with young surfers and Portuguese holiday-makers, frequenting the numerous cafés and restaurants.

Estoril

The major resort along this coast, **ESTORIL** gained a post-war reputation as a haunt of exiled royalty and the idle rich, and it continues to maintain its pretensions towards being a "Portuguese Riviera", with grandiose expatriate villas and luxury hotels. It is little surprise then, that the town's touristic life revolves around an exclusive golf course and **casino**. The latter – within the attractive gardens of the Parque do Estoril – requires a passport and some semblance of formal attire to get in (open 3pm–3am); minimum bet is 1000$00, and you'll have to cough up a few hundred, too, just to get through the door.

Unless you can afford one of the splendid sea-view hotels, the best move in Estoril is out – following the **seafront promenade** to Cascais, a lovely walk that takes about an hour. If you are determined to stay, there's a very helpful **Turismo** (Mon–Sat 9am–8pm, Sun 10am–6pm; ☎01/468 70 44), right opposite the station across the *Avenida Marginal*, which can advise about **private rooms**. Otherwise, upmarket hotels aside, there are just a few **pensions**, of which *Residencial Smart*, Rua Maestro Lacerda 6 (☎01/468 21 64; ②), is perhaps the best, with pleasant rooms and breakfast included. If this is full, other choices include: *Pensão Costa*, Rua de Olivença 2-1° (☎01/468 16 22; ③); *Pensão Chique do Estoril*, Avenida Marginal 60 (☎01/468 03 93; ②); *Pensão Maryluz*, Rua Maestro Lacerda 13 (☎01/468 27 40; ③–④); and *Pensão Casa Londres*, Avenida Fausto Figueiredo 7 (☎01/468 15 41; ③).

Cascais

At the end of the train line, and with three fair beaches along its esplanade, **CASCAIS** is now a major resort. But it's not too large or difficult to get around and has a much younger, less exclusive, feel than Estoril, even retaining a few elements of its previous existence as a fishing village. There's a lively Wednesday **market**, as well as Sunday evening bullfights that draw a largely local crowd.

You'll find the main concentration of bars and nightlife – and consequently most of what makes Cascais tick as a town – on the pedestrian thoroughfare behind the tourist office and the beaches. For a wander away from the crowds, take a right and head into the old, and surprisingly pretty, west side of town. Also worth a look is the afternoon **fish market**, which takes place around 5pm on a promontory between the Ribeira and Rainha beaches.

On the outskirts of town, to the west, is the pleasant **Parque Marechal Carmona**, with its mansion of the counts of Guimarães, preserved complete with its nineteenth-century fittings as a museum. A little further on, around twenty minutes' walk west of the town, is the **Boca do Inferno** – the "Mouth of Hell" – where waves crash against caves in the cliff face. The viewpoints above are always packed with tourists (as is the very tacky market on the roadside) but, frankly, the whole affair is rather unimpressive except in stormy weather. En route, however, taking the coast road past the military-occupied fort, there's a little **beach** with a nice café on a terrace above.

Practicalities

From the **train station**, walk down Estrada Marginal which bears left at the roundabout for the beach and the central Praça do 5 Outubro. On the way you'll pass Rua Visconde da Luz, on the right, along which you'll find the excellent **Turismo** (☎01/486 82 04), where the staff will usually phone around on your behalf for private rooms.

Of the **pensions**, places to try include the highly recommended *Pensão Palma*, at Avenida Valbom 15, across Avenida Marginal from Rua Visconde da Luz (☎01/483 02 57; ④), and the *Estalgem Solar Dom Carlos*, Rua Latina Coelho 8 (☎01/486 51 54; ③), a very attractive sixteenth-century mansion. A cheaper but less scintillating choice is *Pensão Casa Lena*, Avenida do Ultramar 389 (☎01/486 87 43; ④) – from the station, turn right at the roundabout up Avenida 25 de Abril and keep walking until you see Avenida do Ultramar on your right. *Pensão Avenida*, Rua da Palmeira 14-1° (☎01/486 44 17; ②), is basic but tolerable.

RESTAURANTS

Adega Gonçalves, Rua Afonso Sanches 52. Traditional *adega* not yet overwhelmed by tourists, serving huge portions of good food.

Joshua's, Rua Visconde da Luz 19. Slightly pricey, Middle Eastern-style eatery; open late.

Moamba da Galinha, Rua Alexandre Herculano 25a. African food and music, with dishes from around 1500$00.

Os Navegantes, Rua do Poço Novo 17. Splendid local *churrasqueria*; stick to the daily specials and you won't go far wrong.

A Tasca, Rua Afonso Sanches. Pleasant tavern, good for fish dishes.

BARS AND CLUBS

Belbuerguer, Trav. do Visconde de Luz 18. American rock music and burgers, though on Friday and Saturday nights it does good business as a lively bar, open until 2am.

Coconuts, *Hotel Nau*, Rua Dra. Iracy Doyle. Summer disco, full of the trendiest locals and raving tourists. An outdoor dance floor overlooks the sea; there's a minimum consumption charge of 1500$00.

Duke of Wellington, Rua Frederico Arouca. One of three or four English-style pubs in town; this one serves cream teas and Sunday roasts, as well as imported beer.

Fala Who Bar, Rua Afonso Sanches 36. A smart crowd, loud music, pricey drinks and a "Please leave quietly" sign in five languages.

Praia do Guincho

It's a six-kilometre walk from Cascais on the inland route (or there are hourly buses from outside the train station) to **PRAIA DO GUINCHO**, a great sweeping field of beach with body-crashing Atlantic rollers. It's a superb place to surf or windsurf – World Championships have been held here – but also a dangerous one. The undertow is notoriously strong and people are drowned every year: take care.

The beach has become increasingly popular over the years and is fronted by a couple of **hotels** – the deluxe-class *Hotel de Guincho* and slightly more moderate *Estalagem O Muchaxo* (☎01/487 02 21; ⑤) – and a **campsite** (☎01/285 10 14). For **meals**, *O Muchaxo* is acclaimed as one of the best seafood **restaurants** in the Lisbon area; *O Camponês* at nearby Malveira da Serra, toward Colares, is good, too, and rather less expensive.

Sintra and around

Summer residence of the kings of Portugal, and of the Moorish lords of Lisbon before them, **SINTRA**'s verdant charms have long been celebrated. British travellers of the eighteenth and nineteenth centuries found a new Arcadia in its cool, wooded heights, recording with satisfaction the old Spanish proverb: "To see the world and leave out Sintra is to go blind about". Byron stayed here in 1809 and began *Childe Harold*, his great mock-epic travel poem, in which the "horrid crags" of "Cintra's glorious Eden" form a first location. Writing home, in a letter to his mother, he proclaimed the village:

> *perhaps in every aspect the most delightful in Europe; it contains beauties of every description natural and artificial. Palaces and gardens rising in the midst of rocks, cataracts and precipices; convents on stupendous heights, a distant view of the sea and the Tagus . . . it unites in itself all the wildness of the Western Highlands with the verdure of the South of France.*

That the young Byron had seen neither of these is irrelevant: his description of Sintra's romantic appeal is exact – and still telling two centuries later. Move mountains and give yourself the best part of two full days here.

Orientation

Sintra loops around a series of green and wooded ravines, a confusing place in which to get your bearings. Basically, though, it consists of three distinct and separate villages: **Estefânia** (around the train station), **Sintra-Vila** (the main town) and, 2km to the east, **São Pedro de Sintra**. It's ten to fifteen minutes' walk between the station and Sintra-Vila, passing en route the fantastical Câmara Municipal (town hall); and around twenty minutes from Sintra-Vila to São Pedro. The centre of Sintra-Vila is gathered about the extraordinary **Palácio Nacional**, distinguished by a vast pair of conical chimneys. This is the most obvious landmark, dominating the central square. Just downhill is a Turismo (see "Practicalities", below), in Praça da República, which can help with accommodation and provide a useful map of the town.

Getting around **Sintra's environs** involves a fair bit of walking, with the Moorish castle and Palácio da Pena an hour or so's climb above the town, Seteais twenty minutes to the west and Monserrate another forty minutes further on. If time is limited, you might want to make use of **taxis**, which cost roughly 1500$00 one-way to Pena or Monserrate. Alternatively, in summer, you could take one of the **tours** (around 5000$00 per person) arranged by the Sintra Turismo, taking in the Pena Palace, Colares and the Capuchos convent, Seteais, Monserrate and Cabo da Roca.

The Palácio Nacional

The **Palácio Nacional** – or **Paço Real** (daily except Wed 10am–1pm & 2–5pm; 200$00) – was probably already in existence under the Moors. It takes its present form, however, from the rebuilding and enlargements of Dom João I (1385–1433) and his fortunate successor, Dom Manuel, heir to Vasco da Gama's inspired explorations. Its style, as you might expect, is an amalgam of Gothic – with impressive roofline battlements – and the latter king's Manueline additions, with their characteristically extravagant twisted and animate forms. Inside, the Gothic-

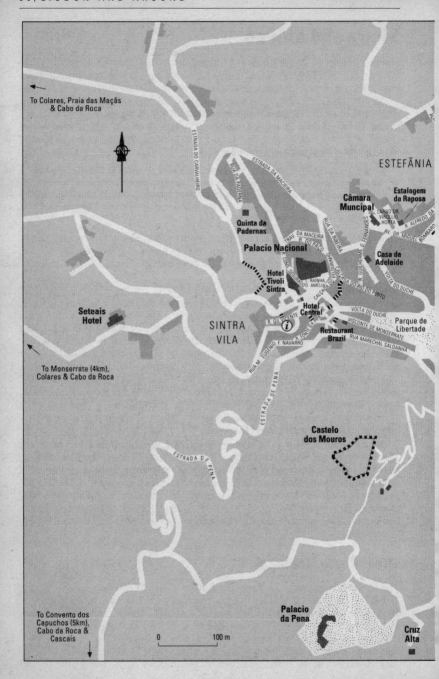

To Colares, Praia das Maçãs
& Cabo da Roca

ESTEFÃNIA

ESTRADA DO CARVALHEIRO

ESTRADA DA MACEIRA

RUA DA PADARNA

Câmara
Muncipal

Estalagem
da Raposa

LARGO DR
VIRGÍLIO
HORTA

R. ALFREDO DA

AV. DR. MIGUEL BOMBARDI

Quinta da
Padernas

TRAV. DA MACEIRA
R. DO PAÇO

RUA DA RIBEIRA

COMD. DA ROCA

R. GUILHERME G. FERNANDES

Palacio Nacional

Casa de
Adelaide

Hotel
Tivoli
Sintra

CONS. SEABRA DO

CALÇADA DO RIO DO PORTO

VOLTA DO DUCHE

L. RAINHA D.
AMÉLIA

Hotel
Central

VOLTA DO DUCHE

Seteais
Hotel

R. GIL VICENTE

i

VISCONTE DE MONSERRATE

Parque de
Libertade

SINTRA
VILA

R. FONTE DA PIPA

RUA MARECHAL SALDANHA

Restaurant
Brazil

RUA M. EUGÉNIO
F. NAVARRO

To Monserrate (4km),
Colares & Cabo da Roca

ESTRADA DE PENA

ESTRADA DE PENA

Castelo
dos Mouros

To Convento dos
Capuchos (5km),
Cabo da Roca &
Cascais

Palacio
da Pena

Cruz
Alta

0   100 m

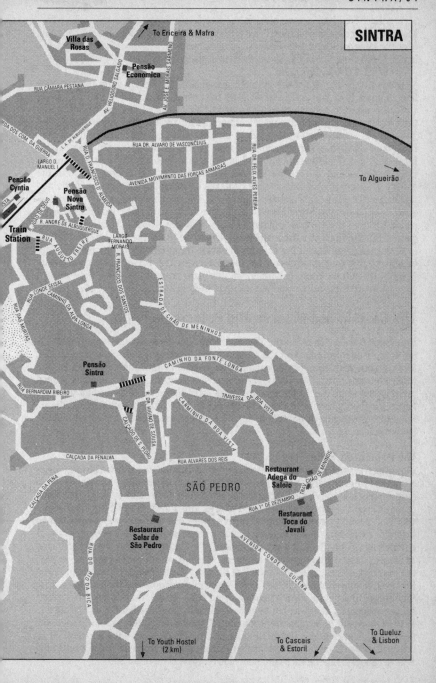

SINTRA

Villa das Rosas

Pensão Economica

To Ericeira & Mafra

RUA CÂMARA PESTANA

AV. HELIODORO SALGADO

AV. JOSÉ E. MORAIS SARMENTO

DA DOS COM. DA GUERRA

L. A. DE ALBUQUERQUE

RUA DR. ALVARO DE VASCONCELOS

RUA DR. FELIX ALVES PEREIRA

LARGO D. MANUEL I

RUA D. FRANCISCO DT ALMEIDA

AVENIDA MOVIMRNTO DAS FORÇAS ARMADAS

To Algueirão

Pensão Cyntia

Pensão Nova Sintra

JOÃO DE DEUS

R. ANDRÉ DE ALBUQUERQUE

Train Station

RUA AUGUSTO FREIRE

LARGO FERNANDO MORAIS

SINTRA

R. FRANCISCO DOS SANTOS

ESTRADA DE CHÃO DE MENINHOS

RUA CONDE SESAL

CAMINHO DA ALFA LONGA

RUA DAS MURTAS

CAMINHO DA FONTE LONGA

Pensão Sintra

RUA BERNARDIM RIBEIRO

R. DR. HIGINO DE SOUSA

TRAVESSA DA BOA VISTA

CAMINHO DA BOA VISTA

CALÇADA DE S. PEDRO

CALÇADA DA PENALVA

RUA ALVARES DOS REIS

Restaurant Adega do Saloio

TRAV. CHÃO DE MININHOS

SÃO PEDRO

CALÇADA DA PENA

RUA 1° DE DEZEMBRO

Restaurant Toca do Javali

Restaurant Solar de São Pedro

RUA DO RIO DA BICA

AVENIDA CONDE DE SUCENA

To Youth Hostel (2 km)

To Cascais & Estoril

To Queluz & Lisbon

Manueline modes are tempered by a good deal of Moorish influence, adapted over the centuries by a succession of royal occupants. The last royal to live here, in the 1880s, was Maria Pia, grandmother of the country's last reigning monarch – Manuel II, "The Unfortunate".

Today the palace is a museum, with informal tours every twenty minutes (it's best to go early or late in the day to avoid the crowds) which allow you a leisurely stroll through the various rooms and patios. You're taken first to the **kitchens**, their roofs tapering into the giant chimneys, and then to the upper floor. First stop here is a gallery above the palace chapel, built perhaps on the old mosque. In a room alongside, the deranged Afonso VI was confined for six years by his brother Pedro II; he eventually died here in 1683, listening to mass through a grid, Pedro having seized "his throne, his liberty and his queen". Beyond the gallery, a succession of state rooms climaxes in the **Sala das Armas**, its domed and coffered ceiling emblazoned with the arms of 72 noble families.

Highlights on the lower floor include the Manueline **Sala dos Cisnes**, so-called for the swans on its ceiling, and the **Sala das Pegas**. This last takes its name from the flock of magpies (*pegas*) painted on the frieze and ceiling, holding in their beaks the legend *por bem* (in honour) – reputedly the response of João I, caught by his queen, Philippa (of Lancaster), in the act of kissing a lady-in-waiting. He had the room decorated with as many magpies as there were women at court in order to satirise and put a stop to their gossip.

The Castelo dos Mouros and Palácio da Pena

From near the church of **Santa Maria**, towards São Pedro, a stone pathway leads up to the ruined ramparts of the **Castelo dos Mouros** (Tues–Sun 9am–sunset, free). Taken with the aid of Scandinavian crusaders by Afonso Henriques, the Moorish castle spans two rocky pinnacles, with the remains of a mosque spread midway between the fortifications. Views from here are extraordinary: south beyond Lisbon's bridge to the Serra de Arrábida, west to Cascais and Cabo da Roca (the westernmost point of mainland Europe), and north to Peniche and the Berlenga islands.

The Palácio da Pena

The upper gate of the castle gives onto the road up to Pena, opposite the lower entrance to **Pena park** (daily 10am–6pm), a stretch of rambling woodland, with a scattering of lakes and follies, ideal for a picnic. At the top of the park, about twenty minutes' walk, rears the fabulous **Palácio da Pena** (Tues–Sun 10am–5pm; 400$00), a wild fantasy of domes, towers, ramparts and walkways, approached through mock-Manueline gateways and a drawbridge that does not draw. A compelling riot of kitsch, it was built in the 1840s to the specifications of Ferdinand of Saxe-Coburg-Gotha, husband of Queen Maria II, and it bears comparison with the mock-medieval castles of Ludwig of Bavaria. The architect, the German Baron Eschwege, immortalised himself in the guise of a warrior-knight on a huge statue that guards the palace from a neighbouring crag. Inside, Pena is no less bizarre, preserved exactly as it was left by the royal family on their flight from Portugal in 1910. The result is fascinating: rooms of concrete decorated to look like wood, turbanned Moors nonchalantly holding electric chandeliers – it's all here. Of an original convent, founded to celebrate the first sight of Vasco da Gama's returning fleet, a chapel and genuine Manueline cloister have been retained.

Above Pena, past the statue of Eschwege, a marked footpath climbs to the **Cruz Alta**, highest point of the Serra de Sintra. Another footpath (unmarked) winds down to the left from Pena, coming out near Seteais (see below).

Seteais, Monserrate and the Convento dos Capuchos

After the castle and Pena, a visit to the palace of **Seteais** and luxuriant gardens of **Monserrate** are the other obvious goals of a Sintra walk. Enthusiastic hikers can make a circuit of these, via the **Capuchos** "Cork Convent"; otherwise, to see everything, you're looking at a taxi-ride at least one-way to at least one of the sights.

The Palácio de Seteais

The **Palácio de Seteais** ("Seven Sighs") stands just to the right of the Colares road, fifteen-minutes' walk from the centre of town. It is one of the most elegant palaces in Portugal, completed in the last years of the eighteenth century and entered through a majestic Neoclassical arch. It is maintained today as an immensely luxurious **hotel**, offering some of the most expensive accommodation in the country; with more modest money to blow, make for the bar and terrace – downstairs to the left, past a distinctly unwelcoming reception.

Beyond Seteais, the road leads past a series of beautiful private *quintas* (manors or estates) until you come upon Monserrate – about another forty minutes' walk away.

Monserrate

With its Victorian folly-like mansion and vast botanical park of exotic trees and subtropical shrubs and plants, **Monserrate** is one of the most romantic sights in Portugal. It would be easy to spend the whole day wandering around the paths laid out through the woods – and the charm of the place is immeasurably enhanced by the fact that it's only partially maintained. The name most associated with Monserrate is that of **William Beckford**, author of the Gothic novel *Vathek* and the wealthiest untitled Englishman of his age. He hired the *quinta* here from 1793 to 1799, having been forced to flee Britain because of homosexual scandal – buggery then being a hanging offence. Setting about improving this "beautiful Claude-like place", he landscaped a waterfall and even imported a flock of sheep from his estate at Fonthill. In this Xanadu-like dreamland, he whiled away his days in summer pavilions, entertaining with "bevys of delicate warblers and musicians" posted around the grounds.

Half a century later, a second immensely rich Englishman, **Sir Francis Cook**, bought the estate. His fantasies were scarcely less ambitious, involving the construction of a great Victorian house inspired by Brighton Pavilion. Cook also spared no expense in developing the grounds, importing the head gardener from Kew to lay out succulents and water plants, tropical ferns and palms, and just about every conifer known. Fernando II, who was building the Pena palace at the time, was suitably impressed, conferring a viscountcy on Cook for his efforts.

The **gardens** are open daily except on public holidays – officially from 9am to 5pm (50$00), though the gates aren't always locked. Cook's **house** is closed but you can still admire the exterior, with its mix of Moorish and Italian decoration (the dome is modelled on Brunelleschi's Duomo in Florence), and peer into a splendid series of empty salons.

The Convento dos Capuchos

One of the best long walks in the Sintra area is to the **Convento dos Capuchos** (daily except Tues 10am–12.30pm & 2–5pm; 200$00), an extraordinary hermitage with tiny, dwarflike cells cut from the rock and lined in cork – hence its popular name of the "Cork Convent". Philip II, King of Spain and Portugal, pronounced it the poorest convent of his kingdom, and Byron, visiting a cave where one monk had spent thirty-six years in seclusion, mocked in *Childe Harold*:

> *Deep in yon cave Honorius long did dwell,*
> *In hope to merit Heaven by making earth a Hell.*

Coming upon the place after a walk through the woods, however, it's hard not to be moved by the simplicity and seclusion of the place. The surroundings, too, beg a startled reaction: the minor road between the convent and Cabo da Roca sports some of the country's most alarming natural rock formations, with boulders as big as houses looming out of the trees.

To reach the convent, the most straightforward approach is by the ridge road from Pena (9km), but there is also an indistinct path through the woods from Monserrate, starting above the fountain opposite the entrance to the gardens.

Further west: Colares, the beaches and Cabo da Roca

About 6km west of Monserrate is **COLARES**, a hill village famed for its wine, which boasts several much-prized vintages. It has a couple of mid-range hotels, if you felt like an alternative base to Sintra, and a fine **restaurant**, *A Bistro* (closed Mon), housed in an old apothecary shop.

Continuing west, the road winds around through the hills to the beach-resort of **PRAIA DAS MAÇÃS** (buses from Sintra train station, or in summer, trams from Colares). This has two pensions and a scattering of restaurants. Nearby **AZENHAS DO MAR**, to the north, with a nice, small beach, and **PRAIA GRANDE**, to the south (again, both accessible on the bus from Sintra) are in similar mould; Praia Grande also has a large **campsite**.

Cabo da Roca

Fourteen kilometres southwest of Colares, **CABO DA ROCA** can be reached by taking a bus to Cruz da Azoia and walking the remaining 3km from there. It's an enjoyable trip, though the cape comprises little more than a lighthouse and a couple of stalls. At one of these, you can buy a certificate recording that you've visited the "Most Westerly Point in Europe" – which indeed you have.

Practicalities

The **train station** is ten to fifteen minutes' walk from the centre of Sintra-Vila; **buses** stop across the street from the station, with services to and from Cascais, Estoril and Mafra. Sintra is a popular resort and you should book ahead or turn up early in the day if you intend to stay. On the spot, accommodation is best arranged through the efficient and helpful **Turismo** (June–Sept daily 9am–8pm, Oct–May daily 9am–7pm; ☎01/923 39 19), just off the central Praça da República. Times when accommodation will definitely be scarce are during the village's annual **festa** in honour of Saint Peter (June 28–29), and in July, when Sintra holds a **music festival**, with classical performances in a number of the town's buildings.

Accommodation

There's a fair range of available **accommodation**: a network of private rooms (best booked through the Turismo; usually ②), half a dozen pensions and hotels, and upmarket bed and breakfast in several local *quintas*, or manorhouses – the best choices are reviewed below.

In addition, there's an attractive youth hostel, the **Pousada de Juventude de Sintra**, at Santa Eufémia (☎01/924 12 10), located in the hills above São Pedro de Sintra. It's a five-kilometre walk from the centre, less if you first catch a local bus to São Pedro. The nearest **campsites** are even further out of town: at *Camping Capuchos* (☎01/86 23 50), near the convent – a ten-kilometre haul to the west, with no bus service – and, more conveniently, on the beach at Praia Grande (☎01/929 05 81; see below).

Casa de Hóspedes Adelaide, Rua Guilherme Gomes Fernandes 11 (☎01/923 08 73). Welcoming and inexpensive place, midway between the train station and Sintra Vila. ②.

Hotel Central, Praça da República 35 (☎01/923 09 63). Characterful and comfortable nineteenth-century hotel, opposite the Palácio Nacional; breakfast included. ⑤.

Pensão Económica, Patio de Olivença 6 (☎01/923 02 29). Lying off Avda. Heliodoro Salgado, this looks like a converted school; fairly basic accommodation, but cheap enough. ②–③.

Estalagem da Raposa, Rua Alfredo Costa 3 (☎01/923 04 65). An old townhouse run as an inn since the last war. Its age is beginning to show, though, and rooms are no longer as clean as they might be. ⑤.

Pensão Nova Sintra, Largo Afonso d'Albuquerque 25 (☎01/923 02 20). Decent rooms and a handy situation, on the square by the train station. Some rooms have fine views. ③–④.

Piela's, Rua João de Deus 70–72 (☎01/924 16 91). Very close to the train station, this café-*pastelaria* has six double rooms available, presided over by a welcoming and informative proprietor. Meals are served, and there's a games room. ②.

Quinta da Paderna, Rua da Paderna 4 (☎01/923 50 53). Highly attractive bed and breakfast accommodation in a lovely old house, just north of Sintra-Vila. ⑤.

Quinta das Sequóias (☎01/923 03 42). Immaculate *Turihab* manor house (formerly the *Casa da Tapada*) with five rooms, out in the Sintra hills beyond Seteais – continue past the Palácio de Seteais hotel for 1km and follow the signposted private road on your left. A lovely antique-furnished place with superb views, gardens, sauna and swimming pool; buffet breakfast included. Recommended. ⑥.

Residencial Sintra, Trav. dos Alvares, São Pedro (☎01/923 07 38). Big, rambling old pension with a garden and swimming pool, and friendly, multilingual owners. Remarkable value – you'll need to book ahead in summer. ④.

Villa das Rosas, Rua António Cunha 4 (☎01/923 42 16). Central villa with a large garden and rooms that feature antique furniture. ⑤.

Eating and drinking

There are some fine **restaurants** scattered about the various quarters of Sintra, with the best concentration at São Pedro, a twenty-minute walk from the centre. Local specialities include *queijadas da Sintra* – sweet cheese pastry-cakes. If you're out for the day, take a **picnic**: the only refreshments out of town are cold drinks from a stall below Pena park (summer only), or exorbitantly priced meals at Seteais hotel. There's a daily **market** in the centre of Sintra-Vila, and a much larger **country market** – with antiques and crafts, as well as food – in São Pedro on the second and last Sunday of every month.

Adega do Saloio, Trav. Chão de Meninos, São Pedro. A fine grill-restaurant, popular enough to have spread to buildings on both sides of the road. Standard Portuguese menu, but notably hospitable owners and a good *arroz de marisco*. Up to 3000$00.

Bar Restaurant Augusto, Rua da Pendôa 9. Boasting an esplanade, this is a good place for a late-night drink (open until 2am), though the food is fairly forgettable.

Casa da Avo, Escadinhas da Audiencia, Sintra-Vila. Slightly soulless but the house wine is cheap enough to drown such thoughts – and it's hard to fault dishes like the *caldeirada* (fish stew). Closed Mon.

Casa da Piriquita, Rua das Padarias 1. Quality tea-room and bakery, busy with locals queueing to buy *qeuijadas da Sintra* and the similarly sticky *travesseiros*.

Restaurante-Bar O Chico, Rua Arco do Teixeira. Open for drinks until 2am, though last food orders are before midnight. Standard Sintra prices and food, but come on Thursdays in summer for the fado.

Piela's, Rua João de Deus 70–72 . Budget meals and late-night drinks, as well as rooms (for which see above).

Restaurante Regional, Trav. do Município 1. Close to the Câmara Municipal, the *Regional* serves imaginative Portuguese food, including a smattering of regional dishes. Dishes at the 1500–2000$00 mark.

Solar de São Pedro, Praça Dom Fernando II 12, São Pedro. Locally renowned French-Portuguese dishes served in an *azulejo*-covered vault. Around 3000–4000$00 per person. Closed Wed.

Toca do Javali, Rua 1º Dezembro 18, São Pedro. Outdoor tables in summer and superb cooking at any time of year. Wild boar (*javali*) is the house speciality. Prices are fairly modest for the quality – up to and around 4000$00 a head.

Restaurante Tulhas, Rua Gil Vicente 4, Sintra-Vila. Behind the Turismo, you'll find imaginative cooking in a fine building, converted from old grain silos. The speciality is veal with madeira at a reasonable 1000$00 or so.

Restaurante Via Brasil, Rua Visconde de Monserrate 60. Budget pizzas, burgers and the odd Brazilian dish.

Palácio de Queluz

The **Palácio de Queluz** (daily except Tues 10am–1pm & 2–5pm; 400$00) lies on the Sintra train line, making it easy to see either on the way out (it's just twenty minutes from Lisbon's Rossío station) or the way back from Sintra. The station is called Queluz-Belas: turn left out of the station and walk down the main road for fifteen minutes, following the signs through the unremarkable town until you reach a vast cobbled square, with the palace walls reaching out around one side.

The building is as perfect a counterpoint to Mafra (see below) as you could imagine: an elegant, restrained structure regarded as the country's finest example of Rococo architecture. Its low, pink-washed wings enclose a series of rambling and beautiful eighteenth-century formal gardens, which, although preserved as a museum, don't quite feel like one – retaining instead a strong sense of its past royal owners. In fact, the palace is still pressed into service for accommodating state guests and dignitaries, and hosts classical concerts in the summer months.

The palace was built by Dom Pedro III, husband and regent to his niece, Queen Maria I, who lived here throughout her 39-year reign (1777–1816), quite mad for the last 27, following the death of her eldest son, José. William Beckford visited when the Queen's wits were dwindling, and ran races in the gardens with the Princess of Brazil's ladies-in-waiting; at other times firework displays were held above the ornamental canal and bullfights in the courtyards. Visits can be greatly enhanced by a meal in the original kitchen, the **Cozinha Velha**, which retains its stone arches and wooden vaulted ceiling. The food is superb, but you're looking at around 5000$00 a head for a full meal.

Mafra

Moving on from Lisbon or Sintra, **MAFRA** makes an interesting approach to Estremadura. It is distinguished – and utterly dominated – by just one building: the vast **Palace-Convent** (daily except Tues 10am–1pm & 2.30–5pm; 400$00) built in emulation of Madrid's Escorial by João V, the wealthiest and most extravagant of all Portuguese monarchs. Arrive at least an hour before closing time to be sure of getting on a guided **tour** (which lasts for one hour).

The palace-convent
Begun in 1717 to honour a vow made on the birth of a royal heir, **Mafra Convent** was initially intended for just thirteen Franciscan friars. But as wealth poured in from the gold and diamonds of Brazil, João and his German court architect, Frederico Ludovice, amplified their plans to build a massive basilica, two royal wings and monastic quarters for 300 monks and 150 novices. The result, completed in thirteen years, is quite extraordinary and – on its own bizarre terms – extremely impressive.

In style the building is a fusion of Baroque and Italianate Neoclassicism, but it is the sheer magnitude and logistics that stand out. In the last stages of construction over 45,000 labourers were employed, while throughout the years of building there was a daily average of nearly 15,000; there are 5200 doorways, 2500 windows and two immense belltowers each containing over 50 bells. An apocryphal story records the astonishment of the Flemish bellmakers at the size of this order: on their querying it, and asking for payment in advance, Dom João retorted by doubling their price and his original requirement.

Parts of the convent are used by the military but an ingenious cadre of guides marches you around a sizeable enough portion. The **royal apartments** are a mix of the tedious and the shocking: the latter most obviously in the **Sala dos Troféus**, with its furniture (even chandeliers) constructed of antlers and upholstered in deerskin. Beyond are the **monastic quarters**, including cells, a pharmacy and a curious infirmary with beds positioned so the ailing monks could see mass performed. The highlight, however, is the magnificent Rococo **library** – brilliantly lit and rivalling Coimbra's in grandeur. Byron, shown the 35,000 volumes by one of the monks, was asked if "the English had any books in their country?" The **basilica** itself, which can be seen outside the tour, is no less imposing, with the multicoloured marble designs of its floor mirrored in the ceiling decoration.

Practicalities
The **town** of Mafra is dull, and with frequent buses heading on to the lively resort of Ericeira, 12km away (see p.108), there seems no point in lingering. Alternatively, you can see the palace as a daytrip from Sintra: there's a mid-morning bus from Sintra station and another back at lunchtime. If you need to stay, the owner of the *Restaurante Primavera* (facing the palace across the main road) lets out clean and comfortable **rooms**; the restaurant here is good, too. Or try the *Solar d'El Rei*, Rua Detras dos Quintas, five minutes' walk from the palace; it's an inexpensive **restaurant** with good food.

South of the Tejo: Costa da Caparica, Setúbal and its coast

As late as the nineteenth century, the southern bank of the Tejo estuary was an underpopulated area used as a quarantine station for foreign visitors; the village of Trafaria here was so lawless that the police only visited when accompanied by members of the army. The huge **Ponte 25 de Abril** suspension bridge, inaugurated as the "Salazar Bridge" in 1966 and renamed after the 1974 revolution, finally ended what remained of this separation between "town and country". Since then, Lisbon has spilled over the river in a string of tatty industrial suburbs that spread east of the bridge, while to the west the **Costa da Caparica** has become a major holiday resort. **Setúbal**, 50km south of the capital, sustains one remarkable church, but little else to delay you. That said, it's not a bad first stop on your way further south and its **coastal** surroundings are particularly attractive.

Across the river: Cacilhas and the Christo-Rei

The most enjoyable approach to the Setúbal peninsula is to take a **ferry** from Lisbon's Fluvial station (by Praça do Comércio) to the suburb of **CACILHAS**. The ferries run every ten minutes, the last returning at 9.35pm (9.10pm at weekends); the crossing takes around ten minutes. The blustery ride itself is fun, though you may well want to come over in the evening to eat seafood. Cacilhas' main street is one long line of reasonably priced **fish restaurants**, popular with Lisbon locals, all offering excellent dishes – *arroz de marisco* is a speciality in most. Eating dinner here, you'll almost certainly miss the last ferry back to Fluvial, but you can still get back to the capital by taking a ferry to Cais do Sodré; these run throughout the night.

The ferry grants you wonderful views of the city, as well as of the enormous **Ponte 25 de Abril** and – on the south bank above Cacilhas – the **Christo-Rei**, a relatively modest version of Rio's Christ-statue landmark. A lift at the statue (summer daily 9am–7pm; 150$00) shuttles you up the plinth, via a souvenir shop, to a highly dramatic viewing platform. On a good day, Lisbon stretches like a map below you and you can catch the glistening roof of the Pena palace at Sintra in the distance.

Bus #10 from Cacilhas (outside the ferry terminal) runs to the statue, or you can come direct from Lisbon on the #52 or #53 (to "Almada"; every 20–30min) from Praça de Espanha in Lisbon (metro *Palhavã*). Get off just over the bridge and cross the road; as you head into town, take the first left – Rua Fernão Mendes Pinto – and it's a ten-minute walk. Driving, cross the bridge and turn left off the highway, following signs for Almada and *Christo-Rei*.

Costa da Caparica

Regular buses from Cacilhas (or the #52 or #53 from Praça de Espanha) run on to **Costa da Caparica**, just over an hour (outside of rush hour) from the capital. It's here that most locals come if they want to swim or laze around on the sand. There are foreign tourists, too, but they're in a minority: this is a thoroughly lively Portuguese resort, crammed with restaurants and beach cafés. It is also –

as far as sea and sand go – more or less limitless. A mini-railway runs along 8km or so of dunes (in season only) and if you're after solitude you need only take this to the end of the line and walk.

Caparica's **beaches**, which take in coves and lagoons as they spread southwards, speak for themselves. It's useful to know, though, that each of the twenty mini-train stops, based around one or two beach-cafés, has a very particular scene or feel. Earlier stops tend to be family oriented, often with a campsite and pool nearby. Later ones are on the whole younger and more trendy, with nudity (though officially illegal) more or less obligatory. One or more stops are predominantly gay – most recently stop no. 17 was the most fashionable.

Practicalities

At **CAPARICA** all buses stop in a dusty depot near the beginning of the sands. If you walk along the beach to the left you come to the main square, where there's a **turismo**, market, cinema and banks.

There aren't very many **hotels** in Caparica. If you strike lucky, a particularly attractive place to stay is the *Hotel-Restaurante Pátio Alentejano*, Rua Professor Salazar de Sousa 17 (℡01/290 00 44; ③), just off the beach to the north of the town centre. Alternatively, the tourist office can book private rooms, and there is a string of **campsites**. Moving north to south along the beach, these are: *Orbitur* (℡01/290 06 61); *Clube de Campismo de Lisboa* (℡01/290 01 00); *Lugar ao Sol* (℡01/290 15 92); *Praia da Saúde* (℡01/290 22 72); *Costa Nova* (℡01/290 30 21); and *Praia da Mata* (℡01/290 26 20). All are pricier than average and crowded in summer. A recommended **restaurant**, among dozens of fish and seafood places along the main street, Rua dos Pescadores, is the *Casa dos Churros* at no. 13.

Setúbal and around

Some 50km from Lisbon, **SETÚBAL** is Portugal's third port and a major industrial centre. Once described by Hans Christian Andersen as a "terrestrial paradise", most of its visual charm is long gone but it's a friendly, enjoyable enough place. If you're heading south and have time to break the journey, it's worth stopping at least for a look at the remarkable Igreja de Jesus. On a more prolonged visit, you could take in its museums, some fine views from local vantage points, and a series of excellent **beaches** nearby.

Around the town

Setúbal's greatest monument is the **Igreja de Jesus**, designed by Diogo de Boitaca and possibly the first of all Manueline buildings. Essentially a late-Gothic structure, with a huge, flamboyant doorway, Boitaca transformed its interior design by introducing fantastically twisted pillars to support the vault. The rough granite surfaces of the pillars contrast with the delicacy of the blue-and-white *azulejos* around the high altar, which were added in the seventeenth century. The church stands on the Praça Miguel Bombarda along the main Avenida 5 de Outubro, about 400m from the train station or the town centre.

Next door to the church, housed in the old monastic quarters, is a small but very fine **municipal museum** (Tues–Sun 10am–12.30pm & 2–5pm) with a superb collection of fifteenth- to sixteenth-century Portuguese art as well as sections dedicated to fifteenth- to eighteenth-century jewellery and to local archaeology. You might also climb up to the **Castelo São Felipe**, to the west of

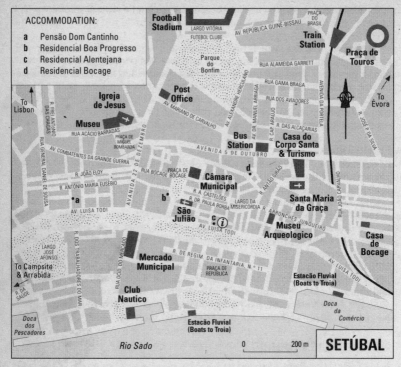

the town. This is now a *pousada*, but the bar is open to non-guests and there are fine views over the mouth of the Sado estuary and the Tróia peninsula.

A half-hour walk along the coast road, west out of Setúbal, takes you to Albarquel, where a magnificently located café-restaurant sits on an outcrop of rock above the sea (reasonably priced café, expensive and highly renowned restaurant).

Tróia and Palmela

Setúbal's traditional **beaches**, reached by frequent ferry from the town (there are long queues for cars in summer), are on the **Península de Tróia**, a large sand spit hemming in the Sado estuary. The peninsula was settled by the Phoenicians and subsequently by the Romans, whose town of *Cetobriga* appears to have been overwhelmed by a tidal wave in the fifth century. There are some desultory remains, including tanks for salting fish, opposite the marina on the landward shore. Originally a wilderness of sand and wildflowers, Tróia must once have been magnificent, but it's now a heavily developed concrete resort. To avoid the worst, and the crowds, be prepared to walk for twenty minutes or so south along the beach.

The small town of **PALMELA**, around 10km north of Setúbal, is worth a visit for the views from the **castle**, which, like that of Setúbal, has been restored and extended as a *pousada*, the *Castelo de Palmela* (☎01/235 12 26; ⑦). A fine place to stay, the castle is also worth a trip for the views, which on a clear day encompass Lisbon, Setúbal, the Sado and Tróia.

Practicalities

You can reach Setúbal by **train**, though since it involves crossing to Barreiro and changing (see p.46), it's quicker to take the **bus** from Lisbon's Praça de Espanha; an hourly service that takes around an hour.

Considering Setúbal's size, **accommodation** is in short supply. However, the **Turismo**, on Praça do Quebedo (Mon–Fri 9am–12.30pm & 2–5pm), runs a helpful accommodation service for **rooms** in private homes. Among **pensions** worth trying are *Residencial Boa Regresso*, Praça de Bocage (☎065/298 12; ②); *Residencial Alentejana*, Avenida Luisa Todi 124 (☎065/213 98; ②); and the *Residencial Bocage*, Rua de São Cristovão 14 (☎065/215 98; ④). The extremely attractive **pousada**, the *São Filipe* (☎065/523 844; ⑥–⑦), occupies the castle, high above the river; and there's a muncipal **campsite**, too (☎065/224 75).

Superb value fish and seafood **restaurants** abound in the dock area and around the western end of Avenida Luisa Todi; *O Capote*, in a small square just off the avenue is one of the best. If you're self-catering, there's a **market** opposite the fountain of Luisa Todi. In midsummer, you'll find the market area considerably expanded with clothes and touristy bric-a-brac.

Evening diversions in Setúbal are reasonably promising. You could start drinking at the *Cactus* on Praça de Bocage and finish at *Torib's* which stays open till about 3am. Between bars you might visit one of the two pool halls or the music club *Absurdia* (usually no entrance charge), or the **Teatro Luisa Todi**, which stages shows at weekends and often runs art-house movies during the week. Alternatively, try the *Seagull* disco, a ten-minute drive along the coast road, or the less pretentious *Leo Taurus*, five minutes' drive along the N10 road.

The Parque Natural da Arrábida

Between Setúbal and Sesimbra lies the **Parque Natural da Arrábida**, whose main feature is the 500-metre granite ridge known as the Serra da Arrábida, visible for miles around and popular for its wild mountain scenery. The twisted pillars of Setúbal's Igreja de Jesus were hewn from here.

The **bus** from Setúbal to Sesimbra takes the main road, well back from the coast, passing through the town of **VILA FRESCA DE AZEITÃO**, where the *José Maria da Fonseca* **wine vaults** can be visited. The free tour is interesting and a good introduction to the local *Setúbal Moscatel*. There is a **campsite**, *Picheleiros* (☎065/208 13 22) just outside town, which is the only site in the park area.

If you have transport, a better route – not covered by buses – is the twisting coast road, the N10-4. Nestling in the cliffs down this road is the sixteenth-century **Convento da Arrábida,** whose crumbling white buildings with their stunning ocean views are the home of a silent Franciscan order. Nearby is the tiny harbour village of **PORTINHO DA ARRÁBIDA**, which has a couple of excellent, clean beaches, wonderful out of season and always quieter than Troia. There are prehistoric cave sites nearby and a good **restaurant** by the water's edge. Next along is **GALAPOS**, arguably the best beach along this whole coast.

Sesimbra

Although in the throes of rapid development as a resort, with apartment buildings and hotels mushrooming on the outskirts, the centre of the little fishing town of **SESIMBRA**, with its steep narrow streets, still manages to retain a semblance of its erstwhile unhurried atmosphere. These days, it's largely a day-trip resort for Lisbon residents, though the wealthier ones have bought second homes here for the summer. A **Moorish castle** dominates the town, a stiff half-hour climb from the centre. Within the walls are a church and various ruins, while a circuit of battlements gives amazing panoramas over the surrounding countryside and coastline. Back in the town, the **municipal museum** in the Palácio do Bispo, features archaeological and historical finds from the area, while the best of the churches, the Manueline **Igreja da Mai**, is on nearby Rua João de Deus.

However, the most attractive corner of town is undoubtedly the original fishing port, **Porto de Abrigo**, with its brightly painted boats, daily fish auctions, and stalls selling a superb variety of shellfish. It's a pleasant walk from the centre, along Avenida dos Naufragos – follow the signs towards the **Forte do Cavalo**, where the local anglers try their hand at sea fishing.

Practicalities

There are regular **buses** from Lisbon's Praça de Espanha; and there are services, too, from Cacilhas and Setúbal. Coming from Lisbon in summer, it's quicker to take the ferry across to Cacilhas and pick up a bus there, as the main bridge road is often jammed solid with traffic. Alternatively, there's a summer **ferry** service from Cacilhas (410$00), with departures every hour.

Accommodation is sparse at any time of year, with just a handful of pensions and pricey hotels. Your best bet is to try for private rooms through the **Turismo** (Mon–Sat 9am–6pm; closed 12.30–2pm in winter; ☎01/223 3304), on the seafront at Avenida dos Náufragos 17. Otherwise, the very central *Residencial Chic*, Travessa Xavier da Silva 2–6 (☎01/223 31 10; ③), will either have, or know about, spare rooms. *Pensão Náutico*, up the hill, off Rua General Humberto Delgado (③), is another comfortable place and a little more secluded; while the *Hotel Espadarte*, Avenida 25 de Abril (☎01/223 31 89; ④), is a decent, fairly upmarket hotel. There's also a well-located **campsite** at *Forte do Cavalo* (☎01/223 39 05), just past the fishing port.

Among the excellent local **seafood restaurants**, try *Sesimbrense*, on the corner of Largo do Município and Rua Jorge Nunes. Rua Latino Coelho, parallel to the seafront, has three or four reasonable places; prices in the restaurants in the main square have increased somewhat over the last couple of years. Best of the **bars** along the seafront is *De Facto*, Avenida dos Naufragos 26; while clubs with a bit of a summer reputation include *Belle Epoch*, off Largo do Calvario, and *Saloon* on Rua Dom Sancho; both stay open till 4am.

Cabo Espichel and Aldeia do Meco

Six buses a day make the eleven-kilometre journey west from Sesimbra to the **Cabo Espichel**, a desolate end-of-the-world plateau where the road winds up at a wide church square. This is enclosed on three sides by ramshackle eighteenth-century pilgrimage lodgings, which are now hardly used. Beyond, wild and wind-swept cliffs drop almost vertically several hundred feet into the Atlantic.

A few kilometres to the north and up the coast from here is the village of **ALDEIA DO MECO** with four buses a day from Sesimbra, providing easy access to the southern beaches of the **Costa da Caparica** (see p.98 for the northern section). Again these are prone to overcrowding in July and August, but they can be almost deserted and extremely warm and pleasant in May or October. Several villages have **rooms** for rent and there is a growing number of official **campsites** – including a particularly good one at Fetais (☎01/223 29 78), between Aldeia and Praia do Penedo. The best strip of beach is by the lagoon at **Lagoa de Albufeira**: it is extremely clean and excellent for windsurfing.

travel details

Trains

Cais do Sodré to Belém (every 15–30min; 7min); Cascais (every 15–30min; 32min); Estoril (every 15–30min; 28min).

Fluvial, via Barreiro, to Albufeira (2 daily; 5hr); Beja (3 daily; 3hr 30min); Évora (3 daily; 3hr); Faro (2 daily; 5hr); Palmela (hourly; 1hr 15min); Setúbal (hourly; 1hr 30min); Tavira (2 daily; 6hr); Vila Real de Santo António (2 daily; 7hr).

Rossío to Caldas da Rainha (13 daily; 2hr–2hr 30min); Figueira da Foz (4 daily; 3hr 45min); Leiria (6 daily; 3hr–3hr 30min); Óbidos (13 daily; 2hr 30min); Queluz (every 15–20min; 20min); Sintra (every 15–20min; 50min); Torres Vedras (13 daily; 1hr 10min–1hr 30min).

Santa Apolónia to Abrantes (6 daily; 2hr 30min); Aveiro (10 daily; 3hr); Badajoz, Spain (4 daily; 6hr); Castelo Branco (6 daily; 3hr 30min–4hr 30min); Coimbra (10 daily; 2hr 30min); Covilhã (6 daily; 4hr 30min–6hr); Elvas (4 daily; 5hr 30min); Guarda (4 daily; 7hr 15min); Portalegre (4 daily; 4hr 30min); Porto, for connections to Spain (10 daily; 3–4hr).

International Trains

Santa Apolónia to Madrid (1 day and 1 night train; 8hr 15min–10hr 30min); Paris (1 daily; 26hr).

Buses

Express buses run daily to all main towns throughout the country; information from the main bus terminal at Avenida Casal Ribeiro (see p.47). Local services include:

Lisbon to Mafra (10 daily; 1hr 30min); Ericeira (10 daily; 1hr 50min); Évora (6 daily; 3hr 30min); Nazaré (3 daily; 4hr); Peniche (8 daily; 3hr); Sesimbra (hourly; 1hr 30min–2hr); Tomar (3 daily; 2hr 30min); Torres Vedras (12 daily; 2hr 30min);

Flights

There are **internal flights** of varying regularity from Lisbon to Bragança, Chaves, Covilhã, Faro, Porto, Vila Real, Viseu and to Madeira and the Azores.

CHAPTER TWO

ESTREMADURA AND RIBATEJO

The **Estremadura** and **Ribatejo** regions have played a crucial role in each phase of the nation's history, and feature the monuments to prove it. Encompassing a comparatively small area, the provinces boast an extraordinary concentration of vivid architecture and engaging towns: **Alcobaça**, **Batalha**, and **Tomar** – comprising the most exciting buildings in Portugal – all lie within a ninety-minute bus ride of each other. Other attractions are equally compelling: ferries sail from Peniche to remote **Berlenga Island**; **Óbidos** is a completely walled medieval village; spectacular underground caverns can be visited at **Mira d'Aire**; and there are tremendous castles at **Porto de Mós**, **Leiria** (itself an elegant town), and on **Almourol**, an islet in the middle of the Tejo.

The Estremaduran coast – the lower half of the Costa de Prata – provides an excellent complement to all this, and if you're simply seeking sun and sand it's not a bad alternative to the Algarve. **Nazaré** and **Ericeira** are justifiably the most popular resorts but there are scores of less developed beaches. For more isolation, try the area around **São Martinho do Porto**, or the coastline west of **Leiria**, backed most of the way by the pine forest of **Pinhal de Leiria**.

Virtually all of these highlights fall within the boundaries of Estremadura, which, with its fertile rolling hills, is second in beauty only to the Minho. The flat, bull-breeding lands of **Ribatejo** (literally "banks-of-the-Tejo") fade into the dull expanses of northwestern Alentejo and there's no great reason to cross the river unless you're pushing on to Évora or can catch up with one of the region's lively traditional **festivals**. The wildest and most famous of these is the *Festa do Colete Encarnado* of **Vila Franca de Xira,** with Pamplona-style bull-running through the streets.

ACCOMMODATION PRICE CODES

All the accommodation prices in this book have been coded using the symbols below. The symbols represent the prices for the cheapest available double room in high season; for a full explanation, see p.23.

① Under 3000$00   ② 3000$00–4000$00   ③ 4000$00–5500$00
④ 5500$00–8500$00   ⑤ 8500$00–12,500$00   ⑥ 12,500$00–20,000$00

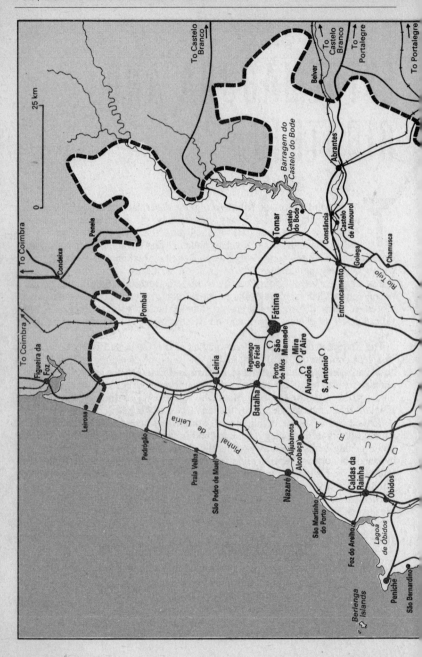

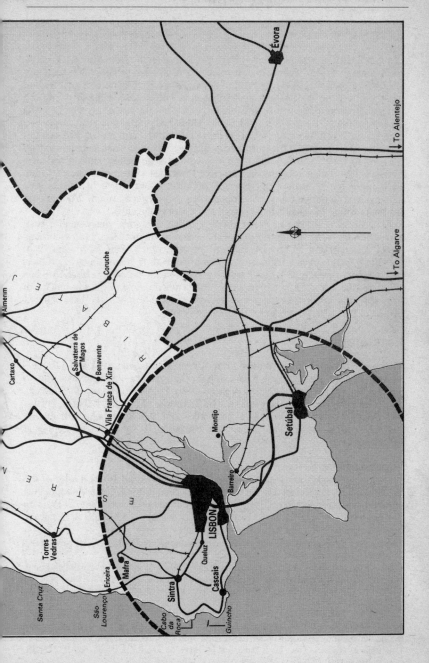

Ericeira

October 5, 1910 marked the end of Portuguese monarchy. Dom Manuel II – "The Unfortunate" – was woken in his palace at Mafra by reports that an angry Republican mob was advancing from Lisbon. Aware of the fate of his father and elder brother, he fled to the small harbour at **ERICEIRA** and sailed into the welcoming arms of the British at Gibraltar, to live out the rest of his days in a villa at Twickenham. Baedeker's guidebook, published the same year, described Ericeira as "a fishing village with excellent sea bathing" and recent development has done little to change the town's original character. The place is undeniably on the way to resort status – the main square has been pedestrianised and new hotels built – but it remains an attractive town. Ericeira is well-known to the Portuguese for its seafood (particularly its lobsters and crayfish) and its very name is said to derive from the words *ouriços do mar* (sea urchin). You can see the tanks where the shellfish are reared at the foot of the cliffs.

At the centre of town is **Praça da República**, the small main square, busy with sidewalk cafés, wonderful pastry shops and a cinema. Bars and restaurants are all concentrated on Rua Dr. Eduardo Burnay, which leads from a corner of the praça to the town's main beach, **Praia do Sul**. A second beach, prettier, much less crowded, and popular with surfers – **Praia do São Sebastião** – lies about 25 minutes' walk north, past the next headland. Otherwise, the bus north from Ericeira passes a fine series of untouched local beaches, the best being at São Lourenço, a peaceful hamlet just 5km away.

Practicalities

There are virtually hourly **buses** to and from Mafra (see p.97) and Lisbon – making Ericeira a useful first or last stop in Estremadura – and services, too, to Sintra. Buses drop you in town at the top of Rua Prudêncio Franco da Trindade, which leads down to the main square. The **Turismo**, at Rua Dr. Eduardo Burnay 33a (Mon–Fri 9am–12.30pm & 3–6pm; ☎061/631 22), may help with finding **private rooms**, which are advertised throughout town above bars and restaurants.

Accommodation

Pensions and hotels are generally good value and pleasant (there's a list of the best below), though most are not open all year round; those that are should be a good deal cheaper in winter. There's a small, but adequate, **campsite** at Praia do São Sebastião (☎061/627 06), and a second at Sobreiro (☎061/525 25), halfway between Ericeira and Mafra; both open all year.

Hospedaria Bernado, Rua Prudêncio Franco da Trindade 17 (☎061/623 78). New, attractive *pensão*, fairly close to the main square. ③.

Casa do Monte, Rua Prudêncio Franco da Trindade 1 (☎061/864 40). A small, but grand, house at the top end of the steep street into town; rooms are small but some have attached bathrooms. Buses to and from Mafra, Sintra and Ribamar stop alongside the shady gardens. ③.

Residencial Fortunato, Rua Dr. Eduardo Burnay 7 (☎061/628 29). Good views from the rooms of Praia do Sul, but a little noisy; an annex copes with the overflow. There's a range of accommodation – and prices – but all rooms come with breakfast included. ③–④.

Hospedaria Gomes, Travessa J. Mola, just off Praça da República (☎061/636 19). Oldish, but clean and fresh with friendly, if somewhat eccentric, staff. ②.

Hotel Pedro o Pescador, Rua Dr. Eduardo Burnay 22 (☎061/86 43 02). Quiet, elegant, pale-blue establishment, with an English seaside hotel feel. Closed Jan. ④.

Hotel Vilazul, Calçada da Baleia 10 (☎061/86 41 01). Just off Rua Dr. Eduardo Burnay, and good value considering the breakfasts, balconies and private bathrooms. Used by upmarket British tour operators. ⑤.

Pensão Vinnu's, Rua Prudêncio Franco Trindade 25 (☎061/638 30). Close to the main square, this is clean, modern and airy with a lively bar to boot. There's also a small supermarket alongside. ③.

Eating

The lively *pastelarias* around Praça da República are recommended for lunch – or tea-time indulgences. In the **restaurants**, seafood is obviously the thing to go for; the local speciality is *açorda de mariscos*, a sort of shellfish stew with bread.

O Barco, Rua Capitão João Lopes. Upmarket seafood restaurant overlooking the harbour; minimum 3000$00 a head. Closed Thurs and Nov.

Snack Bar Bela Sombra, Praia do Sul. A good range of dishes and prices, with very good seafood.

Restaurante Patio dos Marialvas, Rua Dr. Eduardo Burnay, just south of Praça da República. The *ementa turistica* here usually includes *arroz de marisco*, but other dishes are worth trying, too.

Toca do Caboz, Rua Fonte do Cabo. Try the *açorda de mariscos* here; it's very good

Viveiros do Atlantico, corner of Praça da República and Rua Prudêncio Franco da Trindade. Recommended seafood resataurant; under 2000$00 for a meal if you're careful.

Nightlife

Ericeira after dark is surprisingly animated, popular with young *Lisboetas* up for a night out from the capital. *Barzinho*, in Ribamar up the coast, and *Big Surprise*, in Seixal on the Mafra road, are a couple of popular out-of-town venues. In Ericeira itself, a few recommended places include:

Disco-Bar Pirata, attached to the *Hotel Turismo*, Rua Porto de Revez, at the top of Praia do Sul. Biggest disco in town, slightly pricey and exclusive but always a hectic buzz.

Ferro Velho, Rua Dr. Eduardo Burnay. Less trendy, and a shade too cramped, but fun.

Bar Neptuno, Trav. J. Mola. A good-time bar with a two-for-one Happy Hour and frequent live music.

Torres Vedras: battles and beaches

TORRES VEDRAS, 27km north and inland of Ericeira, took its name from the Duke of Wellington's famous defence lines (*Linhas de Torres*) in the **Peninsular War** against Napoleonic France. The "Lines" consisted of a chain of 150 hilltop fortresses, stretching some 40km from the mouth of the Rio Sizandro, directly west of Torres Vedras, to Alhandra, southeast of Torres Vedras, where the Tejo widens out into a huge lake. Astonishingly, they were built in a matter of months and without any apparent reaction from the French. Here, in 1810, Wellington and his forces retired, comfortably supplied by sea and completely unassailable. The French, frustrated by impossibly long lines of communication and by British scorching of the land north of the Lines, eventually had to retreat back to Spain in utter despair. Thus from a last line of defence, Wellington completely reversed the progress of the campaign – storming after the disconsolate enemy to effect a series of swift and devastating victories.

The town

In view of this historical glory, modern Torres Vedras is somewhat disappointing. There are a few ruins of the old fortresses and a couple of imposing sixteenth-century churches, but all this is swamped by a dull sprawl of recent buildings. Yet from the thirteenth to the sixteenth centuries, the **castle** at Torres Vedras was a popular royal residence. It was here, in 1414, that Dom João I confirmed the decision to `take Ceuta – the first overseas venture leading towards the future Portuguese maritime empire. The castle was eventually abandoned and then reduced to rubble by the earthquake of 1755.

Booklets and old maps can be read at the **Turismo**, Rua 9 de Abril, off the Praça 25 de Abril (Mon–Sat 10am–1pm & 2–6pm; ☎061/31 40 94); while across Praça 25 de Abril is the **Museu Municipal**, in the old Convento da Graça (Tues–Sun 10am–1pm & 2–6pm), with a room devoted to the Peninsular War. Unless you get hooked on the local wine, there's not much else to delay your progress.

If you need **somewhere to stay**, there's the *Pensão-Restaurante 1 de Maio*, Rua 1 de Dezembro 3 (☎061/228 75; ③), or *Residencial Moderna*, opposite the cinema on Avenida Tenente Valadim (☎061/31 41 46; ③). For a **meal**, try *Restaurante Barreto Preto*, Rua Praia de Andrada 7, on the way to the train station. In general, however, you'd probably be better off taking one of the many buses on to Peniche, Óbidos, or the popular local resort of Praia de Santa Cruz (see below). The **bus station** is just uphill from the **train station**.

Praia de Santa Cruz and other beaches

Most people at **PRAIA DE SANTA CRUZ** are locals from Torres Vedras and this gives the place a friendly, easygoing feel, as well as some excellent places to eat. The beach itself is long and wide, and features a "screaming rock" – partly covered by the tide – where air and water is forced through a hole in the rock at certain times to produce the distinctive sound. There's a shady **campsite** north of the village, five minutes' walk from the sea. In summer, this fills quickly, but there are also **rooms** available at the *Pensão-Restaurante Mar Lindo*, Travessa Jorge Cardoso (☎061/93 72 97; ④) and at the modern *Hotel de Santa Cruz*, Rua José Pedro Lopes (☎061/93 71 48; ④).

Quieter resorts – uncrowded outside public holidays or summer weekends – are to be found to the north of here and are easily reached on buses heading to Lourinhã or Peniche.

Praia de Porto Novo

At **PRAIA DE PORTO NOVO**, 5km north of Santa Cruz, there's the reliable *Residencial Promar* (☎061/98 42 20; ④), with the beach just across the road. In August 1808, British reinforcements were landed here, at the mouth of the River Maceira. They enabled Wellington, in his first serious encounter with the French, to defeat General Junot at the battle of Vimeiro, following which the French sued for peace.

Lourinhã

In nearby **LOURINHÃ**, 9km to the north, there are banks, restaurants and two pensions: the *Figueiredo*, Largo Mestre Anacleto Silva (☎061/42 25 37; ③) and

Rossio, on Rua Bombeiros Voluntários (☎061/42 30 49; ④) – the latter over a cinema. There's also a very nice *Turihab* property in town, the *Quinta de Santa Catarina*, Rua Visconde de Palma de Almeida (☎061/42 23 13; ⑤)).

Areia Branca and Consolação

Further north, on the Peniche road, is the better known **AREIA BRANCA** ("White Sand"), 21km from Torres Vedras, a small resort with a congenial campsite (☎061/41 21 99) and a good beachside **youth hostel** (☎061/41 21 27). Among the weekend and summer villas here are a couple of upmarket hotels and apartments, though ask at the local **Turismo** (winter Mon, Wed & Fri–Sun 10am–1pm & 2–6pm; summer daily 10am–1pm & 2–7pm; ☎061/42 21 67) about their list of private **rooms**. Locals **eat** at the *Restaurante Dom Lourenço*. Despite the attractive sands here, the sea at Areia Branca is currently considered unsuitable for swimming: the Turismo should know the latest.

Finally, **CONSOLAÇÃO**, just south of Peniche, has a good beach (which is officially safe for swimming) and a small (unofficial) **campsite**.

Peniche and the Ilha Berlenga

PENICHE, impressively enclosed by ramparts and one of Portugal's most active fishing ports, is the embarkation point for the **Ilha Berlenga**. As late as the fifteenth century the town was an island but the area has silted up and is now joined to the mainland by a narrow isthmus with gently sloping beaches on either side and a campsite between them. It's an attractive place for a brief stay, of interest in its own right (above all for the fortress which dominates the south side of town), and with an enjoyable market on the *campo*, held on the last Thursday of the month.

The sixteenth-century **Fortaleza** was one of the dictator Salazar's most notorious jails. Greatly expanded in the 1950s and 1960s to accommodate the growing crowds of political prisoners, it later served as a temporary refugee camp for *retornados* from the colonies. Today it's a **museum** (summer Tues–Sun 10am–noon & 2–7pm; winter Tues–Sun 10am–noon & 2–5pm), with the familiar mix of local archeology, natural history and craft displays, among which you can still see the old cells (on the top floor), the solitary-confinement pens (*segredos*) and the visitors' grille (*parlatório*).

Just outside the city walls, off the fine **north beach** of the peninsula, there's a traditional boatyard. It's fascinating to watch the shipwrights here manoeuvring huge timbers into position to form the skeletal framework of a new fishing vessel. If you've got more time to spare there's a beautiful ninety-minute walk beyond the fortress – out to the tip of **Cabo Carvoeiro**, the rugged, rock-pillared and lighthouse-tipped peninsula beyond Peniche. Another rewarding walk, a few kilometres to the north of Peniche, is to **Baleal**, an islet-village, joined to the mainland by a narrow strip of fine sand.

If you can be in Peniche (and find accommodation) over the first weekend in August, you'll coincide with the **festival** of *Nossa Senhora da Boa Viagem*, where a statue of the Virgin is carried to the harbour in boats to be greeted by people holding candles. After the village priest has blessed the fleet, there are fireworks, bands and dancing in the street.

Practicalities

Buses pull in at the new bus station, on the isthmus just outside the town walls. It's a ten-minute walk into the centre across the Ponte Velha, which takes you to Rua Alexandre Herculano, where you turn left for the **Turismo** (winter daily 9am–1pm & 2–7pm; summer daily 9am–8pm; ☎062/78 95 71).

In summer (particularly in August), **accommodation** can be hard to find, though the tourist office can probably help. Otherwise, look out for *quartos* or *dormidas* signs in the windows; the earlier you arrive, the more reassuring the choice. Out of season, or early in the day, try one of the following pensions: *Residencial Marítimo*, Rua José Estêvão (☎062/78 28 50; ②); *Residencial Katekero*, Avenida do Mar (☎062/787 10; ③); the comfortable and modern *Residencial Félita*, Largo Prof. Francisco Freire (☎062/78 21 09; ③); and the *Residencial Cristal*, Rua 1° de Dezembro (☎062/78 27 24; ③).

If you plan on **camping**, there are several possibilities. The municipal campsite (☎062/78 95 29) is on the way into town, after you've crossed the River Lagôa; well-placed for the bus station. There's a new private campsite (☎062/78 34 60) on the north shore of the peninsula (ask for *Peniche Praia*), and a small campsite at Baleal (☎062/76 93 33), a fair walk northwest of town. In all cases, it's advisable to arrive early in the day in summer as they can be full by midday.

There is a fine array of **restaurants** along Avenida do Mar – most of them good value, and serving huge portions. More upmarket than these is the *Restaurante Nãu dos Corvos*, at Cabo Carvoeiro, with a superb view and a tourist menu for under 2000$00. Just round the corner from the *Residencial Félita*, on the way out of the town centre, a wonderful **bakery/snack bar** is just the place for breakfast or picnic provisions, usually full of fishwives in knitted triangular capes and socks, swinging plastic bags of fish as they sip *bicas* and exchange news.

Ilha Berlenga

The **ILHA BERLENGA**, 10km offshore and just visible from the cape, is a dreamlike place – rather like a Scottish isle transported to warmer climes. Just one square mile in extent, it is the largest island of a tiny archipelago, with a jagged coastline of grottoes, miniature fjords, and extraordinary rock formations. In summer the sea is calm, crystal clear, and perfect for snorkelling and diving – rare in the Atlantic.

The only people permitted to live here are a couple of dozen fishermen, as the whole island has been declared a **Natural Reserve**, the home of thousands upon thousands of seabirds, including gulls, puffins and cormorants, perched in every conceivable cranny and clearly plotting to leave their mark on every possible victim. Makeshift paths are marked out with stones, and guardians watch out for visitors straying into the prohibited areas and disturbing the birds.

Human life revolves around the main **landing dock** with its colour-washed fishing boats and small sandy **beach**. It can get crowded and noisy down here at the height of the season – it takes very few people to make the place seem packed – though the only actual buildings are a cluster of huts, a rather basic shop and a lighthouse. Nearby, there's a **bar-restaurant** with **rooms**: the *Pavilhão Mar e Sol* (☎062/75 03 31; ⑤).

A short walk beyond the lighthouse, on an islet joined by the narrowest of causeways, is the seventeenth-century **Forte de São João Baptista**. It's currently a rudimentary **hostel** (☎062/75 02 44; ①) with a kitchen (you'll need to bring your own food and sleeping gear), for which you must reserve in advance at the *Clube Naval* (Navy Club), near the old harbour in Peniche (☎062/78 25 68). There's also a free **campsite**, which clings to a strictly limited site on the rocky slopes above the harbour. If you want to stay here, you have to book at the Turismo in Peniche – it's best to write in advance.

Rowing boats can be hired at the jetty to explore the intricacies of the coastline, though you may prefer to go in something with a motor if there's any motion on the sea (you can get a guided trip for a few hundred *escudos*). Don't miss the **Furado Grand**e, a fantastic tunnel 75 metres long which culminates in the aptly named **Cova do Sonho** (Dream Cove) with its precipitous cliffs.

Getting there

The **ferry** from Peniche to Berlenga takes one hour – longer if the sea is rough. The service operates from June 1 to September 20; currently, there are three daily ferries in July and August (9am, 11am and 5pm; return at 10am, 4pm & 6pm) and one daily in June and September (10am; return at 6pm in June, 5pm in Sept). A return **ticket** is 2000$00; there's a limit of 300 tickets sold each day; one person can buy up to five at a time. In July and August you may have to get up at 6am to secure a boat ticket for the same day. For more **information**, visit the *Residencial Avis*, near the Turismo on Largo Jacob Periera (☎062/78 21 53).

If the weather is difficult, times will change and boats may be cancelled. In any case, be sure to go without breakfast – it's a rough ride, as evinced by a grim collection of buckets under the seats!

Óbidos

ÓBIDOS, "The Wedding City", was the traditional bridal gift of the kings of Portugal to their queens. The custom was begun in 1282 by Dom Dinis and Dona Isabel, and the town can hardly have changed much in appearance since then. It is very small and completely enclosed by lofty medieval walls: streets are cobbled, houses whitewashed with bright blue and yellow borders, and at all points steep staircases wind up to the ramparts, where you can gaze across a ludicrously fable-like countryside of windmills and vineyards.

It wasn't always like this. Five hundred years ago, when Peniche was an island, the sea also reached the foot of the ridge on which Óbidos stands and boats were moored below its walls. However, by the fifteenth century the sea had retreated leaving a fertile green plain and the distant Lagoa de Óbidos with its narrow, shallow entrance to the sea.

The town is touristy, of course, but perhaps less than you might expect. You can walk right around the town along its perimeter **walls** – a narrow and at times hair-raising walkway with no handrails, and from this vantage point the town still seems to have a private life of its own. If you stay the night, the feeling is reinforced, as the town slowly empties to regain its charm.

Around the town

The most striking building in town is Dom Dinis's massively-towered **Castelo**, which has been converted to a very splendid *pousada* (for which, see

"Accommodation", below). Below the castle, the principal focus of the streets is the parish church, the **Igreja de Santa Maria**, in the central praça – chosen for the wedding of the ten-year-old child king, Afonso V, and his eight-year-old cousin, Isabel, in 1444. It dates mainly from the Renaissance period, though the interior is lined with seventeenth-century blue *azulejos* in a homely manner typical of Portuguese churches. On the left-hand wall is an elaborate tomb designed by Nicolas Chanterene, an influential French sculptor active in Portugal in the first half of the sixteenth century. The *retábulo*, to the right of the main altar, was painted by **Josefa de Óbidos**, one of the finest of all Portuguese painters – and one of the few women artists afforded any reputation by art historians. Born at Seville in 1634, Josefa spent most of her life in a convent at Óbidos. She began her career as an etcher and miniaturist and this remarkable handling of detail is carried through into her later full-scale religious works. Another of her paintings, a portrait, can be seen in the adjacent **museum** in the old town hall (daily 9am–12.30pm & 2–6pm; 100$00).

Every two years (September–November), Óbidos mounts an international **festival of modern art** in a building opposite the tourist office. There's also an annual **festival of ancient music** (first two weeks in October), due to take place in future in the new *Casa da Musica*, just inside the Porta da Vila, the principal town gate at the far end of Rua Direita. On Saturday mornings, the town hosts an small **market** , just outside the gate – still predominantly a local affair. If you're on the lookout for things to buy, there's a range of **shops** on the main Rua Direita, from the *Casa Mourisco* (ceramics, paintings and carvings) to the old people's **handicrafts centre**, which has a good variety of nicely made items.

Practicalities

Buses from Caldas da Rainha (6km to the north) and Peniche (24km west) stop outside the Porta da Vila. From here **Rua Direita** leads straight through the town to the extremely helpful **Turismo** (Mon–Fri 9.30am–1pm & 2–6pm; ☎062/95 92 31). The **train station** is at the foot of the ridge and if you are not too heavily laden, you can cross the tracks and climb the steps, which will bring you to the gate by the Castelo *pousada* – at the opposite end of Rua Direita. Otherwise, follow the road and the easier gradients to reach the Porta da Vila.

Accommodation

Accommodation is on the expensive side, unless you get one of a handful of private **rooms** (usually ②), advertised in windows of a few of the houses and sometimes touted to new arrivals at the bus station. **Pensions and hotels** include:

Albergaria Josefa d'Óbidos, Rua Dr. João de Ornelas (☎062/95 92 28). Modern hotel, outside the walls, with air-conditioning, and TV in every room. Breakfast is included. ⑤.

Albergaria Rainha Santa Isabel, Rua Direita (☎062/95 91 15). Carefully preserved facade, but more of a modern hotel than the others, with lift, lounge, bar and hearty breakfasts. Some of the rooms have balconies looking onto the main street. ④.

Casa da Relógio, Rua da Graça (☎062/95 91 94). Outside the walls, a former eighteenth-century mansion whose "clock" is in fact a stone sundial. Six double rooms available, all with bath. Real value for money. ④.

Casa do Poço, Travessa da Mouraria (☎062/95 93 58). Downhill from the castle, this house has been rebuilt retaining its Moorish foundations and a well in the courtyard. There are only four double rooms, all en-suite, and there's fado in the bar at weekends. ④.

Estalagem do Convento, Rua Dr. João de Ornelas (☎062/95 92 17). A minor convent, converted rather tastelessly into a hotel. Patio dining in summer (expensive) is the best feature. ⑥.

Pousada do Castelo (☎062/95 91 05). Relatively small, but nevertheless one of the country's finest and priciest *pousadas* – visit for morning coffee or afternoon tea at the very least. ⑥.

Residencial Martim de Freitas, Estrada Nacional 8 (☎062/95 91 85). On the road to Caldas da Rainha, this has huge, simply furnished rooms, and breakfast is included. It's generally friendly, although recent reports haven't been so enthusiastic. ③.

Eating

Restaurante Alcaide, Rua Direita. Arrive early, or book, particularly if you want to eat on the balcony. Opposite the *Albergaria Rainha Santa Isabel*. Closed Mon and Nov.

Casa de Ramiro, Rua Porta do Vale. Just outside the walls in an old house, redesigned in Arabic style. It's noted for its grills. Closed Thurs and Jan–Feb.

Estalagem do Convento, Rua Dr. João de Ornelas. Excellent patio dining, but not cheap at 3500$00 for the *table d'hôte* menu.

Restaurante O Conquistador, Rua Josefa de Óbidos, off Rua Direita. Near the Porta da Vila; try the chickpea soup and the duck, or eat from the tourist menu for around 1800$00.

Caldas da Rainha

Six kilometres north of Óbidos, **CALDAS DA RAINHA** ("Queen's Spa") was put firmly on the map by Dona Leonor. Passing by in her carriage, she was so impressed by the strong sulphuric waters that she founded a hospital here, initiating four centuries of noble and royal patronage. That was in 1484 but the town was to reach the peak of its popularity in the nineteenth century when, all over Europe, spas became as much social as medical institutions. The English Gothic novelist, William Beckford, stopping off on his journey to Batalha and Alcobaça (recorded in his *Travels in Spain and Portugal*), found it a lively if depressing place – "every tenth or twelfth person a rheumatic or palsied invalid, with his limbs all atwist, and his mouth all awry, being conveyed to the baths in a chair".

Disappointingly little remains of all the royal wealth poured into the spa, though it is still a pleasant stop on your way to Nazaré or Alcobaça. From the central **Praça da República**, which hosts a fruit market every morning, the **royal spa hospital**, still very much in use, is a short walk downhill. If the idea appeals, you can bathe in a series of warm, sulphurous swimming pools for a nominal entrance fee. Protruding from the back of the spa is the striking Manueline belfry of **Nossa Senhora do Pópulo**, the hospital church. There's a Virgin and Child by Josefa de Óbidos in the sacristy.

In nearby Parque Dom Carlos I, the **Museu de José Malhão** (Tues–Sun 10am–12.30pm & 2–5pm) displays the work of José Malhão and other late-nineteenth-century painters. There are two other museums at the far edge of the park: the **Atelier Museu António Duarte** (daily 9am–12.30pm & 2–5pm), devoted to a minor sculptor, and alongside – and much better – the **Museu da Cerâmica** (Tues–Sun 10am–12.30pm & 2–5pm), which contains some of the original work of local potter and caricaturist Rafael Bordalo Pinheiro; look for his series of lifesized ceramic figures representing the Passion. Indeed, Caldas remains famed for its traditional ceramics, which include peculiar phallus-shaped objects. The **Feira Nacional da Cerâmica** is usually held over the first ten days in July.

Practicalities

It's a short walk from either **bus** or **train station** to **Praça da República**, where you'll find a summer **Turismo** (daily 9am–7pm; closed 1–3pm on Sat & Sun; ☎062/83 10 03); the main office is next to the town hall in Praça 25 de Abril (all year, daily 9am–7pm; closed 1–3pm on Sat & Sun; same phone).

Due to the presence of the spa, there's a fair amount of **accommodation**, most of it reasonably priced. Two of the most convenient places are to be found in Rua Almirante Cândido dos Reis, just off Praça da Republica: the *Residencial Portugal* at no. 24 (☎062/342 80; ④), a longstanding favourite improved by the pedestriani-sation of this busy shopping street, and the modern *Residencial Europeia* at no. 64 (☎062/347 81; ④). For cheaper rooms, try the *Pensão Residencial Estremadura*, Largo Dr. José Barbosa 23 (☎062/83 23 13; ③), on a quiet square next to Praça da República; or the *Central* on the same square (☎062/83 19 14; ③), a little dearer but the birthplace of painter José Malhão. There's also an *Orbitur* **campsite** (☎062/83 23 67; open mid-Jan to mid-Nov), centrally located in the park.

For **food**, it's hard to beat the spit-roasts and grills at the *Zé do Barrete,* at Travessa da Cova da Onça 16–18 (closed Sun), midway down Rua Almirante Cândido dos Reis. There are several other good restaurants along this street, too, while the *Residencial Portugal* also has pretty substantial meals.

North along the coast to Nazaré

Heading **north from Caldas**, buses and trains loop inland, touching the coast only at São Martinho do Porto, 13km south of Nazaré. If you have your own trans-port, bear northwest instead at Caldas along the N360, which takes you past the **Lagoa de Óbidos**, and then out along the coast on a beautiful clifftop route – a much better option than the busy N8.

Foz do Arelho

At **FOZ DO ARELHO**, the first resort you come to, 9km from Caldas, there's a fine beach, and a couple of decent **pensions**: the *Penedo Furado* (☎062/97 96 10; ④) and *Foz Praia* (☎062/97 94 13; ④). One kilometre before the village, and only 500 metres from the lake, the *Quinta da Foz* (☎062/97 93 69; ⑤) is a magnificent county house hotel.

São Martinho do Porto

SÃO MARTINHO DO PORTO is the main resort between Peniche and Nazaré, and was until recently – like the rest of this stretch – hardly developed. Things have been changing fast over the past few years, however, and this is now one of the more exploited Estremaduran resorts. In midseason, or at weekends, it's probably not worth the struggle to find a room – or even a place in the campsite.

The reason for São Martinho's tourist success is its **beach**: a vast sweep of sand which curls around a landlocked bay to form a natural swimming pool. This shelter makes it one of the warmest places to swim on the west coast, with the sands sloping down into calm, shallow, solar-heated water. If you want something more bracing – or less crowded – there's also a a good northern beach, around the bay. But beware of the Atlantic beaches beyond the bay; they can be dangerous. Even within the bay, the beaches are not without their hazards, since water pollution levels have been known to mnake swimming unsafe.

Check with the **Turismo**, at the far end of Avenida 25 de Abril (winter Mon–Fri 10am–1pm & 3–6pm; summer Mon–Fri 9am–7pm, Sat & Sun 9am–1pm & 3–7pm; ☎062/98 91 10), about the possibility of accommodation in **private rooms**. Otherwise, try one of four **pensions**. Popular *Pensão Americana*, Rua D. José Saldanha 2 (☎062/98 91 70; ③), is two blocks from the seafront, and rents out mountain bikes to its guests; while nearer to the beach, and with a good restaurant, is *Pensão Carvalho*, Rua Miguel Bombarda 6 (☎062/98 96 05; ④). *Pensão Parque*, Avenida Marechal Camona 3 (☎062/98 95 05; ④), is a grand hotel fallen on hard times, though its large rooms, gardens, palms and tennis court still make it an attractive option (closed Nov–Feb). Most comfortable, though, is the pine furnished *Residencial Concha*, Largo Vitorino Froís (☎062/98 92 20; ⑤), recently renovated, and with negotiable rates out of season. There's also a **campsite**, *Colina do Sol* (☎062/98 95 88), 2km to the north, off the Nazaré road (N242), and a **youth hostel** (☎062/99 95 06), 4km away and further inland at Alfeizerão, off the Caldas da Rainha/Alcobaça road (N8).

Eating is best done at the restaurants attached to the *Americana* or *Carvalho* pensions; or at *A Cave*, Rua Conde de Avalar, *O Largo* at Largo Vitorino Froís 21, or the *Café Baia*, Rua Vasco da Gama, behind the Turismo. After that, look into the *Bar Bonnie*, near the *Residencial Concha*, open every night and with a disco at weekends.

Nazaré

After years of advertising itself as the most "picturesque" seaside village in Portugal, **NAZARÉ** has finally more or less destroyed itself in the process. In summer, the crowds are way too much for the place to cope with, and the enduring characteristics are not so much "gentle traditions" as trinket stalls and high prices. It's a pity, as local traditions happily coexisted with the tourists for some time, women weaving barefoot through the town bearing immense trays of fish on their heads, and the fishermen sitting unperturbed on the beach, mending their nets beside brilliantly painted sardine boats. Nowadays, however, the boats have all but disappeared to a new harbour, fifteen minutes' walk from the village, where cranes have replaced the oxen once used to haul in the boats. In the old village, mcanwhile, the traditional dress worn by women drying sardines on the beach looks increasingly quaint and phony.

The village and beaches

Nazaré was originally based on a rock face, 110 metres above the present sprawl of towering holiday apartment buildings – the legacy, by most accounts, of pirate raids which continued well into the nineteenth century. Legend tells of a twelfth-century knight, Dom Fuas Roupinho, who, while out hunting, was led up the cliff by a deer. The deer dived off into the void and Dom Fuas was saved from following by the timely vision of **Nossa Senhora da Nazaré**, in whose name a church was subsequently built.

You can reach this church, and the surrounding Sítio district, on a **funicular**, which rumbles up almost continuously from 7.30am to midnight. There is an enjoyable *miradouro* up top, though the shrine itself is unimpressive, despite an icon carved by Saint Joseph and painted by Saint Luke (a handy partnership active throughout Europe). The church does, however, host a well-attended **Romaria** (Sept 8–10) with processions, folk dancing, and bullfights. The Sítio bullring also stages Saturday night *touradas* in summer.

The problem with Nazaré's **beaches** – grand tent-studded sweeps of clean sand, stretching out to the north beyond the headland of Sítio, and south across the narrow Alcoa estuary – is that swimming is dangerous. The Atlantic can be fierce along the Estremaduran coast, so, for safety's sake, stick to the patrolled main beach where the bathers are packed in as tightly as the sardine boats. Alternatively, tramp southwards towards the village of Gralha, where you'll find a number of small coves and one sheltered beach isolated enough to be a popular spot for nude bathing.

Practicalities

On public transport, it's simplest to arrive at Nazaré by bus. There are regular connections with most towns in the region, and the **bus station** is centrally located, halfway down Avenida Vieira Guimarães, which meets the main drag, Avenida da República, at right angles at the foot of the hill. The nearest **train station** is at Valado, 6km inland, on the Alcobaça road; buses from Alcobaça call there on the way into town.

Avenida da República runs the length of the beach and is where you'll find most of the hotels and restaurants, as well as the **Turismo**, near the funicular (July–Aug daily 10am–10pm; Sept–June daily 9.30am–12.30pm & 2–6pm; ☎062/ 56 11 94). There's a second office on Rua Mouzinho de Albuquerque, up the hill and near the town hall, but neither is particularly enterprising.

There are several **banks** on Avenida Vieira Guimarães and outside banking hours **currency** can be exchanged at the *Viagens Maré* travel office on Praça Dr. Manuel de Arriaga and at the larger hotels.

Accommodation

Pensions in Nazaré are heavily booked throughout the summer but **rooms** are plentiful: you'll be accosted at the bus station by their owners; expect to pay around 3500–4000$00 in high season. If you have problems finding a place, consult one of the tourist offices, which hold lists of available rooms. The more promising pension and hotel possibilities are listed below.

There's a **campsite** at Valado (☎062/56 11 11; closed mid-Nov to mid-Jan), near the train station, and another, the *Vale Paraíso* (☎062/56 15 46; open all year), just 2km out of town, on the road to Marinha Grande (N242).

Residencial Beira-Mar, Avda. da República 40 (☎062/56 13 58). Right on the beachfront and very pleasant, as it should be at the price. Large breezy rooms (some with sea views) and private bathrooms. Closed Nov–Feb. ⑤.

Pensão Central, Rua Mouzinho de Albuquerque 83–85 (☎062/55 15 10). Old, but well managed; book in advance if you can. The rooms facing the courtyard are best. Breakfast included. ③.

Residencial Cubata, Avda. da República 6 (☎062/56 17 06). Better than it looks – don't let the exterior put you off. It's between the Turismo and the foot of the funicular. ⑤.

Pensão Europa, Praça Dr. Manuel de Arriaga 24 (☎062/55 15 36). Bright, cramped rooms which can be noisy, in the smaller of the two squares opening on to Avda. da República. There's a restaurant at street level. ③.

Residencial Marina, Rua Mouzinho de Albuquerque 6 (☎062/55 15 41). Down the street from the *Central*, this a good-value, cheerful choice. ④.

Hotel da Nazaré, Largo Afonso Zuquete (☎062/56 13 11). Small rooms, simply furnished. The views from the upper floors are splendid, and the rooftop terrace is even better. Closed Jan. ⑥.

Pensão Restaurante Ribamar, Rua Gomes Freire 9 (☎062/551 58). Across the road from the Turismo, and with some rooms overlooking the beach. The bathrooms are tiled with *azulejos*. ⑤.

Eating

The main concentration of **restaurants** is along Avda. da República and the several squares off the avenue.

Aquário, Largo das Caldeiras 13. One of the best (and cheapest) for a seafood blow-out.

Brisa do Mar, Avda. Vieira Guimarães 10. Opposite the bus station and, after all the seafood elsewhere in town, pleasantly ordinary Portuguese staples.

Carlota e Catarina, Rua Adrião Batalha 162. Good seafood served in an agreeable setting.

Casa Lazaro, Rua António Carvalho Laranjo. Follow the sign from the beachfront near the *Residencial Beira-Mar*. Just off the main drag but all the better for that in terms of price and atmosphere. Great value seafood and house wine.

A Tasquinha, Rua Adrião Batalha 54. Just off Praça Dr. Manuel Arriaga. The prawns and *arroz de marisco* here are particularly good.

Alcobaça

The Cistercian monastery at **ALCOBAÇA** was founded in 1153 by Dom Henrique to celebrate his victory over the Moors at Santarém six years earlier. Building started soon after, and by the end of the thirteenth century it was the most powerful monastery in the country. Owning vast tracts of farmland, orchards and vineyards, it was immensely rich and held jurisdiction over a dozen towns and three seaports. Its church and cloister are the purest and the most inspired creation of all Portuguese Gothic architecture and, alongside Belém and Batalha, are today the most impressive monuments in the country. In addition, the church is the burial place of those romantic figures of Portuguese history, Dom Pedro and Dona Inês de Castro.

The Monastery

The **Mosteiro de Alcobaça** (April–Sept daily 9am–7pm; Oct–March daily 10am–1pm & 3–6pm; 300$00), although empty since its dissolution in 1834, still seems to assert power, magnificence and opulence. And it takes little imagination to people it again with the monks, said once to have numbered 999. Mass was once celebrated here without interruption, but it was the residents' legendarily extravagant and aristocratic lifestyles that formed the common ingredients of the awed anecdotes of eighteenth-century travellers.

Even William Beckford, no stranger to high living, found their decadence unsettling, growing weary of "perpetual gormandising . . . the fumes of banquets and incense . . . the fat waddling monks and sleek friars with wanton eyes, twanging away on the Jew's harp". Another contemporary observer, Richard Twiss, for his part found "the bottle went as briskly about as ever I saw it do in Scotland" – a tribute indeed. For all the "high romps" and luxuriance, though, it has to be added that the monks enjoyed a reputation for hospitality, generosity and charity, while the surrounding countryside is to this day one of the most productive areas in Portugal, thanks to their agricultural expertise.

The Abbey Church

The main **Abbey Church**, modelled on the famous Cistercian abbey of Cîteaux in France, is the largest in Portugal. External impressions are disappointing, as the Gothic facade has been superseded by unexceptional Baroque additions of the seventeenth and eighteenth centuries. Inside, however, all later adornments have been swept away, restoring the narrow soaring aisles to their original vertical simplicity. The only exception to this Gothic purity is the frothy Manueline doorway to the sacristy, hidden directly behind the high altar, and, as at Tomar and Batalha, encrusted with intricate, swirling motifs of coral and seaweed.

The church's most precious treasures are the fourteenth-century **tombs of Dom Pedro and Dona Inês de Castro**, each occupying one of the transepts and sculpted with phenomenal wealth of detail. Animals, heraldic emblems, musicians and biblical scenes are all portrayed in an architectural setting of miniature windows, canopies, domes and towers; most graphic of all is a dragon-shaped Hell's mouth at Inês' feet, consuming the damned. The tombs are inscribed with the motto "Até ao Fim do Mundo" (Until the End of the World) and in accordance with Dom Pedro's orders have been placed foot to foot so that on the Day of Judgement the pair may rise and immediately feast their eyes on one another.

Pedro's earthly love for Inês de Castro, the great theme of epic Portuguese poetry, was cruelly stifled by high politics. Inês, as the daughter of a Galician nobleman, was a potential source of Spanish influence over the Portuguese throne and Pedro's father, Afonso IV, forbade their marriage. The ceremony took place nevertheless – secretly at Bragança in remote Trás-os-Montes – and eventually Afonso was persuaded to sanction his daughter-in-law's murder. When Pedro succeeded to the throne in 1357 he brought the murderers to justice, personally ripping out their hearts and gorging his love-crazed blood appetite upon them. More poignantly he also exhumed and crowned the corpse of his lover, forcing the entire royal circle to acknowledge her as queen by kissing her decomposing hand.

The Kitchen

From one highlight to another. Beckford – Romantic dilettante that he was – stood bewildered by the charms of these tombs when "in came the Grand Priors hand in hand, all three together. 'To the *kitchen'*, said they in unison, 'to the kitchen and that immediately'". They led him past the fourteenth-century Chapter House to a cavernous room in the corner of the cloisters.

This route you can follow. Alcobaça's feasting has already been mentioned but this **kitchen** – with its cellars and gargantuan conical chimney, supported by eight trunklike iron columns – sets it in real perspective. A stream tapped from the River Alcôa still runs straight through the room: it was used not merely for cooking and washing but also to provide a constant supply of fresh fish, which plopped out into a stone basin! At the centre of the room, on the vast wooden tables, Beckford continued to marvel at:

> *pastry in vast abundance which a numerous tribe of lay brothers and their attendants were rolling out and puffing up into a hundred different shapes, singing all the while as blithely as larks in a corn field. "There", said the Lord Abbot, "we shall not starve. God's bounties are great, it is fit we should enjoy them".*

And enjoy them they did, with a majestic feast of "rarities and delicacies, potted lampreys, strange Brazilian messes, edible birds' nests and sharks' fins dressed after the mode of Macau by a Chinese lay brother"! As a practical test for obesity the monks had to file through a narrow door on their way to the **Refectory**; those who failed were forced to fast until they could squeeze through.

The Cloisters and Sala dos Reis

The **Claustro do Silencio** (Cloisters of Silence), notable for their traceried stone windows, were built in the reign of Dom Dinis, the "poet-king" who established an enduring literary and artistic tradition at the abbey. An upper storey of twisted columns and Manueline arches was added in the sixteenth century, along with, in its standard position opposite the refectory, a beautiful hexagonal lavatory.

The **Sala dos Reis** (Kings' Room), off the cloister, displays statues of virtually every king of Portugal down to Dom José, who died in 1777. Blue eighteenth-century *azulejos* depict the siege of Santarém, Dom Afonso's vow, and the founding of the monastery. Also on show here is a piece of war booty which must have warmed the souls of the brothers – the huge metal cauldron in which soup was heated up for the Spanish army before the battle of Aljubarrota in 1385 (for more of which, see "Batalha", below).

The rest of the monastery, including four other cloisters, seven dormitories and endless corridors, is closed to the public. Parts of it are currently occupied by a mental asylum – sad glimpses of which can be caught from some of the windows in the visitable parts. For the best overall view of the monastery, make your way to the ruined hilltop **castle**, about five minutes' walk away.

Practicalities

Though Alcobaça itself is not a hive of activity, it's not a bad place to stay. A useful first call is the **Turismo** (summer daily 9am–7pm, winter daily 10am–1pm & 3–6pm; ☎062/423 77) on the central Praça 25 de Abril, opposite the monastery. They can supply maps of the town and advise on accommodation and transport. The **bus station** is five minutes' walk from the centre of town, across the bridge; coming into town, bear left and head towards the abbey towers. There are reasonably frequent connections to Nazaré and Leiria.

Accommodation

There is a scattering of inexpensive **pensions and hotels**, all just off Praça 25 de Abril, cheapest of which is the *Residencial Mosteiro*, Avenida João de Deus 1 (☎062/421 83; ②), on the corner of the avenida and Rua Frei Estevão Martins – friendly if a bit old and basic. It also has two restaurants, the one downstairs in the basement a noisy *taberna típica* seating 180 – which, nevertheless, fills up at weekends with wedding parties and day trippers. The best inexpensive rooms, though, are at the *Pensão Corações Unidos*, Rua Frei António Brandão 39, just off the main square (☎062/421 42; ③): big rooms, with breakfast included, and decent meals served, too. By way of contrast, the *Hotel Santa Maria*, Rua Dr. Francisco Zagalo (☎062/59 73 95; ④), is a dull modern hotel facing the monastery.

The local **campsite** (☎062/422 65) is 15 minutes' walk north of the bus station, on Avenida Manuel da Silva Carolina, near the covered market; there are some trees for shade, but the ground here is hard and barren.

Eating

In addition to the **restaurants** at the various pensions, consider eating at the *Celeiro dos Frades* ("monks' barn"), under arches alongside the abbey – ask for *Arco de Cister* – where you can dine well for around 1500$00. *Restaurante O Telheiro*, Rua da Levadinha, up the road beyond the *Hotel Santa Maria*, is more expensive but has great views over the abbey.

Leiria

A royal castle hangs almost vertically above the graceful town of **LEIRIA**, a place of cobbled streets, attractive gardens, and fine old squares. If you are travelling around on public transport, you will probably want to make it your base for a couple of nights, as the three big sites of northern Estremadura – Alcobaça, Batalha and Fátima – all make easy day excursions by bus. Not so easy, but still quite feasible, are day trips to Porto de Mós and the caves of Mira de Aire, Alvados and Santa António; or to São Pedro de Moel and the coast. Leiria itself lacks much in the way of culture or nightlife, but it has enough restaurants and bars to keep the evenings occupied.

Leiria's **Castelo** (daily 9am–5.30pm; 100$00) was one of the most important strongholds in Moorish Portugal, reconquered by Afonso Henriques as he fought his way south in 1135. The actual building you see today dates mostly from the fourteenth and eighteenth centuries. Within its walls stands a royal palace, with a magnificent balcony high above the Rio Lis, and the church of Nossa Senhora da Penha, erected by João I in about 1400 and now reduced to an eerie, roofless shell. If you have small children with you, beware: there are several precipitous, unguarded points among the buildings and staircases.

At the heart of the old town is **Praça Rodrigues Lobo**, surrounded by beautiful arcaded buildings and dominated by a splendidly pompous statue of the eponymous seventeenth-century local poet. It's a promising area, too, for bars and restaurants, as well as for rooms (see below).

Practicalities

Arriving by **bus**, you'll be dropped at a modern terminal at the near end of Avenida Heróis de Angola, but with another entrance on Praça Paulo VI. Across the Jardim Luís de Camões, on Praça Goa Damão e Dio, near the bridge, is the **Turismo** (Mon–Fri 9am–6pm, Sat & Sun 10am–1pm & 3–6pm; open an hour later in summer; ☎044/81 47 48), which dispenses maps. The **train station** is 4km north of town – a cheap taxi ride away.

Accommodation

For **accommodation**, make your way to Praça Rodrigues Lobo and look around the restaurants (several of which offer rooms) and pensions here and on the narrow side streets: try Rua Mestre de Aviz and Rua Miguel Bombarda. Other cheap rooms are to be found in Largo Paio Guterres and Largo Cónego Maia, both near the sixteenth-century cathedral. There's also a very well-appointed **youth hostel** – one of the most enjoyable in the country – at Largo Cândido dos Reis 7 (☎044/318 68).

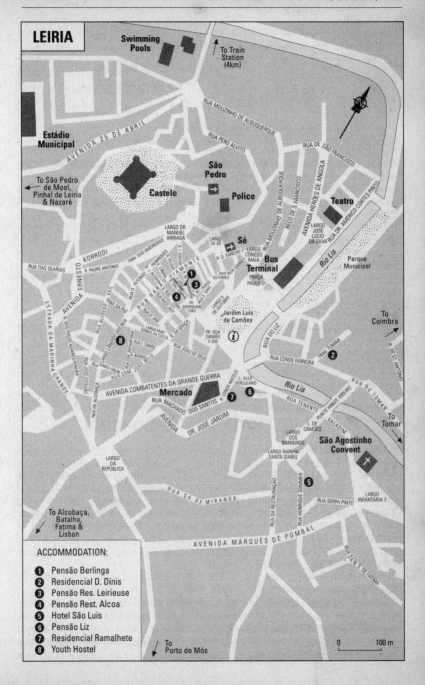

LEIRIA

Swimming Pools

To Train Station (4km)

RUA MOUZINHO DE ALBUQUERQUE

RUA PERO ALVITO

RUA DE SÃO FRANCISCO

Estádio Municipal

AVENIDA 25 DE ABRIL

São Pedro

To São Pedro de Moel, Pinhal de Leiria & Nazaré

Castelo

Police

AVENIDA HERÓIS DE ANGOLA

BECO DE S FRANCISCO

RUA MOUZINHO DE ALBUQUERQUE

Teatro

AVENIDA JOSÉ LÚCIO DA SILVA

RUA DR. AMÉRICO CORTES PINTO

LARGO DR. MANUEL ARRIAGA

LARGO DE SÉ

Sé

R D SANCHO I

LARGO CÓNEGO MAIA

Bus Terminal

PRAÇA PAULO VI

Rio Lis

Parque Municipal

KORRODI

AVENIDA ERNESTO

RUA DAS OLARIAS

R. PADRE ANTÓNIO

TRAV. DAS AMOREIRAS

R. AFONSO HENRIQUES

C. PAIO GUTERRES

RUA BARÃO VIAMONTE

LARGO DE OUTUBRO

Jardim Luís de Camões

ESTRADA DA MARINHA GRANDE

AVENIDA DOS POVOS ALVARES PEREIRA

RUA ALFREDO KEIL

TRAV. DA PAZ

RUA D AFONSO

RUA D JOÃO I

RUA DA GRAÇA

PR. RODRIGUES LOBO

PR. GÇA DAMÃO E DIO

To Coimbra

RUA DO LIZ

LARGO MAR GOMES DA COSTA

RUA D. DINIS

RUA F. TOMÁS

RUA DA GRAÇA

RUA JOÃO DE DEUS

RUA GOMES FREIRE

RUA DR. ARTHUR PAIVA

C. BEIRAL

RUA COM. JOÃO BELO

TRAV. TOMAR

RUA CONDE FERREIRA

LARGO CANDIDO DOS REIS

RUA JOSÉ ESTEVÃO

AVENIDA COMBATENTES DA GRANDE GUERRA

Mercado

RUA MACHADO DOS SANTOS

L. ALEX HERCULANO

L CONDE MATEUS

Rio Lis

RUA TENENTE VALADIM

PONTE HINZE RIBEIRO

RUA DE TOMAR

To Tomar

RUA DE ALCOBAÇA

AVENIDA DR. JOSÉ JARDIM

L. DE CAMÕES

LARGO DOS BARREIROS

LARGO RAINHA SANTA ISABEL

São Agostinho Convent

LARGO DA REPÚBLICA

RUA SÁ DE MIRANDA

RUA DA RESTAURAÇÃO

RUA HENRIQUE SOMMER

RUA SERPA PINTO

LARGO INFANTARIA 7

To Alcobaça, Batalha, Fatima & Lisbon

AVENIDA MARQUÉS DE POMBAL

RUA DA N S DE FÁTIMA

ACCOMMODATION:

1 Pensão Berlinga
2 Residencial D. Dinis
3 Pensão Res. Leirieuse
4 Pensão Rest. Alcoa
5 Hotel São Luis
6 Pensão Liz
7 Residencial Ramalhete
8 Youth Hostel

To Porto de Mós

0   100 m

Pensão Alcôa, Rua Rodrigues Cordeiro 20–26 (☎044/326 90). Large rooms and great views over the town; and considerable reductions outside summer. ③.

Pensão Berlinga, Rua Miguel Bombarda 3 (☎044/82 38 46). Just off Praça Rodrigues Lobo; look for the sign in the corner of the square. It's much better inside than the exterior suggests; rooms with shower fall into the next category. ③.

Residencial Dom Dinis, Trav. de Tomar 2 (☎044/81 53 42). Across the bridge from the Turismo and up a steep side road. This is a very attractive hotel, handy if you're driving since parking is easy. ③.

Pensão Residencial Leirense, Rua Afonso de Albuquerque 6 (☎044/320 61). A firm favourite for some years that's been recently renovated and now offers even better value for money. It's very central and breakfast is included. ③.

Pensão Liz, Largo Alexandre Herculano 10 (☎044/81 40 17). Fairly central and near the bridge by the tourist office. Good value, with breakfast included. ④.

Residencial Ramalhete, Rua Dr. Correia Mateus 30 (☎044/81 28 02). Near the market and not too far from the Turismo, the rooms here are quieter at the rear. Reception is on the first floor. ④.

Hotel São Luís, Rua Henrique Sommer (☎044/81 31 97). Good location, but away from the centre, and inexpensive for its class. Breakfast included. ④.

Eating

Restaurante Aquário, Rua Mouzinho de Albuquerque 17. There's a set menu here for around 2000$00 but you could eat for less, especially if you sit up at the bar. It's on a side street running off Jardim Luís de Camões. Closed Thurs.

Jardim, Jardim Luís de Camões. Seafood and other specialities; popular with students.

Restaurante Montecarlo, Rua Dr. Correia Mateus 32–34. The best on this street, where you can eat for under 1000$00; a *meia dose* should be more than sufficient.

Tromba Rija, Rua Professores Portelas 22 (☎044/32022). Real Portuguese cuisine – slightly more expensive, but worth every penny – can be found at out of town on the Marrazes road; go under the N1 and take a left turning after the *Casa da Palmeira*. Closed Sun, Mon lunchtime and in August.

The Pinhal de Leiria and its beaches

Some of the most idyllic spots on the stretch of coast west of Leiria are in the **Pinhal de Leiria** (or *Pinhal do Rei*), a vast 700-year-old pine forest stretching from São Pedro de Moel to Pedrógão. Although there were always trees here, the "Royal Pine Forest" was planned by Dom Dinis, a king renowned for his agrarian reforms, to protect fertile arable land from the menacing inward march of sand dunes. It has since grown into an area of great natural beauty, with sunlight filtering through endless miles of trees and the air perfumed with the scent of resin.

The **beaches**, for the most part, are superb, and currently the sea is free of pollution from Paredes da Vitória, 12km south of São Pedro de Moel, to Leirosa, 11km south of Figueira da Foz.

São Pedro de Moel

The nearest beach to Leiria is at **SÃO PEDRO DE MOEL**, 22km to the west. Some of the buses from Leiria involve a change at Marinha Grande, about halfway, but even out of season there's a bus each way every two hours or so (first from Leiria at 8am; last bus back at 6.45pm). If you wish to stay, **accommodation** – even in high season – should be no problem, since there are more than a dozen pensions and hotels. However, prices vary considerably and in low season you'll pay half the summer price, or less; whatever the season, a sea view will cost more. It pays to shop around. The youth hostel is closed, with no plans to re-open it, which is a shame because the clifftop site is one of the best in São Pedro. There are two **campsites**, though, north of the village. The nearer is the *Orbitur* site (☎044/59 91 68; open all year); the less expensive, the *Inatel* (☎044/59 92 89; closed mid-Dec to mid-Jan).

Excellent **restaurants** abound, among them *A Conche*, near the church, whose owner once ran a glass factory in Angola. Two others, open all year, are the *Brisamar*, Rua Dr. Nicolau Bettencourt, and *A Forte*, on Praçeta Afonso Lopes Vieira, both of which specialise in seafood.

South of São Pedro, too, you can find sheltered stretches of beach – especially around **PAREDES DA VITÓRIA**, an area popular with Portuguese, camping outside the established campsites – though here you're no longer in the forest.

Praia Velha, Praia da Vieira and Pedrógoã

A couple kilometres north of the lighthouse at São Pedro, **PRAIA VELHA** is a delightful local resort with no accommodation but some great restaurants. Try *O Rei dos Frangos*.

Ten kilometres to the north, **PRAIA DA VIEIRA** and **VIEIRA DE LEIRIA**, the latter 3km inland, are on the estuary of the Rio Liz and are notable for their fish restaurants. There's a **campsite** near the beach (☎044/69 53 34; open July–Sept) – though it's rumoured to be due to close; check with the tourist office in Leiria – and several **restaurants**, including the good *Solemar*. Two *residencials* offer **rooms**: the *Ouro Verde* (☎044/69 59 31; ④) and *Estrela do Mar* (☎044/69 57 62; ④).

At **PEDRÓGOÃ**, 6km to the north, there's another **campsite** (☎044/69 54 03; closed mid-Dec to Jan), a *pensão*, four restaurants, a seasonal tourist office – and little else.

Batalha

Eleven kilometres south of Leiria, the **Mosteiro de Santa Maria da Vitória**, better known as **BATALHA** (Battle Abbey), is the supreme achievement of Portuguese architecture – the dazzling richness and originality of its Manueline decoration rivalled only by the Mosteiro dos Jerónimos at Belém, with which it shares UNESCO world monument status. An exuberant symbol of national pride, it was built to commemorate the battle that sealed Portugal's independence after decades of Spanish intrigue.

With the death of Dom Fernando in 1383, the royal house of Burgundy died out, and in its wake there followed a period of feverish factional plotting over the Portuguese throne. Fernando's widow, Leonor Teles, had a Spanish lover even during her husband's lifetime, and when Fernando died she betrothed her daughter, Beatriz, to Juan I of Castile, encouraging his claim to the Portuguese throne. João, Mestre de Aviz, Fernando's illegitimate stepbrother, also claimed the throne. He assassinated Leonor's lover and braced himself for the inevitable invasion from Spain. The two armies clashed on August 14, 1385, at the **Battle of Aljubarrota**, which despite its name, was actually fought at São Jorge, 10km north east of Aljubarrota and just 4km south of present-day Batalha (see p.128).

Faced with seemingly impossible odds, João struck a deal with the Virgin Mary, promising to build a magnificent abbey in return for her military assistance. It worked: Nuno Álvares Pereira led the Portuguese forces to a memorable victory and the new king duly summoned the finest architects of the day.

The Abbey

The honey-coloured **Abbey** (May–Sept daily 9am–6pm; Oct–April daily 9am–5pm; cloisters 250$00; museum 400$00 in summer, 250$00 in winter) was transformed by the uniquely Portuguese Manueline additions of the late-fifteenth and early sixteenth centuries, but the bulk of the building was completed between 1388 and 1434 in a profusely ornate version of French Gothic. Pinnacles, parapets, windows and flying buttresses are all lavishly and intricately sculpted. Within this flamboyant framework there are also strong elements of the English perpendicular style. Huge pilasters and prominent vertical decorations divide the main facade; the nave, with its narrow soaring dimensions, and the chapter house, are reminiscent of church architecture in the English cathedral cities of Winchester and York.

The Capela do Fundador

Medieval architects were frequently attracted by lucrative foreign commissions, but there is a special explanation for the English influence at Batalha. This is revealed in the **Capela do Fundador** (Founder's Chapel), directly to the right upon entering the church. Beneath the octagonal lantern rests the joint tomb of Dom João I and Philippa of Lancaster, their hands clasped in the ultimate expression of harmonious relations between Portugal and England.

In 1373, Dom Fernando had entered into an alliance with John of Gaunt, Duke of Lancaster, who claimed the Spanish throne by virtue of his marriage to a daughter of Pedro the Cruel, King of Castile. A crack contingent of English longbowmen had played a significant role in the victory at Aljubarrota, and in 1386 both countries willingly signed the **Treaty of Windsor**, "an inviolable, eternal, solid, perpetual, and true league of friendship". As part of the same political package Dom João married Philippa, John of Gaunt's daughter, and with her came English architects to assist at Batalha. The alliance between the two countries, reconfirmed by the marriage of Charles II to Catherine of Bragança in 1661 and the Methuen Commercial Treaty of 1703, has become the longest-standing international friendship of modern times – it was invoked by the Allies in World War II to establish bases on the Azores, and the facilities of those islands were offered to the British Navy during the 1982 Falklands war.

The four younger sons of João and Philippa are buried along the south wall of the Capela do Fundador in a row of recessed arches. Second from the right is the

---

THE ABBEY UNDER THREAT

The N1 motorway from Lisbon to Coimbra runs across an embankment perilously close to the abbey and, besides the question of aesthetics, is altering the structure gradually as vibrations and fumes take their toll. There is talk of "moving" the road, though no plans have yet been forthcoming. In addition, the abbey is showing its age: built largely of limestone, it's being increasingly affected by acid rain.

Tomb of Prince Henry the Navigator, who guided the discovery of Madeira, the Azores and the African coast as far as Sierra Leone. Henry himself never ventured further than Tangiers but it was a measure of his personal importance, drive and expertise that the growth of the empire was temporarily shelved after his death in 1460.

Concerted maritime exploration resumed under João II (1481–95) and accelerated with the accession of Manuel I (1495–1521). Vasco da Gama opened up the trade route to India in 1498, Cabral reached Brazil two years later and Newfoundland was discovered in 1501. The momentous era of burgeoning self-confidence, wealth and widening horizons is reflected in the peculiarly Portuguese style of architecture known (after the king) as Manueline. As befitted the great national shrine, Batalha was adapted to incorporate two masterpieces of the new order: the Royal Cloister and the so-called Unfinished Chapels.

The Claustro Real and Sala do Capítulo
In the **Claustro Real** (Royal Cloister), stone grilles of ineffable beauty and intricacy were added to the original Gothic windows by Diogo de Boitaca, architect of the cloister at Belém and the prime genius of Manueline art. Crosses of the Order of Christ and armillary spheres – symbols of overseas exploration – are entwined in a network of lotus blossom, briar branches and exotic vegetation.

Off the east side opens the early fifteenth-century **Sala do Capítulo** (Chapter House), remarkable for the audacious unsupported span of its ceiling – so daring, in fact, that the Church authorities were convinced that the whole chamber would come crashing down and employed criminals already condemned to death to build it. The architect, Afonso Domingues, could only finally silence his critics by sleeping in the chamber night after night. Soldiers now stand guard here over Portugal's **Tomb of the Unknown Warriors**, one killed in France during World War I, the other in the country's colonial wars in Africa. The **Refectory**, on the opposite side of the cloister, houses a military museum in their honour. From here, a short passage leads into the **Claustro de Dom Afonso V**, built in a conventional Gothic style which provides a yardstick against which to measure the Manueline flamboyance of the Royal Cloister.

The Capelas Imperfeitas
The **Capelas Imperfeitas** (Unfinished Chapels) form a separate structure tacked on to the east end of the church and accessible only from outside the main complex. Dom Duarte, eldest son of João and Philippa, commissioned them in 1437 as a royal mausoleum but, as with the cloister, the original design was transformed beyond all recognition by Dom Manuel's architects. The portal rises to a towering fifty feet and every inch is carved with a honeycomb of mouldings: florid projections, clover-shaped arches, strange vegetables; there are even stone snails. The place is unique among Christian architecture and evocative of the great shrines of Islam and Hinduism: perhaps it was inspired by the tales of Indian monuments that filtered back along the eastern trade routes. Although conveniently referred to as Manueline, it is really in a class by itself and illustrates the variety and uninhibited excitement of Portuguese art during the Age of Discovery.

The architect of this masterpiece was Mateus Fernandes, whose tomb lies directly outside the entrance to the Capela do Fundador. Within the portal, a large octagonal space is surrounded by seven hexagonal chapels, two of which contain the sepulchres of Dom Duarte and his queen, Leonor of Aragon. An ambitious upper story – equal in magnificence to the portal – was designed by Diogo de Boitaca but the huge buttresses were subsequently abandoned after a few years.

Practicalities

The Battle Abbey stands alone, the huddle of cottages that once surrounded it swept away and replaced by a bare concrete expanse. There's not much else here but a sprinkling of tourist shops, bars and restaurants, which all do brisk business during the Fátima weekend in early October, when the place is packed. **Buses** stop on central Largo da Misericórdia.

Accommodation is limited and the best idea is to see Batalha on a day trip from Leiria. If you do want to stay, try *Pensão Vitória*, Largo da Misericórdia (☎044/966 78; ②), a basic place with a small restaurant, by the bus stop. *Casa do Outeiro*, Largo Carvalho 4 (☎044/968 06; ④), near the town hall, is a charmingly converted small house with a swimming pool; while for leisured luxury, the new *Pousada do Mestre Afonso Domingues*, Largo Mestre Afonso Domingues (☎044/ 962 60; ⑤), is impossible to better.

São Jorge: the battle site

The Battle of Aljubarrota was fought on a plain 10km northeast of Aljubarrota itself, at the small hamlet of **SÃO JORGE**, just 4km south of Batalha, and when the fighting was over a **chapel** was built, which still stands. The battle lasted only one hour, but it was a hot day and the commander of the victorious Portuguese forces, Nuno Álvares Pereira, complained loudly of thirst; even today, a jug of fresh water is placed daily in the porch of the chapel in his memory.

Also in São Jorge, the **Museu Militar** (Tues–Fri 2–5pm, Sat & Sun 10am–noon & 2–5pm) deals with the battle itself and the contemporary political intrigue, while nearby there's a frieze commemorating the battle with carved blocks of stone representing, it is said, the archers and foot soldiers.

None of this is particularly any reason to come, though you can always break your journey here on the way to or from Porto de Mós (see below), 5km to the south; indeed, you may have to change buses in São Jorge anyway.

Porto de Mós, Mira de Aire and some caves

High above the small, white village of **PORTO DE MÓS**, just 8km south of Batalha but well off the tourist trail, a grandiose thirteenth-century **castle** stands guard. It was given to Nuno Álvares Pereira in 1385 by the grateful Dom João I in recognition of his victory at Aljubarrota – significantly, the Portuguese army had rested here on the eve of the battle – and was later turned into a fortified palace reminiscent in scale of that at Leiria. Severely damaged in the earthquake of 1755, the castle has been renovated piecemeal since then; four of its original five electric-green conical towers have so far been restored, though the building as a whole is still out of bounds to visitors.

More significantly, Porto de Mós is the nearest base from which to visit three of Estremadura's fabulous **underground caves** – at Mira de Aire, Alvados and Santo António – which lie within the *Parque Natural das Serras de Aire e Candeeiros*. The most scenic driving route through the park is the N362, which runs from Porto de Mós in the north right the way to Santarém, though the caves themselves are all located in the eastern half of the park. There's a convenient **bus to Mira de Aire** which leaves from Porto de Mós' terminal on Avenida Dr. Francisco Sá Carneiro at around 8am (last one back from Mira de Aire around 5pm). This, and other matters, can be checked at the helpful **Turismo** (Mon–Sat 10am–1pm & 3–6pm; ☎044/49 13 23) in the Jardim Público, which is adjacent to the main Largo do Rossio.

If you plan to stay, there are two **overnight** possibilities in town. The *Residencial O Filipe*, Largo do Rossio 41 (☎044/40 22 46; ③), and the *Quinta do Rio Alcaide* (☎044/40 21 24; ④), a converted mill around 1km out of the village on the road to the caves (the N243). Cafés and **restaurants** are grouped around the bus terminal.

On weekdays, there are **buses to Porto de Mós** from Leiria, via Batalha, or from Batalha itself. At other times, you could catch one of the long-distance buses from Leiria or Batalha to Alcobaça or Caldas da Rainha and ask to be set down at São Jorge, just off the main N1 and take a local bus from there to Porto de Mós.

Mira de Aire

The largest, most spectacular and most accessible caves in Portugal are the **Grutas de Mira de Aire** (Jan–March & Oct–Dec daily 9am–6pm; April–June & Sept daily 9am–7pm; July & Aug daily 9am–8pm; 400$00; ☎044/44 03 22), ten minutes' walk from the bus stop in the drab textile town from which they take their name. Discovered in 1947, they comprise a fantasy land of spaghetti-like stalactites and stalagmites and bizarre rock formations with names like "Hell's Door", "Jelly Fish" and "Church Organ". Rough steps take you down and the excellent 45-minute guided tour (in French or Portuguese, or even English on occasion) culminates in an extravagant fountain display in a natural lake 110 metres underground. You might have to wait some time for a group of acceptable size to gather.

Alvados and Santo António

There are similar caves in open country near the hamlets of **ALVADOS** and **SANTO ANTÓNIO** (both Jan–March & Oct–Dec 9am–6pm; April–June & Sept 9am–7pm; July & Aug 9am–8pm; 300$00; ☎044/84 08 76). Three buses a day run between Porto de Mós and Mira de Aire, passing within 3km of Alvados and 7km of Santo António. Hitching along the main road is not too difficult but there's a good chance you'll have to walk part of the way.

Grutas da Moeda

The labyrinthine **Grutas da Moeda** (Oct–May 9am–5pm; June–Sept 9am–8pm; 400$00; ☎044/903 02) at **SÃO MAMEDE** are also well worth seeing, not least because one of the chambers has been converted into a unique bar with rock (!) music, subtle lighting and stalactites nose-diving into your glass of beer. They're best visited from Fátima, 6km away, where, with concerted haggling, you should be able to arrange a reasonably priced taxi.

Fátima

FÁTIMA is the fountainhead of religious devotion in Portugal and one of the most important centres of pilgrimage in the Catholic world. Its cult is founded on a series of six **Apparitions of the Virgin Mary**, in the first of which, on May 13, 1917, three peasant children from the village were confronted, while tending their parents' flock, with a flash of lightning and "a lady brighter than the sun" sitting in the branches of a tree. According to the memoirs of Lúcia, who was the only one who could hear what was said – and the only one of the children to survive into her teens – the Lady announced, "I am from Heaven. I have come to ask you to return here six times, at this same hour, on the thirteenth of every month. Then, in October, I will tell you who I am and what I want".

News of the miracle was greeted with scepticism, and only a few casual onlookers attended the second appearance, but for the third, July 13, apparition, the crowd had swollen to a few thousand. Although only the three children could see the heavenly visitor, Fátima became a *cause célèbre*, with the anticlerical government accusing the Church of fabricating a miracle to revive its flagging influence, and Church authorities afraid to acknowledge what they feared was a hoax. The children were arrested and interrogated but refused to change their story.

By the date of the final appearance, October 13, as many as 70,000 people had converged on Fátima where they witnessed the so-called **Miracle of the Sun**. Eye-witnesses described the skies clearing and the sun, intensified to a blinding, swirling ball of fire, shooting beams of multicoloured light to earth. Lifelong illnesses, supposedly, were cured; the blind could see again and the dumb speak. It was enough to convince most of the terrified witnesses. Nevertheless, the three children remained the only ones actually to see the Virgin, and only Lúcia could communicate with her.

To her were revealed the three **Secrets of Fátima**. The first was a message of peace (this was during World War I) and a vision of Hell, with anguished, charred souls plunged into an ocean of fire. The second was more prophetic and controversial: "If you pay heed to my request", the vision declared, "Russia will be converted and there will be peace. If not, Russia will spread her errors through the world, causing wars and persecution against the Church" – all this just a few weeks before the Bolshevik takeover in St Petersburg, though not, perhaps, before it could have been predicted. The **third secret** has never been divulged – it lies in a drawer of the Pope's desk in the Vatican, read by successive popes on their accession but supposedly too horrible to be revealed, though the present incumbent has hinted that the day may not be far off when he will announce its contents. In 1984, an Irish priest tried to hijack an *Aer Lingus* plane in an attempt to persuade the Pope to reveal the secret, but the crisis was defused with no-one any the wiser.

The Basílica and the town

To commemorate the extraordinary events and to accommodate the hordes of pilgrims who flock here, a shrine has been built, which has little to recommend it but its size. The vast white **Basílica**, completed in 1953, and its gigantic esplanade are capable of holding more than a million devotees. In the church the **tombs of Jacinta and Francisco** – Lúcia's fellow witnesses, both of whom died in the European flu epidemic of 1919–20 – are the subject of constant attention in their chapels on either side of the main exit. Long Neoclassical colonnades flank the basílica and enclose part of the sloping esplanade in front. This huge area, reminiscent of an airport runway, is twice the size of the piazza of Saint Peter's in Rome. On its left-hand side the original oak tree in which the Virgin appeared was long ago consumed by souvenir-hunting pilgrims; the small **Chapel of the Apparitions** now stands in its place, with a new tree a few yards away.

Whatever your feelings about the place, there is an undeniable (and to some people suffocating) atmosphere of mystery around it, perhaps created by nothing more than the obvious faith of the vast majority of its visitors. It's all at its most intense during the great **annual pilgrimages** on May 12–13 and October 12–13. Crowds of up to 100,000 congregate, most arriving on foot, some even walking on their knees in penance. Open-air mass is celebrated at 5am and an image of the Virgin is paraded by candlelight as priests move among the pilgrims hearing confessions. The fiftieth anniversary of the apparitions attracted one-and-a-half million worshippers, including Pope Paul VI and Lúcia – who is still alive, a Carmelite nun in the Convent of Santa Teresa near Coimbra. Lúcia was again part of the vast crowds that greeted John Paul II here in 1982 and 1991.

A multitude of hospices and convents have sprung up in the shadow of the basílica, and inevitably the fame of Fátima has resulted in its commercialisation. As each year goes by, the grotesquely kitsch souvenirs on sale move into hitherto unexplored territories of taste – look out for the Fátima ballpoint pens, which tilt to reveal the Virgin in Glory. Business is particularly brisk on Sunday, when thousands of local families converge by bus, car, lorry and cart – yet the shrine itself is not yet swamped.

There is a pleasant walk up to the place of the **"Apparitions of the Angel"**, outside the village, along which pilgrims follow the Stations of the Cross.

Practicalities

There are regular **bus services** to Fátima from Leiria (25km to the northwest) and Tomar (35km east) making it an easy daytrip. Coming **from Batalha** (20km west) on the N356, you'll pass Reguengo do Fétal, another pilgrimage site that's host to a torchlit procession (lit by burning oil carried in shells) up to a hilltop sanctuary around October 3. **By train**, you'll need to get a taxi or local bus (there's not always an immediate connection) from Estação de Fátima, 10km from town; the station is on the main Lisbon–Porto line.

Pensions and restaurants abound in Fátima, most of them decked out in tasteful shades of Marian blue. But frankly there's little reason to stay except during the pilgrimages (when the pensions are booked months ahead) to witness the midnight processions. At these times people camp all around the back and sides of the basílica. Beware of thieves during the pilgrimages.

However, outside the major pilgrimages – or weekends – there's enough **accommodation** to go round, since many of the older boarding houses are built on monastic lines, with over a hundred rooms and private chapels. *Casa do Beato Nuna*, Avenida Beato Nuno 51 (☎049/53 30 69; ③), is one of the older places; more modern are the *Residencial Santo António*, Rua Francisco Monto 59 (☎049/ 53 14 55; ③), and the *Residencial São Paulo*, Rua de São Paulo (☎049/53 15 72; ③). A particularly good **restaurant** is *O Zé Grande*, Rua Jacinto Mauro 32, on the road up to the básilica; further afield, 4km out of Fátima at Boleiros but worth the trip, is the *Restaurante O Truão*.

Tomar

The Convento de Cristo at **TOMAR**, 34km east of Fátima, is an artistic *tour de force* which entwines the most outstanding military, religious and imperial strands in the history of Portugal. The *Ordem dos Templários* (Order of the Knights Templar) and their successors, the *Ordem de Cristo* (Order of Christ), established their headquarters here and successive Grand Masters employed experts in Romanesque, Manueline and Renaissance architecture to embellish and expand the convent in a manner worthy of their power, prestige and wealth.

In addition, Tomar is an attractive town in its own right, well worth a couple of days of slow exploration. Built on a simple grid plan, it is split in two by the Rio Nabão, with almost everything of interest on the west bank. Here, Tomar's old quarters preserve all their traditional charm, with whitewashed, terraced cottages lining narrow cobbled streets. This pleasing backdrop is seen to best effect during Tomar's famous *Festa dos Tabuleiros*, held at intermittent intervals (see p.136), when the entire town takes to the streets.

The Town

On the central Praça da República stands an elegant seventeenth-century town hall, a ring of houses of the same period and the Manueline church of **São João Baptista**, remarkable for its octagonal belfry, elaborate doorway, and six panels attributed to Gregório Lopes (c. 1490–1550), one of Portugal's finest artists. Nearby at Rua Joaquim Jacinto 73 is an excellently preserved fourteenth-century **Synagogue** (daily except Wed 9.30am–12.30pm & 2–6pm; free), interesting in a town dominated for so long by crusading Defenders of the Faith. Its stark interior, with plain vaults supported by four slender columns, houses a collection of thirteenth- to fourteenth-century Hebraic inscriptions. In 1496 Dom Manuel followed the example of the *Reis Católicos* (Catholic Kings) of Spain and ordered the expulsion or conversion of all Portuguese Jews. The synagogue at Tomar was one of the very few to survive so far south – there's another at Castelo de Vide in the Alentejo. Many Jews fled northwards, especially to Trás-os-Montes where Inquisitional supervision was less hawk-eyed.

Midway between the town and the Convento de Cristo, it's worth taking the time for a look around the unassumingly beautiful Renaissance church of **Nossa Senhora da Conceição**. It is attributed to Diogo de Torralva, architect of the Convento's Great Cloisters. The Turismo has keys for the church.

The Convento de Cristo

The **Convento de Cristo** (Tues–Sun 9.30am–12.30pm & 2–5.30pm; 300$00) is set among pleasant gardens with splendid views, about a quarter of an hour's walk uphill from the centre of town. Founded in 1162 by Gualdim Pais, first and grandest Master of the **Knights Templar**, it was the headquarters of the Order, and, as such, both a religious and a military centre.

One of the main objectives of the Templars was to expel the Moors from Spain and Portugal, a reconquest seen always as a crusade against the Dark Forces – the defence of Christianity against the Infidel. Spiritual strength was an integral part of the military effort and, despite magnificent additions, the sacred heart of

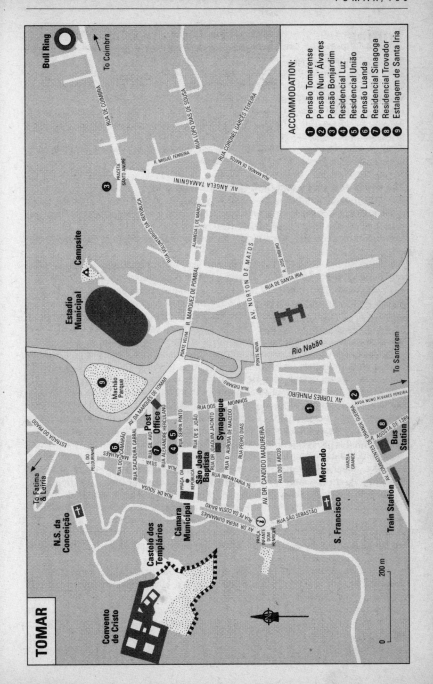

TOMAR

ACCOMMODATION:
1. Pensão Tomarense
2. Pensão Nun' Álvares
3. Pensão Bonjardim
4. Residencial Luz
5. Residencial União
6. Pensão Luanda
7. Residencial Sinagoga
8. Residencial Trovador
9. Estalagem de Santa Iria

Bull Ring

To Coimbra

RUA DE COIMBRA

R. MIGUEL FERREIRA
PRACETA SANTO ANDRÉ
RUA CORONEL GARCÊS TEIXEIRA
RUA LOPO DIAS DE SOUSA
RUA MANOEL DE MATOS
AV. ÂNGELA TAMAGNINI

RUA DOS VOLUNTÁRIOS DA REPÚBLICA
ALAMEDA 1 DE MARÇO

Campsite
Machão Parque
Estadio Municipal

RUA DE SANTA IRIA
AV. NORTON DE MATOS
RUA DE JOSÉ RIBEIRO

R. MARQUEZ DE POMBAL
PONTE VELHA
PONTE NOVA

Rio Nabão

To Santarem

AV. TORRES PINHEIRO
AVDA NUNO ÁLVARES PEREIRA

RUA EVERARD
RUA DOS MOINHOS
Post Office
Synagogue
RUA DA MARQUÊS DE TOMAR
RUA GIL AVO TOMAR
RUA ALEXANDRE HERCULANO
RUA SERPA PINTO
RUA DE S. JOÃO
RUA DR. JOAQUIM JACINTO
RUA D. AURORA DE MACEDO
RUA PEDRO DIAS
RUA DOS ARCOS
AV. DR. CANDIDO MADUREIRA
RUA INFANTARIA 15

To Fátima & Leiria

ESTRADA DO PRADO
LGO PELOURINHO
RUA SACADURA CABRAL
RUA MAÇANILHÃES
RUA DOS CAMARÃO
RUA DR. SOUSA
RUA DA SILVA
PRAÇA DA REPÚBLICA
São João Baptista
Câmara Municipal
N.S. da Conceição

AV. DR VIEIRA GUIMARÃES
RUA DE FÉ DA COSTA BAIXO
PRAÇA INFANTE DOM HENRIQUE

Castelo dos Templários
Convento de Cristo

Mercado
VARZEA GRANDE
AV. COMBATENTES DE GRANDE GUERRA
AV. D. AGOSTA DE 1385
Bus Station
Train Station
RUA SÃO SEBASTIÃO
S. Francisco

0   200 m

the whole complex remains the **Charola** (also known as the Rotunda or Templars' Apse), the twelfth-century temple from which the knights drew their moral conviction. It is a strange place, more suggestive of the occult than of Christianity. At the centre of the sixteen-sided, almost circular, chapel stands the high altar, surrounded by a two-storeyed octagon. Deep alcoves, decorated with sixteenth-century paintings, are cut into the outside walls; the Templars are said to have attended mass on horseback. Like almost every circular church, it is ultimately based on the Church of the Holy Sepulchre in Jerusalem, for whose protection the Knights Templar was originally founded. At the time of writing, the Charola was closed for restoration, with no indication as to when it will re-open; until it does, you can only see it from a distance.

The Order of Christ – and Dom Manuel's additions

By 1249 the reconquest in Portugal was completed and the Templars reaped enormous rewards for their services. Tracts of land were turned over to them and they controlled a network of castles throughout the Iberian peninsula. But as the Moorish threat receded, the Knights became a powerful political challenge to the stability and authority of European monarchs.

Philippe-le-Bel, King of France, took the lead by confiscating all Templar property in his country, and there followed a formal papal suppression of the Order in 1314. In Spain this prompted a vicious witch-hunt and many of the Knights sought refuge in Portugal, where Dom Dinis coolly reconstituted them in 1320 under a different title: the **Order of Christ**. They inherited all the Portuguese property of the Templars, including the headquarters at Tomar, but their power was now subject to that of the throne.

In the fifteenth and sixteenth centuries, the Order of Christ played a leading role in extending Portugal's overseas empire and was granted spiritual jurisdiction over all conquests. Prince Henry the Navigator was Grand Master from 1417 to 1460, and the remains of his **Palace** in the Convento de Cristo can be seen immediately to the right upon entering the castle walls. Henry ordered two new cloisters, the **Claustro do Cemitério** and the **Claustro da Lavagem**, both reached via a short corridor from the Charola and attractively lined with *azulejos*.

Dom Manuel succeeded to the Grand Mastership in 1492, three years before he became king. Flush with imperial wealth, he decided to expand the convent by adding a rectangular **nave** to the west side of the Charola. This new structure was divided into two storeys: the lower serving as a chapter house, the upper as a choir. The **main doorway**, which leads directly into the nave, was built by João de Castilho in 1515, two years before Dom Manuel appointed him Master of Works at Belém. Characteristically unconcerned with structural matters, the architect profusely adorned the doorway with *appliqué* decoration. There are strong similarities in this respect with contemporary Isabeline and Plateresque architecture in Spain.

The crowning highlight of Tomar, though, is the sculptural ornamentation of the windows on the main facade of the **Chapter House**. The richness and self-confidence of Manueline art always suggests the Age of Discovery, but here the connection is crystal clear. A wide range of maritime motifs is jumbled up in two tumultuous window frames, as eternal memorials to the sailors who established the Portuguese Empire. Everything is here: anchors, buoys, sails, coral, seaweed and especially the ropes, knotted over and over again into an escapologist's nightmare.

The windows can only be fully appreciated from the roof of the **Claustro de Santa Bárbara**, adjacent to the Great Cloisters, which unfortunately almost completely obscure a similar window on the south wall of the Chapter House.

A new style: João III

João III (1521–57) transformed the convent from the general political headquarters of the Order into a thoroughgoing monastic community, and he endowed it with the necessary conventual buildings: dormitories, kitchens and no less than four new cloisters (making a grand total of seven). Yet another, much more classical, style was introduced into the architectural mélange of Tomar. So meteoric was the rise and fall of Manueline art within the reign of Dom Manuel that, to some extent, it must have reflected his personal tastes. João III on the other hand had an entirely different view of art. He is known to have sent schools of architects and sculptors to study in Italy, and his reign finally marked the much-delayed advent of the Renaissance in Portugal.

The two-tiered **Great Cloisters**, abutting the Chapter House, are one of the purest examples of this new style. Begun in 1557, they present a textbook illustration of the principals of Renaissance neoclassicism. Greek columns, gentle arches and simple rectangular bays produce a wonderfully restrained rhythm. At the southwest corner a balcony looks out on to the skeletal remains of a second Chapter House, begun by João III but never completed.

Practicalities

The **train** and **bus stations**, on Avenida Combatentes da Grande Guerra, are within easy walking distance of the centre. Head directly north and you'll soon hit Avenida Dr. Candido Madureira, at the top end of which there's a very helpful **Turismo** (June–Sept Mon–Fri 9.30am–12.30pm & 2–6pm, Sat & Sun 10am–1pm & 3–6pm; Oct–May Mon–Fri 9.30am–12.30pm & 2–6pm, Sat 10am–1pm; ☎049/32 26 03); there's no sign, but it faces a fierce statue of Infante Dom Henrique and the gates of a park, which once formed the gardens of the Convento de Cristo.

Accommodation

Tomar has a good range of **accommodation** and finding a room should be pretty straightforward. There's also a pleasant municipal **campsite** (☎049/32 26 07; open all year), out towards the football stadium. With your own transport you could always stay instead at the site at **Castelo de Bode** (14km from Tomar and 7km from the train station at Santa Cita, two stops before Tomar). Bode reservoir is Lisbon's main water source, set amid pine woods and with boats for rent to reach the islands in the lake.

The only time when accommodation will be hard to come by is during Tomar's *Festa dos Tabuleiros*, held in uncertain years during July – see the feature on p.136 for more details.

Pensão Bonjardim, Praçeta de Santo André (☎049/31 31 95). Basic but all right, though some way out, across the river. ③.

Estalgem de Santa Iria, Parque do Mouchão (☎049/31 33 26). In the park, by the river, Somerset Maugham once stayed here, which is recommendation enough – but then he was rich. ⑥.

Pensão Luanda, Avda. Marquês de Tomar 15 (☎049/31 29 29). Modern *pensão* facing the river. All the rooms come with bath. ④.

Residencial Luz, Rua Serpa Pinto 144 (☎049/31 23 17). A notch up the scale and excellent value, especially for multiple-person rooms (for 4–6 people). ③.

Pensão Nun'Álvares, Avda. Nuno Álvares Pereira 3 (☎049/31 28 73). Large, clean rooms (noisy at the front) – book ahead to secure one of just eleven rooms. Breakfast included. ①.

Residencial Sinagoga, Rua Gil Avô 31 (☎049/31 67 84). Near the town hall, this new place has air-conditioning and TV in all rooms. ④.

Pensão Tomarense, Avda. Torres Pinheiro 13 (☎049/31 29 48). Not a first choice, but cheap. Rooms are spartan and, at the front, noisy, but there are fine views of the Convento from the rear rooms. Breakfast included. ①.

Residencial Trovador, Rua de Agosto de 1385 (☎049/32 25 67). Light and airy *residencial* facing the bus station. There's a family atmosphere, which makes a change, but it's not terribly central. ⑤.

Residencial União, Rua Serpa Pinto 94 (☎049/31 28 31). Central and very popular; in July and August advance booking is essential. Nice rooms around a courtyard, all with private bath or shower. Breakfast included. ③–④.

Eating and drinking

Many of the *pensões* in Tomar have attached **restaurants**, of which the *Nun' Álvares* (see below) is the best. Otherwise, two or three other highly rated places are worth looking out for. Midday, the busiest **cafés and bars** are on Avenida Dr. Cândido Madureira and around the Varzea Grande; on a summer's evening there's more action on the riverside.

Bela Vista, Trav. Fonte Choupo 6. The town's most renowned restaurant, with full meals for under 2000$00; try the chicken curry. Closed Mon evening, Tues and Nov.

Restaurante Nabão, Rua Fonte Choupo 3, across the Ponte Velha. Standard Portuguese favourites at moderate prices.

Nun'Álvares, Avda. Nuno Álvares Pereira 3. This has the edge on its pension rivals, with a fine house wine and tasty local dishes.

Restaurante Piri-Piri, Rua dos Moinhos 54. Large portions of occasionally bland food (despite the spice promised by the name), though the grilled trout is good. Closed Sun.

THE FESTA DOS TABULEIROS

Tomar is renowned throughout the country for its **Festa dos Tabuleiros** (literally, the Festival of the Trays). Its origins can be traced back to the saintly Queen Isabel who founded the Brotherhood of the Holy Spirit in the fourteenth century, though some believe it to derive from an ancient fertility rite dedicated to Ceres. Whatever its origins, it's now a largely secular event, held at three- or four-yearly intervals, making it difficult to predict. It was last held in 1991 and is due to take place again in 1995: it's a five-day affair, at the beginning of July, with the highlight – the parade of "trays" – on the final Sunday.

The **procession** (*Procissão dos Tabuleiros*) consists of 400 or so young women wearing white, each escorted by a young man in a white shirt, red tie and black trousers. She carries on her head a tray with thirty loaves threaded on vertical canes, intertwined with leaves and colourful paper flowers, and crowned with a white dove – the symbol of the Holy Spirit. The resulting headdress weighs 15kg, and is roughly person-height – hence the need for an escort to lift and help balance it. As with other festivals, there's music and dancing in the streets, fireworks at dawn and dusk, and a bullfight the night before the procession. The day after the procession, bread, wine and beef are distributed to the local needy, following Isabel's injunction to "give bread to the poor" – needless to say, the bulls providing the beef have their own procession, three days before that of the *tabuleiros*.

Santarém

SANTARÉM, capital of the Ribatejo, rears high above the Rio Tejo, commanding a tremendous view over the rich pasturelands to the south and east. It ranks among the most historic cities in Portugal: under Julius Caesar it became an important administrative centre for the Roman province of Lusitania; Moorish Santarém was regarded as impregnable (until Afonso Henriques captured it by enlisting the aid of foreign Crusaders in 1147); and it was here that the royal *Cortes* (parliament) was convened throughout the fourteenth and fifteenth centuries. All evidence of Roman and Moorish occupation, though, has vanished and with the notable exceptions of two exquisite churches modern Santarém has little to show for its history. Even so, a visit is rewarded by the famous view from the *miradouro* known as the **Portas do Sol**, and, if you can plan your stay to coincide, by a whole series of **festivals** held in the town and region.

Around the town

At the heart of the the old town is **Praça Sá da Bandeira**, overlooked by the many-windowed Baroque facade of the Jesuit **Seminário** (1676), which serves as the town's cathedral (daily 9.30–11.30am & 2.30–5.30pm). Rua Serpa Pinto or Rua Capelo e Ivens lead from here towards the signposted Portas do Sol, about fifteen minutes' walk, with the best of the churches conveniently en route.

First of these is the Manueline **Igreja de Marvila**, at the end of Rua Serpa Pinto, with its brilliant seventeenth-century *azulejos* and lovely stone pulpit, comprising eleven miniature Corinthian columns. From here, Rua J. Araújo, at right angles to the side of the church, descends a few yards to the architectural highlight of Santarém: the early fifteenth-century **Igreja da Graça** (9.30am–1pm & 2.30–5.30pm). A spectacular rose window dominates the church and overlapping "blind arcades" above the portal are heavily influenced by the vertical decorations on the main facade at Batalha. Pedro Álvares Cabral, discoverer of Brazil in 1500, is buried within, but his rather austere tomb-slab is overshadowed by the elaborate sarcophagus of Pedro de Menezes (died 1437), first Governor of Ceuta.

Continuing toward the *miradouro*, a third sidetrack is to the twelfth-century church of **São João de Alporão**, now an archaeological museum. Take a look at the flamboyant Gothic tomb of Duarte de Menezes (died 1464). So comprehensively was he butchered by the Moors in North Africa that only a single tooth was recovered for burial. Avenida 5 de Outubro eventually finishes at the **Portas do Sol** (Gates of the Sun), a large garden occupying the site of the Moorish citadel. Modern battlements look down on a long stretch of the Tejo with its fertile sandbanks. And beyond, a vast chunk of the Ribatejo disappears into the distance – green, flat, and monotonous.

Bulls and festivals

The thinly populated agricultural plain above which Santarém stands is the home of Portuguese **bullfighting**. The very best horses and bulls graze in the lush fields under the watchful eyes of *campinos*, mounted guardians dressed in bright eighteenth-century costume. Agricultural traditions, folk dancing (especially the *fandango*), and bullfighting all come together in the great annual **Feira Nacional da Agricultura**, held at Santarém for ten days starting on the first Friday in June, while dishes from every region in Portugal are sampled at the **Festival de Gastronomia** (10–12 days, ending on 1 Nov). For a fixed price you can eat as much as you like during this event.

More bullfights are staged during the **Milagre Fair** (first two Sundays in April), the **Piedade Fair** (on two Sundays in October), and throughout the summer; and there are **street markets** on the second and fourth Sunday of every month.

Practicalities

The **train station** lies a couple of hundred metres below the town and unless you take a taxi you'll have to walk into the centre. The **bus station** is more central and Rua Pedro Canavarro, across the gardens opposite the bus station, leads into **Rua Capelo e Ivens**, the main pedestrian street of the old town. Excellent maps are available from the **Turismo** at no. 63 (Mon–Fri 9.30am–12.30pm & 2–6pm, Sat & Sun 9.30am–12.30pm & 2–5pm; ☎043/231 40).

Accommodation

Finding a place to stay can be hard during festival times, when your best bet is to turn up early and see if the Turismo can find you a **private room**. There should be little problem at other times of year; try one of the **hotels or pensions** listed below. The cheapest beds are at the **youth hostel** (☎043/33 32 92) on Avenida Afonso Henrique, near the bullring and fairground; while the nearest **campsite** for tents (there's a local campervan park) is across the river, 9km to the east, at Alpiarça (☎043/543 99; open all year).

Hotel Abidis, Rua Guilherme de Azevedo 4 (☎043/220 17). A slice of nineteenth-century style with close on thirty rooms, though only six have a bath. Highly recommended and excellent value. ②.

Hotel Alfageme, Avda. Bernardo Santaremo 38 (☎043/37 08 07). New hotel whose rooms are all en-suite, air-conditioned and double-glazed. Breakfast included. ④.

Residencial O Beirante, Rua Alexandre Herculano 5 (☎043/225 47). Moderately priced rooms, all with private bath, near the town hall. ④.

Residencial Jardim, Rua Florbela Espança 1 (☎043/33 35 54). In Alto da Bexiga, 2.5km out of town, this is plush enough but lacking in character. ④.

Pensão do José, Trav. do Frois 14 (☎043/230 88). A clean, basic pension, on a quiet alley-way just off Rua Capelo e Ivens. ②.

Quinta de Vale de Lobo, Azóia de Baixo, 6km north of town (☎043/422 64). Part of the *Turihab* accommodation scheme, this pleasant house (where the historian Alexandre Herculano spent the last years of his life) is surrounded by gardens. ⑤.

Residencial Vitoria, Rua 2° Visconde de Santarém 21 (☎043/225 73). Fifteen minutes' walk from the centre: decent, if small, rooms – all with bath; breakfast included. ③.

Eating

Santarém has a range of **restaurants**, mainly on – or just off – Rua Capelo e Ivens and in the area around the bullring, out on the road to Cartaxo. Among local fish specialities look out for *fataça na telha*, mullet cooked on a tile.

Castiço, Campo de Feiras. Decorated like a Ribatejo ranch and specialising in meat dishes. Closed Sun.

O Mal Cozinhado, Campo de Feiras. Small place, where you may need to reserve a table, particularly on Friday, which is fado night. Some of the meat comes from bulls recently on

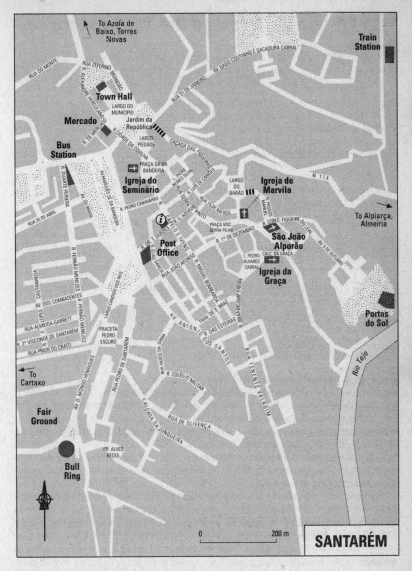

SANTARÉM

duty in the nearby bullring – and, despite the odd restaurant name ("badly cooked"), dishes are good.

Pigalle, Rua Capelo e Ivens. Busy restaurant, with a separate bar. Closed Sun.

Portas do Sol, Jardim das Portas do Sol, inside the castle. Superb views and fine food, though the service can be a little abrupt.

O Saloio, Trav. do Montalvo, off Rua Capelo e Ivens. Popular with local families; plain decor, but very good value for money.

Vila Franca de Xira and the Tejo Nature Reserve

VILA FRANCA DE XIRA, 45km downriver from Santarém, makes a rival claim to be the capital of the Ribatejo, but it's largely a drab, industrial city – a poor second when it comes to historical associations and cultural attractions. On the other hand, Vila Franca is the central point of interest for aficionados of the Portuguese bullfight: the rearing of bulls and horses dominates the local economy. The two great annual events are the **Festa do Colete Encarnado** ("Red Waistcoat Festival", a reference to the costume of the *campinos*) held over several days in the first two weeks of July; and the Feira de Outubro (October Fair), in the first two weeks of the month. On both occasions there are bullfights and a Pamplona-style running of the bulls through the streets – leading to the usual casualties among the bold (and drunk).

Accommodation on these occasions is difficult to find and you're advised to book well in advance or visit the festivals on a day trip from Santarém or Lisbon. Places to stay in town include the *Residencial Ribatejana*, Rua da Praia 2 (☎063/ 229 91; ③), next to the station, and the *Residencial Flora*, Rua Noel Perdigão 12 (☎063/27 12 72; ④), one block from the station and with a good restaurant. There's a shaded **campsite** (☎063/260 31; open all year) on the outskirts, near the municipal swimming pool.

For **eating**, *O Copote* in the station square, on the first floor above a bar, is inexpensive; *Restaurante O Redondel*, Praça de Touros (near the bullring on the Lisbon side of town; closed Mon) is also recommended, though the full works here can cost around 3500$00 per person.

Reserva Natural de Estuario del Tejo

South and southeast from Vila Franca de Xira, the banks of the Tejo are classified as the **Reserva Natural de Estuario del Tejo**, providing protection for the thousands of wild birds that gather in the estuary. It's Portugal's most important wetland and a new headquarters has been established in **ALCOCHETE**, due east of Lisbon (Avenida Combatentes 1; ☎01/234 17 42), from which information and advice is dispensed. With your own transport, the best approach to the reserve is from Alcamé, south of the N10 Vila Franca–Porto Alto road, or – better still – from Pancas, west of the N118.

Alternatively, you can see the reserve from the Tejo estuary itself by **renting a boat** (or a place in a boat). Take the ferry from Lisbon (hourly from Praça do Comércio, in the Baixa) to Montijo, a fifty-minute journey, and once there it's a five-kilometre bus or taxi ride to Alcochete. Contact Domingos Chefe, the boat owner (☎01/236 02 78; best done with the help of a Portuguese speaker), a day in advance to agree on the timing; you'll also need to obtain permission to visit from the reserve headquarters. The boat costs around 6000$00 and can take up to nine people.

The birds on view depend on the time of year of your visit. September to February is best, when you'll be certain to see migrating species, like flamingos, teal and avocet. Later in the year, you'll catch nesting species: black-winged stilt, purple heron and marsh harriers.

Ribatejo: along the banks of the Tejo

Besides Santarém and Vila Franca, there are several smaller towns and villages on both **banks of the Rio Tejo** worth passing by if you have time on your hands and your own transport. The western bank, with its rolling hills and vineyards, is fairly well served by trains and buses; the riverside marshes and rich plain of the eastern bank are not so accessible, though the N118 links the major villages. Accommodation isn't particularly plentiful, but then you're unlikely to want to stop for any great for any great length of time in the various towns and villages – except during their energetic annual **festivals**, when what accommodation there is will be fully booked in any case.

Golegã to Salvaterra de Magos

GOLEGÃ, 30km northeast of Santarém on the west bank of the Tejo, is best known for its **Feira Nacional do Cavalo** (National Horse Fair), held during the first two weeks in November. The fair incorporates celebrations for St Martin's Day on November 11, when there's a grand parade; while other diversions include a running of the bulls, roasted chestnuts and barbecued chickens to eat, and *água-pé* (literally "foot water") to drink – a light wine made by adding water to the crushed grape husks left after the initial wine production. In the evening, people crowd into the *Restaurante Central*, on Largo da Imaculada Conceicão, both to eat and to mingle with haughty *cavaleiros* who have survived the bullfighting. The restaurant has some **rooms** to rent, though they'll be almost certainly occupied during the fair. Otherwise, try the *Casa de Santo António da Azinhaga*, Rua Nova de Santo António (☎049/951 62; ⑤), in the attractive streamside village of Azinhaga, 12km from Golegã on the N365. There's a **campsite** (☎049/942 22) on the edge of Golegã, on the same road.

Chamusca

Across the Tejo from Golegã – 9km by road – **CHAMUSCA** is the most northerly of the east bank's bullfighting towns. Its *Festa da Ascensão* is held during the week incorporating Ascension Day (ie, 40 days after Easter), when bulls are run and fought for six days. Outside these times, things are much quieter: the reconstructed 1930s-style **Casa Rural Tradicional** in the municipal park alongside Largo 25 de Abril is about as exciting as it gets.

Alpiarça

There's a great deal more interest in **ALPIARÇA**, 18km south of Chamusca (and just 10km east of Santarém), where the **Casa Museu dos Patudos** (Wed–Sun 10am–noon & 2–5pm; 300$00), on Rua José Relvas on the outskirts, was originally the home of José Relvas (1858–1929); musician, art collector, landowner, bullfighter, diplomat and politician. Designed by Raul Lino, the exterior of the house is striking, with a colonnade and outdoor staircases to the first floor. Inside, you'll find priceless collections of Portuguese paintings, porcelain, furniture, tapestries and over forty carpets from Arraiolos, including one embroidered in silk, dating from 1701. The **Turismo** in the town hall may be able to help with renting **rooms**; otherwise, there's a **campsite** (☎043/543 99) beyond the museum and off the Almeirim road.

Almeirim

ALMEIRIM's golden days were during the reign of the House of Avis (1383–1580), when the royal family – ensconced at Santarém, just 7km to the northwest – hunted from a summer palace on the riverside here. Nothing remains of the palace today, but you might want to drive out from Santarém for **lunch** at the *Restaurante Tonçinho*, on Rua Macau, whose brick oven and open kitchen adds a certain interest to mealtimes (closed Wed and Aug).

Salvaterra de Magos

SALVATERRA DE MAGOS, 29km south of Almeirim, retains rather more of its historical relics. A palace built for the Bragança monarchs is long gone, but the palace **chapel** still survives, with an outstanding golden altarpiece, as does the falconry, whose 310 niches once housed the royal falcons. In its eighteenth-century heyday, the palace contained a theatre and a bullring, though when the noble Count of Arcos was killed while fighting bulls here, Pombal banned the sport – which was only legally reinstated again in 1920.

Cartaxo and Azambuja

Back on the west bank, 14km southwest of Santarém, **CARTAXO** sits amid some of the Ribatejo's finest vineyards. Junot's troops passed through here in 1808 on their way to Lisbon; they had covered almost 1000km in 30 days and arrived ragged and footsore, finally reaching the capital one day after the royal family had left for Brazil. The town's **Museu Rural e do Vinho** (Tues–Sun 10am–12.30pm & 2–6pm), on Rua José Ribeiro da Costa, leading south out of town, is established as a rural *quinta*, with a couple of traditional houses where you can taste and buy the local, full-bodied, fruity wine. A couple of kilometres east of town, a sixteenth-century manor house, the *Solar dos Chavões*, has been converted into a country **restaurant** serving fish soup, fried eels and other local dishes, all best accompanied by the local wine. It's on the road out to the Santana-Cartaxo train station; look for the sign on the left to Vila Chã de Ourique.

AZAMBUJA, 13km further south, is a dull but prosperous farming town which only really comes alive during its *Feira do Maio*, held during the last weekend in May. The Marquês de Pombal built a 26-kilometre-long canal – the Vala de Azambuja – parallel to the river here, to drain the land when the Tejo was in flood. At its mouth are the ruins of the **Palácio das Obras Novas**, used as a staging post for the steamers plying from Lisbon north to Constância, at the confluence of the Tejo and the Zêzere, in the nineteenth century.

Alenquer and Alhandra

Perched on a hillside 12km northwest of Vila Franca de Xira, **ALENQUER**'s most prominent building is its **Franciscan convent**, founded in 1222 by Dona Sancha, daughter of Dom Sancho I. It's the oldest Franciscan house in Portugal, built while St. Francis of Assisi was still alive, and features a fine thirteenth-century doorway and Manueline cloisters, the latter added in 1557.

ALHANDRA, on the banks of the Tejo and just 4km southwest of Vila Franca, stood at the eastern end of the Torres Vedras lines (see p.109); a statue of Hercules, high above the town, marks Wellington's success, and is fastened with a plaque to commemorate the work of Nevas de Costa, the Portuguese engineer who planned the lines.

Up the Tejo: Almourol and beyond

Forty kilometres **north of Santarém**, the Rio Tejo swings east, flowing past the remarkable castle at Almourol to meet the Rio Zêzere at Constância. Further east, Abrantes is the last significant stop on the river, beyond which road and rail routes branch out for Spain or north and south for the rest of the country.

Almourol and Tancos

As if conjured up by some medieval-minded magician, the **castle of Almourol** stands deserted on a tiny island in the middle of the Tejo, 45km northeast of Santarém. Built by the Knights Templar in 1171, it never saw military action – except in sixteenth-century romantic literature – and its double perimeter walls and ten small towers are perfectly preserved. It's military property but there's no objection to visitors, and once inside you'll be granted a beautiful rural panorama from the tall central keep.

The train line hugs the northern banks of the Tejo at this point and there are two convenient stations, Tancos and Almourol, thirty and fifteen minutes' walk respectively from the island. The latter is stuck in the middle of nowhere but **TANCOS** is actually a small village with a couple of bars catering for a nearby army barracks. To reach the castle from Tancos, strike out along the railway tracks: the river banks are an impassable forest of eucalyptus trees, cacti and assorted bushes. For around 300$00 per person, a ferryman will row you around the island and deposit you on a miniature beach to explore the castle at leisure.

Constância

CONSTÂNCIA, 3km upstream from Almourol, is a useful place to stay the night after a visit to the castle. A sleepy whitewashed village, arranged like an amphitheatre around the Tejo and the mouth of the Rio Zêzere, it is best known in Portugal for its association with **Luís de Camões**, Portugal's national poet. In fact, Camões was here for only three years (1547–50), taking refuge from the court of Dom João III, whom he had managed to offend by the injudicious dedication of a love sonnet to a woman on whom the king himself had designs. Constância, however, is said to have remained dear to the poet's heart until the end of his life. In more troubled times, the town served the Duke of Wellington in 1809: he amassed his forces here and prepared for the Battle of Talavera in Spain.

For Constância, get off the **train** at Praia do Ribatejo-Constância, the stop after Almourol. If you want **to stay**, ask for *dormidas* in the central cafés or try one of the following: *Residencial Casa João Chagas*, Rua João Chagas (☎049/994 03; ④); the more expensive *Casa O Palácio* (☎049/992 24; ⑤), by the water's edge; or the *Quinta de Santa Barbara* (☎049/992 14; ⑤), 1km out of town, off the road to Abrantes. The nearest **campsite** is in an attractive lakeside setting at Castelo de Bode, 9km up the Rio Zêzere.

Abrantes

ABRANTES occupies a position similar to Santarém, perched strategically above the Tejo, 15km upstream of Almourol. But the streets and *praças* here are prettier; the spring and summer flowers on Rua da Barca and in the Jardim da República are a delight; and the views more varied and just as extensive, making the town more of a worthwhile base in its own right. Additionally, the town has useful train connections linking up with the lower Beiras and the Alto Alentejo.

The highpoint – in all respects – is the town's battered **Castelo** (Tues–Sun 10am–12.30pm & 2–5pm), constructed in the early fourteenth century. As at Santarém, Romans and Moors established strongholds here, and the citadel was again sharply contested during the Peninsular War. The chapel of **Santa Maria do Castelo**, within the fort, houses a motley archaeological museum, its prize exhibits being three tombs of the Almeidas, Counts of Abrantes. From the battlements there's a terrific view of the countryside and the rooftops of Abrantes and the gardens around its walls. Two large, whitewashed churches tower above all else; both were rebuilt in the sixteenth century.

Practicalities

The helpful **Turismo** (daily 9.30am–12.30pm & 2–6pm; ☎041/225 55) is on Largo da Feira, with the **bus station** nearby on Rua Nossa Senhora da Conceicão. There are two local **train stations**, both out of town. The main one is 2km south, across the Tejo, and all trains stop there; you could walk into the centre from here, but it's uphill all the way – shared taxis aren't too expensive.

Accommodation is generally easy enough to find, with several decent-priced pensions, a hotel and a *Turihab* lodging, 10km out of town. *Pensão Central*, Praça Raimundo Soares 15 (☎041/224 22; ②), is pleasant and inexpensive; the *Abrantes*, Rua Miguel de Almeida 13, off Praça Raimundo Soares (☎041/221 19; ②), very rundown but with rock-bottom prices. *Pensão Aliança*, Largo do Chafariz 50 (☎041/223 48; ②) is better, with showers in some rooms and hot baths down the corridor. The *Turihab* place, *Quinta dos Vales* (☎041/973 63; ⑤), is at Tramagal, on the southern bank of the river, 10km from Abrantes, or a ten-minute walk from the train station at Tramagal. It's a white country house, with horses available if you want to hack along the river banks.

There are a number of reasonable **restaurants** in Abrantes. One of the best is the *Pelicano*, Rua Nossa Senhora de Conceicão, near the bus station (closed Thurs), though a meal here still shouldn't cost more than 2000$00. Otherwise, try either the *Fumeiro*, Rua do Pisco 9 (closed Sun), or – 3km out of town, at Alferrarede, near the second train station – the *Cascara* (closed Mon), a local favourite.

travel details

Trains

Abrantes to Castelo Branco (5 daily; 1hr 15min–1hr 45min); Covilhã (5 daily; 2hr 30min–3hr 30min); Elvas (3 daily; 2hr 45min); Guarda (3 daily; 5hr); Lisbon (8 daily; 2hr); Portalegre (3 daily; 1hr 45min); Porto (6 daily; 5hr 15min).

Caldas da Rainha to Figueira da Foz (8–9 daily; 1hr 45min–2hr 30min); Leiria (Mon–Fri 9 daily, Sat & Sun 6; 45min–1hr); Lisbon (8 daily; 2hr); Torres Vedras (6–8 daily; 35–45min).

Fátima to Coimbra (6 daily; 1hr 30min); Porto (5 daily; 3hr 45min).

Leiria to Caldas da Rainha (9–10 daily; 45min–1hr); Figueira da Foz (7–8 daily; 50min–1hr 20min); Lisbon (5 daily; 2hr 45min–3hr 30min); São Martinho do Porto (9–10 daily; 50min); Torres Vedras (5–6 daily; 1hr 40min–2hr).

Lisbon to Caldas da Rainha (8 daily; 2hr–2hr 30min); Leiria (5 daily; 2hr 45min–3hr 30min); Torres Vedras (6 daily; 1hr 10min–1hr 30min).

Santarém to Abrantes (6 daily; 1hr 10min); Castelo Branco (5 daily; 2hr 50min–3hr 10min); Coimbra (4 daily; 1hr 35min); Covilhã (5 daily; 3hr 45min–4hr 45min); Guarda (4 daily; 4hr 30min–5hr 15min); Lisbon (17–25 daily; 50min); Tomar (5–9 daily; 1hr–1hr 15min); Viseu (4 daily; 3hr 30min–4hr 10min).

Tomar to Lisbon (4–9 daily; 2hr 10min); Porto (3–5 daily; 3hr 45min); Santarém (5–9 daily; 1hr–1hr 15min).

Torres Vedras to Caldas da Rainha (6–8 daily; 35–45min); Figueira da Foz (2 daily; 2hr 10min–2hr 30min); Leiria (5–6 daily; 1hr 40min–2hr); Lisbon (6 daily; 1hr 10min–1hr 30min).

Vila Franca de Xira to Alhandra (10–16 daily; 6min); Azambuja (6–12 daily; 18min); Coimbra (7–11 daily; 2hr 10min); Lisbon (10–16 daily; 20min); Porto (4 daily; 4hr); Santarém (6–12 daily; 30–40min); Tomar (8–12 daily; 1hr 10min–1hr 45min).

Buses

Abrantes to Coimbra (4–6 daily; 2hr 50min); Fátima (4 daily; 1hr 25min); Leiria (5 daily; 1hr 50min); Santarém (6 daily; 1hr 25min); Tomar (4 daily; 40min).

Alcobaça to Batalha (10 daily; 30min); Leiria (8 daily; 45min).

Batalha to Fátima (4 daily; 25min); Leiria (8 daily; 15min); Lisbon (3 daily; 2hr 5min).

Caldas da Rainha to Leiria (3 daily; 1hr 15min); Nazaré (3 daily; 45min); São Martinho do Porto (7 daily; 25min).

Ericeira to Lisbon (8–12 daily; 1hr 45min); Sintra (8 daily; 45min).

Fátima to Coimbra (2 daily; 1hr 25min–2hr); Lisbon (7–8 daily; 1hr 30min–2hr 15min); Porto (2 daily; 2hr 30min–3hr).

Leiria to Abrantes (5 daily; 1hr 50min); Alcobaça (8 daily; 50min); Batalha (8 daily; 15min); Coimbra (5 daily; 1hr 10min); Fátima (5 daily; 25min); Lisbon (6 daily; 1hr 45min–2hr 15min); Porto de Mós (5 daily; 35min); São Pedro de Moel (6 daily; 50min); Tomar (4 daily; 2hr).

Lisbon to Ericeira (8–12 daily; 1hr 45min); Leiria (6 daily; 1hr 45min–2hr 15min); Santarém (12 daily; 1hr 20min–2hr); Vila Franca de Xira (15 daily; 50min).

Nazaré to Alcobaça (12 daily; 35min); Leiria (10 daily; 1hr 10min).

Peniche to Areia Branca (hourly; 35min); Caldas da Rainha (hourly; 55min); Consolação (hourly; 15min); Óbidos (8 daily; 45min); São Martinho do Porto (hourly; 1hr 20min); Torre Vedras (6 daily; 50min).

Santarém to Abrantes (6 daily; 1hr 25min); Lisbon (12 daily; 1hr 20min–2hr); Tomar (1 daily; 1hr 15min).

Tomar to Abrantes (4 daily; 40min); Coimbra (2 daily; 2hr 10min); Fátima (2 daily; 45min); Leiria (2 daily; 1hr 10min); Lisbon (2 daily; 2hr 20min); Porto (1 daily; 3hr 45min); Santarém (1 daily; 1hr 15min).

Vila Franca de Xira to Évora (1 daily; 2hr); Lisbon (15 daily; 50min).

CHAPTER THREE

COIMBRA AND THE BEIRA LITORAL

T he province of **Beira Litoral** is dominated by the city of **Coimbra**, which, with Lisbon and Porto, forms the trio of Portugal's historic capitals. Sited on a hill above the Mondego river, it's a wonderfully moody place, full of ancient alleys and lanes, spreading around the country's oldest university. As a base for exploring the region, the city can't be beaten, with Portugal's most extensive Roman site, **Conimbriga**, 16km to the southwest, the castle at **Montemor-o-Velho** 32km west on the road to Figueira da Foz, and the delightful spa town of **Luso** and ancient **forest of Buçaco** under thirty minutes' journey to the north.

Beira's endlessly sandy coastline, from Figueira da Foz north as far as Porto, has been dubbed the **Costa de Prata** ("Silver Coast"). Although slowly succumbing to development, most noticeably around **Praia de Mira**, it remains one of the least spoiled coasts in Portugal. Indeed the only resorts of any real size are **Figueira da Foz** and **Aveiro**, and even these have retained an enjoyably old-fashioned feel. In many of the smaller coastal villages, life remains highly traditional, with the whole community still involved in hauling in the fishing boats and their catches.

Inland, the villages and towns of the fertile plain have long been conditioned by the twin threats of floodwaters coming down from Portugal's highest mountains, and silting caused by the restless Atlantic. Drainage channels have had to be cut to make cultivation possible and houses everywhere are built on high ground. At Aveiro, positioned on a complex estuary site, a whole network of canals was developed to cope with the currents, and to facilitate salt production and the harvesting of seaweed – still the staple activities of the local economy. The Beira region also hints at the river valley delights to come, in the Douro and Minho,

---

ACCOMMODATION PRICE CODES

All the accommodation prices in this book have been coded using the symbols below. The symbols represent the prices for the cheapest available double room in high season; for a full explanation, see p.23.

① Under 3000$00	② 3000$00–4000$00	③ 4000$00–5500$00
④ 5500$00–8500$00	⑤ 8500$00–12,500$00	⑥ 12,500$00–20,000$00
	⑦ Over 20,000$00	

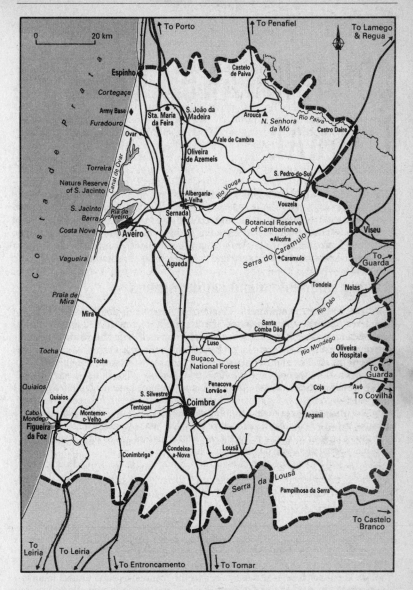

further north. Following the delightful **Rio Mondego** upstream from Coimbra, you'll come to see why it has been celebrated so often in Portuguese poetry as the *Rio das Musas* – River of the Muses. An equally beautiful road journey trails the **Rio Vouga**, from Aveiro, up to the town of **Vouzela** and the spa of **São Pedro do Sul**.

Coimbra

COIMBRA was Portugal's capital for over a century (1143–1255) and its famous **university** – founded in 1290 and permanently established here in 1537 after a series of moves back and forth to Lisbon – was the only one in Portugal until the beginning of this century. It remains highly prestigious (though Lisbon has far more students nowadays) and provides the greatest of Coimbra's monuments. For a small, provincial town, however, there are a remarkable number of other riches: two cathedrals, dozens of lesser churches, and scores of ancient mansions, one housing the superb Museu Machado de Castro.

In addition to these attractions, the town can be a lot of fun: it's a very manageable size, with a population of under 80,000, its streets packed with bars and taverns. Coimbra is at its most lively when the students are in town, and can be decidedly sleepy during the holidays. The best time to be here is in May, when the end of the academic year is celebrated in the **Queima das Fitas**, with graduates ceremoniously tearing or burning their gowns and faculty ribbons. This is also when you're most likely to hear the genuine **Coimbra fado** (though the tourist office organises events throughout the summer), distinguished from the Lisbon version by its mournful pace and romantic or intellectual lyrics.

Arriving, information and getting around

There are three **train stations** – *Coimbra A, Coimbra B* and *Coimbra Parque*. Riverside **Coimbra A station** (often just "Coimbra" on timetables) is right at the heart of things; some of the express through trains call only at **Coimbra B**, 3km to the north, from where you can pick up a local train into Coimbra A. **Coimbra Parque** is for arrivals from and departures to Lousa, to the south (see p.158).

The main **bus station** is on Avenida Fernão de Magalhães, about fifteen minutes' walk from the centre. Almost all long-distance buses operate from here, as do international services to Spain, France and Germany. *Avic* buses, operating along the Costa de Prata to and from Praia da Mira, stop at a station in Rua João de Ruão, near the post office. *Avic* also operates buses to and from Condeixa-a-Nova (for Conimbriga), which leave from a stop just off Largo da Portagem. For more bus information, see "Listings", p.156.

Drivers should beware that driving into Coimbra can be a nightmare, since most of the central streets around Praça do Comércio are closed to cars. Use one of the signposted car parks and walk into town.

Information and getting around

For a free map, call in at the helpful **Turismo** (summer Mon–Fri 9am–8pm, Sat & Sun 9am–12.30pm & 2–5.30pm; winter Mon–Fri 9am–6pm, Sat & Sun 9am–12.30pm & 2–5.30pm; ☎039/330 19), on the triangular Largo da Portagem, facing the Ponte Santa Clara. There are also tourist offices on Praça Dom Dinis and Praça da República (open the same hours as the main office) and a small information kiosk on the platform of Coimbra B. You'll get most out of **walking** around central Coimbra; indeed, you'll have no choice given the complexity and inaccessibility of most of the hillside alleys and streets. Tickets for **town buses** (which include services out to the campsite and youth hostel) are sold at kiosks in Largo da Portagem and Praça da República; buying a book of ten tickets saves money. The best place to find a **taxi** is outside Coimbra A station.

Accommodation

Much of the city's **accommodation** is to be found within a short walk of Coimbra A station. The cheaper pensions are concentrated in Rua da Sota (left and immediately right out of the station) and the little streets off it: a central, if rather sleazy looking location. More expensive places line Avenida Fernão de Magalhães (left and immediately left out of the station), Avenida Emídio Navarro (directly ahead of the station) and Largo das Ameias, between the two.

Budget alternatives to the pensions and hotels listed below include a youth hostel and campsite. The **Pousada de Juventude**, at Rua Henriques Seco 14, above the Parque Santa Cruz (☎039/229 55), is a decent, if not overwelcoming, modern hostel: reception is open 9am–noon and 6pm–midnight. It's about twenty minutes' walk, or take buses #7, #8, #29 or #46 from Coimbra A. The well-shaded **campsite** is at the municipal sports complex (*Camping Municipal*; ☎039/71 29 97; open all year), and has the added attraction of the adjacent town swimming pool. Bus #5 runs there from Largo da Portagem, or, if you're coming from Lousa, you can get off at São José station, 250m from the campsite entrance.

Pensão Alentejana, Rua Henriques Seco 1 (☎039/259 24). Some way out of the centre, this old villa is near Praça da República and the youth hostel. All rooms have bath and the price includes breakfast. ④.

Hotel Almedina, Avda. Fernão de Magalhães 199 (☎039/291 61). New, functional and ugly, the rooms here lack charm but there's parking nearby, and it's handy for the bus station. There's a bar, too. ④.

Pensão Antunes, Rua Castro Matoso 8 (☎039/230 48). Quiet and good value – some rooms look across the river, and most are decently sized, with bathrooms. It's near the botanical garden, some way from the centre, though there are a couple of excellent bars nearby. ③.

Residencial Avenida, Avda. Emídio Navarro 37 (☎039/221 55). In a good position on the riverside, though not as comfortable as it looks and a little pricey. ④.

Hotel Bragança, Largo das Ameias 10 (☎039/221 71). An old hotel across the road from the train station. It looks a little grim but is attractive enough inside. ⑤.

Casa dos Quintais, at Assarfage, 6km south of Coimbra (☎039/43 83 05). Small *Turihab* house with a delightful garden and fine views of Coimbra. There are just three double rooms with a common lounge area; call ahead to reserve a room. ⑤.

Residencial Domus, Rua Adelino Veiga 62 (☎039/285 84). On a narrow street across from the train station, this homely place has rooms with bath and some very confused decor. ③.

Pensão Flor de Coimbra, Rua do Poço 5 (☎039/238 65). Off Rua da Sota, and close to the station, this is definitely nothing special, though it's among the cheapest in town. ②.

Residencial Internacional, Avda. Emídio Navarro 4 (☎039/255 03). Facing the river, this once-grand hotel has divided up its rooms, making them a bit on the small side. But it's a friendly place, and the rooms do at least have a bit of character. Rooms at the front can be noisy, though. ③.

Residencial Kanimambo, Avda. Fernão de Magalhães 484 (☎039/271 51). Upstairs in a new block, this is the best choice near the bus station. The energetic owner hails from Mozambique (the name means "thanks"). ③.

Residencial Larbelo, Largo da Portagem 33 (☎039/290 92). Right by the main Turismo; you can't miss the fancy lime green facade. It's clean, simply furnished and – for single travellers at least – rather overpriced, though handily located. All rooms have private shower. ③.

Residencial Lusa Atenas, Avda. Fernão de Magalhães 68 (☎039/264 12). Clean, spacious rooms, with private bath. Enthusiastic staff keep things running smoothly, though if the *residencial* is full they might try and put you in the annex at no.191, which is not as good. ③.

Residencial Moderna, Rua Adelino Veiga 49 (☎039/254 13). Dull but clean place on the same street as the *Domus* (but nearer Praça do Comércio). ④.

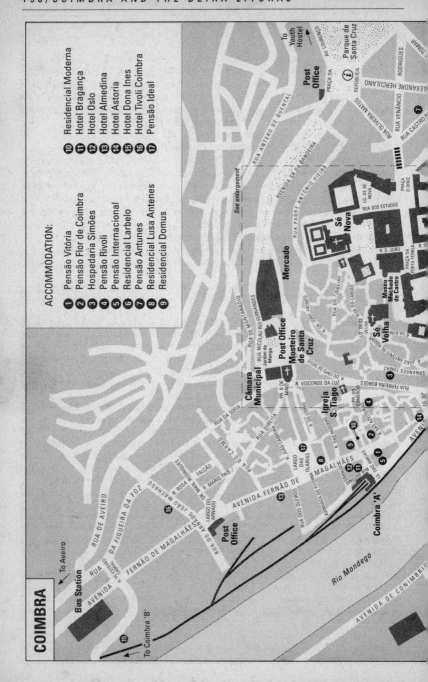

COIMBRA

ACCOMMODATION:

1. Pensão Vitória
2. Pensão Flor de Coimbra
3. Hospedaria Simões
4. Pensão Rivoli
5. Pensão Internacional
6. Residencial Larbelo
7. Pensão Antunes
8. Residencial Lusa Antenes
9. Residencial Domus
10. Residencial Moderna
11. Hotel Bragança
12. Hotel Oslo
13. Hotel Almedina
14. Hotel Astoria
15. Hotel Dona Ines
16. Hotel Tivoli Coimbra
17. Pensão Ideal

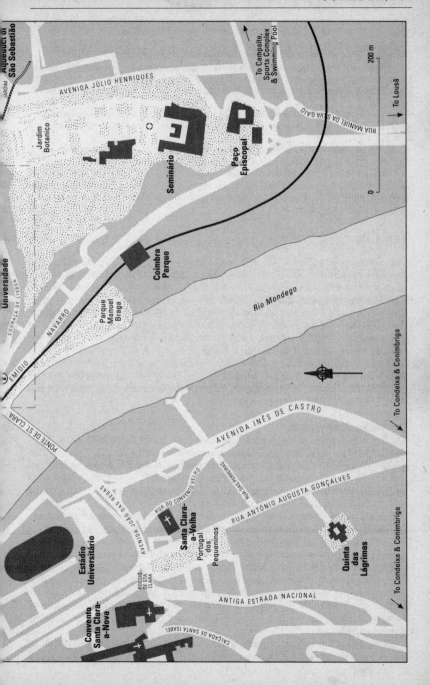

Hotel Oslo, Avda. Fernão de Magalhães 23 (☎039/290 71). Pleasant but rather pompous modern hotel with a restaurant and bar on the top floor. Despite the Scandinavian style, the rooms facing the street feature traditional Portuguese late-night noise. ⑤.

Pensão Rivoli, Praça do Comércio 27 (☎039/255 50). Excellent-value rooms (some with en-suite showers) in a splendid central, pedestrianised location. Rooms are tucked away at the back of the building, which makes them quiet; the only drawback is the less than reliable hot water. ③.

Hospedaria Simões, Rua Fernandes Tomás 69 (☎039/346 38). Simple, clean monastic lodgings above the Arco de Almedina. The ground-floor rooms are noisy but cheaper than in the rest of the building. ①.

Residencial Universal Avda. Emídio Navarro 47 (☎039/224 44). Comfortable and convenient, but overpriced. Its sister establishment, *Pensão Parque*, at no. 42 is currently closed for restoration, but has similar rooms and prices. ③.

Pensão Vitória, Rua da Sota 3–11 & 19 (☎039/240 49). Much the best of the cheap pensions on this street (the others are the *Lorvanese* and *Sota*), closest to the train station and with a good restaurant downstairs. ①.

The City

Old Coimbra straddles a hilly site, with the university crowning its summit, on the right bank of the Rio Mondego. Its slopes are a convoluted mass of ancient alleys around which the modern town has spread, and most of interest is concentrated on the hill or in the largely pedestriansed commercial centre at its foot. Chances are you'll get lost as soon as you start to climb past the remains of the city walls, but it's no problem – continue heading uphill to get to the **Velha Universidade** (old university); come downhill and eventually you'll strike the main shopping street, **Rua Ferreira Borges**, or the river. It's probably best to start your exploration of Coimbra with the Velha Universidade, not least because it's the easiest place to find, and from its balcony the city is laid out below you like a map. Before leaving, set your sights on your next destination and with luck you should be able to find it when you get down.

The Velha Universidade

The main buildings of the **Velha Universidade** (daily 9.30am–12.30pm & 2–5pm; 250$00 for university and library; another 250$00 for Sala dos Capelos) date from the sixteenth century when João III declared its establishment at Coimbra permanent. They're set around the **Patio das Escolas**, a courtyard dominated by the Baroque clocktower nicknamed *A Cabra* – the goat – and a statue of the portly João III.

The elaborate stairway to the right of the main court leads into the administrative quarters and the **Sala dos Capelos**; tickets are sold here for visits to each of the main sections of the university. The hall itself – hung with portraits of Portugal's kings – is used for conferring degrees and has a fine wood-panelled ceiling with gilded decoration in the Manueline style. The highlight of this part of the building, though, is the narrow catwalk around the outside walls. The central door off the courtyard leads past the **Capela**, not the finest of Coimbra's religious foundations but one of the most elaborate – covered with *azulejos* and intricate decoration including twisted, rope-like pillars, a frescoed ceiling, and a gaudy Baroque organ.

To the left is the famous **Library**, a Baroque fantasy presented to the faculty by João V in the early eighteenth century. Its rooms telescope into each other, focus-

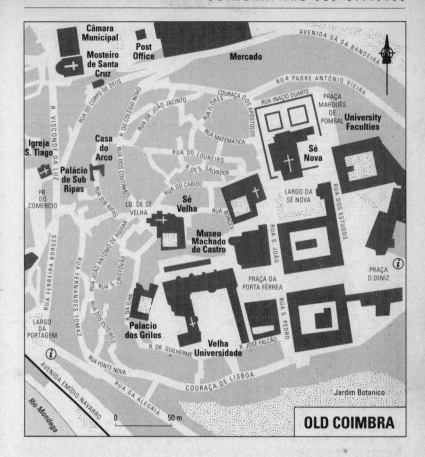

ing on the founder's portrait in a disconcertingly effective use of *trompe l'oeil*. The richness of it all is impressive, such as the expanse of cleverly marbled wood, gold leaf, tables inlaid with ebony, rosewood and jacaranda, Chinese-style lacquer work and carefully calculated frescoed ceilings. The most prized valuables, the rare and ancient books, are locked away out of sight and, impressive multilingual titles notwithstanding, the volumes on the shelves seem largely chosen for their aesthetic value; no one seems likely to disturb the careful arrangement by actually reading anything.

The Museu Machado de Castro

After the university a good first stop is at the **Museu Machado de Castro** (Tues–Sun 10am–1pm & 2.30–5pm; 200$00; free Sun morning, *ISIC* card holders free), just down from the unprepossessing Sé Nova (New Cathedral). The museum, named after an eighteenth-century sculptor, is housed in the former archbishop's palace, which would be worth visiting in its own right even if it were empty. As it is, it's positively stuffed with treasures: sculpture (especially a little medieval knight, riding home with his mace slung over his shoulder), paintings, furniture, and ceramics.

Underneath all this is the Roman **Cryptoportico**, a series of subterranean galleries probably used by the Romans as a granary and subsequently pressed into service for the foundations of the palace.

The Sé Velha

The **Sé Velha**, or Old Cathedral (daily 9.30am–12.30pm & 2–5.30pm), squats about halfway down the hill; an unmistakable fortress-like bulk. Started in 1162, it's one of the most important Romanesque buildings in Portugal, little altered and seemingly unbowed by the weight of the years. The one significant later addition – the Renaissance *Porta Especiosa* in the north wall – has, in contrast to the main structure, almost entirely crumbled away. Solid and square on the outside, the cathedral is also stolid and simple within, the decoration confined to a few giant conch shells holding holy water and some unobtrusive *azulejos* from Seville around the walls. The Gothic tombs of early bishops and the low-arched cloister (150$00) are equally restrained.

Mosteiro de Santa Cruz

Restraint and simplicity certainly aren't the chief qualities of the **Mosteiro de Santa Cruz** (daily 9am–12.30pm & 2–6pm; cloister 200$00), at the bottom of the hill past the old city gates. Although it was originally founded by São Teotónio and pre-dates even the cathedral, nothing remains that has not been substantially remodelled. Its exuberant facade and strange double doorway set the tone. In the early sixteenth century Coimbra was the base of a major sculptural school that included the French artists Nicolas Chanterene and Jean de Rouen (João de Ruão), as well as the two Manueline masters João de Castilho and Diogo de Boitaca, all of whom had a hand in rebuilding Santa Cruz.

These artists designed a variety of projects: **tombs** to house Portugal's first kings, Afonso Henriques and Sancho I; an elaborate **pulpit**; and most famously, the **Cloister of Silence**. It is here that the Manueline theme is at its clearest, with a series of airy arches decorated with bas-relief scenes from the life of Christ. From the cloister a staircase leads to the raised *coro*, above whose wooden benches is a frieze celebrating the nation's flourishing empire.

While at the monastery, try to set aside some time for the small **Jardim da Manga**, alongside. More cloister than garden, it was at one time surrounded by orange trees, and today still retains a cupola and fountain; there's a handy **café** nearby.

The Santa Clara convents

It was in Santa Cruz that the romantic history of Dom Pedro and Inês de Castro (see "Alcobaça", p.120) came to its ghoulish climax. Pedro, finally proclaimed king, had his lover exhumed and set up on a throne in the church, where his courtiers were forced to pay homage to the decomposing body.

Inês had originally lain in the **Convento de Santa Clara-a-Velha**, across the river, her tomb placed alongside the convent's founder and Coimbra's patron, the saint-queen Isabel. Isabel was married to Dom Dinis, whom she infuriated by constantly giving away his wealth to the poor. She performed one of her many miracles when, confronted by her irate husband as she smuggled out yet another cargo of gold, she claimed to be carrying only roses: when her bag was opened that was exactly its contents. The Gothic hall church she built was almost entirely covered by silt from the Mondego river, but the ruin – an amazing sight – is slowly being restored.

The two tombs have long since been moved away, Inês' to Alcobaça and Isabel's to the **Convento de Santa Clara-a-Nova** (daily 9am–12.30pm & 2–5.30pm), higher up the hill and safe from the shifting river. The new convent, built in 1650, doesn't have much of the charm of the old and the fact that the nuns' quarters now house a Portuguese army barracks doesn't help. Its two saving graces, which make the climb worthwhile, are **Isabel's tomb** – made of solid silver collected by the citizens of Coimbra – and the vast **cloister** financed by João V, a king whose devotion to nuns went beyond the normal bounds of spiritual comfort. The army's presence exerts itself in a small **military museum** (daily 10am–noon & 2–5pm; 100$00), displaying bits and bombs retrieved intact from World War II.

Portugal dos Pequeninos to the Jardim Botânico

Between the two convents extends the parkland site of **Portugal dos Pequeninos** (summer daily 9am–7pm; winter daily 9am–5.30pm; 350$00, under 10s, 100$00), a 1950s' themepark where scale models of many of the country's great buildings are interspersed with "typical" farm houses and sections on the overseas territories, heavy with the White Man's Burden. Historically and architecturally accurate it's not, but the place is great fun for kids who can clamber in and out of the miniature houses.

A short distance beyond is a somewhat more sombre little park, the **Quinta das Lágrimas** (Garden of Tears), in which, so legend has it, Inês de Castro was finally tracked down and murdered. Probably the most rewarding garden in Coimbra, though, is the **Jardim Botânico**, on the far side of the hill from *Portugal dos Pequeninos*. Founded in the eighteenth century, these botanical displays once enjoyed a worldwide reputation and, even if they've seen better days, it's still very pleasant to stroll among the formally laid out beds of plants from around the world. Nearby are impressive remains of the sixteenth-century **Aqueduto de São Sebastião**.

Eating, drinking and nightlife

The city's cheapest meals are to be found either in the pensions (like the *Vitória*); in the atmospheric little dives in a trio of tiny alleys – Beco do Forno, Beco dos Esteireiros, or Rua dos Gatos – between Largo da Portagem and Rua da Sota; or in the workers' canteens along Rua Direita. For more sophisticated meals, try one of the **restaurants** listed below.

At some stage of the day, you should visit one of the traditional **coffee houses** along Rua Ferreira Borges and Rua Visconde da Luz, filled with business types and package-laden shoppers. *Arcadia*, on Rua Ferreira Borges, is a favourite, easy to miss but just the place to while away a rainy morning. Praça da República, across town by the Parque de Santa Cruz, is also surrounded by cafés and **bars**, this time popular with students. In particular, look out for the *Associação Académica* on Rua Castro Matoso, open at lunchtime and until late in the evening for drinks and snacks.

Nightlife is less predictable, but you can occasionally find **fado sessions** taking place on the steps of the cathedral at about 11pm. The trendy *Café Santa Cruz*, on Praca 8 de Maio, and *Bar Diligência*, at Rua Nova 30, have regular nightly fado sessions. For up-to-the-minute news on concerts and events, it's best to talk to one of the students in the *Associaçao Acadêmica* (see above).

Restaurants

Dom Pedro, Avda. Emídio Navarro 58. On the river, the decor (including a fountain) is attractive and the waiters attentive, but the food can sometimes disappoint. Around 2000–3000$00.

Esplendoroso, Rua da Sota 29. Very good Chinese restauramnt patronised by locals and tourists alike. Around 1500$00 a head.

O Funchal, Rua das Azeiteiras 18. Just off Praça do Comércio, this reasonably priced place serves generous helpings of chicken or mutton stew and the like in agreeable rustic surroundings.

A Lanterna, Largo da Sota. Bar and disco on the ground floor open until 2am, and a more subdued restaurant on the first floor. A wide, and somewhat traditional, menu; up to 2000$00.

Trovador, Largo da Sé Velha 17. Next to the old cathedral, this is surprisingly good value – around 2000–3000$00. Or you can just drink on the balcony to the accompaniment of evening fado sessions.

Viela, Rua das Azeiteiras. Bright place with good food, overseen by a friendly proprietor. The *carne de porco* is delicious and a gluttonous bargain at 800$00.

Listings

Banks and exchange Banks are grouped along the avenidas west and east of Coimbra A station, Avda. Emídio Navarro and Avda. Fernão de Magalhães. The *Hotel Astoria,* Avda. Emídio Navarro 21 (close to Largo da Portagem), will change currency outside bank hours, as will *Hotel Tivoli*, Rua João Machedo.

Buses All long-distance and some local buses use the bus station at the top end of Avda. Fernão de Magalhães (information on ☎039/270 81). *AVIC*, Rua João de Ruão 18 (☎039/237 69), runs to the Costa de Prata resorts, Figueira da Foz and Aveiro and to Condeixa-a-Nova (for Conimbriga); *Moisés Correia de Oliveira*, Rua João Macheda 23 (☎039/282 63), runs to Montemor-o-Velho and other villages on or close to the Coimbra–Figueira da Foz road (N11) and direct to Figueira itself.

Crafts The *Torre de Anto* (Mon–Fri 9am–12.30pm & 2–5.30pm), at the bottom of the old town near the Arco de Almedina, houses a handicraft co-op with fine, well-priced goods. There are several other craft and antique shops around the Arco de Almedina.

Market The main food market is on Rua Nicolau Rui Fernandes, above the post office. On Saturday mornings, there's an open-air antiques market in Praça do Comércio.

Police Main HQ at Rua Nicolau Rui Fernandes, across from the post office (☎039/220 22).

Post office The main post office is on Avda. Fernão de Magalhães at Largo do Amado (Mon–Fri 8.30am–6.30pm, Sat 9am–12.30pm); other offices are on Rua Nicolau Rui Fernandes, across from the market, and on Praça da República.

Swimming pool The *Piscina Municipale* (summer only 10am–1pm & 2–7pm) is at the municipal sports-complex: take bus #5 from Largo da Portagem.

Telephones It's easiest to make international calls from the main post office or the branch across from the market.

Travel agencies *Abreu*, Rua da Sota 2 (☎039/270 11), and *Intervisa*, Avda. Fernão de Magalhães 11 (☎039/238 73), both sell international bus and flight tickets. Or try *Viagens Mondego*, Rua João de Ruão 16 (☎039/220 25).

Conimbriga

The ancient city of **CONIMBRIGA** (summer daily 10am–12.30pm & 2–6pm; winter closes at 5pm; 150$00), 16km southwest of Coimbra, is by far the most important Roman site in Portugal. It was almost certainly preceded by a substantial Celto-Iberian settlement, dating back to the Iron Age, but the excavated buildings nearly all belong to the latter days of the Roman Empire, from the second to the fourth century AD. Throughout this period Conimbriga was a major stopping point on the road from *Olisipo* (Lisbon) to *Bracara Augusta* (Braga). Although by no means the largest town in Roman Portugal, it has survived better than any other – principally because its inhabitants abandoned Conimbriga, apparently for the comparative safety of Coimbra, and never resettled it. That the city came to a violent end is clear from the powerful wall thrown up right through its heart; a wall thrown up so hurriedly and determinedly that it even cut houses in two.

It is the **wall**, with the **Roman road** leading up to and through it, that first strikes you. Little else, indeed, remains above ground level. In the urgency of its construction anything that came to hand was used and a close inspection of the wall reveals pillars, inscribed plaques and bricks thrown in among the rough stonework. Most of what has been excavated is in the immediate environs of the wall; the bulk of the city, still only part-excavated, lies in the ground beyond it.

What you can see is impressive enough, though. **Houses** with excellent mosaic floors, **pools** whose original fountains and water-ducts have been restored to working order, and a complex series of baths with their elaborate under-floor heating systems have been revealed. To make sense of it all, it's worth investing in the official guidebook at the entrance. In the summer you may find students on site to explain the finer points.

The **museum**, opposite the site entrance (daily except Mon; 150$00), displays fascinating finds from the dig, including bronze jewellery and coins, and fragments of statues. Around the back is an excellent **café** with views from its terrace down into the valley, whose steep sides were for many years Conimbriga's main defence.

Getting there: Condeixa-a-Nova

There's one daily **bus** direct to the site from Coimbra (leaving from Largo da Portagem at 9am); returning from the site at around 1pm (6pm at weekends).

Alternatively, you can take one of the hourly buses from Coimbra (again leaving from Largo da Portagem) to the small town of **CONDEIXA-A-NOVA**, half an hour's walk to the south of Conimbriga. Condeixa is the centre of the Beira's **hand-painted ceramics** industry and eight local factories are open for visits. It's a pleasant place in its own right, too, with several bars and cafés around the central square. Arriving in the early afternoon at Condeixa, you could walk to the site, spend a leisurely few hours there, and then catch the direct bus back to Coimbra.

Montemor-o-Velho

Thirty-two kilometres west of Coimbra, the **castle** at **MONTEMOR-O-VELHO** continues to brood over the flood plain of the Mondego. From the train, or driving along the N111, to Figueira da Foz (see p.166), its keep and crenellated silhouette rivals that of Óbidos, as does its early history. First the Romans, then the Moors, fortified this conspicuous rocky bluff; finally taken from the Moors at the end of the eleventh century, it became a favoured royal residence. It was here in 1355 that Dom Afonso IV met with his council to decide on the fate of Inês de Castro, and here, thirty years later, that João of Avis received the homage of the townspeople on his way to Coimbra to be acclaimed king Dom João I. Despite this royal attention, the town itself never prospered, and today there's little enough to see either inside the castle walls, though the views, naturally enough, are stunning. The sole attraction is the Manueline **Igreja de Santa Maria de Alcáçova**, said to have been designed by Diogo de Boitaca of Belém fame; it has a beautiful wooden ceiling, fine twisted columns and Moorish-style *azulejo* decoration.

There's no particular reason to stay, given the proximity of Coimbra or indeed Figueira da Foz, just 13km further west. But the *Residencial Abade*, Rua Combatentes da Grande Guerra 15 (☎039/68 94 58; ④), a beautiful, converted period town house, just up from the town hall, persuades some to stop. The **Turismo** in the town hall (Mon–Fri 9am–12.30pm & 2–5.30pm; ☎039/68 91 14) could doubtless drum up more reasons to hang around, though perhaps there's no better excuse than a **meal** at the *Restaurante Ramalhão*, Rua Tenente Valadim 24 (closed Sun evening, Mon, and Oct), where all the dishes – eel stew, chicken with rice, duck or rabbit – use ingredients grown, reared or caught around the town. You'll get away for 1500–3000$00 depending on your appetite.

Lousã and the Serra da Lousã

Another popular daytrip is to the medieval-looking village of **LOUSÃ**, 25km southeast of Coimbra, and its surrounding *serra* countryside. Going by train from Coimbra Parque station, sit on the right, facing the engine, for maximum scenic enjoyment of the lush, green valley. From the **station**, a road leads directly into Lousã in around ten minutes.

The village

Wandering along Lousa's main street, you pass a succession of intricately decorated **chapels** and **casas brasonadas** (heraldic mansions), while in the handsome town hall, a little museum doubles up as the **Turismo** (Mon–Fri 9am–12.30pm & 2–5.30pm; ☎039/99 35 02). Customarily helpful, this can supply you with maps of the Serra da Lousã, vital if you want to explore the range, and useful, too, for the walk up to Lousa's ruined **castle**. Following the path up from the village brings you out, after around 3km, at a spot where a tributary of the Mondego curls around a narrow gorge between two splendid wooded hills. On one site a miniature **castle**; on the other is a small hermitage dedicated to **Nossa Senhora da Piedade**. Pilgrims mingle with swimmers, who come to bathe in the chilly river pool between the two; picnickers abound, and there's a café. There are springs midway, bubbling up beautifully clear water that locals drive up to collect.

The village has two **pensions**, both pleasant and moderately priced: the *Residencial Martinho* in Rua Forças Armadas (☎039/99 13 97; ②) and *Pensão Bem Estar* on Avenida Coelho da Gama (☎039/99 14 45; ②). There is also a **campsite** (☎039/99 10 52; open all year). During your stay, don't forget to try the delicious **Licor Beirão** – herb-flavoured "firewater" – which is made locally from a secret recipe developed by a pharmacist from Lousã.

The Serra da Lousã

A hike to the top of the **Serra da Lousã** will reward you with stunning views and a sequence of eerie sights, in the range's abandoned villages. The most direct path runs through the woods above Lousã and is marked, rather intermittently, with yellow and white blazes on the trees.

There are six villages on the range, all of them deserted in the 1950s as a result of rural emigration. It's quite an unsettling experience to wander through the empty streets and into the open houses. In the first village you come to, **CASAL NOVO**, a few of the houses are being renovated as holiday homes and it's possible that you may be able to stay the night; check first with the Turismo in Lousã. Beyond Casal Novo is **TALASNAL**, where more houses are available to rent.

Upriver: Penacova and Lorvão

Northeast of Coimbra, the hilly, wooded valley of the **Rio Mondego** is a delight. The river is trailed by the minor N110 road (Mon–Fri 8 buses daily; fewer at weekends) and in summer it's possible to rent a **kayak** from Coimbra for the trip upriver to Penacova – or downriver if you do the trip in reverse (which is rather easier). For details of the kayaks, contact Coimbra Turismo, or the campsite at Penacova (see below); kayaks leave Coimbra at 10am from the Quinta das Lágrimas.

Penacova

PENACOVA, 22km northeast of Coimbra, is a small town set high above the river, with stunning views of the valley – spoiled only by the scars left by the motorway building taking place on the opposite hillside. There is little enough to the place itself – the appeal is in the river and woods around – though an oddity is the highly elaborate **toothpicks** on sale. These are hand-carved from willow by local women and are genuinely beautiful artefacts; the more delicate are like feathered darts. You can inspect these – buy them, too, if you wish – at the **Turismo** (Mon–Fri 9am–12.30pm & 2–5.30pm; ☎039/47 71 14) in the town hall.

If you fancied a night in these quiet surroundings, there are two **hotels**: the traditional *Pensão Avenida*, Avenida Abel Rodrigues da Costa (☎039/47 71 42; ①–②), and the newer, and beautifully furnished, *Residencial São João* (☎039/47 75 45; ③), downhill from the *Avenida*. The **campsite** (☎039/47 74 64; closed Jan) is on the opposite bank of the river and it's from here that *O Pioneiro do Mondego* arranges the downriver **kayak trips** to Coimbra (April to mid-Oct; 2000$00 per person), leaving Penacova at 11am. For meals, there's a superb **restaurant** – *Restaurante O Panorâmico* – with a view that excludes the motorway, and where a full meal goes for around 2000$00.

Lorvão

A strange side trip from Penacova, or Coimbra, could also be made to the **Convento de Lorvão**, at the village of **LORVÃO**. You'll need to take the bus to Rebordosa, 3km before Penacova, and then walk the remaining 5km to the convent. This very ancient complex was founded by Benedictines in the ninth century, predating the arrival of the Arabs, and later taken over by Cistercian nuns. The abbesses are buried horizontally in the graveyard; the lesser sisters are buried vertically, in twos and threes.

Most of what remains of the convent is the product of heavy restoration in the eighteenth century. If you ring for admission, you can visit the **church**, which displays the skull of an Arab king in its treasury, and with luck climb up to the *zimbório*, or domed roof, with its splendid views over the village. The visit, however, is a disturbing one, as Lorvão serves as a distressingly old-fashioned mental institution; the inhabitants lower paper cups down on pieces of string to visitors in the courtyard, to receive money or cigarettes.

The Buçaco Forest

The **Buçaco Forest** is something of a Portuguese icon. The country's most famous and most revered woods were a monastic domain throughout the Middle Ages, and the site in the Peninsular War of a battle that saw Napoleon's first significant defeat. Today, they are a little uncared for and overvisited, but remain an enjoyable spot for rambling.

Benedictine monks established a hermitage in the midst of Buçaco Forest as early as the sixth century, and the area remained in religious hands right up to the dissolution of the monasteries in 1834. The forest's great fame and beauty, though, came with the **Carmelite monks** who settled here in the seventeenth century, building the walls which still mark its boundary.

In 1643 Pope Urban VIII issued a papal bull threatening anyone who damaged the trees with excommunication; an earlier decree had already protected the monks' virtue by banning women from entering. The monks, meanwhile, were propagating the forest, introducing varieties new to Portugal from all over the world. Nowadays there are estimated to be over seven hundred different types of tree, but the most impressive remain some of the earliest – particularly the mighty Mexican Cedars.

From Coimbra it is easy enough to visit the forest as a daytrip, or en route to Viseu. All of the non-express buses from Coimbra to Viseu take a short detour from the spa town of **Luso**, through the forest, stopping at the old royal forest lodge, now the swanky *Hotel Palace do Buçaco*, and again by the **Portas da Rainha**. Alternatively, you could stay overnight in Luso itself, just a short walk from the forest, or, if you have money to burn, in the *Hotel Palace*.

Walks around the forest

Walks are laid out everywhere in Buçaco: along the **Vale dos Fetos** (Valley of Ferns) to the lake and cascading **Fonte Fria**, for example, or up Avenida dos Cedros to the **Porta da Coimbra**. But you can wander freely anywhere in the forest, and in many ways it's at its most attractive where it's wildest, away from the formal pathways.

The **Via Sacra**, lined with chapels in which terracotta figures depict the stages of Christ's journey carrying the cross to Calvary, leads from the *Hotel Palace* to the **Cruz Alta**, a giant cross at the summit of the hill. From here, as from the Porta da Coimbra, there are magnificent panoramas of the surrounding country. It's a lovely place, if not always the haven of peace the monks strove to create – at weekends and holidays the woods are packed with picnicking Portuguese.

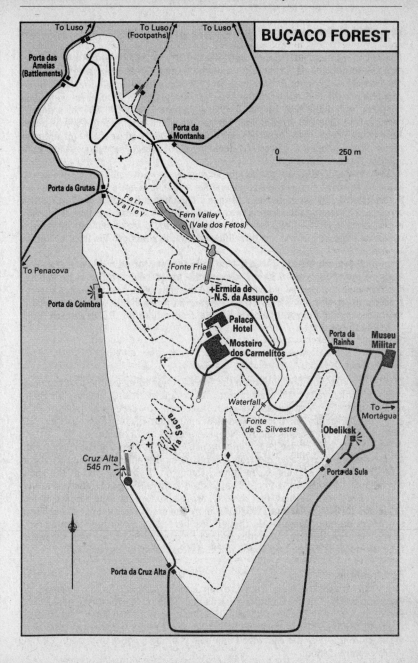

BUÇACO FOREST

To Luso

To Luso
(Footpaths)

To Luso

Porta das
Ameias
(Battlements)

Porta da
Montanha

0   250 m

Porta da Grutas

Fern
Valley

Fern Valley
(Vale dos Fetos)

Fonte Fria

To Penacova

+Ermida de
N.S. da Assunção

Porta da Coimbra

Palace
Hotel

Mosteiro
dos Carmelitos

Porta da
Rainha

Museu
Militar

Waterfall

To
Mortágua

Via Sacra

Fonte
de S. Silvestre

Obeliksk

Cruz Alta
545 m

Porta da Sula

Porta da Cruz Alta

The Hotel Palace and the Battle of Buçaco

The **Hotel Palace do Buçaco** (☎031/93 01 01; ⑦) stands at the heart of the forest, built on the site of the old Carmelite monastery as a summer retreat for the Portuguese monarchy. However, since it was only completed in 1907, three years before the declaration of the Republic, it saw little royal use. An enormous imitation Manueline construction, it charges upwards of 28,000$00 for a double room, but anyone can stroll in and have a drink or a meal. For 100$00, you can view what remains of the Mosteiro dos Carmelítas, and admire the Afonso Mucha prints or the sequence of *azulejos* depicting the Portuguese conquest of Ceuta and the Battle of Buçaco.

The **Battle of Buçaco** was fought largely on the ridge just above the forest, and it marked the first serious reverse suffered by Napoleon in his campaigns on the Peninsula. The French under Massena launched a frontal assault up the hill on virtually impregnable Anglo-Portuguese positions, sustaining massive losses in what for the Duke of Wellington amounted to little more than a delaying tactic, which he exploited in order to give himself time to retreat to his lines at Torres Vedras.

A small **Museu Militar** (March–Nov daily except Mon 9am–5.30pm, Dec–Feb daily except Mon 10am–5.30pm), outside the forest near the Portas da Rainha, contains maps, uniforms and weapons from the campaign. Just above it, a narrow road climbs to the obelisk raised as a memorial to the battle, with vistas inland right across to the distant Serra da Estrêla, from where the **Porta de Sul** leads back into the forest.

Luso

LUSO lies just 3km downhill from the forest. A spa town for the past hundred years or so, its waters still draw crowds of Portuguese, taking the cure for rheumatism and other complaints. As such places go, it's pretty enjoyable, with a series of elegant spa buildings, a wonderful nineteenth-century *Salão do Chá* – all white wicker, potted palms and Art Nouveau decor – and a casino.

Taking the waters can be fun, too. It costs under 1000$00 for the basics, with a full session of massage, electrolysis and other therapies priced up to about 5000$00; the only serious expenditure is incurred if you see one of the spa's consultants. There's also a fine, Olympic-sized **swimming pool**, attached to the *Grande Hotel das Termas* (see below), whose somewhat stiff admission fee (Mon–Fri 750$00, Sat & Sun 1100$00) is more than recompensed if you feel like a few hours basking. Most locals, though, are here to picnic in the surroundings, taking the opportunity to fill bottles and plastic containers for free with spa water from the outdoor **Fonte São João** (which also has its own *Casa do Chá*).

Practicalities

There are **buses** to Luso from the top end of Avenida Emídio Navarro in Coimbra; **trains** (on the Coimbra–Guarda line) stop on the northern outskirts of Luso. The helpful **Turismo** (Mon–Fri 9.30am–1pm & 2–6.30pm, Sat & Sun 10am–12.30pm & 2–6pm; ☎031/93 01 33), on Rua Emídio Navarro (an extension of the *avenida*), near the post office, can help you find a **room** or provide a list of local accommodation.

Budget **pension and hotel** choices include *Pensão Astória*, Avenida Emídio Navarro (☎031/93 91 82; ②), almost opposite the *Grande Hotel*, which has a certain faded charm; the *Pensão Portugal*, Rua Dr. Marinho Pimenta (☎031/93 91 58; ①), which is quite a climb from the town centre and fairly unprepossessing but undeniably value for money; and the friendly *Pensão Lusa*, Rua Costa Simões (☎031/93 92 07; ①), pleasantly situated above the town centre. Considerably more upmarket, but still reasonable value, is *Pensão Alegre*, Avenida Emídio Navarro (☎031/93 92 521; ④), at the top end of town, an impressive building full of nineteenth-century style which was once the residence of the Conde Graciosa. Top-of-the-range is, of course, the *Grande Hotel das Termas do Luso*, Rua dos Banhos (☎031/93 04 50; ⑤), an orange blancmange of a building in need of a lick of paint, though still splendidly furnished inside and surprisingly affordable; it's closed from mid-October to April.

Most of the pensions and hotels have **restaurants** attached, one of the best being that of the *Pensão Central* on Rua Emídio Navarro, which has a rooftop terrace and a good cook. The restaurant at the *Pensão Lusa* is good, too, while at the plain and popular *Cesteiro* on Rua Lúcio Abranches, towards the train station, you can eat well for under 2500$00.

The Dão Valley and the Serra do Caramulo

The route east from Luso to Caramulo leads through the **valley of the Rio Dão**. The road follows the valley assiduously, with the river on the right, and the **Serra do Caramulo** on the left, all the way to Tondela (and on to Viseu). This is the heart of the region where **Dão wines** – some of the country's finest and richest reds – are produced. Where they're not covered with vineyards, the slopes are thickly wooded with pine and eucalyptus trees, though all too often there are bare tracts where forest fires have raged.

To the north stretches the **Reserva Botânica do Cambarinho**, a vast area of great natural beauty. The central **Lafões valley**, again covered by vineyards, is reminiscent of the terraced hills of the Minho and Douro; other parts are densely wooded and dark, more like the Beiras countryside around Luso.

Getting to Caramulo: Tondela

Public transport links to Caramulo **from Luso**, involve something of a detour. You need first to take a bus to **TONDELA**, 40km to the northeast, where you should be able to pick up one of the two daily buses to Caramulo/Águeda, a majestic if rather bumpy drive straight across the centre of the Serra do Caramulo. Coming **from Coimbra**, there are three daily buses to Caramulo, via Águeda. If you're detained by choice or necessity in Tondela, the *Residencial Tondela de Severino Gonçalves* (☎032/822 411; ②) is excellent value, and there's a good restaurant, opposite, in the square.

A rather easier approach to Caramulo is **from Vouzela** (see below). On weekdays, two buses daily run between Vouzela and Varzielas, 4km north of Caramulo; from there you can either walk, hitch or, with luck, pick up a local bus connection. If you are approaching from the south, Vouzela is an obvious next destination after Caramulo.

The Serra do Caramulo

Of the three tiny villages at the heart of the mountain range, **CAMBARINHO**, and **ALCOFRA** are mostly of interest for their environs, full of rhododendrons, brightly coloured azaleas, and thick green shrubs growing wild on the hillside. If you feel like staying off the beaten track, both have **rooms** to rent, since the villagers have wised up to the financial advantages of taking an interest in tourism. Perhaps the best base, though, is the third village, Caramulo.

Caramulo

Tucked beneath the peaks of the high Beiras *serra*, **CARAMULO** is a great walking base – the loftiest Serra de Caramulo peak, **Caramulinho** (1062m), is less than an hour's hike away. It's also a very striking village, a diminutive, rather ghostlike place that seems an almost surreal setting for a couple of the country's finest museums.

Principal of these is the **Fundação Abel Lacerda**, a wonderfully jumbled art collection, with everything from primitive religious sculpture to sketches by the greatest modern masters – minor works by Picasso and Dalí among them. There's an exquisite series of sixteenth-century Tournai tapestries depicting the earliest Portuguese explorers in India, full of weird animals and natives based on obviously very garbled reports. A painting by British portraitist Graham Sutherland, donated to Portugal by the Queen, and symbolising the long alliance with Britain, is accompanied by its letter of authenticity from Buckingham Palace. Elsewhere there's a large *John the Baptist*, painted by Grão Vasco, and quantities of beautiful furniture and jewellery. Next door, and even more incongruous, is a collection of **vintage cars and motorcycles**, including a pack of chrome-plated American dream machines.

Caramulo has a fine **pension**, the *São Cristovão* (☎032/86 13 94; ③), though call first to ascertain whether this is open; it closes during the winter months. The only alternative is the six-bedroom **pousada**, *São Jerónimo* (☎032/86 12 91; ⑤), just outside the village – cheaper than most in the chain and with a swimming pool.

Along the Rio Vouga

The **Rio Vouga** is one of the most beautiful, somnolent rivers in Portugal, a fine route to follow if you feel like taking in a little of backwater Portugal. The old Vouga train line, along the river, has been discontinued, the service replaced by *CP* buses (on which rail passes are valid), which pick up and let down passengers at the disused train stations along the way. Coming from Coimbra or Aveiro, the place to leave the train for the bus is Albergaria-a-Velha, rather than Sernada (which involves some backtracking on the bus). Alternatively, you can approach from the south, from Luso or Caramulo, via Vouzela.

Vouzela

VOUZELA is a small provincial town with an almost palpable sense of civic pride. The locals – and the tourist office – boast of the peculiar sweet cakes, or *pasteis de*

Vouzela (only for the most sweet-toothed), richly flavoured traditional dishes like *Vitela de Lafões*, and the heady local *vinho Lafões* (similar to *vinho verde*). Vouzela also has its own local paper, which is quite a feat for a town with little over two thousand inhabitants.

The old centre is built around a sluggish stream, which serves as the backdrop to the main morning activity – washing clothes. Beneath a low **Romanesque bridge**, garments are spread to dry on the tall grass and soap suds run blue in the clear water. Houses clustered around the bridge are all of the small town manor-type, with granite steps and balconies and whitewashed plaster-work. Topping this scene, a viaduct gracefully loops its way across the roof tops, while beyond it the *serras* of Arada and Caramulo rise up, dark and green, to north and south.

Back along the lane towards the main through-road, the **Turismo** (daily 9am–12.30pm & 2–5pm; ☎032/77 15 15) is housed in a former prison in the small town square. On the floor above, there's a **museum** (free) offering insights into local preoccupations such as weaving, photography and painting. It's a small, rather odd collection, ranging through anthropological and historical exhibits, traditional craftwork and Romanesque fragments, to an array of old dolls. Nearby is the thirteenth-century parish church and the town **Pelourinho**, popularly referred to as the *forca* or scaffold, from its days as a site of executions during the Inquisition.

Practicalities

The *Casa de Camilinha* offers cheap food and is the local *RN* **bus** agent; buses arrive and depart from outside; *CP* buses leave from the old train station. Finding a **room** shouldn't be much of a problem at the *Pensão Marqués*, Rua A. Gouveia 76 (☎032/77 20 29; ②), which has a very good restaurant, popular with local families. Otherwise, try the **meals** at the *Restaurante O Chafariz* or *Restaurante Paulo*. There is a municipal **campsite** with fine views (☎032/77 18 47; open all year), 1km up the road towards **Senhora do Costelo** (a further 1.5km away), a low hill which is the location for much merrymaking and picnicking on the first Sunday after August 5.

There's another **feira** on May 14 when flowers are strewn in the streets in honour of **São Frágil**, and everyone drives up into the hills to witness the blossoming of the rare *loendreiros*, a kind of rhododendron peculiar to this area. Otherwise, note that there's a **street market** every first Wednesday in the month, a good time to be in town.

São Pedro do Sul

Eight kilometres northeast of Vouzela is **SÃO PEDRO DO SUL**, possibly the oldest spa in Portugal. It was a great favourite with the Romans, a popular haunt of Portuguese royalty – Dom Afonso Henriques is said to have bathed his wounded leg here after the battle at Badajoz – and remains among the grandest and most attractive in the country. The spa's position beside the Vouga, and the pine trees all around, certainly lends it charm, and it makes for a pleasant stop between buses or an afternoon trip from Vouzela. Under the central span of the bridge, a small island teems with swans and ducks, while downstream fishermen and young boys fool around on and in the water.

You can pick up bus connections in São Pedro to Viseu and Lamego, but if you plan to stay, you'd be wise to book ahead. The seven **hotels and pensions** are all on the expensive side and frequently full. Among the best options are the *Pensão Pedro* (☎032/71 12 44; ①), *Pensão Ultramarino* (☎032/72 30 11; ④) and *Hotel Vouga* (☎032/72 30 63; ④). In high season, these and the other places may insist on your paying for full board. There's a **campsite** (☎032/71 17 93; open all year) on the eastern outskirts of town.

Figueira da Foz

FIGUEIRA DA FOZ is one of the liveliest towns on the west coast, a major resort and deep-sea fishing port. Sited at the mouth of the Mondego, roughly equidistant from Lisbon and Porto and only an hour by train from Coimbra, it attracts people from all over the country. And with good reason, for Figueira has superb beaches and surf, and the town has a bubbling good humour about it, even when it's packed to the gills. Don't be put off by the somewhat industrial approach from the south: the centre of Figueira is atmospheric, reasonably affordable and as close to a typical Portuguese resort as you'll find.

The town and beaches

The town doesn't offer much in the way of sightseeing – the most impressive sights are the beaches – but there are a couple of places to look out for. The **museum** (daily except Mon 9am–12.30pm & 2–5pm; free), on Rua Calouste Gulbenkian, has an impressive archaeological section, as well as a large number of photographs of nineteenth-century bathing belles. The inside walls of the **Casa do Paço** (Mon–Fri 9.30am–12.30pm & 2–5pm; free), on the waterfront by the marina, are covered with thousands of Delft tiles, part of a ship's cargo which somehow got stranded in Figueira. Just along the river from the latter on Rua 5 de Outubro is the **market**, good for food and just about anything else you might need.

Figueira's **town beach** is enormous, not so much in length as in width: it's a good five-minute walk across the sand to the sea and unless you wear shoes or stay on the wooden walkways provided, the soles of your feet will have been burned long before you get there. If it's **surfing** you're after, then just step over the barrier to the next stretch of sands to the south, where fans gather to admire the breakers. By contrast, **Cabadelo beach**, behind the mole on the Mondego rivermouth's south bank, is small, sheltered and good for families – though to reach it you have to go right out through the town and over the bridge, a long, long hike. The only problem in recent years has been that of pollution; the European Blue Flag, denoting water acceptable to swim in, does not always fly over all of Coimbra's beaches. If this concerns you, an up-to-date appraisal of the water quality at each of the beaches is posted outside the Turismo – tests are carried out weekly in summer and monthly during the winter.

You can always have a dip instead in the fee-paying **swimming pool** on the north side of town: about a 15-minute walk along Avenida Dr. Manuel Gaspar de Lemos or, coming from the beach side, a ten-minute walk along Rua Alexandre Herculano.

Practicalities

It can take time to find a room in Figueira in high season, but with persistence you should be able to get something. There's certainly no lack of places to try. If you need help, the **Turismo** (June–Sept daily 9am–8pm; Oct–May Mon–Fri 9am–12.30pm & 2–5.30pm; ☎033/226 10), on the seafront Avenida 25 de Abril, by the *Hotel Atlântico*, is even more helpful than most. There's a second office (same hours; ☎033/330 19) in **Buarcos**, a fishing village at the northern end of the bay, which has become more or less part of Figueira – it's served by regular buses along the seafront. If you end up staying some way,out of town, you might want to **rent a bike** from *AFGA* at Rua Miguel Bombarda 79 (☎033/289 89), near the post office; it costs 1500$00 per day.

Accommodation

In high season, you might well be met at the train station by people offering **private rooms**, which – provided they're reasonably central – will be the best bargain in town. Otherwise, there are a couple of the cheaper pensions just in front of the train station on Rua Fernandes Tomás and Rua da República, but these are some way from the beach. It's better to keep walking next to the river until you see the sea, then cut down into the town centre. Along here both **Rua Bernardo Lopes** and **Rua da Liberdade** are lined with possibilities, though those nearer to the casino tend to be booked well in advance. You'll also find that **prices** – already comparatively high in Figueira – tend to shoot through the roof in summer; in July and August, you may well be asked to pay more than the price categories given below suggest.

There are three **campsites**. Best bet is probably the municipal campsite, *Camping Municipal de Figueria da Foz* (☎033/330 33; open all year), 2km inland – follow the signs – large and well-equipped, with a swimming pool and tennis courts. Across the river mouth, and close to Cabadelo beach, the *Foz do Mondego* site (☎033/314 96; closed mid-Dec to mid-Jan) is by far the cheapest in the area; while the *Orbitur* site (☎033/314 92) at Gala, 4km to the south, across the estuary, is easily the most expensive – though the ocean is much cleaner for swimming here.

Pensão Bela Figueira, Rua Miguel Bombarda 13 (☎033/22 72 28). Close to the main beach and town centre. Not remarkable in any way, but a reasonable fall-back. ③.

Residencial Bela Vista, Rua Joaquim Sotto-Mayor 6 (☎033/224 64). Out towards the municipal campsite, this is geared strictly towards long-stay holidaymakers, though you might find room at either end of the season; closed Oct–May. ③.

Pensão Central, Rua Bernardo Lopes 36 (☎033/223 08). Between the casino and the waterfront, this spacious *pensão* has high-ceilinged rooms with shower. Good value for money. ③.

Pensão Europa, Rua Cândido dos Reis 40 (☎033/222 65). Very central, near the casino and municipal gardens, and above a fish restaurant. Bare, adequate rooms with basin. ③.

Pensão Figueirense, Rua Direito do Monte (☎033/224 59). Large, light, airy rooms, three minutes' from the station. ③.

Hotel Hispânia, Rua Francisco António Dinis 61 (☎033/221 64). An old established hotel, well-placed for casino, waterfront and main beach; closed Nov–Feb. ④.

Residencial Pena Branca, Rua 5 de Outubro 42 (☎033/326 65). In Buarcos, near the post office and Turismo, and just outside the city wall. Splendid, high-quality set-up with private bathrooms, phone, TV, fridge and balcony; breakfast included. There's a good regional restaurant below. ④.

Hotel Wellington, Rua Dr. Calado 23–25 (☎033/267 67). One block from the beach, this is a genteel sort of place, though with rather small bedrooms. ④.

Eating

The centre of town is packed with **places to eat**, with any number of seafood restaurants offering *ementas turísticas* at reasonable prices. The following are some less obvious alternatives.

Restaurante Bela Figueira, Rua Miguel Bombarda 13. The *pensão*'s restaurant serves fine Indian-Portuguese food. Try the shrimp and rice curry – and eat on the terrace (where prices are slightly higher).

Restaurante Cacarola, Rua Cândido dos Reis. Highly recommended for fish.

Pizzaria Cristal, Rua Académico Zagalo 26–28a. Tasty pizzas and pasta dishes with some vegetarian options. Good house red wine, too.

Dory Negro, Largo Cavas Direitas 16. On the way to Buarcos, this is more expensive than most, but is the place to come for fish.

O Escondidinho, Rua Dr. F.A. Dinis 62. Hidden away (as the name suggests), this is worth seeking out for superb and inexpensive Goan food. Closed Mon.

Snack-Bar Marujo, Rua Dr. Calado 51a. Up the street from the Turismo – decent food in a warm atmosphere.

Café-Restaurante Nicola, Rua Bernardo Lopes 83. A bustling downtown rendezvous, big on snacks.

Restaurante Tahiti, Rua da Fonte 86. Just five minutes from the casino; good food and friendly staff.

Nightlife, entertainment and events

Nightlife, for the wealthy, centres on the **Casino** at Rua Dr. Calado 1 (open 3pm–3am; take your passport for entry), for which semi-formal dress – and an initial outlay on chips – is compulsory. The casino also houses a couple of **cinemas**, which generally have quite up-to-date releases. In the first couple of weeks of September the casino hosts an **International Film Festival** – a little uneven in its organisation, but always with a good selection of new films shown in their original language.

Alternatively, there are several central **discos**, longstanding favourites including *Disco Bergantim*, Rua Dr. Lopes Guimarães 28 (10.30pm–4am; 2000$00 minimum expenditure) and *Silver Spring*, Rua Maestro David de Sousa 42, which is smaller and more select but with similar prices and opening hours. The current locals' choice is *Discoteca Amnistia*, Avenida de Tavanede, near the train station and the bridge over the Mondego, or *Flashen,* a disco in Quiaios, 8km north of Figueira, hidden in the pine trees outside the village.

One of the best of the year's parties is **Saint John's Eve** (June 23/24) with bonfires on the beach and a "Holy Bathe" in the sea at dawn; while **bullfights** are often held during the sumer season.

North of Figueira: Praia de Mira

The coastline immediately **north of Figueira** is remarkable only for its air of total desertion. Beyond Buarcos, there's very little, and for long stretches hardly even a road. Off the main north–south road (N109) you can get to the coast at just three points before Aveiro: at **Quiaios**, **Tocha** and **Mira**, each with their respective beaches. Sadly, the wooded area inland from the dunes suffered badly in the fires of summer 1993; expect charred brush landscapes throughout the region.

Praia de Quiaios and Praia da Tocha

With a car you can find virtually empty beaches around either **QUIAIOS** or **TOCHA**, though the low-lying coastal plain offers no protection against the Atlantic winds. Six buses a day run up the N109, stopping at Tocha (21km from Figueira), from where you'll have to walk the 8km west to the coast. There isn't any accommodation once you get to either beach, other than the excellent **camp-sites** at Praia de Quiaios (☎033/91 04 99; June–Sept), which has its own swimming pool, and at Praia da Tocha (☎031/44 11 43; mid-June to Sept).

Praia de Mira

Set on a small lagoon – the southernmost point of a system of waterways and canals centered around Aveiro – **PRAIA DE MIRA** is the focus of increasing development. Seven kilometres west of the inland town of Mira, it is much more accessible than the beaches at Quiaias or Tocha, with half a dozen buses a day from either Figueira or Coimbra. You couldn't describe Praia de Mira as a beautiful place, despite its traditional wooden stilt-houses, but the beach that stretches around it is seemingly endless and backed by dunes: ideal if your sights extend no further than beach lounging and walks.

There are two official **campsites** a short way from the village – the municipal site (☎031/47 21 73; May–Sept) is closer and considerably cheaper, though less well-equipped, than the *Orbitur* site (☎031/45 15 25; open all year). There is also a new **youth hostel** and campsite (☎031/47 12 75; hostel open all year; campsite June–Sept), though this is at Barrinha de Mira, 2km from the beach. Alternatively pick from a couple of good **pensions**, the *Arco-Iris* (☎034/47 12 02; ③) and *Pensão do Mar* (☎031/47 11 44; ④; closed Feb–March), both overlooking the sea, or any number of places offering cheap, basic *dormidas* along the main street. For the latter, just ask in any bar.

TRADITIONAL FISHING METHODS

Praia de Mira is one of the very few places in Portugal where traditional fishing methods have just about survived. Even if it's too cold to swim, you can spend a day or two on the beach, watching the techniques in action.

There is no real harbour, so the few remaining fishing boats are hauled across the beach, rolled on small tree trunks. They have very high prows and slightly lower sterns, so that they can be launched through the crashing breakers. Once clear of the surf they head out a kilometre or two offshore, drop their nets, and then return – the nets are slowly trawled in, traditionally by teams of oxen marching up and down the beach, though nowadays more usually by tractors. This can take more than an hour and once the haul has come in the fish are taken out, sorted and auctioned there and then on the beach. It's a process that involves the whole village, either in the boats, driving the tractors, coiling ropes, or sorting the catch.

On a good day you can pick up a huge fish for virtually nothing and cook it yourself over a fire on the beach. Not surprisingly the local restaurants also have really good seafood, especially the thick, bouillabaisse-like soups and stews.

Aveiro and around

Like Figueira da Foz, **AVEIRO** is a sizeable resort, with a series of excellent beaches to north and south. However, it's also a place of some antiquity and of interest in its own right. It was a thriving port throughout the Middle Ages, up until the 1570s, when the mouth of the Vouga silted up, closing its harbour and creating vast fever-ridden marshes. Recovery only began in 1808 when a canal was cut through to the sea, re-opening the port and draining much of the water; only the shallow lagoons you see today were left. These form the backbone of a modern economy based on vast **salt-pans**, fishing and the collection of seaweed (*molico*) for fertiliser. The occasional pungent odour wafting across town, seemingly from the lagoon, is actually from the large paper factory nearby – one of Portugal's chief industries.

The town's big annual event is the **Festa da Ria**, celebrated in the last two weeks of August with boat races, folk-dances, and competitions for the best decorated *barcos moliceiro*, the flat-bottomed lagoon boats used to collect seaweed. The other major celebration is the **Festa de São Gonçalinho**, held in honour of the patron saint of fishermen and single women in the second week of January. Those who have made vows during the year, either for the safe return of a fisherman or for the finding of a husband, climb to the top of a chapel and throw down loaves of bread to the crowd below; the aim is to catch as much as possible.

The Town

In town, the only sight of real note is the fifteenth-century **Convento de Jesus**, in which has been installed a museum (Tues–Sun 10am–noon & 2–5pm), whose finest exhibits all relate to Santa Joana, a daughter of Afonso V who lived in the convent from 1475 until her death in 1489. She was barred from becoming a nun because of her royal station and her father's opposition, and was later beatified for her determination to escape from the material world (or perhaps simply from an unwelcome arranged marriage). Her tomb and chapel are strikingly beautiful, as is the convent itself, and there's a fine collection of art and sculpture – notably a series of seventeenth-century naive paintings depicting the saint's life.

Other than this, the main activity in town is hanging around in the **cafés**, watching life on the Ria: try some of the celebrated local sweets, especially *ovos moles*, candied egg yolks which come in little wooden barrels.

The lagoon and beaches

There's no beach in Aveiro itself but the coast to north and south is a more or less a continuous line of sand, cut off from the mainland for much of the way by the meandering **lagoon**. Roaming about this area, note that the pine forests shelter several military bases, so stick to the roads and don't camp outside official sites. During July and August, the Turismo organises **boat trips** around the Ria (usual departure 10am, returning at 5pm; 2000$00), giving you three hours in Torreira (see below), though at any time of year a group of people can rent a boat to tour the river; information, again, from the Turismo.

The most accessible points from Aveiro are **PRAIA DA BARRA**, at the mouth of the Vouga, and **COSTA NOVA**, just to its south, both of which are served by local buses. Neither, however, are anything more than functional daytrip beaches, enormously crowded on summer weekends. If you're headed south, Praia de Mira (see p.169) is a far more preferable place to stay.

Going **north** is rather more fun: take the bus to Forte de Barra (4km) and the ferry from there to **SÃO JACINTO**, a thriving little port with good swimming and dockside cafés. Beautiful it's not, but it is an atmospheric sort of place and backs onto an extensive **bird reserve**, where you can join a two-hour guided tour (assemble at 9–9.30am or 2–2.30pm; 200$00); for more information, consult Aveiro's Turismo or the reserve itself (☎034/33 12 82).

Buses run north from São Jacinto through **TORREIRA**, a lively little resort with several small pensions, a campsite, and a highly recommended restaurant, *Casa Passoiera*, on the main road. The buses at this point loop back round to Aveiro; to head onwards to Furadouro (see p.173) means making a detour through Ovar.

Practicalities

Aveiro is on the main Lisbon–Porto rail line, and **train** is by far the easiest way to arrive; most **buses** use the train station forecourt and adjacent streets as their terminus anyway. From the station, walk straight down the broad main street in front of you – Avenida Dr. Lourenço Peixinho – and you'll eventually hit the river and town centre.

The **Turismo**, in a beautiful Art Nouveau building at Rua João Mendonça 8 (June–Sept daily 9am–9pm; Oct–May Mon–Sat 9am–7pm; ☎034/236 80), by Praça Humberto Delgado, supplies free maps and can help with finding accommodation, but options are distinctly limited. If at all possible, book ahead at one of the places listed below.

Accommodation

Given the high price of accommodation in Aveiro, budget travellers will probably make straight for the **youth hostel** (☎034/38 19 35), on Rua das Pombas, south of Praça Humberto Delgado. Otherwise, the choice is staying in Aveiro itself or out of town, at one of the lagoon- or beach-resorts. The local **campsites** are also out of town, at São Jacinto: either *Orbitur São Jacinto* (☎034/482 84; mid-Jan to mid-Nov), a substantial site with good facilities, or the municipal site nearby (☎034/33 12 20; open all year). You'll find further campsites south of Aveiro, too: at Praia da Barra, Costa Nova and Praia da Vagueira.

AVEIRO

Adega Saõ Gonçalinho, Rua das Salinheiras 28. Cheapest rooms in town, with an annexe at Travessa do Arco 17. ②.

Hotel Arcada, Rua de Viana do Castelo 4 (☎034/230 01). Small, unexciting rooms, though pleasant enough staff. ④.

Residencial Beira, Rua José Estevão 18 (☎034/242 97). Clean, welcoming place just off the praça, with breakfast included. ③–④.

Pensão Residencial Estrela, Rua José Estevão 4 (☎034/238 18). Bare but comfortable rooms in an old, converted house. Some on the top floor are a bit pokey, though. ③.

Hotel Imperial, Rua Dr. Nascimento Leitão (☎034/221 41). Some way from the centre, but with fine views of the lagoon and the nearby Convento de Jesus; breakfast included (and there's a good restaurant, too). ⑤.

Pensão Palmeira, Rua da Palmeira 7–11 (☎034/225 21). In the old quarter, between the praça and the Canal de São Roque to the north. Bright rooms, some with shower or bath, and most with TV. ④.

Residencial Pomba Blanca, Rua Luís Gomes de Carvalho 23 (☎034/225 29). Very pleasant rooms in a gracious, quiet townhouse, near the station. ⑤.

Residencial Santa Joana, Avda. Dr. Lourenço Peixinho 227 (☎034/286 04). One block from the station. Modern and comfortable – all rooms have bath. ③.

OUT OF TOWN

Residencial Albertina, Praia da Torreira (☎034/483 06). A modern block at the beach, with colourful air-conditioned rooms and bar. ③.

Albergue A Mansão, Lugar do Celeiro, Bunheiro (☎034/460 00). A little inaccessible, though worth the effort if you have transport. The French proprietor and chef conjour up a friendly, almost Bohemian atmosphere; the price includes breakfast and evening meal; thoroughly recommended. ④.

Pensão A Marisqueira, Avda. João Corte Real, Gafanha da Nazaré (☎034/36 92 62). Between Praia de Barra and the Ria da Costa Nova, this is good value. ③.

Pensão Moliceiro, Avda. Hintze Ribeiro, between São Jacinto and Torreira (☎034/482 35). Decent enough place that usually has room to spare. ③.

Pousada da Ria, Bico do Muranzel, between São Jacinto and Torreira (☎034/483 32). Mid-priced *pousada*, most of whose 19 rooms have balconies on the water's edge, facing the lagoon. There's a swimming pool and tennis courts, too. ⑥.

Quinta do Paço da Ermida, 3km from Ilhavo, south and off the N109 to Vagos and Mira (☎034/32 24 96). A short distance from one of the lagoon arms, this magificent manor house belongs to the family of the founder of the Vista Alegre porcelain company – one of the oldest in Europe. ⑥.

Eating and drinking

Surprisingly, in a town with pretensions to being a resort, **restaurants** are few, far between, and often full. Good standbys are *El Mercantel*, just off the Rossio, the *Zico Snack Bar* on Rua José Estevão, and the *Sonatura* **vegetarian** restaurant (closes 8.30pm Mon–Fri, 3pm on Sat) across the canal from the Turismo. For slightly pricier meals, try *Centenário* on Largo do Mercado; *Alexandre 2*, at Cais do Alboi 14, with fine river views and meals for under 2000$00; or *Galo d'Ouro* at Travessa do Mercado 2. **Local specialties** include eels and shellfish from the lagoons and powerful *Bairrada* wine.

North: Ovar, Furadouro, Santa Maria de Feira and Arouca

OVAR, 25km north of Aveiro, is on the main train line to Porto. If you're lucky, there'll be a bus waiting to take you into the centre of Ovar; failing that, it's a fifteen-minute walk. The place is an attractive market town, with the asset of a fine beach at Furadouro, 4km walk (or local bus) away. In the main square is a helpful **Turismo** (July–Sept daily 9am–9pm, Oct–June daily 9.30am–12.30pm & 2.30–5.30pm; ☎056/57 22 15), and nearby is a surprisingly good **Museu Etnografica** (daily 10am–noon & 2–6pm), with an international collection of pottery, plus traditional clothing and the usual folklore displays. Perhaps more compellingly, while you're here try some of the local *pão-de-ló* sponge cake – every bit as good as it looks.

FURADOURO marks pretty much the northern extent of the system of waterways, and like its neighbours to the south boasts a long stretch of pine-backed dunes. There may be a few **rooms** available above the *Café Amadeu* and there's a **campsite** (☎056/59 14 71; open all year), too.

Santa Maria da Feira

At **SANTA MARIA DA FEIRA** (or, more simply, Feira), easily reached by bus from Aveiro or Espinho (see p.223), one of the most spectacular castles in Portugal – the **Castelo da Feira** – towers above the town, its skyline a fanciful array of domes. Its principal room is the Great Hall, a magnificent Moorish structure, while beyond the keep, a tunnel links the two parts of the castle in such a way that no direct or easy access can ever have been offered to intruders. In some of the walls you may notice a few stones marked with Roman inscriptions, and you can make out the familiar straight Roman road through the wooded hills above.

On the way down from the castle, you pass the grand **Convento de Loios** (now a conference centre), at the back of which you'll find an incredibly tacky cement grotto and garden of faked bridges and pebble-lined paths. This apart, there's not much else to the place, except during the annual **Festa das Fogaceiras** (Jan 20), when files of little girls parade through the town carrying castle-shaped *fogaça* cakes. It's a custom – much revived in recent years – which dates back to the plague of 1750 when the Infante Pedro made a *vota* to Santa Maria that cakes in the shape of his castle would be baked in thanksgiving for those who survived.

If you want to stay in Feira, the tumbledown *hospedaria* at Dr. Santos Carneiro 5 (①) offers exceptionally cheap **rooms**, though don't expect them to be enormously comfortable. Decent and inexpensive **meals** are to be had at the *Restaurante Parque*, which also has rooms to let.

Arouca

AROUCA, a further 20km or so east of Feira, is a small town overshadowed by a vast and magnificent **convent**. It makes a pleasant trip into the hills, with bus links from Oliveira de Azeméis on the main N1 highway – which, if you get stuck there overnight, has a couple of affordable pensions and a campsite. However, if you can make it, Arouca would be the better place to stay, with the very friendly *Pensão Alexandra* (①), on the main street, and pricier *Residencial São Pedro* (☎056/945 80; ④) further up the street. For meals, try *Cheiro Verde*, beneath the modern shopping complex.

The **Convento da Arouca** (Tues–Sun 9am–noon & 2–5pm; 200$00) was founded as early as 1091, though most surviving parts are from rather later medieval times. In the kitchen there are huge fireplaces along Alcobaça lines; the vast Baroque church holds richly carved choir stalls and a great organ with 1352 notes, played on rare occasions by one of the country's few experts; while off the central courtyard there's an airy Sala Capítula, where the abbesses once held court, lined with *azulejos*.

The convent peaked in importance when Queen Mafalda, of whose dowry it had formed a part, found her marriage to Dom Henrique I of Castille annulled and retired here to a life of religious contemplation. In the extensive **museum** upstairs, you can see some of Mafalda's most prized treasures, including an exquisite thirteenth-century silver diptych, along with a series of paintings by Josefa de Óbidos (see p.114) and Diogo Teixeira, the latter a notable Portuguese Primitivist. Four centuries after Mafalda's death, in 1792, villagers claimed to have witnessed her saving the convent from the ravages of a terrible fire. She was promptly exhumed and beatified.

During the **Festa de Nossa Senhora da Mó**, the whole town turns out for a picnic on the crown of the hill 8km east of the town. Everyone takes food and drink along, plays their own music and parades about enjoying themselves– it's a lot of fun.

The Serra da Arada: rocks that pop

If you have your own transport, consult the Turismo for details about places to visit in the **Serra da Arada**, beautiful nearby countryside, terraced like the Minho and abundantly littered with dolmens, crumbling villages and waterfalls with ancient bridges. While you're in the area, watch (or listen) for the local geological phenomenon of "jumping stones". A "parent" rock literally gives birth to a small disc of "baby" rock, flinging it into the world with an impressive pop.

travel details

Trains

Aveiro to Coimbra (at least hourly; 1hr); Espinho (half-hourly; 50min); Lisbon (11–13 daily; 2hr 40min–4hr 50min); Ovar (half-hourly; 30–40min); Porto (half-hourly; 50min–1hr 30min).

Coimbra to Aveiro (at least hourly; 1hr); Figueira da Foz (17 daily; 1hr 10min–2hr); Guarda (5 daily; 3hr–3hr 20min); Lisbon (15–16 daily; 1hr 10min–3hr 20min); Lousa (7–16 daily; 1hr); Luso-Buçaco (2–3 daily; 45min); Ovar (5 daily; 1hr 30min); Porto (12 daily; 1hr 20min–2hr).

Figueira da Foz to Caldas da Rainha (4 daily; 1hr 25min–2hr 25min); Coimbra (17 daily; 1hr 10min–2hr); Leiria (3–6 daily; 1hr 10min–1hr 15min); Lisbon (3 daily; 3hr 30min); Torres Vedras (3–5 daily; 2hr–3hr 25min).

Buses

All the major towns have an express service at least once a day, and there are frequent, regular bus services throughout the region. Where there's a range of journey times below, the quickest times are those of the express buses. International buses from Lisbon to Paris also pass through Coimbra, though seats must be reserved in advance.

Arganil to Coimbra (5 daily; 1hr).

Aveiro to Figueira da Foz (6 daily; 1hr 15min); Mira (6 daily; 35min).

Coimbra to Arganil (5 daily; 1hr); Braga (6–7 daily; 2hr 40min–3hr); Caramulo (3 daily; 2hr); Condeixa-a-Nova (hourly; 30min); Covilhã (4 daily; 3hr 25min); Fátima (4 daily; 1hr–1hr 25min); Figueira da Foz (10 daily; 1hr–1hr 45min); Guarda (4 daily; 2hr 40min); Leiria (4 daily; 1hr); Lisbon (16 daily; 2hr 20min); Mira (6 daily; 1hr 5min); Montemor-o-Velho (3–9 daily; 1hr 10min); Penacova (4–8 daily; 1hr); Porto (7 daily; 1hr 30min–2hr 45min); Santa Maria de Feira (2 daily; 2hr 45min); Tondela (5 daily; 1hr); Viseu (5 daily; 1hr 20min).

Figueira da Foz to Aveiro (6 daily; 1hr 15min); Coimbra (10 daily; 1hr–1hr 45min); Leiria (9 daily; 1hr 15min); Mira (6 daily; 40min); Tocha (6 daily; 30min).

Mira to Aveiro (6 daily; 35min); Coimbra (6 daily; 1hr 5min); Figueira da Foz (6 daily; 40min).

Penacova to Coimbra (4–8 daily; 1hr).

Santa Maria de Feira to Coimbra (2 daily; 2hr 45min).

São Pedro do Sul to Sernada do Vouga (9–10 daily; 1hr 45min) for trains to Aveiro and Espinho; Viseu (9–10 daily; 1hr).

Vouzela to Sernada do Vouga (9–10 daily; 1hr 35min) for trains to Aveiro and Espinho; Varzielas (Mon–Fri 2 daily; 30min); Viseu (9–10 daily; 1hr 10min).

CHAPTER FOUR

MOUNTAIN BEIRAS

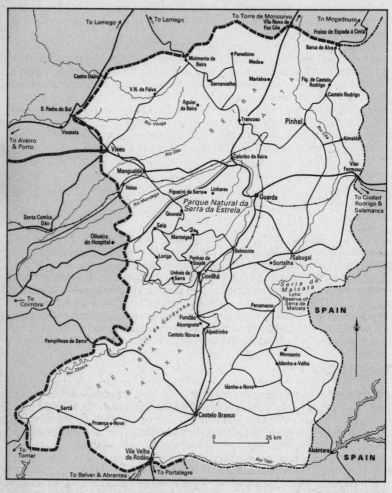

C omposed of two provinces, the **Beira Alta** (Upper) and **Beira Baixa** (Lower), the **Mountain Beiras** region features some of the least explored country in the Iberian peninsula. Arguably, it is also the most quintessentially Portuguese part of the country. Little touched by outside influence, it is historically the heart of **ancient Lusitânia** where Viriatus the Iberian rebel (a symbol of the spirit of independence in Neoclassical literature) made his last stand against the Romans. You'll see many signs of this patriotism in the fine old town of **Viseu**, in Beira Alta, where every other café or hotel is called the *Viriato* or *Lusitânia*. Here, too, in the heights of the stunningly beautiful **Parque Natural da Serra da Estrela**, lies the source of the **Rio Mondego**, that most Portuguese of rivers: the only one (bar the insignificant Zêzere) to run right to the sea without having its origins in Spain. The whole region in and around the park is excellent walking country, especially if you strike off from one of the two main routes which cross the range.

Guarda is perhaps the most fascinating of the Beira Alta towns. Though diminutive in size for somewhere of such renown, it has one of the highest locations of any provincial capital in the country and it bristles with life, especially on *feira* days. To the north and east stretch a whole series of high-sited castle-towns and some of the country's most remote villages. Over to the south lies the more sombre plain of the **Beira Baixa** with its capital at **Castelo Branco** and, its most obvious highlight, the ancient hilltop town of **Monsanto**.

The whole Mountain Beiras region is very little visited by tourists and travellers: if you've spent some days in the fleshpots of Lisbon, Porto, or the Algarve, you'll find a very different **atmosphere** here – and almost exclusively Portuguese company.

Viseu

From its high plateau, **VISEU** surveys the country around with the air of a feudal overlord; and indeed, this dignified little city is capital of all it can see. It's also a place of great antiquity. There was a Roman town here, and on the outskirts you can still make out the remains of an encampment claimed to be the site where Viriatus fought his final battle. In fact, it was almost certainly a Roman fortification and aside from a statue of Viriatus, there's not much there. The heart of the medieval city has changed little, though it's now approached through the broad avenues of a prosperous provincial centre. Parts of the walls survive and it's within their circuit, breached by two doughty gateways, that almost everything of interest lies.

The Old City

A good place to start looking around town are the old streets around the **Praça da Sé**. On the approach here, from central Rossío up through the Porta do Soar, or along the shop-lined Rua Dr. Luís Ferreira, a certain amount of restoration and "beautification" has been undertaken, but the jumble of alleys immediately behind the cathedral remains virtually untouched. You suddenly come upon sixteenth-century stone mansions proudly displaying their coat of arms in the middle of a street of crumbling shacks.

The cathedral square itself is lined with noble stone buildings, most striking of which is the white Baroque facade of the **Igreja da Misericórdia**. Silhouetted against a deep blue sky it looks like a film set without substance – you expect to walk around the back and find wooden props holding it up. There's some truth to that feeling: behind the symmetry of the facade, it's a very ordinary, rather dull church.

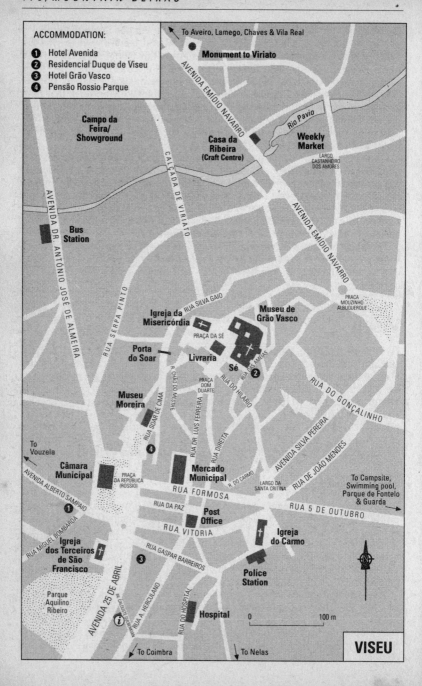

ACCOMMODATION:

1. Hotel Avenida
2. Residencial Duque de Viseu
3. Hotel Grão Vasco
4. Pensão Rossio Parque

To Aveiro, Lamego, Chaves & Vila Real

Monument to Viriato

AVENIDA EMIDIO NAVARRO

Campo da Feira/ Showground

Casa da Ribeira (Craft Centre)

Rio Pavio

Weekly Market

LARGO CASTANHEIRO DOS AMORES

CALÇADA DE VIRIATO

AVENIDA DR. ANTÓNIO JOSÉ DE ALMEIRA

Bus Station

AVENIDA EMIDIO NAVARRO

RUA SERPA PINTO

RUA SILVA GAIO

Igreja da Misericórdia

Museu de Grão Vasco

PRAÇA MOUZINHO ALBUQUERQUE

PRAÇA DA SÉ

Porta do Soar

Livraria

Sé

RUA DAS AMEIAS

RUA DO GONÇALINHO

R. CHÃO DO MESTRE

PRAÇA DOM DUARTE

RUA DO HILÁRIO

RUA SOAR DE CIMA

Museu Moreira

RUA DR. LUIS FERREIRA

RUA DIREITA

AVENIDA SILVA PEREIRA

RUA DE JOÃO MENDES

To Vouzela

Câmara Municipal

PRAÇA DA REPÚBLICA (ROSSIO)

Mercado Municipal

R. DO CARMO

LARGO DA SANTA CRITINA

To Campsite, Swimming pool, Parque de Fontelo & Guarda

AVENIDA ALBERTO SAMPAIO

RUA FORMOSA

RUA 5 DE OUTUBRO

RUA DA PAZ

Post Office

RUA VITORIA

RUA MIGUEL BOMBARDA

Igreja dos Terceiros de São Francisco

RUA GASPAR BARREIROS

Igreja do Carmo

AVENIDA 25 DE ABRIL

RUA A. HERCULANO

Police Station

Parque Aquilino Ribeiro

RUA DO HOSPITAL

Hospital

0   100 m

To Coimbra

To Nelas

VISEU

There's nothing two-dimensional, however, about the **Sé**, a weighty twin-towered Romanesque base on which a succession of later generations have made their mark. The granite frontage, remodelled in the seventeenth century, is stern and makes the church look smaller than it actually is – inside it opens out into a great hall with intricate vaulting, twisted and knotted to represent ropes. The cathedral's Renaissance **cloister**, of which you get no intimation from outside, is one of the most graceful in the country. The rooms of its upper level, looking out over the tangled roofs of the oldest part of the town, house the treasures of the cathedral's art collection, including naive sculptures, two thirteenth-century Limoges enamel coffers and a twelfth-century Bible.

Museu de Grão Vasco

The greatest treasure of Viseu is the **Museu de Grão Vasco** (Tues–Sun 10am–12.30pm & 2–5pm; 200$00; free at weekends), right next door to the cathedral in the Paço dos Três Escalões – once the Bishop's palace. **Vasco Fernandes** (known always as *Grão Vasco*, The Great Vasco) was the key figure in a school of painting which flourished at Viseu in the first half of the sixteenth century. The style of these "Portuguese primitives" is influenced heavily by Flemish masters and in particular Van Eyck, but certain aspects – the realism of portraiture and richness of colour – are distinctively their own. Vasco and his chief rival Gaspar Vaz have a fair claim to being two of the greatest artists Portugal has produced.

The museum is spread over three floors with the works of the Viseu School on the uppermost. The centrepiece of the collection is the masterly *Saint Peter on his Throne*, one of Grão Vasco's last works and painted, it is said, to rival Gaspar Vaz's treatment of the same theme for the church at São João de Tarouca (see p.238). It shows considerably more Renaissance influence than some of the earlier paintings but its Flemish roots are still evident, particularly in the intricately – and sometimes bizarrely – detailed background.

Other works attributed to Vasco include a *Calvary* and a *Pentecost*, but there's considerable argument over what is actually his. Several pictures are clearly the fruits of collaboration – most obviously the fourteen panels of the former cathedral altarpiece. These, now exhibited in a room of their own, depict the life of Christ and some sections are clearly better executed than others – notice *The Adoration of the Magi* in which Balthazar, traditionally an African king, is depicted as an Indian from newly discovered Brazil.

Practicalities

Viseu is no longer on the rail line, though *CP* **buses** still operate along the old routes, linking the town with Guarda, Coimbra and Lisbon on the Beira Alta line at Nelas (30min south of Viseu by bus) and with the Coimbra–Aveiro–Porto line at Sernada do Vouga (2hr 45min west of Viseu). Coming from Porto, an alternative approach is to take the Douro train line to Peso da Régua (2hr) and then the bus via Lamego, Castro Daire and Carvalhal (under 3hr). The **bus station** in Viseu is on Avenida António José de Almeida, a short walk from the centre.

The centre of town is marked by the **Praça da República**, an elongated square that is also known as **Rossío**. The **Turismo** (Mon–Fri 9am–12.30pm & 2.30–6pm, Sat & Sun 9.30am–12.30pm & 3–6pm; ☎032/42 20 14), just south of Rossío on Avenida Calouste Gulbenkian, is helpful for maps and information on the Beira Alta region as a whole.

Accommodation

Most of the places to stay are in the old quarter, though the cheaper pensions in Viseu seem uniformly poor. You might be better off with a **room** in a private house (try Rua Chão de Mestre 107) or above one of the cafés in Rua Direita, for which you'll pay around 3000$00. Among **hotels and pensions**, pick from the list below. There's a well-equipped *Orbitur* **campsite** (☎032/261 46; closed mid-Nov to mid-Jan) in the Parque do Fontelo, ten minutes' walk from Rossío. The campsite has no pool, but there's a municipal pool 500m away, on Avenida José Relvas.

> For an explanation of the **accommodation price codes**, see p.23

Hotel Avenida, Rua Miguel Bombarda 1 (☎032/42 34 32). A fairly pleasant hotel near the Parque Aquilino Ribeiro, with a few cheaper rooms. ④.

Pensão Bela Vista, Rua Alexandre Herculano 510 (☎032/42 20 26). Functional pension in a street near the Turismo; has some cheaper, bath-less rooms. ④.

Casa de Rebordinho, Rebordinho, 6km south on the N231 Nelas road (☎032/46 12 58). *Turihab* property: a converted seventeenth-century manor house on a farm estate. ⑤.

Residencial Dom Duarte, Rua Alexandre Herculano 214 (☎032/42 19 80). Pleasant *residencial*; all rooms with bath. ④.

Residencial Duque de Viseu, Rua das Ameias 22 (☎032/42 12 86). New hotel, right by the cathedral, where all the rooms but one have baths and air-conditioning. ④.

Hotel Grão Vasco, Rua Gaspar Barreiros (☎032/235 11). Viseu's finest – a grand central hotel with bar and swimming pool. Overpriced, though, for what you get. ⑥.

Pensão Rossio Parque, Praça da República 55 (☎032/42 20 85). An old hotel that has seen better days. Some rooms are small and cramped; others have no window or shower. ④.

Pensão Visiense, Avda. Alberto Sampaio 31 (☎032/42 19 00). Off the Rossío and with large clean rooms, despite the shabby appearance. ③.

Eating, drinking and festivals

Viseu is well-known for its gastronomic delights, and wherever you eat, or drink, bear in mind that locally produced **Dão wines**, especially the reds, are some of the best you'll find in the country. For provisions, there's a **weekly market** on Thursday, on the ring road by Largo Castanheiro dos Amores, and a weekday market in the **Mercado Municipal**, off Rua Formosa. The liveliest event is Viseu's **Feira de São Mateus** – held throughout September – which is largely an agricultural show, but is enlivened by occasional bullfights and folk-dance festivals. The showground is at the top end of Avenida António de Almeida, beyond the bus station and across the Rio Paiva. The **restaurants** listed below are all very popular locally; you may have to wait for a table.

O Cortiço, Rua São Hilário 43. In the old town, just down from the statue of Dom Duarte, this is popular enough for tables to be hard to get. Food and decor are *tipicos*, but the service can be a bit sullen. Around 2500$00 a head.

O Hilário, Rua São Hilário 35. Cheaper than *O Cortiço* and not bad for the money; try the *morcela casiera frita* (fried blood pudding).

Rodízio Real, Bairro Santa Eulália (☎032/42 22 32). Out in the suburbs, on the N2 (Coimbra direction), this specialises in Brazilian dishes, for which diners come from far afield; up to 3500$00.

Trave Negara, Rua dos Loureiros 40. Rustic charm doesn't come cheap here, but the food is traditional and well-prepared. The 4000$00 fixed-price menu is excellent value given the quality of the cooking.

East to Celorico

East of Viseu, the high and austere territory of the **Serra da Estrela** spreads itself as far as the eye can see: a landscape of great jagged boulders and rough, dry grass – often singed in patches by summer fires. The wilderness of the area, as so often in mountain regions, belies its inhabitants, who, though a little abrupt, have none of the suspicion of outsiders often encountered in Portuguese cities and coastal regions.

The E80 motorway from Aveiro cuts east through this region, skirting Viseu and running to Guarda. Train travellers first have to backtrack south to Nelas from Viseu in order to follow the **Beira Alta rail line** from Santa Comba Dão to Guarda. By road or rail, the only realistic stop before Guarda is at **Celorico da Beira**, which lies at a nexus of routes, with bus connections to Linhares (p.192), perhaps the most attractive of the *serra* villages.

Celorico da Beira

CELORICO DA BEIRA, 50km east of Viseu, is an unprepossessing town, its one claim to fame is as the birthplace of the aviator Sacadura Cabra. It is certainly not the most attractive *serra* base, split as it is by heavy traffic along the east–west road from Spain and the north–south route to Lisbon. It does, however, have a fine castle and, if you're passing through at the right time, it's the best place to pick up a pungent *queijo da serra*, the famed round cheese of the Serra da Estrela district.

The **Castelo** is open intermittently but if it's closed you can get the key from the *Câmara Municipal* (town hall). Put your trust in the rickety construction strung up outside the large keep and you can climb to impressive views from the roof. On a clear day the Sé and single tower of the castle at Guarda are both visible, while all around stretches the extraordinary wasteland of the mountains, split only by a small river and a couple of Portuguese highways.

The castle has a long military history, forming, together with Trancoso and Guarda, a triangle of defensive fortifications against Spain. In its day, a garrison of three hundred, well equipped with arms and an ample supply of food, were able to hold out with relative ease against border skirmishes. Only on one occasion, in 1198, did they have to call for assistance – which was provided by the stout men of nearby Linhares. **Feiras** – held on alternate Fridays for cheese, and on Tuesdays for the ordinary covered market – are the times to catch the town's cheery provinciality. You'll see some of the more rugged mountain types coming in to sell their *queijo da serra*. Market-going is their only form of income, enabling them to reinvest in their impoverished hilltop farms – the farmers of the Serra da Estrela must have the harshest agricultural lifestyle in Europe.

Practicalities

Celorico's **train station** is 4km north of town; bus connections are erratic, so you'll probably need to take a taxi (if you can find one), hitch or walk. It's more convenient to arrive by bus since many long-distance services pass through Celorico: there are bus stops along the town's main road, in front of the *Residencial Parque* and in front of the *Café Central*, where you can consult timetables. There is a small **Turismo** (Tues–Sat 10am–noon & 2–5.30pm; ☎071/721 09), on the edge of town on the Coimbra road.

The town's best and most central **pension** is the *Residencial Parque* (☎071/721 97; ③), located on the main road through town. There's also a new hotel on the road to the tourist office, the *Hotel Mira Serra* (☎071/726 04; ⑤), with magnificent views from some of the bedrooms. Beyond the tourist office, there are rooms above the *Nova Estrela* (☎071/722 42; ①), whose **restaurant** is excellent, as is the nearby *Boa Hora*. There is a possible freelance **campsite** by the Mondego river, near the station. Further upstream, off the Guarda road, 7km from town, there's an official **site** (☎071/726 45; open April–Sept) at Lajeosa do Mondego.

Guarda

GUARDA, at an altititude of over 1000m, is claimed by its inhabitants to be the highest city in Europe – an assertion to be taken with a modest pinch of salt. It is high enough, though, to be chilly and windswept all year round – and to offer endless views, especially to the east into Spain. The city was founded in 1197 by Dom Sancho I, to guard (as the name implies) his borders against both Moors and Spaniards. It was a heftily fortified place and, despite the fact that castle and walls have all but disappeared, it still has something of the grim air of a city permanently on a war footing. It is known in Portugal as the city of the four Fs: *Fria, Farta, Forte e Feia* – cold, rich, strong and ugly. However, in recent times, the city fathers – unhappy with the last of these – have launched a campaign to substitute either *Fiel* (loyal) or *Formosa* (beautiful). Oversensitive perhaps, though it is true to say that the centre of Guarda, with its arcaded streets and little *praças*, can be distinctly picturesque.

The Town

At the heart of it all is the dour grey **Sé**, one of those buildings which took so long to complete (1390–1540) that several architectural styles came and went during its construction, all of them incorporated somewhere into the work. The castellated main facade, with its two heavy octagonal towers, looks like the gateway of some particularly forbidding castle, but around the sides the design is lightened by flying buttresses, fantastic pinnacles, and grimacing gargoyles – the ones facing Spain are particularly mean-looking. Inside it's surprisingly long and lofty, with twisted pillars and vaulting influenced by the Manueline style of the later stages of its development. The huge carved stone **retábulo** is the work of João de Ruão, a leading figure in the sixteenth-century resurgence of Portuguese sculpture at Coimbra.

It's amazing, for a place of its size and importance, that, the cathedral aside, there's little else to see in Guarda. The displays of local archaeology, art and sculpture in the **Museu Regional** on Rua Alves Roçadas (Tues–Sun 10am–12.30pm & 2–5.30pm) are, frankly, dull; of the **castle**, on a bleak little hill nearby, only the plain square keep (the *Torre de Menagem*) survives, while the **walls** are recalled by just three surviving gates – the most impressive of them the **Torre dos Ferreiros** (Blacksmiths' Tower). The cobbled streets of the old town, though, are fascinating in themselves, and the tangled area between the other two portals – the **Porta da Estrela** and **Porta d'El Rei** – can have changed little in the past 400 years.

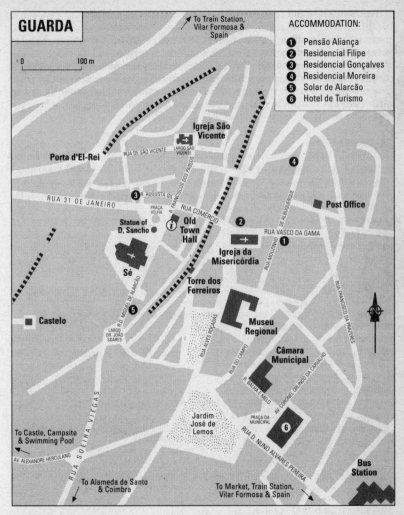

GUARDA

To Train Station, Vilar Formosa & Spain

ACCOMMODATION:
1. Pensão Aliança
2. Residencial Filipe
3. Residencial Gonçalves
4. Residencial Moreira
5. Solar de Alarcão
6. Hotel de Turismo

0   100 m

Igreja São Vicente

Porta d'El-Rei

RUA DE SÃO VICENTE   LARGO SÃO VICENTE

RUA 31 DE JANEIRO   R AUGUSTA GIL

R FRANCISCO DOS PASSOS

PRAÇA VELHA

RUA COMERCIO

Statue of D. Sancho

Old Town Hall

Igreja da Misericórdia

RUA VASCO DA GAMA

RUA MOLIZINHO DE ALBUQUERQUE

Post Office

Sé

Torre dos Ferreiros

R D MIGUEL DE ALARCÃO

Castelo

LARGO DR JOÃO SOARES

RUA ALVES ROÇADAS

Museu Regional

Câmara Municipal

RUA DO CAMPO

R BAIXA E MELO

RUA FRANCISCO DA PRAZERES

AV CORONEL ORLINDO DA CARVALHO

To Castle, Campsite & Swimming Pool

AV. ALEXANDRE HERCULANO

RUA SOEIRA VIEGAS

Jardim José de Lemos

PRAÇA DA MUNICIPAL

RUA D. NUNO ALVARES PEREIRA

Bus Station

To Alameda de Santo & Coimbra

To Market, Train Station, Vilar Formosa & Spain

Markets and festivals

Like Celorico, Guarda has a covered **market** (below the bus station), busiest on Saturdays, where you'll find delicious *queijo da serra*, the local mountain cheese. On the other side of town, below Avenida Monsenhor Mendes do Carmo, is the open-air *Feira Ao Ar Livre*, held every Wednesday. Numerous **festivals** also take place in the Guarda area. The biggest events are the great **Feiras** (June 24 and October 4), extended markets full of life and character. The **Festas da Cidade** (held during the summer months on different dates each year) are more cultural affairs with exhibitions and folk-dancing, a little too highly organised for their own good.

Practicalities

Guarda's **train station** is 3km north of the town centre but there's usually a bus to meet all the major arrivals. The **bus station**, alongside Rua D. Nuno Alvares Pereira, is fairly central and ultra-efficient; services are operated by a variety of companies to most of the neighbouring villages. The only problem is that many buses leave early in the morning and often don't return until late in the afternoon. The **Turismo** (Mon–Fri 9am–12.30pm & 2–5.30pm; ☎071/22 22 51), where you can buy a town map, is on the other side of Praça Velha.

Accommodation

You should have no trouble getting a room at one of the **pensions and hotels** detailed below. Guarda's *Orbitur* campsite (☎071/21 14 06; closed mid-Nov to mid-Jan) is in a park a short way from the castle; beware that in spring and autumn the nights can get extremely cold. The town's heated swimming pool is in the same park.

Pensão Aliança, Rua Vasco da Gama 8a (☎071/22 22 35). Just down the hill from the *Filipe*, this welcoming place has a street-level restaurant. ③.

Residêncial Filipe, Rua Vasco da Gama 9 (☎071/21 26 58). A more upmarket hotel, opposite the Misericórdia. Some of the rooms are a little cramped, but all have private facilities. ④.

Residencial Gonçalves, Rua Augusto Gil 17 (☎071/21 25 01). Centrally located, off the Praça de Camões; clean but a bit down-at-heel. ③.

Residencial Moreira, Rua Mouzinho de Albuquerque 47 (☎071/21 41 31). Central and good value; rooms with showers fall into the next price category. ②.

Solar de Alarcão, Rua Dom Miguel de Alarcão 25–27 (☎071/21 43 92). Magnificent granite manor house dating back to the seventeenth century, with lovely rooms. It's part of the *Turismo de Habitação* scheme. ④.

Hotel de Turismo, Praça da Municpão (☎071/22 33 66). Guarda's grandest, part of the *Best Western* chain: big and reasonably well run. ⑤.

Eating

Most of the town's **restaurants** are to be found in the area between the Porta da Estrela and the church of São Vicente.

Residencial Filipe, Rua Vasco da Gama 9. The first-floor dining room is a shade too florid, but there's no arguing with the generous portions of good food.

Restaurante A Fragata, Rua 31 de Janeiro 17. Near the cathedral and highly recommended, with a tourist menu at around 1300$00; otherwise meals from 2000$00.

Restaurante Julio, Rua Francisco de Passos 22. Recommended local restaurant.

Restaurante Paladium, Rua Francisco dos Prezeres 23. On the way to the bus station (and near *Hotel de Turismo*), this serves daytime snacks and a full menu in the evening. Meals for around 2000$00; the chicken dishes are especially good.

Solar da Beira, Rua Francisco de Passos 9. Highly recommended.

North of Guarda: the *planalto* of Beira Alta

North and east of Guarda stretches a rough and barren-looking territory known as the **Planalto** – tableland – of the Beira Alta. Villages here are spread far apart, with much of the land between untamed by agriculture, strewn with boulders and great slabs of granite. The odd valleys and settlements, though, are fertile, with a local speciality of roast or dried chestnuts. Once a replacement for potatoes, and now a dessert, they come from vast, shady trees growing beside the roads on almost any approach to a village.

In medieval times the region was home to prosperous Jewish settlements such as **Trancoso** and **Sernancelhe**, though their merchant trade went into decline from the Age of Discovery onwards as business moved to the coast. In successive centuries, the *planalto* towns became closely associated with Portuguese independence from Spain, and in particular with Afonso Henriques' march south down the length of the country. Their **castles** are today the highlight of the region. **Penedono**'s Castelo Roqueiro is especially magnificent, with seventeenth-century reconstructions on top of the original article. Spectacular, too, is the star-shaped fortress at **Almeida**, the site of the penultimate battle in the Peninsular Wars against Napoleon.

If you're travelling in **winter**, take to heart the proverb that *O frio almoça em Penedono, merenda em Trancoso e ceia na Guarda* – "The cold lunches in Penedono, takes tea in Trancoso and dines in Guarda" – and come suitably prepared. You will at least be rewarded by some extraordinary landscapes: the frost (*sincelo*) can have an extraordinary effect on the *planalto*, with massive trees linked by boughs of crystal and metre-long icicles hanging from every house.

Trancoso

TRANCOSO, still largely contained within a circuit of medieval walls, is an atmospheric little town, full of dark alleyways and interesting architectural details. The presence of a large **Jewish community** during the Middle Ages is apparent from the facades of the more ancient homes. Each has two doorways – one broad, for trade, on the ground floor, the other narrow and leading to the first floor for the family – and above the carefully crafted and bevelled stonework, some have clumsy crosses, inscribed by the Inquisition to indicate the family's conversion to Christianity. The most striking is the former **rabbi's house** (known as the *Casa do Gato Negro*), near the restaurant *São Marcos*, which is decorated with the Lion of Judea, the Gates of Jerusalem, and a figure of *Preguiça,* which some translate as "Sloth".

At the centre of the fortifications is the **castle**, with its squat, almost triangular, tower – a distinctive silhouette visible from many miles away. It's a Moorish

---

BANDARRA: A COBBLER'S PROPHECY

Trancoso takes its place in Portuguese history through the legend of one **Bandarra**, a shoemaker-prophet who lived in the town in the fifteenth century. The cobbler began his prophetic career with local horoscopes and poems, but after a while moved to more national matters – foretelling, among other things, the end of the Portuguese kingdom. In an age of religious dilemma and disillusionment with monarchical rule, his prophecies struck a chord – and attracted the attention of the authorities. Their circulation was banned and Bandarra condemned to death, a sentence commuted, after popular outcry, to a punishment of walking barefoot around town carrying a massive candle until it burned to the wick.

There the matter might have rested, but twenty years after Bandarrra's death, Dom Sebastião did indeed die – along with most of the Portuguese nobility, in the battle of Alcácer-Quibir – leaving no heir to the throne. Portugal subsequently lost independence to Spain, and Bandarra was pronounced the Nostradamus of his time.

design and a reminder of the Saracen domination of the town in the tenth century, following the town's conquest by al-Mansur. The following two centuries saw frequent siege and battle, with the fortress taken by Fernando Magno in 1033, and finally by Afonso Henriques and Egas Moniz in 1139 – an event celebrated by the construction of the monastery at São João de Tarouca (see p.238). Trancoso's later military history includes the usual invasions and billeting during fourteenth-century Castillian troublemaking and nineteenth-century Peninsular Warring – look out for a charming corner house with an open stone stairway on the central square, with the tellingly British name, *Quartel do General Beresforde*.

An equally historic site is the small **Chapel of São Bartolomeu**, on the side of the dusty avenue leading into town, where Dom Dinis married the twelve-year-old Isabel of Aragon. Outside the walls from here, in front of the law courts, **Celtic tombs** attest to very early origins indeed. Here and there a coffin-cover lies askew; the rest of the mound is a carved mass of human-shaped pits of varying sizes – one obviously for a child.

Practicalities

The town is 44km north of Guarda. **Buses** leave at 10am and 1pm for Pinhel; at 1.45pm for Penedono; and at 3.15pm for Pinhel, Almeida and Figueira de Castelo Rodrigo. Lamego-bound buses, via Sernancelhe, pass by several times a day – though you may have to go out to the main road to catch them. For Guarda and major towns en route to Lisbon there's a 5.15pm weekday service. There is a helpful **Turismo** (Mon–Sat 9am–12.30pm & 2–5.30pm; ☎071/911 47), opposite the Bartolomeu chapel.

The town offers a choice of three **pensions**. *Residencial Portas d'El Rei*, on the main street, Rua Fernandes Vaz (☎071/914 11; ②); the newer *Pensão Vale a Pena*, outside the walls near the hospital; (☎071/919 51; ③); and the *Residencial Dom Dinis* (☎071/915 25; ③), also outside the walls, next to the post office. For **eating**, the *Café Bandarra*, near the main gateway, serves a wide range of dishes; more expensive, but value for money, is the *Restaurante Muralhos* nearby.

Feiras are held on Fridays, with the big annual bash, the **Feira de São Bartolomeu**, on August 8–14, followed by the **Festa de Nossa Senhora da Fresta** on August 15.

Sernancelhe

Sited a couple of kilometres off the Guarda–Lamego road, 30km from Trancoso, **SERNANCELHE** is not exactly the hub of Beira Alta. But it's a quietly impressive place, in the manner of Trancoso, with further reminders of the area's Jewish past and a fine riverside location. The village is also said to have the *planalto*'s finest chestnuts. The trees, broad-boughed and spreading across the road, dominate the landscape as you approach the village. Carnivals, love songs, recipes, and folk tales all centre on the fruit, and if you coincide with the **Festa de Nossa Senhora de Ao Pé da Cruz** on May 1 you'll witness a curious mixture of religious devotion, springtime merrymaking, and, above all, folkloric superstition. There's a dance of the chestnuts, a blessing of the trees, and the exchange of handfuls of blossom by local lovers, aside from the religious procession.

Should you want to know more, the local cultural expert, Padre Cândido Azevedo, in his majestic, castle-like home overlooking the town, is more than pleased to greet a stranger. The walk up there takes you through the **old quar-**

ter of town, now only semi-populated, and coming alive only for the weekly Thursday market. Following the main road, you pass the **Igreja Matriz**, an attractive Romanesque church with a curious facade. Fixed into twin niches on either side of the main doorway, are six weathered apostles – said to be the only free-standing sculptures of the period in the whole of Portugal. Inside the church are several sixteenth-century panels, including a magnificent *John the Baptist*.

Wandering about this part of town you'll see the same features of medieval **Jewish settlement** as in Trancoso – canted lintels, pairs of granite doorways of unequal size, the occasional cross for the converted. Equally noticeable are a number of large **townhouses**, dating from the sixteenth and seventeenth centuries. One of these is the supposed birthplace of the Marquês de Pombal. Another was the birthplace of Padre João Rodrigues, an eminent and influential missionary who founded a series of mission houses in Japan in the sixteenth century. Japanese tourists often make the pilgrimage here to see the building.

Practicalities

The village has two **pensions**, the *Flora* (☎054/553 04; ②) and *Trasmontana* (☎054/552 44; ②) – both fairly basic and inexpensive. Alternatively, you could put a tent up by the river, just outside Sernancelhe, or at the **Barragem do Tavora**, a man-made barrage 3km to the north.

Buses on to Lamego (see p.234) leave from the N226, 4km away – there are four a day in the week, fewer at the weekend. There are also weekday buses to Penedono (1pm and 7pm) and Trancoso (9am).

Penedono

Twenty-five kilometres to the northeast, **PENEDONO** is another one-horse town, but again a likable place, and with a fantastic **Castelo Roquiero** – visible from miles around. The *roqueiro* ("rock") part of the name is due to the castle's emergence from its granite base, as if the rock and the walls were one and the same. From the top, as you might imagine, there are grand views, with the village's old quarter laid out below. Keys are available from the village shop, who will warn you to rattle the doors in order to get the pigeons in the air – rather than flying straight at your face.

The castle, in times of war, and the **Solar dos Freixos** (now the Town Hall), in times of peace, were supposed to have been home to Álvaro Gonçalves Coutinho, the legendary **King Magriço**, ("Lean One"), sung of in Camões' *Os Lusíadas*. It's a claim fought over fiercely with the inhabitants of Trancoso, who likewise are prepared to swear he is their man. Penedono, though, has the edge, as its name, from *pena* and *dono*, means literally "King of the Rock". According to Camões the *Magriço* led eleven other men to England to champion the cause of twelve noble English ladies, who found themselves without knights, and fought a joust on their behalf. Such tales of chivalry made them the subjects of numerous allegorical murals and panels of *azulejos* around the country.

Practicalities

The village has just one **pension**, the *Solneve* (☎054/542 39; ②), with friendly management, though you could also find **rooms** above the *Café Gomes* (☎054/542 35; ②) or the *Café Avenida* (☎054/544 73; ②) on the main road; the latter has excellent food. **Feiras** are held every other Wednesday, and there's a **Romaria** on September 15–16. **Buses** leave at 2pm and 7.30pm on weekdays for Vila Nova de Foz Côa, and at 8.30am for Trancoso (connection to Coimbra).

Pinhel

PINHEL is big enough to run both a wine cooperative (producing an excellent red) and a cake factory (churning out *cavaca* sweetmeats). But, digestibles apart, it's also small enough to have left the old centre of town virtually untouched. You can walk right around the crumbling castle walls, across the top of five intact archways, through vegetable plots and back gardens, and remain almost unaware of the twentieth century. From one corner of the **walls** you look down on the shell of a ruined **Romanesque church** – whose facade alone merits closer inspection. On another stretch you will discover what is left of the original **fortress**, a soaring tower with an intricately carved Manueline window.

Down in town further architectural pleasures are in store, with numerous **manor houses** clustered about magnificent gardens. One of the largest is now the **Câmara Municipal**, its hallway bedecked with a series of excellent photographs of local buildings of interest. An adjacent building houses the town **museum** (Mon–Fri 10am–noon & 2–6pm; free), with a pile of **Celtic tombstones** on the ground floor and, upstairs, remnants of a local convent.

Practicalities

Pinhel has two modest-priced **pensions**: the *Residencial Pinhelense* (☎071/423 73; ②), with superb meals, and the *Residencial Falcão* (☎071/430 04; ②). If you want to **camp**, no one seems to mind tents being pitched around the castle walls.

Buses leave from the centre of the municipal gardens – ask in the museum or nearby shop for schedules. One useful connection is the *Berrelhas* bus which you can flag down at about 4.15pm (every day) to go to Almeida or on to Figueira de Castelo Rodrigo. The local **Festa de Santo Antonio** is held on the Sunday closest to June 13.

Almeida

ALMEIDA is perhaps the most attractive of all the fortified border towns. A beautifully preserved eighteenth-century stronghold, its **walls** are in the form of a twelve-pointed star, with six bastions and six curtain walls within ravelins – a Dutch design, influenced by the French military architect Vauban. A four-kilometre walk around the walls takes in all the peaks and troughs, and if you stay overnight, there's an irresistible charm in watching the sun go down and the lights come on in a hundred tiny villages across the plateau of the Ribacôa. This was one of the last stretches of land to be recognised as officially Portuguese, in the Treaty of Alcañices with the Spanish in 1297, and it's easy to see why boundaries were not clearly staked out in the broad, flat terrain. Indeed, it was occasionally reoccupied by Spain, on the last occasion in 1762 – after which the present stronghold was completed.

Inevitably, perhaps, tourism has been catching up with the place. A new government *pousada* was completed in 1986 and subsequently the number of cafés in town has risen from three to a dozen or more. The locals seem grateful, if intrigued, by the phenomenon of rich tourists and foreign ministers turning up in their long-forgotten town, to fork out more than a villager's weekly earnings to ride in a souped-up pony cart, or to pay through the nose (relatively speaking) for a coffee on the balcony overlooking the humble dwellings below.

The fortifications and the Peninsular War

The arrival of the *pousada* neccessitated the hacking out of a new gateway in Almeida's **fortifications**, though the result isn't as outrageous as feared. However, the original two double gates are amongst the town's most splendid features – long shell-proof tunnels with emblazoned entrances and sizeable guard rooms. In the outer guard room of the São Francisco gateway is a small **museum** (daily 9am–noon & 2–5pm), while in the larger guard room a new **Turismo** office has been established.

Almeida played a key role in the Peninsular War (1807–14). In January 1808 it fell to the French General Junot whom Napoleon subsequently made Governor of Portugal. Later, when the French retreated unscathed following the infamous Convention of Sintra of August 1808, the Portuguese reoccupied the town. The Napoleonic army returned in 1810 and, en route to Buçaco and Torres Vedras, occupied Ciudad Rodrigo in Spain and besieged Almeida. The Luso-Britannic forces held out for seventeen days and then on July 26 the unforeseen happened. A leaky barrel of gunpowder, carried from the cathedral–castle in the centre of town to the *Praça Alta* (an artillery platform on the northern walls), left a fatal trail of powder. Once ignited, this began a fire which killed hundreds, and the survivors gave themselves up to the French. Wellington, on his victorious return from Torres Vedras, defeated the French on May 11, 1811, at Fuentes d'Onoro and subsequently took the fortress at Almeida with no bloodshed. The French army scuttled away during the night, probably making use of one of three *portas falsas* – narrow slits in the ramparts allowing for a discreet exit.

The **Casamatas** (daily 9am–noon & 2–5pm; tip expected), or barracks, is second in size only to Elvas, with a capacity for five thousand men and their supplies. Its layout explains how it withstood lengthy sieges. With its own water supply, rubbish chute, breathing holes, hidden escape routes, munitions chamber (there's a range of cannonballs and gunshot still on view), and dormitory space, the possibilities were limitless.

One other curiosity, opposite the new *pousada* gateway in the walls, is an inscription on the side of a small house declaring it to be the dumping ground for illegitimate children. At the **Rodo dos Eispostos** (literally the "Circle of the Deserted") anyone could come and claim an unwanted child for themselves – a convenient arrangement for both mother and foster parent.

Practicalities

For those with the means, the *Pousada Senhora das Neves* (☎071/542 83; ⑥) provides the town's finest **accommodation**. This apart, staying in the old town is a question of talking with the villagers. A good first stop is the *Casa da Amelinha*, where *ginginha* (morello cherry liqueur) has been served since 1883. It's an unofficial gathering place – ask here, or at any of the neighbouring cafés, whether there are any local rooms to let.

Otherwise, there are two new *residencials* by the crossroads outside the fort – *A Muralha* (☎071/543 57; ③) and *Morgado* (☎071/544 12; ③), alongside which, and under the same management, is the *Restaurante A Tertúlia*. A second good

restaurant, nearer town, is the *Restaurante Portas de Almeida*. A personal favourite of the **cafés** within the fort is the *Terreiro Velho*, near the market stalls; it stays open till 2am most nights and, despite fairly modern tastes in music, seems popular with old as well as young. For **camping**, make your way to the Rio Côa, a 2km stroll downhill on the Pinhel road. Just above the old Romanesque bridge (and its present-day equivalent), you'll find some idyllic spots.

If you can possibly do so, try to coincide with one of the twice-monthly **feiras** (on the 8th day and last Saturday) or – best of all – visit at Pentecost (fifty days after Easter) for the grand picnic at the **Convento da Barca**, a former Franciscan monastery, with a distinctively Tuscan feel about its domed chapel and setting. It's the only time you can visit the former monastery (now a private house), but at other times of the year you can sample the excellent red wine, apples, peaches, nuts and various other produce for which it is famous, at shops in town.

Buses on to the north come from Vilar Formoso twice on weekdays and go as far as Figueira de Castelo Rodrigo. One sure service to catch is the *Berrelhas* bus which passes through on the main road, 200 metres from the gates to Almeida at about 5pm every afternoon. Going south there are local services as far as Vilar Formoso (14km), which has trains to Guarda or Spain, and three daily buses to Sabugal and Castelo Branco.

The Serra da Estrela

The peaks of the **Serra da Estrela** – the highest mountains in Portugal and the last of the four central Iberian *serras* – rise to the southwest of Guarda. The range is basically a high plateau cut by valleys, from within which emanate two of Portugal's greatest **rivers**: the Rio Mondego, the longest Portuguese river with its source in Portugal itself, flows north to Celorico da Beira before swinging southwest to Coimbra and the sea at Figueira da Foz; while the Rio Zêzere flows southwest from near Guarda until it joins the Rio Tejo (Tagus) at Constância. Over the years the *serra* landscape has changed. Once, farmers lived in stone houses with straw roofs, dotted across the peaks and valleys, though now they have moved to more modern dwellings on the valley floor. Originally, too, the whole area was heavily forested, but these days the pines are widely cultivated for timber and shepherds now graze their sheep on the higher ground. Lower down, where the land is more fertile, rye is grown.

For visitors, most of the interest is in the mountain region known as the **Parque Natural da Serra da Estrela**, established in 1976 to preserve the rural character of the *serra* villages and landscape. In 1990, all land over 1200 metres was designated "protected countryside", which means in effect that you're not allowed to camp, light fires or pick flowers – though there are three major (and several minor) **trails** through the park, which take in various authorised camp-sites and villages with accommodation and other facilities. The best time to walk the trails is from May to October; some of them are featured on p.197.

Your **approach** to the park will depend on how much you plan to see of the higher ground, and whether or not you have your own transport. Public transport into the area is erratic at the best of times, though a little easier in winter when Penhas de Saúde has Portugal's only **skiing** facilities.

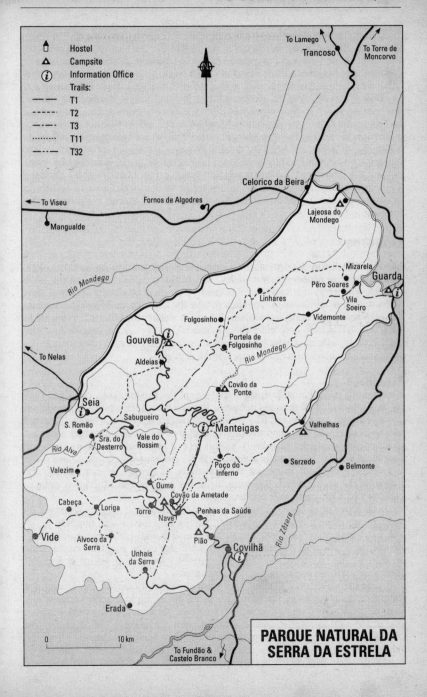

PARQUE NATURAL DA
SERRA DA ESTRELA

From the west and north, you can follow the N17 down from Celorico da Beira, branching off on minor roads to enter the park at the quirky village of **Linhares**, or via the larger (and less interesting) towns of **Gouveia** and **Seia**. Alternatively, from the east and south, the railway and N18 road (between Guarda and Castelo Branco) skirt the eastern slopes, with access to the park from **Belmonte** and **Covilhã**. If you're intent on serious hiking, the best base is **Penhas da Saúde**, just northwest of Covilhã, which has the region's only youth hostel, from where there's access to the valleys north to **Manteigas** or south to **Unhais da Serra**.

For specific details about the *parque natural*, there are **information offices** in Manteigas, Gouveia and Seia; the details are given in the relevant sections below. At each, you'll be able to buy several useful English-language **guidebooks**, invaluable if you intend to delve into the region in any depth: *Discovering the Region of the Serra da Estrela* describes the hiking trails, while *Estrela: uma visão natural* (a natural approach), details all the major habitats and species contained within the park.

Linhares

LINHARES, 20km southwest of Celorico da Beira, perches on a sunny slope overlooking the Mondego river valley, one of the most accessible of the *serra* villages, with a trio of attractions in its castle, a series of troglodyte-like dwellings, and a stretch of Roman road. To reach it, take the Celorico da Beira–Gouveia **bus** and stop at Carrapichana, from where it's a 2km walk to the village. If you want to **stay**, ask at Linares' only café, the *Linharense*, in the central square near the church. They will know who has a spare room or where best to pitch your tent – most probably above the village near a football pitch.

The village
Barely distinguishable at first, the lofty keep of the **Castelo** soon rises into reality, in command of all that lies before it. It dates from 1169 when Linhares, then more of a town, was claimed for Portugal. Afonso Henriques realised its potential as a defensive post, and soon the men of Linhares were trained up and equipped to carry out such feats of bravery as the rescue of Celorico da Beira from the Spaniards in 1198. In the walls are traces of the *cisternas* which would have given the village a constant supply of water at times of siege. You can still see the course of the spring which now runs along the gully beneath the great slabs of rock on which the castle was constructed.

If you arrive in Linhares in the early morning the village appears deserted, its only sounds of life the animals grunting and kicking their stable doors to be let out. Later in the day you'll see the donkeys being brought in from the fields and, depending on the time of year, seeds laid out to dry in the sun, wine casks being washed for the next year's vintage and, whatever the season, village gossips on their doorsteps, keen as ever to meet a stranger.

A little-known secret of the village's **church** is that it contains three paintings almost certainly executed by **Grão Vasco** and belonging to a larger series which is now lost. Propped up behind vulgar wooden statues and, in one case, stuck in one of the side aisles, the panels, depicting the *Adoration of the Magi, Descent from the Cross* and *Annunciation*, shine out in the obscurity. They reveal all the qualities of the great painter – his skill as a portraitist and his deft handling of tone and colour, particularly in the depiction of clothing and folds of material.

The Roman Road

Near the schoolhouse in Linhares a path branches off the road toward Figueiró da Serra. Following it, you'll soon realise that you are walking along an old **Roman road** – part of the one which ran to Braga – with heavy slabs of rock for paving stones looking like something out of an Asterix cartoon. The walk is a beauty, the hedgerows lined with flowers in the spring and blackberries in the autumn.

Gouveia

Another 20km southwest by road, **GOUVEIA** has lost the rural *serra* feel that once constituted its charm, as it has developed into a fair-sized provincial town. However, it has a Thursday market that's worth coinciding with, as well as an information centre for the *parque natural*.

Incongruously, it also has a modern art museum, above the Turismo (see below), the **Museu de Abel Manta** (daily 10am–12.30pm & 2–5.30pm), with a broad selection of contemporary Portuguese pictures all donated by Gouveian-born artist Abel Manta (1888–1982). There's a small room dedicated to the man himself, a figure of some stature who frequented groups which included Amadeo de Sousa Cardoso (see "Amarante", p.229) and Almada Negreiros (see the "Museu da Cidade" in Lisbon) – some of whose works are also here and who represented Portugal in the Venice Biennale. This selection of Manta's work features only one outstanding picture, but the collection as a whole is enjoyable.

Portugal's sense of heraldry comes out in manor houses of every shape and size, where sets of arms are tacked up over doorways, on cornices, beneath the corners of the roof, and any other empty space. Gouveia boasts several examples, the finest of which is the **Câmara Municipal**. This hosts open-air concerts in its courtyard during the summer months, but you are generally free to walk in.

Finally, you may have noticed a **statue** of a shepherd with his dog, at the entrance to the town, which is proudly illuminated at night. Though not perhaps the finest piece of sculpture, it is significant for what it represents. The people in the hills around here live a harsh and impoverished existence and have, as the Portuguese put it, "an unlimited capacity for suffering". There is never a break in the agricultural year, for when the summer is over and the harvest is stored away it is time to begin the cheesemaking, an activity which brings in their only serious income. The shepherd's friend in this harsh lifestyle is his dog, the *Cão da Serra da Estrela* – a fearsome looking breed said to be cross-bred from wolves.

Practicalities

Arriving by bus, walk up from the bridge (where you're dropped), veer right and you'll soon come across the **Turismo** (Mon–Sat 9.30am–12.30pm & 2–6pm; ☎038/421 85), established along with the municipal library in the basement of a *casa brasonada*. They hand out maps of the town and will point walkers towards the **information centre** of the *Parque Natural de Serra da Estrela*, at Rua dos Bombeiros Voluntários 8 (Mon–Sat 9am–12.30pm & 2–5.30pm; ☎038/424 11), which has further maps and leaflets on the area. For a hiking route in the park that passes through Gouveia, see "Hiking in the Parque Natural" on p.197.

Gouveia offers half a dozen **accommodation** possibilities, including the *Café Cruzeiro*, Avenida 25 de Abril (☎038/424 98; ①), on the way up to the Câmara Municipal; pleasant and inexpensive rooms above the café. *Pensão Estrela do*

Parque, Avenida da República 36 (☎038/421 71; ③), is a dusty old hotel with modern prices, but features a **restaurant** with something of a reputation. The town's most upmarket option is the *Hotel de Gouveia*, Avenida 1º de Maio (☎038/ 49 10 10; ④), with decent if not very characterful rooms. The local **campsite** (☎038/49 10 08) is at Curral do Negro, around 3km from the centre of town; to get there, turn right immediately after the Câmara Municipal, then right again, before finally forking to the left for 2km.

Seia and Sabugeiro

Cut out **SEIA** from your itinerary and you would miss very little, but it can be, like Gouveia, a useful jumping-off point, providing bus connections to the Serra da Lousã (see "Beira Litoral", p.158) and access to the Estrela *parque natural*. If you decide to stay, there are three rather upmarket **hotels**: the excellent *Hotel Camelo*, Rua 1º de Maio 16 (☎038/225 55; ④); the *Estalagem de Seia*, Avda. Dr. Afonso Costa (☎038/25 86 66; ④); and the *Albergaria Senhora do Espinheiro*, Lugar do Espinheiro (☎038/220 73; ④).

With enough time, or transport, however, it's better to press on into the park, after first visiting the **information centre** at Praça da República 28 (Mon–Sat 9am–12.30pm & 2–5.30pm; ☎038/255 06). If you don't have the time for an extended trip, you can always make a fleeting visit to **SABUGUEIRO**, 10km east of Seia, said to be Portugal's highest village. Here, there are three small country houses where you can stay: the *Casa do Cruzeiro*, *Casa Nova* and *Casa da Sofia* (all on ☎038/228 25; ⑤). As well as making a good base for walking, you'll also have the chance to see rye bread, local spice sausage and Estrela cheese being made here.

From Sabugeiro you can continue southeast on the N339 to Penhas da Saúde and Covilhã; or take the minor road northeast to the N232, which runs from Gouveia to Manteigas, Valhelhas and Belmonte – for all of which, see below. There is no regular transport on these routes, but you can usually make do with a mix of walking and hitching. Alternatively, two daily buses cover the southern route to Covilhã, looping around the fringes of the park, via the little spa-village of Unhais da Serra on the N230.

Belmonte

Twenty kilometres south of Guarda, **BELMONTE** was the birthplace of Pedro Álvares Cabral, the discoverer of Brazil, and is a village of considerable charm, commanded by a heavily restored thirteenth-century **castle**. It is a pleasant stopping-off point on the route south, and for those with transport, provides access to the Estrela *parque natural* as well as to the barren and medieval region of the Beira Baixa (covered later in this chapter). There are limited bus services, running to the two main Beira Baixa towns of Fundão and Castelo Branco, but not to Sabugal and the Transylvanian-like fortress-village of Sortelha, for which you'd do better to return to Guarda. Despite Belmonte's proximity to both of these, the region between them is deserted and wild with roughly surfaced roads and few cars.

Buses might well drop you on the main road, at the foot of the hill (a junction known as *Ginjal*), from where you'll have to walk 2km uphill to the village. If you want **to stay**, there's the *Pensão Altitude* (☎075/91 11 20; ②) in the village, though you might prefer the *Hotel Belsol* (☎075/91 22 06; ④), with its swimming pool, back down on the main road between the junction and the turn-off for Valhelhas and Manteigas (N232). A few kilometres along the N232 itself, there's a **campsite** at Valhelhas (☎075/481 60) on the Rio Zêzere, open from mid-May to the end of September. Buses for Manteigas, originating in Guarda, pass this way three times daily; you may have to change at *Ginjal*.

Covilhã

Another 20km beyond Belmonte, **COVILHÃ** lies immediately below the highest peaks of the *serra*, and is the most obvious base for exploring the park. In summer, weekend picknickers and campers spread across the hillsides; in winter, ski enthusiasts take over, using Covilhã as a base for trips to the slopes. It's a steeply terraced town, every thoroughfare looking out across the plain below or up to the crags of the Serra da Estrela. A market town since the Middle Ages; it developed a textile industry in the seventeenth century, using wool from the local sheep – who also provide the milk for the renowned local *queijo da Serra*. After industrialisation the woollen industry began to harness water power from the mountain streams; factories today, down on the plain below town, are powered by hydroelectricity.

Covilhã's favourite son is **Pêro de Covilhã** who set out in 1487, on behalf of Dom João II, to search for Prester John (legendary Christian priest and king) in what is now Ethiopia. However, having reached Cairo, de Covilhã sailed instead to India before returning to Cairo and then heading south on his original errand. He never found Prester John and never returned to Portugal, though Vasco da Gama found his report about India useful when he made his own celebrated voyage there, around the Cape of Good Hope, in 1498. In front of the town hall there's a huge, polished granite slab depicting Pêro de Covilhã's voyages and a decidedly queasy looking statue of the man himself.

The **train station** is 4km from the town, at the foot of the hill, while **buses** stop half way up the hill at Largo São João. From either terminus you'll have to walk up into town or take a taxi to the central Praça do Município, where there's a **Turismo** (Mon–Sat 9am–noon & 2–8pm; ☎075/32 21 70) and a bus information office, both on the ground floor of the town hall.

Other than the campsite on the road to Penhas da Saúde (see below), the cheapest **accommodation** is to be found between Largo São João and Praça do Município, where you'll find the *Hospedaria São Francisco*, Rua Almeida Eusebio 35 (☎075/32 22 63; ②); the *Residencial São João*, Rua Nuno Alvares Pereira 76 (☎075/32 46 70; ②); and the *Pensão Regional*, Rua das Flores 4–6 (☎075/32 25 96; ③). On Praça do Município itself, or just off it, are the *Residencial Montalto* (☎075/32 76 09; ③), which has seen better days, and the *Residencial Solneve*, Rua Visconde da Coriscada 126 (☎075/32 30 01; ④), which has a very good **restaurant**. You can also eat well at the *Restaurante Os Arcos*, alongside the *Pensão Regional* and at the *Restaurante Sporting*, Rua Comendador Mendes Veiga, behind the *Solneve*, where 1500$00 will buy you a good meal. For less than half of that, eat pizza or pasta at the *Café Ketchup*, Rua Comendador Campos Melo 44.

Hikers or skiers intending to move on should contact the *Club Nacional de Montanhismo*, Rua Pedro Álvares Cabral 5 (office hours; ☎075/233 64) for up-to-date details of local conditions. Covilhã also has plenty of shops for stocking up on **provisions**.

Penhas da Saúde

The most obvious – and enjoyable – hike from Covilhã is the route up the glacial valley to **PENHAS DA SAÚDE**, an energetic, 11km walk. Leaving Covilhã by Rua Montes Herminios, the road begins immediately to climb in hairpin bends up the barren mountainside, after 4km passing the *Pião* **campsite** (☎075/31 43 12; open all year). There is a bus, but it only runs during the ski season and at weekends from July to mid-September.

At the crest of a rise – and with superb views across the plain to the Serra de Malcata – you reach Penhas' 160-bed **youth hostel** (☎075/253 75), as well as the *Estalgem O Pastor* (☎075/32 28 10; ③) and the modern *Hotel Serra da Estrela* (☎075/31 38 09; ⑥). In July and August there's also large-scale, and unofficial, **camping** across the hillside. But bear in mind that, despite the accommodation here, Penhas da Saúde is not a village and there are no other facilities available here.

Local hikes

From Penhas, you are within striking distance of the chief beauty spots of the *serra*, with the highest peak in Portugal – **Torre** (1993m) – just a few kilometres up the road to the northwest; it can be climbed quite easily. The stone *torre* (tower) here was added in the last century, on the orders of Dom João VI, to raise the height to a more impressive 2000 metres. Nearby is the vast statue of **Nossa Senhora da Boa Estrela**, carved into a niche in the rock, to which there's a massive procession from Covilhã on the second Sunday in August. A little west of Torre is the narrow rock cone known as the **Cântaro Magro** (Slender Pitcher), which conceals the source of the Rio Zêzere; there's an excellent summer **campsite** below it at Covão d'Ametade. One of the natural park hiking routes passes by Torre and through Penhas and Covilhã; see "Hiking in the Parque Natural", opposite.

North to Manteigas

A few kilometres beyond Penhas, you can strike **north** at Nave de Santo António, between Penhas and Torre, and follow the glacial **valley of the Rio Zêzere** down to the spa of **CALDAS DE MANTEIGAS**. Five kilometres beyond is the larger *serra* village of **MANTEIGAS** proper, whose whitewashed houses and red roofs run along the contour above the Rio Zêzere. If you're reliant on buses, you'll have to come from Guarda, 45km to the northeast (3 daily), the route bypassing Belmonte and passing the campsite at Valhelhas (see p.195) on the way. The bus stops on the main street, Rua 1 de Maio, setting you down outside the **main information office** for the *Parque Natural da Serra da Estrela* (Mon–Sat 9am–12.30pm & 2–5.30pm; ☎075/98 23 82), where you can buy books and guides to the park; nearby, there's a regular **Turismo** (Mon–Sat 9.30am–noon & 2–6pm; ☎075/98 11 29).

As for **accommodation**, at the bus stop/Turismo end of the village, and high above the main street, is the *Residencial Estrela*, Rua Dr. Sobral 5 (☎075/982 88; ③), sporting fine views across the valley. A little way along the main street, the *Residencial Serradalto* (☎075/98 11 51; ③) has an attached restaurant and craft shop. Further on, and up a side street, is the *Casa de São Roque*, Rua de Santo

HIKING IN THE PARQUE NATURAL

Several waymarked **hiking trails** cut across the Parque Natural de Serra da Estrela. The map on p.191 shows the main trails, some of which are detailed here. Those described below would take between three and four days to complete (depending, naturally, on your level of fitness, weather conditions, etc), but shorter, alternative routes spin off from the main trails, while each is broken down into segments which could be tackled as half-day or day hikes. Always check with the park information offices before setting off on hikes; and be properly prepared and equipped for what can be quite tough routes.

● T1 (waymarked in red) runs **from Guarda to Vide** (on the N230). The route leads you across high land, first to Videmonte, an inhabited farming area, and then through Portela de Folgosinho on a forest road and to the dammed lake at Rossim. You then reach Torre (see "Penhas da Saúde", p.196), via Cume, after which the route ends either at Loriga (on the N231) or at Vide (N230). You'll need to be self-sufficient after Videmonte; there are no other settlements until you reach Vide.

An alternative route (T11: waymarked in red and yellow) is to leave the trail at Portela de Folgosinho and walk, first through pine woods and then farmed land, to Covoa da Ponte, where there's a campsite. From there you can visit Manteigas (p.196) and return to the T1 at Cume. T14 leaves the trail at Torre instead and runs down to Penhas da Saúde and Covilhã, by way of the Pião campsite.

● T2 (waymarked in yellow) runs from north to south, **from Vila Soeira via Gouveia to Loriga**, along the western edge of the Serra da Estrela. Access to Vila Soeira is from Guarda along the T1, after which the route runs to Linhares (p.192) and Folgosinho village, where there's a grocery store and medical centre. At Gouveia there's a campsite; then the route runs through Cabeça de Velha, with an enormous block of stone weathered into the shape of an old woman, and on to Senhora do Desterro (grocery store), Castro de São Romão (superb vantage point), Valezim – a sizeable village on the N231 – and finally to Loriga.

● T3 (waymarked in yellow) runs **from Videmonte via Verdelhos to Loriga**, this time along the eastern slope of the *serra*, crossing the Mondego and Zêzere rivers. As above, you reach Videmonte from Guarda along the T1 and then walk on to Valhelhas (campsite). Next, at Poço do Inferno, there's a spectacular waterfall; the route then follows the Nave de Santo António, a sandy alluvial plain which was once a glacial lake – it's now natural grassland supporting cattle in the summer. Finally, you pass through Alvoco da Serra on the N231 and, from there, to Loriga.

Alternatively, T32 leaves the T3 at Paço do Inferno and takes the forest road to the Rio Zêzere, after which it passes through Manteigas to the Covão d'Ametade (summer campsite), before rejoining the T3 at the Nave de Santo António.

António 63 (☎075/98 11 25; ③), which dates from the turn of the century. Finally, at the far end of the village, the new *Albergaria Berne* (☎075/98 13 51; ④) comes with a pine-clad interior and restaurant.

Apart from the hotel **restaurants**, there's the reliable, but less ambitious, *O Olival*, on the left on the way into the village; on the main street, *O Maniel* and *Antiga Casa Anita* are more upmarket but not too expensive.

It's worth noting that drivers (or energetic hikers) could continue beyond Manteigas, 12km to the west, where there's a marvellous **pousada**, the *São Lourenço* (☎075/981 50; ⑥). It's only got 21 rooms, so don't turn up without a reservation.

Sabugal, Sortelha and Serra da Malcata

The area **east of Covilha**, over towards the Spanish border, is worth exploring for the chance to visit **Sabugal** and, more particularly, **Sortelha**, whose amazing circuit of walls rises amid one of the bleakest locations in all Portugal. If you're dependent on buses, you'll need to backtrack to Guarda for connections. However, if you have your own transport, the two towns are an easy sidetrip from Covilhã (40km away), and you can continue into the **Serra da Malcata** – wild terrain which, believe it or not, harbours a **lynx reserve**.

Sabugal

SABUGAL, like most towns in Beira Alta, has a **castle**. It's a good one, too, with massively high walls, a vast hollow centre, and a pentagonal tower with three arched chambers piled one on top of the other. Trust the rickety staircase and you could be on top of the world; trust the wobbly stonework and you could walk right around the walls. The village has a couple of **pensions** and, though there's no official campsite, nobody should object if you put a tent up by the river, on its out-of-town stretch. There's a **festa** (June 24) and a grand **feira** (June 29); at other times of year it's all pretty quiet.

Regular **buses** leave from the main square for Guarda, and others go north to Vilar Formoso and south to Penamacor and Castelo Branco. To get **to Sortelha**, 15km west, public transport is limited to school buses, which run in the late afternoon (and, obviously, don't run during the holidays). You may have to walk.

Sortelha

SORTELHA is isolated and rather eerie, especially when mist drifts down from the *serra*. It is an ancient town, with Hispano-Arabic origins, and was also the first *castelo roqueiro* ("rock fortress") to be built this side of the Côa. Mystery and legend have grown up with the castle and its fortifications (*sortelha* means "ring"), with stories spun around the figure of an old lady, *a velha*, whose profile you can see on rocks from outside the top gates. At first sight the town seems nothing special. Walk uphill from the new quarters, however, and you arrive at the fantastically walled old town. Within the grid, take a look at the **Igreja Matriz** (keys from the house next door) with its beautiful ceiling, executed by medieval Moors. Arabic script can be seen, too, on several house lintels near the top of town.

It's also worth taking time to browse around the **antique shop** on the road up to the castle, and the **carpet workshop** on the route back down towards Sabugal. Both offer insights into the way life used to be, but above all they show a healthy attitude to present-day tourism. Even if their continuing existence depends entirely on the foreign visitor, you never get the feeling that the show is laid on just for you. The chance to work with the fine materials and coloured wools seems to be enjoyed by all in the workshop, and the antique dealer is as happy to chat about the curious customs and folk tales as strike a bargain.

Festivals

Sortelha's major event is a **bullfight**, which takes place on August 15, once every two or three years, when the local council has money to stage it. It retains the ancient and peculiar custom of the *forca* – a rudimentary defence against the bull, using branches – which has been handed down from generation to generation. The order of events for the day begins with a *forca* involving all the young boys of the village – at least 25 of whom are needed to carry the device to prevent it from being tipped up by the bull. Later, solo performers strut the stage with their red capes to take the bull's charges. Onlookers are also frequently involved – many a young bull has hopped up onto the terrace of rocks, only to find himself sniffing at discarded hats and bags while nervous laughter rises up from behind the safety of the nearest wall. In non-bullfight years there's still a **festa** on August 15, and a **romaria** in honour of Santo António takes place each June 13.

Practicalities

Sortelha has three superb and inexpensive country **lodgings,** the *Casa do Vento Que Soa, Casa do Pátio* and, best of all, the *Casa da Escadinha* (all ②). For advance booking – which is recommended in summer – phone ahead (☎071/681 82 or 681 13). Each of the houses is a traditional village home in the old town, replete with massive walls, wooden furniture, hot baths, cobwebs – all in all, a splendid mix of modern comforts and medieval surroundings.

If you're out of luck, try asking for **rooms** at the *Restaurante Celta*. Alternatively, there are any number of promising areas to pitch **camp** above and beyond the old town, where the terrain is rocky and sheep take shelter beneath massive boulders. Best bet for **meals** is the wood-beamed *Restaurante Típico*, which often has *javali* (wild boar) on the menu.

Buses back to Sabugal leave at 7.30am on schooldays, and sometimes at 9am on Tuesdays and Thursdays – check times the day before in the café.

The Serra da Malcata

The **Serra da Malcata** has its reserve's headquarters at Penamacor (Rua dos Bombeiros Voluntários), 33km south of Sabugal. They are full of advice about how to approach the area and where best to go at different times of the year. The **lynx** – a graceful spotted feline with the build of a domestic cat but the dimensions of a labrador – is notoriously difficult to see, especially without the aid of the park keepers, but the countryside is compensation enough if you don't get a sighting. If you're fortunate you might also see a wild boar disappearing into the forests of black oak. The reserve also contains a **barragem** (dam), currently a scar on the landscape, though it will hopefully heal in time; it has good swimming spots.

Penamacor

PENAMACOR itself is a rather dull place, split in two by constant noisy traffic, but it has numerous cafés where you can get a snack, the reasonable *Poço* restaurant for meals, and opposite the restaurant, up a side road to the left of the petrol station, an un-named café which lets out pleasant **rooms** (①). There's also a **castle** – nothing out of the ordinary if you've come from Sabugal and Sortelha, though the climb up is rewarded by views over the Serra da Malcata towards Spain, and tremendous sunrises and sunsets.

Unless you are hanging around to explore the Serra da Malcata, you would really do better to move on for the night to rural **MEIMOA**, 12km north, with an ancient bridge and streets as often clogged with cattle and carts as people. There are two *pensões* here, including the *Santos* (①), on Largo D. Tilhena; ask at the adjacent butcher's shop if no-one's around.

South from Covilha: Serra da Gardunha

Fundão and the neighbouring villages of **Alpedrinha** and **Castelo Novo** lie sunk
into a ridge, the **Serra da Gardunha**, south of Covilhã. All have magnificent views
and are healthy, rural places, with delicious local fruit and, at Castelo Novo, healing waters. Without your own transport, a route through Fundão is an easier
approach to Monsanto than cutting across country from Sabugal and Penamacor.

Fundão

FUNDÃO, 17km south of Covilhã by road or rail, is the largest town in the area
and a pleasant place to stock up on supplies. As far as sights are concerned,
though, even the local tourist pamphlet admits that the town has "no monuments
of note". Fundão's rural tranquility, however, does much to make up for its touristic shortcomings, as does its glorious abundance of fresh fruit and vegetables.
The villages around the *serra* are celebrated for their produce and this is the local
market centre. In season you'll find cherries, apples, pears, grapes and chestnuts.

   If you wanted to **stay overnight**, the choice is limited. The small *Pensão
Tarouca*, Rua 25 de Abril 37 (☎075/521 68; ②) is adequate; it is just off Avenida da
Liberdade, which runs from the train station up to Praça do Município. But other
than this, you have to pay much more to stay at either the new five-storey *Hotel
Samasa*, also off the *avenida* (☎075/712 99; ⑤), or at the eighteenth-century *Casa
dos Maias*, Praça do Município (☎075/521 23; ⑤). The **Turismo** on Avenida da
Liberdade (Mon–Fri 9am–noon & 2.30–4pm, Sat 9am–noon & 2.30–6pm; ☎075/32
21 70) might be able to help with **rooms**; or there's a small campsite (☎075/531
18; open all year), 2km west of town on the N238, with some shade and a swimming pool. There aren't many **restaurants** either, though the *Veneluso*, Travessa
das Oliveiras 12, just beyond the *Hotel Samasa*, is recommended.

On to Alpedrinha: Alcongosta

Moving **on to Alpedrinha** is a pleasure in itself: a three-hour walk along an old,
cobbled Roman road via the hamlet of **ALCONGOSTA**, known for its baskets
and wickerwork. Given the fine walk from Fundão, it seems a shame to use the
bus. However, trains will deposit you on the plain below Alpedrinha – with a steep
approach along another section of Roman road.

Alpedrinha

ALPEDRINHA is set into the side of the *serra*, overlooking fields of olives and
fruit trees. In spring the hillside flowers, fruit-tree blossoms and springwater
oozing from every crack in the road make it as idyllic a spot as you could hope to
find – notwithstanding the rumbling lorries crashing through the village on the
main road to the south. It is easy to escape the noise though, once you wander up
to the older quarters or on into the *serra*.

   A good first stop is at the museum in the former **Paços do Concelho**. This
displays an interesting collection of tradesmen's tools – from cobbler to baker to
tinsmith – and traditional clothing, including a striking, black wedding dress, the
customary colour in this part of the world. A short way beyond, the **Capela do
Leão**, in the courtyard of the Casa de Misericórdia, provides Alpedrinha with its

current talking-point. Something of a mystery surrounds a series of valuable sixteenth-century panels which disappeared from the chapel. The panels were last spotted at a Primitivist exhibition in Lisbon, which coincided with renovation work due to be carried out on the chapel.

At the top of the same street, above the plain **Igreja Matriz**, you'll come across Alpedrinha's highlight: an elaborate fountain known as the **Chafariz de Dom João V**. When the king passed through in 1714 he found the water so good that he commissioned the *chafariz* as a sign of royal approval. The little village flourished and grand houses such as the now-deserted **Palácio do Picadeiro**, which towers above the fountain, were constructed during the eighteenth century. In front of this spectre of a palace, the old **Roman road** (from the times when Alpedrinha was called Petratinia) begins to wind its cobbled way up the side of the *serra* toward Fundão.

Other architectural delights abound, all detailed in the "Friends of Alpedrinha" booklet (available from the library below the museum). Above all, don't miss the **furniture workshop**, situated below the main road on the way out of town toward Castelo Branco. Ask inside and someone will show you around António Santos Pinto's **sala de arte**, with some of the most consummate singlehanded marquetry ever produced. Pinto moulded Louis XV chairlegs to Napoleonic dressers and threw the odd carved African page-boy into his structures for good measure. There's even a set of tableaux depicting the first six cantos of Camões' *Lusíadas* – all in the most incredible detail.

Practicalities

Information on **buses** is available from the newspaper kiosk on the side of the main through-road. The Alpedrinha **train station**, on the plain below, is unstaffed but you can buy tickets on the trains.

The best known of Alpedrinha's **pensions** is the *Pensão Clara* (☎075/573 91; ③), run by a sprightly old lady of the same name. There's no sign, but it is on the right as you enter the village on the E802 from the north; its more formal name is the *Quinta das Cerejeiras*. In the village itself, and cheaper, is the *Pensão Sintra da Beira*, Rua Francisco Dias 14 (☎075/578 58; ②), with a reasonable restaurant. **Campers** can pitch tents near the swimming pool, off the main road in from the north.

On the outskirts of the village are two country houses with accommodation: *Casa do Barreiro*, Largo das Escolas (☎075/571 20; ④), off the main road below the *Clara*, a turn-of-the-century house in need of decoration and set amid rambling gardens, but with magnificent views; and the *Casa da Comenda* (☎075/ 571 61; ⑤), above the Igreja Matriz, an early seventeenth-century "fortress house" with a swimming pool and billiards room.

The town hosts a tremendous **feira** (market), on the first Sunday in every month, and a full-blown festival, the **Festa do Anjo da Guarda**, each August 3.

Castelo Novo

In northern Portugal **CASTELO NOVO** is best known as the source of *Alardo*, a bottled mineral water reputed to possess healing properties. At the **spa**, marked by just a single café-restaurant, the water gushes from every crack in the earth's surface. There is no accommodation, but there's scope for camping – and no shortage of sparkling, clear, water.

The village proper, like Alpedrinha, has ancient origins, and a few crumbling remains to prove it: a **castle**, an attractive **Paços do Concelho** (above the main square), and a Manueline **pelourinho**. Off to the sides of the square, narrow alleyways and heavy stonework constitute the village's principal charm. Although there is no **bus** to the village, four daily run along the main N18 road (between Fundão and Castelo Branco); you can be dropped or picked up at the crossroads, 4km out.

Into the Beira Baixa

After the surpassing beauty of most of Beira Alta, the flat plain of the lower province, **Beira Baixa**, comes as something of an anti-climax. For the most part it's monotonous, parched country, dotted here and there with cork and carob trees or the occasional orchard. However, from **Castelo Branco**, the capital of the Beira Baixa and its only sizable town, you can make rewarding and fairly easy excursions to two strange and atmospheric villages – **Monsanto** and **Idanha-a-Velha**.

Castelo Branco

Not much of **CASTELO BRANCO** has survived the successive wars of this frontier area and today it appears as a predominantly modern town – and attractive for it. Set out around wide boulevards, large squares, and small parks, it has an air of prosperity and activity in contrast to the somnolent villages round about.

What's left of its **old town** is confined within the narrow cobbled alleyways and stepped sidestreets leading up to the ruins of the **Castelo**. Around its twelfth-century walls, a garden-viewing point, the **Miradouro de São Gens**, has been laid out. Nearby is the **Palácio Episcopal**, the old Bishop's palace, with its formal, eighteenth-century garden – a sequence of elaborately shaped hedges, Baroque statues, little pools, fountains and flowerbeds. The balustrades of the two grand staircases are peopled with statues – on one, the Apostles; on the other, the kings of Portugal. Two of the latter are much smaller than the rest: the hated Spanish rulers, Felipe I and II. Elsewhere in the gardens other statues represent months of the year, signs of the zodiac, Christian virtues and the then-known continents.

The palace itself houses a **regional museum**, its collections roaming through the usual local miscellany, save for a large and splendid collection of finely embroidered bedspreads, or *colchas*, a craft for which the town is known throughout Portugal. However, the museum is currently closed for long-term renovations and is unlikely to open for several years. The same is true of the elegant sixteenth-century **Câmara Municipal** in the Praça Luís de Camões, though you can still view the exterior and those of the several seventeenth- and eighteenth-century mansions in the streets around it.

Practicalities

There is a **Turismo** (Mon–Fri 9am–12.30pm & 2–5pm; ☎072/210 02) right in the centre of Castelo Branco, in a little park off the Alameda da Liberdade. The **bus station** is on the corner of Rua Rebelo and Rua do Saibreiro, the latter leading straight up to the Alameda. It's a little further to the **train station**, but equally simple – straight down the broad Avenida de Nuno Álvares.

Considering its size, the town has a surprising number of **pensions** (ten or more), though less than half of these merit recommendation. *Residencial Martinho* at Alameda da Liberdade 41 (☎072/217 06; ②) is the most central and the best in its price range; the *Residencial Caravela*, Rua do Sabreiro 24 (☎072/239 39; ③), near the bus station, is adequate. For more comfort, try the well-run *Residencial Arraiana*, Avenida 1º de Maio 18 (☎072/216 34; ④); otherwise, the Turismo can point you towards inexpensive *dormidas* behind the Alameda (①–②). The municipal **campsite** (☎072/216 15; closed mid-Nov to Jan 1) is 3km north of town along the N18.

For somewhere decent to **eat**, head for the *Restaurante Arcadia*, just off the Alameda da Liberdade (and near *Residencial Martinho*). It's open daily and particularly crowded with locals at the weekend, paying around 1500$00 for a fine spread. There's a large covered **market** on Avenida 1º de Maio.

Monsanto

MONSANTO, 48km northeast of Castelo Branco (buses twice daily), claims to be the most ancient settlement in Portugal. It is a claim easy enough to believe, for the old village – there's a newer settlement at the bottom of the hill – looks as if it has barely changed since the Iron Age. Its houses cower beneath a huge fortified granite outcrop, the stone from which they are themselves constructed. From a few hundred yards, they disappear entirely into the grey, boulder-strewn background, with only the odd splash of whitewash, added in these more peaceful times. It is all incredibly basic and beautiful – flowers are everywhere and the streets, barely wide enough even for a mule, are simply carved out of the rock.

The **castle** too is impressive, though tumbledown. As you climb up through the village you're quite likely to meet someone who'll insist on guiding you up, showing you the views and expounding some of the legends. A big celebration takes place every May 3, when the village girls throw baskets of flowers off the ramparts. The rite commemorates an ancient siege when, in desperation and close to starvation, the defenders threw their last calf over the walls: their attackers, so disheartened at this evidence of plenty within, gave up and went home.

Finding food and accommodation is very difficult in Monsanto. You're better off walking (or taking the infrequent local bus) the 8km to Penha Garria, where the *Cafe Isaias* on Rua da Tapada has **rooms** (②) and good **meals**.

Idanha-a-Velha

IDANHA-A-VELHA is another tiny backwater, sited midway between Castelo Branco and Monsanto. It sees just one bus a day (mid-afternoon) from Castelo Branco, which promptly turns around and leaves; however, if you don't have transport, it shouldn't be too hard to hitch from Monsanto.

The village is certainly worth a little effort to reach. It's possibly of a similar age to Monsanto, but has a considerably more illustrious history. Known as Igaetania, it was once a major Roman city, and subsequently, under Visigothic rule, was the seat of a bishopric – which endured even Moorish occupation. Wamba, the legendary King of the Goths, is said to have been born here. During the reign of Dom Manuel, however, early in the fifteenth century, it is said that a plague of rats forced the occupants to move to Monsanto or nearby Idanha-a-Nova.

The village looks much as it must have done when the rats moved in, and not far different to when the Romans left, either. It still retains a section of massive Roman wall, the **Roman bridge** is still in use, and odd Roman relics lie about everywhere. In the very ancient **Basílica**, which is at least part Visigothic, there's a collection of all the more mobile statues and lumps of inscribed stone found about the place; another small chapel contains an exhibition of coins, pottery, and bones, all found more or less by accident. Another oddity, whose history nobody seems to know, is a Moorish-inspired balconied mansion.

travel details

Trains

Castelo Branco to Abrantes (5–6 daily; 1hr 15min); Covilhã (5 daily; 1hr 30min); Guarda (3 daily; 3hr); Lisbon (5–6 daily; 4hr 5min).

Celorico da Beira to Coimbra (5 daily; 2hr 50min); Guarda (5 daily; 50min); Lisbon (4 daily; 4hr 15min); Vilar Formoso (2 daily; 2hr); Viseu (5 daily; 2hr 15min).

Covilhã to Abrantes (5–6 daiuly; 2hr 25min–3hr 15min); Castelo Branco (5–6 daily; 1hr–1hr 30min); Guarda (3 daily; 1hr 15min); Lisbon (5–6 daily; 4hr 20min–6hr).

Guarda to Abrantes (3 daily; 4hr 40min); Castelo Branco (3 daily; 3hr 20min); Coimbra (5 daily; 2hr 50min–3hr 40min); Covilhã (3 daily; 1hr 15min); Lisbon (7 daily; 5hr–7hr 50min); Porto (2 daily; 6hr 20min); Vilar Formoso (3 daily; 50min); Viseu (4 daily; 2hr–2hr 30min).

Vilar Formoso (Spanish border) to Guarda (3 daily; 50min); Lisbon (3 daily; 5hr 40min); Salamanca, Spain (2 onward connections from Portugal daily; 2hr 30min).

Viseu to Coimbra (3 daily; 2hr); Guarda (4 daily; 2hr–2hr 30min); Lisbon (3 daily; 4hr).

Buses

Almeida to Guarda (1 daily; 1hr 30min).

Alpendrinha to Covilhã (2–3 daily; 2hr 35min); Fundão (2–3 daily; 15–25min); Guarda (2–3 daily; 1hr 25min); Lisbon (2–3 daily; 4hr 10min).

Belmonte to Guarda (3 daily; 45min).

Castelo Branco to Covilhã (2 daily; 1hr 5min); Guarda (2–3 daily; 1hr 55min); Lisbon (2–3 daily; 4hr 10min).

Celorico da Beira to Coimbra (2 daily; 2hr 10min); Covilhã (2 daily; 1hr 15min); Guarda (3 daily; 1hr 15min); Lisbon (1 daily; 5hr); Viseu (2 daily; 1hr 15min).

Covilhã to Castelo Branco (2–3 daily; 1hr 5min); Fundão (2–3 daily; 25min); Guarda (2–3 daily; 50min); Lisbon (2–3 daily; 5hr 20min); Penhas da Saúde (July to mid-Sept Sat 2, Sun 4; 35min).

Guarda to Almeida (1 daily; 1hr 30min); Alpendrinha (2–3 daily; 1hr 25min); Belmonte (3 daily; 45min); Castelo Branco (2–3 daily; 1hr 55min); Covilhã (2–3 daily; 50min); Fundão (2–3 daily; 1hr 10min); Lisbon (2–3 daily; 6hr); Manteigas (3 daily; 1hr 15min–1hr 30min); Trancoso (3 daily; 1hr 30min).

Trancoso to Bragança (2 daily; 3hr); Celorico da Beira (2 daily; 1hr 25min); Covilhã (2 daily; 3hr 35min); Guarda (3 daily; 1hr 30min); Lisbon (2 daily; 6hr 10min); Pocinho (2 daily; 1hr 20min); Viseu (2 daily; 1hr 50min).

Vilar Formoso to Guarda (3 daily; 50min); Lisbon (3 daily; 5hr 40min).

Viseu to Celorico da Beira (2 daily; 1hr 25min); Coimbra (4 daily; 1hr 20min–1hr 35min); Covilhã (1 daily; 2hr); Guarda (1 daily; 1hr 30min); Lisbon (1 daily; 4hr 20min); Trancoso (2 daily; 1hr 50min).

CHAPTER FIVE

PORTO AND THE DOURO

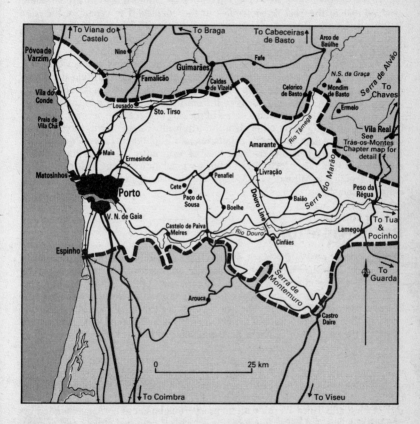

ortugal's second largest city, **Porto** is magnificently situated on the great
gorge of the Douro River, its old quarters scrambling up the rocky north
bank in tangled tiers. It's a massively atmospheric city, almost Dickensian
in parts, though the attention of most visitors is focused firmly on the port-
producing suburb of **Vila Nova de Gaia**, across the river. The coastal waters
either side of the city are shockingly polluted these days, but you don't have to
head that far north to find excellent beaches; those fronting the resorts of **Vila do
Conde** and **Póvoa de Varzim** offer a taste of what's to come as you head into
the Minho.

Above all, though, it's the **Rio Douro** ("river of gold") which dominates every aspect of this region: a narrow, winding gorge for the major part of its long route to the Spanish border, with port wine lodges dotted about the hillsides and a series of tiny villages, visited by few except their inhabitants and seasonal wine trade workers. The valleys and tributaries form some of the loveliest and most spectacular landscapes in the whole of Portugal and even though the wine no longer shoots down the river's rapids in barges, as it once did, a trip up the valley remains one of the best scenic routes in the country. The capital of the Alto Douro province is **Peso da Régua**, a small town with more scope for visiting wine lodges; and just 13km south of here is the delightful Baroque town of **Lamego**, the home of Portugal's champagne-like wine, *Raposeira*.

If you're driving, you can follow minor roads along the river practically all the way from Porto to the border-crossing at Miranda do Douro. Taking the **train**, though, is probably more fun. The **Douro line** joins the course of the river about 60km inland from Porto and sticks to it from then on, cutting into the rockface and criss-crossing the water on a series of rocking bridges: one of those journeys that needs no justification other than the trip itself. To the north, three narrow gauge rail lines follow the river's tributaries into Minho and Trás-os-Montes: the **Tâmega** line to the beautiful riverside town of **Amarante**; the Corgo line connecting with Vila Real (see p.293), a useful bus terminal for exploring Trás-os-Montes; and the **Tua** line to Mirandela (p.300), where you can catch buses on to Bragança in the northeast.

Porto (Oporto)

Although the capital of the north, **PORTO** is a very different city from Lisbon – unpretentious, inward-looking, unashamedly commercial. As the local saying goes: "Coimbra studies; Braga prays; Lisbon shows off; and Porto works". The city's greatest sights are its bridges: four of them, two modern, two nineteenth-century, and each spectacular. The two old ones are the metalwork Maria Pia railway link, designed by Eiffel, and the dizzying, two-tiered Ponte Dom Luís I, which connects the city with **Vila Nova de Gaia**, home of the port wine lodges – all of which offer tours and tastings to visitors.

In the city proper, there are a handful of buildings around which to direct your wanderings: the landmark **Torre dos Clérigos** and the **Sé**, the ornate interiors of the **Bolsa** and church of **São Francisco**, and a clutch of good **museums**. But the fascination of Porto lies very much in the day-to-day life of the place: a bizarre mix of First and Third World, with its prosperous business core, surrounded by opulent suburbs and villas, tempered by a heart of cramped streets and ancient alleys, untouched by the planners. This side of Porto comes into focus if you take a walk along the **quayside** between the Dom Luís and Maria Pia bridges. The improvised sheds and shacks here, clinging to the sides of the gorge, could to all appearances be a Brazilian shanty town.

It's a real shock to discover such poverty in western Europe. However, for all that, it remains hard not to like the city, or to respond to the crowds, tiny bars and antiquated shops. If you can plan a visit to coincide, the place is at its earthiest and finest during the riotous celebration of **Saint John's Eve** (the night of June 23–24). On this night, seemingly the entire population takes to the streets, hitting each other over the head with leeks, plastic hammers, or anything else to hand.

Arrival and Information

From the **airport**, 13km north of the city, bus #56 shuttles to and from Praça de Lisboa, by the Universidade building; the journey usually takes forty minutes, but allow an hour at peak times of day. On the way into Porto, the bus passes the youth hostel and Boavista. Taxis from the airport into the centre cost 1500–2000$00, depending on your final destination. **Drivers** should try to avoid getting caught up in the downtown grid, whose streets are best negotiated on foot or in a taxi. If you're picking up a rental car, it might be better to wait until the day you leave, then pick one up at the airport.

Coming into Porto by train or bus, you'll find yourself deposited fairly centrally, though the various terminals can cause a little confusion. Coming from the south, **trains** drop you at the **Estação de Campanhã**, a few kilometres east of the centre; change here for a local train into **São Bento** station, in the heart of the city – it takes about five minutes and there should never be more than a twenty-minute wait. Most trains from the north run directly to São Bento, though narrow-gauge trains from Guimarães and from the north coast (Vila do Conde/Póvoa de Varzim) use the smaller **Estação da Trindade**, just to the north of Avenida dos Aliados.

Bus companies have no single terminal and a glance at the schedules suggests that each company operates from a different street in a different part of town. Most, though, are fairly central, and a large number operate from a common terminal below the Torre dos Clérigos at **Rua das Carmelitas**. Other services from the south tend to arrive in the streets around **Rua Alexandre Herculano** (just east of São Bento), and those from the north (Viana do Castelo, Barcelos or Braga) from around **Praça Filipa de Lencastre**.

Information

Porto has two central tourist offices, where you can pick up a large-scale city plan as well as information about train and bus departures. The main **Turismo** is at the northern end of the central Avenida dos Aliados, by Praça General Humberto Delgado (summer Mon–Fri 9am–7pm, Sat 9am–4pm, Sun 10am–1pm; winter Mon–Fri 9am–5.30pm, Sat 9am–4pm, Sun 10am–1pm; ☎31 27 40); and there's another, smaller office in Praça de Dom João I (Mon–Fri 9am–12.30pm & 2–5.30pm; ☎31 75 14), which is closer to São Bento station. There's also a tourist counter (daily 8am–8pm; ☎941 25 34) at the airport.

Getting Around

Although modern Porto sprawls for some miles along the north bank of the Douro, most sights of any interest are within the compact and very hilly centre, and all are within **walking** – or perhaps more accurately *climbing* – distance. For trips further afield, there's a reliable network of **buses** and trolleybuses which leave from three main terminals: Cordoaria, by the Universidade building (stops in Campo dos Mártires da Pátria and Praça Gomes Teixeira, across the gardens); the central Praça da Liberdade, at the bottom of Avenida dos Aliados; and Bolhão (stops in front of the theatre on Rua Sá da Bandeira and halfway up at Bolhão itself).

The **telephone code** for the city of Porto is ☎02.

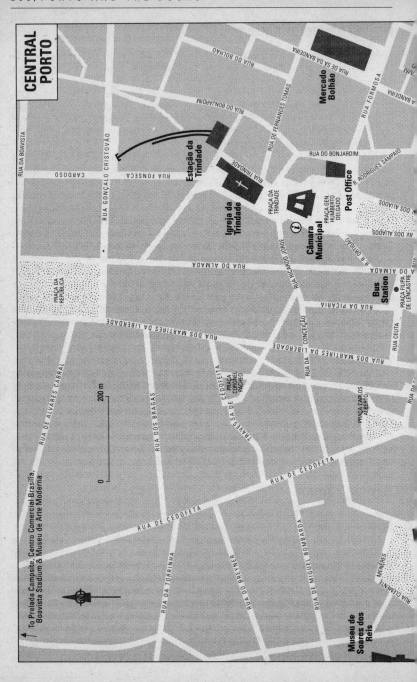

CENTRAL PORTO

RUA DA BOAVISTA

RUA GONÇALO CRISTOVÃO

CARDOSO

RUA FONSECA

RUA DO BONJARDIM

RUA DO BOLHÃO

RUA DE SÁ DA BANDEIRA

RUA DE FERNANDES TOMÁS

RUA FORMOSA

A BANDEIRA

Mercado Bolhão

Estação da Trindade

RUA DO BONJARDIM

R. RODRIGUES SAMPAIO

Igreja da Trindade

RUA TRINDADE

PRAÇA DA TRINDADE

Post Office

PRAÇA GEN. HUMBERTO DELGADO

DOS ALIADOS

AV. DOS ALIADOS

Câmara Municipal

R. DR TIAGO

RUA RICARDO JORGE

RUA DO ALMADA

RUA DA PICARIA

Bus Station

PRAÇA FILIPA DE LENCASTRE

DO ALMADA

PRAÇA DA REPÚBLICA

RUA DOS MÁRTIRES DA LIBERDADE

RUA DA CONCEIÇÃO

RUA DOS MÁRTIRES DA LIBERDADE

RUA CEUTA

RUA DA

RUA DE ÁLVARES CABRAL

TRAVESSA DE CEDOFEITA

CEDOFEITA

PRAÇA CORONEL PACHECO

PRAÇA CARLOS ALBERTO

200 m

0

RUA DOS BRAGAS

RUA DE CEDOFEITA

RUA DE CEDOFEITA

RUA DA TORRINHA

RUA DO BREYNER

RUA DE MIGUEL BOMBARDA

MENERES

RUA CLEMENTE

To Prelada Campsite, Centro Comercial Brasília, Boavista Stadium & Museu de Arte Moderna

Museu de Soares dos Reis

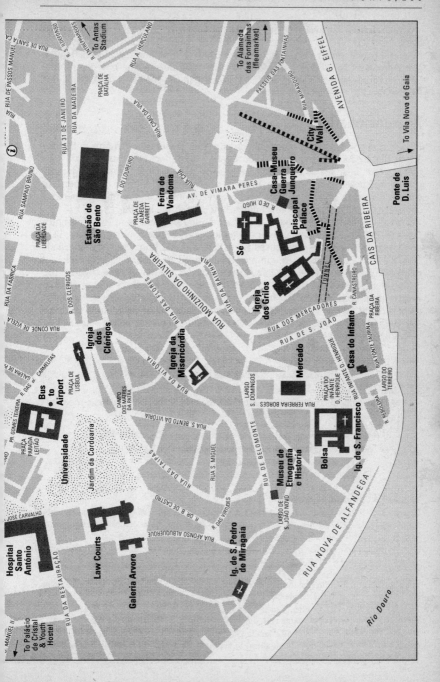

Single **tickets** are available but it works out cheaper to buy them in blocks (20 tickets for 1280$00). If you're intending to use public transport much, consider buying a **travel pass**: a one-day city pass costs 300$00, four-day, 1340$00 and a seven-day pass is 1860$00 – the last two are valid outside the city centre, too. They're all available at kiosks around Porto and in the *papelaria* on Avenida dos Aliados, next to the *Café Imperial*.

Accommodation

Porto's **accommodation** is generally good value. The cheapest rooms in the city are in the area south and east of São Bento station; for rather more salubrious places, your best bet is to ignore bargainers at the stations and head for the *pensões* and hotels detailed below, in areas west or east of Avenida dos Aliados. In winter, it's worth investing in more expensive rooms than you might otherwise choose, or you'll freeze. Very few budget hotels have any heating.

Porto's popular **youth hostel**, the *Pousada de Juventude*, is at Rua Rodrigues Lobo 98 (☎606 55 35; open all year; reception open 9–10am and after 6pm), 2km northwest of the centre; take buses #3, #19, #20 or #52 from Praça da Liberdade (ask for Praça da Galiza). In summer, you'll need to book ahead. The closest **campsite**, *Parque de Campismo de Prelada*, Rua Monte dos Burgos (☎81 26 16), is 3km northwest of the centre and open all year round. Get there on bus #9 from Bolhão until 9pm, or bus #50 from Cordoaria until midnight. There's a second local site, the *Parque de Campismo de Salgueiros*, at Rua de Salgueiros, Canidelo (☎781 05 00; May–Sept), across the river, near the Salgueiros beach – not a place to swim.

ACCOMMODATION PRICE CODES

All the accommodation prices in this book have been coded using the symbols below. The symbols represent the prices for the cheapest available double room in high season; for a full explanation, see p.23.

① Under 3000$00	② 3000$00–4000$00	③ 4000$00–5500$00
④ 5500$00–8500$00	⑤ 8500$00–12,500$00	⑥ 12,500$00–20,000$00
	⑦ Over 20,000$00	

West of Avenida dos Aliados

Pensão dos Aliados, Rua Elísio de Melo 27 (☎200 48 53). Just off Avda. dos Aliados, this very comfortable pension fills quickly in summer; book ahead. It can be noisy, though, so try for a room at the back. Breakfast included. ③.

Pensão Estoril, Rua de Cedofeita 193 (☎200 27 51). Rooms of varying sizes (and sometimes of odd shapes) in a friendly and well-maintained *pensão*, with a café on the ground floor for breakfast. It's on the pedestrianised section of the street, north of Praça Carlos Alberto. ②.

Pensão Europa, Rua do Almada 396 (☎200 69 71). All in all a little gloomy, but with a noisy bar and good restaurant. The cheaper rooms come without shower. ①.

Pensão Residencial d'Ouro, Praça Parada Leitão 41 (☎208 12 01). Off Praça Gomes Teixeira, by the university. Rooms with differing facilities at a range of prices. ③.

Pensão Pão-de-Açucar, Rua do Almada 262 (☎200 24 25). Stylish 1930s' hotel with quiet rooms and private bathrooms; book ahead in summer. It's at the junction with Rua Ramalho Ortigão and close to the tourist office. ④.

Residencial Paris, Rua da Fábrica 27–29 (☎32 13 96). Huge rooms with fine ceilings in a place now showing its age – it's always clean, though. Breakfast is included and taken in a restaurant overlooking a small garden. The *residencial* is one block up from Rua do Almada. ②.

Residencial Porto Chique, Rua Conde de Vizela 26 (☎208 00 69). Reasonable rooms (with and without shower) and only ten minutes' from São Bento station. ②.

Pensão Porto Rico, Rua do Almada 237 (☎31 87 85). Small, homey rooms, quieter at the back than at the front (if you prefer the noise of cats to cars). Opposite the *Pão-de-Açucar*. ③.

Pensão São Marinho, Praça Carlos Alberto 59 (☎31 43 80). Efficient and friendly; all rooms with shower; set in a pleasant, garden square 300m from the Torre dos Clérigos. Breakfast included. ③.

Pensão Universal, Avda. dos Aliados 38 (☎200 67 58). Basic pension, but always clean. You pay for the location, which is ideal, but noisy. Breakfast included. ④.

Pensão Vera Cruz, Rua Ramalho Ortigão 14 (☎32 33 96). Close to the tourist office, this represents a hike in quality, more of a hotel than a pension. It's elegant, if a bit pricey, and breakfast is included. ④.

East of Avenida dos Aliados

Pensão Chique, Avda. dos Aliados 206 (☎200 90 11). Friendly, clean and well-run. Considering its central position, it is a reasonable bargain. ③.

Albergaria Girassol, Rua Sá da Bandeira 131 (☎200 18 91). A tiny little inn, further up the street from the *Peninsular*. There's a good ground-floor restaurant, too. ④.

Grande Hotel do Porto, Rua de Santa Catarina 197 (☎200 81 76). Claiming to be the oldest hotel in Porto, this large place still retains a touch of grandeur. It's on the pedestrianised part of the street and less than ten minutes' from São Bento. ⑤.

Hotel do Imperio, Praça da Batalha 130 (☎200 68 61). An old railway hotel, immediately east of São Bento (though up a steep hill). Modern and comfortable hotel and, despite the dark decor, good value for money. ④.

Pensão Mondariz, Rua Cimo da Vila 139. One of several places down here advertising *dormidas*. Not at all classy, given its location, but cheap enough and with good views over the city. Prices are negotiable out of high season. ①.

Pensão Monte Sinai, Rua Alexandre Herculano 144 (☎200 82 18). Fairly basic rooms with bath, and a noisy location. ②.

Pensão do Norte, Rua de Fernandes Tomás 579 (☎200 35 03). On the junction with Rua de Santa Catarina (opposite an extravagantly tiled church), this pleasant, rambling old place has masses of rooms, with and without facilities. The best have balconies overlooking the street, though these are undoubtedly noisy. ②.

Pensão Paulista, Avda. dos Aliados 214 (☎31 46 92). Well-placed, and with good rooms, but you'll want a room at the back if you're to sleep soundly. Breakfast included. ③.

Hotel Peninsular, Rua Sá da Bandeira 21(☎200 30 12). Central (just uphill from São Bento station) and comfortable two-star hotel. The *azulejos* in the entrance reveal it to have once been the outbuilding of the nearby church. ③.

North: Praça da República and around

Residencial Brasilia, Rua Álvares de Cabral 221 (☎200 60 95). A really friendly hotel (the best of three in a row, and not to be confused with the less attrative *Pensão Brasil*) used by youth groups. It's near Praça da República and some way out, but buses #31, #82 and #84 go to the square. ③.

Pensão Cesar, Rua da Boavista 667 (☎31 49 84). Quite a way from the centre (near Praça da República), but worth the effort. The rooms are smallish, but adequate – there's air-conditioning in summer and heating in winter. Breakfast is included. ④.

Pensão Portugesa, Trav. Coronel Pacheo 11 (☎200 41 74). A converted house, some way out, near Praça da Coronel Pacheo, and consequently quiet. You can pay more for en-suite facilities. ②.

Residencial Rex, Praça da República 117 (☎200 45 48). At the top end of Rua do Almada, facing the garden square. It has the feel of a grand hotel, but was in fact a private house until relatively recently. Rooms are spacious and functional; breakfast is included. Highly recommended. ④.

The City

The "centre" is perhaps best regarded as **Avenida dos Aliados**, the commercial hub of the city, fronted by banks and offices. **Praça da Liberdade** marks the bottom end of this sloping avenue and a little further south, across the busy road (or reached via a pedestrian underpass), is the **Estação de São Bento**, the main train station. South of São Bento, a labyrinth of medieval streets and seedy-looking alleyways tumble below the **Sé**, or cathedral, down to the waterfront **Cais da Ribeira**, which is lined with fish tavernas and cafés. Here, the two-tier **Ponte Dom Luís I** runs across the river to the port wine suburb of **Vila Nova da Gaia**.

The streets leading off Avenida dos Aliados are the city's major shopping areas: to the west, the busy **Rua da Fábrica** with its stationers and bookshops; to the east, **Rua de Passos Manuel**, which runs into **Praça Dom João I**, and beyond into **Rua de Santa Catarina**, full of clothes and shoe shops. The only other areas of interest are all to the west of the centre: you can walk as far as the **Jardim do Palácio de Cristal** and the Solar do Vinho do Porto, though you'll need to use public transport to reach the shopping complex at **Boavista** or Porto's **Museu de Arte Moderna**.

From Avenida dos Aliados to Cordoaria

The broad **Avenida dos Aliados** is as good a starting point as any, though other than a quick squint up the avenue to the Town Hall at the very top and a coffee at the pavement tables of the *Imperial* café at the bottom, there's little reason to linger. If you didn't arrive by train, you may as well cut down briefly to the **Estação de São Bento**, one of the city's grandest buildings in its own right, with magnificent *azulejos* by Jorge Colaço in the entrance hall. These, somewhat arbitrarily, take on two great themes – the history of transport and the battle of Aljubarrota.

The stifled streets of the old town rarely permit any sort of overall view of the city, so it's a good idea to climb the Baroque **Torre dos Clérigos** (Mon–Sat 10.30am–noon & 3.30–5pm, Sun 10.30am–noon & 3–5pm; closed Wed; 50$00), 200m west of São Bento, to get your bearings. This landmark was designed, like the curious oval church beneath it, by the Italian architect Nicolau Nasoni and was once the tallest structure in Portugal. The dizzying vistas from the top take in the entire city, as well as south across the river to Vila Nova de Gaia and sometimes even to the distant mouth of the Douro and the coast.

PORTO'S MUSEUMS

Porto's museums, it seems, are undergoing an almost continuous process of "restoration". Several, including the Soares dos Reis and the Museu de Etnografia e História, have been closed for some time, with little firm indication of when they might re-open or of what the reorganised exhibits will look like. The accounts below rely on the latest available information, but for up-to-the-minute details check with the tourist office.

The *Casa Africana*, Rua dos Clérigos 112, is another delight, a combined **bacalhau and port wine shop** which advertises itself by hanging its wares outside. The *bacalhau* (dried, salted codfish) is bundled up in stacks all around the counter, alongside just about every type of port available.

The area immediately below the tower comprises the older sections of the university, and the gardens of the **Cordoaria**. This area is a fairly prestigious quarter of town, housing, for example, most of the city's commercial art galleries, which are grouped together on Rua Galeria de Paris, leading off to the north, behind the Cordoaria. At the main dealers here, *Galeria Nasoni* at no. 68–80 (closed Aug–Sept), you're free to wander in and take a look at four floors of the best (and priciest) paintings on sale in the country.

There is more modern art across the Cordoaria from here, at the **Galeria Árvore** on Passeio das Virtudes. This is a cooperative of painters, sculptors and designers who run their own art school in close competition with the official *Escola das Belas Artes* (itself housed in a nearby mansion). They pride themselves on the vitality of the teaching and the freedom they allow their pupils – the results of which are on view in a punchy summer show in June/July.

The Sé and down to the Cais da Ribeira

Set on a rocky outcrop a couple of hundred metres up from São Bento station, Porto's cathedral, the **Sé** (9am–noon & 2–5.30pm) is a bluff, austere fortress. Despite attempts to beautify it in the eighteenth century, it retains the hard, simple lines of its Romanesque origins – more impressive from a distance than close up. Inside it's depressing, even the vaunted silver altarpiece failing to make any impression in the prevailing gloom. For 100$00, however, you can escape into the neighbouring cloisters, and climb a Nasoni-designed Renaissance staircase leading up to a dazzling chapterhouse, with more views from the casement windows over the old quarter. There are fine views, too, from the broad flagged courtyard in front of the cathedral.

Beside the Sé stretches the fine facade of the Archbishop's Palace (not open to the public) while around the back, along Rua de Dom Hugo, is the **Casa Museu de Guerra Junqueiro** (Tues–Sat 9am–noon & 2–5pm; 100$00). This is the former home of the poet Guerra Junqueiro, housing his collection of artwork and furniture. The tours around these collections are not very enthralling, though the mansion and its pretty gardens happily outshine their contents.

Rua de Dom Hugo curls back around to the Sé to merge with the crumbling, animated old alleys which lead down to the riverside. From the prancing statue of Vimara Peres, **Calçada de Vandoma** plunges downwards, lined with the stalls of an authentic **flea market** (at its best on Saturday mornings). A few of the stalls sell fruit or homemade foods, but most have a spread of unremitting junk – torn clothes, broken transistor radios, used batteries. This area is the most fascinating and atmospheric part of the city: a medieval ghetto of back streets that would have been demolished or prettified in most other cities of Europe. Tall, narrow, and rickety, the houses have grown upwards into every available space, adapting as best they can to the steep terrain.

Not much goes on down at the waterfront since the big ships stopped calling here, but along the **Cais da Ribeira** old men still sit around as if they expect to be thrown a line or set to work unloading some urgent cargo. Cafés and restaurants line the quayside, too, providing some of Porto's best food (see p.220), alongside a weekday **market**. A post-modern cube of a fountain adds a slightly surreal air to the quarter.

Following the Cais westward, past the Praça da Ribeira, you reach Rua da Alfândega, which leads away from the water, past the **Casa do Infante** (currently closed for restoration), the house where Prince Henry the Navigator is said to have been born. It's an impressive mansion which, when in use, tends to house touring exhibitions.

The Bolsa and around

Away from the water, approached along Rua Infante de Dom Henrique, Porto's Stock Exchange, the **Bolsa** faces a statue of the *Infante* Henry himself, tucked into an eponymously named square. The building is a pompous nineteenth-century edifice with a vast neoclassical facade – and its keepers are inordinately proud of the place. On the **guided tours** (June–Sept Mon–Fri 10am–5.30pm, Sat & Sun 10am–noon & 2–5pm; Oct–May Mon–Fri 9am–noon & 2–5pm; 400$00) they dwell, with evident glee, on the enormous cost of every item, the exact weight of every piece of precious metal, and the intimate details of anyone with any claim to fame ever to have passed through the doors; President Kennedy, apparently, was one. The tour's nadir is the "Arab" Hall, an oval chamber that misguidedly attempts to copy the Moorish style of the Alhambra; here the guide's superlatives achieve apotheosis. Should you not want to bother with the tour you can see the main courtyard, easily the most elegant part, without having to buy a ticket.

Adjoining the Bolsa is the **Igreja de São Francisco** (Mon–Sat 9am–5pm; 250$00), perhaps the most extraordinary church in Porto. From its entrance on Rua de São Francisco it looks an ordinary enough Gothic construction, but the interior has been transformed by an unbelievably ornate eighteenth-century refurbishment. Altar, pillars, even the ceiling, drip with gilded rococo carving which reaches its ultimate expression in an interpretation of the *Tree of Jesse* on the north wall. If it has reopened, don't miss the church's small **museum**, housed in a separate building next door and consisting of artefacts salvaged from the former monastery. Beneath the flags of the cellar is an *osseria* – thousands of human bones, cleaned up and stored to await Judgement Day.

Two other churches in this neighbourhood have small museums. Pride of the **Igreja da Misericórdia**, a couple of blocks to the north, is a remarkable *Fons Vitae*, depicting King Manuel I with his wife Leonor and eight children, richly clothed, kneeling before the crucified Christ. It's an exceptional example of fifteenth-century Portuguese Realism – a style which was heavily influenced by Flemish painters like Van Eyck and Van der Weyden. To gain admission, knock at the government offices next door and ask for permission to enter the *Sala das Sessões*. Over to the west, in the **Igreja de São Pedro de Miragaia**, there's another fine fifteenth-century triptych; the church is kept locked but someone with a key is usually near at hand.

Between these two churches, the **Museu de Etnografia e História** occupies a beautiful noble house in the quiet Largo de São João Novo. It's currently closed, but you should certainly check whether it's reopened, since its collection is marvellous – a fascinating mixture of jewellery, folk costumes, ancient toys and almost anything of interest that has defied easy definition.

Northwest: to Soares dos Reis and the Jardim do Palácio de Cristal

Northwest of the Cordoaria, on Rua de Dom Manuel II, is the **Museu Nacional Soares dos Reis**, Portugal's first designated national museum – dating from

1933. It occupies the former royal *Palácio das Carrancas*; a building that was the French headquarters in the Peninsular War and from where they fled so hurriedly that the Duke of Wellington, leading his troops across the Douro, was able to sit down and eat the celebratory banquet that had been laid out for Marshal Soult and his officers. Again, the museum is temporarily "closed for works", but its excellent collections include glass, ceramics and a formidable display of Portuguese art of the eighteenth and nineteenth centuries. Highlights include the paintings by Henrique Pousão and sculptures by Soares dos Reis (*O Desterrado* – The Exiled – is probably his best-known work) and his pupil, Teixeira Lopes.

Follow the road past the Museu Soares dos Reis, or take any bus from Cordoaria except #6 and #18, and you soon reach the **Jardim do Palácio de Cristal**, a beautiful stretch of park dominated by a huge domed pavilion; this was built to replace the original "Crystal Palace" and now serves as a sports arena. In summer the park hosts hockey matches and pop concerts.

Around the back of the park, down the cobbled Rua Entre Quintas, stands the **Quinta da Macieirinha**, which houses both the **Romantic Museum** (Tues–Sat 10am–noon & 2–5pm), a collection of mid-nineteenth-century furniture and artwork, and – on the ground floor – the **Solar do Vinho do Porto** (Mon–Fri 11am–11pm, Sat 5–11.30pm). Here, in a comfortable lounge, whose terrace overlooks the river, you can sample one of hundreds of varieties of **port wine**, starting at around 150$00 a glass. The list is the same as at the Port Wine Institute in Lisbon but the service is considerably friendlier and the wine, after all, is at home. It's a good prelude to a visit to the port lodges across the river in Vila Nova de Gaia (see below).

Boavista and the Igreja de Cedofeita

The road directly west at the top end of Praça da República, Rua do Boavista, leads to Praça Mouzinho de Albuquerque, popularly known as the **Rotunda da Boavista**. This is overlooked by a huge column, with a lion astride a much flattened eagle, erected to celebrate the victory of the Portuguese and British over the French in the Peninsular War. There's also a flash modern shopping centre near here, the **Centro Comercial de Brasília**, on Avenida Boavista.

A couple of blocks before you reach the Rotunda, you pass the very simple **Igreja de Cedofeita** (from *cito facta*: "built quickly"), a church that is reputed to be the oldest Christian building in the entire Iberian peninsula. It was supposedly built by the Suevian king Theodomir in 556, though the current building is a twelfth-century Romanesque refashioning.

Out of the Centre

The best of the museums outside the centre is the highly contemporary **Museu de Arte Moderna** (Tues–Sun 2–8pm; 200$00), at Rua de Serralves 977, about half an hour's bus journey to the west ; take bus #78 from Cordoaria or from near the Palácio de Cristal. Administered by Lisbon's Gulbenkian Foundation, the museum is housed in a 1930s' palace known as the *Casa de Serralves*, and displays the work of a number of Portuguese architects and designers. No public collection in the country gives you a more accurate picture of Portugal's modern art scene, and the setting manages to be at once majestic and personal. Exhibitions run for a month at a time, and the **gardens** (Tues–Sun 2–6pm; free) remain open, even during the two-week rehanging closures.

Other than this, you might want to ask at the tourist office if the **Casa-Museu de Fernando de Castro** has reopened yet. This extraordinary house is crammed with treasures and in particular with pieces of gilded wood salvaged from the city's convents following the 1910 dissolution of the monasteries. It's maintained by the Soares dos Reis authorities and is at Rua de Costa Cabral 176 (an extension of Rua de Santa Catarina), way to the north of the centre.

Finally, down by the river beyond the Jardim do Palácio de Cristal is Porto's newest museum, the **Tram Museum** (Tues–Sat 9am–noon & 2–5pm; 50$00), housed in an old tram shed. Until recently, trams still ran through the city's streets, though these days you have to be content with the special (and pricey) **tram tours** operated by the museum. These leave Praça Infante Dom Henrique (Tues, Thurs & Sat at 2.30pm; 3000$00) on a three-hour jaunt along the length of Rua do Boavista to Castelo do Queijo, to the west, returning along the waterfront – and passing the museum en route.

Vila Nova de Gaia

The suburb of **Vila Nova de Gaia** is taken over almost entirely by the port trade. Walking across the **Ponte Dom Luís I** from central Porto, the names of the old **port wine lodges,** spelled out in huge white letters across their roofs, dominate the views. The most direct route to the wine lodges is across the bridge's lower level from Cais da Ribeira, but if you've a head for heights it's an amazing sensation to walk over the upper deck some two hundred feet above the river. There's a beautiful view of the tiered ranks of Porto's old town from here and an even better one from the terrace of the **Mosteiro da Nossa Serra do Pilar** high above the bridge. From this former convent, Wellington planned his surprise crossing of the Douro in 1809 and it's a barracks again today. The round church is open to the public, but sadly the unusual circular cloister rests in a sort of no-man's-land between church and army territory; it's currently being restored.

The Origins of the port wine trade

The distinction between **port wine** and the other Portuguese wines was first made at the beginning of the eighteenth century. Many British merchants, engaged in importing English cloth and Newfoundland cod to Portugal, were already living in Porto and were familar with Portuguese wines. When Britain prohibited the import of French wines from 1679 to 1685 and later during the War of the Spanish Succession (1702–1714), Portuguese wines became increasingly popular in Britain, with wines from the Douro region being particularly fashionable. The **Methuen Treaty** of 1703 between Britain and Portugal reduced the duty paid on Portuguese wine in return for the removal of Portuguese restrictions on British woollen goods. As a consequence, the port wine trade became so profitable and competitive that inferior wines, often adulterated and artificially coloured, were passed off as the genuine article – giving port itself a bad name. This led the future Marquês de Pombal to found the *Companhia Geral da Agricultura dos Vinhos do Alto Douro* in 1756 while, at the same time, **demarcating** the area from which port wine could legitimately come. The monopoly and demarcation were contentious for many years; the area was regularly extended, but only recently was permission granted for port to mature elsewhere than the lodges at Vila Nova de Gaia. Even now, strictly speaking, the demarcated area lies on either side of the Douro from Barrô, 8km downstream of Peso da Régua to

FLATTERY WILL GET YOU
ROUND THE WORLD!

"The excellence of the TV series is only surpassed by the books. All who have had any involvement in Rough Guides deserve accolades heaped upon them and free beer for life."
Diane Evans, Ontario, Canada

"I've yet to find a presentation style that can match the Rough Guide's. I was very impressed with the amount of detail, ease of reference and the smooth way it swapped from giving sound advice to being entertaining."
Ruth Higginbotham, Bedford, UK

"What an excellent book the Rough Guide was, like having a local showing us round for our first few days."
Andy Leadham, Stoke, UK

"Thank you for putting together such an excellent guidebook. In terms of accuracy and historical/cultural information, it is head and shoulders above the other books."
John Speyer, Yorba Linda, California

"We were absolutely amazed at the mass of detail which the Rough Guide contains. I imagine the word Rough is a deliberate misnomer!"
Rev. Peter McEachran, Aylesbury, UK

"I have rarely, if ever, come across a travel guide quite so informative, practical and accurate! Bravo!"
Alan Dempster, Dublin, Ireland

"The Rough Guide proved to be a very popular and useful book and was often scanned by other travellers whose own guides were not quite so thorough."
Helen Jones, Avon, UK

"My husband and I enjoyed the Rough Guide very much. Not only was it informative, but very helpful and great fun!"
Felice Pomeranz, Massachusetts, USA

"I found the Rough Guide the most valuable thing I took with me – it was fun to read and completely honest about everywhere we visited."
Matthew Rodda, Oxford, UK

"Congratulations on your bible – well worth the money!"
Jenny Angel, New South Wales, Australia

"Our Rough Guide has been as indispensable as the other Rough Guides we have used on our previous journeys."
Enric Torres, Barcelona, Spain

We don't promise the earth, but if your letter is really useful (criticism is welcome as well as praise!), we'll certainly send you a free copy of a Rough Guide. Legibility is a big help and, if you're writing about more than one country, please keep the updates on separate pages. All letters are acknowledged and forwarded to the authors.

Please write, indicating which book you're updating, to:

Rough Guides, 1 Mercer St, London WC2H 9QJ, England,
or
Rough Guides, 3rd floor, 375 Hudson St, New York, NY 10014-3657, USA

Travel the world
HIV *Safe*

Travel *Safe*

HIV, the virus that causes AIDS, is worldwide.

You're probably aware of the dangers of getting it from unprotected sex, but there are many other risks when travelling.

Wherever you're visiting it makes sense to take precautions. Try to avoid any medical or dental treatment, but if it's necessary, make sure the equipment is sterilised. Likewise, if you really need to have a blood transfusion, always ask for screened blood.

Make sure your travelling companions are aware of the risks and the necessary precautions. In fact, you should take your own sterile medical pack, available from larger high street pharmacies.

Remember, ear and body piercing, acupuncture and even tattoos could be risky, because they all involve puncturing the skin. And although you might not normally consider any of these things now, after a few drinks - you never know.

Of course, the things that are dangerous at home are just as dangerous when you travel. So don't inject drugs or share works.

Avoid casual sex and always use a good quality condom when having sex with a new partner (and each time you have sex with them).

And it's not just a 'gay disease' either. In fact, worldwide, it's most commonly transmitted through sex between men and women.

For information in the UK:

Ring for the TravelSafe leaflet on the Health Literature Line freephone 0800 555 777, or pick one up at a doctor's surgery or pharmacy.

Further advice on HIV and AIDS: National AIDS Helpline: 0800 567 123. (Cannot be reached from abroad).

The Terrence Higgins Trust Helpline (12 noon–lOpm) provides advice and counselling on HIV/AIDS issues: 0171 242 1010.

MASTA Travellers Health Line: 0891 224 100.

Travel *Safe*

Travel the world HIV *Safe*

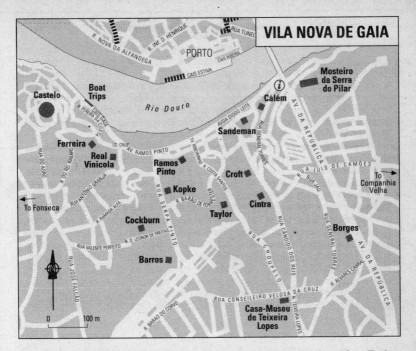

the Spanish frontier at Barca de Alva and on the Portuguese bank north to Freixo de Espada á Cinta and beyond.

Touring the lodges

Most of the **port wine lodges** were established in the eighteenth century, in the wake of the treaty of 1703 between England and Portugal, and although on the whole they have long since been bought by multinational brewing companies, they still try hard to push a "family" image. Almost without exception, they offer free **tasting** and a **tour** of the lodge, though not all are open for visits year-round. Most are usually open Monday–Friday 9.30am to noon and 2–5pm; in summer, some (like *Calém* and *Sandeman)* open on Saturday and Sunday, too. Simply stroll along the waterfront and follow the signs to the various lodges: some have tours at specific times, so you may have to pop back later, but many sit you in a waiting room until enough people have arrived. The **Turismo** in Vila Nova (Mon–Fri 9am–5.30pm, Sat 10am–6pm, Sun 2–6pm; ☎30 19 02) has up-to-date details of tours and visiting hours.

It's interesting to contrast one of the large manufacturers, like **Sandeman** or **Real Vinícola** – which operate virtually a production-line process – with the smaller, more traditional lodges such as **Calem**, **Croft**, or **Kopke**. **Taylor** – a bit of a hike uphill – gives a very informative talk on the processes and is happy to take just a couple of visitors at a time, as is **Fonseca** (whom they own). There are distinct contrasts, too, between the "British" names and the Portuguese-founded establishments, like **Ramos Pinto** or **Borges**. At the **Companhia Velha** lodge, the Swedish Consulate is actually tucked into the grounds; the company led the

MAKING PORT WINE

Grapes from vines in the demarcated region are **harvested** from mid-September to mid-October and then crushed – mechanically nowadays and not by foot, whatever the various lodges say. The grape juice ferments for a couple of days and then, when the natural sugar level is sufficiently reduced, the **fermentation** process is arrested by the addition of grape brandy – in a ratio of four parts wine to one part brandy. The wine then stands in casks in the *armazém* (lodge) of the company **quinta** (estate) until the following March, when it's transported downstream to the shippers' lodges at Vila Nova de Gaia, where it matures.

There are four basic **types of port** – *branco* (white), *tinto* (red), *tinto aloirado* (ruby) and *aloirado* (tawny) – which spend varying times maturing. **Vintages** are only declared in certain years, when a *quinta*'s wine is deemed to be of a sufficiently high quality; when this happens, the wine spends only two years in the cask before being bottled and left to mature. A vintage wine is ready to drink between ten and fifteen years after bottling; it's a darker colour than the other wines, because of the amount of time it spends in the bottle. The label on the bottle will show you the company, the vintage year, the year it was bottled, and sometimes the name of the *quinta*. **Late-bottled vintage wine** (LBV) is wine that's not of vintage quality, but still good enough to mature in bottles, to which it's transferred after five or six years in the cask. All other ports are made from blends of wines, and most are kept in the cask for much longer – at least seven years for a tawny. Wines designated 20-, 30-, or 40-year-old port are also blended and spend, on average, that length of time in the cask, after which time they lose much of their original red colour, becoming lighter the older they are.

first Portuguese challenge to the British port monopoly in the nineteenth century. Also in the grounds are numerous warehouses storing casks for the rich and famous (Generalissimo Franco – or his descendants – among them), as well as a six-kilometre-long tunnel – intended to form part of a rail link but found to be built at the wrong angle – which now serves as a perfect cold storage for Velha's famed sparkling wines and vintage ports.

Casa-Museu de Teixeira Lopes

A more sober visit in Vila Nova de Gaia could be made to the **Casa-Museu de Teixeira Lopes** (Mon–Sat 9am–12.30pm & 2–5.30pm, free), a very steep hike up Rua Cândido dos Reis from the waterfront; or take bus #36 across the bridge as far as "Hospital". Lopes was Soares dos Reis's principal pupil and formed the centre of an important artistic and intellectual set that lived in Gaia at the turn of the century. The circle is well represented in the second part of the museum's display, the first being devoted to Lopes' work – much of it preoccupied with the depiction of children. His masterpiece is considered to be the enigmatic portrait of an Englishwoman, *A Inglesa*.

River trips and walks

The *Cruzeiro das Quatro Pontes* company operates regular **river trips** (May–Oct Mon–Fri on the hour from 10am to 6pm; Sat at 10am, 11am & noon) leaving from the dock outside the *Ferreira Port Company*. The standard 50-minute ride takes you through most of the city, and under all four bridges.

Another rewarding excursion is the **walk downriver** past the port houses to the coast at the small fishing port of **Afurada**. Small ferries, bedecked with *Sandeman* hoardings and pursuing erratic courses against the currents, cut across the rivermouth between here and the grubby Porto suburb of **Foz do Douro**. From there, you can take a #1 or #18 bus back to the centre of town.

Eating

You may be shocked to discover that the city's speciality is *tripas* (tripe) and that the people are affectionately referred to by the rest of the country as *tripeiros* – tripe eaters. Don't let this put you off – there's always plenty of choice on the menu and the cooking is as good as any in Portugal. You'll be able to eat well and cheaply, though the central shopping areas – on either side of Avenida dos Aliados – are surprisingly short of cafés and restaurants; for the best bargains, you have to be prepared to dig into less salubrious areas. At the basic level, Porto has **workers' cafés** galore, all with wine on tap and often with a cheap set menu for the day. They are mainly lunchtime places, though most serve an evening meal until around 7.30pm and a few stay open later; prime areas are the grid of streets north and south of the Cordoaria: especially Rua do Almada (north) and Rua de São Bento da Vitória (south). Moving more upmarket, into the **restaurant** league, the Cais da Ribeira is hard to beat for atmosphere or for its fish, with any number of café-restaurants installed under the arches of the first tier of dwellings.

Unless otherwise stated, all the restaurants listed below are open daily; telephone numbers are given for those where it might be necessary to reserve in advance. You'll be able to eat a full meal with drinks for around 2500$00 a head, often much less than this if you're careful.

If you're **buying your own food**, check "Listings" (below) for the locations of central markets. Also worth seeking out is the **bakery** at Travessa de Cedofeita 20b, one of the oldest in the country, using traditional methods such as burning *carqueja* – a variety of broom which reaches high temperatures while producing very little ash. The speciality is *pão-de-ló*, a round sponge cake.

Central Porto

Aquário Marisqueiro, Rua Rodrigues Sampaio 163 (☎200 22 31). Just off Avda. dos Aliados, one block south of Rua Formosa. One of the city's best seafood restaurants – and not expensive for the quality of cooking. Around 2000–3000$00. Closed Sun.

A Brasileira, Rua do Bonjardim 118. Old of the oldest and most elegant of Porto's restaurants, with an Art Deco interior, pavement café, stand-up bar and smallish dining room with attentive waiter service. Around 3000$00. Closed Sun.

Don Guilon, Rua de Passos Manuel 241. Reliable budget-priced restaurant.

Restaurante O Escondidinho, Rua de Passos Manuel 114 (☎200 10 79). The entrance isn't obvious (*escondidinho* means "the little hidden place"), but once you've located it you're in for a treat – a cluttered, country-house interior and excellent French-influenced Portuguese cuisine. Try the hake in Madeira sauce and a kirsch omelette if you have 3000$00 to spend; more like 5000$00 for a feast. Book ahead.

Pedro dos Frangos, Rua do Bonjardim 219–223. Down to earth grillhouse, where you can sit at the bar or in the upstairs restaurant. A *meia frango* (half chicken), fries, salad and wine won't come to more than 1500$00 – leaving plenty of change for a night's entertainment. Closed Tues.

Cais da Ribeira and Around

Casa Filha da Mãe Preta, Cais da Ribeira 39. Built into the arches – the *azulejo*-decorated upper floor gives you a view over the river. An excellent *ementa turistica* features mackerel, sardines and all the business.

Chez Lapin, Rua Canastreiro 40 (☎200 64 18). Under the arches, near Praça da Ribeira, this deceptively large place is popular locally, particularly on Sundays when many others are closed (reserve in advance then). And, yes, one house speciality is rabbit.

Restaurante Chinês, Avda. Vimara Peres 38. Some of the city's best Chinese food – served in a modern building just at the entrance to the Ponte Dom Luís I. Allow around 2000$000 for the tourist menu.

Dom Tonho, Cais da Ribeira 13–15 (☎200 43 07). Typical of the recent move upmarket for the Cais da Ribeira area is this high-class restaurant owned by pop star Rui Veloso. Expensive.

Mais Um, Avda. Vimara Peres 73. Good, cheap food and friendly management.

Taverna do Bébobos, Cais da Ribeira 24 (☎31 35 65). Established in the nineteenth century, this has a real old *tasca* feel, with its barrels of wine on the walls. Fish and regional specialities – try the pork with wine sauce. Very popular, so book ahead if possible. Full meals will cost up to 3000$00. Closed Sun and the first two weeks of Sept.

Around Praça da Batalha

Casa Meia Lua, Rua Cimo da Vila 151. Small and friendly place where you can eat well for around 1000$00.

Mesa Antiga, Rua Santo Ildefonso 208. Excellent regional specialities in a family-run restaurant – the most typical dish is tripe. Closed Sat.

Montecarlo, Rua de Santa Catarina 17. Hidden away up on the second floor , this looks like a badly neglected 1930s' tearoom, has views over Praça da Batalha, a buzzing television, food that veers from good to indifferent and, particularly at Sunday lunchtime, very noisy locals. It's also very good value for money.

Tropical, Praça da Batalha 132. Simple *churrasqueria* on the square with fine servings of grilled chicken, accompanied by a demon-like *piri-piri* sauce. Other dishes – "underdone meet" and "beef-steak with cheeps" – are less inspired. Friendly and cheap; under 1500$00 for chicken, fries, dessert, wine and coffee.

Cordoaria to Praça de Carlos Alberto

Casa Costa, Campo dos Mártires da Pátria 166. Very cheap workers' diner on the square immediately south of the gardens. Open until 10pm.

Papagaio, Trav. do Carmo 32. French cuisine and bistro decor – old film stars and parrots featuring heavily (*papagaio* means parrot).

Piramide, Rua do Breyner 50. A vegetarian restaurant (and as such, quite a find). The dish of the day is the thing to go for, otherwise you're in for a long wait.

Solar Moinho de Vento, Largo do Moinho de Vento. Largely patronised by locals and moderately priced – around 1500$00. It's at the top of end of Rua da Fábrica.

A Tasquinha, Rua do Carmo 23. "Olde worlde" sort of place, with wine barrels, a block north of the gardens. Only open until 9.30pm and closed Sun.

Restaurant Típico, Trav. de Cedofeita 56. Fairly authentic Portuguese food at reasonable prices – around 1500$00.

Drinking, nightlife and entertainment

Cafés in the city rival Lisbon's, with some lovely old Art Deco survivals in the main shopping streets. Trendier, late-night **bars** are found in the streets around the Cais da Ribeira (Rua de Fonte Taurina, Rua de São João and Rua de Belomonte), where establishments run the gamut from unlicensed (and thus illegal) bars selling cheap beer to designer joints aimed squarely at the club crowd. Many of the latter have a minimum charge of around 800$00. Porto's **discos** are highly regarded, too, although most are way outside the centre – you'll need a taxi. As with Lisbon, most of Porto's clubs stay open until 4–5am or so, with a standard 1000–1500$00 admission levied; at most places you can present the entrance ticket as a voucher for your first couple of drinks.

As for other forms of entertainment, **classical music concerts** are held regularly in the *Auditório Nacional Carlos Alberto*, Rua das Oliveiras 43 (☎200 45 40) and the *Claustros do Convento de São Bento da Vitoria*, Rua São Bento da Vitoria (☎200 65 47); **dance** and other musical events, including major **pop and rock concerts**, in the *Coliseu*, Rua Passos Manuel (☎200 51 96). Current **films** are on show at the *Auditório Nacional* (see above), *Cinema Batalha*, in Praça da Batalha, and *Cinema Novo*, in Rua de Constitação. You can pick up monthly concert **programmes** from the tourist offices; and there are film details and other **listings** in the local edition of *Público*.

Cafés

A Brasileira, Rua do Bonjardim 116. A sister branch to the one in Lisbon, with pavement seats and a good stand-up bar for breakfast and refuelling during the day. Closed Sun.

Imperial, Avda. dos Aliados. Best central spot for watching the world go by, with outdoor seats on the avenida and an interior awash with mirrors and murals.

Majestic, Rua de Santa Caterina 112. Perhaps the nicest of the old Art Deco cafés, the Majestic has recently been refurbished.

Bars

Academia, Rua de São João 80. Modish, oversized disco bar with pretensions.

Aniki Bobo, Rua de Fonte Taurina 58. Cool and spacious bar, sometimes featuring live music – there's a minimum charge here.

O Buraco da Viela, Rua dos Canastreiro. A regular young crowd produces a good atmosphere.

Esta-Se Bem, Rua de Fonte Taurina 70. A nice little *tasca* with a bit of atmosphere as clubbers call in for cheap drinks before moving on.

Gremayo, Rua de São João 76. Top bar with some of the best music in town.

Meia Cave, Praça da Ribeira 6. A prime example of what a bit of prosperity has brought to the area: a smart well-dressed crowd paying premium prices for drinks served up with loud rock.

Porto Fino, Rua de Fonte Taurina 52. Metallic silver modernist bar.

Solar do Vinho do Porto, Rua Entre Quintas, Jardim do Palácio de Cristal. Laid-back venue for port-drinking in civilised surroundings; see p.215.

Discos and clubs

Batô, Largo do Castelo 13. High camp pirates' galleon interior, just needs Errol Flynn sliding down one of the masts. Trendy clientele, and high prices.

Cais 447, Avda. Menéres 447, Matosinhos. Won't appeal to all; the *Cais* seems proud of its go-go-dancers-on-marble-columns image and comparisons with the *Alcântara* in Lisbon.

Griffon's, Centro Comercial Brasília, Avda. da Boavista. Always busy dance bar, overflowing with pretentious types, redeemed by non-stop good music. Free entrance, but dress up for it.

Indústria, Avda. do Brasil 853, Centro Comercial da Foz, Foz do Douro (☎67 68 12). Porto's fashion-conscious at their most vapid.

Labirinto, Rua Nossa Senhora de Fátima 334 . A "bar-arcade" catering for a wide range of tastes with shows, concerts, exhibitions, live music.

Loko Moskito, Rua Eugénio de Castro, Galeria Foco. Small, down-to-earth bar laid out to cater for only a few people. Nice atmosphere and usually good music.

Rocks, 228 Rua Rei Ramiro, Vila Nova de Gaia (☎30 12 08). Built in old port cellars, this does indeed rock. Fantastic terrace with a view over the Douro, and barbecues in the summer.

Swing, Centro Comercial Brasília, Avda. da Boavista (☎69 00 19). The disco-goers no. 1 choice in the city, with a lively clientele bent on enjoying themselves.

Listings

Airlines *TAP*, Praça Mouzinho de Albuquerque 105 (☎69 98 41); *British Airways*, Rua Júlio Dinis 778–2º (☎69 45 75).

Airport information Call ☎948 21 41.

American Express c/o *Star Travel*, Avda. dos Aliados 202.

Banks and exchange Main branches are concentrated around Praça da Liberdade. When they're closed, *Intercontinental*, Rua Ramalho Ortigão 10, just below the main tourist office, will change money, as will the major hotels.

Books and maps There is an English-language bookshop in Rua da Picaria; try also *Livraria Internacional*, Rua 31 de Janeiro 43, or the lovely old shop at 144 Rua dos Clérigos. Maps are available from *Porto Editora*, Rua da Fábrica.

Buses Major companies include: *Rodoviária do Porto*, Praça Filipa de Lencastre, which serves most destinations in northern Portugal, both by express and local bus; *Rodonorte*, Rua Ateneu Comercial do Porto, off Rua de Passos Manuel, for express services to towns in Trás-os-Montes (Vila Real, Chaves, Bragança); and *InterNorte*, which operates international buses to most parts of Europe from their head office on Praça da Galiza and, more conveniently, from Rua das Carmelitas. *Rede Nacional de Expressos (Renex)*, Rua Alexandre Herculano, is the best express service to Lisbon. Before setting out for any of these terminals, it's well worth checking times and details with the tourist office.

Car rental Companies include: *Jumbo Travel*, Rua Ceuta 47 (☎38 15 61); *AutoCerro*, Rua do Monte 130 (☎941 35 13); and *Inter Rent*, Rua do Bolhão 182 (☎38 19 64). Most companies maintain offices at the airport, where cars can usually be booked on the spot.

Car repairs Addresses from the *Automóvel Clube de Portugal*, Rua Gonçalo Cristovão 2 (☎200 92 73), which also operates a breakdown service.

Consulates *UK*, Avda. da Boavista 3072 (☎68 47 89); *Netherlands*, Rua da Reboleira 7 (☎200 48 67). The nearest consulates for all other nationalities are in Lisbon; see p.84.

Cruises Apart from the short river tours detailed on p.218, longer – three-hour – journeys along the Douro leave twice daily from the Cais da Ribeira. In addition, *Endouro Turismo*, Rua da Reboleira 49 (☎208 41 61), operates one- and two-day cruises up the Douro as far as Barca de Alva, on the Spanish border.

Emergencies General ☎115 (free); Red Cross ☎60 720; Police ☎200 68 21.

Hospital *Santo António*, Rua José de Carvalho (☎200 73 54).

Markets There's a general daily market in the *Mercado Bolhão* on Rua Sá da Bandeira, behind the main post office, a must for self-caterers and picnic buyers. Flea markets (best on Saturday mornings) are held along Calçada de Vandoma, below the Sé, and Alameda das Fontaínhas, overlooking the river.

Newspapers English-language papers are available from *Tabacaria Senador* on Praça da Batalha; the subway kiosk below São Bento station; and *Livraria Bertrand* in the Centro Comercial de Brasília, Praça Mouzinho de Albuquerque (bus #3 from Praça da Liberdade). Porto's leading paper, the *Jornal de Notícias*, and the local edition of *Público*, are useful sources of information on cinemas, clubs and sports events, etc.

Pharmacies Late-night services are detailed in the *Jornal de Notícias*.

Post office The main post office (daily 8.30am–9pm) is opposite the town hall in Praça General Humberto Delgado; *posta restante* mail is held here, and you can also make international phone calls.

Shopping Most shops open Monday–Friday only, and those that do open on Saturday close at lunchtime. However, the *Centro Comercial Brasilia* (at the Praça Mouzinho de Albuquerque end of Avda. Boavista) stays open over the weekend.

Sport The city's principal soccer team, F.C. Porto, were winners of the European Cup in 1987 and have alternated with Benfica over recent years in winning the league championship; they play at the 90,000-capacity *Estádio das Antas*; bus #6/78 from "Praça da Liberdade". First Divison football is on view, too, from two other Porto sides: S.C. Salgueiros, who play in Vila Nova de Gaia at the *Sport Comércio e Salgueiros*, on Rua Álvares Cabral, and Boavista F.C., whose *Estádio do Bessa* is on Rua Primeiro de Janeiro.

Telephones You can make international calls at the post office in Praça General Humberto Delgado and at the *Telecom* office in Praça da Batalha.

Trains See "Arrival and Information" for destinations from the various Porto stations. São Bento station information office has timetables for all trains routed from Campanhã; they can tell you the connection you'll need to make from São Bento. If you're leaving Porto on an international connection – Paris especially – in the summer, be sure to reserve a seat several days in advance.

Travel agencies *Jumbo Travel*, Rua Ceuta 47 (☎38 15 61) is useful for budget/student travel.

Around Porto: the coast

The coastline immediately **south of Porto** is one of the worst polluted in Europe, with industrial effluent and inadequate sewage facilities constituting a major health hazard. In recent years, there have been several outbreaks of hepatitis in Porto and Vila Nova de Gaia, linked with bathing in these waters, and it is currently not safe to swim until you reach Espinho or, better still, Esmoriz, Contegaça or Furadouro. The coast **to the north** is little better and you should certainly not swim off Matosinhos; indeed, all the Porto beaches from Pastoras to Castelo do Queijo are officially out of bounds to bathers. However, press on a few kilometres further north from here to **Vila do Conde** or **Póvoa de Varzim** and you may be tempted to stay; indeed, in summer, you might prefer to visit Porto while based at one of these resorts.

South of Porto

Access to Espinho, Esmoriz and Cortegaça from Porto is either by **train** (hourly from São Bento) or **bus** (regular departures from the Praça Filipa de Lencastre terminal).

Espinho
ESPINHO, 18km south of Porto, is a major resort – though not a very attractive one. Windswept and overcrowded, it has a feeling of a suburb rather than a town, with a casino, a few high-rise hotels (more are on the way), hordes of tourist shops, a dull grid of numbered streets and a railway line right through the centre. To be positive, there is an enthusiastic **Turismo** on Rua 6 (June–Sept Mon–Fri 9am–9pm, Sat & Sun 10am–noon & 3–6pm; Oct–May Mon–Fri 9.30am–12.30pm & 2–5.30pm, Sat 9am–noon; ☎02/72 09 11) with some interesting ideas for exploring the hinterland; and **surfing** is possible here, too – advice from the surf shop in the *Centro Comercial California*. **Swimmers** might want to use the pool at the northern end of the esplanade; the Ministry of Health has blacklisted the Silvade beach to the south of town.

Staying overnight can be expensive since the few remaining old buildings on the seafront, some of which were pensions, are being bulldozed to make way for apartments. The cheapest hotel is the *Hotel Mar Azul*, Avda. 8, no. 676 (☎02/72 08 24; ④), with comfortable rooms and reasonable facilities. More interesting is the nineteenth-century *Vila Maria*, Rua 62, no. 667 (☎02/72 03 53; ④), set in its own grounds. There's a **campsite**, *Lugar dos Mochos* (☎02/72 37 18; open all year), inland, on the northern edge of town, not far from the *Vila Maria*.

You'll have no problem finding somewhere to **eat**, the most famous place being *Casa Maretta* on the esplanade, with excellent fish and seafood dishes. At the other end of the scale, *Pá Velha*, at the corner of ruas 16 and 23, serves tea and cakes. Finally, there are a dozen or more **discos and pubs**, whose reputations wax and wane: *Discoteca Spinus*, Rua 9, no. 87, continues to see off most of the competition.

Esmoriz and Cortegaça

The beaches at **ESMORIZ** (6km south of Espinho) and **CORTEGAÇA** (a further 2km south) offer a restful contrast to Espinho, primarily because the road and railway start to move inland as they head further south. This leaves you a walk of a couple of kilometres or so to reach either beach, both of which are backed by sand dunes and groves of pine and eucalyptus; both also have **campsites** (*Esmoriz* ☎02/727 09; *Cortegaça* ☎02/75 21 99), open all year. Just to the north of Praia de Esmoriz there's a small lagoon – one of the reasons that the road and railway were forced inland in the first place – and here you can expect to see waders, ducks and, depending on the season, pigeons and doves.

North of Porto

The stretch of coast around the mouth of the Douro is severely polluted, and you need to head at least as far as **VILA CHÃ**, 18km north of Porto, for a dip in the ocean. Despite encroaching development, this retains a fishing village identity, and has a fine sandy beach with pools at low tide. There's a **campsite** at Praia de Vila Chã (☎02/928 31 63), 1km west of the station. Trains run hourly from Porto's Estação da Trindade, and buses from Praça Filipa de Lencastre, to Vila Chã, before moving on to the larger resorts of Vila do Conde and Póvoa de Varzim.

Vila do Conde

VILA DO CONDE, 27km north of Porto, has become quite a significant resort over the last few years, but it has lost refreshingly little of its character in the process. Partly, this is because the beach (and all its attendant development) is a couple of kilometres south of town – a long stretch of fine sand, with drinks kiosks and restaurants to hand, and a stumpy fortification marking one end. Vila do Conde itself, though, manages to remain an active fishing port with a bustling Friday market and an atmospheric medieval quarter, which juts out into the sea beside the Rio Ave. The narrow streets are at their best on Saints' Days, when the little street corner votive chapels are illuminated by worshippers.

Dominating everything, on a rise behind, is the enormous bulk of the **Convento de Santa Clara** (daily 8am–12.30pm & 2–6pm), which is now a reformatory for boys but is still open for visits. One of the inmates will be designated to show you around its early Gothic church, which contains fine relief carvings, especially on the tombs of the founders. There's an elegant cloister, too, with a fountain fed by the long aqueduct – now partly ruined – which stretches from here into the hills. Below, back in the centre of town, the sixteenth-century **Igreja Matriz** is a beauty, with a soaring, airy interior and – thanks to the Basque workmen who helped with its construction – an unusual but very effective mix of Spanish and Portuguese styles. Vila do Conde is also known for its lace and, with the help of the handicraft centre on Rua 5 de Outubro (or, failing that, the Turismo), you can visit the **lace-making school** on Rua de São Bento. If you're especially interested in Portugal's regional crafts, there's a bonus in the town's annual **crafts fair**, held in the last week of July and the first week of August.

Buses from Porto arrive (and leave from) in front of the Igreja Matriz. The **train station** is a five-minute walk from the centre; follow the river down, past the convent, to the bridge. Just up from the bridge, on the left, is the **Turismo**, an ivy clad house in a rose garden at Rua 25 de Abril 103 (Mon–Fri 9am–6pm, Sat & Sun 1.30–5pm; ☎052/63 14 72). This has a list of private **rooms**, which is likely to be all you'll find in the summer. If you're booking ahead, or travelling out of season, try the *Pensão Patrata*, overlooking the waterfront at Cais das Lavandeiras 18 (☎052/63 18 94; ③); the more modern *A Princesa do Ave* on Rua Dr. Antonio José Sousa Pereira (☎052/64 20 65; ④); or the *Estalagem do Brasão* on Avenida Dr. João Canavarro (☎052/63 20 16; ⑤). All are good value, the last in a converted, seventeenth-century town house, with *pousada*-quality furnishings. The nearest **campsite** (☎052/63 32 25; open all year) is 2km south of town, near the beach.

Of the **restaurants**, recommended places included *La Fruits*, a stylish fondue place on the Cais das Lavandeiras, and *Le Villageois* (closed Mon) for steaks, which overlooks the riverside Praça da República. These are both pricey choices, though, and more reasonable budget meals can be had at *Restaurante Saõ Roque* in Rua do Lidador (closed Mon) and *Restaurante Ramon* in Rua 5 de Outubro (closed Tues).

Póvoa do Varzim

PÓVOA DO VARZIM is within walking distance to the north of Vila do Conde – but the two couldn't be more different. Although Póvoa, too, retains a small harbour, along with the ruins of a fortress, it is very much an out-and-out resort. A casino and a line of concrete hotels open onto the beach, which is crowded throughout the year with Portuguese holidaymakers.

But you shouldn't be discouraged from coming. The crowds here help to create a lively, enjoyable seaside feel, restaurants are plentiful and excellent value and there usually seems to be enough accommodation to go round. The helpful **Turismo**, at Avenida Mouzinho de Albuquerque 166 (May to mid-Sept daily 9am–9pm; mid-Sept to April Mon–Fri 9am–9pm, Sat 9.30am–1pm & 2.30–6.30pm; ☎052/61 46 09), has lists of **rooms**, while the cheaper **pensions** are to be found mostly along Rua Paulo Barreto and Rua Caetano de Oliveira, which run parallel to the beach, one block inland: here, on the former you could try *Pensão Campino* (☎052/62 47 98; ②) or, on the latter, *Pensão Firminho* (☎052/68 46 95; ②). Mid-range options include *Pensão Cego do Maio*, Largo Dr. David Alves (☎052/62 27 98; ③) and *Pensão Avo Velino*, Avenida Vasco da Gama (☎052/68 16 28; ④) or, if you can run to it, the *Residencial Luso-Brasileira*, Rua dos Cafés 16 (☎052/61 51 61; ⑤), 100m from the beach – though you'll need a top-floor room to be able to see it.

Buses operate from the central Praça do Almada; the **train station** is a few minutes walk from here, along the Rua Almirante Reis. To reach the beach from the train station (10min), turn right and, on reaching Praça do Almada, turn left and walk straight ahead – along Rua Dr. S. Campos, across Praça da República and then along Rua da Junqueira, at the end of which is the seafront.

Around Póvoa de Varzim

There are four reasonably accessible sites close to Póvoa, which, given a spare day and rented bikes, or a car, would make a rewarding circuit. It's more difficult by public transport; consult Póvoa's tourist office before setting out.

LAUNDOS, 7km to the northeast, is notable for its windmills which stand on São Felix hill. Trains make a halt here on the line between Póvoa de Varzim and Vila Nova de Famalicão (3–4 daily), and further on there's also a stop at Fontainhas, a couple of kilometres from **RATES**, a village which sports a splendid eleventh-century Romanesque church. Built in granite by the Benedictines for Henry, Count of Burgundy, and dedicated to São Pedro, the three naves are timber-roofed, while inside, a series of fine pillars with carved capitals are lit by a colourful rose window. **RIO MAU**, 8km from Póvoa, is the site of a smaller, but even better decorated, Romanesque church, also granite, completed in 1151 and dedicated to São Cristovão. The carvings on the capitals are reminiscent of those in Braga cathedral and, in this case, are thought to illustrate the Song of Roland. You can reach Rio Mau by bus from Póvoa.

The oldest of the settlements on this circuit is **TERROSO**, just 5km northeast of Póvoa de Varzim. A *citânia* similar to the better known ones at Sanfins (p.227) and Briteiros (p.257) was excavated at the beginning of this century – and the double ring of ramparts can still be traced. The spring here once fed the eighteenth-century aqueduct which carried water over 999 arches to the Convento de Santa Clara in Vila do Conde (see above).

Inland from Porto

Travelling **north** by road or rail from Porto towards the southern Minho towns of Guimarães and Braga, you pass through attractive, rolling countryside: a mix of market gardening in the valleys, vines on the gentle slopes, and wooded hill tops. Santo Tirso is the minor capital of this area, a riverside town which serves as a base for visiting the Romanesque church at nearby Roriz and the *citânia* of Sanfins de Ferreira.

Santo Tirso

Just under 30km north of Porto, **SANTO TIRSO** lies on the steep southern bank of the River Ave, which flows west to meet the sea at Vila do Conde. At the foot of the slope, by the bridge linking the town to its train station, is the former Benedictine monastery and church of São Bento, which now houses an agricultural college and a small **municipal museum** (Mon–Fri 9am–12.30pm & 2–6pm, Sat 9am–12.30pm). This is less than gripping, fielding the usual motley collection of local archeological finds, but take the opportunity to visit the church, whose cloister features a fine double row of galleries dating from the fourteenth century. On the plateau cresting the slope is the town hall, a charmless, concrete block; the **Turismo** (Mon–Fri 9am–12.30pm & 2–5.30pm; ☎052/520 64) occupies an annex.

Buses drop you at the station on Rua Infante Dom Henrique; **trains** (hourly, from Porto's Trindade station) stop on the other side of town, across the river. The train route continues from Santo Tirso to Guimarães. You're unlikely to need to stay – and **accommodation**, in any case, is limited and expensive – but if you do, try the homely *Pensão Familiar Caroco*, Largo Coronel Batista Coelho (☎052/52 823; ④).

Roriz

RORIZ, 10km east of Santo Tirso, is much prettier, but the paucity of local public transport means you'll have to walk at least some of the way. Any bus on the Santo Tirso–Guimarães route can set you down just after Rebordoes, leaving a four-kilometre walk to the church of São Pedro, at the top of the village. It's uphill all the way, but a pleasant enough hike, and you can pause to look out over the valley of the Rio Vizela, which merges with the Rio Ave just before Santo Tirso.

The village itself is a mixture of old, rough granite cottages, whitewashed houses and several fairly kitsch creations built by returned emigrants – one is straight out of Disneyland, a Seven Dwarfs' cottage with brown concrete thatch. The date of the elegant Romanesque **church of São Pedro** is disputed, but it's said to stand on the foundations of a Roman temple, later destroyed by the Moors. It was originally the church of the Benedictine monastery which once stood alongside, of which only one building still stands – and that is in private hands. The fine west door is embellished with an early Gothic rose window, while adjacent is a solitary bell tower.

The Citânia de Sanfins de Ferreira

Another 4km beyond the church of São Pedro, along a track through shady woods and up a gentle slope, is the **Citânia de Sanfins de Ferreira**. Here, on the crest of a hill, you can still trace the outer ramparts and the foundations of circular huts, though other than those there's little to see. But it's a splendidly atmospheric place – the skyline to the south appears infinite and, at the height of summer, the only sound is that of the broom pods popping.

East to Penafiel

One of the surviving northern inland train routes – the **Douro railway line** (*Linha do Douro*) – heads east, out of Porto, although running, in fact, for an initial 40km alongside the Rio Sousa and not the Rio Douro. If you're on one of the slow trains, it will stop at Cête, a dozen stations out of Porto and just a kilometre or so away from the vilage of **PAÇO DE SOUSA**. This was the former headquarters of the Benedictines in Portugal and, set beside the Rio Sousa, is a popular picnic spot for Porto locals.

The principal sight, inevitably, is the old **abbey church**, a dank and dark medieval building in the process of restoration. In one corner is the **tomb of Egas Moniz**, tutor and adviser to the first king of Portugal, Afonso Henriques, and a great figure of loyalty in Portuguese histories. In 1127, shortly after Afonso Henriques had broken away from his grandfather, the king of León, Egas was sent to negotiate a settlement, thus enabling Afonso to concentrate his efforts on the Moors in the south. Within three years, the king of León considered the treaty to be broken on the Portuguese side and threatened all-out war. Egas made his way to León, presented himself and his family, and, as can be seen on the panels around the tomb, offered to receive the punishment due to his master. Mercy was granted and the king sent the loyal minister home unscathed.

There are a couple of **cafés** in the village and plenty of possible **camping** spots. If you're looking for a bed, it's not much further down the line to Penafiel.

Penafiel and around

At **PENAFIEL** you enter *vinho verde* country. The wine's origins lie with the Benedictine monks, who were famed in this region for their laborious terracing of the valley slopes. A further legacy of the Benedictine presence is a dozen of the finest **Romanesque churches** in the country, each gorgeously sited in hamlets hidden away in folds of the countryside.

Despite the new motorway in the Sousa valley to the west, Penafiel itself is still split by main road traffic, and getting to it involves a connecting bus from the **train station** – some way down the hill. But it has a saving grace in its fabulous local **wine**, served from massive barrels in the *adega* in the central Largo do Padre Américo. This also offers basic food, washed down with pints of wine at a time; a stream of old men in black hats moves regularly through its doors. Right next door is a good-value **pension**, the *Casa João da Lixa* (☎055/251 58; ②), while nearby, there's a fine covered **market**. If you are interested in exploring the area's churches, call in at the **Turismo**, housed in a modern complex at Avenida Sacadura Cabral 90 (Mon–Fri 9am–12.30pm & 2–5.30pm; ☎055/71 25 61), which dispenses advice and stacks of leaflets. Just downhill from here is the *Restaurante Relógio do Sol*, which serves good food (at around 1000$00 a head) and has a fine view over the Sousa valley.

Most of the local **churches** are hard to reach without your own transport. The most accessible by bus (departure at 11am; return mid-afternoon) is at **BOELHE**, off the main road to Entre-os-Rios and overlooking the Tâmega valley. This is reputedly the smallest Romanesque church in the country: a simple building, without much architectural detail, which gains its power from a stunning position on the brow of a hill. If it's closed, ask for the key at the nearest house.

The Tâmega: Amarante and beyond

At **LIVRAÇÃO**, about an hour from Porto, the Tâmega train line cuts off for Amarante (see below), hugging the ravine of the **Rio Tâmega**, a Douro tributary. There is scarcely more than the station at Livração, so if you're changing trains, keep your eyes open. The Tâmega line trains terminate at Amarante, from where four buses daily run up into the Serra do Marão – following the course of the Rio Tâmega – to **Celorico** and on to the next crossroads at Fermil, where a local bus picks up passengers for **Mondim de Basto**. To explore the valley, the best idea is to take a bus to Celorico and walk, following the increasingly overgrown tracks, to Mondim: a pleasant two-hour hike, through woods and over viaducts.

If your time is limited, the half-hour trip from Livração to Amarante is worthwhile in itself. From the start it's an impressive, scenic ride, with pine woods and vines clinging to incredible slopes, and goats scrambling across the steep terrace walls to nibble at haystacks constructed to hang from the branches of living trees.

Amarante

AMARANTE is set immaculately along the Tâmega river, the wooden balconies of its old houses leaning over the water. It's a fine place to stop, with any number of bars and cafés along the riverside, mostly on the opposite side from the station. Sadly, the polluted river beaches can no longer be recommended – at least for swimming – though, in summer, pedalboats (*barcos a pedal*) or rowing boats can be hired for an hour or two's dawdling.

The church, and former monastery, of **São Gonçalo**, beside the very elegant town bridge, is Amarante's most prominent monument. It forms the heart of an ancient fertility cult – probably with pagan origins – which still persists here at the grand *Festa de São Gonçalo*, celebrated on the first weekend in June. At this time, traditionally, the local unmarried youth exchange phallus-shaped cakes as tokens of their love. In the church, the saint's tomb is said to guarantee a quick marriage to anyone who touches it – his face, hands, and feet have been almost worn away by hopeful suitors. Another chapel, devoted to Gonçalo's healing miracles, is festooned with wax models of every conceivable part of the body along with entire artificial limbs, bottles full of gallstones, and other votive offerings.

Around the side of the church, in the cloister of the former monastery, is the **Museu Municipal Amadeo de Sousa Cardoso** (Tues–Sun 10am–12.30 & 2–5.30pm; free). This is a surprising exhibition to find out in the sticks – dominated by the Cubist works of local boy Amadeo de Sousa Cardoso, one of the few Portuguese painters of this century to achieve international renown.

Should you happen to be in Amarante on a summer Saturday evening (July–Sept) you could join in one of the **festivals** in the gardens of the Casa da Calçada, with as much food and wine as you can handle for around 3000$00. There's also a year-round Wednesday **market**, held beside the river.

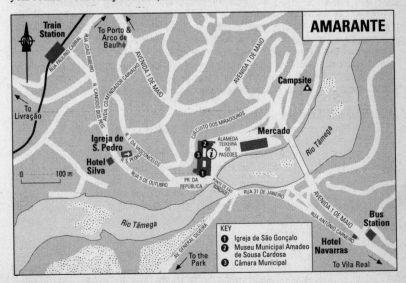

Practicalities

The **train station** is ten minutes' walk northwest of the centre, while **buses** pull up a little closer in, on the other side of the river. For information, and help with accommodation during summer, when rooms can be hard to come by, head for the **Turismo** (summer daily 9.30am–7pm; winter Tues–Sun 9.30am–12.30pm & 2–5pm; ☎055/429 80), housed in the Câmara Municipal, next to the art museum.

The nicest budget **accommodation** in town is at the *Hotel Silva*, on the north side of the river at Rua Cândido dos Reis 53 (☎055/42 31 10; ③) – comfortable and pleasantly sited, with a balcony (and several rooms) overlooking the river. Other choices are all across the river, with the *Residencial Estoril*, Rua 31º de Janeiro 49 (☎055/43 12 91; ①), and the *Casa Avião*, also on Rua 31º de Janeiro (☎055/43 29 92; ①), both very reasonably priced. Further along Rua 31º de Janeiro, and much more upmarket, is the *Casa Zé da Calçada* (☎055/42 20 23;. ⑤), a turn-of-the-century town house, while near the bus station is the modern *Hotel Navarras*, Rua António Carneiro (☎055/43 10 36; ⑤). There is a municipal **campsite** (☎055/43 21 33; open all year) in town, on the riverbank; another is planned a little further upstream.

Most pensions have **restaurants**, of highly varying quality, or try the *Adega Regional* on Rua de Olivença, off the main praça, where the proprietor serves well-spiced dishes washed down with jugs of heavy local red wine. More obvious is the *Café São Gonçalo*, on Praça da República, alongside the church and with the bridge in view, where the food is good but more expensive than usual. Also decidedly pricey, but worth every *escudo* is the restaurant attached to the *Casa Zé da Calçada* on Rua 31º de Janeiro, which dishes up local specialities.

Into the Serra do Marão: the Basto villages

Beyond Amarante you really feel the climb into the **Serra do Marão** on the approach to the villages of Celorico and Mondim de Basto, both set astride the Tâmega. To the north – and technically in the Minho region – is the larger, provincial town of Cabeceiras de Basto, which provides a useful transport link to Braga and the Peneda-Gerês national park (see the Minho chapter). This region, the **Terras de Basto**, is a fertile countryside that produces a strong *vinho verde*. The name ("basto" meant "I claim") comes from a group of Celtic statues, symbols of power, which have been found in several local spots.

Celorico and Mondim de Basto

Thirty kilometres northeast of Amarante, **CELORICO DE BASTO** is an attractive little village, full of civic pride in its neatly laid-out lawns and formal flower beds. It has a single **pension** (the *Progresso:* ☎055/32 11 70; ②), and lots of hiking potential. For a brief foray into the woods, there is a labyrinth of paths, heading off from behind the village church, while in the distance is the prospect of Monte Farinha, the highest peak in the region (see below). The mountain is more easily approached from Mondim de Basto, which is accessible from Celorico on a roundabout eleven-kilometre road (sporadic buses), or by hiking 6km along the old rail line.

Unless you're intent on hiking, there's little enough to **MONDIM DE BASTO**, though the views are majestic enough to wake up to after a night's stay, and there's good river swimming. There are two **places to stay**: the *Residencial Arcadia*, near the bus terminal (☎055/38 14 10; ③), and the *Residencial Carvalho*, by the petrol station on Avenida Dr. Augusto Brito (☎055/38 10 57; ③). There's also an excellent **campsite** – about 1km from the centre along the Vila Real road. For **meals**, try the *Churrasqueira Chasselik*.

There are regular **bus connections** from Mondim to Vila Real (a spectacular ride, skirting the Parque Natural de Alvão), Guimarães and Porto, changing buses at Fermil, just across the Tâmega valley. Alternatively, you could catch a bus – or walk – the 7km on to the lively provincial town of Cabeceiras de Basto (see below), from where there are regular buses to Braga and the Peneda-Gerês national park.

Monte Farinha and the Cabril Valley

Monte Farinha is surprisingly easy to climb – less than three hours' easy walking – and, if the times coincide, you can get a head start by taking the bus to the foot of the ascent, three-and-a-half kilometres from Mondim. Walking, follow the Cerva road out of Mondim, then take a path up to the right shortly after Pedra Vedra. Once on the mountain, follow the road which zig-zags to the summit. The panoramic views well repay your efforts, and at the top is the attractive parish church of **Nossa Senhora da Graça**, centre of a major *festa* on the first Sunday in September.

Another good hike from Mondim is into the **Cabril valley**. Only about twenty minutes beyond the village campsite, the Cabril – more a stream than a river – is crossed by a Roman bridge; impressive in itself and set near a little waterfall, where there's a good swimming hole. From here, follow the stream upstream to a working watermill or take the stone track (about 200m upriver) along what must have been a Roman road. Follow this, cross a road, and you're at the start of a maze of small paths cutting between the fields and vineyards of the Cabril valley, and leading higher into the pine-forested slopes.

Cabeceiras de Basto

CABECEIRAS DE BASTO is at the heart of the *Terras de Basto*, and proudly displays the finest of the *basto* figures – which has sported a French head since a prank during the Napoleonic Wars – in the gardens across from the bus station. The main local monument, just outside the town, is the Baroque **Mosteiro de Refojos** – one of the few religious institutions not to have succumbed to the temptation to bludgeon faith into the populace through a quartet of loudspeakers. If you pay your respects to the sacristan, not only can you visit the treasury (a collection of statues and religious garments) but also gain privileged access to the clocktower, from which you can view the church's highlight – the *zimbório* (dome). From here, too, you can look down over the peeling houses of the region's old landowners, reminders of the glory and elitism of Portugal's Age of Absolutism; they were hard hit by the revolution and its aftermath. Another area of town to explore is beyond a patch of ground set aside for the Monday **feira** – a left turn after the school takes you into the Campo do Guinchoso, where there's a *pastelaria* and **swimming** in the river – past the new housing development, signposted *Praia da Ranha*.

There is reasonable **accommodation** to be had at the *Residencial-Restaurante A Cafrial* on Avenida General Humberto Delgado (☎053/66 26 90; ③), and at the *Residencial-Restaurante São Miguel*, at Campo do Seco (☎053/66 10 34; ①), further out in the modern quarter of the town, near the post office. A short way up the road, at the back of the Refojos monastery, the *Restaurante Cozinha Real de Basto* has very good **meals**.

Buses connect Cabeceiras with Celorico and Mondim de Basto, Póvoa de Lanhoso in central Minho (which has links with Braga and Gerês destinations), Chaves in Trás-os-Montes, and Porto (Mon–Sat only).

Along the Douro: to Peso da Régua and on to the Spanish border

Leaving Porto **by road** and heading for Peso da Régua and port wine country, there are two possibilities: either take the motorway eastwards, leaving it at Penafiel or Amarante, or – with more time – follow the N108 southeast. This road hugs the north bank of the Douro river until Entre-os-Rios (where the Tâmega meets the Douro), after which it forks, allowing you to drive along either river bank. The north bank road is quicker; the south bank more attractive. As for the *Linha do Douro* **train from Porto**, this shadows the motorway, and passes close to Penafiel, but shortly after Livraçao, the line finally turns south to reach the Douro and then heads upstream. At Mesão Frio, the river temporarily leaves its confined channel and broadens into the little plain commanded by the port wine town of **Peso da Régua**. East of here, trains continue as far as **Pocinho**, though to travel any further – and to cross the border into Spain – you'll need to take buses or your own transport. You could always cut north from Régua instead, up the Corgo line, a brief excursion through marvellous vine and granite landscape to Vila Real (see p.293). Régua is also the jumping-off point for buses to the pilgrimage centre of **Lamego**, 13km to the south, at the tip of Beira Alta, and since this is by far the easiest link with the town, Lamego is covered here, along with its immediate region.

Peso da Régua

PESO DA RÉGUA (usually just Régua) is a small and very provincial town that has been known for over two centuries as the "Capital of the Upper Douro", because of its role in the port industry. In fact, the centre for quality port wines has shifted to Pinhão, half an hour further east; Régua is simply the junction and the depot through which all the wine must pass on its way to Porto. Nevertheless, the ornamental *barcos rabelos* anchored on the river, and the sombre *Sandeman* cut-out on the horizon, are a reminder of Régua's previous importance as the first capital of Pombal's demarcated port-producing region.

The small **Turismo** (Mon–Fri 9.30am–12.30pm & 2–5.30pm; ☎054/228 46) on the riverbank, opposite the train station, can inform you about visits to the local **port wine lodges** – open from Monday to Saturday. The easiest to visit are in Régua itself, the *Casa do Douro* and *Ramos Pinto*, each of which runs more personalised and interesting tours than their Vila Nova de Gaia equivalents. Apart from these alcoholic diversions, there's not much to do in Régua except wander through the upper town and along the riverbank. It's as well to be sure of your train connection or next bus out. **Buses to Lamego** run every hour up until 9pm, from in front of the station.

If you need to **stay**, the *Residencial Império,* at the corner of Largo da Estação and Rua Vasques Osório (☎054/32 23 98; ③), very close to the station, has nice

> ### RIVER, RAIL AND RIBBON LAKES
>
> In the eighteenth century, when the port-producing area was first demarcated (see p.216), the **Rio Douro** could not be navigated by the traditional *barcos rabelos* (barges) beyond the rapids of Cachão de Valeira. By the end of the century, engineering works had circumnavigated the worst of the rapids and opened up the Douro as far east as Pocinho, but travel was still slow – it took three days to float wine down from Peso da Régua to Porto. The arrival of the **railway** at the end of the nineteenth century accelerated transport up and down the valley: the track reached Régua in 1880 and arrived at the Spanish border in 1887, with the branch lines up the river's tributaries completed by 1910. Later, road transport replaced rail and the river itself became something of a backwater until the 1970s, when dams were planned along the length of the Douro.
>
> With the completion of the fifth dam in 1985, the river was turned into a series of **ribbon lakes** and thanks to locks along the route, it's now possible to cruise from Porto to Barca de Alva on the Spanish border, a distance of just over 200km. In addition, there are tentative proposals to dam the Coã valley and, more dramatically, the Tua valley, though a lack of funds may yet reprieve these side valleys. In the meantime, tourism is being encouraged as cruising, canoeing and water-skiing opportunities increase along the Douro.

rooms and views. At the other end of town, but cheaper, are the *Residencial Quixote*, Avenida Sacadura Cabral (☎054/32 11 51; ②) and *Pensão Borrajo* on Rua Vasques Osório (☎054/233 96; ①). **Camping** is possible, free of charge, below the swimming pool down by the river just beyond the bridge. There are plenty of **restaurants** along the main street; the *Muxima* is as good as any – and sometimes has rooms to let.

East to the border

Just beyond Régua, and past the massive dam of a hydroelectric power station, you begin increasingly to see the terraced slopes where the **port vines** are grown. They're at their best in August, with the grapes ripening, and in September, when the harvest has begun. Quotas for wine production have been in force around here since the mid-eighteenth century, and some terrace walls from that period have withstood the assault of the diggers and dynamite that are used nowadays to clear the way for the vineyard tractors. Grape-treaders and the traditional *barcos rabelos* have also been replaced by machines and cistern lorries, though there's still a demand for large groups of hand-pickers (*rogas*) when there's a bumper crop.

Pinhão, Tua and Pocinho

The country continues craggy and beautiful, with the softer hills of the interior fading dark green into the distance, past **PINHÃO**, the main centre for quality ports. There are a couple of **pensions** here if you want to stay: the *Pensão Douro*, ☎054/724 04; ②) and the *Pensão Ponte Grande* (☎054/724 56; ③). At **TUA**, 13km to the east of Pinhão, the narrow-gauge **Tua railway** begins its journey north to Mirandela (see Chapter 7, *Trás-os-Montes*), while the Douro line itself ends a further 32km east at the isolated station of **POCINHO**.

Torre de Moncorvo

Train arrivals at Pocinho are met by buses to **TORRE DE MONCORVO**, 10km to the northeast; several of these buses continue on to Mogadouro and Miranda do Douro, deep in Trás-os-Montes. A couple of other daily connections run to remote Freixo de Espada à Cinta, virtually on the Spanish border, and south to Vila Nova de Foz Côa, and thence into Beira Alta. All these buses arrive in and depart from the main square, Praça Francisco Meireles.

Aside from the sixteenth-century cathedral, there's little to see in Moncorvo (as it's known locally), though the narrow medieval streets are handsome enough: with the help of a map from the **Turismo**, on Rua Manuel Sexas (Mon–Fri 9am–12.30pm & 2–5.30pm; ☎079/222 89), you can track down the remains of the old town walls. The town's other attraction is more enduring – its almond trees, which draw crowds of Portuguese in February and March to witness the blossom, and whose nuts are gathered and sugared, and sold in local shops.

Accommodation should be no problem. The best pension is the *Passarinho* at Rua Infante Dom Henrique 23 (☎079/223 19; ②), or, if renovations have been completed, the *Campos Monteiro*, Rua Visconde de Vila Maior 55 (☎079/223 55; ②). More upmarket is a member of the *Turihab* network; the *Casa da Arco*, a town house built in 1880 and conveniently oposite the tourist office, at Rua Manuel Sexas 12 (☎079/224 01; ⑤). There's a **restaurant** attached to the *Residencial Caçula*, just down from the Sé, but otherwise Moncorvo is a bit of a gastronomic desert.

Barca de Alva and the border

Although trains go no further than Pocinho, walkers might enjoy following the rails for the twenty kilometres southeast to **BARCA DE ALVA**, and thence across the frontier to the villages along the Spanish Río Duero. Barca itself is an attractive place, overlooked by mountains on all sides and with a row of whitewashed cottages facing the river. But it's looking a little neglected now since the railway line across the border was discontinued in the 1980: if you're brave enough you can risk the rickety old metal railway bridge into Spain (beware of rotten sleepers and snakes!). **Accommodation** in the village is at the *Baga Douro* (①–②), above the restaurant on the main road along the river; the *Casa de Posto*, a few doors along, also has cheap rooms. The *Baga Douro* is the only place **to eat**, with a fine set meal and excellent breakfasts of coffee, fresh bread and local honey.

Barca makes a good local walking base. Cross the road bridge into Trás-os Montes and follow the quiet road along the Douro, towards Freixo de Espada. This takes you through olive and orange groves, and past the terraced vineyards still providing grapes for the port companies in Porto.

Lamego and Around

Although technically in Beira Alta, **LAMEGO** is isolated at the tip of its mountain province, and much more accessible from Régua and the Douro. The town itself has more in common with the Douro region, too, spreading over gentle slopes of the rich agricultural land fed by the river, a terrain which the locals put to good use in the production of such delights as hams and melons, as well as *Raposeira* – the closest thing to champagne you will find in Portugal.

Lamego is a wealthy place, and long has been, as evidenced by the graceful white *quintas* and villas on the hillsides, and the luxuriant architecture of the centre, where Baroque mansions seem to stand on every corner and lavish decorations are found within the smallest chapel. Lamego also has one of the very greatest Baroque structures in Europe – the shrine of **Nossa Senhora dos Remédios**, which, with its monumental stairway, dominates the west–east axis of the town.

The Town

For all the architectural histrionics of the shrine, it's Lamego's **Sé** that clearly delineates the centre of town. It is basically a Renaissance structure, though with a thirteenth-century tower surviving from a previous building. The mixture works well and the cloister is a beauty. Facing the cathedral, occupying an eighteenth-century palace, is the town's excellent **Museu Regional** (Tues–Sun 10am–12.30pm & 2–5pm), whose exhibits include five of the remaining panels of a polyptych commissioned from Grão Vasco by the Bishop of Lamego in 1506. Judging by the lack of correlation between the various panels – for instance the *Creation of the Animals* and the prodigiously executed *Annunciation* – some of the work must be attributed to the great man's school. Also on show are a series of sixteenth-century Flemish tapestries (including a marvellous *Life of Oedipus* sequence), three curious statues of a conspicuously pregnant Virgin Mary (a genre peculiar to this region), a fine assembly of *azulejos*, piles of ecclesiastical treasure from the Episcopal Palace and a group of chapels rescued from the decaying *Convento das Chagas*.

Across the square, Rua da Olaria, a narrow street of tiny shops, leads into Rua de Almacave, which follows the walls of the old inner town. The route takes you past the **Igreja de Almacave**, a very ancient foundation said once to have been a mosque, to Praça do Comércio. From here you can pass through the walls of the **Old Citadel** and climb up to the **Castelo**, surrounded by a cluster of ancient stone houses. This has been pressed into service as the local scout headquarters and the boys do have a fairly legitimate claim on the place, having – so they say – cleared eighteen lorryloads of garbage away in the 1970s and saved the building from ruin. You're unlikely to be able to gain entry either to the castle or to the thirteenth-century **Cisterna**, below, one of the strangest buildings in the country. An ancient water source, its interior resembles a perfectly preserved Romanesque chapel, its walls still bearing the original stonemasons' marks.

Nossa Senhora dos Remédios

The celebrated shrine of **Nossa Senhora dos Remédios** is a major point of pilgrimage – a reputation for healing miracles draws devotees from all over the country. Standing on a hill overlooking the city, it's approached by a magnificently elaborate eighteenth-century stairway, modelled on the one at Bom Jesus near Braga. Its seven hundred steps – which the most committed pilgrims ascend on their knees – are punctuated by a *via santa* of devotional chapels, *azulejos* and allegorical fountains and statues. After the approach, and its own facade, the church itself is simply a detail in the architectural ensemble: an assembly hall for the ever-present faithful.

The great **pilgrimage** here takes place on September 8, an occasion for several weeks' celebration in Lamego, starting in the last week of August and continuing

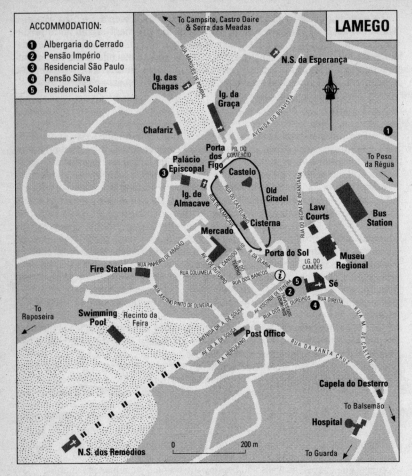

ACCOMMODATION:
- ❶ Albergaria do Cerrado
- ❷ Pensão Império
- ❸ Residencial São Paulo
- ❹ Pensão Silva
- ❺ Residencial Solar

LAMEGO

To Campsite, Castro Daire & Serra das Meadas

N.S. da Esperança

Ig. das Chagas

Ig. da Graça

Chafariz

Porta dos Figo

Palácio Episcopal

Castelo

Old Citadel

Ig. de Almacave

Cisterna

Mercado

Porta do Sol

Law Courts

Bus Station

Museu Regional

Fire Station

Sé

To Raposeira

Swimming Pool

Recinto da Feira

Post Office

Capela do Desterro

To Balsemão

Hospital

0   200 m

N.S. dos Remédios

To Guarda

into mid-September. Apart from the pilgrimage and its associated processions – some with cavalcades of young children in white – there's a traditional "Battle of Flowers", torchlit parades, rock concerts with some of the country's top bands, dances, car races and a fair on the Recinto da Feira, below the sanctuary.

Balsemão

At the hamlet of **BALSEMÃO**, a three-kilometre hike from the back of the Lamego cathedral, is a seventh-century chapel founded by the Suevi. The route requires three left turns in all: the first is at the Capela do Desterro down into the old quarters of town and across a bridge; the second, a fork on to the hillside road; and the third comes a little while later, taking you down into the valley and above a rushing river. After three large curves, a village school, a collection of outhouses and the chapel appear. Alternatively, take any Lamego–Régua bus and jump off at the sign pointing to the *Capelo de São Pedro*, a fifteen-minute walk away.

The undistinguished facade and dark interior of the **Capelo de São Pedro** (Tues–Sun 10am–12.30pm & 2–5pm) give it the air of a family vault, an impression strengthened by the imposing **sarcophagus** of Dom Afonso of Porto. Florid fourteenth-century capitals encircling the tomb make the few remaining Suevi curls on the archway into the choir seem subdued by comparison. A profoundly pregnant statue of *Nossa Senhora do Ó* (that's Ó as in *O! Nossa Senhora, Mãe de Deus . . .*) has recently been restored.

Practicalities

The **bus station** is behind the museum, right in the centre of town. In addition to the Régua connections (hourly until 8.15pm), there are services linking Viseu, Guarda and other points in Beira Alta. The **Turismo** is on Avenida Visconde Teixeira (summer Mon–Sat 9am–12.30pm & 2.30–8pm, Sun 10am–12.30pm & 2.30–8pm; winter Mon–Fri 9am–12.30pm & 2–5.30pm, Sat 9am–12.30pm; ☎054/ 620 05), just off the main square, Largo de Camões.

Accommodation

Accommodation can be tricky to find and is on the expensive side. Booking ahead is strongly advised, though if you turn up on spec, the Turismo may be able to sort you out a **private room**; possibilities include rooms at Rua de Santa Cruz 15 and Rua da Olario 61, above a smoked-ham shop and café (both ①). The local **campsite** (☎054/620 90) is 4km out on the N2 Castro Daire road, just beyond the *Moteis Turisserra* (see below), where there's a weekend of pilgrimages, picnics and general revelry on the second Sunday of every June. There are no buses to the campsite, but hitching in summer is no problem. **Pension and hotel** possibilities include:

Albergaria do Cerrado, on the Régua road, on the outskirts of town (☎054/631 64). Lamego's top hotel – well-equipped but a bit characterless. ⑥.

Pensão Império, Trav. dos Loureiros 6, off Avda. Visconde Teixeira (☎054/627 42). Pleasant if rather overpriced rooms. ④.

Moteis Turisserra, 4km out on the Castro Daire road (☎054/620 80). A modest motel (and very good restaurant), occupying a lofty position on the Serra das Meadas, alongside the campsite. ②.

Hotel Parque, by the church of Nossa Senhora dos Remédios, at the top of the hill (☎054/ 621 05). An unbeatable location and lovely hotel, set in its own gardens. ④.

Residencial São Paulo, Avda. 5 de Outubro (☎054/631 14). Reasonably central and reasonable quality. ④.

Pensão Silva, Rua Trás-da-Sé 26 (☎054/629 29). Decent rooms, though be warned that the cathedral bells strike every quarter of an hour all night long. ②.

Residencial Solar, Avda. Visconde Teixeira (☎054/620 60). A fraction further from the clock – though still with fine views over the cathedral. ①.

Eating and Drinking

Restaurants in Lamego, like pensions, are on the expensive side. The one at the *Pensão Império* is probably the best, if funds will stretch. If not, try the *Novo* (opposite the cathedral), or the *Combinado* on Rua da Olaria 17 (behind the Turismo), which does wonderful trout stuffed with smoked ham. Two other possibilities can be found on Avenida Dr. Alfredo de Sousa; the *Avenida* and the more expensive *Nenúfar*, the latter good for roast suckling pig and trout. A fine **picnic** can be assembled from the ham shop and nearby grocers on Rua da Olaria.

For drinking, a couple of saloon-door **bars** are to be found on the way to the castle – at the top of Rua de Almacave and at Rua do Castelinho 25 – though both close at 9pm. Finally, champagne enthusiasts may want to visit the **Caves Raposeira**, 1km out of town on the Castro Daire road. These are open for free tours and tasting (usually at 10am, 11am, 2pm, 3pm and 4pm); check with the tourist office before setting out.

South from Lamego

Continuing **south from Lamego**, in the direction of Guarda and Viseu, the country of the **Leomil** and **Montemuro** ranges is high, wild and sparsely inhabited. This territory was among the earliest to fall to Afonso Henriques, the first king of Portugal, in his march south against the Moors. It is said that he laid the first stone of the monastery of **São João de Tarouca** after his victories at Trancoso and Sernancelhe in Beira Alta. The region's three other rewarding sights – the monastery of **Salzedas**, the fortified bridge at **Ucanha** and the church at **Tarouca** – were also founded at this time.

São João de Tarouca
The small village of **SÃO JOÃO DE TAROUCA**, off the southeast route from Lamego to Guarda, was the site of the first Cistercian monastery to be founded in Portugal (1124). Only the simple **Romanesque Church** is really intact, and even here the greatest treasure – Gaspar Vaz's renowned altarpiece of Saint Peter – is no longer on display. Villagers complain that the authorities in Lisbon removed the painting for cleaning in 1978 and have refused to return it ever since. Being less portable, the medieval tomb of Dom Dinis' illegitimate son, the Count of

---

THE INSTITUTE OF CULTURAL AFFAIRS

The **Montemuro** district, between Lamego and Castro Daire, suffers enormously from unemployment and depopulation, but sports a long tradition of local handicraft industries, including weaving, knitting, basketry, honey and cheese production, pottery and cape-making. There's still a thriving cultural life, too – from theatre and folk dance to religious festivals – which occupies a central place in Montemuro life.

The **Instituto dos Assuntos Culturais** (*ICA*) is an international development organisation with a staff of six foreign and eight Portuguese workers supporting the initiatives of local people. Some twenty villages, with a total population of about 11,000, are currently involved with the *ICA*'s work. It's based at the village of **Mezio**, about 20km southwest of Lamego on the N2 Castro Daire road.

If you're interested in having a look at what the Institute does – and it seems there's not much it doesn't take an interest in – you might like to stop en route between Lamego and the Mountain Beiras and stay for a day or two: visitors are actively encouraged. Facilities are basic, but there are showers and toilets and plenty of organic food. Contributions are around 3000$00 per person per day, but that's pretty much all-inclusive. If you want to make enquiries in advance, write to the *ICA* at Rua Central 47, Mezio, 3600 Castro Daire or telephone ☎054/68 92 46.

Whether or not you choose to stay, you may find the *ICA* pamphlet *Hiking Trails in the Montemuro* useful. It describes ten half-day **walks** in the region; the *ICA* can provide guides if you wish.

Barcelos, with elaborate hunting scenes carved into the sides, still lies in a side aisle. In summer there are usually students working on the site, who will probably be happy to show you around. There's a pleasant spot for rest and recuperation – and a nice **café** – down by the river, not two minutes' walk from the church.

Buses leave Lamego every Thursday (market day) at 8am and 1.30pm to pick up shoppers from Tarouca. On other days, you have to take one of the Guarda- or Moimenta-bound buses and ask to be dropped just before Mondim da Beira, a half-hour hike from Tarouca, high above the brook that waters the remote valley.

Ucanha

In **UCANHA** – north of Tarouca, on the opposite side of the N226 – life revolves around the water. Down below the main road, two ingenious ducts have been made to tap the river upstream in order to provide adequate washing facilities in the centre of the village. The wash houses are practically in ruins, but the system of one tank for suds and another for rinses, common to the Mediterranean, has been preserved. Running below the pools, the river looks so tempting that on a sunny day, regardless of what trash might be floating by, the village children are constantly nipping in and out.

The real beauty of the scene stems from the majestic **tollgate** and single-arched **bridge**. They date from shortly after 1163, when the diocese of Salzedas was awarded to Teresa Afonso, erstwhile nursemaid to Afonso Henriques' five sons and heirs and widow of Egas Moniz, the first king's tutor and closest adviser. Besides marking and protecting the border of her domain, these structures were also, of course, an ostentatious mark of manorial power. Today, clothes are hung out to dry under the arches.

Salzedas

SALZEDAS lies 4km further along the Ucanha road, past *Murganheira*, another "champagne" cooperative and a rival to *Raposeira*. The **Monastery** here was once the greatest of its kind, grander even than São João de Tarouca. The complex was rebuilt with money donated by Teresa Afonso in 1168, when the order was Augustinian; it became Cistercian during a later period of administration from Alcobaça.

Unfortunately, eighteenth-century renovation has largely altered its original appearance into a clumsy mixture of Baroque and pseudo-Classical styles. The monastery's main facade presides over the small square of the diminutive village. As at Tarouca, students work here in the summer and, though they may seem surprised to see casual visitors, they will follow you around and open the relevant doors. The smell of decay is strong inside and the two dark and dusty **paintings** of *Saint Peregrine* and *Saint Sebastian* by Grão Vasco, either side of the choir, are easily overlooked. More conspicuous are the fifteenth-century tombs of the Coutinho family – dominant nobles in these parts in the early years of the Portuguese nation – near the entrance. Out through a side door, a succession of courtyards, once fronting formal gardens, bear the scars of a period of extensive pillage and decay, which began in 1834 with the dissolution of the monasteries.

travel details

Trains

Amarante to Livração (7–9 daily; 25min); Porto (8–9 daily; 1hr 40min–2hr).

Espinho to Coimbra (11 daily; 1hr 5min–1hr 40min); Lisbon (9 daily; 3hr 35min–4hr); Porto (15–19 daily; 20–40min).

Penafiel to Livração (14–17 daily; 25min); Peso da Régua (12–13 daily; 1hr 20min); Pocinho (4 daily; 3hr 15min); Porto (15–18 daily; 45min–1hr 10min); Tua (5 daily; 2hr 10min).

Pocinho to Penafiel (3–4 daily; 3hr 10min); Porto (3–4 daily; 4hr 30min).

Peso da Régua to Porto (11–12 daily; 2hr 10min–2hr 40min); Vila Real (5 daily; 55min).

Porto to Coimbra (14–15 daily; 1hr 25min–2hr) Espinho (15–19 daily; 20–40min); Lisbon (15 daily; 3hr–4hr 20min); Livração (15–18 daily; 1hr 15min–1hr 40min); Penafiel (15–18 daily; 45min–1hr 10min); Peso da Régua (11–12 daily; 2hr 10min–2hr 40min); Pocinho (3–4 daily; 4hr 30min–4hr 50min); Póvoa de Varzim (roughly every 30min; 1hr); Santo Tirso (11–17 daily; 50min); Tua (6–7 daily; 3hr 15min–3hr 35min); Viana do Castelo (9–10 daily; 1hr 45min–2hr 25min); Vila do Conde (roughly every 30min; 50min).

Tua to Mirandela (4–5 daily; 1hr 50min).

Buses

Amarante to Cabaceiros de Basto (3 daily; 1hr 35min); Fernil (3 daily; 1hr).

Lamego to Peso da Régua (16 daily; 25min); Viseu (1 daily; 1hr 20min).

Peso da Régua to Lamego (16 daily; 25min).

Pocinho to Bragança (2 daily; 1hr 40min); Celerico da Beira (2 daily; 1hr 45min); Coimbra (2 daily; 4hr 55min); Lisbon (2 daily; 7hr 25min); Trancoso (2 daily; 1hr 20min); Viseu (2 daily; 2hr 45min).

Porto to Abrantes (4 daily; 4hr 25min); Amarante (hourly; 1hr 30min); Braga (5–6 daily; 1hr 10min); Coimbra (3 daily; 2hr 45min); Leiria (5–6 daily; 2hr 35min); Lisbon (hourly; 3hr); Tomar (1 daily; 3hr 45min); Viana do Castelo (3 daily; 1hr 10min); Vila do Conde (hourly; 45min); Vila Real (5 daily; 3hr 45min).

CHAPTER SIX

THE MINHO

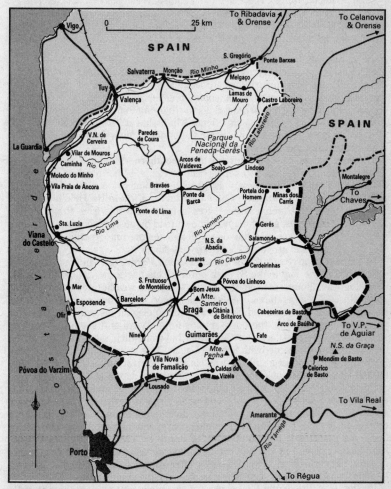

With good reason the Portuguese consider the **Minho** – the province north of Porto – to be the most beautiful part of their country. Its river valleys, wooded hills, trailing vines and barely developed coastline are given prominence in every travel brochure, while much is

---

MINHO MARKET DAYS

Monday: Ponte de Lima (every 2 weeks; p.277).

Tuesday: Braga (p.249).

Wednesday: Arcos de Valdevez (p.280); Caminha (p.269); Ponte de Barca (every 2 weeks; p.279);Valença do Minho (p.271).

Thursday: Barcelos (p.259); Monção (p.273).

Friday: Melgaço (p.275); Guimarães (p.243); Viana do Castelo (p.263).

Saturday: Paredes de Coura (every 2 weeks; p.272); Vila Nova de Cerveira (p.270).

made of the Minho's thoroughly traditional aspect: in a conservative region, deeply suspicious of change, wooden-wheeled ox-carts still creak down cobbled lanes while age-old conventions are maintained at dozens of huge country markets, *festas* and *romarias*. In summer especially, you're likely simply to happen upon these carnivals, though it's worth trying to plan your trip around the larger events if you're keen to experience Minho life at its most exuberant – the main markets are featured above, while the principal festivals are detailed where appropriate throughout the chapter.

The largest towns are concentrated in the southern Minho and any trip should allow time to examine the competing historic claims of **Guimarães**, first capital of Portugal, and neighbouring **Braga**, the country's ecclesiastical centre. Between them lie the extensive Celtic ruins of the **Citânia de Briteiros**, one of the most impressive archaeological sites in Portugal, while from Braga it's also easy to visit **Barcelos**, site of the best-known (and biggest) of the region's weekly markets. It takes place on Thursdays, though for the full experience reserve a room in advance and arrive on Wednesday evening.

At Barcelos, you're only 20km from the **Costa Verde**, the Minho coast, which runs north all the way to the Spanish border. This has some wonderful beaches along the way, though the sea here is cold – and the weather, too, can be uncertain, with cool temperatures even in midsummer. The principal resort is **Viana do Castelo**, an enjoyable and lively town with an elegant historic core, though if you're seeking isolation, there are strands to the north and south that scarcely see visitors. The coast ends at **Caminha**, beyond which the **Rio Minho** runs inland, forming the border with Spanish Galicia. This is a delightful region, featuring a string of compact fortified towns flanking the river on the Portuguese side, their fortresses, in various stages of disrepair, staring across at Spain.

Inland from Viana, the Minho's other major river, the beautiful **Rio Lima**, runs east through a succession of gorgeous small towns where there's little to do but soak up the somnolent scenery. On the whole, much of the Minho is like this – outrageously picturesque and full of quiet charm and interest. In the Lima valley itself, and particularly around the town of **Ponte de Lima**, these characteristics have been exploited by the *Turismo de Habitação* scheme, whereby local manor houses, old farms and country estates offer rooms to tourists on a bed-and-breakfast basis – a highly enjoyable way of seeing the countryside.

Further east, the gentle Minho scenery eventually gives way to the waterfalls, river gorges, reservoirs and forests of the protected **Parque Nacional da Peneda-Gerês**. This is superb camping and hiking territory, stretching from the main town and spa of **Caldas do Gerês** north as far as the Rio Minho and the Spanish border. It's possible to dip into the park from a couple of easily accessible towns, but you really need to devote several days if you're to see the more isolated regions; even by car the going's slow and on foot you could spend weeks exploring the trails.

SOUTHERN MINHO

The **southern Minho**'s two chief cities, **Guimarães** and **Braga**, are both small enough to walk around in a busy day's sightseeing, though a night's stay has greater rewards. This is especially true if you want to explore the the series of religious sites around Braga, including the extraordinary pilgrimage site of **Bom Jesus do Monte**; while you'll need to set aside another half day at least to see the **Citânia de Briteiros**. However, perhaps the best overnight stop is at **Barcelos**, provided you can find a room on a Wednesday night before the weekly market.

Guimarães and Braga are on separate branch lines of the main **train route**, which starts in Porto and passes through Barcelos on its way north to Viana do Castelo. You may need to change at Lousado for Guimarães (though there are also direct trains from Porto) and at Nine for Braga; but it's far quicker to use the direct **bus** between Braga and Guimarães rather than fiddle about with connections between the train lines.

Guimarães and around

Birthplace of Afonso Henriques in 1110, and first capital of the fledgling kingdom of "Portucale", **GUIMARÃES** has a special place in the story of Portuguese nationhood. From here began the reconquest from the Moors and the subsequent creation of a united kingdom which, within a century of Afonso's death, was to stretch to its present borders. Although Guimarães subsequently lost its pre-eminent status to Coimbra – which became the Portuguese capital in 1143 – it never relinquished its sense of self-importance, something that's evident from the careful preservation of an array of impressive medieval monuments. There's a grandeur to the town, and a tangible sense of history in the narrow streets, which conspires to make Guimarães one of the most attractive places in the country.

If you can afford to stay at one of the two local *pousadas* – one in the centre, the other in a former monastery at **Penha**, 5km southeast – then the experience is complete. Otherwise, decent budget accommodation is strangely hard to come by, though this matters little since Braga, or even Porto, is close enough to be able to visit on a day trip. And unless you book well in advance, you'll have to see Guimarães this way if you're here during either of the town's festivals. The major

---

ACCOMMODATION PRICE CODES

All the accommodation prices in this book have been coded using the symbols below. The symbols represent the prices for the cheapest available double room in high season; for a full explanation, see p.23.

① Under 3000$00	② 3000$00–4000$00	③ 4000$00–5500$00
④ 5500$00–8500$00	⑤ 8500$00–12,500$00	⑥ 12,500$00–20,000$00
⑦ Over 20,000$00		

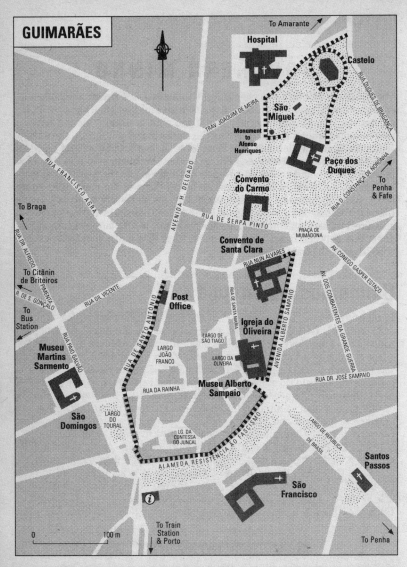

GUIMARÃES

To Amarante

Hospital

Castelo

RUA DUQUES DE BRAGANÇA

São
Miguel

TRAV. JOAQUIM DE MEIRA

Monument
to
Afonso
Henriques

Paço dos
Duques

RUA D. CONSTANÇA DE NORONHA

RUA FRANCISCO AGRA

AVENIDA H. DELGADO

Convento
do Carmo

To
Penha
& Fafe

To Braga

RUA DE SERPA PINTO

RUA D. CONSTANÇA DE...

RUA DR ALFREDO PIMENTA

Convento de
Santa Clara

PRAÇA DE
MUMADONA

AV CONEGO GASPAR ESTAÇO

To Citânin
de Briteiros

RUA NUN ALVARES

RUA GIL VICENTE

AV. DOS COMBATENTES DA GRANDE GUERRA

R. DE S. GONÇALO

Post
Office

RUA DE SANTA MARIA

AVENIDA ALBERTO SAMPAIO

To
Bus
Station

RUA DE SANTO ANTONIO

LARGO DE
SÃO TIAGO

Igreja do
Oliveira

Museu
Martins
Sarmento

RUA PAIO GALVÃO

LARGO
JOÃO
FRANCO

LARGO DA
OLIVEIRA

RUA DR. JOSÉ SAMPAIO

São
Domingos

RUA DA RAINHA

Museu Alberto
Sampaio

LARGO
DO
TOURAL

LARGO DE REPÚBLICA

LG. DA
CONTESSA
GO JUNCAL

DE BRASIL

Santos
Passos

ALAMEDA RESISTÊNCIA AO FASCISMO

São
Francisco

0   100 m

ⓘ

To Train
Station
& Porto

To Penha

event is the **Festas Gualterianas** (for São Gualter, or Saint Walter), which has taken place on the first weekend in August every year since 1452. If you miss this you can catch most of the same stall-holders, and something of the atmosphere, the weekend after in Caldas de Vizela, a spa-town 10km south of Guimarães. Next in importance is the long-established *romaria* to **São Torcato**, 6km northeast of town, on the first weekend in July, which, in the curious language of the Turismo leaflet, "includes a procession with archaic choirs of virgins".

The Town

The old centre of Guimarães is an elongated kernel of small, enclosed squares and cobbled streets. It is buttressed at its southern end by the town gardens and overlooked from the north by the imposing castle, an enduring symbol of the emergent Portuguese nation. In between lie a series of medieval churches, convents and buildings that lend an air of dignity to the streets – two of the convents provide an impressive backdrop to a couple of the country's more illuminating museums.

Around the Castelo

The imposing **Castelo** (Tues–Sun 9am–12.30pm & 2–5pm; free) was built by Henry of Burgundy, though its fame stems from the establishment of the first Portuguese court here, by his son, **Afonso Henriques**. Afonso is reputed to have been born in the great square keep which is surrounded now, as then, by seven castellated towers. It's a fine structure, its marvellous solidity enhanced by its juxtaposition with the diminutive Romanesque chapel of **São Miguel** (same hours as the castle), on the grassy slope below, in whose font Afonso was probably baptised.

Just across from the chapel, the **Paço dos Duques** (daily 9am–5.30pm; 300$00, Oct–May 200$00, *ISIC* card holders free) was once the medieval palace of the Dukes of Bragança. Under the Salazar dictatorship, its ruins were "restored" as an official residence for the president, and today, with such memories fading, it looks rather ludicrous – like a mock-Gothic Victorian folly. Inside is an extensive collection of portraits, furniture and porcelain, around which perambulate lengthy guided tours.

Perhaps more attractive are the **children's toys** – hammered out from old tin and no doubt lethal, but beautiful objects nonetheless – on sale in a number of shops opposite the castle; there's a café here, too.

Along Rua de Santa Maria

From the castle, **Rua de Santa Maria** leads down into the heart of the old town, a beautiful thoroughfare featuring iron grilles and granite arches. Many of the town's historic buildings have been superbly restored, and as you descend to the centre you'll pass one of the loveliest, the seventeenth-century convent of Santa Clara, which today does service as the **Câmera Municipal**.

On a much more intimate scale are the buildings ranged around the delightful central squares at the end of the street, **Largo de São Tiago** and **Largo da Oliveira**. The latter is dominated by the **Colegiada**, a convent-church built (like the great monastery at Batalha) in honour of a vow made by João I before his decisive victory over Castile. Its unusual dedication is to "Our Lady of the Olive Tree" and before it stands a curious Gothic **canopy-shrine**. This marks the legendary spot where Wamba, unwillingly elected king of the Visigoths, drove a pole into the ground swearing that he would not reign until it blossomed. Naturally it sprouted immediately. João I, feeling this to be a useful indication of divine favour, set out to meet the Castilian forces from this very point.

At the heart of the Colegíada is a simple Romanesque cloister with varied, naively carved capitals. This, and the rooms off it, comprise the **Museu Alberto Sampaio** (Tues–Sun 10am–12.30pm & 2–5.30pm; 200$00), essentially the treasury of the collegiate church and convent but, for once, outstandingly exhibited and containing pieces of real beauty. The highlight is a brilliantly composed silver-gilt *Triptych of the Nativity*, said to have been found in the King of Castile's tent after the Portuguese victory at Aljubarrota (1385). Close by this is displayed the tunic worn by João I in the battle. Unfortunately, you have to take a guided tour of the museum, which – if you don't speak Portuguese – becomes reduced to a litany of substances and dates ("wood, sixteenth-century") intoned by someone following two steps behind you, switching on and off the lights.

The Museu Martins Sarmento and the Igreja de São Francisco

Across to the west, over the main Largo do Toural, the **Museu Martins Sarmento** (Tues–Sun 9.30am–12.30pm & 2–7pm) is another superb collection, also housed in a former convent. Here, finds from the neighbouring *citânias* of Briteiros and Sabroso are displayed in the fourteenth-century Gothic cloister of the Igreja de São Domingos. They include a remarkable series of bronze votive offerings (among them, a "coach", pulled at each end by men and oxen), ornately patterned stone lintels and door jambs from the huts; while most spectacular of all are the two *Pedras Formosas* ("beautiful stones") and the so-called *Colossus of Pedralva*. The *Pedras*, once taken to be sacrificial altars, are in fact the portals to funerary monuments, one of which survives *in situ* at the Citânia de Briteiros. The *Colossus* is more enigmatic and considerably more ancient, a vast granite hulk of a figure with arm raised aloft and an oversized phallus. It shares the bold, powerfully hewn appearance of the stone boars found in Trás-os-Montes and, like them, may date from pre-Celtic fertility cults of around 1500 to 1000 BC.

Among the numerous other churches scattered about the centre of Guimarães, the finest is the **Igreja de São Francisco** (flexible opening hours), on the south side of the town gardens. It features a series of huge eighteenth-century *azulejos* of Saint Francis preaching to the fish, and an elegant Renaissance cloister and fountain. Once again, the church was attached to a monastery of considerable size until the 1834 dissolution.

Penha and Santa Marinha da Costa

You have to travel a short way outside Guimarães for the best preserved medieval building in the region, the former monastery – and nowadays *pousada* – of **Santa Marinha da Costa**. It is set on the slopes of **Penha** (617m), 5km southeast of town, and can be reached by taking the São Roque bus from the Turismo (every 30min between 6am and 10pm, 8pm on Sun); get off at "Costa" and follow the signs.

The monastery was founded in 1154 by order of Dona Mafalda, the wife of Afonso Henriques, in honour of a vow to Santa Marinha, patron saint of pregnant women. Originally Augustinian, the foundation passed into the hands of the Order of Saint Jerome in the sixteenth century. In the **chapel** (July–Sept 9am–1pm & 2–7pm), Jerome's twin emblems of the skull and the lion are recurring motifs. They are surrounded by an oddly harmonious mixture of styles – tenth-century doorways on the south wall, sixteenth-century panels in the sacristy (including Jerome beating his breast with a stone against the temptation of women), and an eighteenth-century organ and stone roof in the choir.

Strictly speaking, the rest of the monastic buildings are off limits except to guests of the *pousada* (see below for details), but you can peek into the magnificent **cloister**, with its Mozarabic doorway, while the beautiful **gardens** are open to the public, too. For more of a look around it would be diplomatic to buy a meal, or at least a drink at the bar.

Practicalities

Arriving by **train**, you'll find yourself ten minutes' walk to the south of the centre; head into town past the university (occupying the grounds of a former *palácio*) and you'll pass the **Turismo** at Avenida Resistência ao Fascismo 83 (June–Sept daily 9am–7pm; Oct–May Mon–Fri 9am–12.30pm & 2–5.30pm; ☎053/41 24 50), at the edge of a stretch of gardens, opposite the main town square, **Largo do Toural**.

The **bus station** is a fifteen-minute walk from the centre, at the bottom of Avenida Conde de Margaride (the Famalição road); walk up the avenue, past the market and turn right for the centre. There are express services from Porto and Lisbon, and regular weekday connections with Braga, Amarante, Cabeceiras and Mondim de Basto, and Póvoa do Lanhoso.

Accommodation

Inexpensive **accommodation** is extremely scarce in town, and even more so during Guimarães' main festivals (see p.244). It's best to book ahead – especially if you're planning a splurge in one of the two *pousadas*. Otherwise, nearby Braga (p.249) has a much better choice of budget accommodation.

There are two **campsites** in the locality. Nearest is *Montanha da Penha* (☎053/51 74 51; open all year), sited close to the Penha *pousada*, a pleasant site with a small swimming pool. Buses leave for Penha every half-hour between 6am and 10pm (8pm on Sun) from the Alameda da Resistência, the gardens near the Turismo. Further out, 7km northwest of Guimarães, *Caldas das Taipas* (☎053/57 62 74; June–Sept), by the Rio Ave off the N101, is even more attractive, but more expensive; it also has a swimming pool nearby.

Casa dos Pombais, Avda. de Londres (☎053/41 29 17). Near the bus station, this eight-eenth-century manor house has a limited number off rooms available – book in advance. Despite the town centre setting, it's a peaceful place, with an attractive garden. ⑤.

Casa dos Retiros, Rua Francisco Agra 163 (☎053/41 22 53). The cheapest place in town, this is a clean and functional hostel, run for pilgrims, which means it's sometimes booked up by groups. There's an 11.30pm curfew, fairly stark surroundings and spartan breakfasts. ③.

Albergaria Palmeiros, *Centro Comercial das Palmeiros*, Rua Gil Vicente (☎053/41 03 24). Part of a commercial mall, which can make it difficult to find (and gain entry after shopping hours). But it's modern and good value, with a restaurant. ④.

Pousada de N.S. de Oliveira, Rua de Santa Maria (☎053/51 41 57). Converted from a row of sixteenth-century houses, right in the medieval centre, this sixteen-room *pousada* is beautifully furnished – and worth every *escudo*. ⑦.

Pousada de Santa Marinha da Costa, Penha, 4800 Guimarães (☎053/51 44 53). This is reckoned to be one of the top *pousadas* in the country, set in a medieval monastery, 5km southeast of town; it is also one of the priciest at around 25,000$00 double. ⑦.

Residencial São Mamede, Rua de São Gonçalo 1 (☎053/51 30 92). Very neat and professional approach (which means no character whatsoever), but with bath and TV in all rooms. It's at the junction of Rua Gil Vicente and Rua de São Gonçalo. ④.

Hotel Toural, Largo do Toural (☎053/51 71 84). On the main square (though the entrance is in Largo A.L. Carvalha, at the back), this elegant townhouse has been completely refurbished – not cheap, but very comfortable. ⑥.

Eating and drinking

Guimarães has no shortage of places to **eat and drink**, although (as with accommodation) it's difficult to get particularly excited about the choice – unless you're destined to eat at the town centre *pousada*, in which case you're in for a treat.

Avenida, Avda. D. Afonso Henriques. On the street that runs from the Turismo out of town, this is in fairly unattractive urban surroundings. Still, you get generous helpings of good food at bargain prices – around 1250$00 a head.

Bom Retiro, Rua de Avelino Germano. Don't be put off by the rather touristic look of this place: the food is good and you find yourself effectively sitting in a kitchen, while your meal is prepared around you.

Oriental, Largo do Toural. Central bar-restaurant serving up a standard variety of Portuguese dishes.

Pousada de N.S. de Oliveira, Rua de Santa Maria. Unquestionably the best restaurant in town, with traditional Minho dishes served up in a wonderful antique dining room. You'll need to reserve a table in advance though. Fixed-price menus cost from 2800–3700$00 a head.

Solar da Rainha, Rua da Rainha D. Maria II. The daily set menu here is good value, though don't expect gourmet cuisine.

O Telheiro, Rua Dom João I 39–41. Just down the side of the Museu Martins Sarmento, this popular place serves a great *arroz de marisco*. Prices are reasonable; you may have to wait for a table at busy times.

Vira Bar, Alameda de São Domaso 25. A well-regarded place with choices ranging from a pizza and dessert for under 1500$00 to the full works for 3000$00.

Entertainment and nightlife

Outside festival time, at the beginning of July and August, the only time the town erupts into spontaneous celebration is when the local **soccer** team, FC Guimarães, plays (and wins) at home. The stadium is located to the northwest of the centre, along Rua Dr. A. Pimenta. Otherwise, a trio of **clubs** might reward a visit.

Crocodile Club, Rua de São Gonçalo. The big young hangout, open July–Sept only, Fri–Sun 10.30pm–3am.

Trás Trás, Rua Gil Vicente. Attracts a similar crowd as the *Crocodile*.

Casa do Arco, opposite the Câmera Municipal. Possibly more enjoyable, for foreign tastes, this has an art gallery and live music, too. Open 3–7pm & 9.30pm–2am.

East of Guimarães: towards Trás-os-Montes

Heading **east towards Trás-os-Montes**, the minor N206 runs across country towards the Rio Tâmega, a region covered in the previous chapter. **FAFE** is the first place you happen upon, 14km away. Little more than an overgrown bus station (you'll almost certainly need to change here for Trás-os-Montes destinations), it has a couple of *pensões* and a large revolutionary statue of a worker violently clubbing his bowler-hatted boss.

Beyond Fafe lies some magnificent countryside, dotted with huge boulders, though you'll really need your own transport to get the most out of the region since bus services are less than regular. Driving, you might want to stop at **GANDARELA**, 17km east of Fafe, which is famed for its topiary, while at **ARCO DE BAÚLHE**, 10km further, a road leads 7km north to Cabeceiras de Basto (see p.231). A dozen kilometres or so further east you finally reach the Tâmega river itself, where you're just 30km from the main Vila Real–Chaves road, one of Trás-os-Montes' finest routes.

Braga

BRAGA, the Turismo pamphlet claims, is the Portuguese Rome. This is clearly going a bit overboard – the Portuguese Canterbury might be more appropriate – though it neatly illustrates the city's ecclesiastical pretensions. One of the most ancient towns in Portugal, founded by the Romans in 27 BC, Braga was an important Visigothic bishopric before its occupation by the Moors. Reconquered early in the Christian campaigns, by the end of the eleventh century its archbishops were pressing for recognition as "Primate of the Spains", a title they disputed bitterly with Toledo over the next six centuries.

The city is still Portugal's religious capital – the scene of spectacular **Easter celebrations**, with torchlit processions and hooded penitents – while Braga's outlying districts boast a selection of important religious buildings and sanctuaries, including that of **Bom Jesus**, one of the country's most extravagant Baroque creations. Braga also has a reputation as a bastion of reactionary politics. It was here, in 1926, that the military coup leading to Salazar's dictatorship was launched, while in the more recent past, after the 1974 revolution, the Archbishop of Braga personally incited a mob to attack local Communist offices.

Such memories don't seem so distant when you look around at the weight of church power in Braga, perhaps best represented by an archbishop's palace built on a truly presidential scale. However, the city is an enjoyable place to stay, and it seems recently to have acquired a new energy that reflects less of the church than of its position as a fast-growing commercial centre.

Arrival and accommodation

Braga is a fair-sized city, though the old town – an oval of streets radiating out from the Sé – is a compact area. The main **bus station** is just over five minutes' walk from the centre; follow Rua dos Chãos downhill into Praça da República. The **train station** is west of the centre, a fifteen-minute walk from the old town, reached down Rua Andrade Corvo. The **Turismo** – housed in a wonderful Art Deco building – is at Avenida da Liberdade 1 (June–Sept Mon–Fri 9am–7pm, Sat & Sun 9am–5pm; Oct–May Mon–Fri 9am–5pm; ☎053/225 50), on the corner of the main Praça da República; it offers an impressive large-scale map of the city. If you are heading for Gerês, the **national park headquarters** in Braga is in a large, white house on Avenida António Macedo in the Quinta das Parretas suburb (Mon–Fri 9am–12.30pm & 2–5.30pm; ☎053/61 31 66), a twenty-minute walk from the centre, where you can buy a useful map and booklet.

Accommodation

There are plenty of *pensões* and hotels in Braga (though beware of turning up without a reservation during religious events and local festivals, principally at Easter and in June) and it makes a decent base for touring the southern Minho. An alternative to sleeping in the city is to stay up at Bom Jesus (see p.254), just 3 or 4km from the centre.

The cheapest beds are at Braga's excellent **youth hostel**, Rua de Santa Margarida 6 (☎053/61 61 63), off Avenida Central, which is very popular in the summer with hikers heading for the national park. There's a kitchen and state-of-the-art pressure showers; reception is open 9am–noon and 6pm–midnight.

The nearest **campsite** is *Camping Parque da Ponte* (☎053/733 55; open all year), a two-kilometre walk from the centre, down Avenida da Liberdade; it is right next to the municipal swimming pool. Otherwise, the *Caldas das Taipas* campsite (see "Guimarães and around", above) is 15km southeast of Braga and also makes a reasonable base, provided you have your own transport.

Casa Santa Zita, Rua São João 20 (☎053/234 94). A pilgrim-hostel, hidden behind the Sé; look out for the brass plaque. Large and peaceful, with nice rooms, an altogether religious aura, and curfew and dress code. Not for hell-raisers, but good value. ②.

Hotel Residencial Centro Comercial Avenida, Avda. Central 27–37 (☎053/757 22). Inside the *centro comercial*, there's a lift to reception on the second floor. Big, well-furnished rooms with TV and baths – some have kitchenettes. ④.

Hotel Francfort, Avda. Central 1–7 (☎053/226 48). Just across from Praça da República, this charming and friendly place dates from 1879 and is beginning to show its age – though the Art Deco dining room has recently been redecorated. Simple rooms, some with bath, make this one of the best bargains in town. ②–③.

Grande Residêncial Avenida, Avda. da Liberdade 738 (☎053/229 55). Fine old pension in a great location. Once grand, it too is beginning to fade a little these days, but remains good value for money. Rooms at the rear are quieter than those overlooking the avenida. It fills quickly and reservations are dvisable in summer. ③.

Residencial Inácio Filho, Rua Francisco Sanches 42 (☎053/228 49). Quirky, central, spotless *residencial*, cluttered with antique typewriters, cash registers and telephones. Most rooms come with a bath. You'll find it to the left off Rua do Souto, heading down from the Turismo. Recommended. ③.

Hotel João XXI, Avda. João XXI 849 (☎053/61 66 30). Off Avda. da Liberdade, on the way out of town, this small six-storey hotel has a top-floor restaurant and neat, en-suite rooms. ④.

Albergaria Senhor-a-Branca, Largo da Senhora-a-Branca 58 (☎053/299 38). Facing a garden and attractively furnished, this is only a couple of years old and so one of the smarter choices in town – there's parking space too. ④.

The City

The obvious point from which to start exploring Braga is **Praça da República**, a busy arcaded square at the head of the old town. It's backed by the former town keep, the **Torre de Menagem**, while in the arcade itself you'll find two fine coffee-houses which look out down the length of the long central gardens. From here, almost everything of interest is reached down narrow **Rua do Souto**, the main pedestrianised street which runs past the Sé. The street is Braga's main shopping district, though few commercial centres are like this one, where shoe shops rub shoulders with places selling candles, icons and other religious paraphernalia.

The Sé

The old town centre is dominated by the **Sé**, a rambling structure founded in 1070 after the Christian reconquest. The original Romanesque building encompasses Gothic, Renaissance and Baroque additions, though the cathedral's south doorway is a survival from the building's earliest incarnation, carved with rustic scenes from the legend of Reynard the Fox. The most striking element of the cathedral, however, is the intricate ornamentation of the roofline, commissioned by Braga's great Renaissance patron, Archbishop Diogo de Sousa, and executed by João de Castilho, later to become one of the architects of Lisbon's Jerónimos Monastery, the greatest of all Manueline buildings.

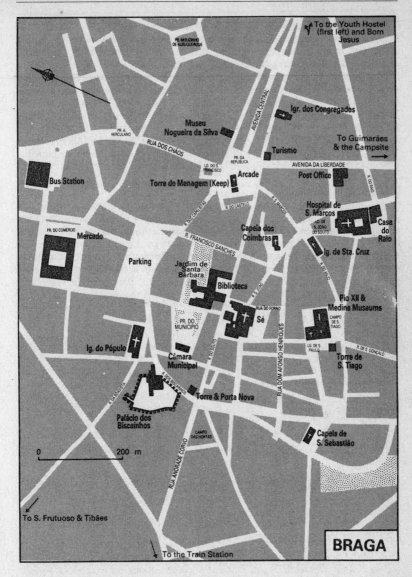

To the Youth Hostel (first left) and Bom Jesus

PR. MOUZINHO DE ALBUQUERQUE

AVENIDA CENTRAL

Igr. dos Congregados

Museu Nogueira da Silva

PR. A. HERCULANO

RUA DOS CHÃOS

Turismo

To Guimarães & the Campsite

LG. DO S. FRANCISCO

PR. DA REPUBLICA

Arcade

AVENIDA DA LIBERDADE

Post Office

R. DO RAIO

Bus Station

Torre de Menagem (Keep)

R. DO CASTELO

R. DA CAPELISTAS

R. S. MARCOS

Hospital de S. Marcos

LG. DE S. JOÃO DO SOUTO

Casa do Raio

PR. DO COMERCIO

Mercado

R. FRANCISCO SANCHES

Capela dos Coimbras

Ig. de Sta. Cruz

R. DO RAIO

Parking

Jardim de Santa Bárbara

Biblioteca

RUA DO FORNO

R. E JOÃO

Pio XII & Medina Museums

PR. DO MUNICIPIO

Sé

CAMPO DE S. TIAGO

Ig. do Pópulo

Câmara Municipal

R. DO SOUTO

LG. DE S. PAULO

R. DE S. GONÇALO

Torre de S. Tiago

R. DA PRANSA

R. DOS BISCAINHOS

Torre & Porta Nova

RUA DOM AFONSO HENRIQUES

Palácio dos Biscaínhos

CAMPO DAS HORTAS

Capela de S. Sebastião

0   200 m

RUA ANDRADE CORVO

To S. Frutuoso & Tibães

To the Train Station

BRAGA

Inside, the cathedral complex is disorientating: you enter through a courtyard fronting three Gothic chapels, a cloister and, most prominently, a ticket desk, where you can gain access to the **Museu de Arte Sacra** (daily 8.30am–12.30pm & 2–6.30pm; winter closes at 5.30pm; 200$00). Essentially the cathedral's treasury, this is one of the richest of such collections in Portugal, and has representative pieces from the tenth to the eighteenth centuries, but the items are unlabelled and confusingly arranged; it all manages to look a little dull. Eventually you emerge alongside the magnificent Baroque twin organs in the **Coro Alto** to gaze down into the cathedral proper – unexpectedly small and, when you descend, remarkably uninteresting.

Of the three outer chapels, the fourteenth-century **Capela dos Reis** (King's Chapel) is the most significant, built to house the tombs of the cathedral's founders, Henry of Burgundy, first Count of Portucale, and his wife Teresa – the parents of Afonso Henriques. Exposed beside them is the mummified body of Archbishop Lourenço, found "uncorrupt" when his tomb was opened in the seventeenth century. He had fought in the great victory over the Castilians at Aljubarrota in 1385, riding around bestowing indulgences on the ranks, and there sustained a scar on his cheek – which he himself is said to have carved proudly on his effigy.

The rest of the old town

Opposite the cathedral, across Rua do Souto, you won't be able to miss the old **Archbishop's Palace**, a great fortress-like building, which in medieval times actually covered a tenth of the city. Today it easily accommodates the municipal library (Mon–Fri 9am–noon & 2–7pm) and various faculties of the university, and inside you can inspect the ornate ceilings of the medieval reading-room and the *Sala do Doctor Manuel Monteiro*. Unless you have an academic interest, you're unlikely to find Braga's other **churches** very inspiring: most, like the cathedral, were stripped and modernised in the late-seventeenth and eighteenth centuries. Probably the most interesting, architecturally, is the small Renaissance **Capela dos Coimbras**, another of Archbishop de Sousa's commissions, on Largo Carlos Amarante, further east up Rua do Souto and off to the right.

On the whole, more inspiring are the numerous **mansions** from earlier ages, with their extravagant Baroque and Rococo facades. The **Câmara Municipal** and **Casa do Raio** – on either side of the cathedral – are both by André Soares da Silva, the archbishop's architect, and look out, too, for the apostle-clad roofline of the **Hospital de São Marcos**, adjacent to the Casa do Raio. Best of all though is the mid-seventeenth-century **Palácio dos Biscaínhos** (Tues–Sun 10am–noon & 1–5.30pm; 200$00), whose flagstoned ground floor was designed to allow carriages through to the stables. Nowadays, it houses a small museum of period furniture; the pretty landscaped gardens out back were again designed by Soares da Silva.

Across town, in Campo de São Tiago, a former seminary has been turned into the **Museu Medina e Pio XII** (Tues–Sun 10am–12.30pm & 3–6pm; 200$00), which consists of two distinct collections: the *Pio XII*, housing dusty religious regalia, and the *Medina*, named after the Portuguese painter and donated on the understanding that it would be housed separately from any other exhibits. Save your energy for the collection of fonts and capitals gathered in a courtyard like standing stones, or for the small excavation of a first-century Roman water tank – and try persuading the guide to hold back on a few of the endless locked doors.

Eating, drinking, nightlife and festivals

The city's most characterful locales are its nineteenth-century **cafés** – busy throughout the day and into the evening. In all of these you can get sandwiches and snacks, and often full meals, though Braga is also well-endowed with tempting **restaurants**; a selection of the best is listed below.

For details of local **cultural events**, get hold of a copy of the *Correio do Minho* newspaper; the Turismo generally has one on the counter and is happy to offer advice. In particular, don't miss out on tickets to anything that's on at the *Teatro Circo* (☎053/224 03), on Avenida da Liberdade, opposite the *Centro Comercial Gold*. As well as theatrical performances, **films** are shown here; as at two cinemas in the *Centro Comercial Avenida* on Avenida Central.

There's a fair **club scene** in Braga, though venues change hands and names reasonably regularly. Most of the action takes place at the bottom end of Avenida da Liberdade, around the *Hotel Turismo*, current favourites being: *Locomotiva*, actually beneath the *Hotel Turismo* and with a reputation that stretches as far as Lisbon; and *Salsa*, Rua de Diu (just around the corner from the *Locomotiva*), featuring a mixed bag of music and an unpretentious crowd.

Cafés

Café Astória, Avda. da Liberdade. By far the best of the old coffee houses, mahogany-panelled and with cut-glass windows, going very beautifully to seed. Occasional live music and invariably tasty snacks add to its attraction.

A Brasileira, Largo Barão de São Marinha. Another superb old-style café, at the top of Rua do Souto, full of crusty old waiters dealing out brandies to a similarly aged clientele. In summer, you can sit in the open window-terrace – virtually on the street.

Miragem, in the gardens of Avda. Central. All Art Deco curved glass, chrome and black leather, serving good pizzas.

Prégão, Largo da Praça Velha 18. Lovely place for a snack and a drink, with a chatty barman, good wines and sangria.

Restaurants

A Ceia, Rua do Raio. This excellent restaurant is always crowded with locals, so arrive early, especially at weekends, or you'll have to eat at the bar. Spit-roast chickens and steaks are served up in enormous portions at moderate prices, and there's a fine wine list. It's not easy to find – look for the sign above the pavement. Closed Mon.

Conde de Agrolonga, Praça de Agrolonga 74. Typical Portuguese restaurant with a 1500$00 *ementa turística*. It's north of Rua do Souto, between it and the Mercado Municipal.

Restaurante Inácio, Campo das Hortas 4. Through the town gate at the end of Rua do Souto and off to the left, this is a pricey and rather cosmopolitan restaurant that doesn't limit itself to Portuguese dishes. It's in an old stone house with rustic decor – and costs around 2600$00 a head and upwards. Closed Mon.

Restaurante A Marisqueira, Rua do Castelo 15. The rather shabby looking interior belies a menu of well-presented seafood dishes at around 1000$00; the tourist menu costs just 1600$00.

Restaurante Moçambicana, Rua Andrade Corvo 8. Just outside the town gate, at the end of Rua do Souto. As the name suggests, a spattering of African dishes feature on the menu. Cheap.

Rio Este, Rua das Barbarosas. This place is convenient for the campsite; take the first left having crossed the river down Avda. da Liberdade. The house speciality – possibly the nastiest dish in Portugal – is *Papas de Sarrabulho*, but they serve seafood dishes as well.

Pizzaria Papalloni, Rua da Taxa 10. Close to the youth hostel, this is a dependable place for inexpensive, tasty pizzas.

Festivals and markets

In addition to the **Semana Santa** (Holy Week) celebrations, the whole city is illuminated for the **Festas de São João** (June 23–24), which provides the excuse for ancient folk dances, a fairground and general partying. The main **pilgrimage to**

Bom Jesus (see below) takes place over Whitsun (six weeks after Easter). Don't expect to find a room at any of these times, unless you book well ahead.

Throughout the year, there's popular entertainment in the **Feira Popular Bracalandia**, 1km out of town on the Bom Jesus road. This is a permanent fairground, with a ferris wheel, rides and the like, popular with locals and tourists in the early evening. There's also a regular **Tuesday market**, held at the exhibition park, at the end of Avenida da Liberdade.

Around Braga: Bom Jesus, São Frutuoso and Tibães

Having soaked up the religious atmosphere in Braga itself, there's a trio of fascinating associated sites in the surroundings. The Baroque stairway and pilgrim church of **Bom Jesus do Monte**, 4km east of Braga, is a good enough reason to come in the first place, while a similar distance to the northwest is the Visigothic church of **São Frutuoso** and a ruined Benedictine monastery at **Tibães**.

Buses to Bom Jesus leave every half-hour (at 10 and 40 minutes past each hour) from near the Hospital de São Marcos on Largo Carlos Amarante. Buses to São Frutuoso/Tibães leave from the corner of Rua do Carvalho/Rua de São Vicente (they are marked *Ruães*). If you want to make things easy by renting a **taxi** for a few hours, António Fanil da Silva (☎053/61 40 19) offers reasonable rates.

Bom Jesus do Monte

BOM JESUS DO MONTE is one of Portugal's best-known images, as much concept as building. Set in the woods high above the city, the glorious ornamental stairway of granite and white plaster is a monumental homage created by Braga's archbishop in the first decades of the eighteenth century. There is no particular reason for its presence – no miracle or vision – yet it remains the object of devoted pilgrimage, with many penitents climbing up on their knees.

Buses run the 3km from Braga to the foot of the stairway. At weekends they are packed, as seemingly half the city piles up to picnic in the woods. Most of the local families, armed with immense baskets of food, ride straight to the top in an ingenious hydraulic **funicular** (100$00). If you resist the temptation and make the climb up the stairway, Bom Jesus's simple allegory unfolds.

Each of the **stairway** landings has a fountain: the first symbolises the wounds of Christ, the next five the Senses, and the final three represent the Virtues. At each corner, too, are chapels with mouldering, larger-than-life wooden tableaux of the Life of Christ, arranged chronologically, leading to the Crucifixion at the altar of the church. As a design it's a triumph – one of the greatest of all Baroque architectural creations – and was later copied at Lamego.

Eating and accommodation

Bom Jesus is a very pleasant place to spend an afternoon or, best of all, early evening. There are wooded gardens, grottoes and miniature boating pools behind the church and, at the far end, several lively **restaurants** – filled on Saturdays with parties from a constant stream of weddings.

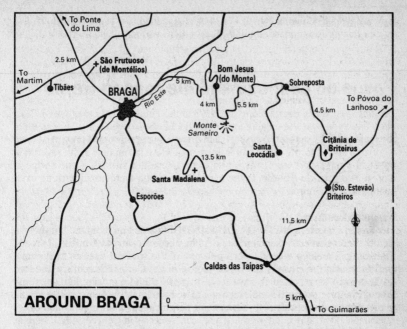

AROUND BRAGA

0 _____ 5 km

You can also stay up on the mount. There are a couple of pricey **hotels**, under the same ownership, the *Hotel do Elevador* (☎053/67 66 11; ⑤) and the larger *Hotel do Parque* (☎053/67 65 48; ⑤), as well as a better-value one-star hotel overlooking the steps, the *Sul-Americano* (☎053/67 67 01; ③), and two simple pensions (②–③), less well sited, over by the restaurants. A further option is the splendid late-eighteenth-century *Casa dos Lagos* (☎053/67 67 38; ④), part of the *Turismo de Habitação* scheme, which has one room and three apartments available for rent.

São Frutuoso and Tibães

Slightly closer in than Bom Jesus – 3.5km northwest of Braga – is another worthwhile church excursion: to **São Frutuoso**, built by the Visigoths in the seventh century, adapted by the Moors, and then restored to Christian worship after the Reconquest. It is a gem of a church, set in open countryside with a flanking eighteenth-century chapel. It should be open Tuesday to Sunday until 5pm; keys are kept in a nearby house if you arrive to find it locked. The approach is from the hamlet of São Jerónimo Real, down a (marked) track to the right.

Half a kilometre beyond the São Frutuoso turning, to the left of the main road, a paved track leads to the monastery of **Tibães** (Thurs–Sun 9am–noon & 2–5pm; free), formerly the grandest Benedictine establishment in the land. A vast and ruined hulk, its abandoned medieval buildings, cloisters and rambling gardens were once occupied by gypsy families, but it is now state-owned and due to become part cultural centre, part *pousada*. It is an evocative place and you can look around the **church**, which has been maintained. On some days there is a guided tour of the monastic buildings, on others you may have to knock for the priest.

Póvoa do Lanhoso and the road to Gerês

Heading **east from Braga** along the N103 to the Peneda-Gerês park (see p.281), after 16km you pass the turning for **Póvoa do Lanhoso**, which lies 3km south of the main road. If you have transport, and time to spare, this small provincial town is worth a detour for its castle and Romanesque church. Another sight, revered in Portugal though perhaps of more peripheral interest to visitors, is the shrine of **Nossa Senhora da Abadia**, to the north of the Braga–Gerês road, turning off at Santa Maria do Bouro.

Póvoa do Lanhoso

The modern quarters of **PÓVOA DO LANHOSO** aren't up to much, but they lie sandwiched between two ancient sites. At the northern end of town (the approach from Braga), a steep mound rises up to one of the smallest **castles** in Portugal and a scattering of chapels and picnic tables. In the fourteenth century, the lord of the shire was reported to have locked up his adulterous wife, her lover and their servants in the castle and ordered it to be burned; it was substantially rebuilt in the eighteenth century. The **restaurant** nearby keeps a set of keys and offers reasonable food and good views, if you can squeeze in between their regular parties of christening and wedding guests.

In the opposite direction, 3km out of town, the small church of **Fonte Arcada** is a short walk from the main road (past the white statue). The simple interior, characteristic of the Romanesque style, is in marked contrast to the complications of the doorway with its centrepiece relief of a large sheep.

The town provides useful transport links to the east into Trás-os-Montes; south to the Douro, via the village of Cabeceiras de Basto; and to Porto, via Famalição. Regular **buses** also connect with Braga, Caldas do Gerês and Guimarães. To pick up one of the four daily Chaves buses, you have to walk the 3km north to Pinheiro, on the main N103.

Nossa Senhora da Abadia

Turning off the Braga–Gerês road at **SANTA MARIA DO BOURO** (Bouro to the locals) – which has a shell of a monastery and a large Baroque church – you arrive at the shrine of **Nossa Senhora da Abadia**. This is said to be the oldest sanctuary in Portugal and, like Bom Jesus, is a centre of pilgrimage: the main festival is on August 15. The focus of devotions is a twelfth-century wooden statue of the Virgin and Child, and while the church itself was largely rebuilt in the eighteenth century, outside are two earlier, elegant wings of monks' cells and, usually, some market stalls. There's no accommodation here but you can **eat** well with the pilgrims at the sizeable *Restaurante Abadia*, which can seat up to 500 people.

Back on the main road at Bouro, there are **rooms** available at the *Residencial Santa Maria* (☎053/37 12 31; ②) and **food** can be had next door at the *Restaurante Cruzeiro*.

The Citânia de Briteiros

Midway between Guimarães and Braga is one of the most impressive and exciting archaeological sites in the country, the **Citânia de Briteiros**. *Citânias* – Celtic hill settlements – lie scattered throughout the Minho: remains of twenty-seven have been identified along the coast, plus sixteen more in the region between Braga and Guimarães alone. Most date from the arrival of northern European Celts in the Iron Age (c.600–500 BC), though some are far older, having merged with an existing local culture established since Neolithic times (c.2000 BC). The site at Briteiros was occupied from about 300 BC and seems to have been a last stronghold against the invading Roman forces, resisting colonisation until around 20 BC.

The Roman historian Strabo gave a vivid description of the northern Portuguese tribes, who must have occupied these *citânias*, in his *Geographia* (c.20 BC). They organised mass sacrifices, he recorded, and consulted prisoners' entrails without removing them. Otherwise, they liked to:

> *live simply, drink water and sleep on the bare earth . . . two-thirds of the year they live on acorns, which they roast and grind to make bread. They also have beer. They lack wine but when they have it they drink it up, gathering for a family feast. At banquets they sit on a bench against the wall according to age and rank . . . When they assemble to drink they perform round dances to the flute or the horn, leaping in the air and crouching as they fall.*

Entrails aside – and they may have been literary licence – none of this seems far removed from the Minho and Trás-os-Montes of recent memory.

Getting there

From Braga, there are four daily **buses** to Briteiros, leaving from near the Turismo. Otherwise you have to walk or hitch, either from Bom Jesus (set out along the road beyond the gardens and pensions; 9km from the site), or from Caldas das Taipas (on the Braga–Guimarães bus route; 6km from the site). Alternatively, you might be able to catch one of the buses which run **from Guimarães** through Caldas das Taipas to Póvoa do Lanhoso. Leaving the *Citânia*, hitching a lift from other visitors, either to Braga or Guimarães, should be fairly easy.

The excavations

The site **excavations** (summer daily 9am–dusk; winter daily 9am–5pm; 200$00) have revealed foundations of over a hundred and fifty **huts**, a couple of which have been rebuilt to give a sense of their scale and design. Most of them are circular, with porches for their fires, though some are rectangular, among them a larger building which may have been a prison or meeting house – it is labelled the *casa do tribunal*. There's also a clear network of paved streets and paths, two circuits of town walls, plus cisterns, stone guttering and a public fountain (the *fonte*). Most of these features are identifiable as you wander around the place, though the site is more evocative in its layout and extent than for any particular sights.

One feature not to be missed, however, is the **funerary chamber** (a fair walk down the hill to the left of the settlement) with its geometrically patterned stone doorway. Similar examples, along with carved lintels from the huts and other

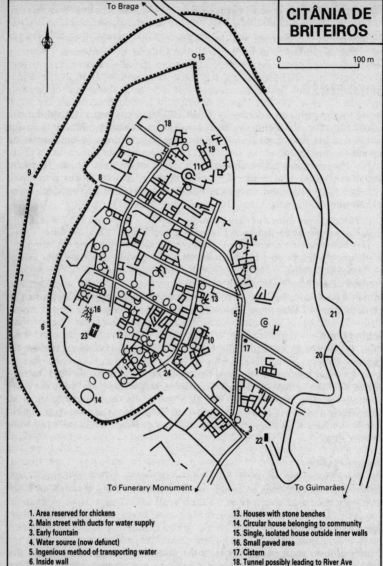

CITÂNIA DE BRITEIROS

0   100 m

To Braga

To Funerary Monument

To Guimarães

1. Area reserved for chickens
2. Main street with ducts for water supply
3. Early fountain
4. Water source (now defunct)
5. Ingenious method of transporting water
6. Inside wall
7. Second (of four) walls
8. Gateway
9. Gateway
10. House with various rooms
11. House with helix
12. Houses reconstructed by Martins Sarmento

13. Houses with stone benches
14. Circular house belonging to community
15. Single, isolated house outside inner walls
16. Small paved area
17. Cistern
18. Tunnel possibly leading to River Ave
19. Law courts(?), prisons(?)
20. Entrance
21. Parking
22. Guard's room
23. Chapel of S. Romão
24. Cross and Christian cemetery

finds from the *citânia*, are displayed at the Museu Martins Sarmento in Guimarães. These indicate that the settlement was abandoned as late as 300 AD and – unlike Conimbriga, another Celtic site near Coimbra – show little Roman influence other than the presence of coins.

Barcelos

It's worth making plans to arrive in **BARCELOS**, 20km west of Braga, for the Thursday market, the **Feira de Barcelos**. The great weekly event of southern Minho, it takes place from around dawn until mid-afternoon on the Campo da República – also known as the Campo da Feira – a vast open square that's about the first place you come upon walking into town from the train station. There are traditional events at other times of the year, too: the *Festa das Cruzes* (Festival of the Crosses) on May 3, and a renowned **folklore festival**, with live music, on the last Saturday of July.

The Feira de Barcelos

The Minho's markets are always interesting and the **Feira de Barcelos**, one of the largest in Europe, is both a spectacle and a crash course in the region's economics. There are stalls selling virtually everything – yokes for oxen, sausage skins and superb fresh bread – whole avenues of ducks and rabbits, as well as row upon row of village women squatting behind baskets of their own produce. Minho is made up of hundreds of tiny, walled smallholdings, rarely more than allotments and many people here are just selling a few vegetables, some fruit, eggs, and maybe even cheese from the family cow. It all looks unbelievably wholesome.

Apart from produce, clothes and kitchen equipment, the *feira*'s big feature is local **pottery and handicrafts**, for Barcelos is at the centre of Portugal's most active *artesanato* region. The pottery ware – *louça de Barcelos* – is characteristically brown with distinctive yellow dots, and has been highly acclaimed since the 1950s, when the imaginative earthenware figurines of Rosa Ramalho began to be collected throughout Europe. In comparison most of today's pieces look as if they fell off a production line (some, indeed, are Far Eastern imports), but there are some good items to be found if you look around, sold at around half the price of outlets elsewhere. Other crafts, too, are impressive – especially the basketwork, traditionally carved yokes (*cangas*) and wooden toys.

The rest of town

At the southwest corner of the Campo is Barcelos' most striking church, the **Templo do Nosso Senhor da Cruz**, fronted by a Baroque garden of obelisks and box-hedges. Built in 1708, its distinctive exterior, created by a simple contrast of dark granite and white plasterwork, was to be influential in the design of churches throughout the region. It's an odd addition to the old part of town, though, which is essentially Gothic and medieval in character – a small, hillside web of streets spun above the Rio Cávado.

THE BARCELOS COCK

A stone cross in Barcelos' archaeological museum depicts the legend of the **Galo de Barcelos**, a miraculous roast fowl which rose from the dinner table of a judge to crow the innocence of a pilgrim he had wrongly condemned to the gallows. The pilgrim, having wisely proclaimed "I'll be hanged if that cock don't crow", got his reprieve. It's a story that occurs in different forms in northern Spain, but the Barcelos rooster has taken a special hold on popular folk art, becoming a national symbol of Portugal and now, usually in pottery form, the ubiquitous emblem of Portuguese tourism.

Heading south from the Campo, you'll soon end up at the **river**, as beautiful as any in the Minho, overhung by willows, fronted by gardens and spanned by a fifteenth-century bridge. Just above it loom the ruins of the **Paço dos Condes**, the former Palace of the Counts of Barcelos, wrecked by the Great Earthquake of 1755 and now providing a shell for the **Museu Arqueologico** (daily 10am–noon & 2–6pm). This is a miscellaneous outdoor assembly of stone crosses, including a sixteenth-century crucifix locally famed for its connection with the legend of *Senhor do Galo* – the Gentleman of the Cock (see feature above); just outside the museum, in the riverside gardens, stands the town's Gothic **pelourinho**. If you wanted to pursue an interest in the local ceramic wares, there's a new ceramics museum, the **Museu de Olaria**, in the Casa dos Mendanhas on Rua Conego Joaquim, 300m from the archaeological museum; check with the Turismo for the current opening hours.

Practicalities

The **train station** is at the eastern edge of town; follow the street straight ahead for fifteen minutes and you'll eventually emerge on the Campo da Feira. **Buses** use a terminal at the southeastern corner of the square; among other services, there's an hourly run to Braga. For more obscure routes and local villages, the services of the *Linhares* bus company may come in handy, departing from the Viana do Castelo road. The **Turismo** is housed in the town's old castle keep, the Torre da Porta Nova, on Largo da Porta Nova (Mon, Tues, Wed & Fri 9am–12.30pm & 2.30–6pm; Thurs 9am–6pm; Sat & Sun 9.30am–12.30pm & 2.30–4pm; ☎053/81 18 82). In addition to its information counter, it features a permanent display and sale of Barcelos handicrafts.

Accommodation

Residencial Arantes, Avda. de Liberdade 35 (☎053/81 13 26). Budget option on the west side of the Campo, ablaze with flowers. ③.

Pensão Bagoeira, Avda. Sidónio Pais 57 (☎053/81 12 36). Located on the southeastern corner of Campo da Feira, this is a real old market inn, with a handful of spotless rooms; phone ahead if you want to secure one on a Wednesday night, before the market. ③.

Casa do Monte, Abade de Neiva (☎053/81 15 19). A country house with large gardens, 3km west of Barcelos on the N103 (Viana do Castelo road). ⑤.

Albergaria Condes de Barcelos, Avda. Alcaides de Feria (☎053/81 10 61). Upmarket hotel on the road in from the station to the Campo. ⑤.

Residencial Dom Nuno, Avda. Dom Nuno Alvares Pereira 76 (☎053/81 50 84). A fancy place, off to the right as you approach Campo da Feira from the station. ④.

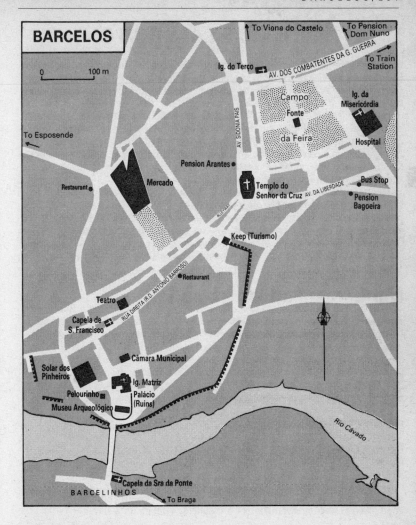

BARCELOS

0   100 m

To Viana do Castelo

To Pension Dom Nuno

To Train Station

Ig. do Terço

AV. DOS COMBATENTES DA G. GUERRA

Campo

Ig. da Misericórdia

Fonte

AV. S.DONA PAIS

da Feira

Hospital

To Esposende

Pension Arantes

Restaurant

Mercado

Templo do Senhor da Cruz

AV. DA LIBERDADE

Bus Stop

Pension Bagoeira

ALLEYWAY

Keep (Turismo)

RUA DIREITA (R.D. ANTÓNIO BARROSO)

Restaurant

Teatro

Capela de S. Francisco

Câmara Municipal

Solar dos Pinheiros

Ig. Matriz

Pelourinho

Palácio (Ruins)

Museu Arqueológico

Rio Cávado

Capela da Sra da Ponte

BARCELINHOS

To Braga

Eating and drinking

On market day, be sure to have lunch at the *Bagoeira*'s **restaurant**, which sees a constant stream of stallholders bringing in pots and pans for takeaways. It's open in the evening, too, and meals – mostly stews, steaks and grills – are excellent value. Both *Dom António*, on the main Rua Dom António Barroso, and *Casa dos Arcos*, in Rua Duques de Bragança, just north of the Solar dos Pinheiros, also have local reputations. Other, cheaper places to eat include a bargain-basement café-restaurant around the corner from the Campo, in the alleyway opposite the Templo; and the grill-restaurant *Furna* on Largo da Madalena (closed Mon). The *Confeitaria Salvação*, Rua Dom António Barreto, is a fifth-generation *pastelaria* still serving its award-winning egg-and-almond sweets.

THE COSTA VERDE

Spurred by the flow of foreign currency into the Algarve, the Portuguese Tourist Board is energetically trying to promote the Minho's almost continuous line of sandy beaches as the **Costa Verde** – a zone which seems to stretch inland along the north bank of the River Minho itself. So far, the seaside element of the campaign hasn't quite worked, for despite the enticing promises of "unpolluted beaches with a high iodine content . . . health for the whole year", Costa Verde is green for a reason. It can be drizzly and overcast right through summer and the Atlantic here is never too warm. Still, if that doesn't bother you and the weather's looking good there's amazing potential; you can pick almost any road, any village, and find a great **beach** virtually to yourself.

The coast between Póvoa de Varzim and Caminha is virtually one long beach, with the road running for the most part 1km or so inland. There are at least four **buses** a day in each direction, most using the resort of **Viana do Castelo** – very much the main event on this coast – as an axis. In addition, there are regular **trains** from Porto, which cut inland to Barcelos before heading back to the coast at Viana do Costelo, from where they run up the coast to Caminha.

North from Porto to Viana

The coast immediately **north of Porto**, as far as Póvoa de Varzim, is accessible by train and covered on p.224. Beyond Póvoa, you really need your own transport, since the train doesn't touch the coast again until Viana do Castelo. There are buses, but it's slow going. The route, however, has its rewards, not least because much of this part of the Costa Verde is protected from development by law: 18km of coastline between Apúlia and the mouth of the River Neiva is designated the *Área de Paisagem Protegida do Litoral de Esposende*.

Esposende and Ofir

The easiest place to reach by public transport is **ESPOSENDE**, 20km north of Póvoa. It's a rather drab sprawl of buildings, with little of interest save the ruins of an eighteenth-century fort now used as a lighthouse. The town itself is actually sited inland on the estuary of the Rio Cávado, with the nearest beaches 4km by road across the estuary at **OFIR**, where a couple of large luxury hotels have been built on a beautiful spit of pine-backed sand. If you are driving, this could be a good place to stop and swim, but it's not enticing enough for a stay.

Mar

North of Ofir, you probably won't see another tourist all the way to the little fishing village of **MAR** (or, more fully, São Bartolomeu do Mar), which fronts one of the best stretches of the Costa Verde. It's just 15km south of Viana do Castelo, but there is still refreshingly little to the place: just a church, shop and café (with a few **rooms** to let), and good unofficial camping amid the pines. As well as fishing, the local economy revolves around gathering **seaweed**. Traditionally, whole families harvest it on the beach using huge shrimping nets, which are then hauled across the sands by beautiful wooden carts pulled by oxen. Although the methods are changing and tractors are supplanting beasts, the seaweed is still stacked at the edge of the village to dry before being spread as fertiliser on the coastal fields.

Viana do Castelo

VIANA DO CASTELO is the one town in the Minho you could describe as a resort – and it's all the more appealing for it. A lively, attractive place, it has an historic old centre, above-average restaurants and, some distance from the town itself, one of the best beaches in the north. It's also beautifully positioned, spread along the north bank of the Lima estuary and shaped by the thick wooded hill of Monte de Santa Luzia, which is strewn with Celtic remains. If this wasn't enough of an incentive to come, Viana's **romaria** at the end of August (see feature on p.267) is the biggest and most exciting festival in the Minho.

The town

Viana has long been a prosperous seafaring town. It produced some of the greatest colonists of the "discoveries" under Dom Manuel and, in the eighteenth century, was the first centre for the shipment of port wine to England. Many of the buildings reflect these times – unusually for the north, you'll notice Manueline mouldings around the doors and windows of Viana's mansions.

At the heart of Viana's old town is the distinctive **Praça da República**, a wonderful square enclosed by an elegant ensemble of buildings. You'll see copies of its showpiece Renaissance fountain in towns throughout the Minho, but few structures as curious as the old **Misericórdia** (almshouse) that lines one side of the square. Built in 1598, this is one of the most original and successful buildings of the Portuguese Renaissance, its upper storeys supported by deliberately archaic caryatids. The adjacent sixteenth-century **Câmera Municpal** has been brightly restored, and stands foursquare above a medieval arcade, while just off the square is the **Igreja Matriz**, Viana's parish church, which retains a Gothic door of some interest.

The **Museu Municipal** (Tues–Sun 9.30am–noon & 2–5pm; 120$00) adds further to these impressions of Viana's sixteenth- to nineteenth-century opulence; it is contained within an eighteenth-century palace and houses a notable collection of ceramics and furniture. It stands near the end of Rua Manuel Espregueira, ten minutes' walk from the square, on the far side of the main Avenida dos Combatentes da Grande Guerra.

If you continue past the museum, you'll eventually reach the old **Castelo** by the sea, in an area known as the Campo do Castelo. Outside the walls, on Fridays, Viana's **market** takes place; it's much smaller than the famous one at Barcelos but attracts many of the same stallholders.

Monte de Santa Luzia

Wherever you stand in Viana, the ugly modern basilica atop **Monte de Santa Luzia** makes its presence felt, glowering from the summit like an evil eye. But don't let this – the ostensible highlight of the town – put you off. It's a great walk up, through the pines and eucalyptus trees (take the shortcut over the railway tracks), or you can be hauled to the top by an old **funicular**. This starts its run (hourly 10am–noon, half-hourly 12.30–7pm; 70$00) from just behind the train station: to reach it, walk through the station and cross the tracks. En route, there are tremendous views down the coast and along the River Lima.

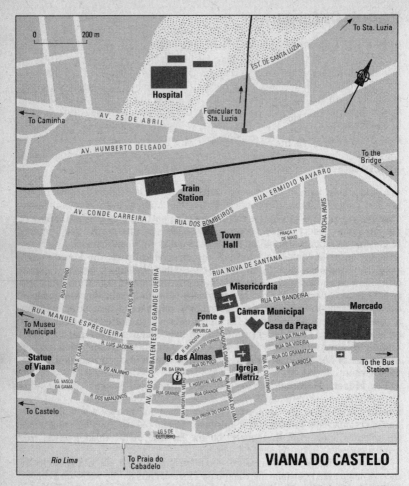

VIANA DO CASTELO

At the summit, there's a café and plenty of wooded walks. While the **basilica** itself is of little interest, look for the side-entrance (marked *Zimbório*), where steps climb right through the building and out on top of the dome itself. It's very narrow, very steep and – at the top – very scary if the wind has picked up, but the views are magnificent.

Behind the basilica, amid the woods and just below the luxury *Hotel Santa Luzia*, lie the ruins of a Celto-Iberian **citânia**, which include the foundations of dozens of small, circular stone huts, a thick village wall and partly paved streets. Occupied from around 500 BC, the settlement was only abandoned with the Roman pacification of the north under Emperor Augustus (c.26 BC). The ruins have been fenced off but there should be access from the approach road to the hotel.

Praia do Cabedelo

Viana's town beach, **Praia do Cabedelo**, lies across the river, reached by a rickety **ferry**, the *Saudade*, which leaves from the harbourside at the southern end of the main avenue (every 30min; 150$00 return); it's a five-minute crossing. Road access from town to beach is over the bridge, east of the centre.

Given sun, the beach is more or less perfect – a low curving bay with good (but not wild) breakers and a real horizon-stretching expanse of sand. There's a bar at the windsurf school, close to where the ferry docks, but other than that nowhere to buy food or drink, so take a picnic. From Viana, the beach extends northwards, virtually unbroken, to the Spanish border at Caminha, and south to Póvoa de Varzim. For the energetic, either of these routes makes a memorable and enjoyable hike and for details of the northern route, see p.268.

Practicalities

The **train station** is at the north end of the main Avenida dos Combatentes da Grande Guerra, which runs right through the town and down to the river at Largo 5 de Outubro. There's a seasonal **Turismo** stand at the station (July & Aug Mon–Sat 9am–6pm, Sun 9.30am–12.30pm), but the main office is in the centre: walk down the avenue and look for the sign pointing to the left; it's in Rua do Hospital Velho, off Praça da Erva (Mon–Sat 9am–12.30pm & 2.30–6pm; Sun 9.30am–12.30pm; ☎058/82 26 20). The building dates from 1468 and was first used by pilgrims travelling to Santiago de Compostela in Spain; later it became a hospital.

Apart from at *festa*-time, there is a **bus stop** on Largo 5 de Outubro, from where you can catch services to Braga. Buses for Ponte de Lima depart from a stop on the main avenue, above its junction with Rua Manuel Espregueira; buses for Porto and Lisbon depart from a little further up the main avenue. Otherwise, all departures in the first instance are from the bus station at the top end of Rua da Bandeira, twenty minutes' walk from the centre.

Accommodation

Pensions – mostly ranged down and off the main avenue – are easy enough to find, although in summer, and particularly during the *romaria*, private **rooms** rather than pensions offer the best deals; ask at the Turismo or look for signs in the windows of houses. However, during the actual festival, expect to pay around 5000$00 for a private room, though they're more like 3000$00 during the rest of the year. You might also ask the Turismo about accommodation at **farms** and **manorhouses** in the surrounding villages, an ideal way to get to know the countryside, provided you have transport; a couple are listed below.

The town's two **campsites** are not very special, but do at least have the advantage of being at the Praia do Cabedelo; take the ferry across the river and walk from there. *Inatel* (☎058/32 20 42; closed mid-Dec to mid-Jan) is for for carnetholders only, and is used by Porto families for summer-long holidays. *Orbitur* (☎058/32 21 67; closed mid-Nov to mid-Jan) is shaded by pine trees, but overcrowded in summer and overpriced for what you get – it's closer to the beach, though.

Hotel Aliança, Avda. dos Combatentes da Grande Guerra (☎058/82 94 98). Eighteenth-century building at the bottom of the avenue that's not entirely lost its period charm. Rooms with bath are at the top end of this category. ④.

Casa Grande da Bandeira, Largo das Carmelitas 488 (☎058/82 31 69). On a little square on the way out of town, heading for Ponte de Lima, this charming seventeenth-century house has a small garden and only three rooms – book ahead. ⑤.

Residencial Dolce Vita, Rua do Poço 44 (☎058/248 60). Excellent-value, spacious rooms, with shared bathroom, above a pizza restaurant; breakfast included. Follow the signs for the Turismo. Recommended. ②.

Pensão Guerreiro, Rua Grande 14 (☎058/82 20 99). Down-at-heel place at the bottom of the main avenue with shared bathrooms. It's friendly, though, and the restaurant (see below) is good. ②.

Residencial Jardim, Largo 5 de Outubro 68 (☎058/82 89 15). Overlooking the river, at the bottom of town, this has spotless, well-furnished rooms with bath and TV. Rooms with a balcony have good views; and prices are at the lower end of this category. ⑤.

Residencial Laranjeira, Rua General Luís do Rego 45 (☎058/82 22 61). A good choice, just off the main avenue (on the right as you walk down to the river), with small, but pleasant rooms, all with bath. Friendly, fresh and comfortable, and with breakfast included in the price. ③.

Residencial Magalhães, Rua Manuel Espregueira 62 (☎058/82 32 93). Twin and triple rooms, with or without bath, furnished in the best Minho tradition, with dark, carved headboards on the beds. ③.

Quinta de Paço d'Anha, Vila Nova de Anha (☎058/32 24 59). Three kilometres south of town on the N3 road to Esposende and the south. The house is on an estate that produces and bottles its own wine; there are four apartments with kitchenette. ⑤.

Hotel Santa Luzia, Monte de Santa Luzia (☎058/82 88 89). Show-piece hotel at the top of the hill above town, refurbished in Art Deco style. It's the priciest place in town, and the most comfortable and best-equipped, though the restaurant is disappointing. ⑥.

Residencial Terra Linda, Rua Luís Jácome 11–15 (☎058/82 89 81). Average and adequate, but tries hard to please. Rooms without bath fall into the lower category. ①–②.

Pensão Viana Mar Avda. dos Combatentes da Grande Guerra 215 (☎058/82 89 62). Another reasonably good place, with warm rooms in winter, and a sunken bar. Half the rooms have baths; the summer overflow of guests is accommodated in two nearby annexes. ④.

Residencial Vianense, Avda. Conde da Carreira 79 (☎058/82 31 18). Comfortable, clean and close to the train station. There's a decent restaurant here, too. ③.

Eating

There's a wide choice of places to eat in town, as you might expect from a busy resort. Some are lunchtime workers' cafés, while there's also a full range of tourist **restaurants**, many of which are extremely good since they cater mostly for demanding Portuguese visitors rather than foreigners. Several of the *pensões* also incorporate restaurants, open to non-residents; a couple of them are definitely worth considering. For general provisions, there is a permanent **market** at the eastern end of town, on Rua Martim Velho.

Casa de Pasto Trasmontano, Rua Gago Coutinho 12. Behind the Câmera Municipal in Praça da República, this low-cost establishment serves basic meals.

Dolce Vita, Rua do Poço 44. The wood-fired pizzas are a bit disappointing, but there's pasta, too, and a fine winelist. Don't worry if it looks full – there is plenty of space downstairs.

Pensão Guerreiro, Rua Grande 14. The first-floor restaurant deceives with its unsubtle pictorial tourist menu; the food is actually very good and fairly inexpensive, and features a bumper serving of *porco à alentejana*. Closed Thurs.

Laranjeira, Rua Manuel Espregueira 24. The restaurant here, below a *pensão*, receives varying reports, partly because it's always busy and sometimes a bit slapdash. It's worth chancing, though, for reasonably priced Portuguese meals.

Marisqueria Almoço, Rua General Luís do Rego. Carefully cooked, generous dishes – highly recommended.

Os Três Arcos, Largo João Tomás da Costa 25. Facing the Jardim Marginal, this is perhaps the best restaurant in town, with excellent food, a full list of *vinhos verdes*, and a bar where you can eat much more cheaply from the same menu – it's mostly seafood, but the turkey is good. If you want a table, call in earlier to book. Closed Mon.

Os Três Potes, Beco dos Fornos 7. Incredibly popular in high season, with national costumes and music at weekends. Good traditional food, but relatively pricey, with full meals running to at least 3000$00. Again, book ahead in summer. Closed Mon.

O Triângulo, Rua dos Manjovos 14. Quiet, pleasant seafood and snack joint.

Viana's Restaurante, Rua Frei Bartolomeu dos Martires 179. The place to pursue an interest in *bacalhau* dishes – simply superb. It's off Avda. Campo do Castelo.

Drinking, nightlife and entertainment

Romaria time aside, there's not an awful lot going on after dark in Viana. But a couple of **cafés** at the bottom of the main avenue are good places for a beer or late-night coffee, and if you're bubbling with energy, a number of clubs are worth a try.

For **cultural** events, consult the *Agenda Cultural,* a quarterly diary issued by the Câmera Municpal; the Turismo should have a copy. There are two **cinemas** in Viana, the *Verde Viana* (Praça 1° de Maio) and the *Cinema Palácio* (Rua de Aveiro); and check the output of the *Teatro do Noroeste* **theatre company**, based at the Teatro Municipal Sá de Miranda, on Rua Major Xavier da Costa (☎058/82 26 44).

Disco-Pub-Clube-Viana Sol, off Largo Vasco da Gama by *Hotel Viana Sol*. A very youthful crowd packs into this place in summer. Open from the afternoon until 3am, 4am on Saturday nights.

Girassol Café, Jardim Marginal. A lovely spot for a *bica*; though it closes at 7pm.

Café Imperial, Praça da República. Art Deco café with stained glass surroundings – and also one of the few places in the centre to open on Sunday afternoon.

Ministério Music Bar, Rua do Tourinho 41. Just off Praça da Erva: groovy music in a dimly lit and vaguely "alternative" youth hangout. There's a pricey cover charge but it's fun.

Pastelaria Paris, Avda. dos Combatentes da Grande Guerra. Great cakes, a pool room and decent toilets for a change!

THE VIANA ROMARIA

Viana's main *romaria*, dedicated to **Nossa Senhora da Agonía** – Our Lady of Sorrows – takes place for three days around the weekend nearest to August 20. A combination of carnival and fair, and fulfilling an important business function for the local communities, it's a great time to be in town.

Events kick off with an impressive **religious parade** on the Friday. But the best day is probably **Saturday**, when there's a massive parade of floats with every village in the region providing an example of a local craft or pursuit: a marvellous display of incongruities, with threshers pounding away in traditional dress while being pulled by a new *Lamborghini* tractor. If you want a seat in the stands, get a ticket well in advance.

On each of the three days there are lunchtime **processions** with *gigantones* (carnival giants), folk dancing, remarkably loud drum bands, pipe bands and, needless to say, concerted drinking. The blessing of the fishing boats on Monday morning is quite moving – women in the fishing quarter decorate their streets with pictures in coloured sawdust on religious and quotidian themes. And there are nightly **firework displays** too, of immense brilliance and noise.

Listings

Banks Main banks are on Praça da República and along the main avenue.

Boat trips Departures from the pier at the bottom of the avenue for trips up the Rio Lima; 2500$00 per person.

Car rental *Avis*, Rua do Gontim (☎058/82 39 94); *Hertz*, Avda. Conde da Carreira (☎058/82 22 50).

Hospital On Avda. 25 de Abril (☎058/82 90 81).

Pharmacy *Nelsina*, Praça da República; *Central*, Rua Manuel Espregueira.

Police Headquarters at Rua de Aveiro (☎058/82 20 22).

Post office Opposite the train station on the main avenue; you can make international telephone calls from here, too.

Swimming pool There's a pool open to the public at the *Hotel do Parque*, Parque da Goliza, east of the waterfront, beyond the train line.

Taxis Available from ranks along Avda. dos Combatentes da Grande Guerra.

Viana to Caminha

North of Viana the train line follows the coast all the way to Caminha. Four trains a day, in both directions, stop at all the villages en route – notably at Carreço, Afife, Gelfa, Vila Praia de Âncora and Moledo do Minho – offering easy access to a sequence of largely deserted beaches. It is possible to **walk** the same route, covering the whole stretch in a couple of days, camping overnight among the sheltered dunes at Afife, 10km north of Viana. Be warned, though, that persistent smuggling takes place on these isolated beaches, which can make the area a dangerous place to be at times, particularly if the local police are pursuing the villains unloading drugs from Spain on the sands.

Carreço, Afife and Gelfa

The small village of **CARREÇO** lies a couple of kilometres east of its beach, where there's a café-bar, toilets and showers. **AFIFE**, another 2km further north is also a good goal: a tiny village with a fort, the small *Residencial Compostela* (☎058/98 14 65; ④) and a useful café-shop at the train station. The dunes – and a particularly wonderful expanse of beach – are fifteen to twenty minutes' walk from the village, the least frequented parts being to the south. If you're looking for a more dramatic place to stay, *Casa do Penedo* (☎058/98 14 74; ③–④) is a typical Minho home, 500 metres inland of the station, on a hillside with sea views.

At **GELFA**, between Afife and Vila Praia de Âncora, there's a **campsite** in the pinewoods (☎058/91 15 37; mid-March to mid-Oct), but it's on the inland side of the train station and hence some distance from the beach.

Vila Praia de Âncora

Six kilometres up the coast from Afife, the next major stop on the train line is **VILA PRAIA DE ÂNCORA**. This is larger than the earlier settlements – almost a real resort – and popular with the locals at weekends. The beach, which is right alongside the train line, is again superb, sheltered by hills and drifting back into a beautiful river estuary, where you can swim enjoyably even when the Atlantic breezes are blowing towels around the sands. For good measure there are two **forts** guarding the bay: the *Fortim de Cão*, south of the estuary and a better-preserved example to the north, just by the little fishing harbour.

The **train station** for Vila Praia is called Âncora-Praia, and is the only station between Viana do Castelo and Caminha at which express trains stop. Finding **accommodation** for a few days here shouldn't be hard. Choices include the *Pensão Verdes Lírios*, Avenida Ramos Pereira (☎058/91 11 13; ③), and the *Hotel Mira*, *at* Rua 5 de Outubro 56 (☎058/91 11 11; ③); as well as **private rooms**, arranged through a seasonal **Turismo** (July–Sept daily 9am–1pm & 2–7pm; ☎058/91 13 84), which is located at the southern end of the seafront. There's also unofficial **camping** on the beach, by the *Fortim de Cão*.

Restaurants are plentiful, as is fresh fish. *Restaurante Forte Nova*, near the church, and the *Café Central*, opposite the train station, are both worth investigating, while *Restaurante Mar Gelfa* (open July–Sept), 20 minutes' walk south down the beach, is recommended for food and sunsets.

Moledo do Minho

North of Vila Praia de Âncora, **MOLEDO DO MINHO** is the train traveller's last chance to swim in the sea. Very much in the same mould as Vila Praia, it too has a fort – this time half-ruined, guarding the river from a long, sandy spit – and is predominantly a Portuguese family resort. If you're heading for Caminha, Valença, or even Spain, you could easily stop off here, wander down to the beach, and catch the following train. If you wanted to stay, the *Pensão Ideal*, Rua Sousa Rego 125 (☎058/72 15 05; ④), might tempt you, and you can eat at the good *Restaurante Praia Sol* on the seafront.

ALONG THE RIO MINHO

At Moledo, the train line finally leaves the coast to follow the south bank of the **Rio Minho**, which meanders northeastwards forming the country's border with Spain. **Caminha** is the first river town, a pleasant stopover, either for a night or for a meal between trains. Beyond here, several small fortified towns guard the Portuguese side of the river, with the Minho train line coming to a halt in perhaps the best of the lot, **Valença do Minho**. This is also the site of a splendid weekly market and a major crossing-point into Spain. However, the best section of the river route is from Valença east to **Monção** and **Melgaço**, which you can only reach by bus. Both towns are also minor border crossings, with buses onwards from the Spanish side.

Caminha

Resembling a smaller version of Viana do Castelo, **CAMINHA** is a quiet river port with a few reminders of better days. These are principally in the main square, Praça Conselheiro Silva Torres (known locally as Largo Terreiro), which sports a battlemented town hall and Renaissance clocktower. Caminha's most distinguished building, though, is the **Igreja Matriz**, a couple of minutes' walk from the main square towards the river; take the street through the arch by the clock tower, past the **Turismo** (Mon–Sat 9.30am–12.30pm & 2.30–6pm; ☎058/92 19 52). The church was built towards the end of the fifteenth century, when the town was reputed to rival Porto in trade, and it still stands within part of the old city walls. Try and find someone with a key, for it has a magnificent inlaid *artesanato* ceiling – a rare burst of Moorish inspiration in the north. Note also the figures carved on the two Renaissance doorways, one on the north side giving the finger to Spain across the river!

A couple of kilometres south of town, the island of **Fortaleza da Ínsua** makes an enjoyable trip – local fishermen run trips across on Sundays from the spit of sand at Foz do Minho. If you want to arrange something during the week (for the next morning), ask in the *Café Valadares* for directions to António Garrafão's house. He will only go if there is a reasonably large – or affluent – group gathered.

Practicalities

The town has a choice of three **pensions**: the excellent-value *Residencial Arca Nova* (☎058/72 14 75; ④), near the train station; the older *Pensão Rio Coura* (☎058/92 11 42; ③), also close to the station; and the rather dreary *Residencial Galo d'Ouro*, Rua da Corredoura 15 (☎058/92 11 60; ②–③), just off the main square. Alternatives include a few private **rooms** in houses (ask at the Turismo or the *Pêro de Caminha* restaurant; see below), and the *Casa de Esteiró* (☎058/92 13 56; ⑤), at the entrance to town, where there is an apartment to rent in a small neighbourhood house with lovely gardens.

There are two nearby **campsites**. The better of them is a little inland at Vilar de Mouros (☎058/72 74 72; open all year), which is nicely positioned, by a small river gorge, and has a swimming pool; there are weekday buses to the site at 11.30am and 6.30pm from outside the café, 200m left out of the train station. The other, which tends to be crowded in summer, is an *Orbitur* site (☎058/92 12 95; open all year), 2km to the south, between the river and the sea, opposite the Fortaleza da Ínsua (weekday buses from the town hall in the main square at 11.30am, 1pm and 6pm stop close by).

Several of the best **cafés and restaurants** are found in the main square: the *Caminhense* has superb regional specialities, the cheerful *Pêro de Caminha* serves pizzas, and the *Pastelaraia Colmeia* is the place for breakfast. There's good, if more expensive food, too, at the *Adega do Chico* on Rua Visconde de Sousa Rego (head up the right-hand side of the main square, away from the clocktower).

The town's **ferry** link across the river to La Guardia in Spain, suspended for several years, is due to be reinstated in the near future. In the meantime, there's still a cross-river service to the east at Vila Nova de Cerveira (see below).

Vila Nova de Cerveira

More or less hourly trains run along the banks of the Rio Minho to **VILA NOVA DE CERVEIRA**, 11km to the northeast of Caminha. A small walled town, this has a car- and passenger-ferry – actually little more than a floating platform – which drifts every half-hour across the river to Goyan in Galicia. The **ferry** (60$00 passengers, 400$00 cars) has turned the village into something of a shopping centre for Spaniards, but it remains a pleasant and accessible place and in many respects is more enticing than the bigger and better known Valença further upstream.

The **Solar dos Castros** on Praça da Liberdade was once a manor house and now serves as a cultural centre. At the back, facing a beautifully well-kept garden, is the **Turismo** (Mon–Sat 9.30am–12.30pm & 2.30–6pm; ☎051/79 57 87) while alongside, in a small garden, is a striking sculpture of a tripod holding aloft a rock. This has become the symbol of the **arts festival** held here every two years in August/September: the remarkable statue depicting men talking, which won first prize in 1984, is displayed just inside the front door of the Solar dos Castros.

Practicalities

If you wanted to stay, there's accommodation available at both ends of the scale. For budget travellers, the pleasant **youth hostel** at Largo 16 de Fevereiro 21 (☎051/79 61 13) boasts its own kitchen and a terrace. And if you have money to burn, there is also an excellent **pousada**, the *Dom Dinis* (☎051/79 56 01; ⑦), built within the old fortress walls and overlooking the ramparts. Although not a historic building itself, this would provide a memorable first or last night in Portugal; not surprisingly, it also has the best restaurant in town. In between these two extremes, regular accommodation is offered at the *Residencial Marinel*, on Largo 16 de Fevereiro (☎051/79 51 14; ②), near the hostel, and *Residencial Rainha Santa Isabel*, Rua Herois do Ultramar (☎051/79 51 69; ③). For **food**, the *Café Restaurant Central* is just one of many good places to eat, while the *Barril Bar*, off the main square, is where much of the evening action takes place.

Valença do Minho and around

The border town of **VALENÇA DO MINHO** (usually just referred to as Valença) is quite absurdly quaint, its old town area clumped amid perfectly preserved multi-layered seventeenth-century ramparts on a hillock above the river. There are great walks here, both down by the river and along the **ramparts** (watch out for hidden stairwells), the design of which was influenced by the work of the seventeenth-century French military architect, Vauban.

On foot, you're likely to approach the old town from the crossroads at the bottom of the hill, where Avenida Espanha – which runs from the train station – enters the new part of town. Climb the hill and you enter through the **Portas da Coroada**, further along from which a causeway leads over a dry moat to the **Portas do Meio**, the bastion's middle gates. Through here, around Largo de São João, there's a rich diversity of buildings lining the narrow, cobbled streets, with sudden views of the surrounding countryside appearing over the lower reaches of the walls. And at the far end sits the town's *pousada*, one of the finest places to stay in the whole of northern Portugal. In the daytime these charms are exploited by myriad souvenir shops, catering for the day-trippers who cross the border from Spain to pick up Portuguese linen, ceramics and electrical goods. Increasingly, the extent of this commercialism is reducing the appeal of the town – Tuy, across the river in Spain, is probably nicer. By late afternoon, though, the crowds are gone and at night Valença is almost a ghost town.

The newer part of town, to the south of the ramparts, has nothing of interest but it's here that you'll track down all the basic necessities. Come on Wednesday and you'll encounter the huge weekly **market,** held on the wooded slopes below the walls.

Practicalities

Now that European cross-border controls have been relaxed, arriving in Valença **from Tuy in Spain**, over the river, is a simple matter of staying on the train for another few minutes as it rattles over the bridge, or simply walking over from Tuy. **Trains from Viana do Castelo** end their run in Valença; to head further east you'll have to take a local **bus**, which arrive at and depart from in front of the train station. There are no obvious signs to the old town; turn right at the avenue that leads away from the station. You'll pass the **Turismo** (Mon–Sat 9am–12.30pm & 2.30–6pm; ☎051/233 74), which isn't outstandingly helpful, but might be able to track down a room.

Accommodation and eating

Private rooms are available in the old town, but otherwise the only place to stay there is at the swanky *Pousada de São Teotónio* (☎051/82 42 42; ⑦), located inside the fortress itself. Even if this is out of your range, a drink in the bar – or lunch in the excellent restaurant (around 3000–4000$00 a head) – is money well spent. Valença also has several **pensions** in the new town, including the *Rio Minho*, on Largo da Estação (☎051/22 33 31; ②–③), down by the train station, which is a bit the worse for wear and often full, though it has a good restaurant. Alternatively, you could **camp** below the ramparts at the western end, as numerous summer travellers do.

Recommended among the **restaurants** is the *Monumental*, under the walls, just inside the Portas da Coroada, which does a wonderful, spicy *arroz de marisco*. Further up, *Bom Jesus*, in Largo Bom Jesus, is popular with the Portuguese and Spanish alike; while *A Gruta*, just inside the Portas do Meio, has an outside bar and an indoor restaurant, under the vaults, where you can see your food being cooked.

Crossing to Spain: Tuy

Just a mile from Valença, Spanish **TUY** is an ancient, pyramid-shaped town with a grand battlemented parish church. It, too, is partly walled and it looks far sturdier than Valença, though the first English guidebook to Portugal (*Murray's* in 1855) reported that "the guns of Valença could without difficulty lay Tuy in ruins". If you're not planning to go on to Spain, at least walk across the frontier bridge to explore Tuy's old quarter by the river. There's no longer any passport control post: walking from the centre of one old town to the other takes around 30 minutes.

By **road** (there's a new bridge over the river) and **train** you can go direct from Valença to Vigo, which is within easy reach of Santiago de Compostela, the ancient and beautiful pilgrimage town of Galicia.

Inland: Paredes de Coura

PAREDES DE COURA, 28km south of Valença, claims to be the oldest village in Portugal, a claim that's just about conceivable and, if you are headed for Ponte da Barca or Ponte de Lima, warrants a detour. You can climb up to the top of the town for views over an almost Swiss landscape, with chalet-style houses and white church spires, or follow the track down beyond the football field to the river for the town's best swimming spot. Every year, over the first weekend in August, there's a **festival** featuring the usual Minho mix of dance, costumed procession and music.

One daily **bus** runs to the town from Valença, leaving at around 5pm. The best **place to stay** is the *Pensão Miquelina* on Rua Conselheiro Miguel Dantas (☎051/78 21 03; ③), which is not far from the **Turismo** (Mon–Sat 9.30am–12.30pm & 2.30–6pm; ☎051/78 35 92), housed in an old prison in Largo Visconde Moselos.

Monção and around

MONÇÃO, 16km east of Valença, preserves yet another Minho **fortress**, though it doesn't quite make the grade – there being little more than a doorway, a section of walling above the bus station and a high defensive walkway that runs along the northern, river-facing, side of town. Perhaps for this reason, Monção has escaped much of the daytime tourist attention that bedevils the towns to the west; the liveliest day to visit is Thursday, market day. But there's an attractive old centre, which always rewards a stroll, and the town's history, in which two local women played a prominent part, provides a colourful backdrop to the surviving fortifications and buildings.

The principal figure in the town's history is **Deu-la-deu Martins**, who is commemorated by a statue and fountain in Largo da Loreto. Her tale, similar to a number of other accounts across Portugal and Spain, recalls a crucial moment in the fourteenth century, when the Spanish troops had besieged the townspeople to the point of starvation. Deu-la-deu baked some cakes, using much skill and next to no flour, and had them presented to the Spanish camp with an offer to "make more if they needed them". The psychological effect of this bluff was so great that the enemy promptly gave up and went away. Local *pãozinhos* (little bread cakes) are still baked in her honour; her birthplace is off the praça, above the butcher's shop on the arched side road.

A second Spanish siege, in the seventeenth-century Wars of Restoration, was relieved in 1659 when the **Countess of Castelo Melhor**, perhaps inspired by earlier example, resorted to psychological warfare once again. The story goes that, having negotiated a ceasefire on condition that full military honours be given to her men, the Countess relinquished her 236 surviving fighters to the Spanish army. Knowing nothing of the town's two thousand fatalities, the enemy assumed they had been kept at bay by this paltry platoon and duly retreated in shame.

In the town, behind the mask of new paintwork and construction, there are a couple of interesting older places that reward a visit. The seventeenth-century **Igreja da Misericórdia** on Praça Deu-la-deu contains some magnificent *azulejos*, as does the Romanesque **Igreja da Matriz** – at the centre of a maze of ancient streets – which houses various tombs, including that of Deu-la-deu herself. The local **festivals** of *Corpo de Deus* (Corpus Christi; June 18) and particularly of *Nossa Senhora das Dores* (Sept 19–22) are interesting times to visit if you can manage it – though you are unlikely to be able to find any accommodation then. The former perpetuates medieval superstition in an elaborate enactment of the

Fight against Evil, a battle that resembles that in the tale of Saint George and the Dragon.

Practicalities

The **bus station** stands in front of the defunct train station, with the town centre straight ahead. There's a first-floor **Turismo** in Largo do Loreto (Mon–Sat 9.30am–12.30pm & 2–6pm; ☎051/65 27 57). For travellers to Spain, there's a simple **car ferry** across the Minho, though this will probably be discontinued once the new **road bridge** across to Salvaterra in Spain is completed.

Pensions raise their rates with each passing day, but you can still find a reasonably priced bed at *Residencial Esteves*, Rua General Pimenta de Castro, near the station (☎051/65 23 86; ②), or at the *Pensão Central*, Rua Dr. Álvares da Guerra 6, near Praça Deu-la-deu (☎051/65 23 14; ③). The former has little atmosphere, but smart modern rooms; the latter is large, musty and rundown, but the balconies offer great views. There are also good-value **rooms** available above the *Pastelaria Raiano* next to the *Central*, or failing that, at the *Casa Constantino*, Rua da Independência 24, where a couple of the rooms overlook the river. More upmarket is the *Pensão Mané*, Rua General Pimenta de Castro 5 (☎051/65 24 90; ④); while better still is the *Casa de Rodas* (☎051/65 21 05; ⑤), a lovely, low eighteenth-century building with four guest rooms, just out of town. The Turismo will find out if there's space and give you directions.

Monção is an excellent place to push the gastronomic boat out. Minho trout and salmon are always tremendous and between January and March the rich, eel-like **lamprey** are in season. The local **wine**, the finest *vinho verde* in the country, is available on draft in a couple of bars off the main square; the most delicious bottled variety is *Palácio da Brejoeira Alvarinho*, which, as a splendid Monção tourist leaflet one-liner puts it, "someone in France once classified as being the best in the world".

Among the best of the budget **places to eat** are the *Boi na Brasa* (opposite the station) for good grilled chicken, and the pleasant *Quinta da Oliveira*, 400m down the road to Braga on Estrada dos Arcos. Probably the best bet in Monção, though, is the *Café Central Restaurant* (not to be confused with the *Pensão Central*'s overpriced restaurant) on the main square, which serves excellent food – the entrance is in the side street at the back.

The Spa, Cortes and Lapela

The presence of a **thermal spa** to the east of Monção (follow the walls) has turned the town into something of a resort for Spanish day-trippers and Portuguese weekenders. Aside from the dubious pleasures of the alkaline water, there's a park and the free *Caldas de Monção* **campsite** by the river; if you swim, take care with the currents.

Further afield, to the west of the town, a pleasant walk trails off into the woods from the stop at *Senhora da Cabeça* to the hamlet of **CORTES**, which was Monção's medieval site. About 3km further west is **LAPELA**, whose river beach is safer for swimmers. The village is dominated by a lofty **tower**, all that remains of a fortress destroyed in 1706 to provide materials for the restoration of the battered walls of Monção.

East to Melgaço

An historic incident in Anglo-Portuguese relations took place on the fragile-looking bridge over the Rio Mouro just before **CEIVÃES**, 10km along the road from Monção to Melgaço. Cascades of garbage tumble down the banks below the spot where John of Gaunt, the Duke of Lancaster, arranged the marriage of his daughter Philippa to King Dom João I in 1386, an arrangement that resulted in the signing of the **Treaty of Windsor** between the two countries. It gave rise to an alliance lasting over six hundred years and to the naming of numerous public places in honour of "Filipa de Lencastre".

Thermal spa enthusiasts might want to stop at **PESO**, another 10km to the east (and just 4km short of Melgaço). This is a tiny spa town, spread along the main road and looking down on a magnificent curve of the river. There's a lovely **campsite** (☎051/423 27; June–Oct) set in lush riverside gardens, and the plush, modern *Residencial Boavista* (☎051/424 64; ④), which has a restaurant, swimming pool and fabulous views.

Melgaço and around

MELGAÇO – the country's northernmost outpost – is a small border town sitting high above the Rio Minho. If its rural origins are somewhat obscured by the modern developments that sprawl along the main road, at its heart not much has really changed. With the exception of a few *festa* days in mid-August, when a display of tractors, an array of the town's long-reputed smoked hams (*presunto*), a craft exhibition, and a performance from the school banjo band are organised, very little happens. Try to arrive for the **Friday market** when chickens, ducks, sticky buns, furniture, pottery, cabbages and corsets cover the stretch of road around the old walls.

At other times the reasons for coming to Melgaço are that it is so obviously off the tourist track, and that it gives easy access to the northern part of the Parque Nacional da Peneda-Gerês and to Spanish Galicia (see below for access details). Its one historic feature is the ruined **fortress**, much fought over during the Wars of Restoration, but now little more than a tower and a few walls handy for hanging out washing.

Short excursions from Melgaço might include the two **Romanesque churches** of Paderne (3km west, off the road to Monção) and Nossa Senhora da Orada (1km east, off the road to the border).

Practicalities

The town's helpful **Turismo** is just out town on the road to Monção. Cheapest **rooms** are with Maria Helena Mouries on Rua Rio do Porto (☎051/421 88; ①), near the Turismo, while **pensions** include the *Flôr do Minho*, south of the central square on Rua Velha (☎051/429 50; ②–③), the cheaper *Pemba* on Largo da Calçada (☎425 55; ②), the modern *Zip Zip*, opposite the town hall (☎051/421 68; ②), or the very nice *Residencial Miguel Peireira*, near the cinema (☎051/422 12; ③).

In the alleys below the fort, a couple of **café-restaurants** offer good food at reasonable prices; and there's a café in the attractive castle gardens overlooking the Minho valley. Try the restaurant below the *Flôr do Minho*, or the *Parisienne*, next door, which both have cheapish tourist menus. *Café-Restaurant O Bilhares*, below the cinema, has an outdoor terrace and a nice feel to it, but is more expensive.

Buses leave for Monção every day (3–5 daily), and connect with services to Braga, Coimbra, Porto and Lisbon; while weekday buses to Lamas de Mouro and Castro Laboreiro for the Peneda-Gerês park leave startlingly early in the morning. Buses to São Gregório, for the Spanish border, leave four times a day, in the afternoon and early evening.

The Spanish border

The **Spanish border post** is at **PONTE BARXAS** (open April–Oct 7am–midnight, Nov–March 8am–9pm), 1km east of **SÃO GREGÓRIO** , which itself is 10km east of Melgaço. Other than taking one of the buses outlined above in "Practicalities", the only way to get there is by taxi, which is reasonably inexpensive.

Across the frontier, buses leave twice daily (not weekends) for Ribadavia and Orense. Ribadavia (along the Minho and with superb local red wine) and Celanova (on a different route to Orense and dwarfed by a vast medieval monastery) must be two of the most lovely and characteristic towns of Spanish Galicia. The Minho itself – or Miño as it becomes known – is more placid in the further reaches, as it is dammed shortly after the point when both of its banks are within Spain.

THE LIMA VALLEY AND PARQUE NACIONAL DA PENEDA-GERÊS

The **Rio Lima**, whose valley is perhaps the most beautiful in Portugal, was thought by the Romans to be the Lethe, the mythical River of Oblivion. Beyond it, they imagined, lay the Elysian Fields; to cross would mean certain destruction, for its waters possessed the power of the lotus, making the traveller forget country and home. The Roman Consul Decimus Junius Brutus, having led his legions across most of Spain, had to seize the standard and plunge into the water shouting the names of his legionaries from the far bank – to show his memory remained intact – before they could be persuaded to follow.

There are roads along both banks of the Lima from **Viana do Castelo** (see p.263), where the river meets the sea. Travelling from Viana on the main N202, regular bus services pass through two highly attractive towns – **Ponte de Lima** and **Ponte da Barca** – from either of which you could take fine walks into the hilly and wooded surroundings, perhaps exploring one or two of the many Romanesque churches in the region, such as that at **Bravães,** between the two towns.

Further east, the Lima runs into the heart of the **Parque Nacional da Peneda-Gerês**, the largest nature reserve in Portugal. The easiest point of access to the central section of the park is from Ponte da Barca or from **Arcos de Valdevez**, 5km to the north, though there's a possible far northern approach, too, from Melgaço on the Rio Minho.

Ponte de Lima

An hour's ride east of Viana do Castelo, **PONTE DE LIMA** lies at the end of a low stone bridge, Roman in origin and said to mark the path of their first hesitant crossing. It's a delightful small town, whose crumbling old centre – as is often the way – has no specific attraction other than its air of sleepy indifference to the wider world. You might disagree if you visit in July or August, when Ponte de Lima begins to show worrying signs of midsummer tourist strain, which the local authorities plan to capitalise on by building a huge golf complex nearby. But at almost any other time of year, the town remains one of Portugal's most pleasing.

The river here offers fine swimming and has wide sandbank beaches where the town's bi-monthly Monday **market**, the oldest in Portugal, has been held since a charter was first granted in 1125. So, too, have the curiously named **"New Fairs"** (second/third weekend of September), a tremendous festival and market, seemingly attended by half the Minho, with fireworks, a fairground, wandering accordionists and *gigantones*, and a large brass band competition. More tradition is on display in early June, when a bull-taunting game, dating back 300 years, is played on the beach near the bridge; needless to say, novice bovine-botherers should take care. The town's main focus is a long riverside **Alameda** shaded by magnificent plane trees, which leads to the rambling old convent of Santo António, which contains a small museum of treasures within its church. In the town, spare an hour to glance around at the handsome buildings: there are several sixteenth-century **mansions** with stone coats of arms, and interesting remains of the old **keep**, used into the 1960s as a prison (the occupants were allowed to hang cups down from the windows for money and cigarettes).

Practicalities

The **bus station** is behind the market, just a minute or so from the river. A few minutes' walk away, in Praça da República in the town centre, the **Turismo** (Mon–Sat 9am–12.30pm & 2.30–6pm, Sun 9.30am–12.30pm; ☎058/94 23 35) hands out a map of town, though you're hardly likely to need one. The tourist office shares its premises with the headquarters of the Minho's **Turismo de Habitação** scheme (see below), which provides some of the finest accommodation you'll find for rent in northern Portugal.

TURISMO DE HABITAÇÃO

The Ponte de Lima **Turismo de Habitação** (*Turihab*) organisation arranges rented accommodation in local manor houses, farms and country estates throughout the Minho. There are nearly thirty properties available in the Ponte de Lima area alone, each with usually just two or three rooms and offered on a bed-and-breakfast basis: you can find yourself staying in some extraordinary historical buildings, and even rubbing shoulders with Portuguese aristocrats who have allowed their ancient seats to become part of the scheme. Bookings are best made through *Turihab* (☎058/94 27 29, fax 058/74 14 44), though you can also make your own reservations or book at local Turismo offices. In high season in certain areas you might find that stays are for a minimum of three nights. Expect to pay around 10,000$00 per room, sometimes a few thousand more for the really exclusive country houses.

Accommodation

There are two **Turihab properties** in town, both seventeenth-century houses: *Casa de Castro* (☎058/94 11 56; ⑤), around 1km out on the N203 to Ponte de Barca, which – legend has it – was partly demolished by the owner in 1896 who was looking for hidden treasure; and *Casa das Pereiras*, on Largo das Pereiras (☎058/94 29 39; ⑤; open June–Oct only), which has a pool and splendid dinners served every Friday evening. If you're driving, other local properties particularly worth enquiring about include the *Moínho de Estorãos* (an old mill); the amazing *Paço de Calheiros* country seat; the stone *Casa do Tamanqueiro*; and the eight-eenth-century *Casa do Outeiro*. All these houses lie one to ten kilometres away from Ponte de Lima, whose Turismo can check on space for you.

Of **pensions and hotels** in the town, the comfortable *Pensão Beira Rio*, Passeio 25 de Abril (☎058/94 34 71; ②), lies on the waterfront, with grandstand views of the comings and goings for the Monday market. The *São João*, in Largo de São João (☎058/94 12 88; ③), near the bridge, is also excellent value and serves good food downstairs in its restaurant. Swankiest choice is the new *Albergaria Império do Minho*, on the Alameda (☎058/74 15 10; ⑤), the centre-piece of a shopping complex and equipped with swimming pool and restaurant.

Alternatively, you could **camp** (unofficially) across the bridge on the river-bank, where during the New Fairs a rainbow-coloured site emerges, with families washing clothes, auctioning cattle, and letting off fireworks throughout the night.

Eating and drinking

There are a few inexpensive **cafés and restaurants** along the riverfront – the *Catrina* is a good one – but the best place to eat traditional local food is the *Restaurante Encanada*, Praça Municipal (closed Thurs), which is close to the market and has a terrace overlooking the river. The food is good and very modestly priced. Also highly recommended is the *Alameda*, at the town end of the bridge, which features more splendid views, photographs of Ponte de Lima at New Fair time, and a good menu that allows you to eat for under 1500$00.

Walks around Ponte de Lima

There's beautiful **walking country** all around Ponte de Lima, especially along both banks of the river east of the town. The Turismo has gone to some pains to produce a set of nominally marked trails, accompanied by the leaflets you pick up from them. Keep your wits about you, however, as directions and left/right details are not all they might be. One walk goes over the bridge and up a winding, dusty road to the TV-mast-topped summit of the hill opposite the town. Here stands the chapel of **Santo Ovidio**, patron saint of ears. If, as is likely, it is closed, you can still peep through the grille and see the walls strung with wax ears and a table covered in them. Each is a model of the afflicted ear of a parishioner, brought here for saintly treatment, or as thanks for relief received.

East to Bravães and Ponte da Barca

From Ponte de Lima, the N203 runs 18km east to **Ponte da Barca**, another Minho market town with a bridge so attractive it, too, has been incorporated into the town's name. On the way, call a halt at **Bravães**, which has a fine Romanesque church, one of several in the Lima region that is simple and rustic in design but features beautiful, naive carvings on the doorways and columns. Most of these churches were built in the twelfth and thirteenth centuries under the supervision of Cluniac monks, who brought their architecture to Spain and Portugal along the pilgrimage routes to Santiago de Compostela in Galicia; the main Portuguese route ran through Braga and so Minho has the highest concentration.

Bravães

At **BRAVÃES**, 14km east of Ponte de Lima, the church of **São Salvador** stands just to the left of the road in the small hamlet. Its two sculpted doorways are perhaps the best in the country, filled with carvings of doves, griffins, monkeys and two of the local wide-horned oxen. If the church is locked ask at the cottage behind and the doors will be flung open for you, lighting up medieval murals of Saint Sebastian and the Virgin.

There's a **bar** in Bravães where local transport-users can debate the chances of a bus going on to Ponte da Barca, 4km further east; it's probably quicker to walk.

Ponte da Barca

Ignoring the modern suburbs of **PONTE DA BARCA**, and heading for the river, the old town quarters form a quintessential pastoral vision. The Lima is spanned here by a lovely, sixteenth-century bridge; alongside is a splendid market and, on the adjoining corner of Largo de Misericórdia, a seasonal **Turismo** (Mon–Fri 9am–12.30pm & 2–6pm, Sat 9am–12.30pm; ☎058/428 99). On alternate Wednesdays there's a superb open-air **market**, which spreads out by the river in an almost medieval atmosphere, drawing hundreds of people from outlying hamlets. Walk down to the other end of the main road and you'll come to the cattle market area. It's also worth noting that the town's annual *Feira de São Bartolomeu* takes place on August 24; don't expect to get any sleep once the party starts.

The finest place **to stay** is unquestionably the *Pensão Maria Gomes*, Rua Conselheiro Rocha Peixoto 13 (☎058/422 88; ②), overlooking the river and bridge, where breakfast is served on the balcony. It's worth phoning ahead to book. On the north bank of the river, opposite the town, the *Quinta da Prova* (☎058/421 63; ⑥) has three apartments with kitchen, each sleeping up to four people, not a bad place to base yourself for longer forays into the region. For **meals**, you could do far worse than eat at *Pensão Maria Gomes*, or try the good-value *Bar do Rio*, close to the Praia Fluvial – a beach on the left bank of the river – which is a nice place to dine watching the sunset.

From the **bus stop** by the bridge, near the arches of the town hall, there are connections to Lindoso (2–4 daily) and Braga (Mon–Fri hourly, fewer at weekends).

Walks from Ponte da Barca

The Ponte da Barca Turismo publishes details of a fine **local walk**, a seven-hour circuit, described from São Miguel near Entre-Ambos-os-Rios (8km east of town), that's highly recommended. It's an uphill hike most of the way, but passes through some gorgeous villages – Sobredo, especially – which seem unchanged from centuries past. There's food available at several points along the way (midway at Germil, for example).

Arcos de Valdevez

As a diversion from the main Minho river route you might contemplate exploring the Rio Vez, which can be reached just 5km north of Ponte da Barca, at **ARCOS DE VALDEVEZ** ("Arches of the Valley of the Vez"). Like almost everywhere in this region, it's ordinarily a sleepy little place, though it shows its true Minho colours during the fortnightly Wednesday **market**. And, as at Ponte de Lima and Ponte da Barca, it only really comes alive during its annual festival, in this case the three-day **Festas do Concelho**, held over the first or second week in August, featuring *gigantones* (giant figures), *zés pereiras* (red-caped drummers), horse races and noisy fireworks. Traditionally these celebrations should take place on the last weekend of the holiday month, but they've been shifted to take account of local emigrants who return to work abroad at the end of August (see the feature below); one of the festival days is actually named the *Dia do Emigrante*.

Practicalities

The **Turismo** is opposite the bridge on Avenida Marginal (Mon–Sat 9am–12.30pm & 2.30–6pm; mid-June to mid-Sept also Sun 9.30am–12.30pm; ☎058/660 01) and has maps to give away. For information on the **bus** service to Lindoso, ask at the depot above Largo da Lapa, from where there are also regular services to Monção, Ponte de Lima and Viana do Castelo. Buses en route to Soajo or Braga (as well as Monção or Lindoso) leave from a stop by the Turismo.

Like Ponte da Barca, Arcos de Valvedez is a useful point of departure for the Parque Nacional da Peneda-Gerês and there's a **park information office** in Arcos on Avenida de Tilias, beside the river (Mon–Fri 9am–12.30 & 2–5.30pm; ☎058/653 38), where you can buy an English-language map of the park.

The town has several good and reasonably priced **pensions**, including the *Pensão Ribeira* on Largo do Milagres (☎058/651 74; ②) and the more expensive *Pensão Tavares*, on Rua Padre Manuel José da Cunha Brito (☎ 058/662 53; ③). A third, attractively sited in the upper part of town, is the small and unpretentious *Pensão Flor do Minho*, at Largo da Valeta 11–15 (☎058/652 16; ①).

There is a cluster of nice **restaurants** in Rua de São João, while other local places that recommend themselves include the *Minho Verde*, Avenida de Tilias, beyond the park office, and *O Lagar*, Rua Dr. Vaz Guedes, in the old quarter. For

---

EMIGRATION AND THE MINHO

Travelling around the Minho, you'll see much new building, even in the smallest and most isolated villages. This is accounted for mainly by **Minho emigrants**, who return to their homes after working abroad in France, Switzerland or Germany, sometimes the United States. Minho, more than any other area of Portugal, suffered severe depopulation from the late 1950s onwards, as thousands migrated in search of more lucrative work.

The new-found prosperity of the emigrants has transformed their homeland in two ways: money sent back from abroad supports the family members left behind and, indirectly, the local economy; while some of the emigrants themselves have returned to enjoy a well-heeled retirement in what they call *minha terra* (my land). August is the time when most people race back from abroad to see their families. If you drop in on a *festa*, don't be surprised to hear groups of well-dressed emigrant kids speaking English, German or French.

a real treat, though, visit *Casa Delfim*, a café down the right-hand side of the church in Largo da Lapa, run by an ageing "world-famous" accordionist and stacked with his instruments, any of which are liable, suddenly, to be snatched up for an impromptu jam session.

Parque Nacional da Peneda-Gerês

The magnificent **PARQUE NACIONAL DA PENEDA-GERÊS** is hardly a secret. Caldas do Gerês, the main centre of the park, attracts more tourists than anywhere else in the Minho, with the possible exception of Viana do Castelo, and at weekends, when Portuguese campers arrive in force, parts of it can seem a bit too close to civilisation. The park as a whole, though, is large enough to absorb the great numbers of visitors. It's split into two distinct parts, based around the southern **Serra do Gerês** and the wilder northern section containing the **Serra da Peneda**; this latter area, in particular (best approached from Melgaço, on the River Minho), remains largely undiscovered.

You can see a great deal of the park under your own steam: at many of the hamlets and villages there's access to accommodation, campsites and food. Trails and paths cover large areas, and there are dozens of hiking opportunities, from short strolls to two-and three-day hikes across whole sections of the park. A long-distance, cross-park trail is planned, too; see the feature on p.287 for more details. If you'd like someone else to take care of the arrangements and plan your walks, contact *Trilhos*, Rua de Belém 94, 4300 Porto (☎02/48 07 40), which may have vacancies on their small hiking group holidays; they'll provide transport, guides, food and accommodation.

Caldas do Gerês and hikes in central Gerês

The national park is centred around the old spa town of **Caldas do Gerês** (commonly known as Gerês), which is reached most easily by bus from Braga – a two-hour journey. From here, there are a couple of interesting and accessible hikes, though, frustratingly, the **central Gerês** section is not well equipped with footpaths and walking off the tracks can be difficult and painful, with small shrubs slashing the legs.

Caldas do Gerês

Weekends aside, when Portuguese picnickers arrive en masse, **CALDAS DO GERÊS** is a relaxed and very elegant base. "The Spa of Gerês", it became fashionable in the early years of the last century – an epoch convincingly evoked by a row of grand Victorian hotels along the sedate old main street, Avenida Manuel Francisco da Costa. The spa still functions, attracting the infirm in the summer season, though most visitors nowadays are younger and healthier, up from the northern cities to picnic in the woods or, in the case of eccentric foreigners, to hike. There's been a lot of recent development in town, but it's not all to the bad and you'll probably appreciate the new public outdoor swimming pool (reached through the park), tennis courts, boating lake and the countless cafés.

Pick up information either at the **Turismo** (Mon & Wed–Sat 9am–noon & 2–6pm; ☎053/39 11 33), at the top end of the main avenue, or the national park office, a little further up (see box on p.284). There is no shortage of **pensions** and some –

PARQUE NACIONAL DA PENEDA-GERÊS

To Celanova & Orense

SPAIN

Bande

SPAIN

Tourém

Fragas da Moura

Cornos da Fonte Fria

▲ 1373 m

1545 m

Pitões das Júnias

Montalegre

Minhos dos Carris

Covelãs

Outeiro

Paredes

Barragem de Paradela

To Chaves

▲ 9 m

Paradela

adouro

Cabril

Pisões

Barragem do Alto Rabagoã

Pincães ião

Rio Cabril

Rio Cávado

Barragem da Venda Nova

Barragem da Salamonde

Venda Nova

	Mirador (viewpoint)
	Hostel
	Campsite
	Mountain Peak
– – –	Footpath
	Main Road
	Road

0   10 km

MAPS AND INFORMATION

A new **map of the park** is available, which details altitudes and all roads (but none of the footpaths). You should be able to pick this up, as well as leaflets, hiking information and other advice from one of three **national park information offices**: the head office in Braga, or either in Arcos de Valdevez or on the spot in Caldas do Gerês (see list below).

Arcos de Valdevez, Avda. de Tilias (Mon–Fri 9am–12.30 & 2–5.30pm; ☎058/653 38).

Braga, Avda. António Macedo, Quinta das Parretas suburb (Mon–Fri

9am–12.30pm & 2–5.30pm; ☎053/61 31 66).

Caldas do Gerês, Avda. Manuel Francisco da Costa (Mon–Fri 9.30am–6pm; ☎053/39 11 81).

Equipment and Dangers

Maps aside, if you plan a long hike, take good boots, warm and waterproof clothes, a compass, food and a water bottle (there are plenty of streams). Beware of fog in spring and winter. Picking flowers and – more importantly – **lighting fires** are forbidden in Gerês. The Portuguese have an alarming habit of lighting them whenever and wherever they picnic, no doubt a contributory factor in disastrous fires such as those that destroyed over 800 square kilometres of forest in 1985 alone.

---

even in the height of summer – are reasonably priced, but note that many are only open from May to October; while in those that do stay open over winter, the restaurants are usually closed. On the main Avenida Manuel Francisco da Costa there are three expensive hotels, though the solitary pension here, the *Central Jardim* (☎053/39 11 32; ④), remains fairly good value. Downstream from here, and across the other side, Rua do Amasso affords ever better views up the valley and boasts a string of decent pensions, namely: the long-established *Pensão da Ponte*, now merged with the *Pensão Príncipe* (☎053/39 11 21; ③) and with nice, old rooms; *Residencial Belo Horizonte* (☎053/39 12 60; ③); the clean and amiable *Pensão Flor de Moçambique* (☎053/39 11 19; ③); *Pensão São Miquel* (☎053/39 13 60; ③), and – with the best views – *Pensão Adelaide* (☎053/39 11 88; ③).

Restaurants at most of the pensions are usually good, with portions healthy enough to satisfy the most jaded hiker. Slightly pricier, but with an entertaining patron and an outdoor patio, is *Casa Santa Comba*, at the bottom end of town, just off the main street on the right as you enter Gerês.

Camping is greatly recommended. The site at Vidoeiro (☎053/39 11 83; April–Oct), well-maintained by the park authority, is just on the edge of town, set alongside a gushing river, with terraced areas for tents and good facilities. Open campfires are permitted here and most evening life takes place around them. There's a second site, *Ponte de Saltos* (☎053/39 13 79; July–Sept) at Vilar da Veiga, 3km south of Caldas, by the water's edge; the *Residencial Manuel da Castro Pires* (☎053/39 11 39; ③), also here, has double rooms available as well as bungalows sleeping four which cost 10,000$00 a night.

West : to Campo do Gerês and around the mountain

This is an exhausting and long day's hike (10–12hr; or camp overnight) but a good one, taking you along the Roman road that began at Braga and stretched ultimately to Rome and Byzantium. The route also runs alongside the **Vilarinho das Furnas** reservoir, with obvious swimming potential. In the height of summer you can see the submerged village of Vilarinho das Furnas itself – turn right after crossing the dam. From there you could reach the Louriça summit (5hr; see p.289) by following the path above the cemetery along the brook and heading for the TV masts.

Setting out from Gerês, follow the road north towards Portela do Homem. You'll have to keep on the road for a while, despite apparent shortcuts, past the defunct campsite at Albergaria and beyond, veering left, by which time the signs are for Campo do Gerês and the reservoir. There is a road off to the reservoir, but the main road heads southwest – first along gladed paths and then suddenly into the open, following stretches of the old Roman road. Fires here have seared the foliage and given the granite crags an almost apocalyptic grandeur. Staying with the road (past an old stone building housing a weaving project run by the park), you veer left into **CAMPO DO GERÊS** (to which there are also six daily buses from Braga).

Here, the friendly *Residencial Stop* (☎053/35 12 91; ②) attracts a young and active crowd, as do the *Cerdeira* **campsite** (☎053/35 10 15; open all year) and the *Vilarinho das Furnas* **youth hostel** (☎053/35 13 39), the latter so-called because, until 1972, it provided accommodation for those who built the dam – hence its bungalows, swimming pool, tennis court and disco. Through any of these establishments you can contact *Equi Campo*, which offers local **horse-trekking** trips.

Soon after Campo do Gerês you come to the crucifix of São João do Campo. Turn off the road here, to the left, on to a dirt track. This will take you around the southern tip of the mountain and, apart from the occasional obsessive car driver, you'll be pretty much alone – eerily so at times, amid the Neolithic boulders. Follow the sign to **Calcedónia**, a Celtic and Roman *citânia* with an impressive cave. This stretch can be hard going in the midday heat, as there is no shelter, so save it for the late afternoon. At the end of the circuit, the way back to Gerês is signposted (right at the first junction, then right again at the water fountain).

The Miradouro, Caniçada reservoir, Rio Caldo and São Bento da Porta Aberta

An hour's walk to the southeast of Caldas do Gerês, the **Miradouro do Gerês** is *the* destination for Portuguese weekend picnickers. And small wonder, with its site overlooking the vast reservoir of Caniçada and a good part of the Gerês range. The only catch, if you're intent on following suit, is the extent of local enthusiasm. This is not a road to walk unless you're immune to inhalation of exhaust fumes and dust; it's better to hitch up and then start hiking. The quickest approach to the Miradouro road is to follow the road behind the service station at Gerês, where it becomes an uphill path. The most obvious, and probably the most attractive, route to follow beyond the Miradouro is **to Ermida** (see below). Just before arriving here, there's a sign pointing you to the *Cascata do Arado*, left off the main track; follow this and a brief walk leads to the magnificent **Arado waterfalls**, with its refreshing pools for swimming.

The best base for the **Caniçada reservoir** is the village of **RIO CALDO**, on its west bank and just 8km south of Caldas do Gerês. Here a number of local houses have been converted for holiday rental and if you turn up and ask around, it may be possible to find space at one. The English-owned *Casa Rio Caldo* (☎053/39 15 98), for instance, may have room. If not, there's a **campsite** at Rio Caldo (☎053/39 12 71; open all year), and numerous **watersports** available locally at the reservoir, with possibilities for both windsurfing and waterskiing; swimming is fine, too.

Beyond Rio Caldo, in the Covide direction, **SÃO BENTO DA PORTA ABERTA** is a small village, high above the reservoir, commanding superb views. Its austere sanctuary is a favourite spot with pilgrims, who gather here at the beginning of July and again a month later; regular buses run out from Braga during this period. The former monastery is now the *Estalgem de São Bento da Porta Aberta* (☎053/39 11 06; ⑤), still a little severe inside, but a winner if you like a fine, well-framed view on awakening; there's a good restaurant, too. An alternative, overlooking the reservoir from the east and considerably more expensive, is the *Pousada de São Bento* (☎053/64 71 90; ⑦), an old timber-beamed hunting lodge. Otherwise, there are cheaper rooms at both the nearby *Casa da Cruz de Real* at Cerderinhas (☎053/64 74 52; ④) and, better, at the *Albergaria do Mosteira* (☎053/64 77 77; ④) on the main road (N103) to Braga. Alongside here you can eat well at the *Restaurante Flórida* for around 1500$00, including local wine.

Ermida and east to Cabril

ERMIDA, despite its proximity to Gerês (90min on foot) and the Miradouro (30min), has an air of seclusion about it. If you're looking for a quiet base, this could be a good choice: there's the *Casa do Criado* (☎053/39 13 90; ②), a scattering of available *dormidas*, an orchard to camp in and a couple of cafés, but it is still very much a farming community.

Continuing **east from Ermida**, along a blackberry-lined lane above the reservoir, you'll pass a small group of waterfalls and cross a distinctly unsafe-looking bridge before coming to **FAFIÃO,** a tiny farming hamlet. Past here the countryside becomes more fertile, terraced with vines and maize, the road winding down to another hamlet, **PINCÃES**, and through it (turn right at the end of the houses) to the slightly larger village of Cabril.

A lovely, isolated place, sat on the Rio Cabril and surrounded on all sides by mountains, **CABRIL** flaunts odd attempts at modernity (100m of tarmac), though its centre is still sauntered through by oxen, goats and flocks of sheep. Parts of the locality have been submerged because of dam construction further up the valley. Consequently, the old bridge is half under water and makes for great swimming, through the bridge arch. There's a **campsite** here, *Outeiro Alto* (☎053/65 98 60; open all year), 1km out on the Pincães road, which is fine provided it's not too busy – there are only two toilets. You can get a good **meal** at the *Restaurante Ponte Novo*, by the bridge, which serves a warming meat stew; the *Café 1 de Maio*, further up the road, also serves food but usually needs advance warning.

On to Montalegre and the Trás-os-Montes: Paradela and Venda Nova

From Cabril, if you're hiking or driving, you could go on to Paradela, Outeiro, Paredes do Rio, Covelães and Pitões das Júnias, the latter with a decaying monastery nearby. There's a *pensão* at Paradela, another at Paredes do Rio and one at Pitões, any of which would make an ideal base for a leisurely exploration of this little-known corner of the Minho.

In particular, the signposted path from Cabril to **PARADELA** – around 23km – is stunningly dramatic, winding along the river valley through the handsome villages of Sirvozelo, Lapela and Xertola. At Paradela, a particularly attractive mountain village whose cobbled streets are lined with vines, you're rewarded by

THE TRILHO DO LONGO CURSO

A long-distance footpath – the **Trilho do Longo Curso** – is planned to run from one side of the Peneda-Gerês park to the other. At present only a couple of sections have been completed (from Cabril to Gerês and from Lamas de Mouro to Castro Laboreiro), but maps in the park already show the final route, which starts in Tourém on the Portuguese-Spanish border, runs down through the Gerês section and then back up through Peneda, ending in Castro Laboreiro. This takes into account most of the main areas of interest in the park and has been designed so that there is always somewhere to stay or camp at the end of a reasonable day's walk. However, if you are looking for the shortest way from A to B, the *trilho* is not your best bet. It often goes out of its way to take in interesting diversions and to avoid following busy roads. Several sections are also very steep and quite hard going.

At the beginning of each section is a large map, showing the route; at every junction along the path, a yellow arrow points the way. On longer stretches, an acorn logo on rocks and trees keeps you on the right track. All the paths the *trilho* follows are old routes, used by generations of villagers; indeed, the *trilho* is particularly good as it passes through villages and hamlets, where it guides you along age-old cobbled paths overhung with trellises and vines.

fine views over the dam and mountains. The *Pensão Pousadinha* (③) is a cosy, friendly place; the *Restaurante Sol Rio*, on the Montalegre road, rather grumpier though boasting marvellous views.

Alternatively, from Cabril or Paradela you can move on to **Montalegre**, via another vast reservoir. Montalegre itself (see p.305) provides a suitably remote and dramatic link with the Trás-os-Montes region, and can be reached by bus from Caldas do Gerês (or from Braga). The appeal lies as much in the road there as in the place itself. Bumpy, narrow, and at all points incomplete, it's one of those journeys that seem to trigger madness in bus drivers, simultaneously delighting and terrifying unaccustomed passengers.

This route takes you through **VENDA NOVA**, a tiny group of houses, with a friendly **pension** (not always open), a rather rundown motel, and a good-value luxury establishment on the shore of the reservoir. There are some lovely walks in the vicinity and exceptionally bracing swimming. Buses from Venda Nova continue regularly to Montalegre, passing the hydroelectric plant of **Pisões** – the largest dam in the country, and an unexpectedly modern development in this otherwise very remote region.

Soajo and Lindoso

The neighbouring villages of **Soajo** and **Lindoso**, midway between the Peneda and the Gerês sections of the park, are reached most easily from (respectively) Arcos de Valdevez and Ponte da Barca. There are buses from both towns (weekdays only from Arcos de Valdevez to Soajo). Approaching from the River Minho, to the north, you can reach Arcos de Valdevez and Ponte da Barca by travelling due south from Monção for 40km down the N101.

Both Soajo and Lindoso are fine centres for hiking, and the walk between the two is enjoyable, too, crossing the dam of the Lindoso reservoir – a route not yet officially open to traffic.

Soajo

SOAJO is a small village tucked into the folds of a hilly landscape. Its highlight is a collection of eighteenth- and nineteenth-century **espigueiros** (grain houses), over twenty of which are clumped together on a stony platform, their roof-crosses (intended to bless the annual crop) giving them the look of a graveyard. In addition to providing a ready-made, breezy threshing ground, the *espigueiros* site offers a degree of protection from rats, though the tall stone mushrooms that raise the houses from the ground do not appear to keep vermin entirely at bay. Their grouping together is a vestige of the days when the isolated village depended heavily on communal effort for its survival. Even now there are several flocks of sheep and goats that belong to the whole community and are tended by the village shepherds. If you set off on a hike at the crack of dawn you will walk up into the hills to the sound of small brass bells.

Changes are not accepted easily and the village takes its traditions very seriously. Folkloric groups are maintained by those who stay behind, while the emigrants all try to inculcate a sense of *minha terra* (my homeland) into their modern-minded (and in many cases American) offspring. The local **festival** (Aug 13–15) has a special feel, with the fun and games spontaneous. Owing to a lack of horses, the *corrida* is a race on foot – balancing blue plastic urns full of water on their heads, the contestants compete for the honour of being ceremoniously drenched by all the others. Large, homemade fireworks are set off all over the place without warning.

Staying in Soajo is simple as long as there aren't many others in town. The only café-restaurant, the *Videira*, at the crossroads next to the bus stop, can direct you to the *Casa do Adro* (☎058/64 73 27; ④), a beautiful eighteenth-century house with nice rooms upstairs. You'll need to book well in advance at festival time.

Lindoso

Set high above the Rio Lima, **LINDOSO** is one of the most attractive villages in Peneda-Gerês. It is easiest reached from Ponte da Barca, though buses also run directly from Braga. Like Soajo, Lindoso is dominated by a cluster of *espigueiros*, and its life is again very traditional. The rearing of **livestock** is central. Every morning starts with the lowing of cows or the clattering of the communally herded sheep and goats, and the smell of animals lies thick in the air. The traditional method of baking bread in these parts involved removing the hot coals and sealing the oven door with an ash and dung mixture, and it's a technique still in use in the old part of the village. If you're at all interested, there's one of these ovens still in place in the heavily restored **Castelo** (daily except Mon 9.30am–noon & 1.30–6pm), whose museum details the results of local excavations.

The former *Pensão Castelo* is currently being converted into a modern *residencial*: when it re-opens it should also have stone cottages for rent. In the meantime, the *Alto Lindoso*, just outside the village on the road to the Spanish border, does reasonable food and can arrange **accommodation** in private houses; or ask around for the local priest, who also rents out rooms. But far and away the best **lodging** prospect in the vicinity is the *Tres Cabanas* (☎058/672 18; ②), 3km out of Lindoso on the Soajo road, across the dam. Run by a charming couple who speak some English, the en-suite rooms are pleasant, if slightly run-down, there are fine views over the valley and River Lima, and breakfast is included. Other meals here are good value, too, with dishes including – strangely – pizzas.

To the east of Lindoso, the **border post with Spain** is open all year round, although it currently closes from midnight to 7am.

A hike across the Serra Amarela

Lindoso is the starting-point for a two-day **walk across the Serra Amarela** via Portela do Homem or Vilarinho das Furnas to Gerês, an adventure for which you should take provisions for three days, in case of fog. The journey is in two stages: a dirt track (13km) from the former youth hostel about 5km above Lindoso town, to the bottom of the **Louriça summit** (1361m), and two less obvious routes across the hills to Portela do Homem (14km) or Gerês (15km). You'll need stout walking boots, a water bottle (last water for the second day is below the road up to Louriça, or up at the top for those going on to Vilarinho das Furnas), a stick (to drive off cattle or wild horses) and something warm (for the night cold).

Setting out from from Lindoso, put your trust in the road and follow its winding course all the way to the deserted cottage below the summit. This is where the two routes split. If you're going on **to Vilarinho**, the forest guard and his family, who live on top of the hill, will point out the reservoir from the plateau in front of the station, and advise you on the best route down. Ignoring their suggestions could get you stuck behind the sheer cliff faces above the deserted, half-sunken village of Vilarinho. Once at the reservoir, you can cross the dam and join the route detailed in the Gerês section to Campo de Gerês.

The alternative route **to Portela do Homem** follows the road (so overgrown as to be barely distinguishable) that lies below the more obvious track from the cottage to the old lookout post. After a large zigzag down into the valley, a wooded patch, and a long stretch pushing through chest-high tree heather along the other side, you break out into a rocky landscape. From here, follow the dry stone wall a short way (700m), turn left (north) along the ridge or just behind it, and walk down into the first valley. Before descending, you'll catch sight of the glacial rounded valley of the Rio Homem (up to Minas dos Carris); a useful landmark away in the distance, Portela do Homem is tucked into a fold of land at its foot.

Cutting across country, you should hit the old road (you can see part of this from back up on the ridge), which ends at the border post. If you're having problems finding your way, use the Spanish border, a stone wall with marker posts (E and P) as a guideline, but cut down to the road as soon as you see it. A couple of hours later you should come upon the border café. At **PORTELA DO HOMEM** there is a collection of Roman milestones. Gerês is 13km further, but you can hitch; don't miss the **river pool** nearby at the bottom of the Minas dos Carris valley.

The northern section: Peneda

Peneda, the northern section of the Parque Nacional da Peneda-Gerês, sees far fewer tourists than Gerês to the south, partly because of the difficulty of access. Without your own transport, you have to rely on the infrequent buses which seem to take a perverse delight in seeing how early they can leave the Minho river town of Melgaço (see p.275). However, the route from here is one of the best approaches to this area of staggering scenery and awesome rock formations.

Weekday **buses** leave Melgaço for Lamas de Mouro and Castro Laboreiro between 5am and 7am (with an additional midday service on Fridays) and return at around 6.45pm – check times with the parcel depot in Melgaço, just around the corner from the *Pensão Pemba*. If you're **driving**, you will find that the route south of Lamas de Mouro into the park, along the valley of the Peneda, has been much improved – you can drive all the way to Soajo with no difficulty.

Lamas de Mouro, Peneda and walks south

LAMAS DE MOURO, 19km southeast of Melgaço, has a beautifully situated **campsite** (☎051/424 40; June–Sept), one of three owned by the national park; it's got hot showers, a bar, and access to the river for swimming. A restaurant at the site is planned, and there's also a *churrasqueiria*, 1km up the road from the campsite – slightly expensive but with generous portions. There is also limited accommodation available at the *Estalagem do Paysan* (☎051/452 23; ②) at the road junction just north of the campsite, where the N202 forks off to Casto Laboreiro.

Nine kilometres beyond the campsite, you reach the sanctuary of **Nossa Senhora da Peneda**, full of devotees at the beginning of September (especially on the 7 and 8), but pretty much deserted the rest of the year, though there are a couple of cafés where you can get a welcome drink. You can take a fairly easy two-hour return walk from the southeast corner of the sanctuary up to the peak of **Penameda** (1258m), where there are freshwater lagoons and extraordinary views across the whole of the Parque Nacional.

PENEDA village itself has cafés and religious artefact shops clustererd around the main square. The *Hotel de Peneda* has rooms available (①), and a decent restaurant. There are slightly pricier rooms at the *Café Star*, while if you don't mind roughing it, you'll probably be allowed to stay in one of the many basic local rooms built for pilgrims who flood the village for the festival in September.

Alternatively, you might consider setting out on the first stage of a two-day hike (approximately 25km, allow an extra day in case of fog) to either **Soajo** or **Lindoso** (both covered earlier), from either of which you can cross the Serra Amarela to Gerês. The Soajo route, which is marginally the easier, follows the Rio Peneda until it meets the Rio Veiga (7km), crosses over to the tiny village of **TIBO**, and takes the road to Soajo (18km). The second trek (for which you'll definitely need a survey map) continues down the Rio Peneda to *Mistura das Águas* (Mixing of the Waters, 11km); from there use the Rio Laboreiro as a guideline down to the Rio Lima (15km), where you can cross over the dam to Lindoso. Alternatively, you can follow the well sign-posted and not too busy lane from Peneda, which joins the Soajo–Lindoso road by the Tres Cabanas.

Castro Laboreiro

The left-hand fork at Lamas takes you up to the ancient village of **CASTRO LABOREIRO** (9km further), a place that's best known for the breed of mountain dog to which it gives its name. The village is practically deserted in summer, being made up of *inverneiras* (winter houses), the pastoral community having gone off to find greener fields and build *brandas* ("soft" houses) for the warmer months. If you can speak Portuguese and want to learn more about the area, contact the village priest, who knows everything. You can eat at the *Estalagem de Laboreiro* (☎051/451 26): this currently doesn't have rooms available, though it's worth a call to check.

To reach the ruins of the town's **castle**, you have a steep twenty-minute walk: left at the roundabout on the other side of the village, then left up a path where the road drops to the right, past a large rock known as the *Tartaruga* (Tortoise), and through heather and between boulders, with sheer drops to each side and steps hacked out of the rock face.

travel details

Trains

Barcelos to Porto (12–14 daily; 1hr 10min–2hr 20min), Valença do Minho (3–4 daily; 1hr); Viana do Castelo (4–6 daily; 20min).

Braga to Lisbon (3 daily; 5hr); Porto (13–16 daily; 1hr–1hr 45min).

Caminha to Porto (5–7 daily; 2hr–3hr 10min); Valença do Minho (6–7 daily; 20–45min); Viana do Castelo (7–9 daily; 20–40min).

Guimarães to Porto (11–15 daily; 1hr 45min); Santo Tirso (11–15 daily; 45min).

Porto to Barcelos (12–14 daily; 1hr 10min–2hr 20min); Caminha (5–7 daily; 2hr–3hr 10min); Guimarães (11–15 daily; 1hr 45min); Nine (12 daily; 1hr; change for Braga); Santo Tirso (hourly; 1hr); Valença do Minho (6–8 daily; 2hr 15min–5hr 30min); Viana do Castelo (12–16 daily; 1hr 30min–2hr 15min).

Valença do Minho to Afife (3–4 daily; 1hr 30min); Barcelos (5–6 daily; 1hr 10min–2hr 20min); Caminha (6–7 daily; 20–45min); Porto (6–8 daily; 2hr 15min–5hr 30min); Vigo, Spain (3 daily; 1hr 10min; connections to Santiago de Compostela and La Coruña); Vila Nova de Cerveira (5–7 daily; 15min); Vila Praia de Âncora (6–7 daily; 30min–1hr).

Viana do Castelo to Afife (4–6 daily; 20min); Barcelos (13–15 daily; 25–45min); Caminha (7–9 daily; 20–40min); Porto (12–16 daily; 1hr 30min–2hr 15min); Vila Nova de Cerveira (6–8 daily; 30min–1hr); Vila Praia de Âncora (5–7 daily; 15–25min).

Vila Nova de Cerveira to Porto (6–8 daily; 2hr–3hr 10min); Valença do Minho (5–7 daily; 15min); Viana do Castelo (6–8 daily; 30min–1hr).

Buses

Arcos de Valdevez to Braga (2–4 daily; 1hr 15min); Ponte de Lima (6–8 daily; 1hr); Soajo (Mon–Fri hourly; fewer at weekends; 30min); Porto (2–4 daily; 2hr); Viana do Castelo (6–8 daily; 1hr 45min).

Braga to Arcos de Valdevez (2–4 daily; 1hr 15min); Barcelos (7 daily; 30–40min); Cabaceiras de Basto (4–5 daily; 1hr 45min); Caldas do Gerês (10 daily; 1hr 30min); Campo do Gerês (6–8 daily; 1hr 20min); Cerdeirinhas (5–9 daily; 45min); Chaves (4 daily; 4hr); Coimbra (4 daily; 3hr); Covide (6–8 daily; 1hr 15min); Guimarães (11 daily; 1hr); Lisbon (4 daily; 8hr); Monção (4 daily; 2hr 30min); Montalegre (4 daily; 2hr 40min); Pisões (5–6 daily; 2hr 15min); Ponte da Barca (14 daily; 1hr); Ponte de Lima (12–16 daily; 1hr); Porto (10–14 daily; 1hr 30min); Póvoa do Lanhoso (5–6 daily; 35min); Terras do Bouro (7–9 daily; 55min); Venda Nova (5–9 daily; 1hr 50min); Viana do Castelo (8 daily; 1hr 30min).

Caldas do Gerês to Braga (10 daily; 1hr 30min).

Campo do Gerês to Braga (6–8 daily; 1hr 20min).

Guimarães to Braga (11 daily; 1hr), Lisbon (1 daily; 5hr 30min); Porto (6 daily; 1hr).

Melgaço to Castro Laboreiro (1–2 daily; 1hr); Lamas de Mouro (1–2 daily; 40min); Monção (3–5 daily; 1hr); São Gregório (4 daily; 30min).

Monção to Braga (4 daily; 2hr 30min); Melgaço (3–5 daily; 1hr) .

Ponte de Barca to Braga (14 daily; 1hr); Lindoso (3–4 daily; 45min); Ponte de Lima (12–16 daily; 20–30min).

Ponte de Lima to Braga (12–16 daily; 1hr); Ponte de Barca (12–16 daily; 20–30min); Viana do Castelo (every 30min; 1hr 20min).

Valença do Minho to Vila Nova de Cerveira (6 daily; 15min); to Spain: Sat to Vigo/Santiago (2hr/4hr 15min); Tues, Thurs, and Fri via Monção and Melgaço for Ponte Barjxas.

Viana do Castelo to Arcos de Valdevez (6–8 daily; 1hr 45min); Braga (8 daily; 1hr 30min); Lisbon (2 daily; 6hr); Ponte de Lima (every 30min; 1hr 20min); Ponte da Barca (6–8 daily; 1hr 30min); Porto (8 daily; 1hr 40min).

CHAPTER SEVEN

TRÁS-OS-MONTES

Trás-os-Montes – literally "Beyond the Mountains" – is Portugal's Lost Domain. For centuries this remote, rural province has been a place to hide and practise one's beliefs in peace: its peculiar traditions and dialects have been formed by a diversity of populations, from the prehistoric tribes who carved the *porcas* (stone pigs) to Jews who sought refuge here from the Inquisition. The extremity of the climate – "Nine months of winter and three months of hell", as the local proverb puts it – and the aridity of much of its land have kept Trás-os-Montes well apart from the mainstream. Even today, with new highways being built and some industry coming to the major towns, the province has a population half the size of that of the Minho in almost twice the area.

A sharp natural divide cuts across the province. In the south is the fertile territory officially entitled the Upper Douro, but known unofficially as the **Terra Quente** (Hot Land). Encompassing the terraced stretches of the rivers Douro, Corgo and Tua, this area produces peaches, oranges, melons and wine. By contrast, the bitter winters of the north have earned it the name of **Terra Fria** (Cold Land). Out beyond Mogadouro, the most visible features of this wild and rugged terrain are the countless pony carts and pigeon houses (*pombais*), while the ubiquitous almond trees, whose fleeting blossom time is in late-February and early March, draws weekenders to the border town of Miranda do Douro.

Travelling into and around the province can be a slow business, with few remaining train services and buses that usually make only short local trips. However, almost any route in Trás-os-Montes has its rewards, and the fortified frontier towns of **Chaves** and **Bragança** should feature on any northern Portuguese itineraries. These two towns aside, Trás-os-Montes' sights are defiantly rural: a succession of hardworking mountain or valley villages, and small, fortified settlements – **Mirando do Douro**, **Mogadouro**, **Freixo de Espada à Cinto** – guarding the border with Spain, whose appeal lies above all in their isolation. The only town of any real size in the entire region is **Vila Real** – a good starting point for a tour of the province, especially for hikers, with its access to the dramatic granite scenery of the **Parque Natural de Alvão**. A second natural park has been designated in the far north of the province, beyond Bragança, in the **Serra de Montesinho**, where walkers can experience Trás-os-Montes at its most rural and remote.

ACCOMMODATION PRICE CODES

All the accommodation prices in this book have been coded using the symbols below. The symbols represent the prices for the cheapest available double room in high season; for a full explanation, see p.23.

① Under 3000$00 ② 3000$00–4000$00 ③ 4000$00–5500$00
④ 5500$00–8500$00 ⑤ 8500$00–12,500$00 ⑥ 12,500$00–20,000$00
⑦ Over 20,000$00

Chaves can be reached, a little tortuously, from the Peneda-Gerês park (see p.281), but the most obvious approach to the region is **from the Douro**, whose eastern reaches (covered in Chapter 5) are technically a part of the province. From the main Douro train line, the **Corgo line** runs through a spectacular winding gorge from Peso da Régua to Vila Real, where you can catch buses north to Chaves; while the **Tua line** runs from Tua to **Mirandela**, from where buses run on to Bragança.

Vila Real and around

VILA REAL is the one break from the pastoralism of the beautiful Rio Corgo, a tributary of the Douro which provides the first link from that region to Trás-os-Montes. The largest industrial town in the northeast, it is bordered on three sides by sprawling suburbs. The broader setting, however, is magnificent, with the twin mountain ranges of **Marão** and **Alvão** (the so-called "Gateway to Trás-os-Montes") forming a natural amphitheatre behind the town. Walkers may well want to make the town a base for a couple of days' exploration of these ranges, while, for more casual exploration, the town gives easy access to a Roman site at **Panóias** and to the **Solar de Mateus** – the country house featured on the *Mateus Rosé* wine label. Compared to the somnolent villages further north and east, Vila Real is actually quite a lively place – especially during the major **festivals** of Santo António (June 13) and São Pedro (June 29), at which time you should book your accommodation well in advance.

The town and its surroundings

The old quarter of Vila Real is attractive enough, built on a promontory above the junction of the Corgo and Cabril rivers, with the main avenue running down the spine of the promontory. The view from the little park at the end, past the fourteenth-century **Capela de São Brás**, is not for vertigo sufferers. There's little else to see in town, save for the **Turismo** building – formerly the palace of the Marquês of Vila Real, and fronted by four Manueline windows – and the **Sé**, over the way, which has modern stained glass windows and a simple, fifteenth-century interior. Back at the bottom of town, by the **Câmara Municipal**, a plaque on the café opposite recalls the birthplace of Diogo Cão, who discovered the mouth of the Congo River in 1482.

Given the paucity of things to do in Vila Real itself, half-day **trips** out to the Solar de Mateus and the Roman remains at Panóias make good use of a night's stopover. Both are easily visited by car, while it's quite feasible to see Mateus by public transport, with regular *Cabanelas* bus services along the Sabrosa road. For Panóias, *Cabanelas* runs a weekday bus at 3pm, though to return you need to walk back down to the stop on the main road.

The Solar de Mateus

The **Solar de Mateus** (signposted "Palácio de Mateus") is just 4km east of Vila Real, along the road to Sabrosa. Described by Sacheverell Sitwell as "the most typical and the most fantastic country house in Portugal", it's certainly the most familiar, being reproduced on each bottle of *Mateus Rosé*, one of Portugal's major wine exports. The facade fits in well enough with the wine's soft-focus image, its

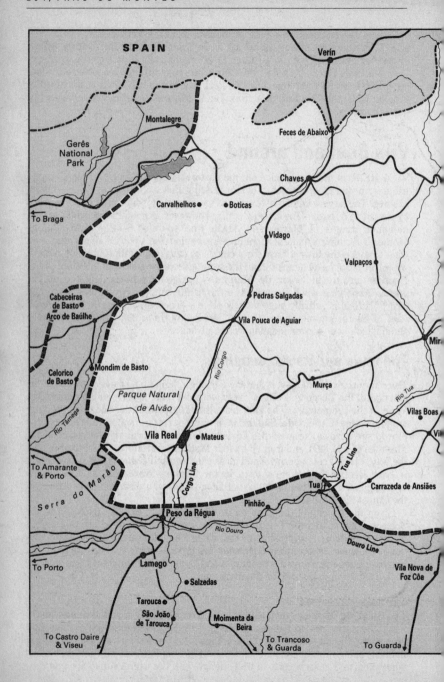

SPAIN

Verín

Montalegre

Feces de Abaixo

Gerês
National
Park

Chaves

Carvalhelhos ● ● Boticas

To Braga

Vidago

Valpaços ●

Pedras Salgadas ●

Cabeceiras
de Basto ●
Arco de Baúlhe

Vila Pouca de Aguiar ●

Mir

Rio Corgo

Celorico
de Basto ● ● Mondim de Basto

Parque Natural
de Alvão

Murça ●

Rio Tua

Vilas Boas ●

Rio Tâmega

Vila Real ● Mateus

Vil

To Amarante
& Porto

Tua Line

Corgo Line

S e r r a   d o   M a r ã o

Tua ●

Carrazeda de Ansiães ●

Pinhão ●

Peso da Régua ●

Rio Douro

Douro Line

To Porto

Lamego ●

Vila Nova de
Foz Côa

● Salzedas

Tarouca ●
São João
de Tarouca ●

Moimenta da
Beira ●

To Castro Daire
& Viseu

To Trancoso
& Guarda

To Guarda

twin wings "advancing lobster-like", as Sitwell put it, across a formal lake. The architect is unknown, though most authorities attribute it to the Italian, Nicolau Nasoni, who built the landmark Clérigos church in Porto; the palace is dated around 1740, the heyday of Portuguese Baroque.

There's a handsome admission fee charged for a somewhat limited tour of the **interior** (summer daily 9am–1pm & 2–7pm; winter daily 9.30am–12.30pm & 2–6pm; house and gardens 750$00, gardens only 550$00). Although there are no special treasures, the building is an enjoyable evocation of its period, full of draperies, aristocratic portraits and rural scenes. The **gardens**, too, are a delight, the spectacular box avenue forming an impressive tunnel about 300m long.

Panóias and Sabrosa

You might combine a visit to Mateus with one to the Roman site of **PANÓIAS**, 5km further along the N322 Sabrosa road. The sole remnant of the once powerful settlement of *Terras de Panóias*, ancient forerunner of Vila Real, it doesn't at first appear much of a site – a few slabs of rock with odd-shaped cavities that are often full of water and rubbish. However, if you know a little French or Portuguese, the tour offered by the old man in the nearby house is worth accepting (tips gratefully received). He brings the three **sacrificial slabs** to life with gory descriptions of the filter systems for the blood and viscera created by the offerings to Serapis, a pre-Roman deity.

As a digression, your guide may elaborate on the harsh times under Salazar, when he was brought up in extreme poverty and lived off potatoes and grass soup. The region, in fact, happens to be where the first potatoes from South America were introduced, and appropriately enough, **Magellan's birthplace** is at nearby **SABROSA**, a village better known nowadays for its wine.

Practicalities

Vila Real is the hub of Trás-os-Montes' regional transport, and home base of the province's major bus company, *Cabanelas*. This operates from the **bus station** behind the *Hotel Cabanelas* on Rua Pedro Castro, just north of the centre; it's worth picking up a timetable here for onward travel. The **train station** (for the Corgo branch line service from Peso da Régua on the Douro line – see p.232) is 500m east of the centre, on the opposite bank of the river; follow the road into town, over the bridge, and turn left for the centre.

The **Turismo** (June–Sept daily 9.30am–7pm; Oct–March Mon–Sat 9.30am–12.30pm & 2–5pm; April & May Mon–Sat 9.30am–12.30pm & 2–7pm; ☎059/32 28 19) is on the central avenue, Avenida Carvalho Araújo, at no. 94. Helpful as ever, it can provide transport and accommodation details, including advice on the various *Turihab* properties in the area. The avenue is the town's main focus, also fronted by the cathedral, main post office and town hall – from outside which most local buses leave (from no. 26).

Accommodation

The pick of the town's **pensions and hotels** is reviewed below. However, the cheapest accommodation is at the **youth hostel**, part of a youth complex on Avenida Dr. Carmona (☎059/32 35 51). There is also a pleasant **campsite**, with a swimming pool, down by the river (☎059/32 47 24; closed Jan). From the centre, follow Avenida 1º de Maio; if you're coming from the train station, take a right

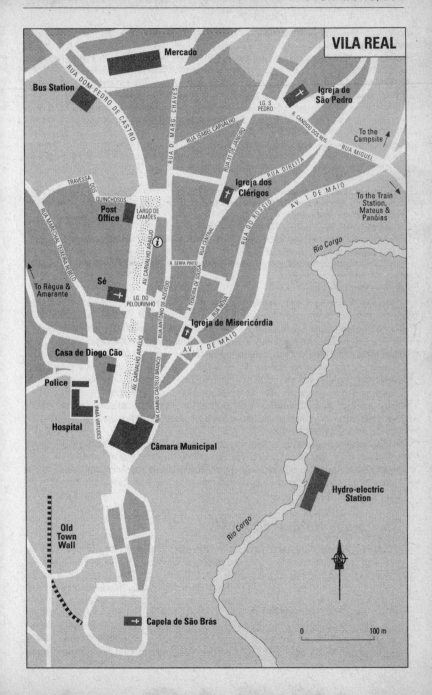

VILA REAL

Mercado

Bus Station

RUA DOM PEDRO DE CASTRO

RUA D MARG CHAVES

Igreja de
São Pedro

LG. S
PEDRO

R. CANDIDO DOS REIS

RUA ISABEL CARVALHO

RUA 31 DE JANEIRO

To the
Campsite

RUA MIGUEL

RUA DIREITA

Igreja dos
Clérigos

AV. 1 DE MAIO

To the Train
Station,
Mateus &
Panóias

TRAVESSA DOS
QUINCHOSOS

Post
Office

LARGO DE
CAMÕES

RUA MARECHAL TEIXEIRA REBELO

AV. CARVALHO ARAUJO

RUA DO ROSSIO

Rio Corgo

R. SERPA PINTO

RUA CENTRAL

To Régua &
Amarante

Sé

LG. DO
PELOURINHO

R. TEIXEIRA DE SOUSA

RUA NOVA

Igreja de Misericórdia

RUA ANTÓNIO DE AZEVEDO

Casa de Diogo Cão

AV. 1 DE MAIO

Police

AV. CARVALHO ARAUJO

RUA CAMILO CASTELO BRANCO

Hospital

R. IRMÃ VIRTUDES

Câmara Municipal

Hydro-electric
Station

Old
Town
Wall

Rio Corgo

N

Capela de São Brás

0   100 m

after crossing the bridge. There's adequate shade here, but arrive early if you want a riverside site.

Residencial Encontro, Avda. Carvalho Araújo 76–78 (☎059/32 25 32). Family-run place with pleasant, apartment-like rooms above a restaurant. It's near the Turismo, and can be a bit noisy at night. ②.

Residencial Excelsior, Rua Teixeira da Sousa (☎059/32 24 22). Clean and good value. ①.

Hotel Mira Corgo, Avda. 1º de Maio 76 (☎059/32 50 01). Vila Real's swankiest hotel is an ugly modern block but its rooms overlook the stepped terraces of the Corgo, far below, and there's an indoor swimming pool. ⑥.

Casa de Hóspedes Mondego, Trav. de São Domingos 11 (☎059/32 30 97). Off Avda. Carvalho Araújo and near the Sé, this has some of the cheapest rooms in town, but it's not for light sleepers – the clock chimes every 15 minutes throughout the night. Largish rooms with strange decor. ②.

Residencial São Domingos, Trav. de São Domingos 33 (☎059/32 20 39). A nice, old-fashioned and friendly pension, that looks as though it's due shortly to collapse – though it's been like this for years. ②–③.

Residencial da Sé, Trav. de São Domingos 19–23 (☎059/32 45 75). Next to the *Mondego*, this new place has a bath in most of the rooms, as well as a restaurant. ③.

Hotel Tocaio, Avda. Carvalho Araújo 45 (☎059/32 31 06). Respectable if a bit gloomy. All rooms come with private bathroom, and the reception area comes with a stuffed wild pig. ④.

Eating and drinking

Good bets for inexpensive **meals** are the cafés in the streets behind the Turismo; particularly recommended here is the *Churraseo*, at Rua António de Azuedo 24, which does wonderful grills and spit-roast chicken (closed Sun). For something a bit fancier, try the *Restaurante O Aldeão*, at Rua Dom Pedro de Castro 70, just down from the bus station. This is popular and very reasonably priced, with a changing daily menu of standards, including a *bife* dish served with absolutely everything: meals cost upwards of 1500$00. The family-run *Bem Star*, in Avenida Carvalho Araújo, opposite the Turismo, is also recommended, while top-of-the-range in town is *Restaurante O Espadeiro*, on Avenida Almeida Lucena, where regional dishes – including stuffed trout and roast kid – are cooked before you; meals here cost 2500$00 upwards.

The liveliest **nightspot** is the unnamed bar at Largo do Pelourinho 11 (open until 1am; Fri & Sat 2am), which, for this part of the country at least, is distinctly *avant garde*. Another good bar, open until midnight, is the *Excelsior* at Rua Serpa Pinto 30–36, a huge, elaborate pool hall featuring the strangest timing meters for your game you'll ever see.

The Parque Natural de Alvão

Portugal's smallest natural park, the **Parque Natural de Alvão**, can be glimpsed if you are travelling by road between Vila Real and Amarante, since the minor N313 and N304 describe a circle through the park, emerging back onto the N15 highway just to the west of Vila Real. Basically a schist basin formed around the **Rio Olo** – a tributary of the Tâmega – the park has some spectacular waterfalls at **FISGAS DE ERMELO**, and a handful of quiet, rural hamlets, whose houses are constructed from the layered rock of the hillsides. The whole district has dramatic, boulder-strewn scenery reminiscent of a Western movie. Good targets would be **LAMAS DE OLO**, on the N313, with its mill and primitive aqueduct; the waterfall (and another mill) at **GALEGOS DA SERRA**; and the dammed lakes of Alvão itself.

Without a car, you're dependent on very sketchy **bus** services to explore the park: *Tâmegatur* goes only as far as Lordelo, and *Rodonorte* to nearby Borbela, from where you're still a fair hike from Lamas de Olo. Serious walkers intending to cross the whole reserve should obtain maps in advance from Porto or Lisbon and consult the **park headquarters** in Vila Real (Rua Alves Torgo 22–3º; ☎059/ 241 38), which can provide information about local campsites.

Northeast: routes to Chaves and Bragança

Beyond Vila Real, Trás-os-Montes begins in earnest, with two main routes heading **northeast**, either to Chaves (64km) or to Bragança (136km). The N2 to Chaves is a particularly fine route, the road constrained by the twists and turns of the **Corgo river valley**, though there's really only one possible stop, at the spa town of **Vidago**. The longer road to Bragança has more of delaying interest, with a good stopover halfway at medieval **Mirandela** in the **Tua valley** (from where the minor N213 cuts north to Chaves); from here, there are also diversions **south** to intriguing towns like Vila Flôr and Carrazeda de Ansiães. The **N15** from Vila Real as far as Mirandela has not yet been upgraded, but beyond Mirandela a fast new highway shoots all the way to Bragança, making this former northern outpost more accessible now than it's ever been.

The Corgo Valley: Vidago

From Vila Real, regular buses run up the N2 through the spectacular **Corgo river valley**, where everything from cowsheds to vine posts is made from granite, and where the luscious green of the vines belies the apparent barrenness of the earth. It's a less dramatic ride than that once provided by the old *Linha do Corgo* train line, long since abandoned to the elements, but it's handsome enough, the road following the valley fairly closely as far as the village of **VILA POUCA DE AGUIAR**, 28km from Vila Real, famous in the north for its bread. Beyond here, the road cuts through the edge of the Serra da Padrela, before reaching the upper valley of the Tâmega river at Vidago, which it then traces for the rest of the route to Chaves.

Vidago
VIDAGO, a summer spa town, is easily the most interesting stop along the way, with some lovely walks in the vicinity and the opportunity to splash about in the local rivers. *The* place to stay was once the sublimely old-fashioned *Palace Hotel*, an Edwardian pile with its own post office, a magnificent pump room, a bandstand amid the trees, and one of the best wine cellars in the country. This is currently being renovated, its top-class place taken for the moment by the *Hotel do Parque*, on Avenida Conde Caria (☎076/971 57; ⑤); more modest lodgings include the *Pensão Alameda*, Rua João de Oliveira (☎076/972 46; ②) and *Pensão Primavera*, also on Avenida Conde Caria (☎076/972 30; ③). It's important to note, however, that the spa, and most of the hotels and pensions, are **closed for the winter** and open only from mid-June to mid-October.

Mirandela and the Tua Valley

It's 71km along the N15 from Vila Real to **MIRANDELA**, an odd little town with a medieval centre, which contains a scattering of Baroque mansions and a brand new modern art gallery. It's a good place to break the journey to Bragança, especially if you've rattled up on the improbably engineered narrow-gauge train from Tua (see p.233), which follows the **Tua valley** for virtually its entire distance.

Mirandela's most striking feature is undoubtedly its Roman **bridge**, renovated in the fifteenth century and stretching a good 200m across seventeen arches. It's now only open to pedestrians, with traffic forced to use the new Ponte Europa downstream, whose weir has widened the river in town into something approaching a lake. Kayaks and pedaloes splash up and down here, while the lakeside gardens and lawns are pleasant places to loaf around.

Parts of the **old town** are in a state of considerable decay. The chapel near the Câmera Municipal, at the summit of the ancient citadel, simply fell down in 1985. Scavengers pilfered the best of the stonework, and what was left was rebuilt in a four-square style that contrasts awkwardly with the grandiose **Câmara Municipal** itself. Formerly the *Palácio dos Távoras*, this was one of several flamboyant townhouses associated with the **Távora** family, who controlled the town between the fourteenth and seventeenth centuries. Pêro Lourenço de Távora rose to power in 1385 at the Battle of Aljubarrota, where he fought against the Castilians at the side of the future João I. Unfortunately, his distant grandson, Luís Álvares Távora, was to accompany Dom Sebastião in 1578 on the disastrous trip to Morocco, and the subsequent decline in the family fortunes went so far that in 1759 Pombal ordered the Távora insignia to be removed from all the palaces.

The modern art gallery, the **Museu de Arte Moderna** (Mon–Fri 2.30–6pm), is combined with the town's library. It has two collections of paintings: one dedicated to local artist Armindo Teixeira Lopes' images of Mirandela and Lisbon; the other, rather more exciting, to a fairly representative display of twentieth-century Portuguese painting and printmaking.

The best time to visit Mirandela is during its **festa** – one of the longest in Portugal (July 25–Aug 15) – or, failing that, for one of the weekday **markets**, held as close as possible to the 3rd, 14th, or 25th of every month.

Practicalities

If you're setting out for Mirandela from Vila Real **by train**, this means backtracking down the branch line to Peso da Régua and heading east along the Douro line to Tua to catch the connection. It's worth the hassle. *CP* **buses** to and from Bragança leave from in front of the train station; *Cabanelas* buses (south down the Tua valley, or north to Chaves) leave from behind the fire station, where Rua da República becomes Rua São Sebastião.

Somewhat surprisingly, Mirandela has half a dozen **pensions and hotels**, so rooms are pretty easy to find, except during the *festa*. *Pensão Praia*, Largo do 1 Janeiro 6 (☎078/224 97; ①), off Rua da República, has attractive lake views from its first-floor rooms, which compensates for the rather elementary facilities. The *Pensão Sá Morena*, also off Rua da República at Rua das Amoreiras 87 (☎078/224 34; ②), is reasonable, though the *Pensão O Lagar*, Rua da República 120 (☎078/227 12; ②), is nicer, furnished in pine and run by friendly people. The local **campsite** (☎078/231 77) is 3km north of town , on the Bragança road.

For **meals**, try the good restaurant at *Pensão Sá Moreno* or one of the first-floor places along Rua da República.

On to Bragança: Macedo de Cavaleiros

At Mirandela the Tua valley broadens and the Bragança road veers east along the Rio Azibo, past **MACEDO DE CAVALEIROS**. Unless the shooting and fishing parties at the exclusive *Estalagem do Caçador* are your bag, this is not much of a place to linger. If you want a lunch stop from driving, or get stranded trying to make a bus connection southeast to Mogadouro, you might check out the delicious **pizzas** at the *Pizzaria d'Italia* at Rua Fonte do Paço 5. There are inexpensive **rooms** available at the *Residencial Churrasqueria*, Rua Pereira Charula 8 (☎078/42 17 31; ②), pricier ones at the *Pensão Monte-Mel*, Praça Agosto Valente 26 (☎078/42 13 78; ④).

South: Vila Flôr and Carrezeda de Ansiães

Travelling by road between Mirandela and the Douro, the main route runs to the southeast of the Tua valley, through **Vila Flôr** and **Carrezeda de Ansiães**. Both are rewarding halts, if you have your own transport and can move on later in the day. Relying on public transport, you may judge the times between bus connections excessive (the most regular services are between Tua train station and Vila Flôr).

Vila Flôr

Twenty-four kilometres south of Mirandela, **VILA FLÔR** was given its name (Town of Flowers) by Dom Dinis, when on his way to meet Isabel of Aragon in the thirteenth century. His favouritism was short-lived though, for soon Vila Flôr was forced to contribute a third of its revenue to rebuilding the walls of rival Torre de Moncorvo, 30km to the south. Nowadays the only striking features of the Vila Flôr townscape are a piece of old wall known as the *Arco Dom Dinis* and a so-called "Roman" fountain.

The place merits a visit principally for its eccentric **Museu Municipal** (Tues–Sun 9.30am–12.30pm & 2–5pm). Three eminent Vilaflôrians donated the contents of their houses to the museum when it was founded in 1946, and the result is an incredible hodge-podge: a much-glued stone *porca* and a few dusty pictures by Manuel Moura are the only items of value. The enveloping clutter contains typewriters, sewing machines, snake skins, a set of broken percussion instruments, religious sculptures, teacups, stuffed animals and an ensemble of zebra-hide furniture.

The town is not a bad place to break a journey. There are three **pensions** at the new end of town, among which *Pensão Campos* on Nova Avenida (☎0789/523 11; ③) is the most pleasant. The municipal **campsite** (☎078/523 50; open all year) is 2km to the southwest, along the N215 Torre de Moncorvo road – one of very few in this area, and equipped with a swimming pool. For **meals**, the best bet is the *Campos*, though they like you to warn them in advance. Otherwise, you may find sustenance at one of the cafés down by the museum. The local red **wines**, from the *Co-Op Vila Flôr*, are regarded as among the best in the country.

The town **festa** runs from August 22–28, with live music and open-air stalls on the last weekend. Couples insist on traditional slow dancing whatever the rhythm of a song. There's also an extensive **street market** on the weekday closest to the 15th and 28th of every month. An important **romaria** takes place at a hilltop sanctuary at nearby Vilas Boas, 8km northwest, on August 15 (Nossa Senhora da Assunção).

Carrezeda de Ansiães

CARREZEDA DE ANSIÃES, 16km southwest of Vila Flôr, is a modern town of little intrinsic interest. However, three-and-a-half kilometres to its south are the intriguing ruins of a medieval **walled town**, known as Ansiães. Little remains within the perimeter of walls except rocks and boulders, but two chapels stand outside, the better preserved of which, twelfth-century **São Salvador**, has a Romanesque portal, extravagantly carved with leaves, animals and human figures.

Local myth has it that a tunnel connects this enceinte to another castle beyond the Douro, 12km distant; a gaping, fly-ridden hole beneath an impressive slab is the principal piece of supporting evidence. What is undoubtedly true, however, is that the town was a base for five different kings, including the King of Léon and Castile, before Portuguese independence; they're listed by the gateway on a plaque unveiled by Mário Soares in February 1987.

People lived in old Ansiães only until the mid-eighteenth century. In 1734, a gentleman named Francisco de Araújo e Costa managed to transfer the official council seat to the new town below – known by then as Carrezeda de Ansiães. He replied to protests by ordering the castle *pelourinho* to be destroyed. With this symbol gone and deprived of a sufficient supply of water, the hill community had no hope of putting up effective resistance. The medieval town went into decline and was soon totally abandoned.

Chaves

CHAVES stands just 12km from the Spanish border and its name, which means "Keys", reflects a strategic history of occupation and ownership. Between 1128 and 1160 the town was an Islamic enclave, and in the following seven centuries it was fought over in turn by the French, Spanish and Portuguese. One of its greatest overlords, **Nuno Álvares Pereira**, was awarded the "keys" of the north by João I for his valiant service at the Battle of Aljubarrota, and from him the town passed into the steady hands of the House of Bragança. However, as recently as 1912 Chaves bore the brunt of a Royalist attack from Spain – two years after Portugal had become a republic.

Today, Chaves is considerably less significant, though it's still a market centre for the villages of the fertile Tâmega plain – the richest agricultural lands in the province – and regional capital for the northern Trás-os-Montes. For visitors, its principal attractions are its splendid setting, a modest array of monuments, a **spa**, and its gastronomy. Chaves is famed in Portugal for its smoked hams, delicious meat cakes (*bôlas de carne*), sausages and a strong red wine. The town also hosts an important **winter fair**, held on November 1.

The town and spa

The old quarter of Chaves is highly compact, grouped above the river, with the spa just below the old walls to the west. Here, in the centre, the town's military past is still much in evidence. There are two seventeenth-century **fortresses**, built in the characteristic Vaubanesque style of the north, and a **Castelo** with a fourteenth-century keep (*Torre de Menagem*), near the bridge. The latter houses a small **Museu Militar** (Tues–Sun 9am–12.30pm & 2–4.30pm; 50$00), which among other things contains the battle colours of the infantry regiment which

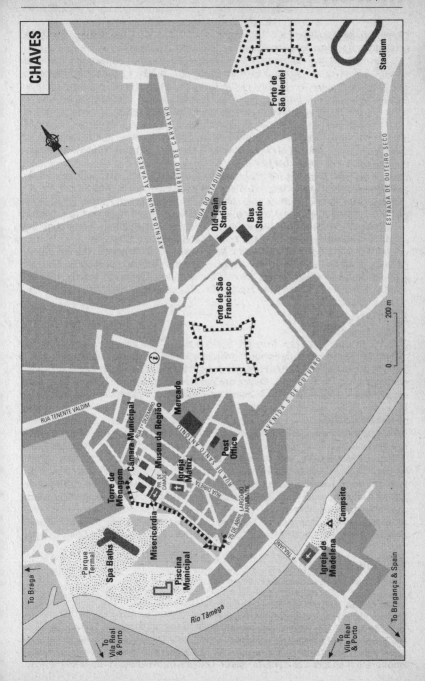

repulsed the Royalist attack from Spain in 1912. That said, the castle gardens and the views from the battlements are the finest attraction here.

The better town museum is the **Museu da Região Flaviense** (Tues–Sun 9am–12.30pm & 2–4.30pm; 50$00) on Praça de Camões, a haphazard assortment of material tracing the history of the town and its customs, including quite an assembly of remains from the old Roman spa settlement. The town was known to the Romans as *Aquae Flaviae*, after its spa waters, and was an important point on the imperial road from Astorga, in Spanish León, to Braga. In the first century AD it was the army headquarters under Aulus Flaviensis, who was responsible for developing the thermal stations here and elsewhere in the region – at Vidago, Carvalhelos and Pedras Salgadas.

You can still take the waters in summer at the Chaves **spa**, built around the *nascente* (spring) below the city walls, toward the river. The water emerges at a piping 73°C and is not very tasty, though the spa is generally full of old ladies with crocheted mug-holders taking a swig. It is reckoned to be particularly good for gout and obesity. Unfortunately, the river itself is polluted – frustrating any chance of a swim – though the gardens are well kept and attractive.

Back in town, further traces of the Roman past are to be seen in the form of the **Ponte Trajano** – the Roman bridge – and its ancient milestones. The two churches in Praça de Camões are worth a look, too: **Igreja de Matriz**, which is partly Romanesque, and the **Igreja da Misericórdia**, distinguished by vast *azulejo* panels.

Practicalities

The **bus station** is a five-minute walk north of the centre; coming into town, follow the main road directly ahead, go straight past the roundabout, and you'll emerge near the **Turismo**, facing the gardens (July–Sept daily 9am–7pm; Oct–June Mon–Fri 9am–7pm, Sat & Sun 10am–12.30pm & 2–6.30pm; ☎076/210 29).

Accommodation

Accommodation is well worth booking in advance in the summer months, when you're quite likely to find the pensions full (and overpriced) and space restricted even in the campsite. Out of season there should be no problem, save for the intense cold in winter if you're in an inexpensive, unheated room. There are **private rooms available** in town, advertised in a number of bars near the castle keep; while the small *São Roque* **campsite** (☎076/227 33; open all year) is across the bridge, on the river.

Residencial Casa das Terras, Largo do Tabolado (☎076/242 80). Modern and well-appointed, near the spa, and typical of the new purpose-built *residencials* that are springing up in town. ④.

Hotel de Chaves, Rua 25 de Abril (☎076/211 18). Late-nineteenth-century hotel which retains a few trappings of grandeur from its better days. Rooms with or without bath, and rather large price differences, depending on what you choose. ②–④.

Hospedaria Flavia, Trav. Cândido dos Reis 12 (☎076/225 13). On a *cul-de-sac*, opposite the *Hotel Trajano*, this has a nice internal, vine-draped courtyard. Some rooms have showers and balcony and are just in the next price category. ①.

Pensão Jaime, Avda. da Muralha (☎076/212 73). Fifty metres from the spa and not much further from the city walls. The reception, and the water, can be cool but it's well-placed and good value at these prices, if a little basic. You might find the price shoots up in summer if the town is full; it's worth bargaining if you're quoted something outrageous. ①–②.

Hotel Trajano, Trav. Cândido dos Reis (☎076/33 24 15). Modern, comfortable and a bit dull, though some of the pleasant rooms have traditional local furniture and good views. There's a renowned restaurant in the basement; see below. ⑤.

Quinta de Santa Isabel, Santo Estêvão (☎076/218 18). This *Turihab* property is 7km from Chaves, 500m off the N103 to Bragança. It's a traditional Trás-os-Montes house, with vineyards, and is where Queen Isabel is said to have slept the night before she married Dom Dinis; the beds are more recent. Rooms and apartments here work out at around 4500$00 per person.

Eating

Some of the pensions and hotels have reasonable **restaurants** attached, but wherever you eat you shouldn't have any difficulty finding good Chaves smoked ham, tasty local sausages and fine Trás-os-Montes red wine.

Adega Faustino, Trav. Cândido dos Reis. Next to the *Hosepdaria Flavia*, this old converted wine cellar with huge wooden barrels on view serves great bean salads and a selection of *petiscos*, which you can turn into an inexpensive meal. And, of course, it has terrific wine.

Restaurante Carvalho, Largo das Caldas. The team which ran the successful *Restaurante Campismo* for years has moved nearer the spa; still highly recommended.

Restaurante Dionisyos, Praça do Município 2. Opposite the *Torre de Menagem*, this serves huge portions at reasonable prices. Try the local speciality, *folar*, an interesting and wholesome pork bread, or the *arroz de tamboril*. There are tables outside in summer.

Restaurante Pote, over the bridge and 1km out on the Bragança road. Serves up generously sized local dishes to an enthusiastic clientele. Closed Mon.

Hotel Trajano, Trav. Cândido dos Reis. A very slick operation in the basement and not too expensive; just the place for Chaves ham and local trout.

Routes on from Chaves: Montalegre and Vinhais

Chaves has useful bus connections west to Braga and the Peneda-Gerês national park via **Montalegre** (45km); east to **Vinhais** (65km), for connections to Bragança; and southeast to Mirandela (53km), on the Tua train line which runs south to the Douro river. Heading **into Spain**, you could pick up an express bus to Orense, via Verin, on a Thursday or Sunday (originating in Porto, these pass through Chaves in the afternoon; book ahead at Chaves bus station if possible). There is no currency exchange at the border post.

West: Montalegre

Approached from Chaves, heading west, **MONTALEGRE** – a ten-kilometre detour off the N103 – looms up suddenly, commanding the surrounding plains. Looking at its isolated position on the map, you might expect a frontier town, with a history rooted in past centuries. In fact, there is a fair amount of modern development, because of the nearby Pisões dam, which is gradually encroaching on the medieval centre and castle. However, it remains quite an atmospheric place and makes an enjoyable night or two's stopover, set amid good walking territory, scattered with dolmens and the odd Templar and Romanesque church.

Accommodation is at the surprisingly fancy *Residencial Fidalgo*, Rua da Corujeira (☎076/524 62; ③), uphill to the left at the main square, Largo do Município. There are nice, clean rooms here, with good views over the valley. Up the hill from the *Fidalgo* is the *Restaurant Floresta*, where it's worth paying the higher than usual prices for good **food** and views. The *Brasilieira* on the southwest side of Largo do Município is also a good bet for an excellent meal, serving large portions. You might ask at the local bars about *Vinho dos Mortos* – Wine of the Dead – so called as it is fermented in bottles buried in the ground at the nearby villages of the Serra do Barroso.

There's a minor **border crossing** into Spain north of Montalegre, at Tourém/Sendim.

East: to Vinhais

To the east of Chaves, five or six weekday buses (one on Sat, none on Sun) roll through the hills along a superb scenic route to Bragança, 96km away. The route becomes ever more barren as you climb and there are fabulous, if bleak, views from various tortuous bends in the road. Two-thirds of the way along is the delightful village of **VINHAIS**, which is dominated by the Baroque convent of **São Francisco**, a vast building incorporating a pair of churches in its facade. The main street runs for 1km or more, with staggering views away to the south at every turn.

If you get stuck in Vinhais, there are three **places to stay**, the least expensive the *Residencial Ribeirinha*, Rua Nova 34 (☎073/724 90; ①), which has lovely old rooms with balconies overlooking the valley. If the bus drops you in the square, it's a long walk back to this; ask to be put off at the *Casa do Povo* (parish rooms) on the way into the village. Otherwise, there are fairly decent rooms at both the *Pensão da Calçada*, above the *Comercial* restaurant at Rua da Corujeira 2 (☎073/72 771; ②), and at *Pensão Leão*, Largo do Arrabalde 20 (☎073/724 50; ①). Alternatively, you could **camp** at Ponte de Soeira, 8km east of the town, where the road crosses the Rio Tuella – it's a picnic and swimming spot, and wild camping is allowed. For **food**, *Restaurant Comercial* has a good menu, and there are several other restaurants as you head out of town on the Chaves road.

Buses to Bragança are few and far between at the weekend. If you really have to move on before Monday, you'll be able to take a taxi from Vinhais for an agreed price of between 3000$00 and 4000$00, depending on the generosity of the driver.

Bragança and around

On a dark hillock above **BRAGANÇA**, the remote capital of Trás-os-Montes, stands a circle of perfectly preserved medieval walls, rising to a massive keep and castle, and enclosing a white medieval village. Known as the Cidadela, this is one of the most memorable sights in Portugal, seemingly untouched by the centuries, with crops still grown within the walls and a hamlet whose size is wonderfully at odds with the royal connotations of the town's dynastic name. The Braganças were the last line of **Portuguese monarchs**, ruling from 1640, when they replaced the Spaniards, until the fall of the monarchy in 1910. To the British, the name is most readily associated with Catherine, queen to Charles II. For the Portuguese, the town represents the defence of the liberty of the people, for the Braganças were the first to muster a popular revolt against Junot in 1808, and have always defended their power to make their own decisions.

The citadel, along with an excellent museum, provides the principal reason for a visit to the town. For anyone interested in a bit of wilderness hiking, though, the nearby **Parque Natural de Montesinho** provides an additional draw (see p.311), while a **cultural festival**, held from August 14 to 22, is another very good reason to be in town. If you're travelling by public transport, you're unlikely – given the paucity of the bus service – to break your **onward journey** from Bragança before the next major town, but drivers can indulge themselves in a variety of fascinating routes, particularly that southeast to Miranda do Douro along the N218.

The Cidadela

At the heart of the **Cidadela** stands the thirteenth-century council chamber, the **Domus Municipalis**. Very few Romanesque civic buildings have survived, and no other has this pentagonal form. Its meetings – for solving land disputes and the like – took place on the arcaded first floor; below was a cistern. Rising to its side is the **Igreja de Santa Maria**, whose interior is distinguished by an eighteenth-century, barrel-vaulted, painted ceiling – a feature of several churches in Bragança. Keys for both are kept locally if you find the doors shut.

Facing these buildings is the town keep, the **Torre da Menagem** (daily except Thurs 10am–noon & 2–5pm; 100$00, free Sun morning), which the royal family rejected as a residence in favour of their vast estate in the Alentejo. It was one of the first works of restoration by the Society of National Monuments in 1928, and houses a fine little craft shop and a collection of military odds and ends. At the side of the keep, a curious **pelourinho** (pillory) rises from the back of a prehistoric granite pig. The town's museum has three more of these crudely sculpted **porcas**, the most famous of which is to be seen at Murça, halfway between Vila Real and Mirandela. They are thought to have been the fertility idols of a prehistoric cult, and it's easy to understand the beast's prominence in this province of wild boars and chestnut forests, where the staple winter diet is smoked sausage.

Look over the furthest walls of the castle and you'll see the Parque Natural de Montesinho stretching to Spain, a view which seems to stress the town's remoteness. One group who made the most of this isolation were the **Jews**, who escaped over the border in the sixteenth century from the terrors of the Inquisition in Spain. Despite the common rule by Spaniards over the two countries during this period, the Inquisition in Portugal was relatively inefficient – administered in municipalities, the organisation spread slowly northwards with ever-decreasing zeal. The Jewish community has left its mark in the names of local families and in the town's cuisine (the *alheira* sausage is made from chicken rather than pork); but the once-thriving synagogue is no more.

You can get a superb **view** of the Cidadela from the bottom of the steps of the church of São Bartolomeu; to get there, follow the signs to the *pousada*, a half-hour walk from the town centre.

The town

Heading back into town from the Cidadela, the narrow, stepped Rua Serpa Pinto leads to the **Igreja de São Vicente**, where Dom Pedro I claimed to have secretly married Inês de Castro (see p.120). A little way to the east is the **Igreja de São Bento**, the town's finest church – a simple Renaissance structure with three contrasting ceilings.

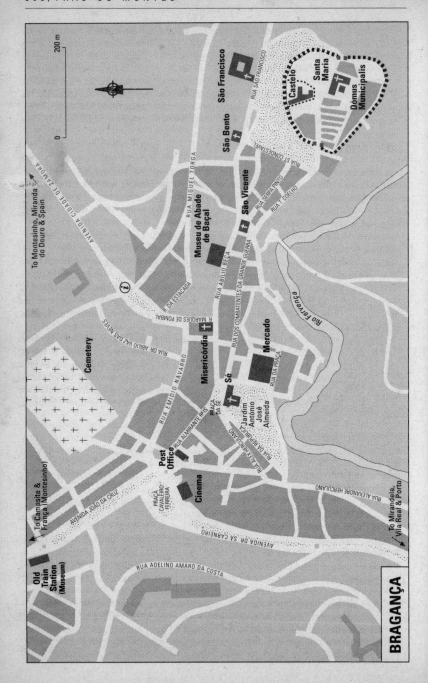

BRAGANÇA

In the other direction is the **Museu do Abade de Baçal**, the town's distinguished museum (Tues–Sun 10am–12.30pm & 2–5pm; 200$00); it's currently being restored. It is installed in the former Bishop's Palace, and in its gardens Celtic-inspired medieval tombstones rub shoulders with a menagerie of *porcas*. Inside, the collection of sacred art and the topographical watercolours of Alberto Souza are the highlights, along with displays of local costumes – especially the dress of the *Pauliteiros* ("stick dancers"), who still perform at festivals around Bragança and Miranda do Douro. Further down the street is a fine Renaissance **Misericórdia**.

One last, incidental sight, which rail buffs will want to check out, is the tiny **transport museum** at the old train station. This features the first steam train operative in northern Portugal, and the royal carriage of Portugal's second-to-last king, Dom Carlos, both brought here from Arco de Baulhe, following the closure of the upper reaches of the Tâmega train line.

Practicalities

Modern Bragança, set along the valley below the Cidadela, is a pleasant enough place, despite an eruption of concrete apartment blocks on the outskirts. Most **buses** operate from outside the old train station, north of the town centre, where the *Cabanelas* company maintains a kiosk, though the bus station itself is out of town on the N103-1 (to França); many buses heading here stop first either outside the *Hotel Bragança* or outside the Turismo. For details of **crossing the border** into Spain, see below.

From the old train station it's a short walk along Avenida João da Cruz to **Praça da Sé**, essentially the centre of town, from where it's a couple of hundred metres north to the very helpful **Turismo** (Mon–Fri 9am–12.30pm & 2–5pm; ☎073/282 73), on Avenida Cidade de Zamora, a wide boulevard split by gardens. Further down the avenue, in a modern development on the left, is the head office of the **Parque Natural de Montesinho** (Apart. 90, Lote 5, Nunes Teizeira, Bairro Salvador; Mon–Fri 10am–noon & 2–5pm; ☎073/287 34).

Accommodation

Pensions and hotels are dispersed around town and above average in cost. Some are unheated, which in winter in these parts is no joke: choose carefully. The nearest **campsite** (☎073/268 20; May–Oct) is 6km north of town, on the França road, and has pretty sparse facilities.

Hotel Bragança, Avda. Dr. Francisco Sá Carneiro (☎073/33 15 79). Box-like concrete structure in a *centro comercial* and popular with visiting businessmen. Comfortable and well-run. ⑤.

Residencial Cruzeiro, Trav. do Hospital (☎073/33 16 33). On an alley off Rua Almirante Reis, this central place has decent rooms with showers. A clean and calm choice. ③.

Residencial Poças, Rua Combatentes da Grande Guerra 200 (☎073/33 11 75). As cheap as it gets in the centre, though pick your room with care – some are very bare and in winter this place is freezing. Check in at the grocery store across the street if no-one's around. ②.

Pousada de São Bartolomeu, Estrada de Turismo (☎073/331 24 93). South of the river, about 1km by road from the centre – follow the signs. Purpose-built in 1959, it's got wood panelling, cork ceilings, great views and a good restaurant. ⑥.

Pensão Rucha, Rua Almirante Reis 42 (☎073/33 16 72). More of a family home than a pension, run by an elderly couple and including a hearty breakfast. You'll have to look hard to spot the sign. Recommended. ②.

Residencial São Roque, Rua da Estacada 267 (☎073/38 14 81). A little out of the centre, but modern and well-furnished, on the top floors of a new block and sporting great views. ③.

Pensão Transmontano, Avda. João da Cruz 168 (☎073/33 18 99). Opposite the train station, this is the cheapest pension in town, but it's brusquely run; look elsewhere if you can. ①.

Residencial Tulipa, Rua Dr. Francisco Felgueiras 8–10 (☎073/33 16 75). Clean, simple place with cramped rooms that, nevertheless, is highly sought after in summer; arrive early or book ahead. ④.

Eating and drinking

Bragança has a promising array of bars and **restaurants** and the places listed below are all recommended. For the town's rather limited **nightlife**, the place to go is *Bô*, a late bar with Brazilian bands and local guitarists in summer, on Rua Combatentes da Grande Guerra .

O Bolha, Jardim Dr. António José de Almeida. Cheap set menus and a homemade pink liqueur which go down very nicely.

Là em Casa, Rua Marquês de Pombal 7. A friendly, convivial place near the Igreja da Misericórdia. Don"t be put off by the over-rustic decor. Full meals for 2500$00 and up.

Restaurante Poças, Rua Combatentes da Grande Guerra 200. Excellent and inexpensive food in the restaurant below the *residencial* – family run and popular enough to fill a couple of floors.

Solar Bragançeno, Praça da Sé. An upmarket but excellent *casa típica*, where you dine in oak-panelled rooms to the accompaniment of classical music. There's a nice bar, too.

Crossing to Spain

If you can get tickets, the easiest way to Spain is by taking the *Internorte* **express bus** from Porto to Zamora, which passes through Bragança in the afternoon (Tues–Sat). Failing that, take a *Cabanelas* bus to the Portuguese border post at **QUINTANILHA** (34km; Mon–Fri departures at 5pm), or the Miranda do Douro bus (6am, 11.30am and 5pm) as far as the border road crossroads and hitch the 12km on to the frontier. At the Spanish frontier village of San Martin del Pedroso, there's a single, combined, pension-restaurant, the *Evaristo*, and an early morning bus to Zamora.

An alternative crossing is to take the road **through the Parque Natural de Montesinho** (see below), through the border villages of **PORTELO** (Portugal) and Calabor (Spain) to the Spanish town of Puebla de Sanabria, which has onwards bus and train services and accommodation. Using public transport, you can catch *Cabanelas* buses to Portelo at 2.15pm (Mon, Wed, Fri) and irregular Spanish buses (Mon–Fri) between Calabor and Puebla de Sanabria; you have to walk or hitch the 6km between Portelo and Calabor.

Southeast: on to Miranda do Douro

Southeast of Bragança, the N218 steers a fine course towards Miranda do Douro and if you're driving you can stop off in some extremely attractive towns and villages on the way. **GIMONDE**, 7km away, would in fact make a fine base if you wanted somewhere quieter than Bragança, a beautifully sited rural village with traditional wooden houses on the edge of the Montesinho park. The rivers Onor, Sabor and Igregas all meet here near a Romanesque bridge, a favourite spot for stork-watching in early summer. There's are **rooms** above the *Restaurante 4* (②), slightly out of town on the Bragança road.

Fifteen kilometres beyond Gimonde, the N218 branches away from the main cross-border road and runs another 10km south to **OUTEIRO**, a once-grand village with a disproportionately huge church, Santo Christo, built in 1755. Outeiro's erstwhile status as defender of Portugal's eastern tranches is confirmed by the presence of a ruined **castle** on the hill above the village. The small bar on the green by the church contains a sketch of this in its heyday, before it was destroyed in the wars with Spain; the barman can tell you the quickest way to climb up if you're tempted. The local water hereabouts is believed to cure breathing problems, its miraculous powers supposedly enhanced after a visitation by Nossa Senhora de Fátima on 11 June 1848.

Between Outeiro and **VIMIOSA**, 22km south, the countryside becomes ever more mountainous and dramatic. The town itself is spectacularly set, though despite some pretty, traditional houses on the steep streets around the Igreja Matriz, there's little of interest in Vimiosa, much of which is swamped by *emigrante*-financed development. There are two modern *residencials* here, the *Central* and more upmarket *Charneca*, signposted off the main Bragança road, but you'd do far better to press on to Miranda, only another 30km to the southeast.

The Parque Natural de Montesinho

Occupying the extreme northeastern tip of Portugal, the **Parque Natural de Montesinho** is the only sector of the *Terra Fria* where the way of life and the appearance of villages have not yet been changed by the new wealth of the emigrant workers. The *Terra Fria*'s predominantly barren landscape is here disrupted by microclimates which give rise to the Serra de Montesinho's heather-clad hills, wet grass plains and thick forests of oak. Another curious feature of the region is the round *pombal* or pigeon house – a structure which, no matter how well-established its position, invariably seems to have dropped in from another world. The ethnographic museum in Miranda do Douro (see p.312) can fill you in on these and other aspects of traditional village life, such as the black cape and the cloaks of straw – as much a protection against heat as against cold.

For leaflets and advice for walkers, contact the **Montesinho park office** in Bragança (see "Practicalities", above), which also has brochures on the local flora and fauna and will recommend **camping** spots. In addition, this is the place to ask about **renting traditional houses** (*Casas Abrigo*), which are scattered throughout the small villages in the park – prices range from around 3000$00 a night, for a studio sleeping two, to 30,000$000 for a property that will hold 25.

The most useful **bus links from Bragança** are to França/Portelo, due north of Bragança (2 *STUB* buses daily from near the old train station), and to Rio de Onor, to the northeast (4–5 daily). It is not too hard to hitch on the França road in summer, and walking beyond here, alongside the **Rio Sabor**, is idyllic, with wonderful and deserted spots for camping and swimming. **Walking to Rio de Onor**, too, is also an option, for more on which see below.

Rio de Onor
RIO DE ONOR, hard by the Spanish border, 25km from Bragança, provides perhaps the most fascinating insight into the village life of the Serra de Montesinho. There are in fact two Rio de Onors – one in Spain, one in Portugal –

but two stone blocks labelled "E" and "P", and a change from cobbles on the Portuguese side to smooth concrete on the Spanish, is all that delineates the frontier. The villagers have come and gone between the two for generations, intermarrying and buying goods; both sides speak a hybrid Portuguese-Spanish dialect known as *Rionorês*. Their extreme isolation encouraged systems of justice and mutual co-operation which are independent of the state and which still exist. The ageing villagers share land, flocks, wine-presses, mills and ovens.

The two villages are set on either side of a stream: the granite steps and wooden balconies of rough stone houses line narrow alleyways, and straw creeps out across the cobbles. The bar in the Portuguese "half" of the village contains a long stick on which locals once marked the number of cattle and sheep they owned. Communal meetings fined troublemakers and miscreants in wine! If you want to **stay**, you can pitch a tent, or there's the possibility of basic shelter in the *Casa do Povo* (parish rooms) provided you contact the village *presidente* on arrival.

STUB **buses**, fluctuating according to local school and market timetables, connect the village four or five times daily with Bragança. But you could always **walk from Bragança** instead, the best part of this 25-kilometre hike coming after the aerodrome, passing through Vargas with its traditional stone houses (where you can camp by the river). The route indicates very clearly how isolated Rio de Onor is – the road has only existed for 15 years, before which time the locals had to walk across open country to and from Bragança.

Miranda do Douro and around

The route from Bragança to **MIRANDA DO DOURO** runs across the *Planalto Mirandês*, a breathtaking journey in late-February and early March, when the sudden blossoming of the almond trees transforms the countryside. Some say that it was the beauty of this vista – and Miranda do Douro itself – that decided Afonso Henriques, the future first king of Portugal, to turn against his Spanish kinsmen, refortify the border and begin his victorious sweep across Lusitânia at the start of the twelfth century. Facing Spain across the deep gorge of the Douro, Miranda do Douro played a key role in all of the country's subsequent wars. After valiant service in the Independence, Spanish Succession, and Seven Year wars, it ended its fighting days in 1762 when an explosion during a Spanish attack destroyed the castle and the town, and killed 400 inhabitants.

The "city"

Today, with a population of less than two thousand, Miranda seems scarcely more than a village. Yet it has the status of a city, and a sturdy sixteenth-century Sé overlooks its cobbled streets and low white houses. This cathedral and the city status dates from a decision by the Portuguese church authorities to make Miranda the capital of the diocese to counteract the feudal power of the House of Bragança in Trás-os-Montes. At the end of the eighteenth century, however, the see was transferred to the larger of the two towns, leaving Miranda cathedral as a cumbersome memento of past glory. To the bitter comment "The sacristy is in Bragança, but the cathedral is in Miranda", the astute Bragançans reply, "If ever you go to Miranda, see the cathedral and come home".

The cathedral aside, Miranda has a certain neat charm, despite a rather off-putting rash of frontier tourist shops. The tidied-up ruins of its Episcopal Palace, now a café, and the medieval facades along **Rua da Costanilha** set the tone, and there is a small medieval bridge, too, over the diminutive Rio Fresno. Beyond here you reach an eighteenth-century fountain, the Fonte dos Canos.

However, the main focus of interest in town is the **Museu de Terra de Miranda** (Tues–Sun 10am–12.15pm & 2–4.45pm), just off Rua da Constanilha. This is literally bursting with curiosities, from lumps of stone to pistols, and features a couple of reconstructed rooms in traditional Mirandês style – an illustration of local life that's inaccurate only in that the agricultural labourers of the region generally live, sleep and die in a single room.

Apart from the local **festa** periods (*Santa Bárbara* on the third Sunday in August; *Romaria Nossa Senhora do Nazo*, Sept 7–8), and the **feira** held on the first weekday of every month, not a lot happens in Miranda.

Accommodation and eating

Of Miranda's **accommodation** options, the *Residencial Flor do Douro*, Rua do Mercado Municipal 7–9 (☎073/421 86; ②), is among the best; in a modern block in a shopping centre, but with fine views from some of its back rooms. *Residencial Planalto*, Rua 1º de Maio (☎073/423 62; ③), is another good choice, with modern, en-suite rooms, but no views. The only pension in the old town is the characterful *Pensão Santa Cruz*, Rua Abade de Bacal 61 (☎073/424 74; ②), near Largo do Castelo, with a family atmosphere, a good restaurant and a chatty pet parrot. The local *pousada*, **Santa Catarina** (☎073/422 55; ⑥), is just outside town, sited on the edge of a gorge, its twelve balconied rooms overlooking the huge Miranda do Douro reservoir. There's a **campsite**, *Santa Luzia* (☎073/421 96; June–Sept), on the southern side of town, by the stadium; it's run by the municipality and is free.

In addition to the pension and hotel **restaurants**, you might like to check out the menus at *O Mirandês* (from 1500$00) or the cheaper *Balbina*; the latter has a collection of grandfather clocks, serves excellent wine and a local *posta assada á mirandesa* (beef) which will feed two or three. The *São Pedro* on Rua Mouzinho de Albuquerque in the old town is also good value, serving excellent *tamboril* and prawn kebabs.

Onwards transport

Moving on from Miranda do Douro, *Santos* operates **buses** from the museum square to Mogadouro, Torre de Moncorvo and Pocinho at 5.45am and 3.15pm (daily) and 11am (Mon–Fri only). The **Spanish border** lies just across the Barragem de Miranda, on the other side of a vast hydroelectric dam – at 528m the highest in the country, and the last before the Portuguese Douro becomes the Spanish Duero. If you have transport, you might take advantage of this crossing (3km to the border post) to approach Zamora; there are no buses along the route.

South to Sendim

The only reason to drive south the 21km along the N221 Mogadouro road to the pleasant, functional town of **SENDIM** is to sample some of the country's top cooking, at the *Restaurante Gabriela*. It is run by Alicia, an award-winning chef who appears on many a Portuguese TV show, and whose speciality is roast veal.

Sadly, though, if she's not there, the food can appear strictly average and over-priced. Provided you strike lucky, and having eaten and drunk your fill, you may be glad of the **rooms** at the restaurant (②–③), or those around the corner at the *Galego* (☎073/732 02; ①).

Mogadouro

For a more unkempt and authentic picture of town life in the *Terra Fria*, take a look at **MOGADOURO**, 47km southwest of Miranda do Douro, and, specifically, head for its castle. This is unexceptional as a monument, but the ground in front is common land where children play and farmers sort out their produce. During the harvest period the area is stacked high with dried *tremoços* bushes, whose seeds are consumed as beer-time snacks and used in soups. The castle hill also commands terrific views over a long, low horizon and a patchwork of fields and *pombais*.

Mogadouro would never be listed for its ancient buildings. The **Câmara Municipal** occupies a former convent, but is treated by the townspeople as their own backyard, herding cows home in the evening, saddling up pony carts, and playing at tossing coins for hours at a time.

The main tree-lined Avenida Nossa Senhora do Caminho has a sports complex and views over the hills on one side, and a row of shops and cafés on the other. The avenue ends at Praça Engenheiro Duarte Pacheco, where **buses** drop you, with the old town and ruined castle beyond. Should you want to **stay**, there are plenty of places from which to choose, including three *residencials* on the road to Freixo (see below) and a string along the main avenue, including *Residencial A Lareira*, at no.58 (☎079/323 63; ④; closed Jan), with a renowned **restaurant** (closed Mon). In addition, there are very cheap rooms at the *Pensão Russo*, Rua 5 de Outubro 10 (☎079/321 34; ①), which also has its own restaurant, and rooms (①) to rent at the otherwise overpriced *Restaurant Estoril*, on Rua da República, off the praça. *Restaurant Kalifa*, on Rua Santa Marinha, also off the praça, is recommended for its steak and superb red wine.

Be warned that the town is busy (and rooms at a premium) in August, when the emigrants are back home with their families. There is an annual **festa** at this time, in honour of *Nossa Senhora do Caminho* (Aug 7–23), with a special *emigrante* weekend on the last Saturday and Sunday of August, before they leave the country again.

Freixo de Espada à Cinta

The twentieth century recedes even further as you travel south to **FREIXO DE ESPADA À CINTA**, reached by changing buses off the Miranda do Douro–Pocinho route at Freixo station, 14km away. The town feels end-of-the-worldish as the bus climbs down to its valley, hidden on each side by wild, dark mountains, a backdrop against which you might glimpse the occasional hawk or black kite. Arrive at dusk and you'll see donkeys being led back to their stables in the lower storeys of the houses.

Curiously, for such a remote outpost, there is a very rich parish church, the **Igreja Matriz** – part Romanesque, part Manueline – with a *retábulo* of paintings by Grão Vasco (see Viseu, p.179). Across the way from the church is a magnificent heptagonal **keep**, a landmark for miles around. Another, unpublicised, attraction is a mansion in Largo do Outeiro, which maintains a garden of mulberry worms for silk production; ask around and you may be taken for a look.

Unexpectedly, too, there are a couple of **places to stay** – a modern *hospedaria* (②), some distance from the square where the bus drops you (ask at the bus stop), and the *Quinta da Boa Vista* (☎079/621 12; ⑤), on the outskirts of town, though this has just three rooms. On Largo do Outeiro, the *pensões Paris* and *Forte*, might also be worth a look, though as often as not the doors are firmly closed at both. For **meals**, the very good *Restaurant Cinta de Ouro* is the place, on the way out of town to the south, up the hill on the left. There's a strong Spanish influence in the cooking, and an outdoor patio. The *Bom Retiro*, nearby, is cheaper, with typical Portuguese dishes.

The road **north of town** passes Lagoaça, a very old village whose houses feature Manueline stone-arched windows, and whose women still wear traditional dress. Pass through the village, beyond the cemetery, and there's a superb viewing platform, looking over the deep Douro valley into Spain.

travel details

Trains
Mirandela to Tua (4–6 daily; 1hr 55min).
Peso da Régua to Vila Real (5 daily; 1hr).
Tua to Mirandela (4–6 daily; 1hr 55min).
Vila Real to Peso da Régua (5 daily; 1h).

Buses
Bragança to Chaves (Mon–Fri 5–6 daily; Sat 1 daily; 3hr); Lisbon (4 daily; 8hr); Macedo de Cavaleiros (3–5 daily; 45min); Miranda do Douro (3 daily; 1hr 30min); Mirandela (3–5 daily; 2hr 15min); Porto (3 daily; 4hr 30min); Vila Real (3 daily; 2hr 30min); Vinhais (6–7 daily; 30min); Viseu (4 daily; 4hr 15min).
Chaves to Braga (4–5 daily; 4hr); Bragança (Mon–Fri 5–6 daily, Sat 1; 3hr); Lisbon (2–4 daily; 8–9hr); Mirandela (1–2 daily; 2hr); Montalegre (Mon–Fri 3 daily, 2hr); Porto (2–6 daily; 3hr); Vila Real (4–11 daily; 2hr).

Freixo de Espada à Cinta to Mogadouro (4 daily; 2–3hr).
Miranda do Douro to Bragança (3 daily; 1hr 30min); Freixo de Espada à Cinta (4 daily; 3hr); Mogadouro (3–4 daily; 2hr 20min).
Mirandela to Bragança (3–5 daily; 2hr 15min); Chaves (1–2 daily; 2hr).
Mogadouro to Freixo de Espada à Cinta (4 daily; 2–3hr); Miranda do Douro (3–4 daily; 2hr 20min); Pocinho (3 daily; 3hr); Torre de Moncorvo (3 daily; 2hr 40min).
Montalegre to Chaves (Mon–Fri 3 daily; 2hr).
Vila Real to Bragança (3 daily; 2hr 30min); Chaves (4–11 daily; 2hr); Coimbra (2 daily; 4hr 30min); Guimarães (3 daily; 1hr 30min); Lisbon (4 daily; 7–8hr); Porto (3 daily; 3hr 30min); Viseu (4 daily; 2hr 30min).

CHAPTER EIGHT

ALENTEJO

The huge, sparsely populated plains of the **Alentejo** are overwhelmingly agricultural, dominated by vast cork plantations – the one crop that is well suited to the low rainfall, sweltering heat and poor soil. This is traditionally one of the poorest parts of the country (indeed, one of the poorest parts of Europe), much of whose sparse population still derives a living from the huge agricultural estates, known as *latifúndios*. However, despite the tedium of the interior landscape, there are unexpected surprises throughout the region, from the strong rural traditions still expressed in a variety of local festivals, to the wealth of ornithological interest – the Alentejo is home to hundreds of types of birds, from black storks to great bustards, all finely adapted to the mix of varied agriculture and marginal wilderness.

For most visitors, understandably, the region's major draws are its few towns and cities, with the standout attraction being historic **Évora**, whose Roman temple and medieval walls and cathedral, have put it very much on the tourist map. Elsewhere in **Alto Alentejo** – the "Upper Alentejo" province – few towns see more than a handful of visitors in a day. Yet there is much to see and enjoy: the spectacular fortifications of **Elvas**; the hilltop sites of **Monsaraz**, **Évora-Monte** and **Marvão**; and the marble towns of **Estremoz**, **Borba** and **Vila Viçosa**, northeast of Évora, where even the humblest homes are made of fine stone from the local quarries. This region is also scattered with **prehistoric remains**, including over a dozen megalithic sites with dolmens, standing stones and stone circles.

South of Évora, the plains of **Baixo** (Lower) **Alentejo** have rather less appeal, and the towns, with the notable exception of **Beja** – once an important Moorish stronghold – can seem rather dull. But the Alentejo **coastline** is almost as exten-

---

LAND REFORM IN ALENTEJO

The Alentejo's structure of **land ownership** has been in place since Roman times, when the new settlers established massive agricultural estates – *latifúndios* – on which they grew imported crops, like wheat, barley and olives. Handed down from generation to generation, these estates remained feudal in character, employing large numbers of farm labourers with no stake in the land they worked. In the wake of the 1974 revolution, much of the land in Alentejo – then a Communist stronghold – was collectivised. However, the workers possessed neither the financial means nor the technical know-how to cope with a succession of poor harvests, and increasingly the original *latifundio* owners have been clawing back their estates at depressed prices. Jobs today are scarcer than ever, as mechanisation has done away with much casual farm labour – a move hastened by European Community grants for modernisation programmes and the introduction of new agricultural methods. Only the Beja district, known in Portugal as the reddest region of the country, has a government still controlled by the Communists, who have gradually lost sway in the rest of Alentejo.

sive as the Algarve's and more than compensates for the lack of urban pleasures. Whipped by the Atlantic winds, its **beaches** can seem pretty wild, but in summer at least the sea is warm enough for swimming, and very few of the resorts attract more than weekend crowds. Particularly enticing are the lagoons of **Melides** and **Santo André** – between Setúbal and the eminently avoidable industrial port of Sines – and the long beaches further south at **Ilha do Pessegueiro**, **Vila Nova de Milfontes** and **Zambujeira do Mar**. If you want to head straight for these southern resorts, there are express buses in summer from Lisbon. Accommodation is somewhat limited, but there are plenty of campsites strategically positioned along the coast.

ALTO ALENTEJO

Unless you are heading south to the beaches, **Évora** provides the easiest starting point in Alentejo, with frequent and fast buses, or rather slower trains, from Lisbon. From here, you're within striking distance of **Estremoz** and the marble towns, beyond which, to the east, lie the superbly preserved walls of **Elvas**, close to the Spanish frontier. The northern part of Alto Alentejo is characterised by more fortified towns – **Portalegre**, **Castelo de Vide**, **Marvão** – any of which would make a splendid night's stopover on your way to points further north.

Évora

ÉVORA is one of the most impressive and enjoyable cities in Portugal, its relaxed provincial atmosphere forming a perfect setting for a range of memorable monuments. A Roman temple, Moorish alleys, a circuit of medieval walls, and a rather grand sixteenth-century ensemble of palaces and mansions are all in superb condition, spruced up by a long-term restoration programme and placed under *UNESCO* protection. Inevitably, they attract a great many summer tourists but despite the crowds, the city is far from spoiled. It still plays its part in the agricultural life of the region, with a produce market on Tuesday mornings; while the university, re-established here in the 1970s, adds an independent side to city life. Évora's big annual event is the **Feira de São João**, a folklore, handicraft and music festival which takes over the city during the last ten days of June.

Arrival and accommodation

Évora's **train station** is 1km southeast of the centre; if you follow Rua da República, straight ahead, you'll reach **Praça do Giraldo**, the city's main square. *CP* **buses** to and from Estremoz, Vila Viçosa and Reguengos de Monsaraz use the train station as a depot; others operate from a **bus terminal** on Rua da República, at the edge of the historic zone. If you're **driving**, you're in for a hard time amid the maze of one-way and narrow streets; try to park as soon as possible, and then walk into the centre.

The **Turismo** (summer daily 9am–7pm; winter daily 9am–12.30pm & 2–5.30pm; ☎066/226 71), on Praça do Giraldo, has maps of the city and province, which include some excellent walking routes. The office can also help with accommodation, which is often stretched to the limit in summer.

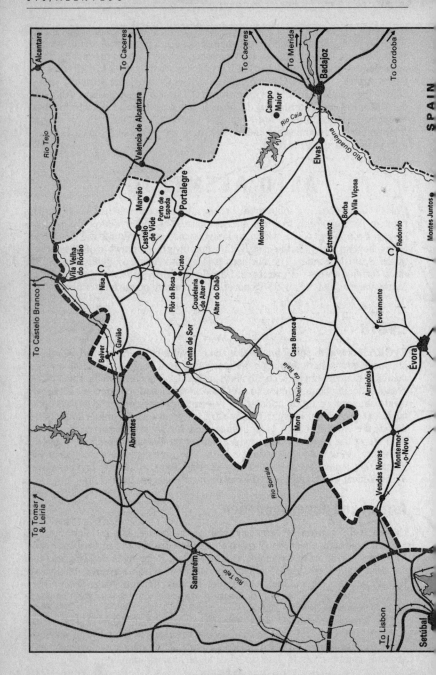

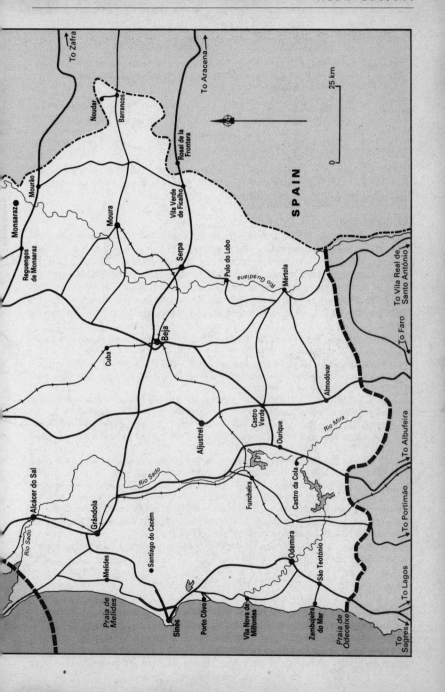

The Turismo can also provide information about **renting bicycles** (or call ☎066/76 14 53), which costs around 1500$00 per day – a good way to reach the megalithic sights in the surroundings (see p.324).

Accommodation

Hotel and pension prices in Évora are higher than usual, more or less comparable with Lisbon. In summer, too, you're advised to book at least a day in advance for any of the places listed below; on the day, **private rooms** (②) can usually be arranged through the Turismo. Évora's *Orbitur* **campsite** (☎066/251 90; open all year) is 2km southwest of town on the N380 Alcáçovas road. There's no reliable bus service and you're best off taking a taxi if you can't face the 45-minute trudge. The campsite itself is clean and well equipped, with a restaurant and swimming pool.

Residencial Diana, Rua Diogo Cão 2 (☎066/220 08). Pleasant enough rooms in a house between the Sé and Praça do Giraldo. ④.

Pensão O Eborense, Largo da Misericórdia 1 (☎066/220 31). A former ducal mansion – elegant, spacious and relaxed. Excellent breakfasts are included in the room rates. You need to walk up the flight of steps to reception. ③.

Pensão Giraldo, Rua dos Mercadores 15 (☎066/258 33). Very pleasant rooms with bath; also some "overspill" rooms available, which are not as nice but much cheaper. ③.

Pensão Os Manuéis, Rua do Raimundo 35 (☎066/228 61). Decent rooms above the restaurant of the same name, just west of Praça do Giraldo. There's a less preferable annexe across the road. ②.

Hotel Planície, Rua Miguel Bombarda 40 (☎066/240 26). An old villa recently modernised by the *Best Western* hotel group, and featuring a good restaurant. ⑤.

Pensão Policarpo, Rua da Freira de Baixo 16 (☎066/224 24). Nice location, in a side-street near the Sé. Comfortable, medium-priced rooms, in a converted sixteenth-century townhouse; most rooms have bathrooms, though there are a few cheaper ones without. ③–④.

Pousada dos Lóios, Largo do Conde de Vila Flor (☎066/240 51). One of the country's loveliest *pousadas*, housed in the old monastery (see below). ⑦.

Pensão Riviera, Rua 5º de Outubro 49 (☎066/233 04). A reasonable if unexciting pension between the Sé and Praça do Giraldo. ⑤.

The City

Évora was shaped by its **Roman** and **Moorish** occupations: the former is commemorated by a temple, the latter by a characteristic tangle of alleys, rising steeply among the whitewashed houses. Most of the city's other monuments, however, date from the fourteenth to the sixteenth centuries, when Évora prospered under the patronage of the ruling **House of Avis**. To them are owed the

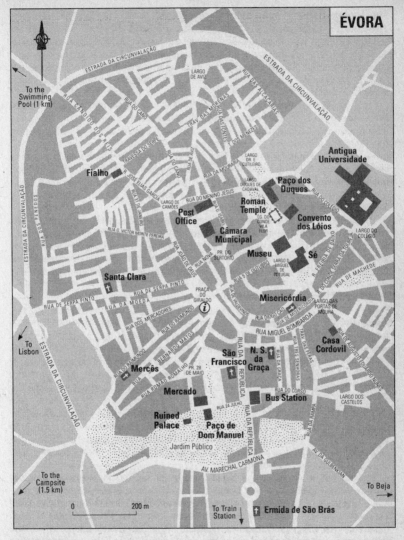

ÉVORA

To the Swimming Pool (1 km)

Fialho

Antigua Universidade

Paço dos Duques

Roman Temple

Post Office

Câmara Municipal

Convento dos Lóios

Museu

Sé

Santa Clara

Misericórdia

To Lisbon

Casa Cordovil

São Francisco

N. S. da Graça

Mercês

Mercado

Bus Station

Ruined Palace

Paço de Dom Manuel

Jardim Público

To the Campsite (1.5 km)

To Beja

0   200 m

To Train Station

Ermida de São Brás

many noble palaces scattered about the city; as are the Jesuit **university**, founded in 1559 by Cardinal Henrique, the future "Cardinal King"; and the wonderful array of Manueline and Renaissance buildings.

That the city's monuments have survived intact was due, in large part, to Évora's decline after the Spanish usurpation of the throne in 1580. Future Portuguese monarchs chose to live nearer Lisbon, and the university was closed down; for the next four hundred years, Évora drifted back into a rural existence as a provincial market centre. Even today, the 40,000-strong population is only half its medieval number.

The Templo Romano and Convento dos Loios

The **Templo Romano** stands at the very heart of the old city. Dating from the second century AD, it is the best-preserved temple in Portugal, despite (or perhaps because of) its use as a slaughterhouse until 1870. The stark remains consist of a small platform supporting more than a dozen granite columns with Corinthian capitals and a marble entablature. Its popular attribution to Diana is apparently fanciful.

Directly opposite the temple, the magnificent fifteenth-century **Convento dos Lóios** has been converted into a top-grade *pousada*. Its cloisters now serve as a dining area in summer, and the hotel staff can be sniffy about allowing in non-residents (or non-diners) to look around. However, dress up as formally as you can – a tie is a help for men – and walk in regardless. The dual horseshoe arches, slender twisted columns and the intricate carvings on the doorway to the chapter house, midway around the cloister, are fine examples of the so-called Luso-Moorish style and have been attributed to Francisco de Arruda, architect of the aqueduct in Évora and the Belém tower in Lisbon.

To the left of the *pousada* lies the former conventual church, dedicated to **São João Evangelista**. This is still the private property of the ducal Cadaval family, who occupy a wing or two of their adjacent ancestral palace. Ring the bell and you should be admitted (100$00) to see the *azulejos* within, the masterpiece of one António Oliveira Bernardes and created early in the eighteenth century.

The Sé and Museu Municipal

Évora's cathedral, the **Sé** (daily 9am–12.30pm & 2–5pm), was begun in 1186, about twenty years after the reconquest of Évora from the Moors. The Romanesque solidity of its original battlemented towers and roofline contrasts sharply with the pointed Gothic arches of subsequent and less militaristic additions, like the porch and central window. The interior is more straightforwardly Gothic, although the choir and high altar were remodelled in the eighteenth century by the German, Friedrich Ludwig, architect of the Convent at Mafra. For a nominal fee you can clamber onto a terrace above the west entrance and take an unusually close look at the towers and the *zimbório* (the lantern above the crossing of the transepts). Don't miss the cathedral **museum** (daily except Mon 9–11.45am & 2–4.45pm; 150$00), either: it's stuffed with treasures and relics, the prize exhibit being a carved statue of the Madonna whose midriff opens out to display layered scenes from the Bible.

Immediately adjacent to the Sé is the former archbishop's palace, now the **Museu Municipal** (Tues–Sun 10am–12.30pm & 2–5pm; 200$00), housing important collections of fifteenth- and sixteenth-century Flemish and Portuguese paintings assembled from the city's churches and convents. These provide a good illustration of the significance of Flemish artists in the development of the "Portuguese School", and reflect the strong medieval trade links between the two countries. Frei Carlos, probably the most important Flemish artist known to have worked in Évora, is well represented, but the centrepiece of the museum is a series of thirteen panels by an anonymous fifteenth-century Flemish artist, portraying scenes from the Life of the Virgin. This was once the cathedral altarpiece.

Up behind the museum, a quick stroll to the north will take you to the beautiful entrance courtyard of the **Antiga Universidade** – one of the liveliest corners of the city.

The rest of the city

As well as artists, great Portuguese and European architects also gravitated to Évora, and the **Ermida de São Brás**, just outside the city walls on the road to the train station, has been identified as an early work by Diogo de Boitaca, pioneer of the flamboyant Manueline style. Its tubular dunce-capped buttresses and crenellated roofline bear scant resemblance to his masterpieces at Lisbon and Setúbal, but they certainly foreshadow the style's uninhibited originality.

No less bizarre is the mid-sixteenth-century facade of the **Igreja da Graça**, out behind the bus station. At each of the corners of its Renaissance pediment, grotesque Atlas-giants support two globes – the emblem of Dom Manuel and his burgeoning overseas empire.

Close by here is perhaps the most memorable monument in Évora – the **Capela dos Ossos** ("Chapel of Bones") in the church of **São Francisco** (Mon–Sat 8.30am–1pm & 2.30–6pm; Sun 10am–1pm & 2.30–6pm, winter closes at 5.30pm; 50$00, plus another $50 for taking photos). A timeless and gruesome memorial to the mortality of man, the walls and pillars of this chilling chamber are entirely covered in the bones of more than 5000 monks. There's a grim humour in the neat, artfully planned arrangement of skulls and tibias around the vaults, and in the rhyming inscription over the door which reads "*Nós ossos que aqui estamos, Pelos vossos esperamos*" ("We bones here are waiting for your bones"). Such macabre warnings to the faithless can be encountered in a couple of other locations in Portugal – at Campo Maior, to the north of Évora, and at Faro in the Algarve.

Another interesting feature of this fifteenth-century church is its large **porch**, which combines pointed, rounded, and horseshoe arches in a manner typical of Manueline architecture. Appropriately enough, the restored **Palácio de Dom Manuel** – the king who gave his name to the style – lies no more than a minute's walk away, in the Jardim Público. Early sixteenth-century, it too incorporates inventive horseshoe arches with strange serrated edges.

Directly opposite São Francisco, on Praça 1° de Maio, the rich craft traditions of the Évora district are well displayed in the **Museu do Artesanato Regional** (daily 10am–noon & 2–5pm). The collections include pottery, weaving, tapestry and carvings in wood cork and bone; modern pieces are on sale, too.

Lastly, it's worth following **Rua do Cano**, north of the old centre, behind the Câmara Municipal. Here, you can travel the course of the medieval **Aqueduto**, into whose arches a row of houses has been incorporated.

Eating and drinking

Évora goes to bed pretty early, as if exhausted by the attentions of the tour-groups. Finding a place to eat, however, is no problem, with a range of decent **restaurants**, to suit most budgets, located around the centre; some of the best are picked out below. There's also a large **market** on the second Thursday of every month in Rossio São Brás. For a late-evening **drink**, in summer you'll find a couple of outdoor cafés in Praça do Giraldo; there's the very pleasant *Gelateria Zoka* at Rua Miguel Bombarda 10; and an occasional event at the university.

Restaurante A Choupana, Rua dos Mercadores 20. Best of a trio of modest-priced restaurants in this central old city street, for standard Portuguese food.

Restaurante Cozinha Alentejana, Rua 5 de Outubro 51. Just off Praça do Giraldo, on the way to the cathedral. Reliable regional cooking. Closed Wed.

Restaurante Cozinha de Santo Humberto, Rua da Moeda 39. Highly recommended by locals, this is on a street which runs downhill from Praça do Giraldo; there's only a small sign. Downstairs, in a converted cellar, you can eat from a fine menu of local dishes for around 4000$00 a head.

Restaurante Fialho, Trav. do Mascarenhas 14. Off Rua Cândido dos Reis, this is reckoned by some to be one of the ten best restaurants in Portugal. Starters, particularly, are superb; prices are high.

Restaurante Guerreiro, Trav. Afonso Trigo 19. At the far end of Rua Cândido dos Reis – spotless and packed with locals, this offers very tasty and inexpensive Portuguese meals.

Liza's Pizza Place, Patio do Salema. Once the stables of a town house, dishes from an extensive menu – and not just excellent pizzas – are served up in a brick-walled, vaulted-ceilinged interior. It's not easy to find; look for *Jovem*, a sort of youth club.

O Portão, Rua do Cano. Popular student haunt for good, inexpensive food, one of several on this street alongside the aqueduct.

Pousada dos Lóios, Largo Conde de Vila Flor. Elegant, upmarket, classic Portuguese dining in the monastery's cloisters. Expect to pay a fortune.

Around Évora

The administrative district of Évora contains over a dozen **megalithic sites** dating from around 3000 BC. The dolmens, standing stones and stone circles found here have their origins in a culture which flourished in the peninsula before spreading north as far as Brittany and Denmark. Two of the most accessible sites lie to the west and northwest of Évora, which makes them possible visits in conjunction with the carpet town of **Arraiolos**. For descriptions of – and directions to – sites other than the couple covered below, ask at the Turismo in Évora for the *Guide to the Megalithic Monuments of the Évora Region* (1000$00). An additional attraction in the district, en route to Estremoz from Évora, is **Évora-Monte**, with its superb Renaissance castle.

Os Almendres

One of the sites nearest to Évora is the **stone circle** and three-metre-high **menhir** (upright stone) at a cork plantation called **OS ALMENDRES**, west of the city, about 3km out of Guadalupe, just south of the N114 Évora–Montemor road. Ask for directions in the village; it's a stiff uphill walk through wild country. Those interested in unusual birds will have the additional pleasure of seeing the **hoopoes** of the area. Back on the N114, you can cut north across country to Arraiolos on the minor N370 road, a journey of around 25km.

Arraiolos

ARRAIOLOS, 22km north of Évora (and connected by bus twice a day), has been famed since the seventeenth century for its superb carpets, and the craft has survived and prospered into modern times. Nowadays the designs tend to be simple and brightly-coloured but the originals were based on elaborate Persian imports. Some of the workshops' most luxuriant eighteenth-century creations can be seen hanging on the walls of Queluz palace, near Lisbon (p.96).

Apart from the carpet shops – where the carpets are expensive, but a lot less so than elsewhere – Arraiolos is a typical Alentejo village with its ruined castle, whitewashed houses and seventeenth-century pillory. While you're here you might as well visit the *Quinta dos Loios* **carpet workshop** in Ilhas, just to the east of Arraiolos on the N370; it has an outlet in Évora itself, *Castelo das Ilhas*, at Rua 5 de Outubro 66, between Praça do Giraldo and the Sé.

Pavia

In the hamlet of **PAVIA**, 20km north of Arraiolos along the N370, is a massive **dolmen**, within which the tiny sixteenth-century chapel of São Dinis was built. The effect is a bit grotesque and out of keeping with Pavia's traditional Alentejan architecture, but impressive nonetheless.

Évora-Monte

Twenty-nine kilometres northeast of Évora, along the N18, the sixteenth-century **castle** at **ÉVORA-MONTE** stands on fortifications going back to Roman times and occupies a spectacular position, atop a steep mound. Its keep is constructed in Italian Renaissance style, with four robust round towers, and is adorned with a simple rope-like relief of Manueline stonework. Within are three vaulted chambers, each displaying intricately carved granite capitals. The town – predominantly medieval in appearance – rings the castle mound.

Estremoz and the marble towns

Northeast of Évora, quarry trucks and tracks announce your entry into marble country. Around **Estremoz**, 46km from Évora, the area is so rich in marble that it replaces brick or concrete as a building material, giving butchers' stalls and simple cottages the sort of luxurious finish you generally see only in churches and the grandest houses. Estremoz itself, and **Borba** and **Vila Viçosa**, are all distinctive marble towns, and the latter has an additional attraction in its ducal palace – the last residence of the Portuguese monarchy.

Estremoz

ESTREMOZ is the largest and liveliest of the three marble towns, and comes into its own every Saturday when the **market** takes over the Rossio, the main square of the **lower town**. This is a classic marketplace of huge dimensions, surrounded by bars, restaurants and churches, and selling – among other things – what are renowned as some of the best cheeses in Portugal, mainly made from ewes' and goats' milk. For centuries Estremoz has also been famous for the manufacture of earthenware jars, the shapes and styles of which have remained basically unchanged since Roman times. You'll see these on sale in the market, too: the most distinctive products are the porous water coolers known as *moringues*, globe-shaped jars with narrow bases, two short spouts, and one handle.

Arriving by bus, you'll be dropped at the Rossio, next to the twin-towered marble facade of the eighteenth-century **Câmara Municipal**. Originally this was one of three convents on the square and is worth a look inside for the grand staircase, decorated with late seventeenth-century *azulejos*. At no.62 on the Rossio, a **Museu Rural** (Tues–Sun 10am–noon & 3–6pm) features a display of earthenware figurines from the town potteries, and has an illuminating ethnographic collection of locally produced artefacts in clay, wood, rush, straw, cork, textile and metal. Nearby, at Rua de Serpa Pinto 87, is a **Museu Agricultura** (Tues–Sun

10am–noon & 2–6pm) with a surprisingly fascinating display of old kitchen equipment.

In its heyday the population of Estremoz was ten times its current size and the town was once one of the most strongly fortified in the country. An army garrison is still stationed here, and the inner star-shaped **ramparts** of the **upper town** are well preserved. On the hill within these fortifications stands a white, prison-like building, easily visible from the Rossio; despite its external austerity, it was once a palace of Dom Dinis, the king famous for his administrative, economic and military reforms. It is now a *pousada*, but you're free to wander in and look around; there's a splendid panoramic view from the tower.

Beyond loom the deep-cut battlements of the thirteenth-century keep, the **Torre de Menagem** – which bears a close resemblance to the great tower of Beja, its exact contemporary. From this part of town the castle of Évora-Monte is clearly visible on the horizon, 30km to the southwest. Opposite the tower, in an old almshouse, is a small **Museu Municipal** (Tues–Sun 10am–noon & 2–6pm), with more displays of Estremoz pottery and Alentejan life.

Practicalities

An enthusiastically-staffed **Turismo** (daily 10am–1pm & 3–7pm; ☎068/227 83) is to be found in a kiosk at the southwestern corner of the Rossio. Unless you're stopping over on Friday night, before the market, **accommodation** should be easy enough to find. Options include the good *Casa Miguel José*, a characterful private house at Travessa da Levada 8 (☎068/223 26; ②); the rooms above the *Café Alentejano*, Rossio 15 (☎068/228 34; ②); *Residencial Mateus*, in the old quarter, at Rua do Almeida 39–41 (☎068/22 22 62; ②); and *Residencial Carvalho*, at Largo da República 27 (☎068/227 12; ②). The *Pousada da Rainha Santa Isabel*, in the upper town (☎068/226 18; ⑦), is one of the grandest Portuguese *pousadas*, with a regal feel to the rooms and stairway.

There's no shortage of **restaurants** in town either. On a budget, the best deal is the tiny, nameless place at Rua Dr. Gomes de Resende Junior 15, on the way to the upper town. Other good alternatives range from the *Residencial Mateus*, which does a wonderful *ensopado de borrego* – the local lamb stew speciality – to the rather pricier *Restaurante Zé Varunca* on Avenida Tomás Alcaide. *Restaurante Aguias d'Ouro*, on the Rossio at no.27, is a little pretentious, with deferential waiters, but the food is good and there's a 2000$00 *ementa turística*. For a real treat, the *pousada*'s restaurant has all you could ask for in atmosphere and cooking, though you're looking at around 4000$00 per head, possibly more.

Borba

Eleven kilometres east of Estremoz is **BORBA**, a dazzlingly white little place, where just about anything not whitewashed is made of white marble. The town seems not to have exploited the wider commercial possibilities of its quarries, though, and with the exception of a fine eighteenth-century fountain there are no particular signs of wealth, no extravagant mansions or remarkable churches. All this only serves to make more extraordinary the extensive use of marble in even the most commonplace cottages, shops and streets. Borba is simply an unassuming town which happens to be built of marble. The town's other main attribute is the **wine** of the local cooperative, which is marketed throughout Portugal. **Rooms** are available at the *Restaurante Lisboeta* at Rua de Mateus Pais 31.

Vila Viçosa

The road from Borba to **VILA VIÇOSA**, 6km to the southeast, is lined on either side with enormous marble quarries, and in town everything from the pavements to the toilets in the bus station are made of the local marble. The town is justly famous, too, for its Paço-Ducal, the last palace-residence of the **Bragança dynasty**. The dukes of Bragança were descended from the illegitimate offspring of João I of Avis, and established their seat here in the fifteenth century. For the next two centuries they were on the edge of the Portuguese ruling circle but their claims to the throne were overridden in 1580 by Philip II of Spain. Sixty years later, while Spanish attention was diverted by a revolt in Catalonia, Portuguese resentment erupted and massive public pressure forced the reluctant João, eighth Duke of Bragança, to seize the throne; his descendants ruled Portugal until the foundation of the Republic in 1910.

The Paço Ducal

Despite a choice of sumptuous palaces throughout Portugal – Mafra, Sintra and Queluz are the most renowned – the Bragança kings retained a special affection for their residence at Vila Viçosa, a relatively ordinary country home, constructed in various stages during the sixteenth and seventeenth centuries. Dom Carlos spent his last night here before his assassination on the riverfront in Lisbon in 1908, and it was a favourite haven of his successor, Manuel II, the last king of Portugal.

The **Paço Ducal** (Tues–Sun 9am–1pm & 2–6pm; 1-hr guided tour; 600$00) has a simple, rhythmic facade. Inside, the standard regal trappings of the more formal chambers are tedious, but the private apartments and mementos of Dom Carlos and his wife Marie-Amélia have a *Hello* magazine fascination. Faded family photographs hang on the walls, changes of clothing are laid out, and the table is set for dinner: the whole scene seems to await the royals' return. In reality, Dom Duarte, present heir to the nonexistent throne, spends his days in experimental eco-farming at his estate near Viseu.

The old town and castle

The **old town**, still enclosed within walls on its hilltop site, was built by Dom Dinis at the end of the thirteenth century and reinforced four centuries later. Originally the population of Vila Viçosa was based within these walls and a few of the cottages are still lived in. The **Castelo** (Tues–Sun 9am–1pm & 2–6pm; 45-min guided tour; 150$00), in one corner of the town, was the seat of the Braganças before the construction of their palace. Its interior has been renovated beyond recognition and houses an indifferent archaeological museum. However, from the roof there's a good view of the Braganças' old **Tapada Real** (Royal Hunting Ground), set within its eighteen-kilometre circuit of walls.

Practicalities

Buses park at the elongated Praça da República, from where the old town is straight ahead of you, and the Paço Ducal beyond. Vila Viçosa is a quiet town and despite its attractions there's very little available **accommodation**. Your best bet is to arrange **private rooms** through the **Turismo** (☎068/983 05) by the town hall on Praça da República. Try those with José da Silva at Praça da República 27 (②) and Maria da Conceição Paixão at Rua Dr. Couto Jardim 7 (☎068/981 69; ②), just off the square. Alternatively, there's an upmarket *Turihab* lodging in an eight-eenth-century manor house, the *Casa dos Arcos*, at Praça Martim Afonso de Sousa 16 (☎068/985 18; ⑤). When all is said and done, probably the simplest bet is to make a daytrip from Évora or Estremoz. Best of the town's **restaurants** is the *Framar* at Praça da República 35.

South to Monsaraz

The road **south from Vila Viçosa** provides great insights into the rural nature of the Alentejo, taking you past Alandroal and Terena, both quite prosperous villages, set below a castle, before entering a region of scattered farming commu-nities. A couple of buses cover the route daily, with numerous diversions along crumbling backroads.

Reguengos de Monsaraz

One of the better targets is the town of **REGUENGOS DE MONSARAZ** (which is also connected by the dull N256 with Évora, to its west). It's known for its fine local *Terras del Rei* white and red wines, and you can visit the *adega* just outside town where the wine is bottled: officially you need written permission, but if you just turn up you may find someone willing to take you around.

From Reguengos, there are six daily buses 17km further east to the dramatic fortified village of Monsaraz. Given this, it's unlikely you'd get stranded in Reguengos, but it's not a bad place to spend the night in any case. There are **rooms** at *Pensão Gato* (③) on the main Praça da Liberdade, and at the cheaper *Pensão Filhão* (②), next door. A better bet might be the rooms (②) advertised in the beautiful old house on Praça de Santa Antónia. Good-value **restaurants** include the *Café Central* on Praça da Liberdade, and *A Grelha*, on Rua do Covalinho, to the left of the church. The best place to sample the local wine is at the unnamed **bar** opposite the market (up the road by the cinema); it's filled with huge barrels, from which the barman dispenses 15$00 glasses of wine.

Monsaraz

MONSARAZ – known to the locals as "Ninho das Águias" (Eagles' Nest) –stands perched high above the border plains, a tiny village, fortified to the hilt and entirely contained within its walls. From its heights, the landscape of the Alentejo takes on a magical quality, with absolutely nothing stirring amid a sensational panorama of sun-baked fields, neatly cultivated and dotted with cork and olive trees. To the east, you can make out the Rio Guadiana, delineating the frontier with Spain.

There's something peculiarly satisfying, too, about such a small village. From the clocktower of the main gateway, the only real street leads past a bar (unmarked, on the left, next to the post office) to the village square. Here you'll find an unusual eighteenth-century pillory topped by a sphere of the universe.

The **Torre de Menagem** stands at the far end of the village, part of a chain of frontier fortresses continued to the south at Mourão, Moura and Serpa, and to the north at Alandroal, Elvas and Campo Maior. When the Moors were ejected in

1167 the village was handed over to the Knights Templar, and later to their successors, the Order of Christ; their fort has now been converted into a bullring.

Practicalities

Rooms are offered along the main street at *Dona Antonia* (☎066/551 42; ③), *Condastavel* (☎066/551 81; ③), and *Dom Nuno* (☎066/551 46; ④). All these places include breakfast in the price and fill quickly in summer; out of season you can probably negotiate a reduction in the room rate. There's also a rather fancy **hotel**, the *Estalagem de Monsaraz*, with a pool and restaurant, at Largo São Bartolomeu 6 (☎066/551 12; ⑤), in the settlement below the castle walls. The *Lumumba*, opposite *Dona Antonia*'s, is the most reasonably priced **restaurant**, with a nice patio and good views; more upmarket options are the attractive, balconied *Casa do Forno*, on a side road between the lower and main roads, and the *Alcaide*, along the lower road.

Buses to Reguengos leave five times daily; to Évora, the once-daily service currently leaves at 5.25pm.

Menhirs around Monsaraz

There are two giant *menhirs* close by Monsaraz, just off the Reguengos road: at **OUTEIRO**, and at **BULHOA**, where the stone is covered with symbolic engravings. A further *menhir* is to be found between Monsaraz and the Guadiana river, at **MONTE DO XAREZ**. This one is four metres high, surrounded by a square of standing stones, and was probably the site of neolithic fertility rites.

Elvas

The hilltop town of **ELVAS**, 40km east of Estremoz, was long one of Portugal's mightiest frontier posts, a response to the Spanish stronghold of Badajoz, just 15km to the east across the Rio Guadiana. Its star-shaped walls and trio of forts are among the most complex and best-preserved military fortifications surviving in Europe. If you make a special detour to see just one Alentejo castle, Elvas is the natural choice; in addition, the town itself is a delight – all steep cobbled streets and mansions.

Elvas was recaptured from the Moors in 1230 and withstood periodic attacks from Spain through much of the following three centuries. It succumbed just once, however, to Spanish conquest, when the garrison was betrayed by Spanish bribery in 1580, allowing Philip II to enter and, for a period the following year, establish his court. The town subsequently made amends, during the war over the succession of Philip IV to the Portuguese territories. In 1644, the garrison resisted a nine-day siege by Spanish troops, and in 1658, with its numbers reduced by an epidemic to a mere thousand, saw off a 15,000-strong Spanish army.

During this period, the fortifications underwent intensive rebuilding and expansion, and they were later pressed into service twice more: in 1801, when the town withstood a Spanish siege during the War of the Oranges, and ten years later, during the Peninsular War, when the fort provided the base from which Wellington advanced to launch his bloody but successful assault on Badajoz. Perhaps out of tradition as much as anything, a military garrison is still stationed in the town.

The Town

Any exploration of Elvas has to start with its **fortifications**. The earliest stretches of the walls date from the thirteenth century, but most of what you see today is a result of the Wars of Succession with Spain in the seventeenth century. Under the direction of the great French military engineer, Vauban, the old circuit of walls was supplemented by extensive moats and star-shaped ramparts, their bastions jutting out at irregular but carefully judged intervals to maximise the effects of artillery crossfire. Echoes of these designs are to be seen at Estremoz and throughout Portugal. Further chains in the fortifications were provided by the **Forte da Graça**, a couple of kilometres north of Elvas, and the superb star-shaped **Forte de Santa Luzia**, a few minutes' walk to the south of the town. The Turismo (see below) will organise a free guided tour of the interior of Forte de Graça for you, provided you inform them a day in advance; you can only see Santa Luzia from the outside.

The Aqueduto Amoreira

With its jagged and ungainly course, the **Aqueduto Amoreira**, at the entrance to the town, looks at first like a bizarre extension of the fortifications. Despite its stark and awkward appearance, it is an imaginative and original feat of engineering: monstrous piles of masonry, distinctive cylindrical buttresses, and up to five tiers of arches support a tiny water channel along its seven-kilometre course, until it is finally discharged at the fountain in Largo da Misericórdia. It was built between 1498 and 1622 to the Manueline designs of Francisco de Arruda.

The town centre

Arruda was also responsible for the **Igreja de Nossa Senhora da Assunção**, dominating Praça da República, which was the cathedral until Elvas lost episcopal status in 1882. Alterations in the seventeenth and eighteenth centuries left a ragged hodge-podge of styles, but its original Manueline inspiration remains evident on the south portal and in the unusual conical dome above the belfry.

Behind the church lies **Largo de Santa Clara**, a tiny cobbled square built on a slope around a splendid sixteenth-century **pelourinho**. Criminals were chained from the four metal hooks toward the top but, aside from the grisly technicalities, it's also a work of art, with a typically Manueline twisted column, and rope-like decorations. Directly opposite stands the strange and beautiful church of **Nossa Senhora da Consolação** (Tues–Sun 9am–12.30pm & 2.30–6pm). From the outside it's nothing more than a whitewashed wall with a mediocre Renaissance porch, but the interior reveals a sumptuous octagonal chapel: richly painted columns support a central cupola and virtually all the surfaces are decorated with magnificent seventeenth-century *azulejos*. The chapel was built between 1543 and 1557, on the site of a Knights Templar chapel – providing the insipiration for its octagonal design.

Largo de Santa Clara tapers upwards to a restored tenth-century archway flanked by fortified towers and surmounted by a **loggia**, or gallery. Originally part of the old town walls, this was built by the Moors, who occupied Elvas from the early eighth century until 1226. The street beneath the gateway leads to the **Castelo** (daily except Thurs 9.30am–12.30pm & 2.30–7pm; winter closes at 5pm), also constructed by the Moors, on an old Roman fortified site, but strengthened by Dom Dinis and João II in the late-fifteenth century.

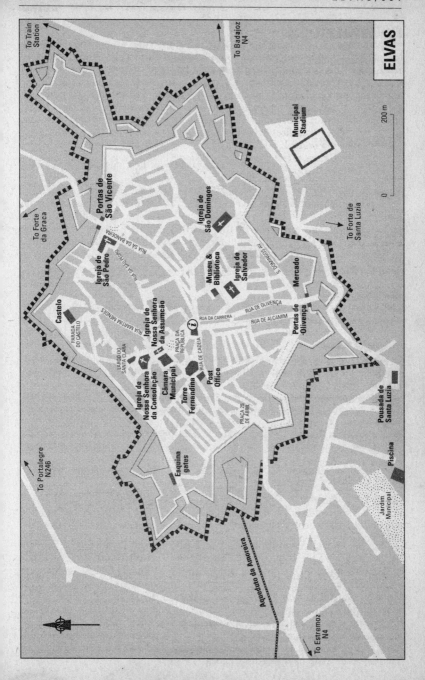

ELVAS

To Train Station

To Forte da Graca

Portas de São Vicente

Igreja de São Pedro

RUA SÃ DA BANDEIRA

RUA DA ALCÁÇOVA

Castelo

PARADA DO CASTELO

Igreja de Nossa Senhora da Consolação

JARDIM DE SANTA CLARA

RUA MARTIM MENDES

Igreja de Nossa Senhora da Assunção

Câmara Municipal

Torre Fernandina

PRAÇA DA REPÚBLICA

RUA DE CADEIA

Post Office

PRAÇA 25 DE ABRIL

To Portalegre N246

Esquina gates

RUA DA CARRIERA

Museu & Biblioteca

Igreja de São Domingos

Igreja de Salvador

AV. DOMINGOS S.

RUA DE OLIVENÇA

RUA DE ALCAMIM

Mercado

Portas de Olivença

To Badajoz N4

Municipal Stadium

To Forte de Santa Luzia

Pousada de Santa Luzia

Piscina

Jardim Municipal

Aqueduto da Amoreira

To Estramoz N4

N

0   200 m

The market and festival

Elvas' weekly event is its **Monday market** – a vibrantly chaotic affair attracting people from miles around, held just outside town behind the aqueduct. Otherwise, the town's big annual bash is its **Festa de São Mateus**, which lasts for a week in late-September and encompasses a programme of agricultural, cultural and religious events. It's well worth coinciding with, although accommodation is at a premium at this time.

Practicalities

The walls make Elvas a pretty easy place to get your bearings. Arriving by **bus**, you'll find yourself right in the centre of town, in Praça da República; the **Turismo** (Mon–Fri 9am–7pm, Sat & Sun 9am–12.30pm & 2–5.30pm; ☎068/62 22 36) is next door. Shuttle buses also run to Praça da República from the local **train station**, 4km down the Campo Maior road at Fontaínhas; the station is on the Lisbon–Badajoz line. **Crossing to the Spanish city of Badajoz**, 15km to the east, is in fact easiest by train, with three daily services taking 15 minutes. Buses to Badajoz leave from Praça da República four times daily, but take at least an hour and you'll have to change to a Spanish bus at the border.

Accommodation

The Turismo can help with **private rooms**, which you may need, given the dearth of decent pensions and hotels within the town. If you want to try on your own, there are currently *quartos* offered with Joaquim Dias, at Rua João d'Olivença 5 (☎068/634 22; ③), and Maria Garcia, Rua Aires Vareza 5 (☎069/62 21 26; ②). Regular **pensions and hotels** include the few places listed below. There is also a **campsite**, on the outskirts of town on the N4 to Estremoz: *Piedade* (☎068/62 37 72; May–Sept).

Casa de Hóspedes Arco do Bispo, Rua Sineiro 4 (☎068/62 34 22). The cheapest guesthouse in town: from Praça da República, turn right down the hill and head past the police station. ①.

Estalagem Dom Sancho II, Praça da República 20 (☎068/62 26 86). The best bet for a hotel in the centre, this characterful hotel in the main square has a fine restaurant downstairs. ④.

Residencial Luso-Espanhola, Rui de Melo (☎068/62 30 92). Comfortable but rather overpriced pension, 2km from town. ④.

Pousada de Santa Luzia, Avda. de Badajoz (☎068/62 21 94). One of the country's more missable *pousadas* – a modern building, outside the town walls, 1.5km from town. ⑤.

Eating

Best of the budget **restaurants** is the invariably packed *Canal Sete* at Rua dos Sapateiros 16, off the main square, opposite the Turismo. More expensive, but with good reputations for cooking, are *O Alentejo* on Rua da Cadeia, *O Aqueduto* on Avenida da Piedade, and the restaurant at the *Estalagem Dom Sancho II* on Praça da República. *Restaurant Flor do Jardim*, in the Jardim Municpal, is also recommended. The *Centro Artístico Elevense*, on Praça da República, next to the bus station, has an attached café-restaurant, with outdoor tables – the *arroz de marisco* here is particularly good. If you want to put your own picnic together, the place to buy supplies is a small, early-morning food **market** held Monday to Saturday at the bottom of Rua dos Chilões.

Campo Maior

The road to the fortress town of **CAMPO MAIOR**, 18km north of Elvas, passes through olive groves and sunflower fields. It's a pleasant enough trip, though the town itself would be unremarkable were it not for the presence of its **Capela dos Ossos** (daily 9am–1pm & 3–7pm), a diminutive version of the Chapel of Bones in Évora. This stands immediately to the right of the large parish church just off Rua 1° de Maio: ask for the key in the church or try the door next to the chapel. Adding to the surreal effect, the entrance is through a neat local government office.

The walls and vaults in the claustrophobic chapel interior are completely covered in human bones, while two skeletons hang from the walls, and three rows of skulls are positioned on the window ledge to inspect passers-by. The chapel is dated 1766 and its purpose is indicated by two verses from the Book of Job traced out in collarbones near the window: "My bone cleaveth to my skin and to my flesh, and I am escaped with the skin of my teeth". Job is complaining of his horrific physical and mental suffering, but takes solace in the knowledge that "though after my skin worms destroy this body, yet in my flesh shall I see God".

The chapel may have been "furnished" following the disaster which devastated Campo Maior in 1732, when a powder magazine in the town's castle was struck by lightning, killing 1500 people and destroying 823 houses. Today the castle is little more than a ruin, though with fine views over the borderlands.

The only other conceivable reason to come to Campo Maior would be for the **festival** in the first week of September, when the narrow, sloping streets are decked with incredibly ornate paper streamers and flowers.

Practicalities

The **bus** journey from Elvas takes just 35 minutes, making it an easy side-trip. There's a **Turismo** in the Câmera Municpal, which may or may not be open depending on whether the renovations are complete. If you wanted **to stay**, *Pensão-Restaurante Francisco Carlos*, at Largo Barão Barcelinhos 5, off Rua 1° de Maio (☎068/68 73 21; ②), is the top choice: owned by a famous fado singer, it's decorated with pictures of the great man, while meals there are often accompanied by some of Francisco's finest renditions. Otherwise, *A Tentadora*, on Rua 1° de Maio itself (☎068/68 62 81; ①), is a simple pension, while *O Ministro*, Travessa da Praça 1 (☎068/68 78 69; ②), is twinned with a restaurant at Rua 13 de Dezembro 41; both places are off Praça da República. In addition, there's another pleasant **restaurant**, *O Faisão*, opposite the parish church.

Portalegre

PORTALEGRE is the capital, market centre and transport hub of the northern district of Alto Alentejo. It is an attractive town, crouched at the foot of the Serra de São Mamede, and endowed with the province's usual contingent of white-washed and walled old quarters, along with some interesting reminders of its industrial history. These include a cork factory, whose great twin chimneys greet you on the way into town, and a tapestry workshop, the last remnant of a thriving period of textile production in the seventeenth and eighteenth centuries. The wealth produced in these years, in particular from silk workshops, has a further legacy in a collection of grand mercantile mansions and townhouses, which give the town an air of faded affluence.

The Town

The town's boom years in the seventeenth century are immediately apparent as you walk up Rua 19 de Junho – the main thoroughfare of the old town – which is lined by a spectacular concentration of late-Renaissance and Baroque mansions. At the southern end of the street, and dominating the quarter, is the **Sé**, an austere building save for a flash of fancy in the pyramidal pinnacles of its towers. To one side of this an eighteenth-century palace houses the **Museu Municipal** (daily except Tues 9.30am–12.30pm & 2–6pm; one-hour tour; 100$00). It's not exactly a compelling visit, with much routine furniture and fittings on display, though there are some lovely ceramics and ivories.

The most interesting visit in town is to the **Fábrica Real de Tapisseria** (Mon–Fri: tours on the half-hour from 9.30–11am & 2.30–4.30pm), the single surviving tapestry factory. It's housed in the new town, in a seventeenth-century former Jesuit training college on Rua Gomes Fernandes, just off the Rossio. The guided tour conducts you through the studios and weaving hall – where 5000 shades of wool are used in the reproduction of centuries-old patterns – and on to a gallery displaying works about to be dispatched to their well-heeled patrons.

Practicalities

All the main roads converge on the **Rossio**, a large square at the centre of the new town. Uphill from here, the Rua 5° de Outubro runs into the walled **old town**. The **bus station** is just a few blocks from the Rossio on Rua Nuno Álvarez Pereira. Shuttle buses to and from here meet **trains** at the Estação de Portalegre, 12km out of town to the south, on the Lisbon–Badajoz line. **Information** is available from an unmarked office in the Galerie Municipal; follow the signs from the Rossio.

Accommodation

There is limited **accommodation** available, and it's advisable to book a day ahead to be sure of a bed. The longstanding budget option is the **youth hostel** (*Pousada de Juventude: Antigo Convento de São Francisco*), on Praça da República (☎045/235 68), housed in a converted Franciscan monastery near the cork factory; reception open 8–10am and 6–11pm. It's in a fairly poor state these days, though, and there's talk of closing it down. **Camping** is quite an attractive alternative. The *Orbitur* site (☎045/228 48; open mid-Jan to mid-Nov) at Quinta da Saúde, 3km into the hills, on the N246-2, is well equipped, with electricity, showers, a few bungalows for rent and a surprisingly good restaurant.

Pensão Alto Alentejo, Rua 19º de Junho 59–63 (☎045/222 90). Comfortable pension in the old town, near the Sé, with reasonably priced rooms with private bath, and heating in winter. ②–③.

Hotel Dom João III, Avda. Dom João III (☎045/211 92). A dull, functional hotel, opposite the Jardim Municipal in the new town. ⑤.

Residencial O Facha, Largo António José Lourinho 3–5 (☎045/231 61). Facing a little square, off the Rossio, this modern place has decent facilities, including a restaurant. It's on the road leading up from the Rossio to the old town. ③.

Pensão Nova, Rua 31º de Janeiro 28–30 (☎045/216 05). Rundown pension, with the same management as the nearby *Pensão São Pedro*, at Rua da Mouraria 14. ④.

Quinta da Fonte Fria, 3km northeast of Portalegre on N359 to Monte Carvalho (☎045/275 75). Attractive *Turihab* property with a great view over the surrounding hills. ④.

Eating and drinking

By day or in the evening, the Rossio is the liveliest place for a drink. There's not much life in the old town, though there is a restaurant or two there worth keeping an eye out for.

Restaurante O Abrigo, Rua de Elvas 74. An inexpensive and reliable choice up in the old town. Closed Tues.

Restaurante O Cortiço, Rua Dom Nuno Alvares Pereira 17. Near the Rossio, the very reasonably priced food here draws nightly crowds of locals; a speciality is the typically Alentejan dish of *migas*. Highly recommended.

Residencial O Facha, Largo António José Lourinho 3–5. There's a good restaurant at this *residencial*, with an *ementa turística* for 1500$00.

Crato, Flôr da Rosa and Alter do Chão

Directly to the west of Portalegre, **Crato** has small-town charms and, nearby, an impressive **dolmen**, as well as the beautiful honey-stone convent of **Flôr da Rosa**. Horse enthusiasts may also want to make the thirteen-kilometre detour south of Crato to **Alter do Chão**, home of a prestigious *coudelaria* (stud farm).

Buses run intermittently from Portalegre to both Crato and Alter do Chão, while the **Estação de Crato** gives access to the Lisbon–Badajoz train line, with connections west to Abrantes and east to Elvas.

Crato

CRATO – 21km west of Portalegre – is an ancient agricultural town which has clearly seen better days and larger populations. A trio of imposing, ornate churches and the elegant **Varanda do Grão Prior** in the main square attest, like Portalegre's monuments, to the textile boom years of the sixteenth century. The *varanda* is the most interesting of the structures – built for the outdoor celebration of mass. Also worth a look is a town mansion a couple of streets away, by the public gardens, which houses a small **museum** (erratic hours) of Alto Alentejo handicrafts and domestic traditions. Well into this century alms were handed out to the local poor from a balcony-chapel upstairs.

The town castle was once among the mightiest in the Alentejo, but today it's a pastoral ruin, overrun by farm animals, fig trees and oregano plants. It is normally locked, but keys are generally kept beneath an abandoned blue cart in the field in front; if they're not there, ask at one of the nearby farm dwellings. From the ramparts, there is a splendid view over the town and across the countless rows of olive trees to the hills of Portalegre.

For a good rural walk from Crato, follow the N363 northwest towards Aldeia da Mata. On the left hand side of the road, about 5km from town, is what is reckoned to be the best-preserved **dolmen** in Portugal. On the corner of the road leading out of town, you'll find an excellent **adega**, with delicious home cooking and a crowded bar where everyone plays *belho* – a kind of miniature version of *boules*.

Practicalities

The town has just one small **pension**, above the *Café Parque* on Avenida Dom Nuno Álvares Pereira (☎045/972 23; ①–②), though the **Turismo** in the Câmera Municipal may be able to fix you up with rooms in private houses. **Campers** can pick their own spots by the old Roman bridge near the train station, or up by the castle.

If you arrive at the **train station**, 3km south of town, the station master will telephone for a taxi, which is not expensive.

Flôr da Rosa

Two kilometres north of Crato lies the village of **FLÔR DA ROSA**, traditionally a centre for **pottery**, with as many as seventy families engaged in the trade in the early part of this century. Today the distinctive *olaria* of the region is made in only two workshops, whose shared kiln is near the convent, high above the broad streets and low houses. Their methods of manufacture haven't changed in centuries, though the clay – yellow for waterproofing, grey for ovenware – has to be sought further and further afield. Purchases break easily, but it's nice to know that these functional (and inexpensive) pieces aren't designed for the tourist trade.

The **Convento de Flôr da Rosa**, founded in the fourteenth century and much endowed over the next two hundred years, was abandoned in 1897, due to leaking roofs and a decaying structure. Over recent years, however, a sizeable injection of state funds has been used to restore the main conventual building, whose church and reception rooms can be visited. Around the main building, you can also make out vestiges of stables and a kitchen, and trace the plan of the gardens, laid out in the insignia of the Order of Malta, in honour of the famous warlord **Nuno Álvares Pereira**, whose family founded the convent.

Father Pereira's tomb (dated 1382) is prominent in the narrow, soaring convent church. Adjoining it, on the ground floor, is the sixteenth-century **Sala do Capítulo**, distinguished by fine brickwork, fan-vaulting and a Gothic cloister. On the first floor are the monks' **dormitories**, whose open casements offer sweeping views across acres of olive trees.

Alter do Chão

ALTER DO CHÂO, 13km to the south of Crato, is another town that did well in the sixteenth-century textile years, as indicated by its attractive Renaissance marble fountain and an array of handsome townhouses. There is a **castle**, too, whose central tower can be climbed for an overview of the region, but the chief reason for a visit is the *Coudelaria de Alter-Real* stud farm, 3km out of town.

The **Coudelaria de Alter-Real** was founded in 1748 by Dom João V of the House of Bragança, and remained in the family until 1910 when the War Office took it over. Today, maintained by the state, it is open for public visits (daily 9am–5pm), though to see the horses in action it's best to arrive in the morning; between 10am and noon you can watch them filing in from the fields to feed, accompanied by the ringing of forty bells.

The tours of the stud are also interesting with a museum display of carriages and horse regalia, through which you are conducted at a stately pace by a retired cavalry officer (tips welcomed). Alter-Real horses have been sought after since the stud's foundation – one is depicted in the equestrian statue of Dom José in

Lisbon's Praça do Comércio, for example – and they remain the favoured breed of the Portuguese mounted police and the Lisbon Riding School at Queluz.

If you can time a visit, April 25 is the best day to be at the *Coudelaria*, when the **annual sale** takes place. The town's main festival – the **Festa de Nossa Senhora da Alegria** – occurs on the following day.

Practicalities

Several **pensions** are clustered in the road opposite the castle in Alter do Chão. Ask for rooms above the *Café Simas* or at the *Pensão Ferreira* (Avda. Dr. João Pestana, ☎045/624 54; ①). Get up before 9.30am if you're interested in seeing the *Coudelaria* coach and horses come in to town to collect the mail.

For **meals**, the *Café Simas* is pretty good, and there are wonderful cakes at the nearby *Pastelaria Ateneia*. **Buses** connect the town with Estremoz and Crato.

Castelo de Vide and Marvão

The upland district **north of Portalegre** is a bucolic landscape, with tree-clad mountain ranges and a series of gorgeous hilltop villages. Among these, the best targets are **Castelo de Vide** and **Marvão**, both with castles, and the former with a spa. Castelo de Vide is the most easily accessible, connected by bus five times daily with Portalegre; Marvão has two daily services, Monday to Friday only. Getting between the two, one morning and one late-afternoon bus from Castelo de Vide to Portalegre connects with buses to Marvão at the main road junction of Portagem.

Castelo de Vide

CASTELO DE VIDE covers the slopes around a fourteenth-century castle, its blindingly white cottages delineated in brilliant contrast to the greenery around. Arriving by bus, you'll be dropped at a pelourinho outside the **Turismo** (Mon–Fri 9am–12.30pm & 2–5.30pm; ☎045/913 61) in the centre of town. From here, half a dozen parallel streets make a sharp climb up to the aptly named **Praça Alta** on the edge of town. The main road, meanwhile, peters out into a narrow path, descending past a tranquil Renaissance fountain to the twisting alleyways of the **Judiaria** – the old Jewish quarter. Amid the cottages, most of which still have Gothic doorways and windows, is a thirteenth-century **synagogue** (daily 9am–7pm), the oldest surviving in Portugal. From the outside it doesn't look very different from the cottages, so you will probably need to ask directions.

On a hill above the Judiaria, the **Castelo** (summer 8am–12.30pm & 2–7pm; winter 9am–12.30pm & 2–5.30pm) squats within the wider fortifications of the original medieval village. While there, chat to the man at the castle door and he'll probably show you the elaborate moving wooden toys that he produces; his neighbour is a lacemaker who trains young women in the art. Samples of both crafts are for sale at a nearby crafts centre, known as *O Ouriço*.

Practicalities

Given its size, the town has a surprising amount of **accommodation**, of which the best-value is the *Pensão Cantinho Particular*, Rua Miguel Bombarda 7 (☎045/911 51; ②) – friendly if a bit on the basic side, though the price includes breakfast. Otherwise, there are better rooms (with bath) at *Pensão Casa do Parque*, Avenida da Aramenha 37 (☎045/912 50; ④), and at the comfortable but soulless *Hotel Sol e Serra*, Estrada de São Vicente (☎045/913 01; ⑤). The **restaurants** at the *Cantinho Particular* and the *Casa do Parque* are both good; for an expensive splurge, try the highly rated *Restaurant Disco Canape*, on the road to Portalegre.

Marvão

Beautiful as Castelo de Vide is, **MARVÃO** surpasses it. The panoramas from its remote eyrie site are unrivalled and the atmosphere even quieter than a population of less than a thousand would suggest. No more than a handful of houses – each as scrupulously whitewashed as the rest – lies outside the seventeenth-century walls. Originally the village seems to have been an outlying suburb of *Medobriga*, a mysterious Roman city which vanished almost without trace. Its inhabitants fled before the Moorish advance in around 715 but later returned to live under Muslim rule, when the place was renamed after Marvan, the Moorish Lord of Coimbra. It fell to the Christians in 1166 and the present **castle** was built by Dom Dinis in 1229 as another important link in the chain of outposts along the Spanish border. The castle stands at the far end of the village, its walls blending into the sharp slopes of the *serra*. It's dauntingly impenetrable and was indeed captured only once, in 1833, when the attackers entered through a secret gate.

The village makes a superb night's stop, as several houses within the walls are rented out under a scheme organised by the **Turismo**, on Rua Dr. António Matos Magalhães (☎045/932 26). In some of these you can get just a room, while others are rented out as a unit; prices, consequently, are extremely varied. Additional **accommodation** is provided by the *Pensão Dom Dinis* (☎045/932 36; ④) and the attractively converted *Pousada de Santa Maria* (☎045/932 01; ⑦).

For **meals**, the *Restaurante Varanda do Alentejo* in Largo do Pelourinho is good (there's no sign), and you can also eat and drink at *Bar da Casa do Povo* or *Bar Marcelino*, both just off the square. The *pousada*'s restaurant serves meals at 3500–5000$00 per head which, even allowing for the grand views, is expensive.

Marvão-Beirã: on into Spain

Lisbon–Madrid trains stop at the station of **MARVÃO-BEIRÃ**, 9km north of Marvão village. Heading for Spain by public transport, this is the easiest way to go; the station *cantina* has a few rooms upstairs if you need to stay overnight between connections. The road border at **GALEGOS**, 14km east of Marvão, is open to traffic but very few cars use it. In addition, there's one daily **bus** from Portalegre direct to the Spanish border town of Valencia de Alcantara.

Northwest of Portalegre: Belver Castle

Travelling northwest from Portalegre, the N18/N118 roads take you up to the Tejo valley, and, of course, the Alentejo border. The most interesting targets on this route are the castles of Abrantes and Almourol in Ribatejo (see p.143–144) and **Belver**, which, although sited with its town on the north bank of the Tejo, is technically a part of Alentejo. If you are dependent on public transport, it is easiest to take a train or bus to Abrantes, and approach Belver from there.

Belver

The **castle** of **BELVER** is one of the most famous in the country, its fanciful position, name and tiny size having ensured it a place in dozens of Portuguese legends. The name comes from *belo ver* (beautiful to see), the supposed exclamation of some medieval princess, waking up to look out from its keep at the river valley below.

The castle dates from the twelfth century, when the Portuguese frontier stood at the Tejo, the Moors having reclaimed all the territories to the south, save Évora, that Afonso Henriques had conquered for his kingdom. Its founder was Dom Sancho I, who entrusted its construction and care to the knight-monks of the Order of Saint John. Its walls form an irregular pentagon, tracing the crown of a hill, with a narrow access path to limit attackers to virtual single file.

If you find the castle locked, search out the guard who lives at no. 1 on the main square in Belver village. For a small fee, he will unlock the **chapel** to show you its formidable fifteenth-century reliquary. All the pieces of bone were stolen during the French invasions in the nineteenth century, but fortunately for the villagers there was still a casket of "spares" hidden away by the priest, and these substitutes are nowadays paraded around town at the **Festa de Santa Reliquária**, held during the last five days in August.

Rooms and transport

You're very likely to track down the castle guard sharing a few jokes over a glass of *bagaceira* (Portugal's cheapest hangover) in Belver's single **café-restaurant-pension**. Rooms (②) are usually available, outside the August festival times.

Buses leave from the praça or from above the **train station**, which is directly below the village beside the river. If you take the train north along the valley towards Castelo Branco, look out for the striking rock faces before Vila Velha de Ródão known as the **Portas do Ródão** (Gates of Ródão).

BAIXO ALENTEJO

The hot, dry inland routes of Baixo Alentejo have little to offer beyond a stop at **Beja** – the most interesting southern Alentejo town – en route to the Algarve, or, if you're heading for Spain, at the frontier towns of **Serpa** or **Mértola**. The coastline, however, is another matter, with resorts like **Vila Nova de Milfontes**, **Almograve** and **Zambujeira do Mar** providing an attractive alternative to the summer crowds on the Algarve. Their only disadvantage – and the reason for a very patchy tourist development – is their exposure to the Atlantic winds, which at times create huge breakers and dangerous swimming conditions. But as long as you're prepared to spend occasional days out of the water, they are enjoyable places to take it easy for a few days by the sea.

All the beaches are situated along minor roads, but there are local **bus services** from Santiago do Cacém and Odemira. Alternatively, coming from Lisbon, you can take the express bus direct to Vila Nova de Milfontes, Almograve and Zambujeira do Mar; it leaves Lisbon twice a day from the Casal Ribeiro terminal (p.47) and, as with all *expressos*, it's wise to buy tickets in advance.

Southeast from Lisbon

Heading southeast into the Alentejo from Lisbon or Setúbal, the main road (and bus) loops around the **Rio Sado estuary**, through **Alcácer do Sal**, at the mouth of the river, and on through the agricultural town of **Grândola**. Heading **towards Beja**, drivers could head instead directly east from Alcácer do Sal, cutting across a succession of country roads and past a couple of huge reservoirs before meeting the main Évora–Beja road.

Alcácer do Sal

Fifty-two kilometres from Setúbal, **ALCÁCER DO SAL** is one of Portugal's oldest ports, founded by the Phoenicians and made a regional capital under the Moors – whence its name (*al-Ksar*, the town) derives. The other part of its name, *do Sal*, "of salt", reflects the dominance of the salt industry in these parts; the Sado estuary is still fringed with salt marshes. Alcácer today is slightly seedy-looking, but fairly attractively so, particularly along its waterfront promenade. At the end of the promenade is the part-ruined Moorish **castle** (daily 10am–noon & 2–5pm), from which there are striking views of the lush green paddy-fields which almost surround the town, and of the storks' nests on the church rooftops.

The *Café-Restaurant Sado* is mid-way along the promenade, near the bus depot at Largo Luís de Camões – try the house speciality, prawns, beer and buttered toast. Here, too, or at one of the town's bakeries, you can sample *pinhoadas,* a honey and pine-seed toffee. If you decide to **stay the night**, there are *dormidas* at Rua Periera 2 (☎065/62 23 55; ②), near the post office, but for a little more you can get a room at *Residencial Silvano*, Rua 1° de Maio 15 (☎065/62 25 90; ②).

At the beginning of October, for four or five days around October 5, the town hosts a **regional fair** featuring an assembly of agricultural machinery, a couple of bullfights and acres of stalls. It's one of the most enjoyable fairs in the south.

Grândola

At **GRÂNDOLA**, 23km south of Alcácer do Sal, the roads diverge: southwest to the coast; east to Beja, Serpa and, ultimately, Spanish Andalucía. As well as the main road through Alcácer to Grândola, there's an enjoyable alternative approach for drivers from Setúbal who can take the ferry to Tróia and make their way down the long sand-fringed **Pensinsula de Tróia** along the N253. The town was made legendary through the song *Grândola vila morena*, the broadcasting of which was the pre-arranged signal for the start of the 1974 Revolution. These days, The Smiths' *Heaven Knows I'm Miserable Now* would be more appropriate.

East towards Beja: Viana do Alentejo

Heading **east** instead from Alcácer do Sal, the minor N5 runs to Torrão, curving around the Rio Sado, past the **Barragem de Vale do Gaio**. Sited on the edge of the reservoir is the *Pousada de Vale do Gaio* (☎065/661 00; ⑤), a fairly simple conversion of the lodge used by the dam engineers.

Continuing east, along the N383, you pass through **VIANA DO ALENTEJO**, a sleepy and typically southern Alentejan village which preserves a highly decorative **castle**, full of Mudejar and Manueline features. The castle walls were built on a pentagonal plan, by Dom Dinis in 1313, and the interior ensemble of buildings was expanded under Dom João II and Dom Manuel I in the late-fifteenth century. To this latter period belong a sequence of elaborate battlements and the parish church, part of a striking group of buildings within the walls, encompassing a Misericórdia, town hall, cistern and pelourinho. **From Viana**, the N384 runs 30km east, past another huge reservoir, to meet the main Évora–Beja road.

Beja

On the inland route through southern Alentejo, **BEJA** appears as a welcome oasis amid the sweltering, featureless wheatfields. South of Évora, it's the most interesting stop on the way to the Algarve, and once past the modern suburbs Beja reveals an unhurried old quarter with a cluster of peculiar churches, a beautiful convent and a thirteenth-century castle. You can take in most of the sights in this compact historic centre in half a day, though in summer the heat will probably turn you towards a bar within an hour or so.

The Town

Beja is best known in Portugal for the love affair of a seventeenth-century nun who lived in the **Convento de Nossa Senhora da Conceição**, just off Largo dos Duques de Beja. Sister Mariana Alcoforado is believed to have fallen in love with Count Chamilly, a French cavalry officer, and is credited with the notorious (in Portugal anyway) *Five Love Letters of a Portuguese Nun*, first published in Paris in 1669. The originals have never been discovered, and a scholarly debate has raged over the authenticity of the French "translation". Nonetheless, English and Portuguese editions soon appeared and the letters became internationally famous as a classic of romantic literature.

Sentimental associations aside, the convent is quite a building. Founded in the fifteenth century, it has a panoply of Manueline fripperies, with elaborate portals and a rhythmic roofline decorated with balustrades and pinnacles. The walls of the cloisters and chapter house are completely covered with multicoloured sixteenth- and seventeenth-century *azulejos*, and present one of the finest examples of this art form. The other highlight is a magnificent Rococo chapel, sumptuously gilded and embellished with flying cherubs.

The convent was dissolved in 1834 and today houses the **Museu Regional** (Mon–Sat 10am–1pm & 2–5pm; 100$00). Compared to the architecture of the building, the museum pieces are comparatively lacklustre, though they include a wide-ranging display on the town's past eras – including items as diverse as Roman and Visigothic stone, fifteenth- to eighteenth-century Portuguese painting, and the grille through which the errant nun first glimpsed her lover.

The Castelo and the rest of town

Beja's **Castelo** (summer Tues–Sun 10am–1pm & 2–6pm; winter Tues–Sun 9am–noon & 1–4pm) rises decoratively on the edge of the old quarter. It was built – yet again – by Dom Dinis and is remarkable for the playful battlements of its *Torre de Menagem*, which costs 100$00 to climb up. Similarly, an exaggerated horseshoe window halfway up hints at the architect's artistic intent. In the shadow of the keep stands the Visigothic basilica of **Santo Amaro**, today a small archaeological museum. The building is a rare survival from pre-Moorish Portugal; the interior columns are carved with seventh-century geometric motifs.

Among other churches in Beja, the most distinctive is the mid-sixteenth-century **Misericórdia** in Praça da República; its huge projecting porch served originally as a meat market and the stonework is deliberately chiselled to give a coarse, "rustic" appearance. Earlier, fortress-inclined Gothic elements are to be seen on the church of **Santa Maria**, in the heart of the old quarter, and on the fifteenth-century **Ermida de Santo André**, on the road out to Lisbon, which is endowed with gigantic tubular buttresses.

Practicalities

The old quarter is a circular tangle of streets, enclosed within a ring road which has replaced the town walls. At its heart is a pair of interlocking squares – Largo de Santa Maria and Largo dos Duques de Beja. The **bus station** lies five minutes' walk southeast of this quarter; the **train station** five minutes' northeast. A very helpful **Turismo** (June–Sept Mon–Fri 9am–8pm, Sat 10am–12.30pm & 2.30–6pm; Oct–May Mon–Fri 10am–6pm, Sat 10am–12.30pm & 2.30–6pm; ☎084/236 93) is located just south of the central squares at Rua do Capitão J. F. de Sousa 25.

Beja has good **transport connections** to the rest of central and southern Portugal, as well as a bus link to Seville in Spain. In most cases you have a choice of bus or train: for Lisbon and the western Algarve take the train, while for Évora, Vila Real de Santo António (for the eastern Algarve) and Santiago do Cacém (for the western Algarve) it's quicker to go by bus.

Accommodation

Most of the town's **accommodation** is to be found within a few blocks of the Turismo. There is not a lot of choice, however, and in summer it is well worth booking ahead. The municipal **campsite** (☎084/243 28; open all year) is located on the south side of town, past the stadium on Avenida Vasco da Gama. It's fairly pleasant and shaded, and adjoins the local swimming pool.

Residencial Bejense, Rua do Capitão J.F. de Sousa 57 (☎084/32 50 01). Not bad quality, close to the Turismo. Doubles all have bath; cheaper singles come without. ③.

Residencial Coelho, Praça da República 15 (☎084/32 40 31). Decent-value pension, with a few rooms overlooking the square; all rooms have private showers. ③.

Residencial Cristina, Rua de Mértola 71 (☎084/230 35). A rather soulless, modern hotel, but Beja's most comfortable, if it's comforts you're after. ④.

Casa de Hospedes Pax Julia, Rua Pedro Victor 8 (☎084/225 75). Marginally superior to the *Rocha*; again, rooms without much in the way of facilities. ①.

Casa de Hospedes Rocha, Largo Dom Nuno Álvares Pereira 12 (☎084/242 71). Basic but clean rooms, without private bathroom. The place is a bit down-at-heel these days, though. ②–③.

Pensão Tomás, Rua Alexandre Herculano 7 (☎084/246 13). Recently renovated pension, with pleasant rooms and a friendly owner. ③.

Eating and drinking

Restaurante Alentejano, Largo dos Duques de Beja. A popular, local restaurant.

Casa Primavera, Largo do Correio. Opposite the post office, this is a real gem: inexpensive, filling meals.

Restaurante Pena, Praça de Diogo Fernandes de Beja 21. Modest prices and dependable cooking. It's between the pedestrian shopping district and the castle.

VERY GOOD

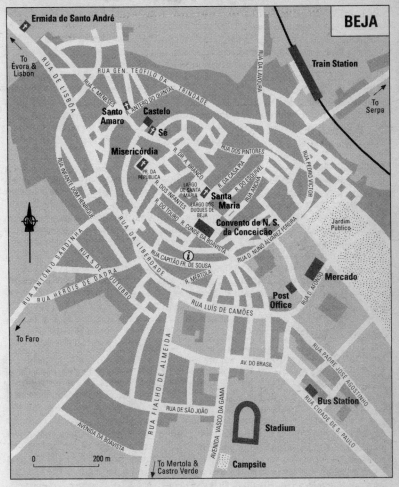

BEJA

Restaurante O Portão, off Rua dos Infantes. Nothing much to look at but serving arguably the best meals in town.

Restaurante Tomás, Rua Alexandre Herculano 7. Excellent restaurant below the *pensão* – the quality is much higher than a "pension restaurant" would suggest.

Serpa

The small market town of **SERPA** lies 30km east of Beja, an enjoyable stop if you are heading towards Spain, or feel like a roundabout but scenic approach to the Algarve, via Mértola. In addition to its classic Alentejan attractions – a walled centre, a castle and narrow whitewashed streets – it offers access (for drivers, anyway) to the Pulo do Lobo waterfall, 18km to the south.

Serpa has at various times been occupied by Celts, Romans, Moors and Spaniards, and inevitably is dominated by its **Castle** (Tues–Sun 9am–12.30pm & 2–5.30pm), predominantly Moorish, and with spectacular vistas of the plain to the north and the hills to the south. There is a tiny archeological museum in the keep and, close by, the thirteenth-century church of **Santa Maria**, containing an altarpiece of intricate wood carving, surrounded by seventeenth-century *azulejos*.

From the castle, you can track the course of the well-preserved eleventh-century **aqueduct**. It is worth a look from close up, too, with the remnants of a chain-pump at one end. If you have time to fill, you might also wander down to the **Museu Etnográfico** (Tues–Sun 9am–noon & 2–6pm), near the hospital, which offers an interesting account of the changing economic activity of the area.

Practicalities

The **bus station** is on the central Largo do Rossio; there are three connections a day to Beja and one through bus to Seville. The only official **place to stay** in town is the smart, new *Residencial Beatriz*, at Largo do Salvador 10 (☎084/534 23; ④), near São Salvador church, though you may well find **private rooms** advertised around the largo, too. At the southwest corner of town there's a new and well-equipped **campsite** (☎084/532 90; open all year) and swimming pool complex. The modern **pousada**, the *São Gens* (☎084/903 27; ⑥), is 2km south of town, on a hill known as Alto de São Gens; it has a swimming pool and wonderful views.

Among Serpa's **restaurants**, *O Zé* at Praça da República 10 is highly recommended for *gaspacho* and delicious local cheese. Opposite, the Art Deco *Café Alentejana* has a very good, if slightly pricey, restaurant above it; alternatively there's a more reasonable, unnamed restaurant at the top of Rua Quente.

The Pulo do Lobo waterfall

If you have transport, the **Pulo do Lobo** (Wolf's Leap) waterfall is an easy half-day's excursion, sited amid stark, rocky scenery, 18km south of Serpa. From Serpa, the road to the falls is signposted behind the Jardim Botanico. It is well surfaced as far as the village of **SÃO BRÁS** (6km); as it climbs into the mountainous countryside, it deteriorates suddenly to a rough track, which becomes narrow and vertiginous as it leads down, around the 16km mark, to a stream – a tributary of the Guadiana. Following the track, after a couple of kilometres you can turn left to arrive very close to the Pulo do Lobo. Around the falls – which you'll probably have to yourself – the river has carved a deep gorge through the hills, and the valley is made up of strikingly eerie rock formations.

North: Pias and Moura

Fifteen kilometres northeast of Serpa, the village of **PIAS** is well known hereabouts for its red wine. There are no particular sights, and the local train station has closed down, but if you're driving it makes an interesting detour for anyone who wants to examine what is still a very traditional Alentejan village. Pias also has a surprisingly good **restaurant**, the *Arroz Doce* in Rua Luís de Camões – try the *migas*. For a **room**, ask for Manuel Brião at the shop on the high street at no.79, or for Senhor José Carvalho Godinho on the road past the *Caixa de Credito Agricular* bank, who has rooms (①) in a lovely old house.

Another 15km north, the thermal spa town of **MOURA** is an opulent place full of grand mansions, houses and pretty squares. The Moors occupied the town from the eighth century until 1233 – it was a Moorish maiden, Moura Saluquia, who ostensibly gave her name to the town – and there still survives an Arabic well in the old town. But it was the discovery of the **thermal springs** that prompted Moura's later wealth; you can visit them, located beside the Jardim Doutora Santiago, which lie beneath the fourteenth-centurty castle, built by Dom Dinis but now in ruins.

The town's main drawback is its lack of **accommodation**. *Pensão Alentejana* in Largo José Maria dos Santos (①) has large and rambling rooms, but is often full; *Residencial Italiano* (②), just up the road, opposite the old station, is less attractive. Best of all is the *Hotel de Moura*, a superbly ornate building complete with *azulejos*, patios, mirrored doors and a rambling garden. It's currently under restoration which, when finished, is likely to double the price of its rooms.

South to the Algarve

There are three main routes **south from Beja to the Algarve**. The most interesting and enjoyable is the **N122** to Vila Real de Santo António (2 buses daily), on the eastern border of the province with Spain; this passes through the old Moorish fortress town of **Mértola** and a scenic stretch of the Guadiana river valley. Alternatives, more convenient if you are heading for western or central Algarve, are to take the N391 across the plains to **Castro Verde**, then the fast E1 to **Albufeira**, or the more mountainous N2 to **Faro** (also two buses daily).

Via Castro Verde

If you're a birder, you may consider the route from Beja to **CASTRO VERDE** (46km south) a must, for the chance to see **great bustards** winging across the plains. This apart, the road has few attractions, with a handful of small agricultural towns set amid interminable parched tracts of wheatfields. Following the N2, directly south of Castro Verde, the route continues in similar vein until you hit the lush greenery of the **Serra do Malhão** and the **Serra do Caldeirão** around Ameixial – just across the border in the Algarve.

To the west, the N264 provides faster access to the Algarve, as well as an interesting detour in the **Castro da Cola**, the remains of a small, Romano-Celtic village, similar to the *citânias* of the north. This is located to the west of the road, a few kilometres beyond the village of Aldeia dos Palheiros. There is a pilgrimage to the site on September 7–8.

Via Mértola

The N122 gets a green edge on the *Michelin* map as it approaches **MÉRTOLA** – a sure sign of rising gradients and an escape from the plains. The town is as beautifully sited as any in the south, set high above the Rio Guadiana, around the extensive ruins of a Moorish frontier castle. It's a quiet, isolated place, certainly worth a night's stopover – more if you feel like a walking or birding base. The region is home to the rare black stork.

The obvious focus for a visit is the **Castelo** (Tues–Sun 9am–12.30pm & 2–5.30pm), views from whose keep sweep across the Guadiana valley. To the north, you may be able to make out the copper mines a few kilometres down the Serpa road at Mina de São Domingos. Until recent decades, these were the principal source of the town's employment, and until World War II they were owned by a British company, which employed a private police force and treated the workers with appalling brutality. Back in town, take time to look around the **Igreja Matriz**, which started life as a Moorish mosque and retains its *mihrab* (prayer niche) behind the altar on the eastern wall. Also worth searching out is the little **Museu Arqueológico** (Mon–Sat 9am–12.30pm & 2–5.30pm), a well-presented collection of recoveries from local digs, notably Roman pottery, jewellery and needles, plus a set of strange-looking religious figures retrieved from the castle.

Practicalities

Orientation is straightforward, with **buses** (to and from Beja and Vila Real de Santo António) stopping by the bridge, close to the **Turismo**, on Rua da República (Mon–Fri 9am–12.30pm & 2–5.30pm, Sat & Sun 10am–12.30pm & 2–5.30pm; ☎086/625 73). **Staying overnight**, you have a choice of two fairly simple pensions – *Pensão Beira Rio*, Rua Dr. Afonso Costa 18 (☎086/623 40; ①), has the edge on *Pensão San Remo*, Avenida Aureliano Mira Fernandes (☎086/621 32; ②) in character and situation – or a *Turihab* property, *Casa das Janelas Verdes*, at Rua Dr. Manuel Francisco Gomes 38–40 (☎086/621 45; ④). The *Restaurante Boa Viagem*, opposite the bus stop, offers a good and inexpensive selection of **meals**. More upmarket, but still very good value, is *Restaurante Alsacrane*, inside the old town walls, overlooking the river at Rua dos Combatentes da Grande Guerra 9; it serves Arabic specialities in its upstairs dining room.

Santiago do Cacém and around

Heading south on the main route from Lisbon or Setúbal, **SANTIAGO DO CACÉM** is the first place that might, realistically, tempt you to stop. A pleasant little provincial town, it is overlooked by a castle, and has on its outskirts – half an hour's walk away – the fascinating Roman ruins of **Mirobriga**. In addition, it's only a short bus journey from the **Santo André** and **Melides lagoons**, forming two of the Alentejo's finest beaches.

The Town

In town, the Moorish **Castle** (daily 8am–8pm) was later rebuilt by the Knights Templar but now serves as a cemetery. There are splendid views over to the sea from the battlements, whose crumbling masonry provides the habitat for a curious species of large golden beetle. It's also worth making your way to the **Museu Municipal** (Tues–Fri 10am–12.30pm & 2.30–5.30pm, Sat & Sun 2.30–5.30pm), one of the most interesting of its kind, housed in one of Salazar's more notorious prisons in a small park just northeast of the centre. A suitably political strain pervades its display: one of the spartan prison cells has been preserved while two others have been converted into a "typical country bedroom" and "a rich bourgeois bedroom". Even a drawing in the section devoted to the local primary school shows a child's impression of the "Great Revolution" of 1974.

Mirobriga

The archaeological section in Santiago's museum should whet your appetite for a visit to Roman **Mirobriga** (Tues–Sat 9am–12.30pm & 2–5pm; 200$00). From the centre, follow Rua de Lisboa for about 1km up the hill, then take the marked turning to the right, and, after another ten-minute walk, turn left at a sign marking the entrance to the site, which lies isolated amid arcadian green hills.

At the highest point of the site a **Temple of Jupiter** has been partly reconstructed, overlooking a small forum with a row of shops built into its supporting wall. A paved street descends to a **villa and bath complex** whose underground central heating system is still intact.

Practicalities

If you want to base yourself in the town, rather than at the beaches, there's a rather thin spread of accommodation, including a few private rooms advertised in windows. The **Turismo** in Largo do Mercado (Mon–Fri 9am–12.30pm & 2–5pm, Sat 9am–12.30pm; ☎069/82 66 96) might be able to help. **Pensions and hotels** include: *Pensão–Restaurante Covas*, by the bus station at Rua Cidade de Setúbal 10 (☎069/226 75; ②); the basic but adequate *Pensão Esperança*, Largo 25 de Abril 17–21 (☎069/221 93; ③); *Residencial Gabriel*, Rua Professor Egas Moniz 24 (☎069/222 45; ②); and, best of all, the *Pousada de São Tiago*, Estrada Nacional (☎069/224 59; ⑤), just out of town on the Lisbon road – a pleasant if not over-memorable *pousada*, with a pool and a decent restaurant.

Two other good **restaurants** – both cheaper than that at the *pousada* – are *O Grelhador*, Rua de Camilo Castelo Branco 26, and *O Braseiro*, Rua Prof. Egas Moniz 15. There's also a fine covered **market** in the centre of town, next to the Turismo, useful for stocking up for a stay at one of the beaches.

The Santo André and Melides lagoons

There are seven buses a day from Santiago do Cacém to **LAGOA DE SANTO ANDRÉ**, and it's a short walk from there along the shore to **LAGOA DE MELIDES**. These two **lagoon beaches**, separated from the sea by a narrow strip of sand, are named after the nearest inland towns, but each has its own small, laid-back community entirely devoted to having a good time on the beach. The **campsites** at both places are of a high standard and there are masses of signs offering rooms, chalets and houses to let. Space is at a premium in July and August, but at other times accommodation should be no problem at all.

At either place, the social scene centres around the beach-cafés and ice-cream stalls. Beyond these is the sand – miles and miles of it, stretching all the way to Comporta in the north and to Sines in the south. The sea is very enticing with high waves and good surf, but be warned and take local advice on water conditions: the undertow can be fierce and people are drowned every year.

Sines, Porto Côvo and Pessegueiro

SINES – the cape just south of Santiago do Cacém – is the one place *not* to go to on this stretch of coast. Vasco da Gama was born here, but he'd probably turn in his grave if he could see the massive oil refinery and the sacrifice of the environment to new roads, railways, pipelines and wells.

The ugliness around Sines is short-lived and just south of here there's a whole set of untouched little beach settlements. The best of all of them is the furthest south, the area around Ilha do Pessegueiro, reached from the road heading down to **PORTO CÔVO** – which is served by three buses daily from Sines. Porto Covo itself is a simple, unassuming little place with a small cove harbour, a pension, the *Boa Esperança*, on Rua Conde Bandeira (☎069/951 09; ③), a few rooms to let, a camping site . . . and a sewage plant right on the oceanfront. The compensation is that Ilha do Pessegueiro is within easy walking distance.

Ilha do Pessegueiro
ILHA DO PESSEGUEIRO (Peach Tree Island) can be reached from the Porto Covo–Vila Nova de Milfontes road, but the nicest approach is to walk, following the coastal path south from Porto Covo. It's only a couple of kilometres.

The resort's name actually applies to the mainland beach; the island itself is less than a kilometre offshore and reachable on local fishing boats. On the mainland, there's the wonderful *Restaurante A Ilha* (☎069/951 13; ③), which has simple but adequate **rooms** to let (which you'll need to book in advance in summer), a small seaside **fort** and a **campsite** (☎069/951 78; open all year). Quite a few people – a good mix of Portuguese and foreign travellers – camp out on the island itself, and although there are no facilities here, it makes an excellent place to hole up for a while if the very simple life appeals.

Odemira and the south Alentejo resorts

On the southern half of the Alentejo coast, **Odemira** – about 15km from the coast – is the main inland base, offering local bus connections to the beach resorts of **Vila Nova de Milfontes**, **Almograve** and **Zambujeira do Mar**.

Odemira

In summer, unless you're camping, you'd be lucky to find accommodation in any of the southern Alentejo resorts, so it's not a bad idea to stay in **ODEMIRA** and take daytrips to the seaside. The town has several **pensions**, best of which are the very good *Residencial Rita*, Largo do Poço Novo (☎083/224 23; ②) and *Residencial Idálio*, Rua Eng. Arantes Oliveira 28 (☎083/221 56; ①), both off to the left when you come out of the bus station. Among **restaurants**, try *O Tarro*, near the main road junction, where 1500$00 will get you a hearty meal.

Vila Nova de Milfontes

VILA NOVA DE MILFONTES lies on the estuary of the Rio Mira, whose sandy banks gradually merge into the coastline. It has an advantage of geography for sailors (the port is reputed to have harboured Hannibal and his Carthaginians during a storm) and swimmers: if the waves of the Atlantic are too fierce you can always swim in the estuary, though beware of very strong currents.

The resort is not exactly undiscovered – the Germans, especially, built villas here through the 1980s – and it is perhaps the most crowded and popular resort in the Alentejo. It's a pretty place, though, with a striking little castle; while

Portuguese families on holiday from the big cities of the north give it a homely atmosphere quite distinct from the cosmopolitan trendiness of the Algarve. If you want to escape some of the crowds, take the ferry from the little jetty to the far side of the estuary to beaches nearby.

All the **pensions** are likely to be fully booked in summer, but off season you can take your pick of excellent and inexpensive rooms. The best lodgings in town – indeed the best on the whole Alentejo coast – are at the *Castelo de Milfontes* (☎083/961 08; ⑦), the fort, which is privately owned and offers highly atmospheric full board (its owner, Dona Margarida, is said to be very picky about her guests). More affordable alternatives include the *Casa dos Arco*s, on Rua dos Carris (☎083/962 64; ③), *Residencial Mil Reis* in Largo do Rossio (☎083/962 23; ④) and the *Cafe-Restaurante Mira Nobre* in Largo do Almada (☎083/962 27; ②). There are two **campsites** just north of the village. The massive *Parque de Milfontes* (☎083/961 04; open all year) has excellent facilities and high prices to match; more modest in every way is the nearby *Campiférias* (☎083/964 09; closed Dec).

Almograve

The coast south of Vila Nova de Milfontes becomes ever more rugged and spectacular. At the tiny resort of **ALMOGRAVE**, 5km west of the Odemira–Vila Nova de Milfontes road, huge waves come crashing down on the rocks and for most of the day swimming is impossible. It can get very crowded at high tide, too, when the beaches are reduced to thin strips with occasional waves drenching everybody's belongings; but, for all that, it's an exhilarating place.

You could camp virtually anywhere back from the beach at Almograve, and there are a few cafés and bars, but the bus service from Odemira is just right for a day-trip. If you are interested in a month-long stay in the village, a Danish woman, Henja Listner (Almograve, 7630 Odemira), offers bed-and-breakfast, catering mainly to writers and painters; write in advance. Otherwise, the *Restaurante Torralta* has **rooms** available.

Zambujeira do Mar and on to the Algarve

At the village of **ZAMBUJEIRA DO MAR**, south of Odemira and 7km west of the main road, a large cliff provides a dramatic backdrop to the beach, which, like that of Vila Nova de Milfontes, can get very crowded in July and August. The scenery more than compensates for the winds and the sea – which can get positively chilly, even in summer – but can't disguise the rundown state of the village and the encircling villas. If you need to **stay** – and the bus schedule from Odemira makes a daytrip impossible – there's the *Residencial Mar-e-Sol* (☎083/611 71; ③), a few *quartos* (try at the *Restaurante Miramar*), and a couple of bars. A reasonable **campsite** (☎083/611 72; March–Oct), about 1km from the cliffs, has showers and a café-bar.

Zambujeira is the southernmost Alentejo beach, and an attractive road twists its way into the hills of the Algarve from the river crossing at Odeceixe. For the most dramatic approach, however, take the road from Odemira through the **Serra de Monchique**, descending to the Algarve coast at Portimão.

travel details

Trains

Alcácer do Sal to Lisbon (3 daily; 1hr 10min–1hr 45min).

Beja to Évora (3–5 daily; 2hr); Faro (2 daily; 3hr 45min); Lisbon (4 daily; 2hr–2hr 25min).

Elvas to Lisbon (4 daily; 5hr); Portalegre (4 daily; 50min).

Évora to Beja (3–5 daily; 2hr); Faro (1 daily; 6hr); Lisbon (5 daily; 2hr 15min).

Lisbon to Alcácer do Sal (3 daily; 1hr 10min–1hr 45min); Beja (4 daily; 2hr–2hr 25min); Belver (4–6 daily; 3hr); Crato (3 daily; 5hr 20min); Elvas (4 daily; 5hr); Évora (5 daily; 2hr 15min); Portalegre (4 daily; 3hr 15min); Sines (2 daily; 3hr 20min).

Portalegre to Crato (3–4 daily; 20min); Elvas (4 daily; 50min); Lisbon (4 daily; 3hr 15min).

Buses

Alcácer do Sal to Lisbon (3 daily; 1hr 30min).

Almograve to Lisbon (2 daily; 4hr 10min); Porto Covo (2 daily; 1hr); Vila Nova de Milfontes (2 daily; 35min); Zambujeira do Mar (2 daily; 25min).

Beja to Elvas (1 daily; 3hr 25min); Évora (8–10 daily; 1hr 20min–1hr 50min); Faro (5 daily; 3hr 50min); Lisbon (6–8 daily; 3hr 20min); Portalegre (2 daily; 4hr 30min); Santiago do Cacém (3 daily; 2hr 30min); Serpa (2–3 daily; 40min).

Borba to Campo Maior (2 daily; 50min); Elvas (1 daily; 30min); Estremoz (3 daily; 15min); Évora (1 daily; 1hr); Vila Viçosa (3–4 daily; 10min).

Campo Maior to Borba (2 daily; 50min); Elvas (5 daily; 20min); Estremoz (2 daily; 1hr); Lisbon (2 daily; 4hr 10min).

Castelo de Vide to Portalegre (5 daily; 35min).

Elvas to Elvas train station (5 daily; 20min); Beja (1 daily; 3hr 25min); Borba (1 daily; 30min); Campo Maior (Mon–Sat 5 daily, Sun 2; 20min); Évora (10 daily; 1hr 35min–2hr); Lisbon (5 daily; 4hr); Portalegre (2 daily; 1hr 30min); Vila Viçosa (1 daily; 35min).

Estremoz to Borba (3 daily; 15min); Campo Maior (2 daily; 1hr); Évora (7 daily; 1hr 15min); Portalegre (8 daily; 1hr 10min–1hr 30min); Viana do Alentejo (4 daily; 1hr); Vila Viçosa (3 daily; 25min).

Évora to Albufeira (1 daily; 5hr 25min); Arraiolos (2 daily; 35min); Beja (8–10 daily; 1hr 20min–1hr 50min); Borba (1 daily; 55min); Coimbra (2 daily; 4hr 30min); Elvas (10 daily; 1hr 35min–2hr); Estremoz (7 daily; 1hr 15min); Faro (5 daily; 5hr 30min); Lisbon (7 daily; 2hr 30min); Monsaraz (2–3 daily; 55min); Portalegre (2 daily; 2hr 20min); Santarém (2 daily; 4hr 30min).

Lisbon to Alcácer do Sal (3 daily; 1hr 10min–1hr 45min); Almograve (2 daily; 4hr 10min); Beja (6–8 daily; 3hr 20min); Belver (4–6 daily; 2hr 40min); Campo Maior (2 daily; 4hr 10min); Crato (3 daily; 4hr 50min); Elvas (5 daily; 4hr); Évora (7 daily; 2hr 30min); Odemira (2 daily; 3hr 45min); Portalegre (3 daily; 5hr 30min); Porto Covo (2 daily; 3hr 10min); Santiago do Cacém (2 daily; 2hr 25min); Serpa (2–3 daily; 4hr); Sines (2 daily; 3hr 20min); Vila Nova de Milfontes (2 daily; 3hr 35min); Zambujeira do Mar (2 daily; 4hr 25min).

Portalegre to Portalegre train station (4 daily; 15min); Beja (2 daily; 4hr 30min); Castelo do Vide (5 daily; 35min); Elvas (2 daily; 1hr 30min); Estremoz (8 daily; 1hr 10min–1hr 30min); Évora (2 daily; 2hr 20min); Lisbon (3 daily; 5hr 30min); Viseu (1 daily; 5hr).

Porto Covo to Almograve (2 daily; 1hr); Lisbon (2 daily; 3hr 10min); Santiago do Cacém (2 daily; 1hr); Vila Nova de Milfontes (2 daily; 30min); Zambujeira do Mar (2 daily; 1hr 15min).

Santiago do Cacém to Lisbon (2 daily; 2hr 25min); Porto Covo (2 daily; 1hr); Sines (1 daily; 35min).

Serpa to Beja (2–3 daily; 40min); Lisbon (2–3 daily; 4hr).

Sines to Lisbon (2 daily; 3hr 20min); Santiago do Cacém (1 daily; 35min).

Vila Nova de Milfontes to Almograve (2 daily; 35min); Lisbon (2 daily; 3hr 35min); Porto Covo (2 daily; 25min–35min); Zambujeira do Mar (2 daily; 45min–1hr).

Vila Viçosa to Borba (3–4 daily; 10min); Elvas (1 daily; 30min); Estremoz (3 daily; 25min).

Zambujeira do Mar to Almograve (2 daily; 25min); Lisbon (2 daily; 4hr 25min); Porto Covo (2 daily; 1hr 10min–1hr 25min); Vila Nova de Milfontes (2 daily; 45min–1hr).

CHAPTER NINE

THE ALGARVE

With its long, sandy beaches and picturesque rocky coves, the **Algarve** has attracted more tourist development than the rest of the country put together. In parts, this has all but destroyed the charms that it was intended to exploit. The strip of coast from Faro west to Lagos has suffered most, with its endless villa complexes creating a rather depressing Mediterranean-style suburbia. On the fringes, though, especially around Sagres and Tavira, things are far better, with small-scale and relaxed resorts and the odd undeveloped beach or island sandbank.

The coastline in fact has two quite distinct characters. To the **west of Faro** you'll find the classic postcard images of the province – a series of tiny bays and coves, broken up by weird rocky outcrops and fantastic grottoes. They're at their most exotic around the major resort towns of **Lagos** and **Albufeira**. For fewer crowds, better bases include the beach village of **Salema**, the historic cape of **Sagres** – site of Henry the Navigator's naval school – or one of the string of villages along the rougher west coast as far as **Odeceixe**.

East of Faro, there's a complete change as you encounter the first of a series of sandy offshore islets, the *ilhas*, which front the coastline virtually all the way to the Spanish border. Overall, this is the quieter section of the coast – developers haven't yet overrun the islands – and it has the bonus of much warmer waters than those further west. First-choice bases along this stretch would be Faro itself, **Olhão** and **Tavira**, all of which offer access to sandbank-islands.

Inland, there are scattered attractions in the Roman ruins of **Estói** and the market town of **Loulé**, both north of Faro; and the old Moorish town of **Silves**, easily reached from Portimão. The outstanding area, however, is the **Serra de Monchique**, the highest mountain range in the south, with cork and chestnut woods, remote little villages and a beautiful old spa in **Caldas de Monchique**.

Practicalities

The Algarve is an all-year-round destination, with sunny and relatively mild winters. In many respects the region is at its best in **spring** or **winter**. Most pensions and restaurants stay open, so rooms are easy to find. Indeed, **off-season travel** in the Algarve will get you some of the best deals in the country, with luxury hotels offering all-in packages at discounts of up to seventy percent; check out the latest deals at the local tourist offices. May has an added attraction in the Algarve's **International Music Festival**, sponsored by the Gulbenkian Foundation and hosting major classical artists.

If you come in the **summer**, without a booking, finding accommodation can be a real struggle. Over the last few years, there has been scarcely a hotel vacancy on the coast in July or August and little on offer from the touts for private rooms (*quartos*). Your own transport is a great help at these times, with more vacancies inland, though car rental, again, is best booked in advance. Be prepared, too, for very high summer prices relative to the rest of the country.

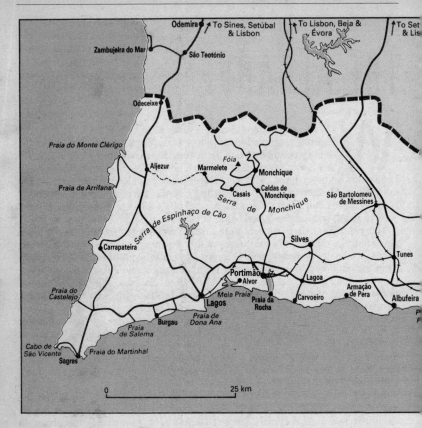

Getting around by **public transport** is easier here than anywhere else in the country, and since the coastline is only 240km long from east to west, you could see an awful lot in just a few days. The Algarve rail line runs from Lagos in the west to Vila Real de Santo António on the Spanish border, calling at most major towns; buses link all the resorts and main inland villages. **Driving** is often more trouble than it's worth. It's undeniably useful if you want to reach the more out-of-the-way inland villages and inaccesssible cove beaches (or head further into Portugal) but driving the main east–west N125 can be a pain since it's constantly being upgraded to cope with increasing traffic: expect roadworks, diversions and traffic jams.

THE EASTERN ALGARVE

All flights to the Algarve land at **Faro**, the administrative capital of the region and by far the largest town along the coast. Although no great holiday destination in itself – holidaymakers are met by bus and sped out to their resorts – the centre of the town is considerably more attractive than the concrete suburbs might suggest; and there are some fine beaches and interesting local villages within easy reach.

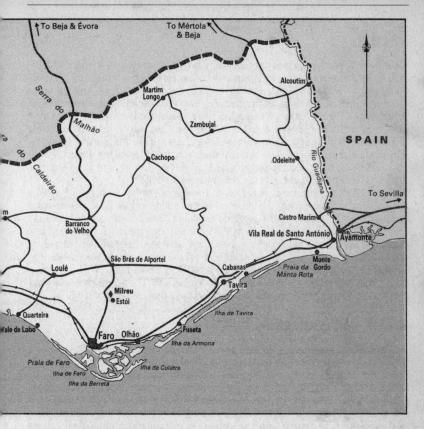

It's also not a bad place to start or finish a tour of the rest of the Algarve: Faro is connected with Lisbon by fast express coaches and offers efficient access to most Algarve towns by bus and – a little slower – on the Algarve rail line.

Faro marks a geographical boundary on the Algarve. The **coastline** east from here to Manta Rota, near the Spanish border, is protected by thin stretches of mud flats, fringed in turn by a chain of long and magnificent sandbanks, or *ilhas*. Often accessible only by boat, they're usually far less crowded than the small rocky resorts of the western Algarve. The towns of **Olhão**, **Tavira** and **Vila Real de Santo António** preserve a fair bit of character, while most of the resorts – with the exception of **Monte Gordo** – are fairly small-scale. Ornithologists should take binoculars, as the shores are thick with various types of wading bird in winter and spring.

Inland, the eastern Algarve offers few diversions, though a couple of day trips provide some distraction: from Faro to the Roman remains at **Estói** and the small country town of **São Brás de Alportel**; and along the Spanish border from Vila Real de Santo António to **Castro Marim** and **Alcoutim**. With longer detours in mind, you might find equal rewards in travelling across the frontier **into Spain**, with Seville only a couple of hours from Vila Real.

Faro

FARO has been transformed from a sleepy provincial town into a centre of tourism, trade and commerce within three decades. However, although the international airport delivers visitors right to its door, the town has a job holding on to them, since most are whisked immediately away to the out-and-out resorts on either side of Faro. This is a little unfair: there's an attractive harbour, backed by a bustling, pedestrianised shopping area, and boats and buses run out to a couple of excellent local beaches. In summer, too, there's quite a **nightlife** scene, as thousands of travellers pass through on their way to and from the airport. There are certainly better places to spend a holiday on the Algarve, but for a night or two's stay at either end, it can be an enjoyable enough base.

Faro's Roman predecessor was 8km to the north – at Ossonoba –(see p.360); the present city was founded by the Moors, under whom it was a thriving commercial port, supplying the regional capital at Silves. Following its conquest by the Christians, under Afonso III in 1249, the city experienced a checkered few centuries, surviving a series of conquests and disasters. Sacked and burned by the Earl of Essex in 1596, and devastated by the Great Earthquake of 1755, it is no surprise that the modern city has so few historic buildings. What interest it does retain is contained within the **Cidade Velha** (Old Town), which lies behind a series of defensive walls, across the harbour from the main part of town.

Arrival and orientation

In the summer months, flights land at Faro's international **airport**, 6km west of the town centre, 24 hours a day. Here, you'll find a police and first aid post, bank, post office and tourist office (daily 10am–midnight; ☎089/81 85 82), but no shops to speak of and nothing much in the provisions line apart from a poor airport restaurant. A number of **car rental** companies (see "Listings", p.359) also have offices at the airport.

The quickest way to get **into the centre** is by taxi, which should cost about 1000$00, slightly more at night; check the fare before getting in. Two buses also run from the airport to the centre, a twenty-minute ride: the #16 (roughly hourly 8am–9pm, July to mid-Sept until 11pm) and the #14 (4 daily), both stopping outside the bus terminal (see below) and further on, at the Jardim Manuel Bivar (known as *Jardim* on the timetables) by the harbour. In the other direction, the #16 runs to the beach and campsite at Praia de Faro, just 3km from the airport (see below). There are timetables posted at the airport bus stop; buy tickets on board.

The **bus terminal** is located on Avenida da República, behind the *Hotel Eva*, just across the harbour from the old part of town. The **train station** is a few minutes' walk further up the avenue, facing Largo da Estacão.

Information

As well as the office at the airport, there's a main **turismo** in town, close to the harbour front at Rua da Misericórdia 8–12 (daily 9am–7pm; ☎089/80 36 04), which can provide a map and some help with accommodation. Noticeboards here deal comprehensively with local and long-distance boat, bus and train timetables, too.

The compact town centre is simple to negotiate **on foot**, and all the pensions and hotels are extremely central. There is a **town bus service**, but you'll only need to use it to get to the beach and campsite (for which, see below) and the airport.

Accommodation

Like most of the Algarve, Faro's accommodation is stretched to the limit in summer. If you fly in without a reservation, it's worth asking the airport tourist office to try and book you a place; otherwise the main office in town can give you an idea of where to look for rooms. Most of the city's **pensions and hotels** – the best of which are picked out below – are concentrated in the area just north of the harbour.

In summer, Faro's **campsite** at Praia de Faro is always full and very cramped; if you want to stay, phone ahead (☎089/81 78 76); it is open all year (reception 8am–9.30pm). Take bus #16, either direct from the airport, or from the stop opposite the bus terminal in town; the site is a ten-minute walk from the bus stop at Praia de Faro.

Casa da Lumena, Praça Alexandre Herculano 27 (☎089/80 19 90). Highly attractive townhouse with a courtyard bar and pleasing, individually furnished rooms with shower. Advance bookings recommended. ④.

Pensão Condado, Rua Gonçalo Barreto 14 (☎089/82 20 81). Recommended *pensão* which often cuts its prices for backpackers. ③.

Pensão Dandy, Rua Filipe Alistão 62 (☎089/82 47 91). Rooms with and without shower in an impeccably clean and polished interior. The prices fall out of season, too. ③–④.

Hotel Eva, Avda. da República 1 (☎089/80 33 54). The town's best hotel, with a superb harbourfront position and rooms whose balconies look across to the old town. There's a pool, too, and a courtesy bus to the local beach. Breakfast included. ⑤–⑥.

Pensão O Farão, Largo da Madalena 4 (☎089/82 33 56). Well-kept *pensão*, opposite the *Madalena*, overlooking a lovely little square. The rooms are not as impressive as the grand marble entrance hall and potted plants, but they are clean and spacious; the ones with showers creep into the next price category. ③.

Hotel Faro, Praça Dom Francisco Gomes 2 (☎089/80 32 76). The only other hotel on the waterfront, this is cheaper than the *Eva* and just as comfortable, with harbour views from the front rooms and from the first-floor bar. Breakfast included. ⑤.

Pensão Madalena, Rua C. Bivar 109 (☎089/208 06). One of the better budget places to stay – good, clean rooms, some overlooking the street, and a friendly reception. ③.

Pensão Nautilus, Rua C. Bivar 38 (☎089/82 25 57). Half a dozen largish rooms, sparsely furnished but comfortable enough at the price; separate bathroom. ②.

Residencial Pinto, Rua 1 de Maio (☎089/82 28 20). Small place with a few rooms sharing a common bathroom. You'll save around 500$00 per room out of season. ②.

ACCOMMODATION PRICE CODES

All the accommodation prices in this book have been coded using the symbols below. The symbols represent the prices for the cheapest available double room in high season; for a full explanation, see p.23.

① Under 3000$00	② 3000$00–4000$00	③ 4000$00–5500$00
④ 5500$00–8500$00	⑤ 8500$00–12,500$00	⑥ 12,500$00–20,000$00
	⑦ Over 20,000$00	

The Old Town

The only part of town to have survived the various violent historic upheavals is the **Cidade Velha** (old town), across the harbour, an oval of cobbled streets and restored buildings set within a run of sturdy walls. The old town is entered through the eighteenth-century town gate, the **Arco da Vila**, next to the tourist office. From here, Rua do Municipio leads up to the majestic Largo da Sé, flanked by the cathedral and a group of palaces – including the former bishop's palace – and lined with orange trees. The Sé itself (Mon–Fri 10am–noon, Sun 8am–1pm) is a squat, white mis-match of Gothic, Renaissance and Baroque styles, all heavily remodelled after the 1755 earthquake. It's worth looking inside mainly for the fine eighteenth-century *azulejo* tiling.

More impressive is the **Museu Municipal** (Mon–Sat 9.30am–noon & 2–5pm; 120$00) in nearby Praça Afonso III, an archeological collection installed in a sixteenth-century convent. The most striking of its exhibits is a superb third-century AD Roman mosaic of Neptune surrounded by the four winds, unearthed a few metres back near the Faro train station. Other items include a collection of Roman statues from the excavations at Estói (see p.360), and a selection of local paintings, militaria and sixteenth-century naive multicoloured tiles, upstairs in the art gallery.

For the rest, the old town streets have mostly been scrubbed clean of interest, though some of the cobbled side streets provide entertaining strolling, with their decorative balconies and tiling.

The rest of town

Having done your historical duty in the old town, the **harbour** is the most interesting area. The town gardens and a cluster of outdoor cafés overlook the moored yachts, while in the back streets around **Rua de Santo António**, shops, bars and restaurants do their best to keep you off the local beach. The most intriguing of Faro's museums is here too: the **Museu Etnográfico** (Mon–Fri 9.30am–noon & 2–6pm; 120$00) on Rua Pé da Cruz, which has a display of local crafts and industries, including reconstructions of typical cottage interiors, and models of the net systems still used in fishing for tuna.

By far the most curious sight in town, though, is the twin-towered, Baroque **Igreja do Carmo** (Mon–Sat 10am–1pm & 3–5pm, Sun during services), near the central post office on the Largo do Carmo. A door to the right of its altar leads to the sacristy where you buy a ticket (50$00) to view the macabre **Capela dos Ossos** (Chapel of the Bones), set in an overgrown garden out back. Like the one at Évora, its walls are decorated with human bones – in this case disinterred from the adjacent monks' cemetery. Nearby, in Largo de São Pedro, the sixteenth-century **Igreja de São Pedro** is infinitely more attractive as a church, its finest decorative work an altar (to the left of the main altar) whose central image is a gilded, wooden *Last Supper* in relief.

The beaches

Faro's "town beach" – **Praia de Faro** – is typical of the sandspit *ilha* beaches of the eastern Algarve; a long sweep of beautiful sand with both a sea-facing and more sheltered land-facing side. It's less characteristic in being both overcrowded and overdeveloped, with bars, restaurants, villas and a campsite jammed onto a

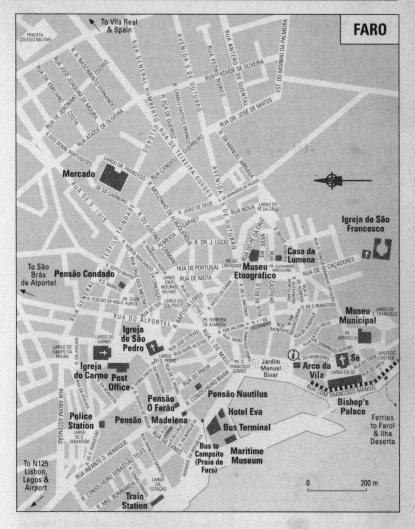

sandy island far too narrow to cope in the height of summer. Still, if you just want a few hours away from the centre of Faro, it's more than adequate; out of season you'll probably have the sands to yourself. Bus #16 runs hourly (8am–8.40pm; until 10.40pm in summer) from the harbour gardens, or from the stop opposite the bus terminal, on a rather circuitous nine-kilometre trip that calls in at the airport first.

Alternatively, **ferries** shuttle through narrow marshy channels to a couple of other local sandbar beaches, between Faro and Olhão. They depart from the jetty below the old town: either to **Farol** on the Ilha da Culatra (June–Sept Mon–Fri 4 daily, Sat & Sun 7; 200$00 return; 45min), which is covered on p.362; or to the nearby **Ilha Deserta** (3 daily; 1000$00 return).

Eating, drinking and nightlife

The heart of the town is a modern, pedestrianised shopping area on either side of Rua de Santo António, where you can find innumerable **restaurants, cafés and bakeries** – the latter stocked with almond delicacies, the regional speciality. Most of the pavement restaurants have similar menus (and similar prices); if you're prepared to scout around the backstreets, you can often find cheaper, better food, though without the accompanying streetlife that makes central Faro so attractive.

Restaurants *Very Good*

Adega Nova, Rua Francisco Barreto 24. Near the train station, this is an old-fashioned *adega* with classic Portuguese food and jugs of wine. An inexpensive choice.

Café Aliança, Rua F. Gomes 7–11. Along the lines of a down-at-heel coffee house, the *Aliança* has seats outside in summer, and a full menu of breakfasts, burgers, salads and omelettes.

Café Boémio, Travessa da Mota 10. Off Rua Vasco da Gama, this small place adds an occasional African touch to its Portuguese cooking. Try the African *bacalhau* or one of the other colonially inspired dishes. Around 2000$00 and upwards. Closed Mon.

Caldinho, Rua Cruz de Mestras 51. On a road leading east from the Largo de São Pedro, the *Caldinho* is a small, plain restaurant which serves highly rated Portuguese food, popular with locals. Around 1500$00. Closed Sun.

Cidade Velha, Rua Domingos Guieiro 19 (☎089/271 45). The only restaurant in the old town – by the Sé – this serves elegant French and Portuguese cooking in a fine eighteenth-century building. At least 4000$00 a head; reserve in advance.

Restaurant Dois Irmãos, Largo Terreiro do Bispo 13–15. Next to Praça Ferreira de Almeida, this is one of the oldest of the city's fish and seafood restaurants, a moderately priced place which specialises in tasty *cataplanas*. Try the sardines, too. Around 2500$00 a head and upwards.

Esplanada Parreiras, Rua Rebelo da Silva 22. An outdoor patio shaded by grape-bearing vines, where you choose from a shortish menu of meat or fish grills – the *frango no churrasco* is good. You'll get away with around 1500$00 a head.

Florida, Rua Ivens 16. English breakfasts served all day for under 1000$00, plus all the usual Portuguese meat and fish specials. Closed Sun.

Sol e Jardim, Praça Ferreira de Almeida 22–23. Associated with (and next door to) the *Dois Irmãos*, this is a junk shop turned restaurant – flags of the world, old agricultural equipment, baskets, and pots and pans suspended from the ceiling of a barn-like "garden" dining room. From 1500$00 a head, though more like double that if you stray into the shellfish and specialities.

Bars and discos

The best of Faro's nightlife is concentrated in the grid of pedestrianised and cobbled streets close to the Hotel Faro – **Rua Conselheiro Bivar** has café-bars with outdoor seating, while later on, in **Rua do Prior**, things get going around midnight; soon afterwards, as the bars fill up, drinkers tumble out onto the cobbled alleys to party. Apart from the many bars which feature loud, late-night music as a matter of course, Faro also occasionally hosts big name rock and pop gigs at the football stadium – check flyposters around town, and ask at the tourist office.

Adega dos Argos, Rua do Prior 15. Large, late-opening bar which gets packed out as drinkers sing along to live Portuguese music.

Bar Chaplin, Rua do Prior 37. A large bar with a club-like feel; drink prices are slightly above average, as, usually, is the DJ.

Kingburger Bar, Rua do Prior 40. A small and relaxed bar, one of the first to open up along here, and one of the last to close.

Megahertz, Rua do Prior 38. Glitzy disco open until 4am.

Sheherazade, at the *Hotel Eva*, Avda. da República 1. Established disco nights in the club to the side of the hotel; usually every Wed, Fri and Sat.

Versailles, Rua Ivens 7–9. Restaurant-bar that's good for a drink post-restaurant/pre-club, with outdoor seating and a youthful, local crowd. Open until midnight.

Listings

Airlines *Air Europe* (☎089/81 84 45); *British Airways* (☎089/81 81 81); *KLM* (☎089/81 89 10); *Lufthansa* (☎089/81 82 69); *TAP* (☎089/81 85 39).

Airport Flight information on ☎089/81 89 82.

American Express c/o *Star Travel*, Rua C. Bivar 36 (Mon–Fri 9am–12.30pm & 2–6pm; ☎089/80 55 25).

Bus Terminal There's an English-speaking information office inside the terminal; bus information on ☎089/80 37 92.

Car Rental *Avis* (airport; ☎089/81 85 38); *Budget* (airport; ☎089/81 79 07; *Hotel Eva*, Avda. da República 1; ☎089/80 34 91); *Eurodollar* (airport; ☎089/81 82 94); *Europcar* (airport; ☎089/81 87 77); *Hertz* (Rua 1 de Maio; ☎089/82 48 77); *Kenning* (airport; ☎089/81 83 51).

Consulate The only British consulate in the Algarve is in Portimão (p.376), at Largo Francisco A. Mauricio 7 (☎082/478 00; Mon–Fri 9.30am–12.30pm & 2.30–5pm). All other consulates are in Lisbon.

Hospital *Hospital Distrital* (☎089/80 34 11).

Left Luggage At the bus terminal; open 8.30am–1pm & 2–6pm.

Police Rua Serpa Pinto (☎089/82 20 22).

Post Office Largo do Carmo (Mon–Fri 9am–12.30pm & 2–6pm, Sat 9am–12.30pm); poste restante here, too.

Sport The Algarve's only First Division soccer team, *Sporting Club Farense*, play at the Estádio de São Luís, in the north of the city, a twenty-minute walk from the centre. Matches are on Sundays.

Taxis There's a rank in front of the *Hotel Faro*, by the town gardens. Or call ☎225 37.

Telephones You can make international calls from the post office.

Travel Agencies *Abreu*, Avda. da República 124; *Marcus & Harting*, Rua C. Bivar 69; *Star*, Rua C. Bivar 36; *Wagon-Lits*, Rua do Pé da Cruz.

Inland: Estói and São Brás de Alportel

Apart from the beach, other worthwhile day-trips from Faro are to the couple of villages in the gentle hills to the north. At **Estói**, you can divide your time between a delightful eighteenth-century country estate and the remains of a Roman settlement at **Milreu**, just below the village. Further north, the hilltop town of **São Brás de Alportel** also makes a pleasant excursion. Travelling by bus, unless you make a fairly early start it's difficult to see both villages on the same day. However, if you feel reasonably energetic it's perfectly feasible to take the bus to São Brás and walk the 7km down to Estói, catching the late-afternoon bus back to Faro from there.

Estói

Regular buses make the twenty-minute journey 11km north of Faro to **ESTÓI**.
Buses drop you in the village square, just off which is the **Palácio do Visconde
de Estói**, a diminutive version of the Rococo palace of Queluz near Lisbon. At
present, only the attractive grounds are open to the public (Tues–Sat 9am–
12.30pm & 2–5.30pm; free); long term renovations of the palace itself are still
underway. The main reason for a visit to Estói, however, is the Roman site at
Milreu (Tues–Sun 10am–12.30pm & 2–5pm; free), a ten-minute walk downhill
from the square. Known to the Romans as *Ossonoba*, the town that once stood
here predated Faro and was inhabited from the second to the sixth century AD.
The surviving ruins are associated with a peristyle villa – one with a gallery of
columns surrounding a courtyard – and dominated by the apse of a temple, which
was converted into a Christian basilica in the third century AD, making it one of
the earliest of all known churches. The other recognisable remains are of a bathing complex with fragments of mosaic. The site was finally abandoned in the
eighth century AD, after which date the Moors founded Faro to the south.

São Brás de Alportel

Seven kilometres north of Estói, **SÃO BRÁS DE ALPORTEL**, in a valley of the
Serra do Caldeirão, also makes an appealing detour for those with a couple of
hours to spare. Buses pull up in the main square, where – in a little circular booth
– the **Turismo** (Mon–Fri 9.30am–12.30pm & 2–5pm, Sat 9.30am–noon; ☎089/84
22 11) dishes out a map, which you won't need since everything lies within a
three-minute walk. Checking out the sights doesn't take long: walk to the bottom
of town to the church of **Senhor dos Passos** (signposted *Igreja da Matriz*), for
its views of the surrounding valleys, and then on to the **Museu Etnográfico do
Trajo Algarvio**, at Rua Dr. José Dias Sancho 61 (Tue–Fri 10am–noon & 2–5pm,
Sat & Sun 2–5pm; 100$00). The museum, housed in an old mansion, is quite the
best reason to come to São Brás. It has a series of alcoves and corridors full of
traditional costumes and farming and domestic equipment.

The quiet surroundings entice a few visitors to make this their Algarve base.
Accommodation isn't the good value it might be, but try for rooms at the
Residencial São Brás, Rua Luis Bivar 27 (☎089/84 22 13; ④), which runs off the
main square; the rooms have showers and breakfast is included. Big-spenders
might want to stay at the very comfortable *Pousada de São Brás* (☎089/84 23 05;
⑥), two kilometres north of town. The views from here are splendid, and there's
an (expensive) restaurant, too; as there are only 29 rooms, advance booking is
essential in summer. **Bars** and **restaurants** are sparse but try *A Horta*, a *churrasqueria* about five minutes out of town on the Faro road, or the *Savoy* (closed Sun
lunch), further up Rua Luis Bivar, past the *residencial*. *Bar Roflin*, just around the
corner on Rua Capitão Caiado, attracts a vibrant crowd, occasionally puts on live
music, and stays open late (closed Mon).

Olhão and its ilhas

OLHÃO, eight kilometres east of Faro, is the largest fishing port on the Algarve
and an excellent base for visiting the surrounding sandbank *ilhas*. It's an otherwise uneventful place, notwithstanding the somewhat surreal prose of the local
brochure, which proclaims Olhão home of the "amazing poodle of the Algarve . . .

muscular and strong. . .[and] of valuable assistance to the fishermen for whom it dives into the water. . . to a depth of over four metres, to guide the fish into the nets". Unfortunately, the aquatic poodles were abandoned for more modern methods in the 1950s.

Once past the built-up outskirts, Olhão is quite an attractive town. There are no sights as such, but the flat roofs, outdoor stairways and white terraces of the old town are striking and give a North African look to the place. No surprise, then, that Olhão has centuries-old trading links with Morocco, as well as a small place in history for its uprising against the French garrison in 1808. Following the French departure, the local fishermen sent a small *caíque* across the Atlantic to Brazil to transmit the news to the exiled king João VI. The journey, completed without navigational aids, was rewarded after the king's restoration to the throne by the granting of a town charter.

The best view of the whitewashed cube-houses is from the belltower of the seventeenth-century parish church of **Nossa Senhora do Rosário** (Tues–Sun 9am–noon & 2–5pm), right in the middle of town. Outside, at the back of the church, an iron grille protects the chapel of **Nossa Senhora dos Aflitos**, where traditionally, townswomen gather when there's a storm at sea to pray for their sailors amid candles and curious wax models of children and limbs.

The other obvious focus of the town is the **market**, held in the two large buildings on the harbourside at the bottom of town. Open from the crack of dawn every day except Sunday, there's meat, fruit and vegetables on one side, fish on the other, the latter hall full of such delights as swordfish heads propped up on the marble counters and squid ink running off the tables into the gutter.

Practicalities

The **train station** is at the northeastern edge of town, off Avenida dos Combatentes da Grande Guerra; the bus terminal is a few minutes away on Rua General Humberto Delgado. From either, it's a quick walk down to the main Avenida da República, a wide boulevard which leads into the city centre, a further five-minute walk away. At the parish church, the avenue forks into two: follow Rua do Comércio, the main (pedestrianised) shopping street, and when it rounds the corner you'll find the **Turismo** (Mon–Fri 9am–12.30pm & 2–5pm, Sat 9am–noon; ☎089/71 39 36), which can provide a town map, advice on accommodation and sailing times for boats to the *ilhas*.

Accommodation

There are no *quartos* in town and consequently accommodation can be hard to find in the height of summer, despite a fair scattering of **pensions**. Of these, first choice should be the *Pensão Bela Vista*, Rua Teófilo Braga 65–67 (☎089/70 25 38; ③), which has a range of bright rooms arranged around a tiled, flower-filled courtyard; from the tourist office, turn left, then first left, and its sign is directly opposite. Other central places include two on Rua Vasco da Gama, the other fork off Avenida da República: the *Pensão Bicuar* at no. 5 (☎089/71 48 16; ②–③), cheerful enough for the price and with smart communal areas; and the *Pensão Vasca de Gama* opposite, at no. 6 (②). The tourist office highly recommends the *Pensão Boémia*, Rua da Cerca 20 (③), three blocks further up Rua 18 de Junho: rooms come with shower and it's quieter than the others. If all else fails, you should find room at the *Hotel Ria Sol*, Rua General Humberto Delgado 37

(☎089/70 52 67; ④–⑤), an upmarket and rather functional fifty-room hotel, by the bus station. The local **campsite** (☎089/70 54 02) is at Marim, three kilometres east of town, and has a pool and good views of Armona. Buses from the terminal run hourly until around 8pm (6.30pm at weekends).

Cafés and restaurants

Rua do Comércio has its share of **cafés** with outdoor seating, and streets on either side harbour a few **restaurants**; the *Taiti* at Rua Vasco da Gama 24 (closed Tues) is reasonably good. For cheaper eating, there are two simple *casas de pasto* in the small square in front of the market, open for lunch and dinner, while the best places for local **fish** dishes are the nearby restaurants on Avenida 5 de Outubro, past the market towards the harbourside gardens. Here, *Papy's* is terrific, its *arroz de marisco* a mammoth serving of prawns, crabs and clams.

The ilhas: Armona and Culatra

Ferries leave for the *ilhas* of Armona and Culatra from the jetty at the eastern end of Olhão's municipal gardens, five minutes' walk from the market. There's a time-table posted at the kiosk; if it isn't open, you can buy tickets on the ferries. The **Ilha da Armona**, a fifteen-minute ride away, is reasonably accessible all year round (July & Aug 8–11 daily; June & Sept 8–9 daily; rest of the year 3 daily; 160$00 each way); Culatra (35min) and Farol (45min), on the **Ilha da Culatra**, are easy enough to see in July and August (9 daily; 200$00), though during the rest of the year (3–4 daily) the service is drastically reduced; you may have to spend more hours than you'd care to on the island. You can also reach Farol in summer from Faro; see p.357.

Ilha da Armona

Ferries drop their passengers at the southern end of the single settlement on **Ilha da Armona** – a long, crowded strip of holiday chalets and huts that stretches right across the island on either side of the main path. It's a fifteen-minute walk to the ocean, where the beach disappears into the distance; a short walk will take you to attractive stretches of sand and dune – the further you walk, the greater the privacy. There are a few **bar-restaurants** by the jetty, while at the other end, the self-service *Santo António* has a terrace overlooking the beach where you can tuck into sardines, salad and beer. There are no campsites, pensions or hotels on Armona, and camping on the beach is frowned upon, but if you want to stay, ask at the tourist office in Olhão about renting **chalets** – though you'll be lucky to find anywhere in high season.

Ilha da Culatra

The **Ilha da Culatra** is another huge sand spit, though very different in character from Armona, its northern shore dotted with a series of fishing settlements, mixed with an incongruous sprinkling of holiday chalets. The ferry's first port of call, **CULATRA**, is the largest settlement, though **FAROL**, the second stop, is far more agreeable. A rather commonplace, untidy village of holiday homes, it is edged by beautiful tracts of beach on the ocean side, though the mainland-facing beach is grubby. Once again, **camping** on the island is not encouraged, and in any case tends to be conspicuous among the fishing villages. Basic **rooms** and **food** at not-so-basic prices are available at the *Hotel Bar Tropical*.

Tavira and around

TAVIRA is one of the most beautiful towns on the Algarve and – at just 30km east of Faro – is a clear winner if you are looking for a base on the eastern stretch. It's sited on both sides of the broad Rio Gilão, which is overlooked by ancient balconied houses and straddled by two low bridges, one of Roman origin. This is an eminently attractive ensemble, which persuades many to stay longer than planned – particularly those intent on lounging around on the superb island beach of the **Ilha de Tavira**, which lies within easy reach of the town. Ferries to the island only operate from May to mid-October, but you can reach other local beaches, like that at **Pedras de El Rei**, all year round. In any case, Tavira itself is certainly worth visiting, at any time of the year. Despite ever-increasing visitors and encroaching development, it continues to make its principal living as a tuna-fishing port, and fish dinners at restaurants along the palm-lined river are in themselves a powerful incentive to stop.

The Town

Founded as long ago as 400 BC, Tavira's greatest period of prosperity came in the sixteenth to eighteenth centuries, the age which produced most of its graceful array of churches and mansions. In the old town streets on both sides of the river, numerous houses retain fine old doorways and coats-of-arms.

From the arcaded **Praça da República**, by the river, it's a short climb up to the **Castelo** (Mon–Fri 8am–5.30pm, Sat & Sun 10am–7pm; free), half hidden on a low hill in the centre of town. From the walls you can look down over the peculiarly Oriental rooftops and the town's thirty-seven churches (most of which, sadly, are kept locked). Adjacent to the castle, the whitewashed **Santa Maria do Castelo** contains the tomb of Dom Paio Peres Correia, who reconquered much of the Algarve from the Moors, including Tavira in 1224. Fittingly, the church stands on the site of the former mosque.

The best part of Tavira is the **river**. Gardens lined with cafés run as far as the lively harbourside **market** (open mornings only), beyond which are moored the fishing boats that still operate out of the river port. This is a great place to wander, among the nets and marine clutter, stopping at one of the restaurants or more basic fishermen's bars, most of which serve up memorable meals, generally involving big tuna steaks.

Practicalities

Tavira has a new **bus terminal**, by the river, from where it's a two-minute walk to the old bridge and Praça da República. The **train station** is 1km from the centre of town, straight up the Rua da Liberdade. There's a **Turismo** (Mon–Fri 9am–12.30pm & 2–5.30pm, Sat 9am–noon; ☎081/225 11) in the Praça da República, which has details of **bike and moped rental** if you want to explore the coast.

Accommodation

The tourist office can sometimes help with **private rooms** if you have no luck at the pensions listed below. As throughout the Algarve, be warned that places are at a premium during the summer season; if a tout offers you a room, take it, at least for the first night, and look around on your own later on. A couple of places

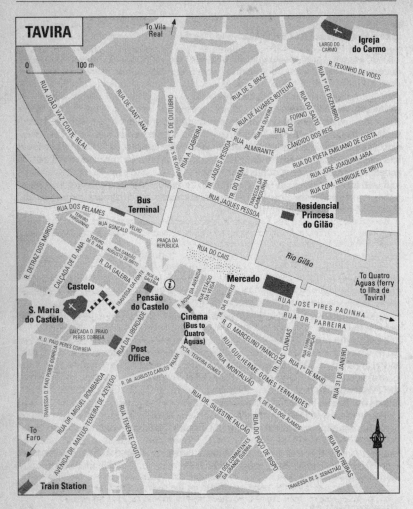

to check out first are at Rua José Pires Padinha 44, opposite the market, and at Rua da Liberdade 74, close to the post office (both ①). The nearest **campsite** is on the Ilha de Tavira, for which see below.

Pensão do Castelo, Rua da Liberdade 4 (☎081/239 42). Very centrally located, across from the tourist office, and with views of the castle and river. Clean, good-value rooms, with separate bathroom; rates drop out of season. ③.

Residencial Lagôas, Rua Almirante Cândido dos Reis 24 (☎081/222 52). Situated on the north side of the river, across the bridge from Praça da República, this has attractive rooms and rooftop views, and the bonus of the top-notch budget restaurant, *Bica*, below. Rooms with shower fall into the next category up. ②.

Residencial Mendonça, Rua dos Bombeiros Municipales (☎081/817 43). An excellent choice, run by the Mendonça family; it's south of the river on the western edge of town. ②–③.

Residencial Mirante, Rua da Liberdade 83 (☎081/222 55). Sporting a tiled red facade, this place is alright, but some of the rooms overlooking the street are a bit noisy. ③.

Residencial Princesa do Gilão, Rua Borda de Agua de Aguiar 10–12 (☎081/32 51 71). A modern, white building, decorated inside with cool Portuguese tiles, this friendly *residencial* stands right on the quayside. Go for a room at the front, with a balcony overlooking the river. Breakfast included. ④.

Cafés and restaurants

A succession of **cafés and restaurants** front the gardens along the riverbank, while further down, on Rua José Pires Padhina, tables edge out on to the riverside. For a drink, there are a couple of cafés in the main square, plenty of nameless backstreet bars with matchstick-chewing old-timers for company, and a couple of trendier spots north of the river.

Aquasul, Rua Dr. Augusto da Silva Carvalho 11–13. Pizza restaurant on the north side that makes a pleasant change. It also has French-influenced main dishes and amenable staff. Under 2000$00 for pizza and drinks.

A Barquinha, Rua José Pires Padhina. This unpretentious bar-restaurant, along the riverfront from the market, has seats outside and serves a good túna steak, with stewed onions and fries. A plateful, wine and coffee comes to under 15000$00.

Restaurante Bica, Rua Almirante Cândido dos Reis 22–24. Inexpensive, excellent Portuguese meals on the north side of the river, under the *Residencial Lagôas*. From around 1400$00 a head.

Cad'Oro, Rua José Pires Padinha. Upmarket riverfront fish restaurant with live music on certain summer evenings. Around 2500$00 and up.

Churrasqueira Grill, Rua Almirante Cândido dos Reis 6. Reliable Portuguese grill restaurant near the *Bica*.

Restaurante Imperial, Rua José Pires Padinha 22. Just back from the riverside gardens, the *Imperial* is well-known for its seafood, including clams and tuna. A decent meal here will cost around 3000$00.

Bars and nightlife

Anazu, Rua Jacques Pessoa 11–13. This large and friendly bar-restaurant on the riverfront is a good place to sit and watch the sun set.

Arco Bar, Rua Almirante Cândido dos Reis 67. Friendly Portuguese bar on the north side of the river, attracting a laid-back crowd.

Coco-Coco, Rua Dr. August do Silva Carvalho 22. Also north of the river, this bar is aimed at those who don't mind shelling out for pricey cocktails.

UBI. Tavira's best disco. You reach it by following Rua Almirante Cândido dos Reis to the outskirts of town; look for the huge warehouse on the right, which conceals *UBI* within a shiny, metallic hangar. Open 11pm–4am; check posters around the town for events.

Ilha de Tavira

The **Ilha de Tavira** stretches southwest from Tavira almost as far as Fuzeta, some fourteen kilometres away. For most of its length the landward side of the island is a dank morass of mud flat, but at the eastern tip the mud disappears and the *ilha* ends in an expanse of sand and sea. The beach is enormous, backed by tufted dunes, and over the years its growing popularity has led to a certain amount of development: at the end of the main path, which runs from the jetty through a small chalet settlement, there are watersports facilities, beach umbrellas and loungers, and half a dozen bar-restaurants facing the sea. Rather than spoiling things, this has fostered something of a good-time feel at the beach.

The **campsite** (☎081/235 05; open all year), a minute from the sands and with a well-stocked mini-market, shelters a youthful crowd, and the bars pump out music into the night. The *Sunshine Bar* serves a tasty tuna steak, and has a full breakfast menu and vegetarian options, too.

Buses (July to mid-Sept hourly 8am–8pm; June Mon–Fri 5 daily, weekends hourly) leave from outside the cinema in Tavira for the ten-minute trip to the jetty at **Quatro Águas**, 2km east of town. Out of season, you've the choice of a half-hour walk from the town (along the river, past the market, and just keep going) or a taxi. The **boats** to the island (May to mid-Oct; 130$00 return) run half-hourly in July and August, hourly on the months either side, with the first departure at around 7.30am. Last boats **back from the island** are at 9pm in May and mid-September to mid-October; 10pm in June; and 11.45pm from July to mid-September.

In the past, during high season, there have also been direct boats to the island from the quayside just downstream from the fish market in town; up to six daily departures for 150$00 return.

Pedras de El Rei and Barril

If you're after a little more space in summer, it's better to head 4km west from Tavira to **PEDRAS DE EL REI**, a holiday village, which while a bit sterile, is not too big and is very pleasant for its type. The sands spread for miles if you feel like laying down a sleeping bag for the night. Alternatively, chalets can be hired on a short-term basis at reasonable prices for small groups, though the complex is usually full in July and August. Fairly regular **buses** (Mon–Fri only) connect the resort with Tavira, or you can walk from the main coastal highway to Pedras in about fifteen minutes.

From Pedras de El Rei, you cross a causeway and then catch a miniature train (100$00) which shuttles backwards and forwards across the mud flats to the beach of **BARRIL** on the Ilha de Tavira. It's a few minutes' walk right or left to escape the tourist facilities at the terminus, and there you are: miles of beautiful, peaceful, dune-fringed beach. Take your own food and drink, though, since the relative isolation means high prices in the couple of café-bars here. This whole area constitutes the **Parque Natural da Ria Formosa**, a nature reserve where you can watch tens of thousands of fiddler crabs, scuttling about, silently waving their claws at the sky.

Tavira to Vila Real

Just to the east of Tavira, the sand spit that protects much of the eastern Algarve from the developers starts to thin out, merging with the shoreline beach at Manta Rota. The result is predictable: **CABANAS**, **MANTA ROTA** and **ALAGOA** have all been intensively developed, robbing the coast of much of its allure. Nevertheless, the beaches at all three resorts are splendid, if crowded in summer. **PRAIA VERDE**, just past Alagoa, is perhaps the best of all, with its sands backed by attractively wooded hills.

The last resort before the Spanish border is **MONTE GORDO**, the most built-up of the eastern holiday towns, with a casino and beachfront gardens. White hotels overlook the wide sands, on which are scattered a profusion of beach café-restaurants with studiously similar menus. You'll be hard pushed to find anywhere at all to stay in these resorts during the summer, except perhaps in Monte Gordo, site of the last **campsite** (☎081/441 88) on this stretch of the Algarve. For rooms, consult the **Turismo** (Mon–Thurs 9.30am–12.30pm & 2–8pm, Fri 9.30am–12.30pm & 2–7pm, Sat & Sun 9.30am–12.30pm & 2–5.30pm; ☎081/444 95), next to the casino on the seafront.

You can reach Cabanas and Monte Gordo by **bus** from Tavira; for Manta Rota, the only services are from Vila Real (or Monte Gordo); and for Praia Verde, the best you can do is get off any bus to Vila Real on the highway and walk down the side road.

Cacela Velha

There's one surprise on this part of the coast. For some reason, the small hamlet of **CACELA VELHA** (not to be confused with Vila Nova de Cacela, 2km inland) is barely untouched by tourism. Perched on a rocky bluff overlooking the sea, surrounded by olive groves, and home to an old church and the remains of a fort, it is spectacularly pretty – a reminder of how the Algarve must have looked half a century ago. Naturally enough, the hamlet is short on facilities, but it's got a little restaurant, a couple of cafés and a handful of **rooms** that are snapped up quickly in the summer. The beach below the village is a delight and it's possible to arrange a lift over to the sand bar just offshore.

Cacela Velha is roughly half way between Tavira and Monte Gordo. To get here, you need to jump off the Tavira–Vila Real bus on the highway, just before Vila Nova de Cacela, from where it's a fifteen-minute walk down a side road to the village.

Vila Real de Santo António

The border town and harbour of **VILA REAL DE SANTO ANTÓNIO** has suffered a marked change in character since the completion of a bridge across the Rio Guadiana, 4km to the north of town. Fewer cars and tourists now clog the streets in summer since anyone bound for Spain can now drive (or catch a bus) straight there. Still, you may want to call in anyway, not least because it's one of the more architecturally interesting towns on the Algarve. The original town was demolished by a tidal wave at the beginning of the seventeenth century, and the site stood empty until it was revived in 1774 by the Marquês de Pombal. Eager to apply the latest concepts of town planning, Pombal used the same techniques he had already pioneered in the Baixa quarter of Lisbon and rebuilt Vila Real on a grid plan. The whole project only took five months – a remarkable achievement, but a startling waste of resources, as it transpired that the hewn stone that Pombal had dragged all the way from Lisbon could have been quarried a couple of miles up the road.

Vila Real is the eastern terminal of the Algarve railway, and **trains** pull up at the station on the riverfront. **Buses** stop just in front of here, while across the way, the **Turismo** (daily 8am–8pm; ☎081/432 72) can be persuaded to phone around for a vacant *quarto*, if you intend to stay. Two of the more pleasant places, worth trying to book ahead for are the *Residencial Felix*, across from the tourist office at Rua Dr. Manuel Arriaga 2 (☎081/347 91; ②), and *Residencial Baixa Mar*, Rua Teófilo de Braga 3 (☎081/435 11; ③), two blocks to the west. Alternatively,

there's a **youth hostel** at Rua Dr. Sousa Martins 40 (☎081/445 65; breakfast included), five blocks up from the tourist office; it's open all year round but again fills easily in summer.

Among **restaurants**, the *Caves do Guadiana*, fronting the fishing port at Avenida da República 90 is outstanding and fairly modestly priced. There are also some good seasonal seafood restaurants on the dunes: follow the road along the riverfront, past the sardine canning factory, and head towards the beach.

Crossing the border

Four daily **buses** run from Vila Real across the bridge to Ayamonte in Spain, currently at 10am, 11.15am, 2pm and 8pm. The 10am departure connects in Ayamonte with the service on to Huelva and Sevilla. **Coming from Spain**, the 3.15pm from Ayamonte connects in Vila Real with services on to Faro and Lagos.

If you just want to make a day trip, it's more fun to use the **ferries**, which still cross the river every half-hour or so, seven days a week (8am–1am), from the terminal next to the train station. The ferry trip takes about fifteen minutes and costs 130$00 per person.

Inland: up the Rio Guadiana

The little village of **CASTRO MARIM**, tucked away 5km north of Vila Real (several buses daily), was once a key fortification protecting Portugal's southern coast. Marim was the first headquarters of the Order of Christ (1319) and the site of a huge **castle** built by Afonso III in the thirteenth century. The massive ruins are all that survived the earthquake of 1755, but it's a pretty place with fine views of the impressive new bridge to Spain.

The marshy area around Castro Marim has been designated as a **nature reserve**, so there's no danger of its being despoiled; a nature reserve office inside the castle has more information. One of the area's most unusual and elusive inhabitants is the extraordinary, ten-centimetre-long, swivel-eyed, opposing-toed, Mediterranean chameleon – a harmless, slow-moving lizard that's severely threatened elsewhere by habitat destruction. Following the footpaths through the nature reserve is an enjoyable way to work up an appetite.

Up the river: Foz de Odeleite and Alcoutim

Boat trips up the Rio Guadiana to the traditional village of **FOZ DE ODELEITE**, 20km to the north of Vila Real, are a good way to see some of the less spoiled parts of the region. At around 6000$00 per person (booked through Vila Real's tourist office), they're not especially cheap, but you do get a huge barbecue lunch, unlimited wine and plenty of swimming opportunities along the way. Departures are usually on Monday, Wednesday, Friday and Sunday during the summer, and on Thursday the rest of the year. Buses from Vila Real travel this way, too, though they follow the N122, which runs inland of the river.

If you're feeling particularly energetic, you could walk the 15km north along the riverside road from Foz de Odeleite to **ALCOUTIM**, a beautiful route. The village is extremely attractive, too, with another ruined castle, and there's a brand new fifty-bed **youth hostel** (☎081/460 04) for overnight stays – or you can **camp** inside the castle walls. A small Turismo and all the bars and cafés are located in the main square, at the bottom of the village by the river. Two **buses** a day run back down to Vila Real, and there are services north to Mertola (p.345) and Beja (p.341).

Across the river lies the **Spanish village of Sanlúcar**, a mirror image of Alcoutim, with its own ruined castle; there's a ferry (foot passengers only). This was once an infamous smuggling route and there are still dark tales of contraband finding its way across at night, in particular tax-free TV sets from Ceuta.

THE WESTERN ALGARVE

The **western Algarve** stretches for a hundred kilometres from Faro to Sagres and encompasses Portugal's most intense tourist developments. The most extreme section is between Faro and Lagos, where the beaches and coves are fronted by an almost continuous stretch of villas, apartments and hotels. The purpose-built resorts feature marinas, golf links and tennis centres – all fine if you've booked a holiday, but not especially inviting for casual visitors.

Albufeira is one of the biggest – and most enjoyable – resorts and other decent stops include **Portimão**, nearby **Praia da Rocha** and **Lagos**, the last of which still retains a bit of local character. All of these places are packed to the gills in summer and, particularly if you have transport, you might do better to seek a base inland at the old market towns of **Loulé** or **Silves**, and drive down to the nearest strip of beach. **Caldas de Monchique**, a nineteenth-century spa town, and neighbouring **Monchique** are other inland options, though these are a good forty minutes' drive from the sea.

Until recently, the coast **west of Lagos** was the place to escape the worst of the crowds, but development – in the shape of a fast new road and burgeoning enclaves of holiday villas – has been horrifically quick. However, erstwhile fishing villages like Burgau and Salema still teeter on the edge of complete exploitation. Beyond these villages the road cuts high above the sea, across a cliff-edged plateau, and down to **Sagres**, with its dramatic scenery and busy nightlife.

The coast **north of Sagres**, heading towards Alentejo, is the last undeveloped swathe of the Algarve – partly because the sea is distinctly colder and often pretty wild. If you can brave the climate, you might like to try low-key villages such as **Vila do Bispo**, **Carrapateira**, **Aljezur** and **Odeceixe**, all of which have magnificent local beaches. These attract a somewhat more youthful and "alternative" crowd than resorts on the Algarve proper – including, it seems, just about every German campervan in Portugal; their combination of nude sunbathing, surf and parties is not everyone's idea of an idyll.

Quinta do Lago to Vilamoura

The coast immediately northwest of Faro is unremitting holiday village territory, with little promise for anyone simply in search of a quiet beach and an unsophisticated meal. This is territory for those into "Sportugal" – as the tourist board promotes the lesiure complexes – and none too fussy about a local environment. You have to head inland for even the barest whiff of the old Algarve, best encountered at the historic market town of **Loulé**.

If you are staying on the Quarteira strip of coast, Loulé makes for a pleasant lunchtime or evening break. Independent travellers might find it the best place for a night away from the crowds, though it's probably more realistic to stay in Faro and see all the places below by **bus**; departures are roughly hourly throughout the day.

Quinta do Lago, Vale do Lobo and Quarteira

The first of the resorts, **QUINTA DO LAGO** is a vast, luxury holiday village with its own sports complex and opulent hotel. There's more of the same at **VALE DO LOBO**, next door, with serious-money hotels, golf courses, a riding school, and a swish tennis centre run by former Wimbledon-pro Roger Taylor. The first place you can reach by bus from Faro is **QUARTEIRA**, 22km away, which is actually quite a pleasant town, with a good weekly market and an attractive beach – though development increasingly threatens to overwhelm it. The bus station is a couple of blocks back from the beach; and there's a **campsite** (☎089/30 28 21) a kilometre east of town. Any bus to or from Faro runs right past it.

Vilamoura

Based around a king-sized marina, **VILAMOURA** is a constantly expanding resort, with a bewildering network of roads signposted to upmarket new hotels and leisure facilities, including some highly exclusive **golf courses**. The beach is impressive – as it should be considering all the development – and, if you're not bothered by the crowds, enjoyable enough. The bus drops you next to the casino, one block from the beach, the Praia da Marina. The enormous *Vilamoura Marinotel* is visible, two minutes away, overlooking the marina – really, the only other reason to stop off here. Bristling with yachting hardware, this makes for an interesting stroll, and you can settle down at one of the cafés backing the marina and watch the leisured set fooling around on their boats.

Inland to Loulé

LOULÉ, 11km inland from Quarteira, has a history similar to most of the towns in southern Portugal – Roman and Moorish occupation – and **castle ruins** to match. The castle walls are the best point to begin a look around town. They have been restored as a walkway and enclose a **Museu Municipal** of vaguely diverting historical bits and pieces. Between the museum and the thirteenth-century Gothic parish church nearby, a grid of whitewashed cobbled streets reveals numerous handicraft shops in which you're free to watch the craftsmen at work – lacemaking, in particular, is a flourishing local industry. On Saturdays, the town is transformed as the whole region seems to arrive en masse for a busy **country market** that still owes surprisingly little of its animation to the tourist trade.

Loulé's most curious sight is a beehive-shaped monument on a nearby hilltop, out in the direction of Boliqueime, which you can't help but notice as you arrive in town. It turns out to be the abandoned skeleton of a modern church; adjacent is the faded sixteenth-century chapel of **Nossa Senhora da Piedade**.

The **bus terminal** is just off the main Avenida 25 de Abril, a five-minute walk from the old town area; there are regular services from Quarteira and from Faro. The **Turismo** (Mon–Fri 9am–12.30pm & 2–5pm, Sat 9am–12.30pm; ☎089/639 00) is inside the castle walls, at Largo Dom Pedro I, and can help you to find **accommodation**. Two decent places are the *Pensão Santa Teresa*, Rua do Comércio (☎089/955 25; ②), off the main Praça da República, and the *Pensão Iberica* at Avenida José da Costa Mealha 40 (③). If you have the money, a clear first choice is the comfortable *Loulé Jardim Hotel* on Largo Manuel de Arriaga (☎089/41 30 94; ④).

There's a good choice of **places to eat**. Among a cluster of restaurants around the parish church, the *Casa de Pasta* serves salads and vegetarian meals, while *Aux Bons Enfants*, is known for its carefully prepared and pricey French cuisine (dinner only; closed Sun). For a real treat, try the intimate *Bica Velhas*, at Rua Bica Velhas 17 (closed Sun); or there's the cheap and cheerful *Ja Está*, Rua Miguel Bombarda 60, and the *Cavaco*, a couple of hundred metres further along the street, where the *cataplanas* are popular.

SUPERNATURAL FORCES ON THE ROAD TO LOULÉ

The following account comes from an impeccably reliable correspondent:

"Driving with a Portuguese friend along N270 from Poço de Boliqueime to Loulé, heading downhill after the *Eurocampina* factory, we noticed that the car began to slow down erratically, as if due to some mechanical failure. As this continued we felt the sensation of driving into some 'other force'. Putting the car into neutral, we slowed down and actually stopped before reaching the bottom of the hill! No brakes! After a few seconds of our stunned exclamations, the car began to move backwards, unaided, up the hill. We actually reached about 20mph until a lorry appeared on the horizon, at which point we slipped into gear and accelerated through "the force".

"I personally experienced this phenomenon on three separate occasions. Locals have no explanation – they prefer to create a mystery to amuse themselves and others. Non-believers are usually of the opinion that it is an optical illusion, and that the rock formations and horizon play tricks with the mind. Of this, I am somewhat dubious. I prefer the other, more inspired idea that some sort of magnetic force is in the area, created by friction at the quarry located further along the road. In fact many heavy-duty lorries use the road, so do pay attention while experimenting. If you can't get hold of a car try hitching a lift with holidayers in 'the force'."

Albufeira and around

Every inch a resort, **ALBUFEIRA** tops the list of package-tour – especially British package-tour – destinations in the Algarve. It was once an unusually pretty village, with narrow, twisting lanes of whitewashed houses criss-crossing the high grey-red cliffs above a beautiful spread of beaches. These still exist, but they are all but engulfed by hundreds of new apartment buildings strung across the local hillsides. If you're looking for unspoiled Portugal, this isn't it – whatever the brochures might say. Nevertheless, Albufeira is still one of the nicer resorts, attracting a varied mix of holidaymakers: an ageing, well-heeled clientele who frequent the more expensive restaurants, and a younger contingent who seem to devote themselves to downing as much beer as is humanly possible.

There's still a Moorish feel to parts of central Albufeira, as well as the more tangible remnants of a Moorish castle – the original Arabic name of the town, *Al-Buhera*, means "Castle-on-the-Sea". But the 1755 earthquake did for much of the town, and most of the modern centre is nondescript, though enlivened somewhat by a small fishing harbour.

None of this is of any consequence whatsoever to the summer crowds, who sleep and eat in town but spend their days at one of a dozen excellent cove-beaches in the vicinity. The **beach** fronting Albufeira itself – reached through a tunnel from the main Rua 5 de Outubro – is as good as any of these, flanked by strange tooth-like rock formations. If it's too crowded here, a relatively short bus (or taxi) ride can open up a number of other possibilities, the best of which are detailed on p.375. At night, the focus switches to Albufeira's central, pedestrianised streets and squares, lined with pavement cafés, bars and restaurants fronted by eager touts and waiters keen to entice you in.

Practicalities

If you're in Albufeira on a package holiday, you might well not be staying in the town at all, but in one of the handful of small resort-villages on either side, like Montechoro, Areias de São João or Praia da Oura. However, all have access to their own beaches and are, in any case, within two or three kilometres of the town centre, which you can reach on regular local buses or by taxi. Everyone else will arrive in Albufeira at the **bus terminal** on Avenida da Liberdade, at the top of town, five minutes' walk from the central Largo Eng. Duarte Pacheco, just to the west of which is the main street, Rua 5 de Outubro. At the end of here is the tunnel that's been blasted out of the rock to give access to the town beach. The **Turismo** (daily 9.30am–8pm; ☎089/51 21 44) is on Rua 5 de Outubro, close to the tunnel. Albufeira's "local" **train station** is actually 6km north of town at Ferreiras; a bus runs to and from the bus station roughly hourly (7am–10pm).

Accommodation

Finding a room can be difficult in high season since most of the **hotels and pensions** are block-booked by package holiday companies. Those listed below are a few exceptions, which may have "independent" vacancies. Otherwise the tourist office can help you find a **private room**, though they'll charge you for any phonecalls they make. Perhaps the best bet, when all is said and done, is to accept the offer of a room from one of the touts who lurk around the bus station; you can always look around on your own later if it's not up to scratch.

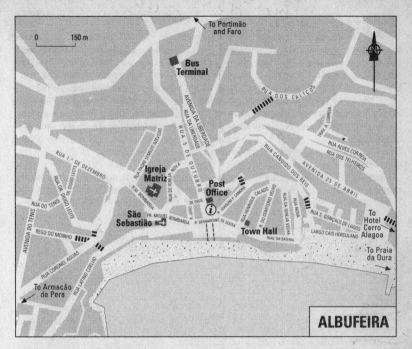

ALBUFEIRA

An attractive alternative is the finely appointed (and expensive) **Camping Albufeira** (☎089/58 95 05; open all year) – complete with swimming pools, restaurants, bars, shops and tennis courts – 2km to the north of town, off the N396, with regular connections from the bus station (any bus to Portimão/Lagos passes it).

Pensão Albufeirense, Rua da Liberdade 18 (☎089/51 20 79). A modern, comfortable *pensão*, with fairly reasonably priced rooms, with and without bath. ③–④.

Hotel Cerro Alagoa, via Rápida, Apartado 2155 (☎089/58 82 61). Extremely comfortable modern hotel on the hill above town, ten minutes' walk from the centre (take the steps at the eastern end of Avda. 25 de Abril), with its own pool, gardens and gym, and courtesy bus to the local beaches. Buffet breakfast included. ⑥.

Residencial Limas, Rua da Liberdade 25–27 (☎089/51 40 25). A good, central choice, though the ten rooms fill quickly. Prices almost halve outside peak season. ④.

Residencial Polana, Rua Cândido dos Reis 32 (☎089/558 59). A large, package-tour hotel, right in the thick of things – it's on a very noisy street full of bars. Rooms come with shower, and breakfast is included. ④.

Pensão Silva, Rua 5 de Outubro 18 (☎089/526 69). Very close to the tourist office, in an alleyway to the right as you face the beach, this is among the cheapest of the places to stay. It only has six rooms so call early. ③.

Residencial Vila Bela, Rua Coronel Águas 15 (☎089/51 21 01). Situated on the west side of the centre (at the junction with Avda. do Ténis), this is an attractive *residencial* with balconied rooms overlooking a small swimming pool and the bay. Open April to October only. ④.

Residencial Vila Branca, Rua do Ténis 4 (☎089/58 68 04). A three-star *residencial* up in the modern part of town, ten minutes from the beach; worth trying if central options are full. ③.

STAYED AURAMORA condo 7000 1 ESCUATOES

Eating

Albufeira has **restaurants** to match every budget – and most tastes. As well as Portuguese restaurants, there's also a whole range of places serving pizzas, Chinese and Indian food, even fish and chips. Naturally, you tend to get what you pay for, but for the better bargains head for the area behind the fishing harbour, to the east of the main beach. Stand around outside, perusing the menu, and you'll often be presented with enticements in the form of drinks vouchers and the like. The morning-after-the-night-before is well catered for in most restaurants and bars, with massive **English-style breakfasts** available until the sensible hour of 2pm.

Restaurants

A Ruina, Praia dos Pescadores, Largo Cais Herculano. Rustic old restaurant on the beach, serving fish fresh from the market. Eat on the beach, inside on one of two floors, or on the roof-terrace. Sardines and salad make a reasonably inexpensive lunch, but otherwise you're looking at 3500$00 and up for a full dinner.

Cabaz da Praia, Praça Miguel Bombarda 7. Just up the hill from the main street and overlooking the beach, this serves excellent but expensive meals. The menu is mainly French-inspired, and the roof terrace offers fine views – for which you're paying higher than usual prices, say 3000–4000$00 a head.

Cantinho Algarvio, Trav. Cais Herculano. Mid-range restaurant where you can fill up on cuts of meat and other standard Portuguese dishes. Around 2000$00.

Louisiana, Largo Cais Herculano. On the terrace above the fisherman's beach, drink cocktails at the outdoor seats and then repair upstairs for selections from the grill menu.

very good

Sotavento, Rua São Gonçalo de Lagos 16. Behind the fishing harbour, this small bar-restaurant serves an affordable selection of Portuguese standards. Around 1500–2000$00.

OUT OF TOWN

A Curva, Rua da Moinheta 25, Algoz. Ten kilometres inland of Albufeira, on the other side of the main N125 highway, this village restaurant has a deservedly high reputation for remarkably good-value country cooking. Closed Sun.

La Cigale, Olhos de Água. Nine kilometres east of Albufeira, and right on the beach, this renowned restaurant has a lovely terrace and high-quality food, including great seafood. Open for dinner only; expect to pay around 3500$00.

Drinking and nightlife

Like the restaurants, Albufeira **bars** are into promotion. There's not much to choose between them, and you may as well frequent those offering the cheapest drinks at the time. In this important connection, keep your eyes open for local free sheets, which carry a great number of Happy Hour (or more) coupons. The main areas for carousing are along Rua São Gonçalo de Lagos, around Largo Eng. Duarte Pacheco and – for more of a late-night scene – along Rua Cândido dos Reis and Travessa Cândido dos Reis. **Discos**, too, are much of a muchness; all stay open until around 4am.

Classic Bar, Rua Cândido dos Reis 10. Loud and young, outside or in – one of the essential stops on the nightlife circuit.

Jo Jo's, Rua São Gonçalo de Lagos. Pub with British soccer and other sports on satellite TV, and London DJs to jolly the crowd along.

Kiss, Montechoro. Out of town, at the southern end of Montechoro, this is regarded as the best club around. The music is good, but the club tends to be overcrowded and very glitzy; watch for flyposters advertising events.

Silvia's, Rua São Gonçalo de Lagos. Central Albufeira disco on a street full of late-opening bars. The entry price includes one drink.

Sir Harry's Bar, Largo Eng. Duarte Pacheco 37–38. Long-standing tourist institution on the square, with English breakfasts and draft British beer.

Sol Dourado, Largo Cais Herculano. Perched above the square, this is one of the nicer terrace-bars from which to watch the sun set over the water.

Zansi Bar, Rua Miguel Bombarda. Live music, *karaoke* and good-value food served day and night.

The local beaches

The rocky red headlands just to the **west of Albufeira** are beautiful – and were largely inaccessible until the 1980s, when the development of a strip of villa resorts very much changed the landscape. There are no direct buses to these resorts, though the Albufeira–Portimão service drops passengers on the main road, a steep 2km walk distant. The main resorts – **SÃO RAFAEL, CASTELO** and **GALÉ** – spread back from small cove beaches with craggy, eroded rock faces. Each is dominated by villa developments, though not all have been finished and the whole area can occasionally resemble a building site, with great gashes of red earth exposed by the bulldozers.

Overall, it's better to head **east of Albufeira**, where you have several more choices. Immediately east of town, ochre-red cliffs divide the coastline into a series of bays and beaches, all reached on local buses (6–9 daily) from the bus station. You can walk to the first, **PRAIA DA OURA**, just 2km from Albufeira, by heading up the steps at the end of Avenida 25 de Abril and following the road out of town; signposts point you down to the beach after 25 minutes. This, though, has been extensively developed and you might want to push on by bus to **OLHOS DE ÁGUA**, 7km further east, an erstwhile fishing village with a smaller beach. If this, too, is crowded, you can walk beyond it to other more isolated coves.

At **PRAIA DA FALÉSIA**, 10km east of Albufeira, and 20 minutes away by bus, the character of the coastline changes to produce one long tremendous stretch of sand, backed by unbroken red cliffs. Just before Falésia, the bus passes through Aldeia das Açoteias, a bewildering chalet and villa complex, from where four daily buses depart for Vilamoura and Quarteira (see p.370).

Inland

If you have transport, you can explore further **inland**, though you're not going to get much off the beaten track. Twenty kilometres to the north, the small town of **SÃO BARTOLOMEU DE MESSINES** preserves a sixteenth-century parish church, remodelled in Baroque style and incorporating interior columns decorated with twisted stone rope. From here, it's 18km southwest to Silves (p.379), one possible lunch stop, or only about half that to the pretty village of **ALTE**, to the east, along the winding N124. Tacked across the hillside, a series of narrow, cobbled, mostly pedestrian streets lead up to the *Fonte Grande*, where there's a stream and an old mill, now converted into a restaurant that caters largely to the "safari" tours that stream out of Albufeira in jeeps into the surrounding countryside in search of the "real" Portugal. You can eat better at the *Cafe Central*, next to the church, back in the centre.

West towards Portimão

Heading west from Albufeira along the main N125, you'll pass through **PORCHES**, about halfway between Alcantarilha and Lagoa. This is where the most famous of the Algarve's handmade **pottery** comes from. Thick, chunky and handpainted, it has a good heavy feel, and if you're looking for thoroughly impractical and ridiculously cheap presents to take home, this is the place to stop. Further on, **LAGOA** is best known for its wine; tours of the vineyards are arranged through local tourist offices.

Down to the coast: Armação de Pêra and Praia da Marinha

Off the main road, down on the coast, is the resort of **ARMAÇÃO DE PÊRA**, about which little complimentary can be said, except for the fact that it claims the largest beach in the Algárve (not a unique claim in these parts, by any means). The bus terminal (little more than an old shed) is at the eastern end of the town and there are regular services from Albufeira and Silves.

There are better things to report about **Praia da Marinha**, however, reached from a turning south between Porches and Lagoa (no bus services). A path leads from a parking area on the clifftop down to an immaculate sandy beach with a string of secluded coves, beautifully warm sea even in winter, and relatively few people to share it with. There's a café of uncertain hours on the sand by the path.

Carvoeiro and Estômbar

Further west, the small resort of **CARVOEIRO** can be reached by bus from Lagoa. Cut into the red sea cliffs, it remains quite an attractive place, despite a line of villa-apartments draped across the surrounding hills. The beach, however, is much too small to cope with the summer influx, and rooms are virtually out of the question in high season. The resort also has quite a number of bars and restaurants, a tourist office and boats offering fishing or beach trips. Accessible by the coast road, a kilometre east, are the impressive rock formations of **Algar Seco**, where the cliffs form dramatic overhangs above narrow beaches – though there's a monstrous hotel a little further along. By way of contrast, a few kilometres inland is **ESTÔMBAR** (a stop for slow trains on the Algarve line), an unremarkable little town that was birthplace of the eleventh-century Moorish poet Ibn Ammãr. The town straggles down a steep hill in a confusion of narrow lanes – nothing very special, though at least you feel you're in Portugal.

Portimão and around

PORTIMÃO is one of the largest towns on the Algarve, with a population of 30,000 plus. It has made its living from fishing since pre-Roman times and with its site on the estuary of the Rio Arade, remains today a sprawling port, a major sardine-canning centre, and a base for the construction industries spawned by the tourist boom. Its appearance is undistinguished – most of the older buildings were destroyed in the 1755 earthquake – and it is pedestrianised shopping streets and graceless high-rises that dominate. However, the riverfront and fishing harbour is a hive of activity with bars and open-air restaurants, serving grilled sardine lunches, and there's a huge **market** on the first Monday of each month, held on the open land beyond the train station.

Most visitors are just here for a day's shopping, taking time out from the resort of **Praia da Rocha**, three kilometres south of Portimão. This more or less merges with the town these days, though keeps a highly distinct identity of its own as a fairly upmarket resort. Just across the estuary to the east of Portimão is the workaday town of **Ferragudo**, with a much smaller and less fancy beach. The coast road west of Praia da Rocha, towards Lagos, has been engulfed by a series of massive and graceless tourist developments of very little interest; only **Alvor** retains any charm at all.

Practicalities

The **train station** is inconveniently located at the northern tip of town and there's no connecting bus into town; a taxi costs about 400$00 or it's a twenty-minute walk. **Buses** pull up much more centrally, on the Largo do Duque, close to the river, from where it's a five-minute walk to the **quayside**, which stretches as far as the bridge over to Ferragudo. The **Turismo** at the top of the central Largo 1 de Dezembro (Mon–Sat 9.30am–12.30pm & 2–6pm; ☎082/236 95) helps with **accommodation**, but it's scarcely worth staying when much nicer Silves or Lagos are so close. Still, if you do get stuck, better value options include the *Pensão O Pátio*, Rua Dr. João Vitorino Mealha 5 (☎082/242 88; ③), near the tourist office, or the spick-and-span *Pensão Arabi*, Praça Manuel Teixeira Gomes 13 (☎082/260 06; ④), closer to the port. There's also a local **youth hostel** (☎082/857 04) at Lugar do Coca Maravilhas, to which the tourist office can direct you.

Any of the stalls that line the quayside, underneath the bridge, will charcoal-grill half a dozen huge **sardines**, and serve them up with a plate of chips and half a bottle of the local wine for under 1000$00. For regular **restaurant** surroundings, try the friendly *Bom Apetite Restaurant*, Rua Júdice Fialho 21, which serves authentic Portuguese cooking, including a splendid *arroz de marisco*.

Praia da Rocha

PRAIA DA ROCHA, ten minutes' south by bus, was one of the first Algarve tourist developments and it's easy to see why. The **beach** is one of the most beautiful on the entire coast: a wide expanse of sand framed by jagged sea cliffs and the walls of an old **fort** (housing a café-restaurant) that once protected the mouth of the River Arade. It was more beautiful still before a great chunk of cliff was blown away to improve access, and the high-rise hotels, discos and sports complex were built alongside the casino.

Bus connections from Praia da Rocha are excellent, with a half-hourly shuttle to Portimão; the stop is outside the *Hotel Jupiter*. Surprisingly, **accommodation** is rarely hard to find, with an array of private rooms arranged through the **Turismo** (Mon–Sat 9am–12.30pm & 2–5.30pm; ☎082/222 90), on the main street, Rua Tomás Cabreira, near the fort. On the cliffs above the beach you'll find the attractive *Solar Penguin* (☎082/243 08; ④), an old mansion with rooms overlooking the sea; the prices drop in winter. If you have thousands of *escudos* burning a hole in your pocket, however, *the* place to stay (if it's open after restoration) is the seafront *Hotel Bela Vista*, a pseudo-Moorish mansion built in 1903 as a wedding gift by the wealthy Magalhães family; the interior is an exquisite mixture of carved woods, stained glass and yellow, white and blue *azulejos*.

Restaurants are plentiful. The *Safari*, Rua António Feu, overlooks the beach and serves Portuguese dishes with an Angolan influence. *O Cloque* (follow the signs for *Rocha dos Castelos*) is a large candlelit venue, complete with several bars, a restaurant and a patio overlooking the sea. **Bars** include *Coconuts*, on Rua Bartolomeu Dias, and *Farmers*, behind the *Jupiter Hotel*, which are both as good (or bad) as they sound, depending on your viewpoint.

Ferragudo

FERRAGUDO, facing Portimão across the estuary, and connected by a regular bus service, is very different in character. Stuck on the side of a hill, it's a rundown little place of narrow streets and tiny houses that has only recently begun to be fancied up for tourists. It sprawls around a fort – the partner to that in Praia da Rocha, built in the sixteenth century to defend Portimão against attack. The town has a couple of small pensions and a few private rooms for rent through the local bars or at the tourist office (if it's open). There are a couple of lively bars – check out the *Caldeirão* which has jazz some nights – and an excellent **restaurant**, *A Lanterna* (closed Sun), which is to be found just across the bridge from Portimão; the smoked swordfish is particularly tempting.

The Ferragudo **beach** is about a kilometre to the south of town. It is popular in a small-scale way, with a windsurfing school and a scattering of restaurant-bars. A large **campsite** (☎082/64 11 21) slouches next to the road ten minutes further to the south of the beach.

Alvor and Quinta da Rocha

Much of the appeal of the ancient port of **ALVOR**, 6km west of Praia da Rocha, has been washed away under a tide of tourists from the surrounding hotels and holiday villages: the town's narrow streets and its multitude of bars and restaurants can hardly cope. Whitewashed houses and lovely views of the estuary are the last vestiges of Alvor's charm. Nonetheless, the **beach** is enormous and if it's a bit on the dull side, at least you can escape the crowds. The west end is also an excellent place for catching *conquilhas* (shellfish). At low tide wriggle your feet under the sand in the shallows until you feel one move, then reach down and grab it – or simply copy the Portuguese who will be out there with you. *Conquilhas* are good fried for a few minutes with oil and garlic (until they open).

In season, **rooms** at Alvor are hard to come by, but there are two **campsites**: one near the beach (*Parque d'Alvor*, ☎082/45 91 78) and the more pleasant *Campismo Dourado* about 1km north, toward Montes de Alvor. The beach **café** *Rosemar* does good fish and basic meals.

Quinta da Rocha

The **Quinta da Rocha nature reserve** lies in the peninsula between the mouths of the rivers Alvor and Odiáxere, northwest of Alvor's huge beach. It is an extensive area which, in the parts not given over to citrus and almond groves, consists of copses, salt marsh, sandy spits and estuarine mudflats, forming a wide range of habitats for different plants and animal life – including twenty-two species of **wading bird**. A Christian environmental group, *A Rocha*, runs a bird-ringing programme from a field centre known as *Cruzinha*, in the middle of the reserve.

The centre also has limited full-board accommodation, in shared rooms, though as its aims are to increase the awareness in Portugal of the environment and Christianity, precedence is given to Portuguese visitors. Access to *Cruzinha* is from a turning south at Mexilhoeira Grande on the coastal N125 highway.

Silves

Eighteen kilometres northeast of Portimão, **SILVES** – the medieval residence and capital of the Moorish kings of the al-Gharb – is one of the few inland towns in this province that really merits a detour. It has a superb castle and a highly dramatic approach, with its red ring of walls gradually revealing their course as you emerge from the wooded hills. Under the Moors, Silves was a place of grandeur, described in contemporary accounts as "of shining brightness" within its three dark circuits of guarding walls. Such glories and civilised spendours came to an end, however, in 1189, with the arrival of **Sancho I**, at the head of a mixed army of Portuguese and Crusaders. Sancho himself was a devout king, at least by the standards of his day, but, desperately in need of extra fighting force, had recruited a rabble of "large and odious" northerners, who had already been expelled from the holy shrine of Saint James of Compostela for their irreligious behaviour. The army arrived at Silves toward the end of June and the 30,000 Moors retreated to the citadel. There they remained through the long, hot summer, sustained by huge water cisterns and granaries, until September, when, the water exhausted, they opened negotiations.

Sancho was ready to compromise, but the Crusaders had been recruited by the promise of plunder, and were not prepared to accept the king's financial inducements to forgo the pleasure of wrecking the town. The gates were opened after Sancho had negotiated guarantees for the inhabitants' personal safety and goods; all were brutally ignored by the Crusaders, who duly ransacked the town, killing some six thousand Moors in the process. Silves passed back into Moorish hands two years later, but by then the town had been irreperably weakened, and it finally fell to Christian forces in 1249.

The Town

The **Moorish Fortress** (always open) remains the focal point of Silves, dominating the town centre with its impressively complete set of sandstone walls, detached towers and elaborate communication system. The interior is a bit disappointing: aside from the great vaulted water cisterns that still serve the town, there's nothing left of the old citadel, which is planted with modern gardens. However, you can circuit the walls for impressive views over the town and surrounding hills. There's a "traditional festival" held here every Saturday night in summer, and a lively annual **beer festival** in June.

Silves' cathedral, or **Sé** (daily 8.30am–1pm & 2.30–6pm), sits below the fortress, built on the site of the Grand Mosque. Flanked by broad Gothic towers, it has a suitably defiant, military appearance, though the Great Earthquake and centuries of impoverished restoration have left their mark within.

Below the Sé, in Rua das Portas de Loulé, is the town's **Museu Arqueologia** (Mon–Sat 10am–12.30pm & 2–6pm; 300$00). It's engaging enough, despite a lack of English-language labelling, and romps through the history of Silves from the year dot to the sixteenth century, through displays of local archeological finds. At the centre of the museum is an Arab water cistern, left *in situ*, which boasts a ten-metre-deep well.

Strolling around the rest of Silves is a pleasure. There's a **market** on the river-front, near the narrow thirteenth-century bridge. This is a fine place to sit out at at one of the grill-cafés (see below) and watch life go by.

Practicalities

The **train station** – an easy approach from either Lagos or Faro – lies two kilo-metres out of town; there is a connecting bus, but it's a pleasant walk if you're not weighed down with luggage. Arriving by **bus**, you'll be dropped on the main road, near the riverfront at the foot of town.

The **Turismo** on Rua 25 de Abril (Mon–Fri 9.30am–12.30pm & 2–5pm, Sat 9.30am–12.30pm; ☎082/44 22 55), in the heart of the town, will help arrange **private rooms**. Recommended are those with Isabel Maria da Silva at Rua Cândido dos Reis 36 (☎082/44 26 67; ②), which are spotless and share the use of a kitchen and a little outdoor terrace; a second choice are the rooms in the same street at no. 9. Alternatively, there are a couple of **pensions**, including the comfortable old *Residencial Sousa*, Rua Samora Barros 17 (☎082/44 25 02; ②); and a **hotel**, the *Albergaria Marisqueira Rui*, just across the river on the south bank (☎082/44 31 06; ④). This is an excellent modern hotel, which incorporates one of the best restaurants to be found anywhere on the Algarve; the hotel drops its prices out of season, too.

For **eating**, the *Restaurante Marisqueira Rui*, above the *Albergaria* (closed Tues), continues to attract residents and tourists from all over the Algarve; if you manage to squeeze in – and you should try – order shellfish, the restaurant's speciality. At the other end of the price scale, and just as enjoyable in its way, is the *Churrasqueria Valdemar*, the best of a handful of grill-cafés on the riverfront road in front of the market. Sit outside and tuck into *piri-piri* chicken, chips, salad and wine for around 1300$00. The *Café Inglês*, by the fortress, sells delicious homemade snacks, ice cream and fruit juices, as well as full meals, and also has seats outside; while *Café Rosa*, in the Praça do Municipio, serves drinks and cakes all day (closed Sun).

Inland to the Serra de Monchique

Nine buses a day leave Portimão for the 24-kilometre, ninety-minute journey north to **Monchique** via **Caldas de Monchique**. Once clear of Portimão's ugly suburbs, the main road crosses the coastal plain, flanked by endless orchards of apples, pears, figs, almonds, pomegranates and citrus fruits. At Porto de Lagos the road divides, east to Silves and north into the foothills of the **Serra de Monchique**; a green and wooded mountain range of cork, chestnut and eucalyptus that provides the western Algarve with a natural northern boundary. It is ideal **hiking country**, or – with a bike or car – a superb route to take if you want to cut across afterwards to the wilder reaches of the western Algarve coast (see p.392).

Caldas de Monchique

CALDAS DE MONCHIQUE, set in a ravine and surrounded by thick woods, has been a celebrated spa since Roman times. In 1495 Dom João II came here to take the waters (though he nevertheless died soon afterwards in Alvor), and in the nineteenth century the town became a favourite resort of the Spanish bourgeoisie. A casino from these times still stands in the main square, serving now as an excellent **handicraft centre**, surrounded by lovely, fading nineteenth-century buildings. The setting is as beautiful as any in the country, though the tiny village's peace and quiet is shattered daily by the busloads of day-trippers who stop for a wander around and a cup of coffee. At times, the buses queue nose-to-tail on the way into the village.

The modern Thermal Hospital sits below the main square, on the edge of a ravine, flaunting its well-kept gardens; below is the ugly *Oficina de Engarrafamento* where the famous water is bottled for sale around the country. But at least this maintains the town's tradition, and Caldas remains an active spa rather than being simply quaint. Climbing up from the spa, behind the square, you can follow the stream to sit under giant eucalyptus trees and picnic. Try taking along some of the local arbutus-berry-derived *aguardente* (fire water), on sale in the handicraft centre, which nicely complements the spring water.

There are two cheap **pensions** in town. The better of the two is the ochre-coloured *Hospedaria Central* (☎082/922 03; ②), backing onto the main square. The other, the *Nova Pensão Internacional* (②), is 100 metres further back, on the road into town. Both are basic, but both also have a wonderful air of melancholic decay which seems to hang over these old spas, especially out of season. A third, more comfortable option is the *Albergaria do Lageado* (☎082/926 16; ④; May–Sept only), which has a pool and garden, and an excellent **restaurant** where you can eat for under 2000$00. The *Central* also has a restaurant, similarly priced and there's another, *1692*, on the square. Out of season you may well find all these places closed.

Not all the **buses** from Portimão call into the centre of Caldas, stopping instead on the main road just out of town before continuing up to Monchique. Note, too, that there's a once-daily summer tourist service from Albufeira (with connections from Vilamoura, Quarteira and Faro) via Silves.

Monchique and around

MONCHIQUE, 6km to the north of Caldas de Monchique, and 300m higher up the range, is a small market town with a huge monthly agricultural fair, famous for its smoked hams and its furniture. There's not a great deal to see, but it's a busy town and makes a nice enough excursion. Of the buildings, the most impressive is the **Igreja Matriz**, the parish church, up a steep cobbled street from the main square, which has a Manueline porch and, inside, a little chapel with a facade of *azulejos*. The most evocative sight, though, is the ruined seventeenth-century monastery of **Nossa Senhora do Desterro**. Only a roofless shell of this Franciscan foundation survives, apparently quite uncared for, but it's in a great position overlooking the town and shows a beautiful blend of classical Renaissance facade with Moorish-influenced vaulting.

The **bus terminal** is in the main square, at the bottom of town. Close by, there are a couple of **places to stay** (though it's difficult to see why you'd need to).

First choice, if you can afford it, is the very welcoming *Residencial Estrela de Monchique*, Rua do Porto Fundo 46 (☎082/931 11; ④), a stone's throw to the right of the bus terminal. Otherwise, the *Bela Vista*, in the main square, is cheaper but noisier and a bit unappealing.

Monchique also has a handful of **restaurants** which soak up the passing tourist trade. *Restaurante A Charrette* on Rua Samora Gil is highly recommended, while *Café Montanha*, Rua do Revez Quente, is fairly inexpensive, serving typical Algarvian meat and fish dishes.

Fóia

Fóia, 8km west of Monchique, is – at nearly 900m – the highest of the Serra's peaks. There are no buses but you might be lucky in hitching a lift from a daytripper. At the top there's a concrete obelisk, a radio tower, a few stalls selling knick-knacks and knitwear (it can be cool up here), a pension-café, *O Planalto*, a hotel, the *Estalagem de Santo António*, and a lot of bus tours . . . What draws the latter is a panoramic view of the Algarve, taking in Portimão, Lagos, the foothills stretching to the Barragem da Bravura, and Cabo de São Vicente. The poet Robert Southey claimed to have caught a glimpse of the hills of Sintra, beyond Lisbon, but that must have been one of those legendary "clear days" – or maybe the air is never as clear now as it was in 1801.

Picota

Reaching 770 metres, **Picota** comes second in altitude to Fóia, though it's much more interesting in terms of its botany, and easier to reach without transport. You can reach the peak from Monchique in around one and a half hours, a walk that takes in cork trees (and cork collection points), eucalyptus and pines, peach, lemon and orange orchards, and even wild goats scurrying about the heights. At the top there's nothing save a rickety watchtower occupied by a solitary guardian with a pair of binoculars. From here you can see the coastline stretching all the way to Sagres, and take in another magnificent view of the Monchique mountain range.

West to the coast

Back down the road from Monchique towards Caldas, the minor N267 cuts west towards the coast, passing through **MARMELETE** after 14km. There are two buses a day from Monchique, but no real point in coming since, unless you're lucky enough to flag down a lift, you won't get any further – and it's another 20km to Aljezur (p.393) and ten more to the coast beyond that. In a car, though, it's a fine route, heading through tranquil countryside before swinging down through the hills and forests to the west coast.

North to Santa Clara

Heading north from Monchique on the main N266 road, it's 20km to the border with Alentejo province through forests of eucalyptus and around another 20km to the huge **Barragem de Santa Clara** – the largest artificial dam in Portugal. After here, the route cuts across the flatlands of the Alentejo to a fork with turnings for Odemira and the west coast, or Beja and the eastern Alentejo.

Just west of the dam, **SANTA CLARA-A-VELHA** (1–2 daily buses from Monchique) makes a pleasant break in the journey, a compact little town with a surviving Roman bridge, rooms and a few café-restaurants where you can get a meal of fresh fish from the Barragem. There's also a **pousada** here, the *Santa Clara* (☎083/98 250; ⑥), a tiny place close to the dam, with just six rooms and a swimming pool; book ahead.

Lagos

LAGOS is one of the most ancient settlements in the Algarve, founded by the Phoenicians, who were attracted to its superb natural harbour. Under the Moors it became an important trading post until its reconquest by Christian armies in 1241. Its attractions today are less the historical associations – though there are a couple of fine churches and a circuit of medieval walls – than the fact that it remains a real town; a fishing port and market centre with a sense of independence and a life of its own. It has, of course, over the last two decades, also developed into a major resort, attracting the whole gamut of visitors, from backpackers to moneyed second-homers. They come for some of the best beaches of the whole Algarve coast: to the east of the town is a long sweep of sand – Meia Praia – where there's space even in summer, while to the west is an extraordinary network of coves, sheltered by cliffs, pierced by tunnels and grottoes, and studded by weird and extravagantly weathered outcrops of purple-tinted rock.

Arriving and accommodation

Lagos is the western terminal of the Algarve railway line and its **train station** is across the river, twenty minutes' walk from the centre; taxis are usually available if you can't face the walk. The **bus station** is a bit closer in, a block back from the main estuary road, Avenida dos Descobrimentos, and almost opposite the bridge to the train station. If you're just passing through Lagos on your way to Sagres, check at the train station before marching into town, since the bus on to Sagres from Lagos tends to call there first.

For those that are staying, it's probably wise to make straight for the **Turismo** in the Largo Marquês de Pombal (Mon 9.30am–12.30pm & 2–8pm, Tues–Thurs 9.30am–8pm, Fri 9.30am–12.30pm & 2–7pm, Sat & Sun 9.30am–12.30pm & 2–5.30pm; ☎082/76 30 31), which is the square adjacent to the central Praça Gil Eanes. They will help with booking private rooms, as well as dishing out maps, leaflets and timetables.

Accommodation

Most of the town's hotels and pensions are fully booked through the summer and unless you turn up very early in the day, your only chance of a bed will be a **room** in a private house, for which you'll pay 3000–4000$00 double, depending on the time of year. The tourist office will phone around and try to find you a space, if there's anything left on their books; arriving early in the day you'll probably be met by touts at the bus or train stations. It's a good idea to take whatever's going (as long as it's central), and look round later at your leisure. Out of season, or booking in advance, you could try for space at one of the established **pensions** and **hotels**, a selection of which are listed below. Prices are comparatively high in season; in winter, however, there are bargains to be had at many of the beach hotels west of town – ask at the tourist office for details.

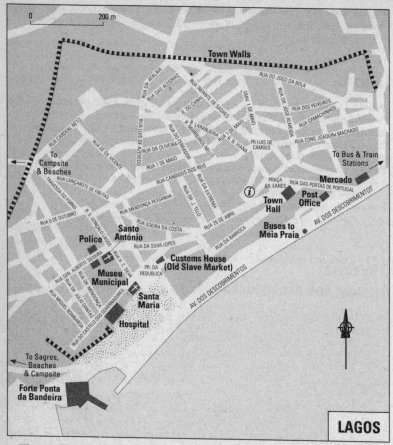

There's a new **youth hostel** (see listings below) in town, while Lagos also has two **campsites**, both to the west of the centre, close by the Praia de Dona Ana. *Parque de Campismo Imulagos* (☎082/76 00 31) is the larger of the sites – huge, in fact, with good facilities, lots of shade and access to a private beach. *Campismo da Trindade* (☎082/76 38 13) is marginally closer to town and beach, but is much more cramped (though it's only half the price of the *Imulagos*). In season a bus marked "D. Ana/Porto de Mós" runs to the sites from the bus station, while the *Imulagos* site provides its own free bus from the train station (hourly 8am–10.30pm). On foot, follow the main Sagres road around the old town and it's about ten to fifteen minutes from the Forte Ponta da Bandeira to the sites.

Residencial Baia, Rua da Barroca 70 (☎082/76 22 92). A slightly less expensive alternative to the *Rubi Mar*, located on the ground floor of the same building, but not as nice or as friendly. ④

Pensão Caravela, Rua 25 de Abril 16 (☎082/76 33 61). Reasonable rooms on the town's main pedestrianised street. Doubles come with or without bath; breakfast included.③

Pensão Dona Ana, Praia de Dona Ana (☎082/76 23 22). Situated at Lagos' finest beach, a 20-minute walk from town across the clifftops. In summer, you'll need to book well in advance for one of the 11 rooms. ③.

Hotel de Lagos, Rua Nova da Aldeia (☎082/76 99 67). The finest hotel in the centre and boasting a remarkable landscaped, "village-style" design – separate compounds of rooms, bars, restaurants and sports facilities joined by glassed-in corridors and walkways. There's a courtesy bus service to its own beach club at Meia Praia, too; and hefty off-season price reductions. ⑤–⑥.

Pensão Lagosmar, Rua Dr. Faria e Silva 13 (☎082/76 37 22). Upmarket *pensão*, close to Praça Gil Eanes, and reliable enough for the money. ⑤.

Residencial Mar Azul, Rua 25 de Abril 13 (☎082/76 97 49). The better establishment on this street, but at the top end of the price scale. A few of the rooms have their own shower and terrace; and breakfast is included. ④.

Pensão Rubi Mar, Rua da Barroca 70 (☎082/631 65). There are only nine rooms here, but if you can find space it's a treat; some have sea views and breakfast is included. The street is off the main Rua 25 de Abril. ③–④.

Pousada de Juventude de Lagos, Rua de Lançarote de Freitas 50 (☎082/76 19 70). The new youth hostel has a few double rooms with shower available (breakfast included), though you'll have to book in advance. The road is a right turn off Rua Cândido dos Reis, walking southwest. ①–②.

The town

Lagos was a favoured residence of Henry the Navigator, who used the town as a base for the new African trade, to which is owed the town's least proud relic – Europe's first **slave market**, whose arcades survive alongside the old **Customs House** in the **Praça da República** near the waterfront. On the other side of this square is the church of **Santa Maria**, through whose whimsical Manueline windows the youthful Dom Sebastião is said to have roused his troops before the ill-fated Moroccan expedition of 1578. Fired up by militant Catholicism, the dream-crazed king was to perish on the battlefield of Alcácer-Quibir (modern Ksar el Kbir, between Tangier and Fes) along with almost the entire Portuguese nobility. It was a disaster that enabled the Spanish to absorb Portugal for sixty years, but it did Dom Sebastião's reputation a world of good among the aggressively devout. He's commemorated in the centre of Lagos, in **Praça Gil Eanes**, by a fantastically dreadful modern statue – pink, ridiculous and looking like a flowerpot man.

Much of the old town was devastated by the 1755 earthquake, though one rare and beautiful church that survived for restoration was the **Igreja de Santo António**. This really demands a look, even if you don't normally venture into churches. Decorated around 1715, its gilt and carved interior is wildly obsessive, every last inch filled with a private fantasy of cherubic youths struggling with animals and fish. Next door is the **Museu Municipal** (Tues–Sun 9.30am–12.30pm & 2–5pm; 200$00), whose bizarre displays range from Roman mosaics and folk costumes to misshapen animal foetuses.

The Praça da República, and the waterfront Avenida dos Descobrimentos, are the best vantage points for the remains of Lagos' once impregnable **walls** and fortifications, which include the squat seventeenth-century **Forte Ponta da Bandeira** (Tues–Sat 10am–1pm and 2–6pm, Sun 10am–1pm; 200$00), guarding the entrance to the harbour.

The beaches

The promontory **south** of Lagos is fringed by extravagantly eroded cliff faces that shelter a series of postage stamp-sized cove-beaches. All are within easy walking distance of the old town, though the beach tracks are increasingly confused by a multitude of paths leading to the hotels and campsites. In addition, the concentration of resort hotels near the beaches means that you may find the least crowded strand is the **town beach** itself, just beyond the Forte Ponta da Bandeira.

Cove beaches to the south

The easiest access on foot to the cove-beaches is to follow the Avenida dos Descobrimentos up the hill (toward Sagres) and turn left just opposite the fire station, where you see the signs to the tiny **Praia do Pinhão**. This is the first of the coves – around a twenty-minute walk from town. Five minutes further, across the cliffs, is the **Praia de Dona Ana** – one of the most photogenic of all the Algarve's beaches, with a good restaurant, the *Mirante*, built into the cliffs.

Beyond here, despite the jostling hotels, you can follow a path around the cliffs and coast to **Praia do Camilo** – sometimes a bit less crowded – and right to the **Ponta da Piedade**, the point, where a palm-bedecked lighthouse makes a great vantage point for the sunset.

Meia Praia

To the **east** of Lagos, flanked by the railway line, is **Meia Praia**, a vast tract of sand that extends for 4km to the delta of the rivers Odiáxere and Arão. A regular **bus service** leaves from the Avenida dos Descobrimentos and travels the length of the beach; alternatively there's a seasonal **ferry** from the side of the Forte Ponta da Bandeira.

Eating

The centre of Lagos is packed with **restaurants**, most found along ruas Afonso d'Almeida and 25 de Abril. Where the Avenida dos Descobrimentos meets Rua das Portas de Portugal, there's a diverting **fish and vegetable market** (Mon–Sat mornings), in front of which is a line of good fish restaurants. Menus are of a similar standard and price almost everywhere, though Lagos does also have a couple of highly regarded places where it's worth pushing the boat out at least once.

Alpendre, Rua António Barbosa Viana 17. One of the oldest restaurants in the Algarve and serving memorable smoked swordfish and decent *arroz de marisco*. The *crepes* are still the best reason to come though – flambéd at your table. At least 3500$00.

Casa do Zé, Avda. dos Descobrimentos. Just around the corner from the market, this does excellent fish dishes at very fair prices. Very much a locals' choice at lunchtime, with the outdoor seating soaking up a brisk trade.

O Cantinho Algarvio, Rua Afonso d'Almeida 17. Centrally located, this is again popular with locals for its wide range of modestly-priced Algarvian food. Around 1500–2500$00.

A Capoeira, Rua 25 de Abril 76. Tiny restaurant ("The Chicken Coop") serving a mixture of Portuguese and continental food – good fish and a fine Mozambican pork dish.

Dom Sebastião, Rua 25 de Abril 20–22. Arguably the town's finest restaurant, with outdoor seating, a stylish interior, superlative seafood, and a fabulous selection of starters. Call in to reserve a table. A full meal runs to about 4000$00, though careful selection would let you get away for less.

Esplanada Ao Natural, Rua Silva Lopes 27. Lively restaurant-bar with mainstream vegetarian dishes at reasonable prices. It also serves healthy breakfasts, from 10am.

Galeão, Rua de Laranjeira 1. A little hidden away, but usually packed out with people who recognise good food when they taste it; you may have to wait for a table. All the Algarvian classics and superb steaks at eminently reasonable prices. Under 3000$00.

Restaurante Piri Piri, Rua Afonso d'Almeida 10. Fresh fish served daily, as well as the spicy chicken dish that gives the restaurant its name. Inexpensive, given its central location, and with a pretty interior.

Pouso do Infante, Rua Afonso d'Almeida 9–11. Mid-range restaurant offering classic Portuguese and Algarvian cookery in a cool, white interior overwhelmed by rustic decoration. Around 2500$00.

Drinking and nightlife

There are lots of **bars** around town, many of them owned by expatriates – in particular Irish and British. Cocktails are unusually popular in Lagos and measures are almost universally generous. Pick up fliers as you do the rounds and you'll be enticed into places by two-for-one offers and special events. Most bars stay open until at least 2am, some even later if the party is in full swing.

Adega Portuguesa, Trav. dos Tanoeiros, just off Rua 25 de Abril. More of a bar than its "wine cellar" name would suggest, but retains a cosy atmosphere.

Lords Tavern, Rua Ant. Crisogono Santos 56. Opposite the *Hotel de Lagos*, this British-style pub has live music most nights (dismal crooners – including the chef – a speciality) and sports channel TV for the big games and fights. Open until at least 2am, more like 4am on occasions.

Mullens, Rua Cândido dos Reis 86. The late-night choice, this warehouse-like bar-restaurant serves meals, plays jazz on the sound system, and stays open until 2am.

Phoenix, Rua 5 de Outubro 11. The best club in Lagos; two dancefloors play contemporary sounds. Stays open till 4am.

Roskos, Rua Cândido dos Reis 79. Opposite *Mullens*, an Irish bar with a 7–10pm Happy Hour and serious cocktails.

Shots in the Dark, Rua 1 de Maio 16. Loud rock and roll bar whose low ceiling and dark interior makes for a sweaty drinking session.

Vee Jay's Bar, Trav. 1 de Maio. Cheap beer, more than fifty cocktails and a dartboard.

Whites, Rua do Ferrador 7. Split-level bar, dancing and more lurid cocktails.

Zanzibar, Rua 25 de Abril 93. Modern, upbeat bar with good music and occasional bouts of "1500$00 all-you-can-drink" madness.

Listings

Bike and motorbike rental *Motoride*, Rua José Afonso 23 (☎082/76 17 20), near the new town hall; *Safari Moto*, Rua Lucinda A. Santos (☎082/76 43 14), behind the bus station.

Boat trips Trips around the coast are easy to arrange with the fishing boats that gather around the Forte Ponta da Bandeira, or you can book a "cruise" at the tourist office.

Bullfights Held most Saturday afternoons in the summer, though they are run strictly for the tourists and their "famous horsemen" are in reality quite unknown.

Buses Travel information for all destinations from the bus terminal (☎082/76 29 44). Note that buses to Portimão leave from Avda. dos Descobrimentos.

Car rental *Avis*, Largo das Portas de Portugal 11 (☎082/636 91); *Luz Car*, Largo das Portas de Portugal 10 (☎082/610 16); *Auto Ourique*; Avda. dos Descobrimentos (☎082/612 52).

Consulate The only British consulate in the Algarve is in Portimão (p.376), at Largo Francisco A. Mauricio 7 (☎082/478 00; Mon–Fri 9.30am–12.30pm & 2.30–5pm). All other consulates are in Lisbon.

Doctor For an English-speaking doctor, call ☎082/78 98 66; you'll pay for the service.

Hospital Rua do Castelo dos Governadores, adjacent to the church of Santa Maria (☎082/76 30 34).

Police Rua General Alberto Silveira (☎082/76 29 30).

Post Office Behind the town hall, just off Avda. dos Descobrimentos; open Mon–Fri 8am–6pm, Sat 8am–1pm.

Taxis There are ranks in front of the post office or call ☎082/76 24 69 or 76 35 87.

Telephones It's easiest to make long-distance calls at the *Telecom* office, next to the post office (Mon–Fri 8.30am–10pm, Sat 9am–1pm & 5pm–midnight, Sun 6–10pm).

Travel Agency Tickets (including bus tickets) and tours from *Clubalgarve*, Rua Marreiros Neto 25 (☎082/76 23 37).

Watersports There's a windsurfing school at Meia Praia. For slides, pools and aquatic fun, take the bus from the bus station (around 9.30am) to *Slide & Splash*, N125, Vale de Deus, Estômbar, a theme park 45 minutes away; adults 2200$00, children 1400$00.

West to Sagres

Once one of the least spoiled parts of the Algarve, the coast **west of Lagos**, to Vila do Bispo and Sagres, is currently facing a barrage of development. A new highway is in the throes of construction, which at times slows traffic down to a crawl through dust and rubble; while on the completed sections of new road, vehicle speed and volume has increased significantly. Villa development along the road continues apace and the erstwhile small settlements on the coast itself (Luz, Burgau and Salema) are also seeing an increasing amount of construction. Among them, **Salema** – a superb beach and still recognisable as a former fishing village – promises most.

Buses run from Lagos several times daily to Luz and Burgau; only twice daily to Salema (though there are much more frequent services to Salema from Sagres/Vila do Bispo).

Luz, Burgau and Salema

Five kilometres west of Lagos you reach the resort of **LUZ**, an unappealing mass of chalets and villas that spreads in all directions from the beach, swamping the old village. There's a large luxury campsite, the *Valverde* (☎082/78 92 11), 1500 metres or so from the seafront, with the full range of tourist facilities, but it's a charmless place.

It's another five kilometres or so to **BURGAU**, another intensively developed, very British holiday spot, though one which still retains a semblance of its former fishing village life. There are bars and restaurants here, including the *Beach Bar Burgau* which rents out watersports equipment as well as serving food and drink (restaurant closed Tues).

SALEMA – 20km west of Lagos – was, until the mid-1980s, still primarily a fishing community, with its old village trailing up the hill. Now, sadly, a vast amount of apartment and villa construction has engulfed the whole area between the N125 main road and the sea. Still, the **beach** – a wide, rock-sheltered bay – is magnificent, and the development could have been worse. Most of the accommodation in Salema is in apartments, though there is a fair-sized and quite attractive hotel, the *Estalagem Infante do Mar* (⑤). Cheaper alternatives include **private**

rooms in the old village – ask at the bars and the post-office shop, or just stroll along the street – and a pleasantly landscaped **campsite** (*Quinta dos Carriços*; ☎082/652 01) up towards the main road. Best of the restaurants is the *Mira-Mar*, signposted off the main street in the village; this serves up barbecued fish and meat on a terrace above the beach.

On towards Sagres

At the road village of **FIGUEIRA** on the N125 (the point at which the highway most closely approaches the coast between Lagos and Sagres) there's the very welcoming *Bar Celeiro* by the bus stop. From here, paths lead off to the lovely **Praia da Figueira** (a twenty- to thirty-minute walk) which is often more or less deserted except for a few campers.

Two other worthwhile beaches are accessible by road from the village of **RAPOSEIRA** (which also has a great-value restaurant, the *Artisanale*), though they are more of a walk. The turning to look out for is signposted "Ingrina": about 1km down the road, take the left fork that passes through Hortas do Tabual and after another 3km or so you'll reach two isolated, craggy beaches – **Praia do Zavial** and **Praia da Ingrina**. These have a minimum of tourist facilities, though there's a **campsite** (☎082/662 42) at Ingrina, and there are no public transport connections from the main road. Zavial is large and sandy, with tumbles of rock at either end and a café-restaurant open daily (except Wed) in season. Ingrina is completely stony but good for beach-combing amid the rock pools.

West of Raposeira the road passes Vila do Bispo and the turn-off for the west coast (see p.392), before heading across the flattened landscape for Sagres.

Sagres and Cabo de São Vicente

Wild and windswept, **SAGRES** and its cape were considered by the Portuguese as the far limit of the ancient and medieval worlds. It was on these headlands in the fifteenth century that Prince Henry the Navigator made his residence and it was here, too, that he set up a school of navigation, gathering together the greatest astronomers, cartographers and adventurers of his age. Fernão de Magalhães (Magellan), Pedro Álvares Cabral and Vasco da Gama all studied at Sagres, and from the beach at Belixe – midway between the capes of Sagres and **São Vicente** – the first long caravels were launched, revolutionising shipping with their wide hulls, small adaptable sails, and ability to sail close to the wind. Each year new expeditions were dispatched to penetrate a little further than their predecessors, and to resolve the great navigational enigma presented by the west coast of Africa, thereby laying the foundations of the country's overseas empire.

After Henry's death here in 1460, the centre of maritime studies was moved to Lisbon and Sagres slipped back into the obscurity from which he'd raised it. In the early 1980s, the forlorn one-street village began to attract a growing number of young backpackers and windsurfers from Europe and North America, drawn by the string of magnificent, isolated local beaches. Now, a decade later, the building of a fast new road from Lagos has put Sagres within easy reach and the inevitable trail of villas and apartments is threatening to overwhelm the place entirely. It can still be a great place to stay, especially in winter, when the wind blows hard and there's a bleak, desolate appeal to the scenery, with hardly a tourist to be seen. Throughout the summer, by contrast, the sprawling village draws quite a lively and oddball social scene: the young beachgoers still flock here, well catered for by an evergrowing array of rooms for rent, restaurants and bars, rubbing shoulders these days though with families in villas and guests from one of the Algarve's two *pousadas*, which overlooks the village.

Sagres village, the Fortaleza and local beaches

Sagres village, rebuilt in the nineteenth century over the earthquake ruins of Henry's town, has nothing of architectural or historical interest and is little more than a line of houses connecting the fishing harbour with the square. Back from the main road, built to transport tourists straight to the headlands, a virtual new town of white villas and apartments spreads into the distance, much of it still under construction.

Henry the Navigator's **Fortaleza** dominates the whole scene near the village. An immense circuit of walls – only the north side survives intact – once surrounded its vast shelf-like promontory, high above the Atlantic. With such explicit demands of secrecy and security, together with its wild remoteness, it must have seemed a kind of Aldermaston or Los Alamos of its day.

You enter through a formidable tunnel, before which is spread a huge pebble **Rosa dos Ventos** (wind compass) unearthed beneath a church in 1921 and said to have been used by Henry himself. Historians disagree – and are equally unimpressed by the claims of the adjacent tourist office to have been the **prince's house**. Still, it is a wonderful, wild setting and the simple, much-restored chapel of **Nossa Senhora da Graça** is at least contemporary with Henry's explorations.

Local beaches

However impressive the fortress, most people's days in Sagres are spent on one of the excellent nearby beaches, five of which are within easy walking distance of the village. Three of them are on the more sheltered coastline east of the fortress: **Praia da Mareta** is just below the square, and the **Praia da Baleeira** is by the harbour, from where it's a five-minute walk to the longest and best beach, the **Praia do Martinhal**, an ideal spot for windsurfing. West of the fortress, the beaches are longer and more impressive, and the one nearest the village is a good spot. It's a longer walk to the beautiful **Praia de Belixe**, 2km down the road from Sagres to Cabo São Vicente, where you are usually guaranteed plenty of sand to yourself.

Whichever beach you choose, the water is very cold and swimming must be approached with caution – there are some very strong currents. Before setting off for the more distant strands, stock up with drinks and picnic supplies since there are virtually no facilities. The village supermarket can oblige with most provisions, plus five-litre flagons of the local wine for evening parties.

Cabo de São Vicente

The exposed **Cabo de São Vicente** – Cape Saint Vincent – across the bay from Sagres, was sacred to the Romans, who believed the sun sank hissing into the water beyond here every night. It became a Christian shrine when the relics of the martyred Saint Vincent arrived in the eighth century; watched over (some say piloted) by ravens, the remains were transferred by boat to Lisbon in 1173.

It was almost certainly at the cape that Henry established his School of Navigation, founded a small town, and built his Vila do Infante. Today only a **lighthouse**, flanked by the ruins of a sixteenth-century Capuchin convent, are to be seen. The other buildings, already vandalised by the piratical Sir Francis Drake in 1597, came crashing to the ground in the Great Earthquake of 1755, the monks staying on alone until the Liberal suppression of the monasteries in 1834.

The cape is nonetheless a dramatic and exhilarating six-kilometre walk from Sagres, a path skirting the tremendous cliffs for much of the way. This is a wonderful spot for **bird life** and at the right time of year you should be able to spot blue rock thrushes and peregrines nesting on the cliffs. Walking on the road is easier, and there's always the chance of a lift – if one doesn't materialise it'll take less than an hour and a half, with glorious views all the way. Try to be at the cape for sunset, which is invariably gorgeous, though frequently also very windy.

Practicalities

Buses from Lagos generally call in at Lagos train station in summer on the way to Sagres, where they stop in the village square; timetables for onward connections are posted in various bars and shops. The service station on the roundabout rents out **bicycles** and **scooters** for getting around the cape and local beaches. Orientation is straightforward, with the walls of the fortress standing at the end of the road, directly ahead of the village. There is a **Turismo** in the village square and another at the Fortaleza.

Accommodation

There are places to stay everywhere in and around Sagres village, and in high season, at least, it's basically a question of turning up and seeing what you're offered. Generally, you'll be approached by people offering **rooms** (around 2500–3500$00 double) and, if you want it, access to a kitchen too. There's little point in giving specific recommendations, since there's not much diference as far as price and location goes. However, if you have the time and inclination, ask around for directions to *Casa da Lidia*; her pleasant rooms and equipped kitchen are often touted by an old man called Francisco – quite a character – who drives new arrivals in the back of his motor-trike and insists you wear a Biggles-like flying helmet to foil the attentions of the zealous local gendarmerie.

Sagres's youth hostel seems to have closed for good and the only alternatives are a scattering of regular **pensions** and **hotels**; as with the private rooms, prices come down considerably out of season. *Residencial Pinheiro*, Rua São Vicente (☎082/641 14; ②), has good clean rooms, while the *Residencial Dom Henrique* (☎082/641 33; ④–⑤) is located right on the village square and is perfectly adequate. Best of all is the **pousada**, the *Pousada do Infante* (☎082/642 22; ⑥), an attractive clifftop mansion with Moorish elements and splendid views of the fortress from its bar-terrace. It's a wonderful location and offers special rates out of season. Equally upmarket is a small, four-room hotel, the Fortaleza do Belixe (☎082/641 24; ⑥), an annexe of the Sagres *pousada*, perched high on the cliff edge, 2km out of town at Belixe.

The nearest **campsite** (☎082/644 41) is 2km east of the village, along the main road; it is convenient for Praia do Martinhal. Camping rough on the beaches is definitely not an option; the local police don't like it and, given the number of rooms available, you can see their point.

Eating, drinking and nightlife

Sagres' main street is lined with restaurants and bars, catering for a range of tastes and budgets. For **breakfast**, try either *Café Cochina* or *A Rosa dos Ventos*, both on Praça da República, the main square. **Restaurants** run the gamut from travellers cafés to more upmarket places specialising in fish. *A Grelha* is typical, with an inexpensive tourist menu; *Atlântico* is an excellent choice on the main street, with good grilled fish; and the *Bar O Pescador* also has meals at prices much more reasonable than you'd expect from the sight of the lobsters patrolling their tanks at the entrance. Elsewhere, *A Tasca*, down by the fishing harbour, serves marvellous seafood, tuna and *caldeirada* (fish stew) at fairly reasonable prices; while the central *Mar A Vista* is a bit pricier, though with excellent sea views, as the name suggests. *Bossa Nova*, Rua Comandante Matoso, off the main street, is noted for its pizzas, pasta, salads and imaginative vegetarian meals; and *Dromedário* is an energetic bistro that serves drinks and snacks all day.

Of the **bars**, the two longstanding favourites, both packed with the travelling youth contingent, are *A Rosa dos Ventos*, on the village square – lively, loud, and drunken – and *The Last Chance Saloon*, around the corner, overlooking the sea. When it's falling down time, everyone moves on to the *Disco Caravelo*, in a strange mosque-like building, a short walk north of the village.

Vila do Bispo and the coast to Odeceixe

Unlike the southern stretches of the Algarve, the **west coast**, stretching north from Sagres to Odeceixe, is still relatively undeveloped. There are several reasons: the coast is exposed to strong Atlantic winds, the sea can be several degrees cooler and swimming dangerous. However, if you can brave the climate, you might like to base yourself at low-key resorts such as **Vila do Bispo**, **Carrapateira**, **Aljezur** and **Odeceixe**, all of which have plenty of beach, plus an inexpensive network of private rooms and scope for freelance camping. Like Sagres, these resorts attract a predominantly young and/or alternative crowd. At a few resorts – Odeceixe, in particular – this can be overwhelming, with summer crowds of German campervan-hippies strutting about nude on the beach. If this sounds more like purgatory than a holiday, you've been warned.

Vila do Bispo

VILA DO BISPO, at the junction of the west and south coast roads, is a pretty little town with a lovely parish **church**, every surface of which has been painted, tiled or gilded. Nothing much happens here, but the town could make a pleasant base if you have transport for daytrips to the beaches. There are some **rooms** above the restaurant in the square and a couple of **pensions** – *Pensão Mira-Sagres* (②) on Rua do Hospital and *Pensão Casal da Vila* on Rua General Carmona (③). In the evening, *Café Correia*, opposite the church, is packed with travellers, while around the corner, down a small alley, is the much cheaper *Oasis*, a locals' haunt, where the house speciality is chicken.

The nearest beach, the cliff-edged **Praia do Castelejo**, is reached by a rough road – no buses and a backbreaking hike – leading 5km west, across a stretch of bleak moors and hills. In summer, there's a little bar-restaurant here.

Carrapateira

Fifteen kilometres to the north of Vila do Bispo (and connected with it by two daily buses) is the village of **CARRAPATEIRA**. This is better positioned for the beach but is itself rather dilapidated and not terribly inviting. It's possible to get a **private room** if you ask around the main square or at the *Bar Barroca*. However, the best accommodation is a couple of kilometres northeast of town at the *Residencial Casa Fajara* (⑤), a spruce modern villa with neat gardens, overlooking an empty river valley. It's a great location, open in the summer months only.

Carrapateira's local beach, a kilometre's walk from the *Casa Fajara*, is the **Praia da Bordeira**, a spectacular strand with dunes, a tiny river and crashing surf. The sandbanks provide shelter from the wind for a sizeable community of freelance campers, who seem to be tolerated by the local police. There is a seasonal café on the beach. A second beach – quieter and with no facilities – is the **Praia do Amado**, 4km south of the Praia da Bordeira, around the Carrapateira headland.

Aljezur and Vale da Telha

The village of **ALJEZUR** (2 buses daily from Vila do Bispo; 3–5 daily from Lagos) is divided into two distinct halves: to the west of the river is a rather drab old quarter, Moorish in origin and straggling along the side of a hill below ruins of a tenth-century **castle**, while across the river to the east lies a more modern settlement. The **Turismo** (Mon–Fri 9.30am–12.30pm & 2–5pm, Sat 9am–noon; ☎082/982 29), by the river, can sometimes help with private **rooms** – the only alternative if you find the town **pension**, the *Residencial Francisca Sirominho* (③) full.

A kilometre south of Aljezur, a road heads through a recently fire-ravaged landscape to the local **beaches** of **MONTE CLÉRIGO** (8km) and **ARRIFANA** (10km). The latter is magnificent, though its village, perched on the cliffs above, is a rather grubby affair, with a couple of lacklustre bars and restaurants. Midway between the beaches is the **VALE DA TELHA** tourist complex, which has planning permission for expansion to a site of 2500 chalets and villas. At present it's nowhere near that size, nor a great commercial success, with just a modest **hotel**, the *Residencial Vale da Telha* (☎082/981 80; ③) and a **campsite** (☎082/986 12) up and running.

Odeceixe

ODECEIXE, hunched on a hill and cramped by the river, is the last village before the Alentejo. Situated near the head of a delightful curving estuary, it is a fairly quiet little place, at least outside July and August. At this time of year, it seems to attract just about every German hippy on the Algarve, a clientèle that creates its own rather exclusive presence. If you hit town outside the hippy season, though, it could be very pleasant, with a couple of simple restaurants, a number of houses offering **rooms**, and some small villas for rent by the beach. There's a campsite here, too.

The beach – **Praia de Odeceixe** – is a high-cliffed cove, stretching north of the estuary. It is one of the most sheltered beaches on this stretch of coast, with a minimum of tourist development and wonderful surf.

travel details

The Algarve rail line

The Algarve rail line runs from Lagos to Vila Real de Santo António, but only three or four services daily operate along the whole route; you may have to change at Tunes or Faro, depending on your destination. For journeys from one end of the rail line to the other, it's worth catching one of the express services rather than the slow local stopping trains.

Faro to Albufeira (13 daily; 30–40min); Lagos (9 daily; 1hr 20min–2hr 20min); (Monte Gordo (5 daily; 1hr 20min); Olhão (15 daily; 15min); Portimão (8 daily; 1hr–1hr 45min); Silves (8 daily; 1hr–1hr 20min); Tavira (15 daily; 40min); Vila Real de Santo António (12 daily; 1hr 30min).

Lagos to Albufeira (9 daily; 1hr–1hr 30min); Alvor (5 daily; 25min); Faro (8 daily; 1hr 30min–2hr); Loulé (8 daily; 1hr 15min–1hr 45min); Portimão (13 daily; 30min); Silves (13 daily; 50min); Tunes (13 daily; 50min–1hr).

Other train services

The hub for services north of the Algarve is Tunes, midway between Lagos and Faro.

Tunes to Lisbon (4 daily; 4–5hr), add on 2hr or so for connections from Vila Real, Faro or Lagos; and to Beja (2 daily; 3hr 20min), with connections for Casa Branca (4hr 40min); change for Évora (5hr).

Algarve buses

Albufeira to Areias de São João (9–13 daily; 8min); Armacão de Pêra (Mon–Sat 5 daily, Sun 2; 35min); Faro (hourly; 1hr 15min); Montechoro (9–13 daily; 15min); Olhos d'Água (hourly; 10min); Portimão (Mon–Fri 8 daily, Sat & Sun 2; 40min); Quarteira (hourly; 45min); São Bartolomeu de Messines (4–6 daily; 30min); Silves (3–6 daily; 45min).

Faro to Albufeira (hourly; 1hr 15min); Estói (Mon–Fri 12 daily, Sat 6, Sun 3; 20min); Loulé (Mon–Fri at least hourly, Sat 8, Sun 5; 30min); Monte Gordo (Mon–Fri hourly, Sat & Sun 7 daily; 1hr 30min); Olhão (Mon–Fri every 15–30min, Sat & Sun roughly hourly; 15–20min); Quarteira (Mon–Fri hourly, Sat & Sun 9 daily; 30min); São Brás de Alportel (Mon–Fri 11 daily, Sat 7, Sun 4; 35min); Tavira (Mon–Fri hourly, Sat & Sun 7 daily; 1hr); Vilamoura (Mon–Fri hourly, Sat & Sun 9 daily; 40min); Vila Real (7–8 daily; 1hr 40min).

Lagos to Aljezur (Mon–Fri 4 daily, Sat 1; 50min); Burgau (9 daily, only 4 on Sun in winter; 25min); Luz (9 daily, only 4 on Sun in winter; 15min); Odeceixe (Mon–Fri 4 daily, Sat 1; 1hr 20min); Portimão (hourly; 40min); Sagres (8–11 daily; 1hr 10min); Salema (6 daily; 40min); Vila do Bispo (8–11 daily; 45min).

Portimão to Albufeira (5–6 daily; 1hr 10min); Alvor (Mon–Fri hourly; Sat & Sun roughly every 2hr; 20min); Caldas de Monchique (3–4 daily; 30min); Faro (5–6 daily; 2hr); Ferragudo (hourly; 10min); Lagos (hourly; 40min); Monchique (8–9 daily; 30–45min); Praia da Rocha (every 15–30min; 10min); Silves (Mon–Fri hourly, Sat & Sun 8 daily; 35min).

Sagres to Lagos (8–10 daily; 1hr); Salema (4–5 daily; 35min); Vila do Bispo (8–10 daily;15min).

Vila do Bispo to Aljezur (Mon–Fri 1 daily; 45min); Carrapateira (Mon–Fri 1 daily; 15min).

Vila Real de Santo António to Ayamonte, Spain (4 daily; 20min); Castro Marim (6–10 daily; 10min); Manta Rota (2–5 daily; 30min); Monte Gordo (Mon–Fri half-hourly, Sat & Sun 10–11 daily; 7min).

Long-distance buses

Several companies operate regular daily express buses between Lisbon and the Algarve: ask at travel agencies or bus terminals. Journey times are approximately as follows:

Lisbon to Albufeira (4hr); Faro/Lagos/Vila Real (5hr 30min); Olhão/Tavira (5hr).

Flights

Faro to Lisbon (5–6 daily); with connections to Porto.

PART THREE

THE

CONTEXTS

PORTUGAL'S HISTORY

The early history of Portugal – as part of the Iberian Peninsula – has obvious parallels with that of Spain. Indeed, any geographical division is somewhat arbitrary, independent development only really occurring following Afonso Henriques' creation of a Portuguese kingdom in the twelfth century.

EARLY CIVILISATION

Remnants of pottery and cave burials point to tribal societies occupying the Tagus valley, as well as parts of the Alentejo and Estremadura, as early as 8000 to 7000 BC, but as yet there have been no finds in Portugal comparable to the Paleolithic caves of Altamira and northern Spain. More, however, is known of **Neolithic** Portugal and its *Castro* culture based on hilltop forts, a culture that was to be developed and refined after the arrival of Celtic peoples in around 700 to 600 BC. These forts, the first permanent settlements, were concentrated in northern Portugal, and particularly in the Minho, where excavations have revealed dozens of **citânias**, or fortified villages. The most impressive is at Briteiros (p.257), near Braga, with its paved streets, drainage systems and circuits of defensive walls; like many of the *citânias* it survived, remarkably unchanged, well into the Roman era. Settlements in neighbouring Trás-os-Montes, in contrast, reflect less of a defensive spirit – but all that remains

of this more pastoral **Verracos** culture are the crude granite *porcas*, stone figures venerating wild sows as objects of a primitive fertility cult.

The potential for new trading outlets and the quest for metals, in particular tin for making bronze, attracted a succession of peoples from across the Mediterranean but most of their settlements lay on the eastern seaboard and so fell within "Spanish" history. The **Phoenicians**, however, established an outpost at Lisbon around 900 BC and there were probably contacts, too, with Mycenaean Greeks. In the mid-third century BC, they were followed by **Carthaginians**, who recruited Celtic tribesmen for military aid against the Roman empire. Once again, though, their influence was predominantly on the eastern seaboard and in the south; with defeat in the Second Punic War (218–202 BC) they were to be replaced by a more determined colonising force.

ROMANS, SUEVI AND VISIGOTHS

Entering the peninsula in 210 BC, the **Romans** swiftly subdued and colonised the Mediterranean coast and the south of Spain and Portugal. In the interior, however, they met with great resistance from the Celtiberian tribes and in 193 BC the **Lusitani** rose up in arms. Based in central Portugal, between the Tagus and Lima rivers, they were, in the words of the Roman historian Strabo, "the most powerful of the Iberian peoples, who resisted the armies of Rome for the longest period." For some fifty years, in fact, they held up the Roman advance, under the leadership of **Viriatus**, a legendary Portuguese hero and masterful exponent of the feigned retreat who, on several occasions, brought the Romans to accept his autonomous rule. He was betrayed after a successful campaign in 139 BC and within two years the Lusitani had capitulated as the legions of Decimus Junius Brutus swept through the north. Still, over a century later their name was given to this most westerly of the Roman provinces, while in the northern Celtic villages Roman colonisation can scarcely have been felt.

Integration into the Roman Empire occurred largely under Julius Caesar, who in 60 BC established a capital at Olisipo (Lisbon) and significant colonies at Ebora (Évora), Scallabis

(Santarém) and Pax Julia (Beja). In 27 BC the Iberian provinces were further reorganised under Augustus, with all but the north of Portugal being governed – as Lusitania – from the great Roman city of Merida in Spanish Extremadura. The Minho formed part of a separate province, later added to northwest Spain to create Gallaecia, with an important regional centre at Bracara Augusta (Braga). In general, though, it was the south where Roman influence was deepest. Here they established huge agricultural estates (the infamous *Latifundia* which still survive in Alentejo) and changed the nature of the region's crops, as they introduced wheat, barley, olives and the vine to the area.

There are no great **Roman sites** in Portugal – at least nothing to compare with Spanish Merida, Tarragona, or Italica – though both Évora (p.317) and Conimbriga (p.157) have individual monuments of interest. The mark of six centuries of Roman rule consists more in a network of roads (used well into the Middle Ages) and bridges, many of them still in use today. There is a more basic legacy, too, the Portuguese language being very heavily derived from Latin.

The **decline of the Roman Empire** in Portugal echoes its pattern elsewhere, though perhaps with greater indifference, the territory always being something of a provincial backwater. **Christianity** reached Portugal's southern coast toward the end of the first century AD and by the third century bishoprics were established at Braga, Évora, Faro and Lisbon. But the state was already disintegrating and in 409 the first waves of barbarian invaders crossed the Pyrenees into Spain. Vandals, Alans, Suevi and Visigoths all passed through Portugal, though only the last two were of any real importance.

The **Suevi**, a semi-nomadic people from eastern Germany, eventually settled in the area between the Douro and Minho rivers, establishing courts at Braga and Portucale (Porto). They seem to have coexisted fairly peacefully with the Hispano-Roman nobility and were converted to Christianity by Saint Martin of Dume, a saint frequently found in the dedications of northern churches.

Around 585, however, the Suevian state disappeared, having been suppressed and incorporated into the **Visigothic** empire, a heavily Romanised yet independent force which for two centuries maintained a spurious unity and rule over most of the peninsula. The Visigothic kings, however, ruled from Toledo, supported by a small and elite aristocratic warrior-caste, so in Portugal their influence was neither great nor lasting. And by the end of the seventh century their divisions, exacerbated by an elective monarchy and their intolerance (including the first Iberian persecution of the Jews), resulted in one faction appealing for aid from Muslim North Africa. In 711 a first force of **Moors** crossed the straits into Spain and within a decade they had advanced and conquered all but the mountainous reaches of the Asturias in northern Spain.

THE MOORS AND CHRISTIAN RECONQUEST

In Portugal, Aveiro probably marked the northernmost point of the **Moorish advance**. The Moors met with little resistance but the dank, green hills of the Minho held little attraction for the colonisers-to-be and over the following century seem to have been severely depopulated. Most of the Moors were content to settle in the south: in the Tagus valley, in the rich wheat belts around Évora and Beja, and above all in the coastal region of the **al-Gharb**. Here they established a capital at Shelb, modern Silves, and, by the middle of the ninth century, an independent kingdom, detached from the great Muslim emirate of al-Andalus which covered most of Spain.

The Moors in Portugal were a mix of ethnic races – for the most part consisting of Berbers from Morocco, but also considerable numbers of Syrians and, around Faro, a contingent of Egyptians, some of them probably Coptic Christians. In contrast to the Visigoths, the Moors were tolerant and productive, their rule a civilising influence. Both Jews and Christians were allowed freedom of worship and their own civil laws, while under Muslim law small landholders continued to occupy lands that they themselves cultivated. For most of these **"Moçárabes"** – Christians subject to Moorish rule – life must have improved. Roman irrigation techniques were perfected and the Moors introduced the rotation of crops and cultivation of cotton, rice, oranges and lemons. Their culture and scholarship led the world – though less from al-Gharb than from Cordoba and

Seville – and they forged important trade links, many of which were to continue centuries after their fall. Perhaps still more important, **urban life** developed, with prosperous local craft industries: Lisbon, Évora, Beja and Santarém all emerged as sizable towns.

The Christian **"Reconquista"** began – at least by tradition – at Covadonga in 718, when Pelayo, at the head of a small band of Visigoths, halted the advance of a Moorish expeditionary force. The battle's significance has doubtless been inflated but from the victory a tiny kingdom of the Asturias does seem to have been established. Initially only 40 by 30 miles in extent, it expanded over the next two centuries to take in León, Galicia and the "lands of Portucale," the latter an area roughly equivalent to the old Swabian state between the Douro and the Minho.

By the eleventh century **Portucale** had the status of a country, its governors appointed by the kings of León. In 1073 Alfonso VI came to the throne. It was to be a reign hard-pressed by a new wave of Muslim invaders – the fanatical Almoravides who crossed over to Spain in 1086 after appeals from al-Andalus and established a new Muslim state at Seville. Like many kings of Portugal after him, Alfonso was forced to turn to European crusaders, many of whom would stop in at the shrine of Saint James in Compostela. One of them, Raymond of Burgundy, married Alfonso's eldest daughter and became heir-apparent to the throne of León; his cousin Henry, married to another daughter, Teresa, was given jurisdiction over Portucale. With Henry's death Teresa became regent for her son, **Afonso Henriques** and began to try to forge a union with Galicia. Afonso, however, had other ideas and having defeated his mother at the battle of São Mamede (1128), he established a capital at **Guimarães** and set about extending his domains to the south.

The reconquest of central Portugal was quickly achieved. Afonso's victory at Ourique in 1139 was a decisive blow and by 1147 he had taken Santarém. In the same year Lisbon fell, after a siege in which passing crusaders again played a vital role – though not sailing on to the Holy Land before murderously sacking the city. Many of them were English and some stayed on; Gilbert of Hastings became Archbishop. By now Afonso was dubbing himself the **first King of Portugal**, a title

tacitly acknowledged by Alfonso VII (the new king of León) in 1137 and officially confirmed by the Treaty of Zamora in 1143. His kingdom spread more or less to the borders of modern Portugal, though in the south, Alentejo and the Algarve were still in Muslim hands.

For the next century and a half Afonso's successors struggled to dominate this last stronghold of the Moors. Sancho I (1185–1211) took their capital, Silves, in 1189, but his gains were not consolidated and almost everything south of the Tagus was recaptured the following year by al-Mansur, the last great campaigning vizier of al-Andalus. The overall pattern, though, was of steady expansion with occasional setbacks. Sancho II (1223–48) invaded the Alentejo and the eastern Algarve, while his successor **Afonso III** (1248–79) moved westwards, taking Faro and establishing the kingdom in pretty much its final shape.

THE BURGUNDIAN KINGS

The reconquest of land from the Muslims also incorporated a process of **recolonisation**. As it fell into the king's hands, new territory was granted to such of his subjects that he felt would be able to defend it. In this way much of the country came to be divided between the church, the Holy Orders – chief among them the Knights Templar – and a hundred or so powerful nobles (*ricos homens*). The entire kingdom had a population of under half a million, the majority of them concentrated in the north. Here there was little displacement of the traditional feudal ties, but in the south the influx of Christian peasants blurred the distinction between serf and settler, dependent relationships coming instead to be based on the payment of rent.

Meanwhile a **political infrastructure** was being established. The land was divided into municipalities (*concelhos*), each with its own charter (*foral*). A formalised structure of consultation began, with the first **Cortes** (parliament) being held in Coimbra in 1211. At first consisting mainly of the clergy and nobility, it later came to include wealthy merchants and townsmen, a development speeded both by the need to raise taxes and by later kings' constant struggles against the growing power of the church. The capital, which Afonso Henriques had moved to Coimbra in 1139, was transferred to **Lisbon** in about 1260 by Afonso III.

The Burgundian dynasty lasted through nine kings for 257 years. In the steady process of establishing the new kingdom, one name stands out above all others, that of **Dom Dinis** (1279–1325). With the reconquest barely complete when he came to the throne, Dinis set about a far-sighted policy of stabilisation and of strengthening the nation to ensure its future independence. During his reign, fifty fortresses were constructed along the frontier with Castile, while at the same time negotiations were going on, leading eventually to the Treaty of Alcañices (1297) by which Spain acknowledged Portugal's frontiers. At home Dinis established a major programme of forest planting and of agricultural reform; grain, olive oil, wine, salt, salt fish and dried fruit became staple exports to Flanders, Brittany, Catalonia and Britain. Importance, too, was attached to education and the arts: a **university**, later transferred to Coimbra, was founded at Lisbon in 1290. Dinis also helped entrench the power of the monarchy, forcing the church to accept a much larger degree of state control and, in 1319, reorganising the Knights Templar – at the time being suppressed all over Europe – as the **Order of Christ**, still enormously powerful but now responsible directly to the king rather than to the pope.

Despite Dinis' precautions, fear of **Castilian domination** continued to play an important part in the reigns of his successors, largely due to consistent intermarrying between the two royal families. On the death of the last of the Burgundian kings, Fernando I, power passed to his widow Leonor, who ruled as regent. Leonor, whose only daughter had married Juan I of Castile, promised the throne to the children of that marriage. In this she had the support of most of the nobility, but the merchant and peasant classes strongly opposed a Spanish ruler, supporting instead the claim of João, Grand Master of the House of Avis and a bastard heir of the Burgundian line. A popular revolt against Leonor led to two years of war with Castile, finally settled at the **Battle of Aljubarrota** (1385) in which João, backed up by a force of English archers, wiped out the much larger Castilian army.

The great abbey of **Batalha** (p.125) was built to commemorate the victory. **João I**, first king of the **House of Avis**, was crowned at Coimbra the same year, sealing relations with England through the 1386 Treaty of Windsor – an alliance which lasted into the twentieth century – and his marriage to Philippa of Lancaster, daughter of John of Gaunt, the following year.

DOM MANUEL AND THE MARITIME EMPIRE

Occupying such a strategic position between the Atlantic and the Mediterranean, it was inevitable that Portuguese attention would at some stage turn to **maritime expansion**. When peace was finally made with Castile in 1411, João I was able to turn his resources toward Morocco. The outpost at Ceuta fell in 1415, but successive attempts to capture Tangier were not realised until the reign of Afonso V, in 1471.

At first such overseas adventuring was undertaken partly in a crusading spirit, partly to keep potentially troublesome nobles busy. The proximity of North Africa made it a constant feature of foreign policy, giving a welcome boost to the economy of the Algarve. The first real advances in exploration, however, came about through the activities of **Prince Henry "the Navigator"**, third son of João and Philippa. As Grand Master of the Order of Christ, he turned that organisation's vast resources towards marine development, founding a School of Navigation on the desolate promontory of Sagres (then regarded as the end of the world) and staffing it with Europe's leading cartographers, navigators and seamen. As well as improving the art of offshore navigation, they redesigned the caravel, making it a vessel well suited to long ocean-going journeys. **Madeira** and the **Azores** were discovered in 1419 and 1427 respectively and by the time of Henry's death in 1460 the **Cape Verde Islands** and the **west coast of Africa** down to Sierra Leone had both been explored.

After a brief hiatus, overseas expansion received a fresh boost in the reigns of João II, Manuel I and João III. In 1487 **Bartolomeu Dias** finally made it around the southern tip of Africa, christening it "Cabo da Boa Esperança" in the hope of good things to come. Within ten years **Vasco da Gama** had sailed on past it to open up the **trade route to India**. This was the great breakthrough and the Portuguese monarchy, already doing well out of African gold, promptly became the richest in Europe, taking a fifth of the profits of all trade and controlling important monopolies on some spices. The small cargo of pepper brought back by Vasco on his first expedition was enough to pay for the trip three times over. Meanwhile Spain was opening up the New World and by the **Treaty of Tordesillas** in 1494 the two Iberian nations divided the world between them along an imaginary line 370 leagues west of the Cape Verde Islands. This not only gave Portugal the run of the Orient but also, when it was discovered in 1500, Brazil (though its exploitation would have to wait nearly 200 more years). By the mid-sixteenth century Portugal dominated **world trade**; strategic posts had been established at Goa (1510), Malacca (1511), Ormuz (1515) and Macau (1557), and the revenue from dealings with the East was backed up by a large-scale **slave trade** between West Africa and Europe and Brazil.

The reign of **Manuel I** (1495–1521) marked the apogee of Portuguese wealth and strength. It found its expression at home in the extraordinary exuberance of the "**Manueline**" style of architecture – an elaborately decorative genre which found its inspiration in marine motifs. Notable examples can be seen in the Convent of Christ at Tomar and the monastery and tower of Belém in Lisbon (see p.67), while the best examples of civil architecture are probably the extensions made by Manuel to the royal palace at Sintra.

Enormous wealth there may have been, but very little of it filtered down through the system, and in the country at large conditions barely improved. The practice of siphoning off a hefty slice of the income into the royal coffers effectively prevented the development of an entrepreneurial class and, as everywhere else in Europe, financial matters were left very much in the hands of the Jews, who were not allowed to take up most other professions.

Portugal had traditionally been considerably more tolerant than other European nations in its treatment of its **Jewish citizens** (and towards the Moorish minority who had been absorbed after the Reconquest). However, popular resentment of their riches, and pressure from Spain, forced Manuel – who had

initially welcomed refugees from the Spanish persecution – to order their **expulsion** in 1496. Although many chose the pragmatic course of remaining as "New Christian" converts, others fled to the Netherlands. This exodus, continued as a result of the activities of the **Inquisition** (from 1531 on), created a vacuum which left Portugal with an extensive empire based upon commerce, but deprived of much of its commercial expertise. By the 1570s the economy was beginning to collapse: incoming wealth was insufficient to cover the growing costs of maintaining an empire against increasing competition, a situation exacerbated by foreign debts, falling prices and a decline in the productivity of domestic agriculture.

SPANISH DOMINATION

In the end it was a combination of reckless imperialism and impecunity which brought to an end the dynasty of the House of Avis and with it, at least temporarily, Portuguese independence. **Dom Sebastião** (1557–78), obsessed with dreams of a new crusade against Morocco, set out at the head of a huge army to satisfy his fanatical fantasies. They were crushed at the battle of **Alcácer-Quibir** (1578), where the Portuguese dead numbered over 8000, including Sebastião and most of Portugal's nobility. The aged **Cardinal Henrique** took the throne as the closest legitimate relative and devoted his brief reign to attempting to raise the crippling ransoms for those captured on the battlefield.

The Cardinal's death without heirs in 1580 provided Spain with the pretext to renew its claim to Portugal. **Philip II** of Spain, Sebastião's uncle, defeated his rivals at the battle of Alcântara and in 1581 was crowned Felipe I of Portugal, inaugurating a period of Hapsburg rule which lasted for another sixty years. In the short term, although unpopular, the union had advantages for Portugal. Spanish wheat helped alleviate the domestic shortage and Spanish seapower helped protect the far-flung empire. Philip, moreover, studiously protected Portuguese autonomy, maintaining an entirely separate bureaucracy and spending long periods in Portugal in an attempt to win popular support. Not that he ever did – throughout his reign pretenders appeared claiming to be Sebastião miraculously saved from the Moroccan desert, tapping a strong vein of resentment among the people. And in the long run, Spanish control proved disastrous. Association with Spain's foreign policy (part of the Armada was prepared in Lisbon) meant the enmity of the Dutch and the British, Portugal's traditional allies, losing the country an important part of its trade which was never to be regained.

Philip's successors made no attempt at all to protect Portuguese sensibilities – cynical and uninterested, they attempted to rule from Madrid while raising heavy taxes to pay for Spain's wars. The final straw was the attempt by Philip IV (Felipe III of Portugal) to conscript Portuguese troops to quell a rising in Catalonia. On December 1, 1640, a small group of conspirators stormed the palace in Lisbon and deposed the Duchess of Mantua, Governor of Portugal. By popular acclaim and despite personal reluctance, the Duke of Bragança, senior member of a family which had long been the most powerful in the country, took the throne as **João IV**.

THE HOUSE OF BRAGANÇA

At first the newly independent nation looked pretty shaky, deprived of most of its trade routes and with the apparently imminent threat of invasion from Spain hanging over it. As it turned out, however, the Spanish were so preoccupied with wars elsewhere that they had little choice but to accept the situation, though they did not do so formally until 1668 under the **Treaty of Lisbon**. João IV used the opportunity to rebuild old alliances and although the Portuguese were often forced into unfavourable terms, they were at least trading again. Relations with Britain had been strained during that country's Commonwealth, especially by Oliver Cromwell's particular brand of Protestant commercialism, but were revived by the marriage of Charles II to Catherine of Bragança in 1661.

At home Portugal was developing an increasingly centralised administration. The **discovery of gold and diamonds in Brazil** during the reign of Pedro II (1683–1706) made the crown financially independent and did away with the need for the Cortes (or any form of popular representation) for most of the next century. It was **João V**, coming to the throne in 1706, who most benefited from the new riches, which he squandered in an orgy of lavish Baroque building. His massive convent at **Mafra**, built totally without regard to expense, employed at times as many as 50,000 workmen, virtually bankrupting the state. Meanwhile nothing was being done to revive the economy, and what little remained from João's grandiose schemes went mainly to pay for imports. The infamous **Methuen Treaty**, signed in 1703 to stimulate trade with Britain, only made matters worse: although it opened up new markets for Portuguese wine, it helped destroy the native textile industry by letting in British cloth at preferential rates.

The accession of João's apathetic son, **José I** (1750–77), allowed the total concentration of power in the hands of the king's chief minister, the **Marquês de Pombal**, who became the classic "enlightened despot" of eighteenth-century history. It was the **Great Earthquake of 1755** that sealed his dominance over the age; while everyone else was panicking, Pombal's policy was simple – "bury the dead and feed the living."

Pombal saw his subsequent mission as to modernise all aspects of Portuguese life, by establishing an efficient and secular bureaucracy, renewing the system of taxation, setting up export companies, protecting trade and abolishing slavery within Portugal. It was a strategy that made him many enemies among the old aristocracy and above all within the Church, whose overbearing influence he fought at every turn. Opposition, though, was dealt with ruthlessly and an assassination attempt on the king in 1758 (which some say was staged by Pombal) gave him the chance he needed to destroy his enemies. Denouncing their supposed involvement, Pombal executed the country's leading aristocrats and abolished the Jesuit order, which had long dominated education and religious life in Portugal and Brazil.

Although Pombal himself was taken to trial (and found guilty but pardoned on the grounds of old age) with the accession of Maria I (1777–1816), the majority of his labours survived him, most notably the reform of education along scientific lines and his completely rebuilt capital, Lisbon. Further development, however, was soon thwarted by a new invasion.

FRENCH OCCUPATION AND THE MIGUELITE YEARS

With the appearance of **Napoleon** on the international scene, Portugal once more became embroiled in the affairs of Europe. The French threatened to invade unless the Portuguese supported their naval blockade of Britain, a demand that no one expected them to obey since British ports were the destination for most of Portugal's exports. Only the protection of the British fleet, especially after the victory at Trafalgar in 1805, kept the country's trade routes open. General Junot duly marched into Lisbon in November 1807.

On British advice the royal family had already gone into exile in Brazil, where they were to stay until 1821, and the war was left largely in the hands of British generals **Beresford** and **Wellington**. Having twice been driven out and twice reinvaded, the French were finally forced back into Spain in 1811 following the Battle of Buçaco (1810) and a long period of near starvation before the lines of Torres Vedras.

Britain's prize for this was the right to trade freely with **Brazil**, which together with the declaration of that country as a kingdom in its own right, fatally weakened the dependent relationship that had profited the Portuguese treasury for so long. Past roles were reversed, with Portugal becoming effectively a colony of Brazil (where the royal family remained) and a protectorate of Britain, with General Beresford as administrator. The only active national institution was the army, many of whose officers had absorbed the constitutional ideals of revolutionary France.

In August 1820, with Beresford temporarily out of the country and King João VI still in Brazil, a group of officers called an unofficial Cortes and proceeded to draw up a new **constitution**. Inspired by the recent liberal advances in Spain, it called for an assembly – to be elected every two years by universal male suffrage – and the abolition of clerical privilege and the traditional rights of the nobility. The king, forced to choose between Portugal and Brazil, where his position looked even more precarious, came back in 1821 and accepted its terms. His queen, Carlota, and younger son **Miguel**, however, refused to take the oath of allegiance and became the dynamic behind a

reactionary movement which drew considerable support in rural areas. With João VI's death in 1826, a delegation was sent to Brazil to pronounce Crown Prince Pedro the new king. Unfortunately Pedro was already Emperor of Brazil, having declared its independence some years earlier. He resolved to pass the crown to his infant daughter, with Miguel as regent provided that he swore to accept a new charter, drawn up by Pedro and somewhat less liberal than the earlier constitution. Miguel agreed, but once in power promptly tore up any agreement, abolished the charter and returned to the old, absolutist ways. This was a surprisingly popular move in Portugal, certainly in the countryside, but not with the governments of Britain, Spain, or France who backed the liberal rebels and finally put Pedro IV (who had meanwhile been deposed in Brazil) on the throne after Miguel's defeat at Évora-Monte in 1834.

THE DEATH OF THE MONARCHY

Pedro didn't survive long. The rest of the century – under the rule of his daughter Maria II (1834–53) and his grandsons Pedro V (1853–61) and Luís (1861–89) – saw almost constant struggle between those who supported the charter and those who favoured a return to the more liberal constitution of 1822. In 1846 the position deteriorated virtually to a state of **civil war** between Maria, who was fanatical in her support of her father's charter, and the radical constitutionalists. Only a further intervention by foreign powers maintained peace, imposed at the Convention of Gramido (1847).

In the second half of the century, with relative stability and the two warring factions to some extent institutionalised into a revolving two-party system, the economy began at last to recover, with the first signs of widespread industrialisation and a major public works programme under the minister Fontes Pereira de Melo. The monarchy, however, was almost bankrupt and its public humiliation over possessions in Africa – Britain and Germany simply ignored the Portuguese claim to the land between Angola and Mozambique – helped strengthen growing republican feelings.

Republicanism took root particularly easily in the army and among the urban poor, fuelled by falling standards of living and growing anger at government ineptitude. **Dom Carlos** (1898–1908) attempted to rule dictatorially after 1906, alienating most sectors of the country in the process and was assassinated, along with his eldest son, following a failed Republican coup in 1908. Finally, on October 5, 1910, the **monarchy was overthrown** once and for all by a joint revolt of the army and navy. Dom Manuel went into exile and died, in Britain, in 1932.

THE "DEMOCRATIC" REPUBLIC

After a provisional government of Republican Unity, **elections** took place in 1911, showing a marked swing towards Afonso Costa's **Democratic Party**, which remained the most dominant political force in the country until 1926. However, the divisions among the Republicans, the cyclical attempts at violent overthrow of the new regime by the monarchists, and the weakening of the country's economic, social and political structures, kept the Republic in permanent turmoil. Political life was in chaos and the hopes, perhaps unrealistically high, of the Republic's supporters never began to be realised. There were 45 changes of government in 16 years and several military uprisings.

The forces that had brought the Republic were supported largely by the urban and rural poor, yet new electoral laws based on a literacy test led to a smaller electorate than under the monarchy, disenfranchising most of the Republic's strongest supporters. Successive governments failed to fulfil the least aspirations. Anticlericalism had been a major plank of Costa's platform, arousing massive hostility in the countryside. Legalising the right to strike merely gave workers a chance to voice their discontent in a massive wave of work stoppages, but the new regime proved to be less than responsive to workers' rights and the repression of union activities was a constant theme. Further fuel was given to the reaction by Portugal's economically disastrous decision to enter **World War I** on the side of the Allies in 1916 and by the vicissitudes of the postwar recession. By 1926 not even the trade unions were prepared to stand by the Republic, preferring to maintain "proletarian neutrality" in the face of what at first seemed no more significant a military intervention than any other.

SALAZAR AND THE "NEW STATE"

While the military may have known what they wanted to overthrow in 1926, they were at first divided as to whether to replace it with a new Republican government or a restored monarchy. From the infighting a Catholic monarchist, **General Carmona**, eventually emerged as president (which he remained until his death in 1951) with the Republican constitution suspended.

In 1928 one **Dr. Salazar** joined the Cabinet as Finance Minister. A professor of economics at Coimbra University, he took the post only on condition that he would control the spending and revenue of all government departments. His strict monetarist line (helped by a change in the accounting system) immediately balanced the budget for the first time since 1913 and in the short term the economic situation was visibly improved. From then on he effectively controlled the country, becoming prime minister in 1932 and not relinquishing that role until 1968.

His regime was very much in keeping with the political tenor of the 1930s and while it had few of the ideological pretensions of a **fascist** state, it had many of the trappings. Members of the National Assembly were chosen from the one permitted political association, the National Union (UN); "workers' organisations" were set up, but run by their employers; education was strictly controlled by the state to promote Catholic values; and censorship was strictly enforced. Opposition was kept in check by the *PIDE* – a secret police force set up with Gestapo assistance – which used systematic torture and long-term detention in camps on the Azores and Cabo Verde islands to defuse most resistance. The army, too, was heavily infiltrated by *PIDE* and none of the several coups mounted against Salazar came close to success. Despite remaining formally neutral throughout the **Spanish Civil War**, Salazar had openly assisted the plotters in their preparations and later sent unofficial army units to fight with Franco. Republican refugees were deported to face certain execution at Nationalist hands.

At home Salazar succeeded in producing the infrastructure of a relatively modern economy but the results of growth were felt by only a few and agriculture, in particular, was allowed to stagnate. Internal unrest, while widespread, was surprisingly muted and apparently easily controlled; the New State's downfall, when it came, was precipitated far more by external factors. Salazar was an ardent imperialist who found himself faced with growing **colonial wars**, which proved costly and brought international disapprobation. India seized Goa and the other Portuguese possessions in 1961 and at about the same time the first serious disturbances were occurring in Angola, Mozambique and, later, in Guinea-Bissau. The regime was prepared to make only the slightest concessions, attempting to defuse the freedom movements by speeding economic development.

The government's reign came to an end in 1968 when Salazar's deck-chair collapsed, and he suffered brain damage. Incapacitated, he lived for another two years, deposed as premier – though such was the fear of the man, no one ever dared tell him. His successor, **Marcelo Caetano**, attempted to prolong the regime by offering limited democratisation at home. However, tensions beneath the surface were fast becoming more overt and attempts to liberalise foreign policy failed to check the growth of guerilla activity in the remaining colonies, or of **discontent in the army**.

It was in the African-stationed army especially that opposition crystallised. There the young conscript officers came more and more to sympathise with the freedom movements they were intended to suppress and to resent the cost – in economic terms and in lives – of the hopeless struggle. From their number grew the revolutionary **Movimento das Forças Armadas** (MFA).

REVOLUTION

By 1974 the situation in Africa was deteriorating rapidly and at home Caetano's liberalisation had come to a dead end; morale, among the army and the people, was lower than ever. The **MFA**, formed originally as an officer's organisation to press for better conditions, and which had become increasingly politicised, was already laying its plans for a takeover. Dismissal of two popular generals – Spínola and Costa Gomes – for refusing publicly to support Caetano, led to a first chaotic and abortive attempt on March 16. Finally on April 25, 1974, the plans laid by **Major Otelo Saraiva de Carvalho** for the MFA were complete and their virtually bloodless **coup** went without a hitch, no serious attempt being made to defend the government.

The next two years were perhaps the most extraordinary in Portugal's history, a period of continual **revolution**, massive politicisation and virtual anarchy, during which decisions of enormous importance were nevertheless made – above all the granting of independence to all of the overseas territories. At first there was little clear idea of any programme beyond the fact that the army wanted out of Africa. Though the MFA leadership was clearly to the left and at first associated with the PCP (Portuguese Communist Party), the bulk of the officers were less political and **General Spínola**, whom they had been forced to accept as a figurehead, was only marginally to the left of Caetano and strongly opposed total independence for the colonies. Spínola's dream was clearly to "do a De Gaulle" in Portugal, while the army was above all determined not to replace one dictator with another.

In the event their hands were forced by the massive popular response and especially by huge demonstrations on May Day. It was clear that whatever the leadership might decide, the people, especially in the cities, demanded a rapid move to the left. From the start every party was striving to project itself as the true defender of the "ideals of April 25." Provisional governments came and went but real power rested, where it had begun, with the MFA, now dominated by Saraiva de Carvalho and Vasco Gonçalves. While politicians argued around them, the army claimed to speak directly to the people, leading the country steadily left. It was a period of extraordinary contradictions, with the PCP, hoping to consolidate their position as the "true" revolutionary party, opposing liberalisation and condemning strikes as counterrevolutionary, while ultra-conservative peasants were happily seizing their land from its owners.

Sudden **independence** and the withdrawal of Portuguese forces from the former colonies – while generally greeted in Portugal with relief – did not always work so well for the countries involved. Guinea-Bissau and Mozambique, the first to go, experienced relatively peaceful transitions, but **Angola** came to be a serious point of division between Spínola and the MFA. When independence finally came, after Spínola's resignation, the country was already in the midst of a full-scale civil war. The situation was even worse in **East Timor**, where more than ten percent of the population was massacred by invading Indonesian forces following Portuguese withdrawal. In Portugal itself the arrival of more than half-a-million colonial refugees – many of them destitute, most bitter – came to be a major problem for the regime, though their eventual integration proved one of its triumphs.

At home, the first **crisis** came in September 1974, when Spínola, with Gonçalves and Saraiva de Carvalho virtual prisoners in Lisbon's Belém Palace, moved army units to take over key positions. The MFA, however, proved too strong and Spínola was forced to resign, General Costa Gomes replacing him as president. By the summer of 1975 more general reaction was setting in and even the MFA began to show signs of disunity. The country was increasingly split, supporting the revolution in the south, while remaining deeply conservative in the north. The Archbishop of Braga summed up the north's traditional views, declaring that the struggle against communism should be seen "not in terms of man against man, but Christ against Satan." Nevertheless the revolution continued to advance; a coup attempt in March failed when the troops involved turned against their officers. The Council of the Revolution was formed, promptly nationalising banking and private insurance; widespread land seizures went ahead in the Alentejo; and **elections** in the summer resulted in an impressive victory for Mário Soares' Socialist Party (PS).

On November 25, 1975, elements of the army opposed to the rightward shift in the government moved for yet another **coup**, taking over major air bases across the country. Otelo Saraiva de Carvalho, however, declined to bring his Lisbon command to their aid; nor did the hoped-for mass mobilisation of the people take place. Government troops under Colonel Ramalho Eanes moved in to force their surrender and – again virtually without bloodshed – the revolution had ended.

DEMOCRACY AND EUROPE: THE 1980S

The period since November 1975 has been one of slow and sometimes shaky-looking, **retrenchment**. The Socialist Party was still in power at the end of 1975 and won further ground in the elections that followed, helping to shape the post-revolutionary constitution – a mildly Socialist document, though providing for a fairly powerful president. Early fears of a right-wing coup led by Spínola failed to materialise, helped by the election of Colonel Eanes, a man whom the army trusted, as president. Saraiva de Carvalho came in second, despite the fact that no major party supported him – a token of the degree of popular following enjoyed by the MFA during the revolution.

Although parties of the right and centre have consistently polled higher votes, the Socialists had effective control until 1980 when Dr. Sá Carneiro managed to create the **Democratic Alliance**, uniting the larger groupings on the right. But within a few months he died in a plane crash. His successor as prime minister, Francisco Pinto Balsemão, barely managed to maintain the coalition for the two years of the term remaining and then only because the rightist parties were united in their determination to amend the constitution "to eliminate clauses which were appropriate in the post-revolutionary atmosphere of 1976 but not to today's needs."

The most enigmatic figure throughout this period remained **President Eanes**, a career soldier who supported the MFA in its early days, later led the forces who ended the revolution and is now accused by the right of being a "Marxist sympathiser". He above all seemed to be the figure of stability, with enormous popular support though (at least until recently) apparently little ambition, being happy to concentrate on developing Portugal's links with Africa, Asia and Latin America and overseeing a gradual normalisation process.

In **elections** held on the ninth anniversary of the revolution, April 25, 1983, Mário Soares' Socialist Party again became the largest single party in the national assembly, though requiring the support of the Social Democrats to maintain a coalition government. Soares' premiership was dogged by the unpopularity of his **economic austerity measures** (in part insisted on by the IMF) and by constant delays and breakdowns in the talks over Portuguese and Spanish **entry into the European Community**. These problems did have one positive result, namely closer relations with the traditionally hostile government in Madrid. But the government's economic problems led eventually to the withdrawal of Social Democratic support and to the collapse of the coalition.

New elections in October 1985 were barely conclusive: the left-wing vote split three ways and the Socialists lost their position as largest party to the **Social Democrats** (PSD), whose flamboyant leader, **Dr. Aníbal Cavaco Silva**, became prime minister. But the main feature of the election was disillusionment with the government and the choices on offer to the electorate. There was massive, countrywide abstention and, in rural districts (where people worried most about the effects of EC membership), attacks occurred on polling booths.

In the months that followed, the revolutionary leader, Lt-Colonel Otelo Saraiva de Carvalho, was arrested and put on trial in Lisbon accused of being the leader of 73 suspected terrorists in the **FP-25** urban guerilla group. Proceedings were postponed following the shooting of one of the key witnesses and it was not until 1987 that Saraiva de Carvalho was sentenced to 15 years' imprisonment (50 others also received prison sentences). He was later conditionally released after a Supreme Court ruling that there had been irregularities at his trial. In February 1990 he renounced the armed struggle and requested an amnesty.

President Eanes, meanwhile – the other great figure at the end of the revolution – had been forced to resign the presidency on completion of his second term in January 1986. He was replaced by former socialist Prime Minister **Mário Soares** who, with the reluctant support of the Communists, narrowly defeated the candidate of the centre-right, becoming the first civilian president for 60 years.

Portugal's entry into the **European Community** in 1986 brought with it the most important changes since the revolution. With the help of a massive injection of funds to help modernise infrastructure and increased foreign investment, Portugal enjoyed unprecedented **economic growth**, running at above four percent per year, greater than most of its European partners. For many Portuguese this resulted in greater material wealth, but behind the trappings of the new prosperity remained pockets of deeply entrenched poverty.

Prime Minister Aníbal Cavaco Silva's early attempts to introduce an economic reform programme were hampered by his lack of a majority, but in April 1987 a censure motion defeat caused the prime minister to resign, bringing about general elections. The PSD (Social Democrats) were returned to power in surprising numbers, enjoying the first absolute majority since the 1974 revolution and the strength to implement real changes. The centre-right government's free enterprise drive for the removal of Socialist structures and privatisation did not run unchallenged: the late 1980s were marked by **industrial unrest**. In March 1988 1.5 million workers took part in a 24-hour general strike in protest against labour reform laws freeing up employers to lay off workers. The law was eventually approved by both the assembly and the president, but strikes continued throughout 1989 in various sectors of the workforce, attempting to bring wages in line with inflation. The government was also able to reach an eventual agreement with the opposition to remove Marxist–Leninist elements from the constitution in August 1989.

The Portuguese **Green Party** won its first seat in the **European Parliament** elections in Strasbourg in June 1989 and the ruling PSD was successful in retaining most of its own seats, but suffered an enormous set-back six months later in municipal elections. The socialist opposition gained control of the capital, Lisbon; the northern industrial centre, Porto; and other significant cities. Four years of economic growth had benefited a new yuppie class, but voters were aware of accentuated social inequality and the continued inadequacy of health and education structures. Public opinion had also been influenced by **financial scandals** involving government ministers. Aníbal Cavaco Silva, however, avoided any dirt rubbing off on him personally and survived a motion of censure questioning the government's ethics. The ministers involved were summarily replaced in a surprise end-of-year reshuffle, along with three other ministers, in a move which was taken to indicate Cavaco Silva's firm grip on the reins.

INTO THE 1990S: THE PROSPECTS

Scandal was also in the air surrounding **President Mário Soares** in early 1990, when the Socialist governor of Portuguese-administered **Macau** (Hong Kong's enclave neighbour), a man personally appointed by Soares, was accused of receiving back-handers from a German company trying to secure the contract for the building of an airport. The incident called Soares' staffs' integrity into question and strained relations with the prime minister, Cavaco Silva, but the president, popular for his down-to-earth image and his dislike of ceremony, retained his public support and won a landslide victory in presidential elections in January 1991. At Cavaco Silva's insistence, the PSD had not put forward a candidate for the presidency, partly in acknowledgement of a successful relationship between the government and the incumbent president and partly to avoid any further humiliation of a figure who was guaranteed to win. In turn, Cavaco Silva won a convincing mandate in the elections of October 1991, when the **PSD returned to government** with over fifty percent of the vote.

The new decade took Portugal into the second stage of its ten-year transition phase for EC entry and into its **presidency of the European Community** in 1992, the year when (on December 31) all remaining trade and employment barriers were removed. The country adopted its EC task with considerable imagination, and expense, staging a superb exhibiton of its culture – *Europalia* – in Brussels, and building a grand presidency HQ in the Lisbon suburb of Belém. On the domestic front, the PSD continued with privatisation and forged plans for the conversion of state-run banks in preparation for joining the European Monetary System in the mid-1990s.

Dealing with **inflation**, currently running at ten percent, remained – and remains – at the top of their agenda. The government has to do this while coping with increased discontent over social issues, as the opposition calls it to account for statistics that show Portugal still has the highest **infant mortality** and **illiteracy** rates in Europe. Unemployment figures, too, although officially less than four percent, hide a high proportion of underpaid and part-time workers and disguise the fact that wages have failed to increase in real terms in spite of impressive economic growth. There are fears, too, that now the European Community brought down its trade borders completely, fiercer competition is likely to force more Portuguese out of work. Portugal's social security system is incapable of assimilating large numbers of **unemployed**, something which could lead to social unrest. Matters are further strained by the demanding efforts to comply with the Maastricht Treaty's targets and the new GATT agreements.

The **opening up of Eastern Europe** has also exposed Portugal to fiercer competition for trade and investment, although a modernised infrastructure and improved transport networks mean that it continues to be attractive to foreign investors. **Tourism**, which accounts for nearly a tenth of the country's GNP and over a quarter of all foreign investment, has flourished and one challenge will be finding alternatives to the Algarve, where restrictions have been imposed to control the industry's all too disturbingly obvious side-effects.

One of the main headaches for the government, though, continues to be the inefficiency of **Portuguese agriculture**, which employs nearly one-fifth of the workforce but produces only a fraction of the country's wealth. So far, help from Brussels has buffered the less advantageous effects of EC membership, but the honeymoon period is over and although some modernisation has taken place, there is still a huge gap between Portuguese **prices** and European Community prices – a gap that is not likely to be eliminated until the end of the decade and one which will tend to keep Portugal among Europe's poorest nations. A slightly alarming shift, too, has been the takeover of large areas of banking, real estate and the financial sectors by Spanish companies, while EC funds still play a dominant role in Portugal's development, thus blurring the true extent of real economic growth.

On a happier note, Lisbon is the **Cultural Capital of Europe** for 1994, thus bringing renewed interest to this somewhat neglected city and resulting in the restoration of buildings and the redesign of parks. It's also anticipated that Lisbon will host Expo 98, a very costly exercise that's viewed with mixed feelings – it would bring enormous prestige, as it did for Seville in Spain in 1992, but would have huge financial implications for the country.

MONUMENTAL CHRONOLOGY

2000 BC– 1500 BC	**Neolithic** settlements in the north of the country – **Verracos Culture** in Trás-os-Montes.	*Porcas* (stone boars) of Bragança, Murça, etc.
700 BC– 600 BC	**Castro Culture** of fortified hill-towns, or *citânias*, concentrated in the Minho; refined by the **Celtic** Iron Age invasions.	**Citânia de Briteiros** (near Braga) and other sites; best collection of artefacts in Museu Martins Sarmento, Guimarães.
210 BC	**Romans** enter peninsula and begin colonisation; northern Portugal not finally pacified until 19 BC.	**Conimbriga**, 4th c BC Celtic town near Coimbra, adapted to Roman occupation (survives until 5th c AD).
60 BC	Julius Caesar establishes a capital at Lisbon and towns at Beja, Évora, Santarém, etc.	Walls and other remains at Idanha, in Beira Baixa; temple and aqueducts of Évora; bridges at Chaves, Ponte de Lima, Leiria and elsewhere.
4th c AD	Bishoprics founded at Braga, Évora, Faro and Lisbon.	
409–411	**Barbarian** invasions: Suevi settle in the north.	
585	**Visigoths** incorporate Suevian state into their Iberian empire.	Isolated churches, mainly in the north, include 7th-c São Pedro de Balsemão (near Lamego) and São Frutuoso at Braga.
711	**Moors** from North Africa invade and conquer peninsula within seven years.	Fortresses/walls survive at Silves, Lisbon, Sintra, Elvas, Mértola, Alcácer do Sal, etc.
9th c	**Al-Gharb** (Algarve) becomes an independent Moorish kingdom, governed from Silves.	Moorish legacy also includes *azulejos* (ceramic tiles), later designed by Muslim (Mudejar) craftsmen for royal palace at Sintra, etc.
868	Porto reconquered by Christian kings of Asturias-León.	
11th c	Country of **Portucale** emerges and (1097) is given to Henry of Burgundy.	Cluniac monks, administering pilgrimage route to Santiago, bring Romanesque architecture from France. 12th-c churches at Bravães, Tomar, etc. Council chamber at Bragança.
1143	**Afonso Henriques** recognised as first king of Portucale at the Treaty of Zamora.	Guimarães castle built.
1147	Afonso takes Lisbon and Santarém from the Moors; followed in 1162 by Beja and Évora and in 1189 (temporarily) Silves.	Fortress-like **Romanesque cathedrals** of Lisbon, Coimbra, Évora, Braga and Porto.
1212	First assembly of the Cortes (parliament) at Coimbra.	1153: Cistercians found abbey of **Alcobaça**: in this and other Cistercian churches, notably at Coimbra, Gothic architecture enters Portugal.
1249	Afonso III completes reconquest of the Algarve.	

1279–1325	Reign of **Dom Dinis** 1297: Castile recognises Portuguese borders.	Over fifty castles built along Spanish border, including Beja and Estremoz. Pinhal Real forest planted. Coimbra University founded.
1385	Battle of Aljubarrota: João I defeats Castilians to become first king of **House of Avis.**	Abbey of **Batalha**, the great triumph of mature Portuguese Gothic, built in celebration of victory. Paço Real built at Sintra.
1415	**Infante Henriques** (Henry the Navigator; d 1460) active at Sagres. 1419: Madeira discovered. 1427: Azores discovered. 1457: Cape Verde Islands discovered.	Navigation School at Sagres; Lagos fort. Painters: Flemish-influenced "Portuguese Primitives" include Nuno Gonçalves.
1495–1521	Reign of **Dom Manuel I** ("The Fortunate"). 1497: Vasco da Gama opens up sea route to India. 1500: Cabral discovers Brazil. 1513: Portuguese reach China.	Late Gothic **Manueline style** develops, with strong marine motifs and flamboyance anticipating art nouveau. Greatest examples at Tomar, Batalha, Lisbon (Belém) and Sintra. By 1530s Renaissance forms are introduced and merged.
1521–57	Reign of João III.	Painters include Grão Vasco (see Viseu).
1557–78	Reign of **Dom Sebastião**. 1578: Disastrous expedition to Morocco, loss of king and mass slaughter of nobility at Alcácer-Quibir.	Important sculptural school at **Coimbra** (1520–70) centred on French Renaissance sculptors Nicolas Chanterenne, Filipe Hodart and Jean de Rouen.
1581–1640	Philip II brings **Spanish** (Hapsburg) rule.	
1640	**João IV**, Duke of **Bragança**, restores independence.	Severe late Renaissance style: São Vicente, Lisbon (designed by Felipe Terzi), etc.
1706–50	Reign of **Dom João V**. Gold and diamonds discovered in Brazil, reaching a peak of wealth and exploitation in the 1740s.	Baroque palace-monastery of **Mafra** (1717–35). Decoration of Coimbra University Library. High Baroque carved, gilt church interiors. Also simpler, more rustic Baroque style of plaster/granite – **Lamego** and **Bom Jesus**. Rococo Palace of **Queluz** (1752).
1755	**Great Earthquake** destroys Lisbon and parts of the Alentejo and Algarve.	"Pombaline" neoclassical rebuilding of Lisbon (Baixa).
1843–53	Maria II holds throne with German consort, Fernando II.	**Pena Palace** folly built at Sintra.
1908 1910	Assassination of Carlos I in Lisbon. Exile of Manuel II ("The Unfortunate") and **end of Portuguese monarchy**.	Cubist painter Amadeu de Sousa Cardoso (d 1918); museum devoted to him at Amarante.
1910–26	"Democratic" Republic.	
1932–68	**Salazar** dictatorship. Goa is seized by India; colonial wars in Africa.	
1974	April 25 **revolution**.	Permanent gallery of modern Portuguese artists at Lisbon's Gulbenkian Foundation.
1986	**Entry to European Community** (EC)	
1994	Lisbon is European city of Culture.	

BOOKS

Portugal has been covered very sparsely by British and American writers and publishers, and many of the works that do exist in English are out of print (o/p) and available only in libraries. Publishing details below are in the form: British/ American publisher, where both exist. Where books are published in one country only, UK, US or Portugal follows the publisher's name.

GENERAL, TRAVEL AND GUIDES

Marion Kaplan *The Portuguese: the Land and its People* (Penguin/Viking). Published in 1991, this is a readable, all-embracing volume, covering everything from wine to the family, poetry and the land. The style is a bit old-fashioned, but it's the best general introduction to the country available.

Rose Macaulay *They Went to Portugal* (Penguin/Clarke, Irwin). The book covers British travellers to Portugal from the Crusaders to Byron, weaving an anecdotal history of the country in the process. A serious study if you take it as such; a good read if you just feel like dipping into the stories.

William Beckford *Recollections of an Excursion to the Monasteries of Alcobaça and Batalha* (o/p); *Travels in Spain and Portugal (1778–88)* (Centaur Press/Albert Saifer). Mad and enormously rich, Beckford lived for some time at Sintra and travelled widely in Estremadura. His accounts, told with a fine eye for the absurd, are a lot of fun.

Lord Byron *Selected Letters and Journals* (Pimlico in UK). Only a few days of Portuguese travel but memorable ones – beginning with romantic enthusiasm, ending in outright abuse.

Almeida Garrett *Travels in My Homeland* (Peter Own/Dufour). A classic Portuguese writer, Garrett was exiled to Europe in the 1820s, came into contact with the Romantics and later returned to play a part in the liberal government of the 1830s. This is a witty, discursive narrative ramble around the country.

Oleg Polunin and B.E. Smythies *Flowers of South-West Europe: A Field Guide* (Oxford University Press in UK and US). The best available guide to the Portuguese flora.

Sacheverell Sitwell *Portugal and Madeira* (Batsford/Clarke, Irwin; both o/p). Mix of art history, observation and rather pompous upper-class travelogue from the 1950s. Sitwell's great enthusiasm is Portuguese Baroque. He also "discovers" Mateus Rosé wine for the British.

HISTORY AND POLITICS

David Birmingham *A Concise History of Portugal* (Cambridge University Press in UK and US). The most recent available book is also the best for the casual reader; concise indeed, but providing straightforward and informative coverage from the year dot to 1991.

Harold Livermore *A New History of Portugal* (Cambridge University Press in UK and US; o/p). Covering events through to 1976, this is thorough, if not exactly inspiring, but was revised a little too soon after the 1974 revolution to be authoritative.

Daniel J. Boorstin *The Discoverers* (Penguin o/p/Vintage). Old, standard text on the Discoveries that you might find in libraries.

C.R. Boxer *The Portuguese Seaborne Empire 1415–1825* (Carcanet Press/Knopf). Entertaining account by a prolific writer on the region.

António de Figueiredo *Portugal: Fifty Years of Dictatorship* (Penguin in UK and US; o/p). An illuminating study which takes as its starting-point the 1926 military coup that brought Salazar to power and goes through to the 1974 revolution.

Lawrence S. Graham and Douglas L. Wheeler, eds. *In Search of Modern Portugal: The Revolution and Its Consequences* (University of Wisconsin Press in UK and US). An academic study published in the early 1980s; heavy going but ultimately rewarding.

A.H. de Oliveira Marques *History of Portugal* (Columbia University Press in UK and US). Accessible general history.

Dan L. Raby, *Fascism and Resistance in Portugal* (Manchester University Press/St Martin's Press). Scholarly account of the subject.

ART AND ARCHITECTURE

Júlio Gil and Augusto Cabrita *The Finest Castles in Portugal* (Beaufort Publishing in UK). A superb illustrated survey of Portuguese castles, let down a little by a highly pedestrian translation/text.

Marcus Binney *Country Manors of Portugal* (Antique Collector's Club/Scala Books; o/p). Again, excellent photos are the main reason to buy this solid volume.

Helder Carita and Homem Cardoso *Portuguese Gardens* (Antique Collector's Club in UK and US). A huge and beautiful tome, lavishly illustrated with photos and plans, with a scholarly text.

FICTION

Fernando Pessoa *The Book of Disquiet* (Serpent's Tail in UK and US). The country's best known poet (see below) wrote just this one work in prose: a kind of autobiography, set in Lisbon, and posthumously compiled from a trunkload of material. Regarded as a modernist classic, the book's admirers include Jorge Luís Borges.

Eça de Queiroz *The Mandarin* (Dedalus/Hippocrene); *The Reliquary* (Dedalus/Noonday Press o/p); *The Sin of Father Amaro* (Black Swan in UK o/p); *The Maias* (Carcanet Press in UK); *Cousin Bazilio* (Carcanet Press in UK); *The Illustrious House of Ramires* (Quartet Books in UK). Queiroz is the classic Portuguese novelist, responsible for a string of nineteenth-century narratives, recently available in new translations. The two best are *The Illustrious House of Ramires* and *The Maias*, entertaining narratives which give a comprehensive account of nineteenth-century Portuguese society.

António Lobo Antunes *An Explanation of the Birds*, *The Natural Order of Things* and *Act of the Damned* (Secker & Warburg in UK); *South of Nowhere* (Chatto/Random House; o/p in both). Many consider Antunes to be Portugal's leading contemporary writer, notwithstanding the increasing worldwide acclaim for José Saramago (see below). The two writers couldn't be more different, however. Antunes is a psychologist and writes helter-skelter prose, notably in the recent *Act of the Damned*, whose narrative voice changes ceaselessly.

José Saramago *Baltasar and Blimunda* (Cape/Ballantine); *The Year of the Death of Ricardo Reis*, *The Gospel According to Jesus Christ* and *The Stone Raft* (Harvill/Harcourt Brace). Saramago has been mooted as a Nobel winner and at last has a number of titles available translated into English. The one to start with is *Ricardo Reis*, a magnificent novel which won The Independent foreign fiction award. Its theme is the return of Dr Reis, after sixteen years in Brazil, to a Lisbon where the Salazar dictatorship is imminent and where Reis wanders the streets to be confronted by the past and the ghost of the writer Fernando Pessoa.

José Cardoso Pires, *Ballad of Dog's Beach* (Dent in UK; o/p). Ostensibly a detective thriller but the murder described actually took place during the last years of Salazar's dictatorship and Pires' research draws upon the original secret-police files. Compelling, highly original and with acute psychological insights, it was awarded Portugal's highest literary prize and also filmed.

Maria Isabel Barreno, Maria Teresa Horta and Maria Velho da Costa *New Portuguese Letters: The Three Marias* (Abacus/Doubleday; both o/p). Published (and prosecuted) in 1972, pre-Revolution Portugal, this collage of stories, letters and poems is a modern feminist parable based on the seventeenth century "Letters of a Portuguese Nun".

POETRY

Luís de Camões *The Lusiads* (Penguin in UK and US). Portugal's national epic, celebrating the ten-month voyage of Vasco da Gama which opened the sea route to India. This is a good prose translation.

Fernando Pessoa *Selected Poems* (Penguin in UK). Pessoa, who died in 1933, wrote startling, lyrical verse in over twenty quite different personas. Virtuoso stuff – and remarkable in the way he produces very simple poems from highly complex themes.

FOOD AND WINE

Edite Vieira *The Taste of Portugal* (Robinson in UK). A delight to read, let alone cook from. Vieira combines snippets of history and passages from Portuguese writers (very well translated) to illustrate her dishes; highly recommended.

Jan Read *The Wines of Portugal* (Faber and Faber in UK and US). Very full descriptions of every region and particularly of soon-to-be-internationally recognised wines. Clear explanations, too, of why each region has its own flavour and much interesting social and historical background.

Alex Liddell and Janet Price *Port Wine Quintas of the Douro* (Philip Wilson/Sotheby's).

Highly erudite account of the wines and history; superb photos put it beyond specialist interest.

RESIDENCE

Rachael Robinson and Victoria Pybus *Live and Work in Spain and Portugal* (Vacation Work in UK). Invaluable handbook packed with details on permits, business, teaching, health, schools, renting and buying property, etc.

TREKKING

Bethan Davies and Ben Cole *Walking in Portugal* (Footprint Guides in UK). New and dependable guide to trekking in the national parks of Gerês, Serra da Estrela, Montesinho, and Serra de São Mamede. An excellent supplement to our own coverage.

MUSIC

Portugal has a rich musical culture, with roots harking back to Provençal troubadours, continuing through ballads and the unique "blues" of the *fado* and encompassing, more recently, the rhythms of the country's five former African colonies.

Each of these elements has a currency in the sounds that you hear today – from the French Provençal strain in the folk music played at northern festivals, to the cosmopolitan rock and jazz of the larger cities. An additional element is added by the wealth of singer-songwriters, most of them from the highly political "New Song" movement fostered by the dramatic events of the 1970s, as the country threw off the 36-year dictatorship of Salazar and was forced to withdraw from its colonies.

INSTRUMENTS, VOICES AND RHYTHMS

There is a startling variety of Portuguese **folk instruments**: bagpipes, harmonicas, accordions, flutes, assorted drums (*caixas, bombos, adufes, pandeiros, sarroncas*) and countless percussion instruments (*reco-reco, ferrinhos, genebres, trancanholas*). But the country's pride and glory is strings, which include violins, the classic twelve-stringed "Portuguese guitar," and six varieties of "**viola-guitars**", unknown elsewhere in Europe. Each of these has a character, tuning and design of its own. Best known are the little four-stringed *cavaquinho* and the bigger *guitarra portuguesa*, the standard accompaniments to Lisbon *fado*.

Others range through elaborate combinations of single, double and triple strings.

One of the most common combinations of instruments is the **zés-pereiras**, made up of a large *bombo*, a *caixa* and a bagpipe or fife (depending on whether you're in the Minho or Beiras region) and often used to announce grand occasions. Another traditional combination popular throughout the country is the **rancho**, made up of violins, guitars, clarinets, harmonicas and *ferrinhos*, with the later addition of the accordion.

If the folk traditions are rich in instruments, its **singers** are unrivalled. In every town and district there is an amateur choir. After a good meal someone will start an **à desgarrada** (a cappella) song, followed intuitively by the other guests. It is not at all unusual, if you go to a **fado** performance, to find the entire staff of the establishment taking part, from the owner to the cloakroom attendant. To listen to a vocal ensemble of three women from Manhouce, or a rural male choir from Alentejo, is to hear genuinely popular roots music. Alentejo is home also to the *saia*, sung by women accompanying themselves on the *pandeireta*.

Since Portugal remains in large part a rural society, a great many **songs** survive reflecting the cycles of nature, such as *natal, reis* and *janeiras* – lullabies and tilling, sowing and harvest songs. They remain very much within a living tradition. Equally authentic, if less harmonious, are the **singing contests** in which rival performers exchange improvisations on a theme, or the *fandango*, a dance where two men match their footwork. Among other popular **traditional dances** are *modas, despiques, chulas, rusgas, corridinhos, viras*, waltzes and the ritual steps of the *pauliteiros* (stick-dancers) of Miranda in the Douro region.

FADO

The *fado* is Portugal's most famous – though perhaps also its least accessible – music. Lyrical and sentimental, it is thought to have origins in African slave songs, though the influence of Portugal's own maritime and colonial past is equally apparent. After the 1974 revolution, when the empire disintegrated, it went through something of a crisis. Today, it has come to be identified with a general sense of frustration and, some would have it, with an endemic and peculiarly Portuguese fatalism.

There are two versions of the *fado*. That of the humble **Alfama and Mouraria districts of Lisbon** (performed mainly in the Bairro Alto clubs, these days) is highly personal and full of feeling. The more academic strand from **Coimbra** reflects that city's ancient university traditions and is performed mainly by students and Coimbra graduates. In both versions, the theme is usually love, though *fados* have been composed on all kinds of subjects.

By far the most famous of the *fado* singers and arguably its greatest performer, is **Amália Rodriguez**. She can be seen at prestige clubs and concerts in Lisbon, though keep in mind that in recent years she has strayed into other genres, even variety.

Other big traditional names include Florencio Carvalho, Alberto Prado, José de Câmara and Castro Rodrigo. Recent performers have adapted the form to a more modern rhythm, including, most recently, Manuel Osório and (a name to look out for in the clubs) **Carlos do Carmo**. The singer-songwriters, too, have looked toward *fado*. Following the lead of José Afonso (see below), nearly all the stars have produced one or two of their own interpretations of the form.

THE BALLAD

It was an attempt to update the Coimbra *fado* that resulted in the modern Portuguese **ballad** and which in turn, in the last years of the dictatorship, gave way to "New Song." This, from the revolution of April 25, 1974 onwards, became a genuine political song movement, broadening in recent years to a movement known as *Música Popular* – essentially contemporary folk music, composed and performed by an impressive roster of singer–songwriters.

The **lyrics** generated by this movement were – and are – as significant as the music. Many artists turned to modern poetry that dealt with contemporary social and cultural issues. They also drew on music rooted in popular tradition, both rural and urban, that reflected influences of various kinds – colonial, French, English, or Spanish – but avoided the easy rhythms of commercial pop.

One of the forerunners of the genre was the 1956 LP *Canções Heróicas – Canções Regionais Portuguesas* ("Heroic Songs – Portuguese Regional Songs"), arranged by Fernando Lopes Graça and performed by the Choir of the Amateur Musicians' Academy. Although the harmonisations are a long way from New Song, two basic elements are already present: committed lyrics and respect for genuine **regional music**.

Another LP, *Fados of Coimbra* by José Afonso and Luís Gois, appeared in May of the same year. The *fado* was out of favour in radical circles at the time. It had become just another branch of "national song," with overtones of vulgar soap-opera.

José Afonso gradually abandoned the Portuguese guitar for the Spanish, which allows for more freedom in the accompaniment. His first solo records came out in 1960, including *Balada do Outono* (Autumn Ballad), which gave its name to the new genre and made it respectable. He was soon joined by Adriano Correia de Oliveira and the **poets** Manuel Alegre, Ary dos Santos and Manuel Correia, whose work provided the text for numerous songs.

After the onset of the **colonial wars** censorship began to wreak havoc. *Menino do Bairro Negro* (Black Slum Kid) and *Os Vampiros* (The Vampires), both by José Afonso, were withdrawn from the market and only instrumental versions allowed to be sold. Some singers chose to go into exile. Luís Cília released several records in Paris under the general title of *A Poesia Portuguesa de Hoje e de Sempre* (Portuguese Poetry of Today and All Times), on which he sung his own arrangements of poems by Camões, Pessoa, Saramago and others.

The release in 1968 of José Afonso's *Cantares do Andarilho* (Songs of the Road) marked the coming of age of the ballad. By now Adriano was making his first LPs, as were Manuel Freire, José Jorge Letria, José Mário Branco, Father Fanhais and soon afterwards Fausto, Pedro Barroso and the Angolan Rui Mingas. At the same time, the **social climate** was becoming increasingly suffocating. These singers were banned from television and hardly ever heard on the radio. There were very few venues and permits were granted sparingly. They had to take other jobs to make a living.

NEW SONG

José Afonso's *Cantigas de Maio* (Songs of May), José Mário Branco's *Mudam-se os Tempos, Mudam-se as Vontades* (Changing Times, Changing Wishes) and Adriano Correia de Oliveira's *Gente d'Aqui e de Agora* (People Here and Now) show an improvement in the quality of the material. The lyrics went further in their reflections on living conditions and were more open in their **protest**. The music explored new forms, rhythms and means of expression. José Mário Branco made a key contribution as an arranger and producer. Preproduction **censorship**, however, continued to be strictly imposed and some singers stopped recording to avoid it. Others, like José Afonso, resorted to ever more cryptic lyrics.

This was how things stood on the night of **April 24, 1974**. At 10.55pm João Paulo Dinis of the "Associates of Lisbon" radio programme played *E Depois do Adeus* (After the Goodbyes), Paulo de Caravalho's Eurovision Song Contest entry for the year. At midnight came the final signal – Leite Vasconcelos played *Grândola Vila Morena* on Radio

PORTUGUESE FOLK: THE KEY FIGURES

JOSÉ AFONSO The "father of modern Portuguese popular music" made a key contribution to song from the 1950s onwards and won fame far beyond his country's borders. He was born in Aveiro and as the son of a civil servant visited several colonies as a child, but it was not until later, when he made a trip to Angola as a student, that he became aware of the colonial realities.

His first records were collections of *fado* made with Luís Góis in 1956. In the 1960s he began to write songs on social issues. His records were censored and he was persecuted by the secret police. His whole life was dedicated to song and his personal crusade against fascism.

After the revolution, he continued to work prolifically and to consistently high standards, composing music for films and the theatre as well as producing nearly twenty LPs. His work was constantly evolving, yet his first compositions are still fresh today. With their careful attention to music, lyrics, arrangement and voice, any of his records is a miniature work of art. He lived modestly and died after a long illness in 1987.

FAUSTO The work of this singer combines the most diverse influences – modern and traditional, Portuguese and African – with a marked urban slant and a lyrical delivery. His skill lies in the subtlety with which he links African rhythms to Portuguese melodies and instruments and the delicacy of his singing.

His early songs provide a poetic analysis of the uncertain post-revolutionary period. Later ones use tales of the deeds of *conquistadores*, sailors and other Portuguese heroes to reflect on the country's history.

SÉRGIO GODINHO Born in Porto, Godinho went into exile as an economics student to avoid military service in the colonial war. He travelled in France, Switzerland and Canada, working at one time as an interpreter for the musical *Hair* and at another as a member of *Living Theatre*.

Due to these influences he is one of the more modern, cosmopolitan singers of his generation. His songs are usually narrative and he has a particular knack for affectionate character sketches. When dealing more directly with political issues he employs a fine sense of humour. His music is both loud and cheerful, intimate and sophisticated.

LUÍS CÍLIA Of the new songwriters, Luís Cília is the one who has devoted most attention to setting his poems to music. His work is rigorous and serious, showing a pronounced French influence. He is good at capturing the essence and general atmosphere of a given political moment in his lyrics. Musically, he has worked in two apparently contrasting fields: traditional song and experimental work with synthesizers from which he has produced a solo album.

JOSÉ MÁRIO BRANCO Another native of Porto, Mário Branco's chief contribution has been as an arranger and producer of records, though he has made important records himself, both individually and as a member of the *Grupo de Acção Cultural*. His skill in the studios has given an added dimension to the records of Portuguese singers.

VITORINO The songs of Vitorino are inextricably linked with the Alentejo region and its farming cooperatives and rural communities, though recently he has made more contact with the city. His early records were uneven in their development, a mixture of Alentejo folk songs, revolutionary anthems and love songs. It is with the latter genre that he has had most success in his recent work.

JANITA SALOMÉ Brother of Vitorino, he also has links with Alentejo, though he has concentrated increasingly on the Arab heritage there and in the Algarve. His music, full of percussion and gentle touches, also betrays the influence of José Afonso, with whom he worked closely in his last years.

Renascença's "Limit" programme. The army captains went into action and on the following day the coup was a reality: Portugal was returning to democracy.

There began an uncertain period during which it was unclear who held power. Singers like Sérgio Godinho, Luís Cília, José Mário Branco and Father Fanhais returned from exile. Now that censorship had been lifted, New Song gave way to **political song**. Everyone had slogans, analyses and solutions to offer in the process of clarification which followed.

Singers were suddenly in constant demand for the political and cultural events being improvised with a minimum of technical resources all over the country, giving performances in factories, cooperatives and squatters' settlements. They set up various groups according to their political leanings: Free Song (*Canto Livre*), the October Group (*Grupo Outubro*) and the Group for Cultural Action – Voices for the Cause (*Grupo de Acção Cultural Vozes na Luta*, or *GAC*). The latter, in mixing traditional songs with its sloganeering political ones, set an unconscious pattern for future developments. Other artists slowly branched out into work with the numerous theatre groups of the time and on soundtracks for films. Some singers and musicians also formed cooperatives, such as *Eranova* (New Age) and *Cantarabril* (Sing of April).

FOLK GROUPS

As time passed and things returned to normal, **traditional music** enjoyed a revival, bringing with it the first commercial folk groups. In the 1960s, much work had been done in studying and recording traditional Portuguese music, most notably by Fernando Lopes Graça and Michel Giacometti, who produced a five-volume *Antologia de Música Regional Portuguesa*. Over the last decade, the group **Almanaque** of Lisbon has followed in their footsteps, producing a series of records from the oral tradition, as well as reworking the traditional themes in a more modern form.

The **Brigada Victor Jara** of Coimbra also began by collecting folk tunes but soon turned to new directions, adapting the work of other folk writers. Although none of its original members are still in the line-up, this group is one of Portugal's best, producing well-crafted work based on sound ideas. Other active folk groups, adopting similar approaches, include *Raizes* (Roots) from Vila Verde (Braga); the *Grupo Etnográfico de Cantares e Trajes* (Ethnographic Song and Costume Group) from Manhouce; *Terra Terra* (Land, Land); *Vai de Roda*, an ethnic arts cooperative from Oporto; *Trigo Limpo* (Clean Wheat) from Alentejo; and *Ronda dos Quatro Caminhos* (Crossroads) from Lisbon.

A more **contemporary** and ambitious folk music has also emerged over the last decade. **Trovante**, which was formed in 1975, is highly acclaimed in Portugal and has worked extensively with José Afonso and Fausto. Its work is full of uneven swayings and sudden changes of direction. Interesting, too, though less successful, are *Charanga*, *Pedra d'Hera*, *Construção*, *Disto e Daquilo* and *Rosa dos Ventos*.

Música Popular – as more recent folk has become known – owes much of its renewed popularity, however, to the work of some singer-songwriters who have dedicated themselves exclusively to it and to musicians who have made records devoted to individual folk instruments.

Among **instrumentalists**, perhaps the most outstanding figure is the guitarist **Carlos Paredes**. He explores both the folk and the classical sides of the Portuguese guitar, with surprising results; his records are a rare treat. Pedro Cabreira Cabral, very much the next generation after Paredes, also continues the tradition of using indigenous instruments – apart from being an exceptional guitarist and learned musicologist, he also makes and restores instruments and has composed original pieces for the Portuguese guitar. Another excellent instrumentalist is **Júlio Pereira**, who began as a songwriter but became interested in traditional string instruments and has recently experimented to great effect in combining them with synthesizers, rhythm boxes and samplers in compositions inspired by folk tradition.

ROCK, JAZZ AND AFRICAN

Though Portuguese rock and jazz cannot even begin to match the maturity of its songwriting tradition, there have been some interesting developments recently. Two names to watch out for are the blues singer **Rui Veloso** and the pop singer **Mafalda Veiga**. Among groups, the most established include **GNR**, **Heróis do Mar**, **Madredeus**, **Chutos e Pontapés**,

Rádio Macau, Sétima Legião and Trovante. An intriguing figure, midway between jazz and "New Age," is the saxophonist **Rão Kyao**. As for jazz proper, there is the great vocalist **Maria João**, the **Lisbon Jazz Sextet**, the experimental trio **Shish**, and the ensembles led by **António Pinho Vargas** and **Mário Laginha**.

On the contemporary Portuguese rock scene, by far the most exciting development is the appearance of groups from the former African colonies of **Angola**, **Mozambique**, **Cabo Verde**, **Guinea-Bissau** and **São Tomé e Príncipe**. Many musicians, particularly from Cabo Verde (Cape Verde Islands), settled in Lisbon during the very hard years following the colonial wars and independence. Others spend part of the year based in Portugal, recording and touring Europe, drawn by the comparatively high fees to be made.

Staying in Lisbon, you're most likely to get a chance to see Cabo Verde groups, which include among their styles *morna*, similar to the Portuguese *fado* and the more danceable *moradeira*. The big moma star of the moment is **Cesaria Evora**, a fabulous diva who is beginning to gain an international following. From **Guinea-Bissau** the sounds are an unusual mix of African and Latin, akin to zouk. Big names to look out for that may be in the country include **Justino Delgado**, **Super Mama Diombo**, **Manecas**, **Africa Libre** and **Jetu Katem**. Finally, two outstanding southern African groups to see are **Guem** from **Angola** and **Fernando Luís** from **Mozambique**.

Manuel Dominguez

RECORDS

Portuguese music is hard to obtain outside the country, save for a few fado recordings (including some excellent reissues of old classics), so our advice is buy when you're there. CDs are broadly similar in cost to the UK, and pricier than in the US; records, by contrast, are excellent value. The following is a personal selection of the most interesting.

Folk

Almanaque *Desafiando Cantigas; Sementes.*
Brigada Victor Jara *Marcha dos Foliões.*
Ronda dos Quatro Caminhos *Fados Velhos.*
Vai de Roda *Vai de Roda.*

Fado

Amália Rodrigues *O Melhor.*
Carlos do Carmo *Um Homem na Cidade; Um Homem no País.*

Portuguese Guitar

Carlos Paredes *Guitarra Portuguesa; Movimento Perpétuo; Concerto em Frankfurt; Espelho de Sons.*
Pedro Caldeira Cabral *Encontros; A Guitarra Portuguesa nos Salões dos sec. XVIII.*

Singer-Songwriters

Adriano Correia de Oliveira *Memória de Adriano.*
Fausto *Madrugada dos Trapeiros; Por Este Rio Acima; Despertar dos Alquimistas.*
Janita Salomé *Lavrar em teu Peito; Olho de Fogo.*
José Afonso *Cantigas de Maio; Venham Mais Cinco; Coro do Tribunais; Com as Minhas Tamanquinhas; Fura Fura; Fados de Coimbra e Outras Canções; Como se Fora Seu Filho; Galinhas do Mato.*

José Maria Branco *Ser Solidário.*
Julio Pereira *Cavaquinho; Braguesa; Cadoi; Os Sete Instrumentos; Miradouro.*
Luís Cília *Cancioneiro; Penumbra.*
Sérgio Godinho *De Pequenino se Torce o Destino; Coincidências; Na Vida Real.*
Vitorino *Romances; Negro Fado; Frol de la Mar.*

Rock/Pop

G.N.R. *Os Homens não se querem Bonitos.*
Heróis do Mar *Mãe.*
Madredeus *Os Dias da Madredeus.*
Radio Macau *Rádio Macau.*
Sétima Legião *Mar d'Outubro.*
Trovante *Terra Firme.*

Jazz

António Pinho Vargas *Variações.*
Maria João *Conversa.*
Rão Kyao *Fado Bailado; Danças de Rua.*
Sexteto de Jazz de Lisboa *Sexteto.*

African

Cesaria Evora *Miss Perfumado* (Cabo Verde).
Kaba Mane *Kunga Kungake* (Guinea-Bissau).
Guem *Dans Voyage* (Angola).
Fernando Luís *Bassopa* (Mozambique).

LANGUAGE

If you have some knowledge of Spanish and/or French you won't have much problem reading Portuguese. Understanding it when it's spoken, though, is a different matter: pronunciation is entirely different and at first even the easiest words are hard to distinguish – the sound is more like that of an East European language than of the Romance tongues in which it has its roots. If you're stuck, most people will understand Spanish (albeit reluctantly) and in the cities and tourist areas French and English are also widely spoken. Even so, it's well worth the effort to master at least the rudiments; once you've started to figure out the words it gets a lot easier very quickly.

PRONUNCIATION

The chief difficulty with **pronunciation** is its lack of clarity – consonants tend to be slurred, vowels nasal and often ignored altogether.

CONSONANTS

The **consonants** are, at least, consistent:

C is soft before E and I, hard otherwise unless it has a cedilla – *açucar* (sugar) is pronounced "assookar."

CH is somewhat softer than in English; *Chá* (tea) sounds like Shah.

J is pronounced like the "s" in pleasure, as is *G* except when it comes before a "hard" vowel (A, O and U).

LH sounds like "lyur" (Batalha).

Q is always pronounced as a "k."

S before a consonant or at the end of a word becomes "sh," otherwise it's as in English – Cascais is pronounced "Kashkaish," Sagres is "Sahgresh."

X has the same sound – *caixa* (cash desk) is pronounced "kaisha."

VOWELS

Vowels are worse – flat and truncated, they're often difficult for English-speaking tongues to get around. The only way to learn is to listen: accents, ã, ô, or é, turn them into longer, more familiar sounds.

When two vowels come together they continue to be enunciated separately except in the case of *EI* and *OU* – which sound like a and long o respectively.

E at the end of a word is silent unless it has an accent, so that *carne* (meat) is pronounced "karn," while *café* sounds much as you'd expect.

The **tilde over Ã or Õ** renders the pronunciation much like the French -an and -on endings only more nasal.

More common is **ÃO** (as in *pão*, bread – *são*, saint – *limão*, lemon), which sounds something like a strangled yelp of "Ow!" cut off in midstream.

A FEW KEY WORDS . . .

Even if you speak no Portuguese at all there are **a few key words** which can help you out in an enormous number of situations.

● *Há* (the H is silent) means "there is" or "is there?" and can be used for just about anything. Thus: "*Há uma pensão aqui?*" (Is there a pension here?), "*Há uma camioneta para . .?*" (Is there a bus to . . .?), or even "*Há um quarto?*" (Do you have a room?).

● More polite and better in shops or restaurants are **"*Tem . . .?*"** (Do you have . . .?) or "*Queria . . .*" (I'd like . . .).

● And of course there are the old standards "Do you speak English?" (*Fala Inglês?*) and "I don't understand" (*Não compreendo*).

PORTUGUESE WORDS AND PHRASES

BASICS

sim; não	yes; no	grande; pequeno	big; little
olá; bom dia	hello; good morning	aberto; fechado	open; closed
boa tarde/noite	good afternoon/night	senhoras; homens	women; men
adeus, até logo	goodbye, see you later	lavabo/quarto de banho	toilet
hoje; amanhã	today; tomorrow	banco; câmbio	bank; change
por favor/se faz favor	please	correios	post office
está bem	it's all right/OK	(dois) selos	(two) stamps
obrigado/a*	thank you	sou Inglês/Inglesa	I am English
onde; que	where; what	Americano/a	American
quando; porquê	when; why	Irlandês/Irlandesa	Irish
como; quanto	how; how much	Australiano/a	Australian
não sei	I don't know	Canadiano/a	Canadian
sabe . . .?	do you know . . .?	Escocês/Escosesa	Scottish
pode . . .?	could you . . .?	Galês/Galesa	Welsh
desculpe; com licença	sorry; excuse me	Como se chama?	What's your name?
aqui; ali	here; there	(chamo–me . . .)	(my name is . . .)
perto; longe	near; far	Como se diz isto em	What's this called in
este/a; esse/a	this; that	Português?	Portuguese?
agora; mais tarde	now; later	O que é isso? Quanto	What's that? How
mais; menos	more; less	é?	much is it?

* *Obrigado* agrees with the sex of the person speaking – a woman says *obrigada*, a man *obrigado*.

GETTING AROUND

Para ir a . . .?	How do I get to . . .?	A que horas parte?	What time does it leave?
esquerda, direita, sempre em frente	left, right, straight ahead	(chega a . . . ?)	(arrive at . . . ?)
Onde é a estação de camionetas?	Where is the bus station?	Qual é a estrada para . ?	Which is the road to . ?
a paragem de autocarro para. . .	the bus stop for . . .	Vou a (Para onde vai?)	I'm going to (Where are you going?)
a estação de comboios	the railway station	Está bem, muito obrigado/a	That's great, thanks a lot
Donde parte o autocarro para. . .?	Where does the bus to . . . leave from?	Pare aqui por favor	Stop here please
É este o comboio para Coimbra?	Is this the train for Coimbra?	bilhete (para)	ticket (to)
		ida e volta	round trip

ACCOMMODATION

Há uma pensão aqui perto?	Is there a pension near here?	Posso/podemos deixar os sacos aqui até . . ?	Can I/we leave the bags here until . . ?
Queria um quarto	I'd like a room	Há um quarto mais barato?	Is there a cheaper room?
É para uma noite (semana)	It's for one night (week)		
É para uma pessoa (duas pessoas)	It's for one person (two people)	Com duche (quente/frio)	With a shower (hot/cold)
Posso ver?	May I see/look around?		Can we camp here?
Está bem, fico com ele	OK, I'll take it	Pode-se acampar aqui?	key
Quanto custa?	How much is it?	chave	
É caro, não o quero	It's expensive, I don't want it		

DAYS AND MONTHS

domingo	Sunday	janeiro	January	agosto	August
segunda-feira	Monday	fevereiro	February	setembro	September
terça-feira	Tuesday	março	March	outubro	October
quarta-feira	Wednesday	abril	April	novembro	November
quinta-feira	Thursday	maio	May	dezembro	December
sexta-feira	Friday	junho	June		
sábado	Saturday	julho	July		

THE TIME

que horas são ?	what time is it?	dez para as duas	one-fifty
é/são . . .	it's . . .	meio-dia	midday, noon
a que horas	(at) what time?	uma da tarde	one in the afternoon
à/às . . .	at . . .		(1pm)
meia-noite	midnight	sete da tarde	seven in the evening
uma da manhã	one in the morning (1am)	(dezanove)	(7pm)
uma e dez	ten past one	nove e meia da noite	nine-thirty (pm)
uma e quinze	one-fifteen	(vinte e uma e trinta)	
uma e vinte	one-twenty	meio-dia e quinze	quarter past noon
uma e meia	one-thirty	meia-noite e dez	ten past midnight
quinze para as duas	one-forty-five		

NUMBERS

1	um	8	oito	15	quinze	30	trinta	100	cem
2	dois	9	nove	16	dezasseis	40	quarenta	101	cento e um
3	três	10	dez	17	dezassete	50	cinquenta	200	duzentos
4	quatro	11	onze	18	dezoito	60	sessenta	500	quinhentos
5	cinco	12	doze	19	dezanove	70	setenta	1000	mil
6	seis	13	treze	20	vinte	80	oitenta	2000	dois mil
7	sete	14	catorze	21	vinte e um	90	noventa	1,000,000	um milhão

PORTUGUESE WORDS AND TERMS: A GLOSSARY

ARCHITECTURAL, HISTORICAL & RELIGIOUS TERMS

AFONSINO Relating to the reign of Dom Afonso Henriques, first king of Portugal.

AZULEJO Glazed and painted tile; originally used as geometric decoration around the base of doorways of a church or mansion; by the late sixteenth century whole pictorial blocks were created. From the late seventeenth until the mid-eighteenth century – the main period – tiles were exclusively blue and white.

CAPELA Chapel; Capela-Mor is a chancel or sanctuary.

CITÂNIA Prehistoric/Celtic hill settlement.

CLAUSTRO Cloister.

CONVENTO Convent, though just as often an old church.

CORO Central, often enclosed, part of church built for the choir.

DOM, DONA Courtesy titles (sir, madam) usually applied to kings and queens.

ERMIDA Remote chapel – not necessarily a hermitage.

IGREJA Church; Igreja Matriz is a parish church.

INFANTA Princess.

INFANTE Prince.

MANUELINO Flamboyant, marine-influenced style of late Gothic architecture developed in the reign of Manuel I (1495–1521).

MOÇÁRABE Moorish-Arabic (usually of architecture or a design).

MOSTEIRO Monastery, or just as often an old church since most orders were suppressed in 1834–38.

MUDÉJAR Moorish-style architecture and decoration.

NOSSA SENHORA (N.S.) Our Lady – the Virgin Mary.

RETÁBULO Altarpiece – usually large, carved and heavily gilt.

SALA DO CAPÍTULO Chapter house.

TORRE DE MENAGEM Keep of a castle.

GENERAL TERMS AND WORDS

ALAMEDA Promenade.

ALBUFEIRA Reservoir.

ALDEIA Village.

BAIRRO Quarter, area (of a town); Alto is upper, Baixo lower.

BAIXA Commercial, shopping centre of town.

CÂMARA MUNICIPAL Town hall.

CAMPO Square or field.

CASTELO Castle.

CENTRO COMERCIAL Shopping centre.

CHAFARIZ Public fountain.

CIDADE City.

CORREIO Post office, abbreviated *CTT*.

ELÉCTRICO Tramcar.

ELEVADOR Elevator or funicular railway.

ESPLANADA Seafront promenade.

ESTAÇÃO Station.

ESTRADA Road; Estrada Nacional is a main road, designated EN on maps.

FEIRA Fair or market.

FESTA Festival or carnival.

FONTE Fountain.

GRUTAS Caves.

HORÁRIO Timetable.

LAGO Lake.

LARGO Square.

MERCADO Market.

MIRADOURO Belvedere or viewpoint.

PAÇO Palace or country house.

PAÇOS DO CONCELHO Town hall.

PALÁCIO Palace or country house; Palácio Real, Royal Palace.

PARQUE NACIONAL/NATURAL National/ Nature Park or Reserve.

PASTELARIA Bakery, pastry shop.

PELOURINHO Stone pillory, seen in almost every northern village.

POUSADA Luxury state-run hotel, sometimes converted from a castle or monastery.

PRAÇA Square.

PRAÇA DE TOUROS Bullring.

PRAIA Beach.

QUINTA Country estate, or its manor house.

ROMARIA Pilgrimage-festival.

SÉ Cathedral.

SENHOR Man, Sir, or Mr.

SENHORA Woman, Madam, Ms or Mrs.

SOLAR Manor house or important town mansion.

INDEX

HELP US UPDATE

We've gone to a lot of effort to make this new edition of *The Rough Guide to Portugal* as up-to-date and accurate as possible. However, things do change – places get "discovered," opening hours are notoriously fickle – and any suggestions, comments or corrections would be much appreciated.

As a small incitement we give free copies of the next edition (or any other *Rough Guide* if you prefer) for the best letters. Please mark letters "Rough Guide Portugal Update" and send them to:

Rough Guides, 1 Mercer Street, London WC2H 9QJ, or
Rough Guides, 375 Hudson Street, 4th Floor, New York NY 10014.

THANKS

As indicated above, letters advising us of changes and errors are hugely appreciated. We're especially grateful for contributions from the following readers of the last edition:

Dixon Adams, Mary and John Alexander, M.R. Andrews, Felix Ansell, Sam Anthony, Michaela Aspden, James Barr, Hettie Barra, Kathy Bayer, Julie Belfield, Anders Berglund, Kathleen Billingham, Jutta Bogenschutz, Nigel Brown, Stephen Brown, Susanna Bryant, Tim Burford, M.L. Buss, Aaron Cahill, Lara Cameron, Mark Carubia, Mark Cathcart, Emily Catto, Kate Chacksfield, David Clark, Derek A. Clarke, Tony Clarke, Jean Coopey, Richard Cotton, Merle Crosdale, James Curtis, Simon Dadd, Mrs P. Dagg, John Dallimore, Keith Dillingham, L.J. Doughty, David Doerr, Christine Douglas, Phil Edwards, Tony English, Frank Evans, Meryl Evans, John Fallon, Rona Ferguson, Steve Garner, Joseph D. Garrison, John Gilmour, Nicholas Gilroy, Kurt Gingold, Mark Glaisher, Dr. and Mrs J.H. Gorvin, Michael Graubert, Cathy Gray, Lynda Gray, Malcom Gunter, H. Hall, Jocelyne Hamadaoui, Lee Harling, Henry Harrison, Bill Hart, Michael James Heath, Stephen Heneghan, Joanna Hewitt, Peter Hoult, Gerdi Houterman, Vince Hunt, Paul Anthony Jay, Paul Jayne, Sue Jones, M.A. Keneally, Julia Kerner, John Kerr, Judith Kinsman, Matthew Lacey, Séamus Laffon, Maria Lageblad, Joanna Lawrie, Simon Lee, Steven Lenos, Michael Levine, Bill Lorch, Jane Luck, A.R. Macer, Charles McDonald, Penny McFadden, Jane McKenzie, Kathy McLeod, Ian L. McNichol, James Miyazawa, Scott Moen, D.W. Money, Ruth Morgan, Rosemary Morlin, Claire Mullan, Rod Murdison, John Murray, Liz Naylor, Alison Norman, Fitch and Michelle O'Connell, Marje van Oostendorp, S.C. Pearce, M.S.T. Price, A.S.L. Rae, Stephen Rainham, Susan Mountford Reis, Mr and Mrs J.H. Rendall, Arthur Riding, Liette Robin, Jane Robinson, Vivienne Scupham, Tiana Sidey, Katherine Slay, John W. Smith, Penny Smithers, Damon Speller, Anita Stadelman, Judy Staynes, Deborah A.Sumby, D. Thomas, Jim Thomas, Pete Tomsett, Derek Twine, Richard and Jacqueline Wakely, Geoff Wallis, Rosie Warren, G.B. Wilkins, Brian and Jennifer Willet, Annie Williams, Rona Williams, Francis Williamson, Tony Woods, Christine and Trevor Young.

DIRECT ORDERS IN THE USA

Title	ISBN	Price
Amsterdam	1858280869	$13.59
Andalucia	185828094X	$14.95
Australia	1858280354	$18.95
Barcelona & Catalunya	1858281067	$17.99
Berlin	1858280338	$13.99
Brazil	1858281024	$15.95
Brittany & Normandy	1858281261	$14.95
Bulgaria	1858280478	$14.99
California	1858280907	$14.95
Canada	185828130X	$14.95
Classical Music on CD	185828113X	$19.95
Corsica	1858280893	$14.95
Crete	1858281326	$14.95
Cyprus	185828032X	$13.99
Czech & Slovak Republics	185828029X	$14.95
Egypt	1858280753	$17.95
England	1858280788	$16.95
Europe	185828077X	$18.95
Florida	1858280109	$14.95
France	1858281245	$16.95
Germany	1858281288	$17.95
Greece	1858281318	$16.95
Greek Islands	1858281636	$14.95
Guatemala & Belize	1858280451	$14.95
Holland, Belgium & Luxembourg	1858280877	$15.95
Hong Kong & Macau	1858280664	$13.95
Hungary	1858281237	$14.95
India	1858281040	$22.95
Ireland	1858280958	$16.95
Italy	1858280311	$17.95
Kenya	1858280435	$15.95
London	1858291172	$12.95
Mediterranean Wildlife	0747100993	$15.95
Malaysia, Singapore & Brunei	1858281032	$16.95
Morocco	1858280400	$16.95
Nepal	185828046X	$13.95
New York	1858280583	$13.95
Nothing Ventured	0747102082	$19.95
Pacific Northwest	1858280923	$14.95
Paris	1858281253	$12.95
Poland	1858280346	$16.95
Portugal	1858280842	$15.95
Prague	1858281229	$14.95
Provence & the Côte d'Azur	1858280230	$14.95
Pyrenees	1858280931	$15.95
St Petersburg	1858281334	$14.95
San Francisco	1858280826	$13.95
Scandinavia	1858280397	$16.99
Scotland	1858280834	$14.95
Sicily	1858280370	$14.99
Spain	1858280818	$16.95
Thailand	1858280168	$15.95
Tunisia	1858280656	$15.95
Turkey	1858280885	$16.95
Tuscany & Umbria	1858280915	$15.95
USA	185828080X	$18.95
Venice	1858280362	$13.99
Wales	1858280966	$14.95
West Africa	1858280141	$24.95
More Women Travel	1858280982	$14.95
World Music	1858280176	$19.95
Zimbabwe & Botswana	1858280419	$16.95

Rough Guide Phrasebooks

Title	ISBN	Price
Czech	1858281482	$5.00
French	185828144X	$5.00
German	1858281466	$5.00
Greek	1858281458	$5.00
Italian	1858281431	$5.00
Spanish	1858281474	$5.00

Rough Guides are available from all good bookstores, but can be obtained directly in the USA and Worldwide (except the UK*) from Penguin:

Charge your order by Master Card or Visa (US$15.00 minimum order): call 1-800-253-6476; or send orders, with complete name, address and zip code, and list price, plus $2.00 shipping and handling per order to: Consumer Sales, Penguin USA, PO Box 999 – Dept #17109, Bergenfield, NJ 07621. No COD. Prepay foreign orders by international money order, a cheque drawn on a US bank, or US currency. No postage stamps are accepted. All orders are subject to stock availability at the time they are processed. Refunds will be made for books not available at that time. Please allow a minimum of four weeks for delivery.

The availability and published prices quoted are correct at the time of going to press but are subject to alteration without prior notice. Titles currently not available outside the UK will be available by July 1995. Call to check.

* For UK orders, see separate price list

DIRECT ORDERS IN THE UK

Title	ISBN	Price
Amsterdam	1858280869	£7.99
Andalucia	185828094X	£8.99
Australia	1858280354	£12.99
Barcelona & Catalunya	1858281067	£8.99
Berlin	1858280338	£8.99
Brazil	1858281024	£9.99
Brittany & Normandy	1858281261	£8.99
Bulgaria	1858280478	£8.99
California	1858280907	£9.99
Canada	185828130X	£10.99
Classical Music on CD	185828113X	£12.99
Corsica	1858280893	£8.99
Crete	1858281326	£8.99
Cyprus	185828032X	£8.99
Czech & Slovak Republics	185828029X	£8.99
Egypt	1858280753	£10.99
England	1858280788	£9.99
Europe	185828077X	£14.99
Florida	1858280109	£8.99
France	1858280508	£9.99
Germany	1858281288	£11.99
Greece	1858281318	£9.99
Greek Islands	1858281636	£8.99
Guatemala & Belize	1858280451	£9.99
Holland, Belgium & Luxembourg	1858280877	£9.99
Hong Kong & Macau	1858280664	£8.99
Hungary	1858281237	£8.99
India	1858281040	£13.99
Ireland	1858280958	£9.99
Italy	1858280311	£12.99
Kenya	1858280435	£9.99
London	1858291172	£8.99
Mediterranean Wildlife	0747100993	£7.95
Malaysia, Singapore & Brunei	1858281032	£9.99
Morocco	1858280400	£9.99
Nepal	185828046X	£8.99
New York	1858280583	£8.99
Nothing Ventured	0747102082	£7.99
Pacific Northwest	1858280923	£9.99
Paris	1858281253	£7.99
Poland	1858280346	£9.99
Portugal	1858280842	£9.99
Prague	185828015X	£7.99
Provence & the Côte d'Azur	1858280230	£8.99
Pyrenees	1858280931	£8.99
St Petersburg	1858281334	£8.99
San Francisco	1858280826	£8.99
Scandinavia	1858280397	£10.99
Scotland	1858280834	£8.99
Sicily	1858280370	£8.99
Spain	1858280818	£9.99
Thailand	1858280168	£8.99
Tunisia	1858280656	£8.99
Turkey	1858280885	£9.99
Tuscany & Umbria	1858280915	£8.99
USA	185828080X	£12.99
Venice	1858280362	£8.99
Wales	1858280966	£8.99
West Africa	1858280141	£12.99
More Women Travel	1858280982	£9.99
World Music	1858280176	£14.99
Zimbabwe & Botswana	1858280419	£10.99

Rough Guide Phrasebooks

Czech	1858281482	£3.50
French	185828144X	£3.50
German	1858281466	£3.50
Greek	1858281458	£3.50
Itallan	1858281431	£3.50
Spanish	1858281474	£3.50

Rough Guides are available from all good bookstores, but can be obtained directly in the UK* from Penguin by contacting:

Penguin Direct, Penguin Books Ltd, Bath Road, Harmondsworth, West Drayton, Middlesex UB7 0DA; or telephone our credit line on 0181-899 4036 (9am–5pm) and ask for Penguin Direct. Visa, Access and Amex accepted. Delivery will normally be within 14 working days. Penguin Direct ordering facilities are only available in the UK.

The availability and published prices quoted are correct at the time of going to press but are subject to alteration without prior notice.

* For USA and international orders, see separate price list

Passport to Portugal

Published in October 1994, this 208-page anthology includes the best of contemporary Portuguese writing, with work from:

José Saramago

The winner of *The Independent* Foreign Fiction prize for *The Year of the Death of Ricardo Reis* is represented by two newly translated stories: 'The Centaur' and 'The Chair'. These stories, the first of which is Saramago's own favourite, are appearing for the first time in English, translated for this anthology by Saramago's approved translator, Giovanni Pontiero.
Passport to Portugal also includes an interview with José Saramago

Antonio Lobo Antunes

An extract from *The Return of the Caravels*, not previously published in English, in which this controversial novelist deals with the *retornados*, the Portuguese who returned home in the 1970s when the African colonies gained their independence

Jose Cardoso Pires

A new story, 'Tomorrow, God Willing', from the author of *Ballad of Dog's Beach*

Vergilio Ferreira

First publication in English for this distinguished author whose work has appeared previously in French, Spanish, German, Greek, Polish and Russian. Ferreira's work has won many prizes in Portugal, including the most important, the Prize of the Portuguese Association of Writers

Helena Marques

Helena Marques rose to prominence in Portugal recently when she published her first novel at the age of almost sixty. *O Ultimo Cais (The Last Quay)* won three literary prizes in its first year of publication, and *Passport to Portugal* includes the first English-language translation of an extract from the novel, plus a new short story from this author

And: Lidia Jorge - Mia Couto - João Aguiar

To order your copy of *Passport to Portugal*, published October 1994, send £6.99 to Passport, 5 Parsonage Street, Wistow, Huntingdon, Cambs PE17 2QD

Or send £12 and receive *Passport to Travel*, featuring Bill Bryson, Lawrence Millman, Nicolas Bouvier, Lieve Joris on Naguib Mahfouz and travel fact and fiction from around the world, plus *Passport to Portugal* on publication

You are
A STUDENT

You **travel**
THE WORLD

You **want**
TO SAVE MONEY

Here's
how

The International
Student Identity Card

Available at Student Travel Offices Worldwide.

Entitles you to discounts and special services worldwide.